The Improvisation Studies Reader

Improvisation is a performance practice that animates and activates diverse energies of inspiration, critique, and invention. In recent years it has coalesced into an exciting and innovative new field of interdisciplinary scholarly inquiry, becoming a cornerstone of both practical and theoretical approaches to performance.

The Improvisation Studies Reader draws together the works of key artists and thinkers from a range of disciplines, including theatre, music, literature, film, and dance. Divided by keywords into eight sections, this book bridges the gaps between these fields. The book includes case studies, exercises, graphic scores, and poems in order to produce a teaching and research resource that identifies central themes in improvisation studies. The sections include:

- Listening
- Trust/Risk
- Flow
- Dissonance
- Responsibility
- Liveness
- Surprise
- Hope.

Each section of the Reader is introduced by a newly commissioned think piece by a key figure in the field, which opens up research questions reflecting on the keyword in question.

By placing key theoretical and classic texts in conversation with cutting-edge research and artists' statements, this book answers the urgent questions facing improvising artists and theorists in the mediatised twenty-first century.

Rebecca Caines is an award-winning interdisciplinary artist and scholar. She is currently an assistant professor in Creative Technologies in the Faculty of Fine Arts at the University of Regina.

Ajay Heble is Director of the International Institute for Critical Studies in Improvisation and Professor of English in the School of English and Theatre Studies at the University of Guelph.

The Improvisation Studies Reader

Spontaneous Acts

Edited by
Rebecca Caines and Ajay Heble

Routledge
Taylor & Francis Group

LONDON AND NEW YORK

First published 2015
by Routledge
2 Park Square, Milton Park, Abingdon, Oxon OX14 4RN

and by Routledge
711 Third Avenue, New York, NY 10017

Routledge is an imprint of the Taylor & Francis Group, an informa business

British Library Cataloguing in Publication Data
A catalogue record for this book is available from the British Library

Library of Congress Cataloguing in Publication Data
A catalog record for this title has been requested

ISBN: 978-0-415-63871-5 (hbk)
ISBN: 978-0-415-63872-2 (pbk)
ISBN: 978-0-203-08374-1 (ebk)

Typeset in Sabon
by Taylor & Francis Books

For Sheila and John

Contents

List of Figures

Acknowledgements

We would like to acknowledge the support and contribution of the international research network that has sustained us throughout our work as editors and scholars, the Improvisation, Community, and Social Practice (ICASP) project, which has recently transitioned into the International Institute for Critical Studies in Improvisation (IICSI). They have been not only a driving force for innovative research in the field, but also a focal point that's given us the opportunity to be energised by a wonderful and like-minded community of friends and colleagues. These research initiatives are generously funded by large-scale grants by the Social Sciences and Humanities Research Council of Canada (SSHRC), and supported by a global partnership of independent researchers, universities, institutional, community, and artistic organisations. Huge thanks to SSHRC's Major Collaborative Research Initiatives (MCRI) and Partnership Grant programmes.

The work of ICASP/IICSI scholars (many of whom contributed to this volume in some way), postdoctoral fellows, students, and staff has made this book possible. In particular, we would like to acknowledge the amazing support we've received from Rachel Shoup. Rachel's remarkable attention to detail, project management skills, dedication, and persistence made her a key force in this book reaching publication. We would also like to acknowledge the work of graduate student, improvising bassist, and writer David Lee who composed the biographies that introduce each author. Thanks, too, to ICASP's (and now IICSI's) incredible Project Manager, Kim Thorne, and to our wonderful graduate research assistants Leslie Allin, Ned Bartlett, Greg Fenton, Katia Hildebrandt, and Christie Menzo for helping us at various stages of this project. We must also thank the artists/scholars who contributed new works to this volume, as well as those who allowed us to reprint sections of their pre-published work. Due to space restrictions, we have had to excerpt some pieces, but we hope we have given a representative sample that will pique your interest in following up on these important scholars and artists.

It is with much gratitude that we recognise the work of the Routledge team, particularly Ben Piggott, in believing from the get-go in such an ambitious project and working with us to bring together such a diverse body of artistic scholarship. And we are grateful to the peer reviewers whose assessments for the press provided us with helpful feedback.

Rebecca Caines would like to thank the Faculty of Fine Arts at the University of Regina, particularly Randal Rogers, for mentoring her in so many ways as a new scholar, and also acknowledges the collegial support of the wonderful interdisciplinary team in the new Creative Technologies area. Ajay Heble would like to acknowledge the support he's received from the Office of the Vice-President (Research) at the University of

Guelph, and offers special thanks to Dr Kevin Hall for his ongoing commitments to the work of ICASP and IICSI. Ajay also extends a deep personal thank you to Dr Eric Schnell.

Most importantly, we thank our families, including those who are scattered across the globe, and our life-partners, Sheila O'Reilly and John Campbell, for their love, their wisdom, and their friendship.

Permissions

2. Jean Luc Nancy. "On Listening." *Listening*, translated from *À l'écoute* (Paris: Éditions Galilée, 2002) by Charlotte Mandel (New York: Fordham University Press, 2007): 1–22. Reprinted, in excerpted form, by permission of Fordham University Press.

3. Jacques Lecoq. "Improvisation." *The Moving Body: Teaching Creative Theatre*, in collaboration with Jean-Gabriel Carasso and Jean-Claude Lallias, translated from *Le Corps Poétique* by David Bradby (New York: Routledge/Theatre Arts Books, 2001): 29–65. Reprinted, in excerpted form, by permission of Routledge.

4. Mattin. "Going Fragile." Reprinted from *Noise & Capitalism*, edited by Mattin and Anthony Iles. (Donostia/San Sebastián, Spain: Arteleku Audiolab [Kritika saila], 2009): 19–23. Anti-copyright.

5. Ingrid Monson. "Music, Language, and Cultural Styles: Improvisation as Conversation." *Saying Something: Jazz Improvisation and Interaction* (Chicago and London: University of Chicago Press, 1996): 73–96. Reprinted by permission of the University of Chicago Press and the author.

6. Pauline Oliveros. "Deep Listening Meditations: Egypt (1999)." *Deep Listening: A Composer's Sound Practice* (New York: iUniverse, 2005): 39–40. Reprinted by permission of the author.

7. Jeff Schlanger, musicWitness®. "Really Listening." (Guelph, Ontario, Canada, 2013). Reprinted by permission of the author.

9. Constantin Stanislavski. "Improvisation." *An Actor's Handbook: an Alphabetical Arrangement of Concise Statements on Aspects of Acting*, edited and translated by Elizabeth Reynolds Hapgood (New York: Routledge/Theatre Art Books, 1963): 78–79. Reprinted by permission of Routledge.

10. Keith Johnstone. "Afterthoughts." *Impro for Storytellers* (New York: Routledge/Theatre Arts Books, 1999): 337–42. Reprinted by permission of Routledge.

11. Bruno Nettl. "Thoughts on Improvisation: A Comparative Approach." *The Musical Quarterly*, Vol. 60, No. 1, (1974): 1–19. Reprinted, in excerpted form, by permission of Oxford University Press and the author.

12. Augusto Boal. "Theatre of the Oppressed." Originally published as part of "Poetics of the Oppressed." *Theatre of the Oppressed* (London: Pluto Press, 2000 [1997]): 131–42. Reprinted, in excerpted form, by permission of Pluto Press and the Theatre Communications Group.

13. Keith Sawyer. "Group Creativity: Musical Performance and Collaboration." *Psychology of Music*, Vol. 34, No. 2 (April 2006): 148–65. Reprinted, in excerpted form, by permission of Sage Journals and the author.

14. Petra Kuppers. "Community Performance: Improvising Being-Together." A revised version of "Community Arts and Practices: Improvising Being-Together." *Culture Machine*, Vol. 8 (2006). Open access. Revised text (2013) and images printed by permission of Petra Kuppers.

15. Judith Malina and Julian Beck. "'Paradise Now': Notes." *TDR – The Drama Review*, Vol. 13, No. 3 (Spring, 1969): 90–107. Reprinted, in excerpted form, by permission of New York University and the Massachusetts Institute of Technology.

16. Yvonne Yarbro-Bejarano. "Chicanas' Experience in Collective Theatre: Ideology and Form." *Women in Performance: A Journal of Feminist Theory*, Vol. 2, No. 2 (1985): 45–58. Reprinted, in excerpted form, by permission of Routledge and the author.

17. Sally Banes. "Spontaneous Combustion: Notes on Dance Improvisation from the Sixties to the Nineties." *Taken By Surprise: a Dance Improvisation Reader*, edited by Ann Cooper Albright and David Gere (Middletown, CT: Wesleyan University Press, 2003): 77–85. Reprinted by permission of Wesleyan University.

18. Wadada Leo Smith. "Luminous Axis, Blade-form Panel" (Graphic Score). Reprinted by permission of the author.

20. Mihaly Csikszentmihalyi. "A Theoretical Model for Enjoyment." *Beyond Boredom and Anxiety: The Experience of Play in Work and Games* (San Francisco and London: Jossey-Bass, 1975): 35–54. Reprinted by permission of John Wiley & Sons.

21. Anthony Braxton. "Keynote Presentation (Guelph) 2007" (Graphic Score). 2007. Reprinted with permission of the author.

22. Cunningham, Merce. "The Impermanent Art." *7 Arts, Number 3*, edited by Fernando Puma (Indian Hills, Colorado: Falcon's Wing Press, 1955): 69–77. Reprinted by permission of the Merce Cunningham Trust.

23. Michael Chekhov. "Improvisation and Ensemble." *To the Actor: On the Technique of Acting.* (New York and London: Routledge, 2013): 35–46. Reprinted by permission of Routledge.

24. Guy Debord. "Theory of the Dérive." *Situationist International Anthology*, Revised and Expanded Edition, edited and translated by Ken Knabb. (Bureau of Public Secrets, 2006). Available at www.bopsecrets.org/SI/2.derive.htm. Copyright free and reprinted by permission of Ken Knabb.

25. Tricia Rose. "'All Aboard the Night Train': Flow, Layering, and Rupture in Post-industrial New York." *Black Noise: Rap Music and Black Culture in Contemporary America* (Middletown, CT: Wesleyan University Press, 1994): 21–61. Reprinted, in excerpted form, by permission of Wesleyan University.

26. Rob Wallace. "Writing Improvisation into Modernism." Orignally published as a part of "Introduction: Writing Improvisation into Modernism." *Improvisation and the Making of American Literary Modernism* (New York: Continuum/Bloomsbury, 2010): 1–24. Reprinted, in excerpted form, by permission of the author and Bloomsbury Publishing.

27. Germaine Liu. "Stone Sketch" (Graphic Score). *Hearing-Visions-Sonores*. 2009. Reprinted by permission of the author.

28. Jack Kerouac. "Essentials of Spontaneous Prose." *The Portable Beat Reader*, edited by Ann Charters (New York: Viking, 1992 [1958]): 57–58. Reprinted by permission of John Sampas, executor, the estate of Jack Kerouac.

30. Rustom Bharucha. "Phantoms of the Other: Fragments of the Communal Uncon-scious." *The Politics of Cultural Practice: Thinking Through Theatre in an Age of*

Globalization. (Hanover, CT, and London: Wesleyan University Press, 2000): 102–22. Reprinted, in excerpted form, by permission of Wesleyan University.

31. Daniel Belgrad. "Bebop as Cultural Alternative." Originally published as a part of "Bebop." *The Culture of Spontaneity: Improvisation and the Arts in Postwar America*. (Chicago and London: University of Chicago Press, 1998): 179–95. Reprinted, in excerpted form, by permission of the University of Chicago Press and the author.

32. Allan Kaprow. "Happenings in the New York Scene." *ARTnews*, Vol. 60, No. 3 (1961): 36–39, 58–62. Reprinted by permssion of ARTnews, LLC (www.art news. com).

33. Nathaniel Mackey. "Other: From Noun to Verb." *Representations*, No. 39 (Summer 1992): 51–70. Reprinted by permission of University of California Press Journals.

34. Julie Dawn Smith. "Playing Like a Girl: The Queer Laughter of the Feminist Improvising Group." *The Other Side of Nowhere: Jazz, Improvisation, and Communities in Dialogue*, edited by Daniel Fischlin and Ajay Heble (Middletown, CT: Wesleyan University Press, 2004): 224–43. Reprinted by permission of Wesleyan University.

35. Charlie Todd. "Frozen Grand Central." *Causing a Scene: Extraordinary Pranks in Ordinary Places with Improv Everywhere* (New York: HarperCollins, 2009): 94–111. Reprinted by permission of HarperCollins and the author.

37. George E. Lewis. "Gittin' To Know Y'all: Improvised Music, Interculturalism, and the Racial Imagination." *Critical Studies in Improvisation/Études critiques en improvisation*, Vol. 1, No. 1 (2004). Available at www.criticalimprov.com/article/view/6. Reprinted by permission of the author.

38. Joseph Roach. "Kinship, Intelligence and Memory as Improvisation: Culture and Performance in New Orleans." *Performance and Cultural Politics*, edited by Elin Diamond (New York and London: Routledge, 1996): 217–36. Reprinted, in excerpted form, by permission of Routledge.

39. Amiri Baraka [LeRoi Jones]. "Swing: From Verb to Noun." *Blues People: Negro Music in White America* (New York: William Morrow, 1963): 142–65. Reprinted by permission of Sterling Lord Literistic, Inc. Copyright by Amiri Baraka.

40. Malcolm X. "OAAU Founding Rally." *By Any Means Necessary: Speeches, Interviews, and a Letter by Malcolm X*. (New York: Pathfinder Press, 1992 [1970]): 63–64. Copyright © 1970, 1992 by Betty Shabazz and Pathfinder Press. Reprinted by permission.

42. Philip Auslander. "Liveness." Originally published as "Conclusion." *Liveness: Performance in a Mediatized Culture* (London and New York: Routledge, 1999): 158–62. Reprinted by permission of Routledge.

43. Gil Scott-Heron. "The Revolution Will Not Be Televised." *So Far, So Good*. (Chicago: Third World Press, 1990): 46–48. Reprinted by permission of Third World Press, Inc.

44. Hans Thies Lehmann. "The Present of Performance." Originally published as a part of "Performance." *Postdramatic Theatre* (London and New York: Routledge, 2006): 134–44. Reprinted, in excerpted form, by permission of Routledge.

48. Richard Schechner. "Playing." Reprinted from *The Future of Ritual: Writings on Culture and Performance* (New York: Routledge, 1993): 24–44. Reprinted, in excerpted form, by permission of Routledge and the author.

49. Susan Foster. "Taken By Surprise: Improvisation in Dance and Mind." *Taken By Surprise: a Dance Improvisation Reader*, edited by Ann Cooper Albright and David

Gere (Middletown, CT: Wesleyan University Press, 2003): 3–10. Reprinted by permission of Wesleyan University.

50. Viola Spolin. "Seven Aspects of Spontaneity." Originally published as part of "Creative Experience." *Improvisation for the Theatre: A Handbook of Teaching and Directing Techniques* (Evanston, Illinois: Northwestern University Press, 1963): 3–17. Reprinted, in excerpted form, by permission of Northwestern University Press and Carol B. Sills.

51. Margaret Thompson Drewal. "Yoruba Play and the Transformation of Ritual." *Yoruba Ritual: Performers, Play, Agency* (Bloomington and Indianapolis: Indiana University Press, 1992): 12–28. Reprinted, in excerpted form, by permission of Indiana University Press.

52. Tim Etchells. "Play On: Collaboration and Process." *Certain Fragments: Contemporary Performance and Forced Entertainment* (London and New York: Routledge, 1999): 50–70. Reprinted, in excerpted form, by permission of Routledge and the author.

53. Nicholas Humbert and Werner Penzel. "Step Across the Border" (DVD Liner Notes). (Winter & Winter, 2003 [1990].) Reprinted by permission of the authors.

54. Wayde Compton. "DJ." *49th Parallel Psalm* (Vancouver: Arsenal Pulp Press, 1999): 24–26. Reprinted by permission of Arsenal Pulp Press.

Prologue: Spontaneous Acts

Rebecca Caines and Ajay Heble

Rebecca Caines is an award-winning interdisciplinary artist and scholar, with a PhD in Performance Studies from the University of New South Wales. Her artistic practice, teaching, and research work explores creative technologies, contemporary performance, site-specific art practices, community-engaged art, and place-based new media audio art. She completed two consecutive SSHRC-funded postdoctoral research fellowships at the University of Guelph's Improvisation, Community, and Social Practice initiative (ICASP), and is now the Director of the IICSI University of Regina site, the Regina Improvisation Studies Centre. She has created professional community-based performance, visual art, new media, and sound art projects in Australia, Northern Ireland, the Netherlands, and Canada, and is the co-director of the University of Regina iPad and Tablet Orchestra. She has published articles in a series of books, including the *Routledge Reader in Community Performance*, as well as papers in journals such as *Afterimage, Performance Research*, and the Australian cultural studies journal *M/C*. She is currently Assistant Professor in Creative Technologies in the Faculty of Fine Arts at the University of Regina.

Ajay Heble is Director of the International Institute for Critical Studies in Improvisation and Professor of English in the School of English and Theatre Studies at the University of Guelph. He is the author or editor of several books, and a founding co-editor of the journal *Critical Studies in Improvisation/Études critiques en improvisation* (www.criticalimprov.com). He is also Project Director for Improvisation, Community, and Social Practice (ICASP), a large-scale major collaborative research initiative, funded by the Social Sciences and Humanities Research Council of Canada. As the Founder and Artistic Director of the Guelph Jazz Festival, Heble has jolted the citizens of Guelph into an appreciation of improvised and avant-garde music and delighted aficionados from around the world with his innovative and daring programming. Under his visionary leadership, the Festival—winner of the prestigious Premier's Award for Excellence in the Arts (2010), and a three-time recipient of the Lieutenant Governor's Award for the Arts (1997, 2000, 2001)—has achieved a rock-solid international reputation as one of the world's most inspired and provocative musical events. Recent projects include two new books both published in 2013 by Duke University Press: *People Get Ready: The Future of Jazz is Now!* (co-edited with Rob Wallace), and *The Fierce Urgency of Now: Improvisation, Rights, and the Ethics of Cocreation* (co-authored with Daniel Fischlin and George Lipsitz). As a pianist, he has released three CDs: *Different Windows*, a live recording of improvised music with percussionist Jesse Stewart (on the IntrepidEar label), and two recordings with his improvising quartet The Vertical Squirrels: *Hold True/ Accroche toi* (on Ambiances Magnétiques) and *Winter's Gate* (on Barcode Free).

In an interview with Reuters marking the occasion of the 50th anniversary of Dr Martin Luther King's profoundly influential 1963 "I Have a Dream" speech, Clarence Jones, Dr King's speechwriter and attorney, remarked that the celebrated words "I have a dream" "were not written in the text that King prepared and began to read that day" (Bernstein, 2013). Instead, Jones recalls, Dr King went off script in response to a prompt from gospel singer Mahalia Jackson, and improvised what has arguably become the most famous political speech in world history, a speech that would "change the course of race relations in the United States" (Bernstein, 2013).

"Tell 'em about the dream, Martin," Jackson yelled out from the stands, according to Jones, "Tell 'em about the dream!" (Bernstein, 2013). In response to Mahalia's prompt, King, as Jones remembers, "moves the text of the speech to the left side of the lectern, grabs the lectern, looks out on those more than 250,000 people assembled and thereafter begins to speak completely spontaneously and extemporaneously" (Bernstein, 2013). It's telling, we think, that such a powerfully important and iconic moment in world history was improvised. Telling that Dr King's most famous words emerged in response to an unforeseen prompt from a member of his audience—from a musician, moreover. Telling that the improvised remarks were about a dream.

Dr King, of course, was dreaming in colour. He was dreaming of a world where people—of all cultures—would get along. Yet in the face of the egregious and monumental degradations that beset aggrieved populations both in the United States and around the world, such a dream (especially at the time of King's speech, but admittedly—and sadly—even today) must have seemed so far out of reach.

We've chosen to introduce *The Improvisation Studies Reader: Spontaneous Acts* with this dream, this improvisation, from what was literally a life-changing moment in world history, because it offers so compelling an example of how spontaneous acts of creativity can offer resources for hope and social transformation, because it speaks powerfully to the deep connections among improvisation and critical issues in politics, social organisation, alternative community formation, and human rights. In short, it offers a telling example of how the social and creative practices associated with aggrieved peoples confronting systems of oppression can be enduring documents of hope, resilience, and determination. Isn't improvisation, after all, about the right to dream publicly? And isn't one of the most urgent lessons that we can learn from improvisation about enacting the very possibilities that we envision (see Fischlin, Heble, and Lipsitz, 2013)? We believe that the documentation and analysis of artistic and social improvisatory acts, and the words of improvisers themselves, are thus extremely important.

Improvisation: a social activity that cannot readily be scripted, predicted, or compelled into orthodoxy. Improvisation: a vital phenomenon occurring across all forms of artistic practice. Improvisation: a key feature of interpersonal communication and social practice. As the pieces we've collected in *The Improvisation Studies Reader: Spontaneous Acts* should make clear, improvisation is a vital life-force and performance practice that has animated and activated diverse energies of inspiration, critique, and invention. In recent years, it has, significantly, also coalesced into an exciting and innovative new field of interdisciplinary scholarly inquiry. As a form of artistic practice that accents and embodies real-time creative decision-making, risk-taking, trust, surprise, and collaboration, improvisation has much to teach us about listening—*really* listening—to what's going on around us, much to tell us about responsibility and hope, about how we can adapt to change, about how we might, as Dr King's words remind us, choose to create a shared future. "There is," after all, "no script for social and cultural life," as anthropologists Elizabeth Hallam and Tim Ingold (2007, p.1) note in the Introduction to their volume *Creativity and Cultural Improvisation*. Drawing on such issues, as well as on questions about the role that spontaneous acts of creativity might play in shaping notions of community, and in fostering new forms of social organisation, this reader presents key scholars and practitioners investigating the psychological, sociological, and cultural roots and implications of improvisatory creative activity. Arguing that the social force of improvised performance practices resides, at least in part, in their capacity to trouble the assumptions (and the expectations of fixity) fostered by dominant systems of knowledge production, the pieces we've collected here will broaden our understanding of how performance studies research and pedagogy can be animated by an analysis of the social impact of process-oriented models of creative practice. The theoretical texts in this Reader provide a solid grounding in contextualising improvisation in the creative arts, at the same time as they present some of the urgent questions facing improvising artists and theorists in the mediatised twenty-first century. Readings include pieces by many of the major artists and scholars working in the field. In addition, the Reader brings together important thinkers whose landmark essays, whilst not directly utilising the term "improvisation", have nevertheless had a major influence in shaping our understanding of the field.

Improvisation is a practised action, but the texts, scores, diary entries, and critical reflections that mark and analyse its presence have historically been circulated in locally specific frameworks and tied to specific artistic or scholarly disciplines. Whilst excellent textbooks and surveys are increasingly available based on disciplinary frameworks (see Albright and Gere, 2003; Fischlin and Heble, 2004; Frost and Yarrow, 2007; Hallam and Ingold, 2007), and there is important analytical work occurring in the emerging discipline of improvisation studies, there are few sustained interdisciplinary resources for students, scholars, and artists working in the field of improvisation (with some exceptions, see Smith and Dean, 1997). Also generally absent are interdisciplinary resources that focus on the social implications of the improvisatory. We have attempted to bring together works by artists and scholars who have shaped the field, where possible showcasing primary material that has had significant impact in its area. We have chosen pieces that speak across disciplinary boundaries, drawing from music, theatre, dance, film, philosophy, performance studies, literature, sociology, and interdisciplinary studies.

Of course, choosing what to include has been incredibly difficult. As editors, we both share the vision that improvisation is a complex phenomenon with sociocultural implications; that sociocultural focus (and our interest in improvisation as a force for political change) has been an important factor in influencing many of our choices. Space restrictions have, unfortunately, meant that so many important artists and texts could not be included. We have also found that primary materials from some areas are just not available, and that the key players are understandably less interested in generating complex text forms than in focusing on their improvising practices. As improvising theatre artist Ruth Zaporah states, "I have planned nothing, and that has kept me very busy" (Zaporah, n.d.). Rather than utilising secondary analyses of important artists, we have, where possible, returned to primary art and scholarship that has taken the field in exciting directions. We have also focused on the twentieth and twenty-first centuries for reasons of space, despite the knowledge that scholarship around historical practices such as mask and theatre, storytelling forms, religious and spiritual practices, ancient games, and so forth continues to inspire work in this area. As we were searching for text forms with an English translation, continuing restrictions on who has economic and social access to publish and disseminate texts in English have constrained us, although we hope that the publication of texts, scores, and words from important scholars and artists from across the globe in this book may continue both to mark and to contest these barriers.

Divided into eight sections (Listening, Trust/Risk, Flow, Dissonance, Responsibility, Liveness, Surprise, and Hope), the Reader contains a balance of theoretical articles/book excerpts and artist statements/documentation of artistic practice including scores, poems, exercises, and descriptions. Case studies and texts are internationally relevant, including Australasian, European, African, Asian, and North and South American perspectives. Each section of the Reader is introduced by a newly commissioned think piece (by major figures in the area) that opens up key research questions reflecting on the keyword in question. Each article in the Reader is also prefaced by a short critical headnote placing the artist/author in context with the field.

Critical Studies in Improvisation is an emerging interdisciplinary field of inquiry that enlarges on the working models of creative practitioners and the knowledge gained in studying creative improvisation in order to examine how it may model innovative forms of social interaction. Under the leadership of research projects and curriculum foci in Canada, the US, Europe, and Australia, as well as the recent launch of journals such as *Critical Studies in Improvisation/Études critiques en improvisation,* this emerging theoretical node is proving increasingly fertile ground for interdisciplinary research into vital questions of liveness, responsibility, intermediality, collaboration and community, critical listening, risk-taking, and experimentation. And as Performance Studies is rapidly advancing as a discipline, this volume will place improvisational practices (from a multiplicity of cultural, historical, and disciplinary vantage points) at the centre of that field. We hope that this volume will also support disciplines such as music, theatre, film, dance, and interdisciplinary studies as they continue to mark the importance of improvised art forms and their social implications in both their syllabi and research. We hope, too, that this Reader may act as an interdisciplinary conversation, a tool-kit, and a source of critical and creative inspiration. It seems increasingly important that society continues to grow resources that track local and intercultural collectivity, that understand and support new forms of history-making through artistic work, and that build tools for negotiation in order to respect difference and cultivate the urgently needed ability to listen and to adapt to unprecedented change. Such resources for hope, as Dr King's improvisations during his "I Have a Dream" speech should remind us, are in direct contrast to the culture of acquiescence or non-participation which asks us to resign ourselves to the way things are because (or so we are too often told), no other future is possible.

Improvisatory practices teach us otherwise. They encourage us to dream about other possible futures, "to discern multiple futures latent inside the constrained present" (Lipsitz, "Listening to the Lambs," this volume), and, as we suggested earlier, they teach us to enact the possibilities we envision: what key US improvising artist Rachel Rosenthal famously calls "doing by doing" (Rosenthal, 2009). Our hope is that students, scholars, artists, and lovers of improvisation will find these texts useful and inspiring as they imagine new ways to create these spontaneous acts that have such potential.

Works Cited

Albright, A. C. and Gere, D. 2003. *Taken by Surprise: A Dance Improvisation Reader*. Middletown, CT: Wesleyan University Press.

Bernstein, S., 2013. Famed King speech almost didn't include 'I have a dream': author. *Reuters,* [online], 26 August. Available at www.reuters.com/article/2013/08/26/us-usa-dream-speech-idUS-BRE97P0EV20130826 [Accessed 18 December 2013].

Fischlin, D. and Heble, A., eds. 2004. *The Other Side of Nowhere: Jazz, Improvisation, and Communities in Dialogue.* Middletown, CT: Wesleyan University Press.

Fischlin, D., Heble, A., and Lipsitz, G. 2013. *The Fierce Urgency of Now: Improvisation, Rights, and the Ethics of Cocreation.* Durham, NC: Duke University Press.

Frost, A. and Yarrow, R. 2007. *Improvisation in Drama.* Second edition. New York: Palgrave Macmillan.

Hallam, E. and Ingold, T., eds. 2007. *Creativity and Cultural Improvisation.* Oxford: Berg.

Rosenthal, R. 2009. *The DbD Experience: Chance Knows What it's Doing!* Edited by K. Noonan. New York: Routledge.

Smith, H. and Dean, R. 1997. *Improvisation, Hypermedia, and the Arts since 1945.* New York: Routledge.

Zaporah, R. n.d. Action Theatre Home Page. *Action Theatre.* Available at http://actiontheatre.com/ [Accessed 12 December 2013].

Part 1

Listening

1   Improvised Listening: Opening Statements
Listening to the Lambs

George Lipsitz

George Lipsitz's writings on an enormous range of subjects are informed by his overriding concern with social justice and his fascination with the politics of culture. An American Studies scholar and a professor in the Department of Black Studies at the University of California, Santa Barbara, his research interests span social movements, urban culture, inequality, the politics of popular culture, and Whiteness Studies. A special interest in music has led him to collaborations on the auto-biographies of Johnny Otis and Preston Love, and studies of the St Louis-based Black Artists Group and Ken Burns' *Jazz*. His recent books include *The Fierce Urgency of Now: Improvisation, Rights, and the Ethics of Cocreation*, co-authored with Daniel Fischlin and Ajay Heble (2013), *How Racism Takes Place* (2011), *Midnight at the Barrelhouse: the Johnny Otis Story* (2010), *Footsteps in the Dark: the Hidden Histories of Popular Music* (2007), and *Time Passages: Collective Memory and American Popular Culture* (2001). Countless scholars have been influenced by Dr Lipsitz's views of popular culture as a repository of history and as a historical force in itself. In "Listening to the Lambs," he evokes the legendary musician Johnny Otis' reactions to the 1965 Watts rebellion, and in doing so frames improvisation as "an alternative academy crucial to preparing ourselves for … the struggle to keep sorrow from degenerating into despair."

Key words: Black Studies; jazz; USA

When the Watts rebellion broke out in Los Angeles during the summer of 1965, politicians, the press, and much of the public expressed surprise at the sudden eruption of rage and fury. But rhythm and blues musician Johnny Otis was not surprised. He knew that Black people in Los Angeles had been crying out for justice for years, but their cries had not been heard. As Otis witnessed the destruction of the community that he loved, he thought of the gospel song "Listen to the Lambs." In the song the lambs are crying for the Lord to come by. Looking at the destruction all around him in Watts, Otis (2009, p.5) thought to himself, "They wouldn't listen to the lambs … The lambs cried, and finally one day the lambs turned into lions."

Johnny Otis had learned how to listen to the lambs from his experiences as a working musician. Afro-diasporic cultural production teaches its practitioners to engage in improvisation in order to discern the hidden possibilities disguised in proximate appearances. A jazz musician has to listen carefully, to recognise not only what the music being played *is*, but also what it *could be*, to listen for the prophetic foreshadowing in even the simplest phrase. Improvisational art questions surface appearances. It cultivates the capacity, as

Robert Farris Thompson (1984, p.19) explains, to "view things from all sides before we make a judgment." This ability guided Johnny Otis's response to the riot. At a time when most outsiders considered the Black community in Los Angeles to be serene, satisfied, and submissive, the music that Otis played taught him to look beyond appearances, to see that his community was critical, resentful, and filled with rage. When the riot came, Otis was not caught off guard. He simply wondered why others had not heard the cries of the oppressed or recognised what they foreshadowed as he had. How could people not know that the very longevity and continuity of white supremacy required its victims to improvise, to interrupt the status quo and challenge its legitimacy?

In the wake of this violent rebellion that convulsed Watts, Otis offered an improvisational response. He published a book titled *Listen to the Lambs* that challenged dominant understandings of the past, present, and future. Because white Americans had not listened to the lambs, he argued, they lacked the prophetic vision that would have enabled them to know that the riots were coming, to see that one day the suppressed anger and frustration of an oppressed people would erupt into violence. Otis had been predicting just such a conflagration for years. He had warned about it in newspaper columns, radio broadcasts, speeches, and direct action demonstrations. He developed his insight and foresight, this ability to listen to the lambs, from his experiences as an improvising musician. Afro-diasporic improvisation is an art of interruption. It teaches performers to prepare for rupture and to respond to it. It is not simply an aesthetic practice but rather an epistemological and ontological imperative. Improvisation entails distinct ways of knowing and ways of being. It emerges from insubordinate spaces and creates emancipatory temporalities. Playing improvised music enabled Otis to discern multiple futures latent inside the constrained present, to recognise how the blasted hopes and cumulative frustrations of the past pervade the present in covert yet powerful ways.

In the year that he published *Listen to the Lambs,* Otis was a high school dropout in his mid-thirties. He held no elected or appointed office. He represented no organised political group. But he had learned how to listen as a working musician and improviser, and that ability positioned him to write a profound and insightful book. The intergenerational networks of musical instruction and apprenticeship that had guided him as an artist helped make him a perceptive and prescient political thinker. Just as Otis recognised the great potential latent in unrecognised and untrained artists, he recognised enormous untapped possibilities in people trapped inside ghetto neighborhoods. As a musician, Otis often attributed his success as a talent scout and producer to his ability to hear what was not yet evident to others. He discovered and developed an astounding number of talented artists including Etta James, Little Esther Phillips, Charles Brown, Sugar Pie DeSanto, Linda Hopkins, Barbara Morrison, and Hank Ballard. This was not a matter of luck, but rather of recognising latent potential. "I can hear the raw talent before it develops," he explained (qtd. in Lipsitz, 2010, p.37). Similarly, he perceived the ghetto to be filled with talent, seeing it as a repository of social insights, ideas, and abilities that society sorely needed. In both cultural and social life, Otis found great value in listening to what Fred Moten (2003, p.223) describes as "the piercing insistence of the excluded."

Johnny Otis spoke out for and from that insistence in his music and in *Listen to the Lambs*. Resonant with what Cedric Johnson aptly describes as the culture of the soapbox, the pamphlet, and the bullhorn, *Listen to the Lambs* placed blame for the riots on the very existence of ghetto conditions rather than on the alleged deficiencies of ghetto residents. Otis argued that while Black people certainly needed and deserved improved opportunities and life chances, the ghetto was not simply a zone of deprivation. Instead, he explained, the ghetto was home to valuable alternative academies, to sites of instruction and apprenticeship replete with knowledge that white society sorely needed. From his perspective, the short-comings of dominant groups were most evident to their aggrieved victims. White society, he argued, needed to learn about itself from the perspective of ghetto residents. But to do so, whites had to learn to listen. They did not yet realise what Otis believed to be the importance of their historical moment. To him, the riots announced that the nation had come to a crossroads and had to make a choice: "It is either *really* the beginning of the end of the color line and all its ramifications, or race war. Anything short of full freedom is unacceptable" (Otis, 2009, p.238).

Johnny Otis knew that in social life as well as in musical life much can be lost by not listening. Hearing just happens, but listening entails attention and interpretation. Listening is an act of deliberation and discernment, a capacity that gets cultivated through experience. Music is an interactive practice. It is a dialogue, not a monologue. There can be no good players unless there are good listeners. Improvisation plays a crucial role in creating the capacity for an augmented sense of listening because at its core, improvisation is an art that opens doors. It creates new understandings of previousness and futurity in order to explore hidden possibilities. It privileges temporary and ephemeral resolutions over per-manent and set in stone closures, recognising that yesterday's solutions always require renegotiation and adaptation tomorrow as situations and conditions change (Small, 1998, p.44). Armed with improvisational knowledge, trash can become treasure. For example, Afro-diasporic quilt makers, yard decorators, and assemblage artists rescue objects that have been discarded by their original owners who view them as useless. Spare rags, empty bottles, and broken ceramic pieces no longer function as clothing, beverage containers, or pottery. But cultural creators able to imagine multiple uses for the same object give them new life through imaginative repositioning. Similarly, musical improvisers con-stantly explore the hidden possibilities inside conventional notes, chords, harmonics, and rhythms (Thompson, 1984, p.158). The unpredictable creativity of improvisation that can forge new relationships among different sounds in music serves as an alternative academy teaching people ways of envisioning and enacting new relationships among different people (Small, 1998, p.63).

An ethics of co-creation emerges out of the aptitude for improvisation (Fischlin, Heble, and Lipsitz, 2013). Johnny Otis learned about this many times during his years as a working musician. In the mid-1940s, for instance, his band's lead alto saxophone player, Rene Bloch, suggested that Otis add Earle Hagen's composition "Harlem Nocturne" to their ensemble's repertoire. Bloch had enjoyed the opportunity the song offered for a saxophone solo when he played it previously with a band in Seattle, so he suggested that Otis place the Ray Noble arrangement of the tune in the band's "book." Initially, Otis thought that Bloch had brought him a "Mickey Mouse arrangement of a Mickey Mouse song." But as he practised the number with his orchestra, Otis thought that if he slowed down the pace of the song and added blues chords to the arrangement, the number might work for his group. One night when the band played the song live at the Club Alabam on Central Avenue, however, something unexpected happened. When the music started, many of the chorus girls and shake dancers in the room flocked to the stage and surrounded the musicians. They swayed slowly and sensuously to the song. Following their lead, Otis slowed down the rhythm even more to match the moves of the dancers. Couples in the audience quickly got up to move to the slow beat. Soon, Johnny Otis's version of "Harlem Nocturne" became a national hit record and the basis for many subsequent covers of the song by other artists (Bloch, 1995, p.45; Robinson, 1997). To this day, the version of "Harlem

Nocturne" that popular music listeners know is the one improvised in the Club Alabam by the dancers, Otis, and Bloch, not the original composition by Hagen or the arrangement by Noble.

Otis recognised that improvisational co-creation also could draw on extra-musical experiences and interactions. Looking back in 1993 on his more than fifty years as a working musician, Otis recalled that he never once had to tell his horn players how to phrase a passage, that he never had to instruct a singer how to phrase a song. Once he provided them with the basic musical elements, the band members improvised on the basis of what they had learned from their lives in vibrant Black communities. Their art, Otis explained (1993), came from listening and watching "the African American way of life" which he encapsulated as:

> The way Mama cooked, the Black English grandmother and grandfather spoke, the way Daddy disciplined the kids—the emphasis on spiritual values, the way Reverend Jones preached, the way Sister Williams sang in the choir, the way the old brother down the street played the slide guitar and crooned the blues, the very special way the people danced, walked, laughed, cried, joked, got happy, shouted in church.
>
> (Otis, 1993, 117)

An emphasis on improvisation enables us to revise the terms of listening and learning. Most contemporary forms of musical instruction inhibit our ability to understand listening as an active social practice. In the western art music tradition—and in much of commercial culture—the audience is thought of as a passive entity that watches, hears, and applauds a performance, but does not do anything to create it. Yet listening should not be so narrowly conceived. Musicians listen as well as play. They craft their notes, chords, and rhythms in response to what they hear from other musicians, in reply to the demeanour of people sitting in auditorium seats, and in reaction to the movements of dancers. Even when music is recorded, it is played and engineered differently for different contexts. Music that is expected to be played on stereo systems or iPods gets engineered differently from music intended for play on car radios or boom boxes. The physical and social spaces musicians share as listeners as well as players turn performances into events that last long after the last note has been played. Under some circumstances, shared sounds can call communities into being and serve as markers of new social identities and social relations.[1] It was a long history of previous listening that enabled gospel singer Marion Williams to create phrases, melodies, and rhythms that seemed to arise solely out of the moment, that frequently brought tears to the eyes of the musicians in Ray Charles's band when they heard his plaintive vocal and blues oriented instrumentals, that made Horace Tapscott realise that he liked playing for community audiences so much that he never really felt comfortable playing until he heard a baby cry (Heilbut, 1992, p.222; Love, 1997, p.160; Isoardi, 2006, p.268).

The dynamic and quintessentially social nature of listening is often occluded by the traditions of cultural creation, curation, evaluation, and conservation in the west. These traditions teach people to privilege the created artifact over the creative act, to conceive of music as an object rather than an activity (Small, 1998, p.12–13). This objectification and reification of live cultural processes into static cultural objects produces what Jon Cruz (1999, p.22) calls "disengaged engagement," an approach to listening that detaches the cultural aesthetics of musical pieces from the larger social, cultural, and political contexts from which they emerge and to which they speak. Yet when reflecting on their actual practices, musicians and audiences often enact a hidden transcript that recognises the difference between disengaged hearing and active and creative listening.[2] For example, jazz bass player Ira Coleman identifies working with—and listening to—vocalists as an important part of his development as a musician. He explains that a singer's range can impose limits on what can be played on the bass, sometimes compelling the accompanist to learn to play in difficult keys and therefore develop new command of the instrument (Bauer, 2003). In this way, obstacles become opportunities. For Miles Davis, listening to other musicians in an ensemble and anticipating audience reception opened up opportunities for strategic silences that could make what was *not* played as important as what was played. "I always listen to what I can leave out," he explained (Pareles, 1991). A similar sense of creative omission guided Max Roach's theory of the importance of silences to a drummer. "Even though I can just play constantly and never stop," he explained in one interview, "the silence is just as important as the sound—silence separates sounds and makes them a language, the way we use words" (Berman and Wah Lee, 1991, p.23).

Rock 'n' roll guitarist Keith Richards found that his experiences as music listener shaped his approach to his instrument. "One of the first lessons I learned with guitar playing," he wrote in his autobiography:

> was that none of these guys were actually playing straight chords. There's a throw-in, a flick-back. Nothing's ever a straight major. It's an amalgamation, a mangling and a dangling and a tangling thing. There is no 'properly.' There's just how you feel about it. Feel your way around it. It's a dirty world down here. Mostly I've found, playing instruments, that I actually want to be playing something that should be played by another instrument. I find myself trying to play horn lines all the time on the guitar. When I was learning how to do these songs, I learned there is often one note doing something that makes the whole thing work. It's usually a suspended chord. It's not a full chord, it's a mixture of chords, which I love to this day.
>
> (Richards, 2010, p.107)

Jazz alto saxophonist Preston Love also valued the unpredictable and dynamic social interactions that shaped his performances. He explained that one of the great joys of backing up the singing of Billie Holiday came from her interactions with the band. She told the musicians that their playing inspired her to sing better. Love remembered occasions during performances when Holiday would move away from the microphone and back up to the band so she could tell him over her shoulder "Junior, you sure are singing back there on that alto" (Love, 1997, p.219).

Learning to listen enables musicians to make singular contributions as improvising performers. As a young girl singing in the alto section of church choirs, Betty Carter had few opportunities to sing solo parts. Yet section singing helped form her approach to her subsequent efforts as a solo singer because it advanced her ability to listen to the harmonic relationships in a song. Section singing gave her the discipline needed to resist a drift to the melody line. These practices and the talents they cultivated helped Carter know what she wanted from her accompanists when she went on to become a skilled and innovative jazz singer (Bauer, 2003, p.12). Saxophonist Charlie Parker once gave Walter Bishop Jr a valuable lesson in listening when he advised the pianist to learn the lyrics of the songs they played as instrumentalists "so you know what you're saying when you solo" (qtd. in Bauer, 2003, p.29).

Musicians often recall their experiences and tastes as listeners as ways of explaining their later development as players. Alto saxophonist Preston Love remembered how a particular kind of listening launched his career as a section player in big bands. Love's brother brought home some recordings by the Count Basie Orchestra and played them for him. Love savored the powerful swing rhythms and the infectious melodies played by the musicians, but one sound particularly stood out for him. The alto saxophone sounded strident and incisive on the fast numbers but pretty and elegant on the slow ones. Even when the reed section played unison notes, the tones played by one alto sax player could be heard distinctly. Enraptured by the sound he heard, Love discovered that the musician producing it was Earle Warren. He set out on a quest to learn all he could about this artist and the music that he made. Love borrowed his brother's saxophone and tried to play like his hero. A little more than a decade later, Preston Love temporarily took Earle Warren's chair in the reed section of the Basie Orchestra when a stomach ailment compelled Warren to leave a tour (Love, 1997, p.23).

Keith Richards similarly credits his listening habits as a novice fan of rock 'n' roll music for his advanced understanding of accompaniment and ensemble playing later in life. "As impressed as I was with Elvis," Richards remembers:

> I was even more impressed by Scotty Moore and the band. It was the same with Ricky Nelson. I never bought a Ricky Nelson record, I bought a James Burton record. It was the bands behind them that impressed me as much as the front men ... I was just impressed by ensemble playing. It was how guys interacted with one another, natural exuberance and seemingly effortless delivery.
>
> (Richards, 2010, p.60)

The interactive and dialogic potentials of listening can be undermined by instrumental and monologic practices of hearing. Jon Cruz (1999, p.59) presents a useful typology that makes distinctions among incidental hearing, instrumental hearing, and pathos oriented hearing. Incidental hearing reduces music to mere noise on the assumption that there is nothing to be learned from unintentional encounters with disorganised sounds. Instrumental hearing transforms music into an asset for the listener, but ignores the origins, evolution, and intent of the sound. Pathos oriented hearing utilises music as raw material for producing ethno-sympathy and ethno-pity, as a way of making the listener feel generous, intelligent, and moral by deigning to enjoy music made by inferiors. As Cruz shows in his extensive inquiry into the promotion of Black folk forms by putatively sympathetic whites, these forms of hearing without listening can do terrible harm. When the lambs are crying for the Lord to come by, hearing them will not help, but listening to them will.

Johnny Otis learned how to listen to the lambs from long experience with different forms of Afro-diasporic improvisation, from people who could not afford to let their sorrow slip into despair. Centuries of spirit-crushing slavery, segregation, and subordination required Black people to develop deep reservoirs of resilience and creativity. The pathology of white supremacy could not be defeated once and for all, but instead had to be confronted over and over again, day after day, year after year. The work and willingness needed for survival had to be cultivated continuously. As Christopher Small (1998, p.86) explains, improvisational music helped equip individuals for this ceaseless struggle by requiring them to communicate and work together. He explains that the African ability to adapt and endure conflict and contradictions rested on the idea "that the supreme value lies in the preservation of the community; without a community for support the individual is helpless, while with it he or she is invincible" (Small, 1998, p.86). That collective spirit permeated Otis's book, so much so that *Listen to the Lambs* was itself an exercise in communal improvisation. Its author turned over nearly a quarter of the book's pages directly to community residents so that they could bear witness to the things they observed during the rebellion. These different voices disrupted the narrative of the book and gave it an uneven and cacophonous tone that no doubt frustrated some readers. At the same time, however, the interplay of voices in *Listen to the Lambs* filled it with energy and authority, revealing more in concert than any of the individual stories could have shown in isolation. *Listen to the Lambs* was not just a book, but also an improvisational act designed to interrupt business as usual in the hope of imbuing the world with an enhanced ability to recognise its repressed potential.

In a world where cultural practice is often reduced to mere recreation and ornamentation of otherwise unhappy lives, improvisation can serve as the source of new epistemologies and ontologies. We cannot create a radically different future unless we learn to think differently about futurity. As James Baldwin (2011, pp.47–49) explains, our society encourages us to savour plots when what we really need are stories. Plots have beginnings, middles, and ends. They lead to narrative and ideological closure. They promote the pursuit of permanent solutions that close down possibilities. Stories, on the other hand, leave us with questions, obligations, and aspirations. They teach that every resolution is temporary, that what we have been taught to think of as the top of the mountain is only another plateau. The western art tradition stokes desires for closure. Audiences break into tumultuous applause at the end of a symphony, motion picture, or play. They are relieved that their journey is over. The Afro-diasporic tradition, on the other hand, imbues artists and audiences with a passion for new dialogues and challenges that broaden horizons and intensify aspirations.

Johnny Otis did not succeed in getting the nation and the world to listen to the lambs in the wake of the Watts Riots. We have all paid a terrible price for that failure. But the Afro-diasporic tradition teaches us that just as jazz has no final chord, social life entails no once and for all failures or successes. The struggle to keep sorrow from degenerating into despair must be waged over and over again, day after day, year after year. Improvisation can be an alternative academy crucial to preparing ourselves for that struggle. Today, in many places around the world, places close to home and far away, the lambs are still crying for the Lord to come by. It is up to us to learn how to listen to them.

Notes

1 See for example Frantz Fanon's description of how nationalist movements often emerge in culture before they take political form in *The Wretched of the Earth* (New York: Grove Press, 1968), 243.
2 See for example Susan Crafts, Daniel Cavicchi, and Charles Keil (1993), *My Music: Explorations of Music in Daily Life* and Deborah Wong (2001), "Finding an Asian American Audience: The Problem of Listening."

Works Cited

Baldwin, J., 2011. *The Devil Finds Work*. New York: Vintage.
Bauer, W. R., 2003. *Open the Door: The Life and Music of Betty Carter*. Ann Arbor, MI: University of Michigan Press.
Berman, M., and Wah Lee, S., 1991. Sticking Power. *Los Angeles Times*, 15 Sep., p.23.
Bloch, R., 1995. Interviewed by Steven Isoardi. Central Avenue Sounds Oral History Collection, Record ID 4230389, UCLA Libraries and Collections.

Crafts, S., Cavicchi, D., and Keil, C., 1993. *My Music: Explorations of Music in Daily Life*. Hanover, CT: Wesleyan University Press/University Press of New England.

Cruz, J., 1999. *Culture on the Margins: The Black Spiritual and the Rise of American Cultural Interpretation*. Princeton, NJ: Princeton University Press.

Fanon, F., 1968. *The Wretched of the Earth*. New York: Grove Press.

Fischlin, D., Heble, A., and Lipsitz, G., 2013. *The Fierce Urgency of Now: Improvisation, Rights, and the Ethics of Cocreation*. Durham, NC: Duke University Press.

Heilbut, A., 1992. *The Gospel Sound: Good News and Bad Times*. New York: Limelight Editions.

Isoardi, S. L., 2006. *The Dark Tree: Jazz and the Community Arts in Los Angeles*. Berkeley, CA: University of California Press.

Lipsitz, G., 2010. *Midnight at the Barrelhouse: The Johnny Otis Story*. Minneapolis, MN: University of Minnesota Press.

Love, P., 1997. *A Thousand Honey Creeks Later: My Life in Music from Basie to Motown and Beyond*. Hanover, CT: Wesleyan University Press/University Press of New England.

Moten, F., 2003. *In the Break: The Aesthetics of the Black Radical Tradition*. Minneapolis, MN: University of Minnesota Press.

Otis, J., 1993. *Upside Your Head! Rhythm and Blues on Central Avenue*. Hanover, CT: Wesleyan University Press/University Press of New England.

———, 2009. *Listen to the Lambs*. Minneapolis, MN: University of Minnesota Press.

Pareles, J., 1991. Miles Davis, Trumpeter, Dies: Jazz Genius, 65, Defined Cool. *New York Times*, 29 Sep. Available at: www.nytimes.com/1991/09/29/nyregion/miles-davis-trumpeter-dies-jazz-genius-65-defined-cool.html.

Richards, K., 2010. *Life* (with James Fox). New York: Black Bay Books.

Robinson, B., 1997. Preacher Man. *Pacific Sun*, 9–15 Apr. p.14.

Small, C., 1998. *Music of the Common Tongue: Survival and Celebration in African American Music*. Hanover, CT: Wesleyan University Press/University Press of New England.

Thompson, R. F., 1984. *The Flash of the Spirit: African & Afro-American Art & Philosophy*. New York: Vintage.

Wong, D., 2001. Finding an Asian American Audience: The Problem of Listening. *American Music*, 19, pp.365–84.

2   On Listening

Jean-Luc Nancy

Translated by Charlotte Mandell

Born in Caudéran, France, in 1940, Jean-Luc Nancy has published works on Lacan, Kant, Hegel, Descartes, and Heidegger. As a professor in philosophy, he worked extensively with the French Ministry of External Affairs in delegations to Eastern Europe, Great Britain, and the USA. His continued productiveness as a writer, and the translation of his work overseas, contributed to a growing international reputation. In his forties, Nancy underwent a heart transplant and battled cancer, but continued to write. He published an account of his experience, *L'intrus* (*The Intruder*), which in 2004 was adapted by Claire Denis into a film. His best-known book is *La communauté désoeuvrée* (*The Inoperative Community*, 1991), which explores themes he continues in *Le sens du monde* (*The Sense of the World*, 1993). In *Être singulier pluriel* (*Being Singular Plural*, 2000) Nancy questions the concept of a "we," indeed of plurality itself. "On Listening" celebrates, among other things, the broader dissemination of musical models, of an internationalised listening, as a social practice leading towards "a musical-becoming of sensibility and a global-becoming of musicality ... the creation of a global sonorous space or scene whose extraordinarily mixed nature ... has no real equivalent in other domains."

Key words: pedagogy; deep listening; France

[...] "To be all ears" [*être à l'écoute,* to be listening] today forms an expression that belongs to a register of philanthropic oversensitivity, where condescension resounds alongside good intentions; thus it often has a pious ring to it. Hence, for example, the set phrases "to be in tune with the young, with the neighborhood, with the world," and so on. But here I want to understand it in other registers, in completely different tonalities, and first of all in an ontological tonality: What does it mean for a being to be immersed entirely in listening, formed by listening or in listening, listening with all his being?

There is no better way to do this than to look beyond present usages. After it had designated a person who listens (who spies), the word *écoute* came to designate a place where one could listen in secret. *Être aux écoutes*, "to listen in, to eavesdrop," consisted first in being in a concealed place where you could surprise a conversation or a confession. *Être à l'écoute*, "to be tuned in, to be listening," was in the vocabulary of military espionage before it returned, through broadcasting, to the public space, while still remaining, in the context of the telephone, an affair of confidences or stolen secrets. So one aspect of my question will be: What secret is at stake when one truly *listens*, that is, when one tries to capture or surprise the sonority rather than the message? What secret is yielded—hence also made public—when we listen to a voice, an instrument, or a sound just for itself?

And the other, indissociable aspect will be: What does *to be* listening, *to be* all ears, as one would say, "to be in the world," mean? What does it mean to exist according to listening, for it and through it, what part of experience and truth is put into play? What is at play in listening, what resonates in it, what is the tone of listening or its timbre? Is even listening itself sonorous?

The conditions of this double interrogation refer first of all simply to the meaning of the verb *écouter*, "to listen." Consequently, to that kernel of meaning where the use of a sensory organ (hearing, the ear, *auris*, a word that gives the first part of the verb *auscultare*, "to lend an ear," "to listen attentively," from which *écouter*, "to listen," comes) and a tension, an intention, and an attention, which the second part of the term marks, are combined.[1] To listen is *tendre l'oreille*—literally, to stretch the ear—an expression that evokes a singular mobility, among the sensory apparatuses, of the pinna of the ear[2]—it is an intensification and a concern, a curiosity or an anxiety.

Every sensory register thus bears with it both its simple nature and its tense, attentive, or anxious state: seeing and looking, smelling and sniffing or scenting, tasting and savoring, touching and feeling or palpating, hearing and listening.

This last pair, however, the auditive pair, has a special relationship with *sense* in the intellectual or intelligible acceptance of the word (with "perceived meaning" [*sens sensé*], if you like, as opposed to "perceiving sense" [*sens sensible*]). *Entendre*, "to hear," also means *comprendre*, "to understand,"[3] as if "hearing" were above all "hearing say" (rather than "hearing sound"), or rather, as if in all "hearing" there had to be a "hearing say," regardless of whether the sound perceived was a word or not. But even that might be reversible: in all saying (and I mean in all discourse, in the whole chain of meaning) there is hearing, and in hearing itself, at the very bottom of it, a listening. Which means: perhaps it is necessary that sense not be content to make sense (or to be *logos*), but that it want also to resound. My whole proposal will revolve around such a fundamental resonance, even around a resonance as a foundation, as a first or last profundity of "sense" itself (or of truth).

If "to hear" is to understand the sense (either in the so-called figurative sense, or in the so-called proper sense: to hear a siren, a bird, or a drum is already each time to understand at least the rough outline of a situation, a context if not a text), to listen is to be straining toward a possible meaning, and consequently one that is not immediately accessible.[4]

We listen to someone who is giving a speech we want to understand, or else we listen to what can arise from silence and provide a signal or a sign, or else we listen to what is called "music."[5] In the case of these first two examples, one can say, at least to simplify (if you forget voices, timbres), that listening strains toward a present sense beyond sound. In the latter case, that of music, it is from sound itself that sense is offered to auscultation. In one case, sound has a propensity to disappear; in the other case, sense has a propensity to become sound. But here there are only two tendencies, precisely, and listening aims at—or is aroused by—the one where sound and sense mix together and resonate in each other, or through each other. (Which signifies that—and here again, in a tendential way—if, on the one hand, sense is sought in sound, on the other hand, sound, resonance, is also looked for in sense.)

When he was six years old, Stravinsky listened to a mute peasant who produced unusual sounds with his arms, which the future musician tried to reproduce: he was looking for a different voice, one more or less vocal than the one that comes from the mouth; another sound for another sense than the one that is spoken. A meaning with frontiers or one on the fringes of meaning, to paraphrase Charles Rosen.[6] To be listening is always to be on the edge of meaning, or in an edgy meaning of extremity, and as if the sound were precisely nothing else than this edge, this fringe, this margin—at least the sound that is musically listened to, that is gathered and scrutinized for itself, not, however, as an acoustic phenomenon (or not merely as one) but as a resonant meaning, a meaning whose *sense* is supposed to be found in resonance, and only in resonance.[7]

But what can be the shared space of meaning and sound? Meaning consists in a reference [*renvoi*]. In fact, it is made of a totality of referrals: from a sign to a thing, from a state of things to a quality, from a subject to another subject or to itself, all simultaneously. Sound is also made of referrals: it spreads in space,[8] where it resounds while still resounding "in me," as we say (we will return to this "inside" of the subject; we will return to nothing but that). In the external or internal space, it resounds, that is, it re-emits itself while still actually "sounding," which is already "re-sounding" since that's nothing else but referring back to itself. To sound is to vibrate in itself or by itself: it is not only, for the sonorous body,[9] to emit a sound, but it is also to stretch out, to carry itself and be resolved into vibrations that both return it to itself and place it outside itself.[10]

Indeed, as we have known since Aristotle, sensing [*sentir*] (*aisthesis*) is always a perception [*ressentir*], that is, a feeling oneself-feel [*se sentir-sentir*]: or, if you prefer, sensing is a subject, or it does not sense. But it is perhaps in the sonorous register that this reflected structure is most obviously manifest,[11] and in any case offers itself as open structure, spaced and spacing (resonance chamber, acoustic space,[12] the distancing of a repeat [*rentoi*]), at the same time as an intersection, mixture, covering up in the referral [*rentoi*] of the perceptible with the perceived as well as with the other senses.

One can say, then, at least, that meaning and sound share the space of a referral, in which at the same time they refer to each other, and that, in a very general way, this space can be defined as the space of a *self*, a subject. A *self* is nothing other than a form or function of referral: a *self* is made of a relationship *to* self, or of a presence *to* self, which is nothing other than the mutual referral between a perceptible individuation and an intelligible identity (not just the individual in the current sense of the word, but in him the singular occurrences of a state, a tension, or, precisely, a "sense")—this referral itself would have to be infinite, and the point or occurrence of a *subject* in the substantial sense would have never taken place except in the referral, thus in spacing and resonance, at the very most as the dimensionless point of the *re*-of this resonance: the repetition where the sound is amplified and spreads, as well as the turning back [*rebroussement*] where the echo is made by making itself heard. A subject *feels*:[13] that is his characteristic and his definition. This means that he hears (himself), sees (himself), touches (himself), tastes (himself), and so on, and that he thinks himself or represents himself, approaches himself and strays from himself, and thus always feels himself feeling a "self" that escapes [*s'éch-appe*] or hides [*se retranche*] as long as it resounds elsewhere as it does in itself, in a world and in the other.

To be listening will always, then, be to be straining toward or in an approach to the self (one should say, in a pathological manner, *a fit of self*: isn't [sonorous] sense first of all, every time, a *crisis of self*?).[14]

Approach to the self: neither to a proper self (I), nor to the self of an other, but to the form or structure of *self* as such, that is to say, to the form, structure, and movement of an infinite referral [*renvoi*], since it refers to something (itself) that is nothing outside of the referral. When one is listening, one is on the lookout for a subject, something (itself) that identifies *itself* by resonating from self to self, in itself and for itself, hence outside of itself, at once the same as and other than itself, one in the echo of the other, and this echo is like the very sound of its sense.[15] But the sound of sense is how it refers to *itself* or how it *sends back to itself* [s'envoie] or *addresses itself,* and thus how it makes sense.

But here it is a question of being on the watch [*être aux aguets*] for a way that is precisely not that of a *watch* [guet] in the sense of a visual surveillance.[16] The sonorous here makes clear its singularity in relation to the optical register, where the relationship to the intelligible as a *theoretical* relationship (*theoretical* is linked, in Greek, to seeing) is more manifestly, if we can use this word, in play.[17] In terms of the gaze, the subject is referred back to itself as object. In terms of listening, it is, in a way, to itself that the subject refers or refers back. Thus, in a certain way there is no relationship between the two. A writer notes: "I can hear what I see: a piano, or some leaves stirred by the wind. But I can never see what I hear. Between sight and hearing there is no reciprocity."[18] In the same way, I would say that music floats around painting much more than painting is outlined around music. Or, in semi-Lacanian terms, the visual is on the side of an imaginary capture (which does not imply that it is reduced to that), while the sonorous is on the side of a symbolic referral/*renvoi* (which does not imply that it exhausts its amplitude). In still other words, the visual is tendentially mimetic, and the sonorous tendentially methexic (that is, having to do with participation, sharing, or contagion), which does not mean that these tendencies do not intersect. A musician writes: "How is it that sound has such a particular impact, a capacity to affect us, which is like nothing else, and is very different from what has to do with the visual and with touch? It is a realm we still do not know."[19]

In these statements, which I adopt for my own, there is no doubt more empiricism than theoretical construction. But the challenge in a study of the senses and of perceptible qualities is necessarily the challenge of an empiricism by which one attempts a conversion of experience into an a priori condition of possibility … of the experience itself, while still running the risk of a cultural and individual relativism, if all the "senses" and all the "arts" do not always have the same distributions everywhere or the same qualities.

Still, what we are thus calling "relativism" in turn constitutes an empirical material that makes a condition of possibility for any "sensation" or for any "perception" as well as for any "culture": it is the referral of one to the other that makes both possible. The difference between cultures, the difference between the arts, and the difference between the senses are the conditions, and not the limitations, of experience in general, just as the mutual intricacy of these differences is, as well. Even more generally, one could say that *the difference in sense* (in the "perceived" [*sensé*] sense of the word) *is its condition, that is, the condition of its resonance.* But nothing is more remarkable, in this order of consideration and experience, than the history of music, more than any other artistic technique, in the course of the twentieth century: the internal transformations following Wagner, the increasing importations of references outside of music labeled "classical," the arrival of jazz and its transformations, then that of rock and all its variations up to their present hybridizations with "scholarly" music, and throughout all these phenomena the major transformation of instrumentation, down to the electronic and computer production of sounds and the remodeling of schemes of sonority (timbres, rhythms, notations), which itself is contemporaneous with the creation of a global sonorous space or scene whose extraordinarily mixed nature—popular and refined, religious and profane, old and recent, coming from all continents at once—all that has no real equivalent in other domains. A musical-becoming of sensibility and a global-becoming of musicality have occurred, whose historiality remains to be thought about, all the more so since it is contemporaneous with an expansion of the image whose extent does not correspond to equivalent transformations in the perceptible realm.

To be listening is thus to enter into tension and to be on the lookout for a relation to self: *not,* it should be emphasized, a relationship to "me" (the supposedly given subject), or to the "self" of the other (the speaker, the musician, also supposedly given, with his subjectivity), but to the *relationship in self,* so to speak, as it forms a "self" or a "to itself" in general, and if something like that ever does reach the end of its formation. Consequently, listening is passing over to the register of presence to self, it being understood that the "self" is precisely nothing available (substantial or subsistent) to which one can be "present," but precisely the resonance of a return [*renvoi*].[20] For this reason, listening—the opening stretched toward the register of the sonorous, then to its musical amplification and composition—can and must appear to us not as a metaphor for access to self, but as the reality of this access, a reality consequently indissociably "mine" and "other," "singular" and "plural," as much as it is "material" and "spiritual" and "signifying" and "a-signifying."[21]

This presence is thus not the position of a being-present: it is precisely not that. It is presence in the sense of an "in the presence of" that, itself, is not an "in view of" or a "vis-à-vis." It is an "in the presence of" that does not let itself be objectified or projected outward. That is why it is first of all presence in the sense of a *present* that is not a being (at least not in the intransitive, stable, consistent sense of the word),[22] but rather a *coming* and a *passing,* an *extending* and a *penetrating.* Sound essentially comes and expands, or is deferred and transferred. Its present is thus not the instant of philosophico-scientific time either, the point of no dimension, the strict negativity in which that mathematical time has always consisted. But sonorous time takes place immediately according to a completely different dimension, which is not that of simple succession (corollary of the negative instant). It is a present in waves on a swell, not in a point on a line; it is a time that opens up, that is hollowed out, that is enlarged or ramified, that envelops or separates, that becomes or is turned into a loop, that stretches out or contracts, and so on.

The sonorous present is the result of space-time: it spreads through space, or rather it opens a space that is its own, the very spreading out of its resonance, its expansion and its reverberation. This space is immediately omni-dimensional and transversate through all spaces: the expansion of sound through obstacles, its property of penetration and ubiquity, has always been noted.[23]

Sound has no hidden face;[24] it is all in front, in back, and outside inside, *inside-out* in relation to the most general logic of presence as appearing, as phenomenality or as manifestation, and thus as the visible face of a presence subsisting in self. Something of the theoretical and intentional scheme tuned to optics vacillates around it. To listen is to enter that spatiality by which, *at the same time,* I am penetrated, for it opens up in me as well as around me, and from me as well as toward me: it opens me inside me as well as outside, and it is through such a double, quadruple, or sextuple opening that a "self" can take place.[25] To be listening is to be *at the same time* outside and inside, to be open *from* without and *from* within, hence from one to the other and from one in the other. Listening thus forms the perceptible singularity that hears in the most ostensive way the perceptible or sensitive (*aisthetic*) condition as such: the sharing of an inside/outside, division and participation, de-connection and contagion. "Here, time becomes space," is sung in Wagner's *Parsifal.*[26]

In this open and above all opening presence, in acoustic spreading and expansion, listening takes place *at the same time* as the sonorous event,[27] an arrangement that is clearly distinct from that of vision (for which, incidentally, there is no visual or luminous "event" either, in an entirely identical meaning of the word: visual presence is already there, available, before I see it, whereas sonorous presence *arrives*—it entails an *attack,* as musicians and acousticians say). And animal bodies, in general—the human body, in particular—are not constructed to interrupt at their leisure the sonorous arrival, as has often been noted. "The ears don't have eyelids" is an old theme that is often repeated.[28] Moreover, the sound that penetrates through the ear propagates throughout the entire body something of its effects, which could not be said to occur in the same way with the visual signal. And if we note also that "one who emits a sound hears the sound he emits," one emphasizes that animal sonorous emission is necessarily also (here again, most often) its own reception.

> A *sound* makes into a semi-presence the whole system of *sounds*—and that is what primitively distinguishes *sound* from *noise. Noise* gives ideas of the causes that produce it, dispositions of action, reflexes—but not a state of imminence of an intrinsic family of sensations.[29]

In any case, as soon as it is present, the sonorous is omnipresent, and its presence is never a simple being-there or how things stand, but is always at once an advance, penetration, insistence, obsession, or possession, as well as presence "on the rebound,"[30] in a return [*renvoi*] from one element to the other, whether it be between the emitter and the receptor or in one or the other, or, finally and especially, between the sound and itself: in that between or antrum [*entre ou antre*] of sound where it is what it is by resounding according to the play of what acoustics distinguishes as its components (volume, length, intensity, attack, harmonics, partials, long-distance noises, etc.) and whose major characteristic is not to form merely the results of an abstract decomposition of the concrete phenomenon, but just as actually to *play* some against others *in* this phenomenon, in such a way that sound sounds or resounds always beyond a simple opposition between consonance and dissonance, being made of an intimate harmony and disharmony among its parts: being made, one should perhaps end by saying, *of the discordant harmony that regulates the intimate as such* ... (And without forgetting, although without being able to speak of it knowingly, the very singular role played in listening by what we call "acoustic oto-emissions" produced by the inner ear of the one who is listening: the oto- or self[*auto*]-produced sounds that come to mingle with received sounds, in order to receive them ...)

All sonorous presence is thus made of a complex of returns [*renvois*] whose binding is the resonance or "sonance" of sound, an expression that one should hear—hear and listen to—as much from the side of sound itself, or of its emission, as from the side of its reception or its listening: it is precisely from one to the other that it "sounds." Whereas visible or tactile presence occurs in a motionless "at the same time," sonorous presence is an essentially mobile "at the same time," vibrating from the come-and-go between the source and the ear, through open space,[31] the presence of presence rather than pure presence. One might say: there is the *simultaneity* of the visible and the *contemporaneity* of the audible.

This presence is thus always within return and encounter. It *returns* (refers) to *itself*, it *encounters* itself or, better, occurs against itself, both in opposition to and next to itself. It is co-presence or, again, "presence in presence," if one can say that. But insofar as it does not consist in a being-present-there, in a stable, fixed being, yet is not elsewhere or absent, it is rather in the rebound of "there" or in its setting in motion, which makes it, the sonorous place ("sonorized," one is tempted to say, plugged into sound), a place-of-its-own-self, a place *as* relation to self, as the taking place of a self, a vibrant place as the diapason of a subject or, better, as a diapason-subject. (The subject, a diapason? Each subject, a differently tuned diapason? Tuned to self—but without a known frequency?)

We should linger here for a long while on rhythm: it is nothing other than the time of time, the vibration of time itself in the stroke of a present that presents it by separating it from itself, freeing it from its simple *stanza* to make it into *scansion* (rise, raising of the foot that beats) and *cadence* (fall, passage into the pause). Thus, rhythm separates the succession of the linearity of the sequence or length of time: it bends time to give it to time itself, and it is in this way that it folds and unfolds a "self." If temporality is the dimension of the subject (ever since Saint Augustine, Kant, Husserl, and Heidegger), this is because it defines the subject as what separates *itself,* not only from the other or from the pure "there," but also from self: insofar as it waits for *itself* and retains *itself,* insofar as it desires (itself) and forgets (itself),[32] insofar as it retains, by repeating it, its own empty unity and its projected or ... ejected [*projetée, ou ... jetée*] unicity.[33]

So the sonorous place, space and place—and taking-place—*as* sonority, is not a place where the subject comes to make himself heard (like the concert hall or the studio into which the singer or instrumentalist enters); on the contrary, it is a place that becomes a subject insofar as sound resounds there (rather, mutatis mutandis, as the architectural configuration of a concert hall or a studio is engendered by the necessities and expectations of an acoustic aim). Perhaps we should thus understand the child who is born with his first cry as himself being—his being or his subjectivity—the sudden expansion of an echo chamber, a vault where what tears him away and what summons him resound at once, setting in vibration a column of air, of flesh, which sounds at its apertures: body and soul of some *one* new and unique. Someone who comes to himself by hearing him*self* cry (answering the other? calling him?), or sing, always each time, beneath each word, crying or singing, *exclaiming* as he did by coming into the world. [...]

Notes

1 The origin of *culto* is unknown; its intensive or frequentative quality, incidentally, is well vouched for.

2 As if the expression were taken from observing certain animals, like rabbits and many others, always listening and "on the lookout" ...

3 This is characteristic of certain Latin languages. *Intendere* is Latin for "tend toward." The first use in French was in the sense of *tender l'oreille* ["stretching the ear," listening]: although, in *écouter,* the ear goes toward the tension, in *entendre,* the tension wins over the ear. Moreover, it would be worthwhile to examine other associations in other languages: the Greek *akouï,* with the meanings of "understanding," "following," or "obeying"; the German *hören,* which gives us *hörchen,* "to obey"; the English *to hear,* the sense of "to learn," "to be informed of," etc.

4 Tension that, without any doubt, is in relation to the "intension" that François Nicolas speaks of in "Quand l'œuvre écoute la musique," in Peter Szendy, ed., *L'écoute* (Paris: Ircam/L'Harmattan, 2000), where the first version of the present essay was published: between the two texts, there is more than just correspondence, a remarkable counterpoint.

5 Perhaps we are permitted to consider two positions or two destinations of music (whether it's the same music or two different genres): music heard and music listened to (or, as they used to be called, background music and concert music). The analogy would be difficult to make in the domain of the plastic arts (except perhaps with decorative painting).

6 Charles Rosen. *The Frontiers of Meaning: Three Informal Lectures on Music* (New York: Hill and Wang, 1994).

7 Indeed, the same is true, formally, for the visible: to understand a piece of music or a painting is to admit or recognize the uniquely pictorial or uniquely musical meaning; at least it's to *strain* toward such a uniqueness or toward its inaccessibility, toward the characteristic of the

inappropriable. The difference is still there, and it is not merely an extrinsic different of "media": it is a difference of meaning and in meaning (and we should deploy it for all perceptible registers). What confers a particular distinction on the sonorous and the musical (without its becoming a privilege) can only emerge little by little, and no doubt with difficulty ... although nothing is clearer to us, or more immediately perceptible.

8 We'll risk saying: because of the considerable difference in speeds (or, for Einstein, in the limited nature of the speed of light), while sound spreads, light is instantaneous: the result of this is a quality of presence of the visual distinct from the coming-and-going quality unique to the sonorous.

9 Which is always at once the body that resounds and my body as a listener where that resounds, or that resounds with it.

10 That, in fact, is the perceptible condition in general: sounding operates as "gleaming" or "smelling" in the sense of emitting a smell, or else as the "palpating" of touching (palpating, palpitating—*palper*, *palpiter*: a small, repeated movement). Each sense is both an example and a differencing in such a "vibrating (itself)," and all senses vibrate among themselves, some against others and some with others, including the sense of meaning [*sens sensé*] ... Which we still have to ... understand. (How many, incidentally, senses there are, or whether they are actually uncountable, is another question.) But, at the same time, we still have to discern how each perceptible system makes a different model and resonance for all the others ... We'll note here for the moment how much sonorous amplification and resonance play a determining role (which it may not be possible to transpose exactly onto the visual plane) in the formation of music and of its instruments, as André Schaeffner points out in his *Origine des instruments de musique* (Paris: Mouton, 1968; 2nd ed., Paris, École des hautes études en sciences sociales, 1994; I thank Peter Szendy, who helped me find this work): "In every case [treatment of the voice or fabrication of instruments by amplification or alteration of sounds] it is much less a question of 'imitating' than of surpassing something—the already known, the ordinary, the relatively moderate, the natural. Hence the extraordinary inventions, a propensity for acoustic monstrosities that would perplex physicists" (25).

11 Once it is agreed that touching gives the general structure or fundamental note of self-sensing [*se sentir*]: in a way, every sense touches itself by sensing (and touches the other senses). At the same time, every perceptible mode or register exposes one of the aspects of "touching (itself)," separation or conjunction, presence or absence, penetration or retraction, etc. The "singular plural" structure and dynamics of all the senses, their way of being precisely "together" and touching themselves while still distinguishing themselves, would be the subject of another study. Here, I am only asking that we never lose sight of the fact that nothing is said of the sonorous that must not also be true "for" the other registers as well as "against" them, "next to" as well as in opposition, in a complementarity and in an incompatibility that are inextricable from each other as well as from the very meaning of perceived sense [*sens sensé*] ... (This text was written and published in its first version before Jacques Derrida published *Le toucher, Jean-Luc Nancy* [Paris: Galilée, 2000], translated as *On Touching: Jean-Luc Nancy*, trans. Christine Irizarry [Stanford: Stanford University Press, 2005].)

12 *Espaces acoustiques* is the title of a composition by Gérard Grisey, who explores the realms of sonorities and their amplifications or intensifications.

13 *Se sentir*, a reflexive verb, literally "to feel oneself," means "to feel, to sense." English has no equivalent for the reflexive form of this verb.—Trans.

14 The pun here is on the word *accès*, "access, approach," which in a phrase like *un accès de colère* means "a fit of anger," or in *un accès de tristesse*, a wave of sadness. Nancy is contrasting *un accès au soi* ("an approach to the self") with *un accès de soi*, translated here as "a fit of self."—Trans.

15 "Echo of the subject": first resonance of a title by Philippe Lacoue-Labarthe to which I will refer later on.

16 This is the not the exclusive characteristic of the word *guet* (whose origin is in the direction of awakening, vigilance), but it is revealing that it is linked to surveillance more spontaneously in a culture where recognition of forms dominates ...

17 Among a hundred different possible distributions and combinations of the "senses," I can, for my argument, outline this one: the visual (and the gustative) in relationship to *presence*, the auditory (and olfactory) in relationship to the *sign* (and the tactile beyond them both). Or else, two Greek examples of brilliance or glory: the visual, *doxa*, appearance in keeping with an

expectation; and the acoustic, *kleos,* renown spread by word. But in this way, we will in any case have said nothing about the other senses (movement, tension, time, magnetism ...).

18 Michelle Grangaud, *État civil* (Paris: P.O.L., 1999).

19 Pascale Criton, interview with Omer Corlaix, in *Pascale Criton: Les univers microtempérés* (Champigny-sur-Marne: Ensemble 2e2m, 1999), 26. On the mimetic comprehension of music and its issues, see Philippe Lacoue-Labarthe, "L'écho du sujet," to which I will have other occasions to refer (Philippe Lacoue-Labarthe, *Le sujet de la philosophie* [Paris: Aubier-Flammarion, 1979]; *Typography: Mimesis, Philosophy, Politics,* ed. Christopher Fynsk, introd. Jacques Derrida [1989; rpt. Stanford: Stanford University Press, 1998]). In fact, I am pursuing here what the declared intention of that text was: to penetrate just a little the "overwhelming power" (294 in the French, 203 in the English) of music, or to go back to the "ante-musical," where "the self / detects the sound of a voice that doubles its own," in the words of Wallace Stevens (from "The Woman That Had More Babies than That," *Opus Posthumous*) with which this text ends. I am concerned only with the resonance of such a voice, prolonging its reverberation into the thinking of Lacoue-Labarthe (isn't his name already echoing itself? La ... La ... : he hears me, he understands me ...).

20 In speaking of "presence to self," one obviously places oneself where Jacques Derrida located the heart of his undertaking, principally starting from *La voix et le phénomène* (Paris: Presses Universitaires de France, 1967; translated as *Speech and Phenomena,* trans. and introd. David B. Allison [Evanston, Ill: Northwestern University Press, 1973]). In fact, one could reopen here the whole *chantier* ["construction site": there is a play on words here, since the word *chant,* or "song," is contained in *chantier*—Trans.] of this "voice": demonstrating that its sonority and its musicality come back to making *différance* "itself" resonate differently. But one should also quite simply remark that the philosophical privilege accorded by Husserl, after many others, to the silent resonance of a voice, as subject of the subject himself, is certainly not foreign (even by reversal) to the singular quality of sonorous penetration and emotion. [...]

21 Hearing and the sonorous do not, however, win from this a privilege in the strict sense of the term, although they draw from it a remarkable particularity. In a sense—and this bears repeating—all perceptible registers make up this approach to "self" (which is also to say, to "sense"). But the fact that they are many—and without any possible totalizing—marks this same approach, at once, of an internal diffraction, which perhaps in turn lets itself be analyzed in terms of repeats [*renvois*], echoes, resonances, and also rhythms. One would have to prolong this analysis elsewhere, which also branches out, as we see, to an analysis of the plurality of the arts (cf. Jean-Luc Nancy, *Les muses* [Paris: Galilée, new enlarged edition, 2001], esp. "Les arts se font les uns contre les autres").

22 For it is suitable to reserve the possibility, demanded by Heidegger, of a transitivity of the verb *to be.*

23 Cf. esp. Erwin Strauss, *Le sens des sens,* trans. G. Thines and J. P. Legrand (Grenoble: Jérôme Millon, 1989), 602 ff.

24 Cf. "Musique" in Jean-Luc Nancy, *Le sens du monde* (Paris: Galilée, 1993), 135.

25 Despite proximities, it would not be possible to apply completely such a description to the other modes of perceptible penetration, which are smell and taste, and even less to luminous penetration.

26 Act 1, scene 1, Gurnemanz, "Du siehst, mein Sohn, / zum Raum wird hier die Zeit [You see, my son, / here time becomes space]," when the scene shifts from outside the forest to inside the Grail Hall, with a great orchestral swell in which the major themes of the work return.

27 Cf. Strauss, *Le sens des sens.* See also, in the paper by Michel Chion that I heard at the Ircam conference, the themes of the impossibility of a *recoil* or a *coming closer* of the sonorous subject, as opposed to the visible subject, or the impossibility of an *overall view* as soon as the sonorous subject has lasted a certain amount of time.

28 In these exact words, by Pascal Quignard, *La haine de la musique* (Paris: Calmann-Lévy, 1996), 107.

29 Paul Valéry, *Cahiers II* (Paris: Gallimard, 1974), 974.

30 Ibid., 68.

31 Or, to insist again on the singular community of "senses": the "sonorous" dimension is the dimension of the dynamics of a come-and-go, manifest also, but differently, in visual or tactile intensity—the "visual" dimension would be that of the obviousness of the aspect or form; the

"tactile" dimension, that of the impression of the texture, each manifesting just as much, but differently, in a certain intensity or modality of the others.

32 One can support this rhythmic constitution of the "self" more precisely with Nicolas Abraham, *Rythmes* (Paris: Flammarion, 1999; translated as *Rhythms: On the Work, Translation, and Psychoanalysis*, trans. Benjamin Thigpen and Nicholas T. Rand [Stanford: Stanford University Press, 1995]).

33 Cf. the analyses of primary retention and of the Kantian "I" that Bernard Stiegler carries out in *La technique et le temps, 3: Le temps du cinéma et la question du mal-être* (Paris: Galilée, 2001).

3 Improvisation

Jacques Lecoq

Translated by David Bradby

"Rhythm is at the root of everything, like a mystery." Born in Paris, Jacques Pierre Lecoq (1921–99) came to theatre through a boyhood interest in sports, especially gymnastics. He taught physical education before forming his own drama group and then joining Jean Dasté's Comédiens de Grenoble, where he was introduced to the work of Jacques Copeau, who had revolutionised French theatre earlier in the century. During his work with the Comédiens, and with the Commedia dell'arte in Italy, Lecoq confirmed his fascination with movement, masks, and mime which— as he relates in "Improvisation: Silence Before Words" (1997)—he sees as essential tools through which artists can connect with themselves, with their peers, and with the world around them. His fascination with the physics and geometry of the moving body was life-long: in 1956 he established l'École Internationale de Théâtre Jacques Lecoq, to which, in 1977, he added le Laboratoire d'Étude du Mouvement (Laboratory for the Study of Movement). Among its many graduates, his school lists international stars such as Julie Taymor, Toby Jones, and Geoffrey Rush; Lecoq continued to teach there until days before his death in 1999.

Key words: pedagogy; theatre; the body; France

Silence Before Words

Replay and Play

We approach improvisation through psychological *replay*, which is silent. Replay involves reviving lived experience in the simplest possible way. Avoiding both transposition and exaggeration, remaining strictly faithful to reality and to the student's own psychology, with no thought for spectators, students bring a simple situation to life: a classroom, a market place, a hospital, the metro. *Play* [acting] comes later, at the point when, aware of the theatrical dimension, the actor can shape an improvisation for spectators, using rhythm, tempo, space, form. *Play* may be very close to *replay* or may distance itself through the most daring theatrical transposition, but it must never lose sight of the root anchoring it to reality. A large part of my teaching method involves making students understand this principle.

We begin with silence, for the spoken word often forgets the roots from which it grew, and it is a good thing for students to begin by placing themselves in the position of primal naïveté, a state of innocent curiosity. In any human relationship two major zones of silence emerge: before and after speech. Before, when no words have been spoken, one is in a state of modesty which allows words to be born out of silence; in this state strength comes from avoiding explanatory discourse. By taking these silent situations, and working on human nature, we can rediscover those moments when the words do not yet exist. The other kind of silence comes afterwards: when there is nothing more to be said. For us that one is not so interesting.

First improvisations allow me to observe the quality of each student's acting: How do they play very simple things? How do they keep silent? Some feel under constraint, forbidden to speak, whereas in fact I forbid nothing, I simply ask them to keep silent, the better to understand what *lies beneath* language.

There are only two ways out of this silence: speech or action. At a given moment, when silence becomes too highly charged, the theme breaks loose and speech takes over. So one may speak, but only where necessary. The other way is action: 'I'll do something.' At the start all the students are so keen to act that they throw themselves into situations irrespective of motivation. In so doing, they overlook the other players and fail to act *with them*. But true play can only be founded on one's reaction to another. They have to understand this essential fact: to react is to throw into relief suggestions coming from the external world. The interior world is revealed through a process of reaction to the provocations of the world outside. The actor cannot afford to rely on an interior search for sensitivities, memories, a childhood world.

Paradoxically, 'The Childhood Bedroom' is one of the oldest themes for improvisation, which I suggest at the beginning of the year.

> You return after a long absence and revisit your childhood bedroom. You have had to travel a long way, you arrive at the door, you open it. How will you open it? How will you go in? You rediscover your bedroom: nothing has changed, each object is in its place. Once again you find all your childhood things, your toys, your furniture, your bed. These images of the past come alive again within you, until the moment when the present reasserts itself. And you leave the room.

The theme is not the bedroom of *my childhood*, but a childhood bedroom, which you play at rediscovering. The dynamics of memory are more important than the memory itself. What happens when you find yourself confronted with a place that you think you are discovering for the first time? Suddenly, a memory is triggered: 'I've already seen that!' You are in an image of the present and suddenly an image of the past appears. Out of the interplay between these two images comes the improvisation. Naturally, anyone who improvises draws on his own memory, but that memory can also be imaginary.

I remember setting this improvisation during a short course in Germany. A girl had performed the rediscovery of a ring in her old jewellery box. Instinctively, she tried it on one finger, but it was too small, so she put it onto her little finger. Her improvisation had given rise to great emotion. Had she invented the ring? Was it a genuine memory? Improvisation sometimes stirs up things that are very intimate, but they belong to the person who performs them. I never ask students to search within themselves for the true memory. I have no wish to enter into their intimate secrets.

This exercise is played solo, in front of the other students. Since it is a performance given in front of spectators, I set no time limit, but am sensitive to the dramatic rhythm which is established, noting where it strikes true. The improvisation is mimed: in this way sensitivity to objects is renewed and many objects can be conjured up without the encumbrance of a single real object.

Waiting is the guiding theme which informs the first silent improvisations. The chief motivating force lies in the look: to *watch* and *be watched*. Much of life is spent waiting; we wait with strangers at the post office, at the dentist. Waiting is never abstract. Different points of contact feed into it – actions and reactions. We seek to rediscover this through our improvisations, but also through observing real life. For acting requires more than memories drawn from life. We must constantly go back to live observation: watching people as they walk down the street, or waiting in a queue, attentive to the behaviour of others in the queue.

The theme I suggest is 'The Psychological Encounter', which I prefer to set in a clichéd context, very bourgeois, but which could also take place in any other space, even one that is undefined.

> *You have been invited, by a very rich lady, to take cocktails at around 5pm on a Friday. The guests have never met each other before. The floor is covered with a huge Persian carpet, a Venetian glass chandelier hangs from the ceiling, on one side of the room is a Renaissance painting, no doubt a forgery. On the other, a beautiful piece of Chinese porcelain stands on a little column. The apartment is on the second floor (the smartest floor to live on in Paris) doubtless in the seizième arrondissement, with a big 1920s bay window looking out over an avenue. At the back, a sideboard with cocktails, whisky, fruit juice, nibbles …*
>
> *Five characters present themselves, one after the other, at the entrance. A majordomo has let them in, they have come through a door, along a corridor and have been told: 'It's there!' The first to come in doesn't know that he will be the first, he arrives and there's no one else, just him. A second person arrives, then a third, a fourth, a fifth. The lady, of course, never appears! So they find themselves confronted with a silent situation, not daring to speak, rather as if they were in a waiting room.*

Work of this kind brings to light a number of possible *detours* or *digressions*. On the one hand there are the 'pantomimic' aspects, when the students replace the words they cannot say with gestures, or when they pull faces in order to express themselves. On the other hand, they often try to show that they have seen something before they have genuinely seen it. They are merely going through the motions. They perform the gesture before having found the sensation which motivates it. The first person to come in doesn't know he is the first. So this very important moment of surprise is established, and with it the timing that is essential to the art of acting. The actor knows the end of the play, but the character doesn't.

Another problem to emerge is the result of an actor copying the timescale and the physical distance established by the previous entries. The first two actors who enter establish a tempo, which must of necessity be disrupted by the third if the scene is to stay alive. They must find a *rhythm* rather than a *tempo*. Tempo is geometrical, rhythm is organic. Tempo can be defined, while rhythm is difficult to grasp. Rhythm is the result of an actor's response to another live performer. It may be found in waiting, but also in action. To enter into the rhythm is, precisely, to enter into the great driving force of life itself. Rhythm is at the root of everything, like a mystery. Of course I don't say that to the students, or they would no longer be able to do a thing. They must discover it for themselves.

Very often, in this type of situation, people take up symmetrical positions. They stand at an equal distance from one another, either in a line, side by side, one behind the other, or in a circle: it's similar to when they enter to the same tempo. Such positions can only serve military or ritual purposes; they are not dramatically playable. Every group will tend to arrange itself according to a geometrical pattern (not to be confused with dynamic geometry). Each character must be both part of the group and separate, must find his own rhythmic beat and his specific space.

The opposite situation also presents itself: someone enters and, wanting to seem original at all costs, behaves like a psychiatric case, adopting the most extravagant behaviour. This is at the opposite extreme from the fault of sheep-like mimicry. Of course it is not what we are looking for. But it may have an interestingly provocative effect on the others, giving them the opportunity to react, however awkward the situation may be. Their reaction is a group one: 'all against one'. A kind of chorus is born, out of the confrontation with this injured hero.

Towards the Structures of Play

After we have worked through this theme once, we return to a stripped-down version of the exercise. Ignoring its anecdotal interest, we turn the theme inside out in order to discover the *motor* which drives it. In this way other themes, images, situations, characters are introduced.

> Two characters pass, each one meets the other's eye and comes to a stop, and a silent dramatic situation arises from this meeting. Then a third person comes along and observes the first two. Then a fourth who watches the first three, etc.

Little by little, the theme is rediscovered by accumulation, but only in its structure. There is no imagery or background given in advance, simply a dramatic motor which can be taken apart and analysed. From this basic structure, we can draw out and demonstrate a number of different sub-themes which can be grouped under the general theme of 'The Person Who ... ' Reduced to this motor, psychological themes lose their anecdotal elements and reach a status of heightened play. They enable us to observe with great precision a particular detail which then becomes the major theme: 'The person who believes that ... but no!' – the person who believes that someone is waiting for him, the person who believes he is hated, the person who believes he is the stronger, the person who believes he is being smiled at.

> You are sitting in a café. Opposite you, at another table, someone makes a small hand gesture in your direction. You wonder if you know her or not. Out of politeness, you respond in the same way. The person opposite, put at ease, begins to gesture more wildly, making large movements, playing with an object, smiling. Little by little a complicity grows between you, a dialogue conducted in gestural signs or facial expressions. In the end the person gets up and comes towards you, smiling. You too get up to greet her ... but she passes beside you and goes on to someone behind you.

The important thing here is the rising dynamic *scale* [like a musical scale] which must be played for every nuance. Progressive playing of this situation leads to the building up of a genuine framework which, if taken further, resembles the performance structures of the commedia dell'arte. Situations are pushed to their limit: 'Someone is afraid, he draws back; Harlequin is afraid, he hides under the carpet or withdraws into himself!' We always try to push the situation beyond the limits of reality. We aim for a level of aesthetic reality which would not be recognisable in real life in order to demonstrate how theatre prolongs life by transposing it. This is a vital discovery for the students.

The notion of the *scale* clarifies the different phases in the progression of a dramatic situation. I have incorporated it in the theme of the 'Six Sounds' which we use as a technical improvisation in class.

> *You are in the middle of a manual task which involves the body in repetitive action (e.g. sawing wood, painting a wall, sweeping), and you will hear six sounds, each of which will have a different importance for you. The first one you do not hear (which does not mean there will be no reaction). The second, you hear, but without paying any special attention to it. The third one is loud and you listen to see if it will repeat. Since it does not, you cease paying attention. The fourth is very loud, and you think you know where it comes from, which reassures you. The fifth fails to confirm what you had thought. Finally the sixth and last is a jet plane which passes over your head.*

This highly structured scale will become a reference point for all the other scales we shall meet subsequently, in a variety of dramatic situations. The exercise is especially useful for understanding the progressive dynamics of a movement, but also for the technical knowledge of the movements imposed by a scale. How is the action changed by the volume of the sounds? Are the gestures you make different according to the importance given to what you hear? What are the links between action and reaction?

In reply to these questions, we conclude that action must always precede reaction. The longer the interval between action and reaction, the greater will be the dramatic intensity and the more powerful will be the dramatic performance if the actor can sustain this level. Dramatic power will be commensurate with length of reaction time. The principle of the *scale*, which we use a great deal, is an excellent means for revealing this law and for demonstrating the levels of acting.

In the course of this work, I first point out the different articulations of the theme to the students, before they perform, then I beat out the sounds myself on a tambourine. I become the director of the exercise, which forces me to give a rhythm to the succession of different sounds. I cannot just beat them out at regular five-second intervals. I have to find the rhythm which is favourable to the performance: if I wait too long, or if I go too fast, the exercise is a failure. The teacher has to become a director for this class.

The aim of these initial exercises, taken as a whole, is to delay the use of the spoken word. The imposition of silent performance leads the students to discover this basic law of theatre: words are born from silence. At the same time they discover that movement, too, can only come out of immobility. 'Be quiet, play, and theatre will be born!', that could be our motto. It would provide a paradoxical echo to the statues erected at the entrance to Khmer temples, one with an open mouth, the next closed. 'First you speak, then you keep silent,' they say. My teaching claims the exact opposite. […]

4   Going Fragile

Mattin

In celebrating what he calls the "fragile moments" of improvisation, Basque artist Mattin draws significant parallels between the playing of music and the high wire act that is everyday life. In doing so he refers to Radu Malfatti, an underappreciated virtuoso of the European improvising community. Mattin began playing electric bass in Bilbao indie rock bands in the early 1990s. Shortly afterwards he moved to London where, while completing an MA in Art Theory at Goldsmiths College, he encountered Eddie Prévost's improvisation workshop and the work of the London Musicians' Collective. In 2000 he moved his musical activities from guitar to computer. Shortly afterwards, he formed the ensemble Sakada with percussionists Prévost and Rosy Parlane. He has made 70 recordings and runs the record labels w.m.o/r and Free Software Series, and the netlabel Desetxea. As well as publishing writings on improvisation and free software, Mattin has argued extensively against the concept of intellectual property. He is co-editor with Anthony Iles of the book *Noise and Capitalism* (available in pdf form as a free download).

Key words: music; improvisation; safety; copyright; Europe

> Of course it is not easy to get out of your own material, and it can be painful; there is an insecurity aspect to it. This actually is probably the most experimental level. When do you think real innovation and experimentation are happening? Probably when people are insecure, probably when people are in a situation very new to them and when they are a bit uncertain and afraid. That is where people have to push themselves. People are innovative when they are outside of their warm shit, outside of the familiar and comfortable ... I don't know exactly what I want, but I do know exactly what I do not want.
>
> (Conversation with Radu Malfatti)

Improvised music forces situations into play where musicians push each other into bringing different perspectives to their playing. Improvised music is not progressive in itself, but it invites constant experimentation. When players feel too secure about their approaches, the experimentation risks turning into Mannerism. What I would like to explore here are the moments in which players leave behind a safe zone and expose themselves in the face of the internalised structures of judgment that govern our appreciation of music. These I would call fragile moments.

During the summer of 2003 I had the opportunity to spend time in Vienna researching the political connotations of improvised music. Not that I found a direct relationship, but through conversations, going to concerts and playing with other musicians, I became aware of some of the potentials and limitations that improvisation has in terms of political agency within the space of music production. For this text, I draw from the conversations I had with the trombonist Radu Malfatti as part of my research. While Malfatti's roots are in the chaotic-sounding improvised free jazz of the 1970s, he is currently more focused on ultra quiet and sparse playing. His approach to performance runs against the stagnation that might occur in sustained improvisation. In his quest to avoid stagnation, Malfatti looks for those insecure situations that I mention above – situations that can call into question the dominant structures of music appreciation. How could you anticipate what you might achieve if you do not know what you will find on the way? To be open, receptive and exposed to the dangers of making improvised music, means exposing yourself to unwanted situations that could break the foundations of your own security. As a player you will bring yourself into situations that ask for total demand. No vision of what could happen is able to bring light to that precise moment. Once you are out, there is no way back; you cannot regret what you have done. You must engage in questioning your security, see it as a constriction. You are aware and scared, as if you were in a dark corridor. Now you are starting to realise that what you thought of as walls existed only in your imagination.

While your senses alert you to danger, you are also going to use them to deal with it. Keep going forward toward what you do not know, to what is questioning your knowledge and your use of it. Keep pushing yourself, knowing that the other players will be pushing you, replacing traces of comfort. This is an unreliable moment, to which no stable definition can be applied. It is subject to all the particularities brought to this moment. The more sensitive you are to them, the more you can work with (or against) them. You are breaking away from previous restrictions that you have become attached to, creating a unique social space, a space that cannot be transported elsewhere. Now you are building different forms of collaboration, scrapping previous modes of generating relations.

Something is happening here, but what is it? It is hard to say, but certainly there is intensity to it. These moments are almost impossible to articulate; they refuse pigeonholing, and evade easy representation.

We are forced to question the material and social conditions that constitute the improvised moment – structures that usually validate improvisation as an established musical genre. Otherwise we risk fetishising 'the moment' and avoid its implications.

> When we talk about stagnation and progression there is just one instrument to help us explain what we mean, and this is time, history.

> (Radu Malfatti)

When Radu Malfatti talks about the breaks that some musicians have made from musical orthodoxy, he looks at the ways that they have dealt with these breaks. Some seek to consolidate or re-metabolise the fragile moments they have encountered; others simply return to the safety of their previous practices. Only very few manage to keep searching for fragility; it requires musicians to make multiple breaks from their own traditions. It's easier to develop coherence within one's practice: There is a fine line between being persistent in pursuing a particular line of research, and getting comfortable within one's methods.

> When something new happens, people do not like it. It's as simple as that … There is nothing I can do about it.

> (Radu Malfatti)

When something different and hard to place appears within the dichotomy of the new and the old of mainstream values, attention cannot easily be drawn to it. While nobody might recognise the importance of what you have done, you need to keep your confidence. It is difficult to be alone in working toward something and yet not know where it will take you; something which threatens to destroy your artistic trajectory, which you have worked so hard to build up. Of course when one uses music, not as a tool for achieving something else (recognition, status …) but in a more aggressively creative way, it is going to produce alienation. But what do you want to do as an improvised musician? Work toward the lowest common denominator, making music which more people can relate to?

Improvised music has the potential to disrupt previous modes of musical production, but it is up to the players to tear them apart in order to find a way in. Opening new fields of permissibility means to go fragile until we destroy the fears that hold us back. We are not talking here about changing the labour conditions of a majority of people, but, being aware that culture, creativity, and communication are becoming the tools of the 'factory without walls,' we need to be suspicious of ways in which cultural practices can be exploited by capital. Because of this we must constantly question our motives, our *modus operandi* and its relation to the conditions that we are embedded in, to avoid recuperation by a system that is going to produce ideological walls for us. To be antagonistic to these conditions means danger and insecurity. To go through them will mean commitment and some of what Benjamin described as the 'Destructive Character':

> The destructive character has the consciousness of historical man, whose deepest emotion is an insuperable mistrust of the course of things and a readiness at all times to recognize that everything can go wrong. Therefore the destructive character is reliability itself. The destructive character sees nothing permanent. But for this very reason he sees ways everywhere. Where others encounter walls or mountains, there, too, he sees a way. But because he sees a way everywhere, he has to clear things from it everywhere. Not always by brute force; sometimes by the most refined. No moment can know what the next will bring.
>
> (Walter Benjamin, 'The Destructive Character', 1931)

Anti-copyright.

5 Music, Language, and Cultural Styles

Improvisation as Conversation

Ingrid Monson

In this chapter from *Saying Something: Jazz Improvisation and Interaction*, Ingrid Monson takes on the considerable challenge of discussing music through such difficult-to-quantify terms as irony, poise, and "talking back." In doing so, she helps to illuminate how musical performance "effectively fuses the social and the musical in the same interactive moment." After studies at the New England Conservatory, and an active professional career as a trumpet player in several different genres of music, in 1985 Dr Monson traded the rigours of life on the road for the different rigours of academia, receiving her PhD in musicology from New York University. She has consistently proven herself an astute researcher who gravitates to original sources—the musicians themselves—to construct "jazz histories" that do not always agree with the histories constructed by critics, scholars, and the music industry, contrasting idealised pictures of jazz with the pragmatic realities—as well as the activist politics and humanistic philosophies—of the music's creators. She edited the 2000 volume *The African Diaspora: A Musical Perspective*, and won the 1998 Irving Lowens Prize for the best book on American music for *Saying Something*. Ingrid Monson is currently Quincy Jones Professor of African-American Music at Harvard University.

Key words: jazz; African-American culture; critical theory

[...] On one level, the image of conversation has structural affinities with interactive improvisational process; on another, the stylistic and affective aspects of conversation raise the issue of music and cultural style. Since jazz musicians have been nearly as famous for their talk—their so-called jargon, the subject of much stereotyping since the swing era—as for their music, the linking of music and language in issues of cultural identity seems especially germane. The ironic, double-edged predicament of African American cultural practices is everywhere in evidence: linguistic and musical practices that have been the cause of cultural celebration and valorization since the 1960s retain their power to stereotype when they are not situated within the history of ethnic interaction and politics in the United States.

The informal, sociable, and metaphorical modes of speaking about music favored by many jazz musicians challenge traditional presumptions about both the nature of the musical object and the definition of musical analysis. In their differences from and overlaps with traditional Western musical theory, the commentaries of professional musicians suggest that musical theories developed for the explication of scores are not fully appropriate to the elucidation of improvisational music making. This is not to say that Western analytical tools are completely inappropriate, only that we need to be aware of their limits. I argue here that meaningful theorizing about jazz improvisation at the level of the ensemble must take the interactive, collaborative context of musical invention as a point of departure. This context has no parallel in the musical practice of Western classical composers of the common practice period, and it should not be surprising that jazz musicians choose to talk about music making in different terms.

In the following [...] work, I develop a perspective on these various linguistic metaphors (especially improvisation as conversation) and on the more general issue of music as a cultural discourse that considers both close analysis of the music and cultural analysis of how improvisation has been part of the construction of meaning, identity, and critique in twentieth-century African American and American society. If musicians are saying something, by what musical and cultural processes do they succeed?

Music and Language

Translating musical experience and insight into written or spoken words is one of the most fundamental frustrations of musical scholarship. Charles Seeger (1977) called this dilemma the *linguocentric predicament*—no matter how elegantly an author writes, there is something fundamentally untranslatable about musical experience. The relationship between music and language, however, has been a continual source of speculation for music theorists and ethnomusicologists and a part of everyday metaphors about music in many cultures.[1] Seeger viewed music and language as two principal means of auditory communication, fundamentally linked through sound but differentiated in their cognitive perception of reality. If language emphasized the "intellection of reality," music stressed its "feeling" (35). Steven Feld has also spoken of music as a "special kind of feelingful activity," but he has not shared Seeger's pessimism on the impasse between speech and music. Seeger, in [Feld's] view, concentrated too heavily on the referential functions of language and too little on the figurative capacities of both language and music. For Feld, the way in which people talk about music—especially their metaphors—contributes a "parallel stream" of figurative information regarding the conceptualization and interpretation of sound, and mediates between speech and music as feelingful activities (Feld 1984).

In discussing the Kaluli of Papua New Guinea, Feld (1981) has placed particular emphasis on the role of metaphor in encoding musical theory. Feld noted the way in which metaphors recur in semantic fields from contrasting cultural domains (22–23) and discussed music itself as a metaphoric process (Feld 1982, 38–43: 1984, 14–15). He argued that "an analysis of musical theory ... relies in part on understanding linguistic mediation of concepts of the musical system" (1981, 23). This linguistic mediation then becomes a means for thinking about the cultural aesthetics of Kaluli society. In a consideration of how to extend this perspective to jazz, the differences between a small, relatively isolated cultural group such as the Kaluli and the heterogeneous musical, cultural, and linguistic systems of urban North America are obvious. Most professional jazz musicians have great proficiency in aspects of Western musical theory—particularly in harmonic and melodic analysis—and can speak its language with great fluency when they choose. Like other African Americans, jazz musicians may speak at one moment in the styles of everyday African America and at another in white, middle-class, school English. The ability to draw from both worlds, which W. E. B. Du Bois long ago termed *double consciousness,* is arguably one of the most significant aspects of the culture of Africans in America (Du Bois 1969). In the community of jazz performers, non-African American musicians must also become familiar with both worlds, for the leadership in this musical tradition has always flowed most heavily from the African American side. How these worlds collide, intersect, and overlap, and what implications these culturally as well as musically interactive processes have on the way in which jazz is perceived and understood as a cultural force, are questions that underlie the following discussion.

Metaphors and Tropes

Anthropologists, too, have long recognized the importance of figurative tropes in cultural interpretation, including those of metaphor, metonymy, synecdoche, and irony. As James Fernandez (1986) has argued, "the analysis of metaphor seems to me to be the very nature of [anthropological] inquiry" (6). Metaphors point to similarities between contrasting cultural domains or activities, while metonyms suggest part-to-whole (contiguous) relationships within cultural domains. Ironic tropes, on the other hand, assert incongruity, especially between apparent meaning and deeper ironic reversal of that meaning. While cultural theorists have devoted their attention mainly to the metaphor, recent work on the theory of tropes has emphasized the relationships among these figurative ways of speaking in cultural practice. Terence Turner (1991) has augmented Fernandez's discussion of metaphor by presenting a theory of the relationships among metaphor, metonymy, and synecdoche. In brief, Turner argues that a metaphor (such as "improvisation is conversation") links cultural domains by selecting an attribute in one domain (improvisation as part of music) similar to an attribute from another (conversation as a part of language). Turner argues that a metonymic (part-to-whole) relationship is therefore implicit in any metaphoric association. The metaphoric association of contrasting domains may in turn construct a more encompassing, higher-level category that "assumes the essential character of its parts," or becomes an example of synecdoche (Turner 1991, 148). Charles Seeger's (1977) view of music and language as subsets of aural communication provides an example of one such larger whole.[2] To return to the metaphor we're examining, if improvisation is like conversation (subsets of music and language), then sociable, face-to-face communication (subset of communication) may be the larger category at stake.

[Consider] Richard Davis's description of an imitative exchange during improvisation: "That happens a lot in jazz, that it's like a conversation and one guy will ... create a melodic motif or a rhythmic motif and the band picks it up" (Davis 1989). This association could be taken as either a structural or a textual metaphor in Fernandez's definition of the terms:

> In the case of structural metaphor the translation between realms is based on some isomorphism of structure or similarity of relationship of parts. By textual metaphor we mean an assimilation made on the basis of similarity in feeling tone.
>
> (Fernandez 1986, 12)

There are structural aspects of the music (the trading of different musical voices) and textual aspects (the feeling or tone of sociability) united in Davis's image. The utility of thinking about these two aspects of the metaphor of conversation lies in the links that can be clarified between music in the moment of performance and the cumulative construction of cultural feeling and tone over time, which Steven Feld (1988) terms an "iconicity of style." [...]

Musical Affinities with Conversation

While sitting in the Gibralter Transmission garage in Machito Square in November of 1989, I played a tape for drummer Ralph Peterson of his composition "Princess" (Peterson 1988). Pianist Geri Allen soloed with the accompaniment of Peterson and bassist Essiet Okon Essiet. Peterson's accompaniment was very dense, and there were several instances in which Allen and Peterson traded ideas with each other. After one rhythmic exchange I remarked,

"Salt Peanuts!" since Geri Allen's piano figure (musical example 11, mm. 9–11) reminded me of Gillespie's famous riff (musical example 12). Peterson commented:

> Yeah! "Salt Peanuts" and "Looney Tunes"—kind of a combination of the two. Art Blakey has a thing he plays. It's like: [he sings measures 1 and 2 of musical example 13]. And Geri played: [he sings measures 3 to 5 of musical example 11]. So I played the second half of the Art Blakey phrase: [he sings measures 3 and 4 of musical example 13].

Figure 5.1 Musical Example 11 – Excerpt from Geri Allen's piano solo on "Princess"

Figure 5.2 Musical Example 12. "Salt Peanuts." Kenny Clarke. (*Groovin' High with Dizzy Gillespie.* Savoy SV–0152. Recorded: New York, NY, 28 February 1945.)

dink dink   dink dink   dink dink di dink   dink dink   ah

Figure 5.3 Musical Example 13 – Ralph Peterson Jr. singing Art Blakey rhythm

Peterson then offered this interpretation:

> But you see what happens is, a lot of times when you get into a musical conversation one person in the group will state an idea or the beginning of an idea and another person will *complete* the idea or their interpretation of the same idea, how they hear it. So the conversation happens in fragments and comes from different parts, different voices.
>
> (Peterson 1989b)

In associating the trading of musical ideas with conversation, Peterson stressed the interpersonal, face-to-face quality of improvisation. The circulation of the Art Blakey rhythm was not only a significant musical moment but an instance of musical dialogue between Peterson and Allen. The exchange of the idea not only established an abstract succession of sounds and rhythms but linked Allen and Peterson as musical personalities (with some experience playing together) at a particular moment in time. At the time I interviewed him, Peterson particularly enjoyed working with Allen because spontaneous moments of musical communication such as this one just seemed to happen without a lot of effort. Peterson felt Allen's contribution to his group was "pivotal," even to the point of saying that if Allen couldn't make a performance, "I'd rather have another instrument. I feel that strongly about her playing" (Peterson 1989a).

These moments of rhythmic interaction could also be seen as negotiations or struggles for control of musical space. One player's interjection, for example, might be experienced by another as an interruption or a challenge. Peterson told me that there were times when Allen felt uncomfortable with some of his interjections and that they had discussed the difference between enhancing a solo and obliterating it (Peterson 1989b). In the "Princess" example we have been discussing, Peterson's Art Blakey rhythm could potentially be perceived as an intrusive rhythmic idea, but Allen's quick reaction communicates that she is strong enough to respond to almost anything he can put forth. In other words, Peterson's completion of the Art Blakey rhythm in measures 7 and 8 (musical example 11) could be seen as an interruption of Allen's phrase that begins in measure 6. His interjection could have caused her to abandon the completion of her melodic idea in measures 7 and 8. Once he has completed his idea, however, she immediately asserts a new and forceful one of her own (m. 9), to which he responds in measure 12. There is a great deal of give and take in such improvisational interaction, and such moments are often cited by musicians as aesthetic high points of performances.

The indivisibility of musical and interpersonal interaction underscores the problem of thinking about jazz improvisation as a text. At the moment of performance, jazz improvisation quite simply has nothing in common with a text (or its musical equivalent, the score) for it is music composed through face-to-face interaction.[3] Musicologists familiar with the eighteenth century will counter that contemporary writers also referred to the conversational and rhetorical aspects of music making. Friedrich Wilhelm Marpurg spoke of subject and answer in his description of the baroque fugue (Mann 1986, 154–55), while Heinrich Christian Koch likened the relationship of antecedent and consequent in periodic phrasing to the subject and predicate of a sentence (Ratner 1956, 441). Language metaphors are in fact extremely common in many musical periods and many cultures.[4] An eighteenth-century score, however, is far more like a novel in Mikhail Bakhtin's (1981) sense than a conversation: if a novel portrays multiple characters and points of view all refracted through a single author's pen, a musical score presents multiple musical lines, instruments, counterpoints, textures, and harmonies coordinated by the composer. Performance of these musical texts—transformation of the notation into sound—includes multiple participants, but in Western classical music performers are generally not allowed to alter or (in some repertories) even embellish this musical notation.

In jazz improvisation, as we have seen, all of the musicians are constantly making decisions regarding what to play and when to play it, all within the framework of a musical groove, which may or may not be organized around a chorus structure. The musicians are compositional participants who may "say" unexpected things or elicit responses from other musicians. Musical intensification is open-ended rather than predetermined and highly interpersonal in character—structurally far more similar to a conversation than to a text. Herbie Hancock put it this way when talking about his experience with the Miles Davis Quintet in the early 1960s:

> We were sort of walking a tightrope with the kind of experimenting that we were doing in music. Not total experimentation ... we used to call it "controlled freedom" ... just like conversation—same thing. I mean, how many times have you *talked* to somebody and ... you got ready to say, make a point, and then you kind of went off in another direction, but maybe you never wound up making that point but the conversation, you know, just went somewhere else and it was fine. There's nothing wrong with it. Maybe you *like* where you went. Well, this is the way we were dealing with music.
>
> (Obenhaus 1986)

When musicians use the metaphor of conversation, they are saying something very significant about musical process.

Sociolinguists define *conversation* as talk occurring between two or more participants who freely alternate turns (Levinson 1983, 284). The process of turn taking builds larger units of talk that Marjorie Goodwin calls *participant frameworks*. Arguments, storytelling, instigating, and a gossip dispute process called "he-said-she-said" are among the types of participant frameworks Goodwin identified for African American children in Philadelphia (Goodwin 1990, 9–10). In their conversations, participants situate themselves in relationship to other participants through language or depict a party (present or absent) as a character within the discussion (10). Through close analysis of conversational interactions, Goodwin observed that during turn taking, individuals display their own interpretation of the talk in which they participate.

> Participants in conversation have the job of providing next moves to ongoing talk which demonstrate what sense they make of that talk. It therefore is possible to see how group members themselves interpret the interaction they are engaged in.
>
> (6)

From these ideas it is apparent that the jazz ensemble, with its rhythm section and soloist roles, is itself a musical framework for participation. This framework balances the relatively fixed rhythm section roles against the freer role of improvising soloist. Composer Olly Wilson has argued that this division into what he calls "fixed" and "variable" rhythmic groups is characteristic of African music:

> Though musical ensembles in African cultures follow a variety of different formats, a general principle appears to govern the division of a musical ensemble into at least two functional groups. The first is one that I refer to as the "fixed rhythmic group," so called because its instruments maintain a fixed rhythmic pulsation throughout the duration of the composition with little variation. The group has a time-keeping or metronomic function; it is frequently manifest in a relatively complex rhythmic form and serves, according to Nketia, as the "time line." The second is the "variable rhythmic group," so named because the rhythms performed by these instruments change.
>
> (Wilson 1992, 331)

There is a considerable degree of flexibility even in the relatively fixed instrumental roles of the jazz rhythm section, but the primary function of the rhythm section is nevertheless to provide the timeline against which the soloist can interact and build. The quality of swinging or grooving is itself produced by this dynamic tension between the relatively fixed and variable elements of the ensemble. Samuel Floyd has suggested that musicians who swing are "Signifying on the timeline" (Floyd 1991, 273). Soloists often change the character of what they play from chorus to chorus, and sensitive rhythm sections change the character of accompaniment in response. [...]

In reacting to the continuous changes in an improviser's solo, rhythm section members display their hearings of the musical events and their understandings of appropriate musical responses. Their responses also indicate what musical events they take to be most significant. Musicians who miss opportunities to respond to or enhance their accompaniment [...] are often said to be "not listening" to what is going on in the ensemble. In other words, it is not enough for a musician to play through a tune with only its melody and harmonic structure in mind, as many jazz pedagogy books would have us believe; the player must be so thoroughly familiar with the basic framework of the tune that he or she can attend to what everyone else in the band is doing.

Nearly every musician who talked to me mentioned the importance of listening in good ensemble playing. Listening in an active sense—being able to respond to musical opportunities or to correct mistakes—is implicit in the way that musicians use this term. It is a type of listening much like that required of participants in a conversation, who have to pay attention to what is transpiring if they expect to say things that make sense to the other participants. Listening affects what musicians decide to play at a particular moment, which is why Cecil McBee was so sure that in good jazz performance, "you're not going to play what you practiced ... Something else is going to happen" (McBee 1990). This spontaneity is absolutely central in the jazz improvisational aesthetic.

To say that a player "doesn't listen" or sounds as though he or she is playing "something he or she practiced" is a grave insult. Such a musician may play ideas that fulfill the minimal demands of the harmony or chorus structure but fail to respond well to the other players in the band. Don Byron commented:

> I hate hearing them bands where like … one cat's playing some shit that he practiced. Another cat's playing some shit that he practiced. Everybody's playing some stuff that they practiced … On a certain level there's like a feeling, "Well, I like playing with you," but I mean, what does that mean? … You know, we didn't play shit together. We didn't do nothing together. I played my stuff, you played your stuff, we didn't screw up the time.
>
> (Byron 1989)

Good jazz improvisation is sociable and interactive just like a conversation; a good player communicates with the other players in the band. If this doesn't happen, it's not good jazz.

The importance of communicativeness and the ability to hear is underscored by another type of language metaphor used by musicians: "to say" or "to talk" often substitutes for "to play." […] Aesthetic evaluations frequently include this usage. To suggest that a soloist "isn't saying anything" is an insult; conversely, to say that he or she "makes that horn talk" is very high praise. The perception of musical ideas as a communicative medium in and of themselves can be most effectively understood against the background of aural recognition of elements of musical tradition […]. A secondary meaning of the talking horn image relates to the ability of horn players to mimic a vocal quality through articulation, attack, and timbre. A very literal imitation of arguing voices can be heard on Charles Mingus's "What Love" (1960). Eric Dolphy on bass clarinet and Mingus on bass sound as though they are having a very intense verbal argument. The musical image of the talking horn personifies the horn, once again refusing to separate the sound from the person who makes it.

A third type of metaphor uses the term *language* to mean "musical style and syntax." When Jerome Harris (1989) explained that he went through periods in which he was less interested in his own instrument than in what trumpeters and sax players and pianists were doing because "the language seemed to be more developed there on those instruments," and Sir Roland Hanna spoke of being able to anticipate Richard Davis's musical "words" (Hanna 1989), they were distinguishing jazz as a unique musical and aesthetic system from other musical genres. This type of language metaphor occurs in a broad spectrum of music traditions throughout the world.

The salience of language metaphors in talk about jazz is clear at this point in our discussion. It is important to realize that there is a coherence among the three types of musical language metaphors as well. Saussure used the terms *langue* and *parole* to distinguish generally between ideas about language as a system and language as it is performed (Saussure 1986). When musicians speak of the "jazz language," they are talking about a musical and aesthetic system that contrasts with others—a usage comparable to *langue*. When they refer to playing music as "talking," they emphasize communication through the act of performing music—a usage akin to *parole*. When they compare performance in the ensemble to "conversation," they refer to a specific genre of musical talk that requires listening carefully to the other participants.[5] The interpersonal character of this process is emphasized very clearly by the conversation metaphor, for what could be more social than a musical or verbal conversation?

I am certainly not the only writer who has noted the pervasiveness of language images in African American music. Ben Sidran, for example, entitled his book on jazz *Black Talk* (1986). Lester Young used of the image of storytelling to describe improvisation (Daniels 1985; Porter 1985, 34), as have many of the musicians who used the metaphor of conversation. Pianist Roland Hanna, for example, talked about technique from this perspective:

Technique is a living process ... It's a kind of storytelling that utilizes everything in your life up to that moment.

(Stix 1978)

Drummer Roy Haynes put it this way:

I like to paint some sort of picture ... you know, tell a musical story according to how I feel.

(DeMichael 1966, 19)

A great deal of the most recent work on African American music has also drawn upon the pervasiveness of these images in African American cultural life (Floyd 1991; Hartman 1991).

African American literary theorists have likewise emphasized an ethos of communication in recent years: bell hooks entitled a collection of essays *Talking Back* (hooks 1989), and the work of Henry Louis Gates Jr. has inspired many to take the African American notion of signifying as a point of interpretive departure (Gates 1988). Prior to the work of Gates, academic discussion of this concept was confined primarily to the literatures of socio-linguistics, folklore, and linguistic anthropology. Among the contributors to this literature are Claudia Mitchell-Kernan (1986), Thomas Kochman (1981, 1983, 1986), William Labov (1969, 1972), Geneva Smitherman (1977), and Roger Abrahams (1970). In the earliest academic literature, most of the attention was focused on the genres of verbal dueling, variously termed *sounding, woofing, playing the dozens, marking,* and *jiving*.[6] Claudia Mitchell-Kernan was among the first to include along with genres of verbal dueling what sociolinguists term *indirect modes of discourse:*

A number of individuals interested in black verbal behavior have devoted attention to the "way of talking" which is known in many black communities as *signifying.* Signifying can be a tactic employed in game activity—verbal dueling—which is engaged in as an end in itself. ... Signifying, however, also refers to a way of encoding messages or meanings in natural conversation which involves, in most cases, an element of indirection. This kind of signifying might best be viewed as an alternative message form, selected for its artistic merit, and may occur embedded in a variety of discourse.

(Mitchell-Kernan 1986, 165)

Signifying as a speaking style defined in this manner includes both formal verbal games and individual statements in which two-sided or multiple meanings are embedded. Often these are statements that indirectly tease, provoke, or potentially insult one or more addressees, who are then challenged to respond in a way clever enough to save face. The difference between these two aspects of signifying corresponds roughly to Bakhtin's distinction between external and internal dialogism. Externally dialogical discourse is compositionally marked—that is, structured like actual dialogue between two or more individuals (Bakhtin 1981, 279, 283). The notion of internal dialogism, by contrast, involves two issues: (1) multiple semantic meanings that vary according to and are defined in relationship to one another and the socio-cultural context in the present and (2) the temporal context in which ideas are expressed and defined in relation to a history of competing social or cultural discourses. The second sense of internal dialogism is often glossed as *intertextuality* in literary circles.[7] In recent years, the common use of the term *signifying* in studies of

African American literature has stressed these internally dialogic aspects of intertextuality and double-sidedness. What is lost sometimes in the extension of this metaphor to texts with a single author is a sense of how signifying is an aesthetic developed from interactive, participatory, turn-taking games and genres that are multiply authored. The particular logic of turn taking in the construction of participatory verbal and musical frameworks is something I wish to stress. Their entextualization through "writing down" or recording is a separate but related matter.

Face-to-Face Verbal and Musical Interaction

Sociolinguist Thomas Kochman described the interactional strategy in the verbal dueling genres of sounding, woofing, and playing the dozens (all of which Gates includes in the idea of signifying) as "indeterminate strategic ambiguity" (Kochman 1986, 156). He observed that whether a particular statement in a verbal duel is taken as a serious insult depends more on the receiver's reaction than on the sender's intentions. From this perspective, the interaction between the speakers is more important than any pre-existing strategic intention in determining whether a given statement leads to play or fighting (157–59). In fact, fighting might ensue only when one party is unable to keep up with the invention of creative responses. One of the chief functions of such verbal exchanges is to sustain the sociability as long as possible. The challenge of the verbal game, as it were, is to keep the interaction at the highest possible pitch of creative intensity.

From an African American perspective, the essence of a "cool" or "hip" response includes reacting with poise and balance to these potentially unsettling verbal teases and challenges. Work by Goodwin (1990) and Morgan (1991) has shown that the sociolinguistic issues Kochman discusses also apply to African American women and children—not just to men, as the work of Kochman, Labov, and Abrahams has implied. The non-African American unfamiliar with these norms of interaction might interpret such teases and challenges as rudeness. This is precisely the type of situation Gumperz had in mind when he suggested that differences in discourse norms and contextualization cues are more likely to be interpreted as attitudinal than linguistic (Gumperz 1982, 132).

In musical aesthetics informed by African American cultural aesthetics, the idea of response is just as important as in verbal communication. [...] Richard Davis commented:

> Now what occurred to me at the moment [of performance] was responding to what I heard the leader voice doing. And then the drummer might pick it up and it might be a whole thing of triplets going back to the second eight; you never know where it's going to go. Sometimes you might put a idea in that you think is good and nobody takes to it. ... And then sometimes you might put an idea in that your incentive or motivation is not to influence but it does influence. It's a very subtle, ESP kind of thing going with people who have traditionally created a ethnic kind of music.
>
> (Davis 1989)

The response of musicians is clearly crucial to whether a particular musical idea is picked up on, developed, or ignored. Samuel Floyd has recognized the critical importance of this principle in African American music and suggested that it be named *call-response,* the equivalent of Gates's signifying as a "master musical trope" for black music (Floyd 1991, 276). I am interested here in its particular realization in the context of jazz improvisation, where it is a crucial component in the large-scale momentum of improvised performances.

It is a fundamentally social, conversational, and dialogic way to organize musical performance. Frequently an exchange will begin with the repetition of a particular musical passage or a response with a complimentary musical interjection, although these are certainly not the only possibilities. I want to underscore the importance of repetition here, since it has been something Western classical music commentators have often disparaged in jazz improvisation and African American music more broadly. The function of repetition in creating a participatory musical framework against which highly idiosyncratic and innovative improvisation can take place has often been lost upon otherwise sympathetic commentators.[8]

Goodwin (1990) has discussed the function of repetition in face-to-face verbal interaction. She notes in her study that a participant in an argument will frequently make use of the sentence structures of the opposing party in responding to and transforming an exchange. She calls this process *format tying* (177–88). In the following example,

> Billy, who has been teasing Martha about her hair, has just laughed.
>
> Martha: I don't know what you laughin' at.
> Billy: I know what I'm laughin' at. Your head.

Goodwin points out that "Your head" would be a sufficient response if all that were needed were an informational reply to Martha's question. "I know what I'm laughin' at" reiterates Martha's sentence structure but transforms it into a reply that escalates the interaction—in effect, using her words against her. This transformative reuse of material is something that Gates emphasizes in his definition of signifying: "repetition with a signal difference" (Gates 1988, 51). Structurally, Goodwin's idea of format tying is very much like the musical process occurring in the rhythmic exchange between Ralph Peterson and Geri Allen in musical example 11. The rhythmic redundancy is used to construct a reply and to reassert the leadership of the soloist. The repetition emphasizes the face-to-face character of the musical interaction.

Goodwin also articulates the relationship between sentence structure and the social action it accomplishes:

> While it is possible to escalate an argument with a subsequent action whose structure is unrelated to that of the action being dealt with, the utterances [she previously cited] ... display their status as escalations of prior actions ... by making use of the talk of the prior speaker and transforming it to their advantage; in essence, they turn the prior action on its head. Indeed there is a very nice fit between the social activity of escalating a sequence and challenging a prior move, and the syntactic structure of these utterances, in which the prior move becomes an embedded subcomponent of the sentence used to answer it.
>
> (Goodwin 1990: 180–81)

Goodwin emphasizes here the dialectic between the microcommand of language structures and their employment for interactional competitive or cooperative purposes, which are both social and aesthetic in character.

This relationship between formal linguistic devices and their practical use in social interactions offers us an important point of comparison to the relationship between formal musical structures and their emotional, aesthetic, and cultural feeling. In the process described by Richard Davis, the same set of musical details (an imitative passage) functions both to create a formal musical shape and to establish a playful dialogue between the soloist and the bassist. The process by which that communication takes place—the choice to pick up on a particular musical opportunity or not—effectively fuses the social and the musical in the same interactive moment. As Cecil McBee emphasized, a process of collectivization occurs when musicians walk out on stage: the interdependence of the members of the ensemble ensures that each individual must adjust to the presence and activities of the other band members.

Feeling and Tone

The metaphor of conversation directs our attention not only to the structural aspects of interactive music making but also to the feeling and tone of particular styles of conversation. Because the musical leadership of jazz has been primarily black, African American cultural sensibilities and ideas of sociability have defined the ideal social and interactional values within multi-ethnic performing and listening communities. In this context, it is not surprising that many non-African Americans in the jazz world have emulated and deeply identified with these musical and social ideals.

During the mid-to late 1930s, popular magazine articles about jazz and swing music began to include definitions of the terms supposedly used by jazz musicians (Chapman 1935; Harvey 1936).[9] An article appearing in *Esquire* magazine in 1936 (Poling 1936, 92) attempted to explain to the reader the meaning of terms such as *breaks, licks, riffs,* and *groove.* That these published definitions are not entirely reliable is apparent when the writer defines *in the groove* as "to play in a dull, unimaginative rut" (92)—certainly the opposite of the term as used by the musicians. In 1938 *Life* magazine pondered the definitions of *jitterbugs, cat,* and *ickey* ("Speaking of Pictures" 1938). In November of that year, *Metronome* reprinted an editorial that had appeared in the *Tulsa Tribune:* "We're getting pretty sick of 'swing'" it says, because "there is very little that is new about swing except the name and the bewildering vocabulary which accompanies it" ("They're Killing Swing" 1938).

The focus on jazz terminology seems to have come with the swing era, a time when African American–based dance music was popularized on a mass scale by white big bands. To non–African Americans who had little familiarity with African American speaking norms, these terms were amusing, confusing, fascinating, and exotic—not at all what they had expected.[10] This fascination with African American speaking styles was sometimes accompanied by a deprecation of African Americans and their fellow travelers who spoke in this manner. Sociological writings from the 1950s and early 1960s are perhaps the worst offenders in this regard. William Cameron described jazz musicians as "non-literate," "non-verbal," and "totally unable to translate their most important feelings into more generally conventional symbols" (Cameron 1954, 180). Merriam and Mack wrote that the jazz musician "remains illiterate with respect to the verbal expression of his own art" (Merriam and Mack 1960, 216).

That the verbal inventiveness of African American speakers could be interpreted as nonverbal is highly ironic in view of the tremendous efforts undertaken by some white jazz musicians to learn how to speak as cleverly as black musicians. Leonard quotes alto saxophonist Art Pepper in this regard:

> I used to stand around and marvel at the way [African American musicians] talked. Having really nothing to say, they were able to play those little verbal games back

and forth. I envied it but was too self-conscious to do it. What I wouldn't give to just jump in and say those things. I could when I was joking to myself, raving to myself in front of the mirror at home, but when it came time to do it with people, I couldn't.

(Leonard 1987, 92)

This combination of fascination with black verbal and musical inventiveness and deprecation of the intelligence and knowledge necessary to produce it has proved to be a tenacious feature of the American reaction to African American presence in society more generally. The presumption that indirect, multisided, and metaphorical modes of speaking require less development of the mind reflects a Western cultural ideology about language that prefers the nonambiguous and non-playful delineation of ideas in intellectual discourse as well as the separation of these ideas from emotions (Lutz 1988, 53–80). In the Western classical music tradition, this preference has manifested itself in the long tradition of separating musical theory from practice, which is perhaps fitting for a musical tradition in which composition has in principle been separated from the moment of performance. In improvisation, composed through face-to-face interaction, however, the separation of sounds from the human beings who produce them makes far less sense. What Christopher Waterman has argued in the case of Yoruba musicians deserves exploration with reference to jazz musicians:

> The tendency in Western analytical thought to divorce structure from content finds its counterpart in musicological approaches which presume a radical distinction between reified musical structures (forms, scales, melodic and rhythmic modes) and qualitative parameters such as timbre, texture, gesture, and flow. This is not a meaningful distinction for Yoruba musicians and listeners. The experiential impact of the base metaphor "good music is good consociation" depends upon the generation of sensuous textures.
>
> (Waterman 1990, 376)

Jazz musicians stand in a particularly betwixt and between relationship to standard musical analysis. Most are quite able to talk about harmony, scales, melodic ideas, and rhythmic precision in terms familiar to students of Western music theory; many, in fact, have had extensive training in classical music and music theory. When describing the effective deployment of these musical resources with other musicians in the context of jazz performance, however, they often prefer metaphorical description for its ability to convey the more intangible social and aesthetic dimensions of music making. The analytic vocabulary of Western musical theory seems "soulless" to many.

Waterman's commentary refers to the equivalent of the groove in neotraditional Yoruba music and emphasizes the idea that "good music is good consociation." The aesthetics of jazz improvisation, as we have seen, also uphold this idea. Since groove is a concept that simultaneously refers to interdependent musical structures and an aesthetic ideal larger than any one individual, it is not surprising that social metaphors figure prominently in musicians' definitions of groove: "playing good time *with* somebody" (Byron 1989); "walking down the street with somebody" (Davis 1989; Washington 1990); "when you meet somebody and you find a compatibility of personalities" (Weiss 1990); "a mutual feeling of agreement on a pattern" (Bowler 1989). The importance of human personality and individuality is conveyed through metaphors that unify sound and the human beings who make the sound through collaborative musical activity.

When Michael Carvin likened groove to "getting into a bubble bath" (Carvin 1990) and Phil Bowler said that the bass is "like the earth—you walk on the earth" (Bowler 1989), each selected a vivid image with which to compare a particular musical process. Such images tend to be personal and individual. In Carvin's case, the image of "hot water around your body" communicates relaxation, which he later cited as an essential component for the establishment of groove. Bowler's comment highlighted through images from nature two essential musical functions of the bass: contributing the bottom of the harmony and providing a walking bass line. Drummer Michael Carvin also spoke of his left hand:

> But I hear the left hand as brass. Short, staccato, spurts or like a boxer, jabbin', jabbin', always keeping something happening.
>
> (Carvin 1990)

"I always speak in parables," Carvin added, because it "helps for people to understand" (Carvin 1992). There is nothing inarticulate or analytically vague about these statements; metaphorical images are in many cases more communicative than ordinary analytical language.

Sociability and Competition

While the musicians I interviewed tended to emphasize positive aspects of musical communication and sociability, Richard Davis did point out that things aren't always perfect:

> But you'll find, just like any other relationship—man and wife, child and parent, friend and friend—[musicians are] not always on the same level all the time. You have fights, you hate each other, you love each other ... you scream at each other ... but all that is part of the natural ingredients that come out of the music.
>
> (Davis 1989)

Sometimes things can even be hostile:

> That's why I won't make music with people that I don't like. ... I'd rather starve to death than play with a son of a bitch that I don't like. Because then I ain't gonna make no music.[11]

Because sociability includes the possibility for discord, the bandstand is an arena in which jealousies and competition—as well as harmony and brotherhood—can occur. A pianist who doesn't respect the musicality of a bass player, for example, may feel frustrated when the bass player doesn't pick up on the harmonic direction the pianist would like. A drummer might find that a particular pianist is always rushing and in an attempt to hold the pianist back must limit his or her musical ideas in the interest of rhythmic cohesion. A usually reliable player may have an off night, causing frustration for the rest of his or her band mates.

Musicians sometimes feel that other musicians are not sufficiently worthy to play with them. An "unworthy" musician can transform this image by performing well, which may include responding well to the potentially confusing musical interjections of other musicians. Such interjections challenge the soloist in much the same way as an opening insult in a verbal duel. An improviser can choose to respond to or ignore these musical ideas, but some of the most magical moments in jazz have occurred when the soloist is, as clarinetist Don Byron has put it, "poised enough to do something about them" (Byron 1987). This poise is essential for defending and defining one's reputation within the fiercely competitive world of professional jazz. The positive feelings musicians report for their peers generally occur between players who respect one another professionally. Musicians are constantly being evaluated both by one another and by audience members. [...]

We have moved from the structural aspects of the metaphor of conversation to the social ethos of jazz talk in music and words. The importance of interaction in jazz improvisation and the reasons why musicians have found language metaphors so attractive in their theorizing should be clear. [...]

Notes

1 The literature on the relationship between music and language is vast. There are several useful overviews, including Powers 1980; Feld 1974; and Nattiez 1990a, 1990b.

2 Turner gives the example of "the frontispiece to Hobbes's *Leviathan*, in which the giant body of the sovereign is made up of the bodies of his subjects" (Turner 1991, 158). For more on Charles Seeger's framework, see Feld 1984.

3 Once improvisations are recorded, however, they become sonic texts [...]. I am limiting my discussion here to the playing that occurs during improvised solos, although there is much improvised interaction from the rhythm section during the playing of the tune or composition as well. For a detailed discussion of the relationship between composition and improvisation, see Berliner 1994, 63–94, 170–91.

4 For a cross-cultural overview of language and music, see Powers 1980.

5 Other cultures make a *langue* and *parole* distinction as well. Feld and Schieffelin (1982) discuss this concept in relation to language in the culture of the Kaluli of Papua New Guinea.

6 Gates's summary of the sociolinguistic literature on signifying is perhaps the most concise currently available (Gates 1988, 44–88).

7 For a discussion of the concept of intertextuality in literary theories, see Hutcheon 1991, 23, 37, 87.

8 Schuller's criticisms of Count Basie's "riff-cum-blues" formats, for example, center on the problems of repetition, lack of harmonic innovation, and clichés (Schuller 1989, 222–62).

9 Most of these articles can be found in the Institute for Jazz Studies (IJS) clippings files under "Jazz Terminology."

10 In 1946 Cab Calloway published a "Hepster's Dictionary" (Calloway 1946) that some (Feather 1952) have credited for encouraging the trend of jazz word lists, dictionaries, or lexicons that was to intensify in the 1950s and 1960s (Shaw 1950; Morris 1954; "Jive Talk" 1954; Burley 1955; Horne 1961; Lees 1962; Gold 1975).

11 The musician requested that this quote be unattributed.

Works Cited

Abrahams, Roger D. 1970. *Deep Down in the Jungle: Negro Narrative Folklore from the Streets of Philadelphia.* 1st rev. ed. Originally published 1964. Chicago: Aldine Publishers.

Bakhtin, Mikhail. 1981. "Discourse in the Novel." In *The Dialogic Imagination: Four Essays*, edited by Michael Holquist, 259–422. Originally published 1935. Austin: University of Texas Press.

Berliner, Paul F. 1994. *Thinking in Jazz: The Infinite Art of Improvisation.* Chicago: University of Chicago Press.

Bowler, Phil. 1989. Interview by author. Tape recording. New York, NY, 17 April 1989.

Burley, Dan. 1955. "Time Out for Cool Talk: The Dilemma of Little Louie Hopp." *Tan* 5(7): 10–11+.

Byron, Don. 1989. Interview by author. Tape recording. Bronx, NY, 10 April 1989.

———. 1987. Interview by author. Tape recording. New York, NY, 8 May 1987.

Calloway, Cab. 1946. "Cab Calloway's Hepster Dictionary." *Disc* 1 (August 1946).

Cameron, William B. 1954. "Sociological Notes on the Jam Session." *Social Forces* 33: 177–82.

Carvin, Michael. 1992. Interview by author. Tape recording. Chicago, IL, 12 December 1992.

——. 1990. Interview by author. Tape recording. New York, NY, 10 October 1990.

Chapman, John. 1935. "Mainly About Manhattan." *Chicago Tribune*. Clippings files. Institute for Jazz Studies. Rutgers University, Newark, NJ.

Daniels, Douglas Henry. 1985. "Lester Young: Master of Jive." *American Music* 3(3): 313–28.

Davis, Richard. 1989. Interview by author. Tape recording. New York, NY, 6 July 1989.

DeMichael, Don. 1966. "The Varied Peripteries of Drummer Roy Haynes or They Call Him Snap Crackle!" *Down Beat* 33(26): 18–19+.

Du Bois, W. E. B. 1969. *The Souls of Black Folks*. Originally published 1903. New York: New American Library.

Feather, Leonard. 1952. "Feather's Nest." *Down Beat* (October 8): 16.

Feld, Steven. 1988. "Aesthetics as Iconicity of Style or 'Lift-Up-Over Sounding': Getting into the Kaluli Groove." *Yearbook for Traditional Music* 20: 74–113.

——. 1984. "Communication, Music and Speech About Music." *Yearbook for Traditional Music* 16: 1–18.

——. 1982. *Sound and Sentiment*. Philadelphia: University of Pennsylvania Press.

——. 1981. "'Flow Like a Waterfall': The Metaphors of Kaluli Music Theory." *Yearbook for Traditional Music* 13: 22–47.

——. 1974. "Linguistic Models in Ethnomusicology." *Ethnomusicology* 18: 197–217.

Feld, Steven, and Bambi B. Schieffelin. 1982. "Hard Works: A Functional Bias for Kaluli Discourse." In *Analyzing Discourse: Text and Talk*, edited by Deborah Tannen, 350–70. Washington, D.C.: Georgetown University Press.

Fernandez, James. 1986. *Persuasions and Performances: The Play of Tropes in Culture*. Bloomington: Indiana University Press.

Floyd, Samuel Jr. 1991. "Ring Shout! Literary Studies, Historical Studies, and Black Music Inquiry." *Black Music Research Journal* 11(2): 265–87.

Gates, Henry Louis Jr. 1988. *The Signifying Monkey: A Theory of African-American Literary Criticism*. New York: Oxford University Press.

Gold, Robert. 1975. *Jazz Talk*. Indianapolis, IN: The Bobbs-Merrill Company, Inc.

Goodwin, Marjorie H. 1990. *He-Said-She-Said: Talk as Social Organization among Black Children*. Bloomington: University of Indiana Press.

Gumperz, John J. 1982. *Discourse Strategies*. New York: Cambridge University Press.

Hanna, Sir Roland. 1989. Interview by author. Tape recording. New York, NY, 25 October 1989.

Harris, Jerome. 1989. Interview by author. Tape recording. Brooklyn, NY, 29 May 1989.

Hartman, Charles O. 1991. *Jazz Text: Voice and Improvisation in Poetry, Jazz, and Song*. Princeton: Princeton University Press.

Harvey, Holman. 1936. "It's Swing." *Delineator* (February): 10–11+.

hooks, bell. 1989. *Talking Back: Thinking Feminist, Thinking Black*. Boston: South End Press.

Horne, Elliot. 1961. "The Words for the Music." *New York Times* (25 June 1961): section VI, 39.

Hutcheon, Linda. 1991. *A Theory of Parody*. Originally published 1985. New York: Routledge.

"Jive Talk." 1954. *Rhythm and Blues* (December 1954 and February 1955): 15.

Kochman, Thomas. 1986. "Strategic Ambiguity in Black Speech Genres: Cross-Cultural Inference in Participant-Observation Research." *Text* 6(2): 153–70.

——. 1983. "The Boundary between Play and Nonplay in Black Verbal Dueling." *Language in Society* 12(3): 329–37.

——. 1981. *Black and White Styles in Conflict*. Chicago: University of Chicago Press.

Labov, William. 1972. "Rules of Ritual Insults." In *Rappin' and Stylin' Out': Communication in Black Urban America,* edited by Thomas Kochman, 265–314. Urbana: University of Illinois Press.

——. 1969. *The Logic of Nonstandard English*. Monograph Series on Languages and Linguistics. Washington: Georgetown University.

Lees, Gene. 1962. "A Show Business Lexicon. *Show Business Illustrated*: 57.

Leonard, Neil. 1987. *Jazz: Myth and Religion*. New York: Oxford University Press.

Levinson, Stephan C. 1983. *Pragmatics*. Cambridge: Cambridge University Press.

Lutz, Catherine A. 1988. *Unnatural Emotions: Everyday Sentiments on a Micronesian Atoll and Their Challenge to Western Theory*. Chicago: University of Chicago Press.

Mann, Alfred. 1986. *The Study of the Fugue*. Originally published 1958. New York: Dover Publications.

McBee, Cecil. 1990. Interview by author. Tape recording. New York, NY, 24 May 1990.

Merriam, Alan, and Raymond Mack. 1960. "The Jazz Community." *Social Forces* 38(3): 211–22.

Mitchell-Kernan, Claudia. 1986. "Signifying and Marking: Two Afro-American Speech Acts." In *Directions in Sociolinguistics: The Ethnography of Communication*, edited by John J. Gumperz and Dell Hymes, 161–79. Originally published 1972. Oxford, Basil Blackwell.

Morgan, Marcyliena H. 1991. "African American Women's Discourse." Unpublished paper.

Morris, William. 1954. *The Real Gone Lexicon*. New York: Self-published.

Nattiez, Jean-Jacques. 1990a. "Can One Speak of Narrativity in Music?" *Journal of the Royal Musical Association* 115: 240–57.

——. 1990b. *Music and Discourse: Toward a Semiology of Music*. Translated by Carolyn Abbate. Princeton: Princeton University Press.

Obenhaus, Mark. 1986. *Miles Ahead: The Music of Miles Davis*. Film.

Peterson, Ralph Jr. 1988. *V*. New York: 19–20 April 1988. Blue Note CDP 91730 2.

——. 1989a. Interview by author. Tape recording. New York, NY, 17 April 1989.

——. 1989b. Interview by author. Tape recording. New York, NY, 28 November 1989.

Poling, James W. 1936. "Music After Midnight." *Esquire* (June): 92, 131–32.

Porter, Lewis. 1985. "John Coltrane's *A Love Supreme*: Jazz Improvisation as Composition." *Journal of the American Musicological Society* 38: 593–621.

Powers, Harold S. 1980. "Language Models and Musical Analysis." *Ethnomusicology* 24: 1–60.

Ratner, Leonard. 1956. "Eighteenth-Century Theories of Musical Period Structure." *Musical Quarterly* 42(4): 439–54.

Saussure, Ferdinand de. 1986. *Course in General Linguistics*. Translated by Roy Harris. Originally published 1922. LaSalle, IL: Open Court.

Schuller, Gunther. 1989. *The Swing Era: The Development of Jazz, 1930–1945*. New York: Oxford University Press.

Seeger, Charles. 1977. *Studies in Musicology 1935–1975*. Berkeley and Los Angeles: University of California Press.

Shaw, Arnold. 1950. *Lingo of Tin-Pan Alley*. New York, NY: Broadcast Music, Inc. (BMI).

Sidran, Ben. 1986. *Black Talk*. Originally published 1971. New York: Da Capo.

Smitherman, Geneva. 1977. *Talkin' and Testifyin': The Language of Black America*. Boston: Houghton Mifflin.

"Speaking of Pictures ... Swing Music Produces These." 1938. *Life* (21 February): 4–5+.

Stix, John. 1978. "Roland Hanna: Versatile Mainstream Pianist." *Contemporary Keyboard* 4(5): 10+.

"They're Killing Swing: More Editorial Blah on the Subject of Swing." 1938. *Metronome* (November).

Turner, Terence. 1991. "'We Are Parrots.' 'Twins Are Birds': Play of Tropes as Operational Structure. In *Beyond Metaphor: The Theory of Tropes in Anthropology,* edited by James W. Fernandez, 121–58. Stanford: Stanford University Press.

Washington, Kenny. 1990. Interview by author. Tape recording. Brooklyn, NY, January 1990.

Waterman, Christopher, A. 1990. "'Our Tradition Is a Very Modern Tradition': Popular Music and the Construction of Pan Yoruban Identity." *Ethnomusicology* 34(3): 367–79.

Weiss, Michael. 1990. Interview with author. Tape recording. Brooklyn, NY, 13 August 1990.

Wilson, Olly. 1992. "The Heterogeneous Sound Ideal in African-American Music." In *New Perspectives on Music: Essays in Honor of Eileen Southern*, edited by Joesphine Wright, 327–38. Warren, MI: Harmonie Park Press.

6   Deep Listening Meditations: Egypt (1999)

Pauline Oliveros

The following "meditation" is a prime example of Pauline Oliveros' principle of Deep Listening: where listening is key to living. In her long career, Oliveros has gone from being a pioneer of tape and electronic music to the founder of the Deep Listening Institute in Kingston, NY. Born in Houston, Texas, she studied music in Houston and San Francisco, where she participated in collectively devised musics in the 1950s and was a founding member of the San Francisco Tape Music Center. When the Center moved to Mills College in Oakland, Oliveros became the first director of what is now called the Center for Contemporary Music. Her ideas of "sonic awareness," an acknowledgement of the many ways that sound shapes and permeates the human landscape, were the basis of "Sonic Meditations" that were the precursors to the Deep Listening projects. Oliveros' books include *Sounding the Margins: Collected Writings 1992–2009*, *Initiation Dream*, *Software for People*, *The Roots the Moment*, and *Deep Listening: A Composer's Sound Practice*. Accordionist, pioneer of electronic music and an adventurous composer, she has collaborated with several generations of improvisers including Terry Riley, Roscoe Mitchell, Anne Bourne, and Jesse Stewart.

Key words: USA; new music; interdisciplinary; electronics; collaboration

The following meditations were composed especially for the March process journey to Egypt led by Ione with Andrea Goodman, Alessandro Ashanti and Pauline Oliveros. It was intended that there would be one listening meditation given each day. The meditations should be done one at a time.

Imagine a sound that you want to hear. During a designated time, such as a day or night, take note of when and where you hear the sound.

From the field of sound that you are hearing, select a sound. Focus on it and amplify it with your imagination. Continue to hold and amplify the sound, even if the real sound has stopped. When you are done, scan your body/mind and notate your feelings.

Listen to any sound as if it had never been heard before.

Listening—I am sound. (Try listening to the words in different ways).

If you are looking—what are you listening to or for?

Focus on a sound that attracts your attention. Imagine a new or different context or field for that sound.

Listen all day to your own footsteps.

Where does sound come from?

Imagine that your ears have extended range above and below the normal range of 16hz to 20khz. What could you be hearing?

Can you find an unusual melody?

If you are feeling sound, where does it center or circulate in your body—psyche?

Listen for a heart sound. (Affective)

In a group or crowd can you hear with their ears?

What is the longest sound you heard today?

What is the sound of our group—of belonging—of not belonging? How do you listen to the field sound of the group? What does the leader listen for? The group member? How do you tune in or out?

Center through what is sounding.

If you could ride the waves of your favorite sound, where would it take you?

Are sounds going out or coming in?

Imaginary improvisation: You are holding the possibility of making the first sound.

Sounds are coming and going and yet creating a field of sound.

Where have you heard the most sounds? The most variety? The most diverse?

As you listen, the particles of sound (phonons) decide to be heard. Listening affects what is sounding. The relationship is symbiotic.

As you listen, the environment is enlivened. This is the listening effect.

7 "Really Listening"

Original art, 30 x 44", made live @ World Percussion Summit September 3, 2013

Jeff Schlanger, musicWitness®

Since the 1970s, Jeff Schlanger has carried on his musicWitness® series of visual art projects in the interrelated subjects of Music, War, and Peace. Including an extended series of paintings, drawings, and prints created during live performances of improvising musicians, his work has been seen at every annual New York City Vision Festival, on the covers of over 30 record albums, and at the Guelph Jazz Festival. Schlanger has collaborated with countless musicians the world over, and has brought musicWitness® to Berlin, Paris, and Tampere, Finland. This artwork, "Really Listening," was created at the Guelph Jazz Festival's 20th anniversary edition (2013) during the launch of the International Institute for Critical Studies in Improvisation. It is a visual response to a live improvised performance by Pandit Anindo Chatterjee, Dong-Won Kim, Hamid Drake, and Jesse Stewart.

Key words: art; musicWitness®; liveness; listening; documentation

Figure 7.1 Really Listening

Part 2

Trust/Risk

8   Improvised Trust: Opening Statements

Ellen Waterman

Ellen Waterman is a scholar and a flautist specialising in creative improvisation and contemporary music. Her SSHRC-funded *Sounds Provocative: Experimental Music Performance in Canada* is a comparative study of experimental music festivals across Canada. Waterman's work on gender, sound, and technology includes a special issue of the journal *Intersections: Journal of Canadian Music* 26.2 (2006), co-edited with Andra McCartney. She is editor of *Sonic Geography Imagined and Remembered* (2002), and she has published extensively on the work of R. Murray Schafer, with whom she worked for ten years. With Gillian Siddall, she is co-editing the anthology *Sounding Bodies: Improvisation, Representation, and Subjectivity* for Duke University Press, and she is a founding editor of the online journal *Critical Studies in Improvisation/Études critiques en improvisation*. Waterman is part of a collaborative project led by Pauline Oliveros involving ICASP/IICSI team members, the Deep Listening Institute, and Rensselaer Polytechnic Institute to develop, document, and study the AUMI—an adaptive-use musical instrument for people with disabilities. She is currently Dean of the School of Music at Memorial University in St John's, Newfoundland. In "Improvised Trust," Waterman highlights the social and interactive aspects of improvisation at their most personal and most essential: "in the end," she writes, "trust is worth the risk."

Key words: music; interdisciplinarity; environmental sound; Canada

Improvisation is often perceived as risky, and it is this very risk that renders the practice virtuosic. Musicians who practise free improvisation work without a safety net. All their decisions are made in the moment, complex responses to external stimuli, internal impulses, memory, and context. The possibility of failure is always imminent, because the process demands such a high degree of self-exposure. Improvisation is most satisfying when the conditions of trust exist that allow participants to risk everything in the moment of performance. This means that improvisation is an arena of social interaction and accountability. It also positions improvisation as a site of dialogism-in-action, where we bring our personal histories and values into contact with others in a spirit of openness to change. What's at stake in improvisation, then, is nothing less than the possibility of personal transformation.

Risk manifested as fear of failure is a fatal distraction. If an actor in an improvisational sketch is worried about his timing, nervous as to whether he'll be sufficiently quick-witted in response to the fast-moving events on stage, he has already compromised his chances of communicating effectively. However, risk manifested as boldness is exciting. A high tolerance for risk is associated with Wall Street financiers, dot com innovators, and extreme sports enthusiasts. Risk takers stand to win big. Placing other people at risk, however, is often a side product of such aggressive energy, while mitigating and managing risk is a growth enterprise for petty bureaucrats. In fact, there is a genuine risk in not taking risks because undue fear of risk results in stasis, containment, and isolation.

Turned on its ear, what seems like virtuosic risk-taking in improvisation is actually the skillful exercise of trust. Contact dancers trust that they can move within a writhing mass of other dancing bodies and that they will come into intimate contact with, but not hurt, or be hurt by, other dancers. The only way to practise such improvising is to take a leap of faith and do it. It is exactly akin to Douglas Adams's (1979) recipe for learning to fly in *The Hitchhiker's Guide to the Galaxy*: jump off a tall building and forget to fall. (As soon as you remember that you are falling, you really do begin to plummet towards the earth.) The analogy to this in theatre is the famous exercise where an actor must fall backwards, trusting that the arms of colleagues are waiting to catch her.

Trust, then, involves the willingness to take a risk that someone or something is trustworthy. Most of us are willing to take risks in exact proportion to how much we trust in the outcome. We trust that the airplane will take off and land safely; that our spouses will still love us when we're old and ugly; that we'll wake up from the anaesthetic after the operation; that cars will stop at the red light while we cross the road. The evening news is constituted by the dramatic consequences that occur when our trust is betrayed. Despite the risk, we take comfort in trusting others and we cultivate trustworthiness because these are the foundations of our humanity.

The delicate negotiation of trust and risk within improvisation may thus be understood in terms of social interaction and accountability. For example, there are numerous kinds of musical improvisation that are far from free form. Many types of improvisation such as Baroque organ fantasies and big band swing jazz are bound by strict genre rules. Straying too far outside these genre rules renders the style unrecognisable. North Indian devotees of Hindustani classical music spend a long apprenticeship with a guru learning all the traditions and musical gestures of a particular *gharana*, or school, before they begin to improvise. Good improvisers in this cultural framework exemplify the musical traditions to which they belong while simultaneously extending them (Napier, 2006). Similarly, masters of traditional Persian *musiqi-e assil* never talk to their students about improvisation. Lessons focus on learning the *radif*, an exacting repertoire of modes and musical figures. Only after completely absorbing the *radif* may one begin to improvise on this material, a process of sophisticated variation (Nooshin, 2003). Trust in earned skill and long tradition nevertheless carries a risk: we may, after all, only be good imitators. We may fail to add to the tradition and thus weaken it. Whatever the social context, it is all too possible to improvise badly, to be banal, repetitive, and boring.

Overcoming this fear, achieving a trusting state, is a necessary condition of effective improvisation that Julie Dawn Smith (2013, p.59) has termed "the listening trust." The listening trust is a social compact—that I will listen to you deeply and respectfully and that you will also listen to me in the same way even if we can't agree. The listening trust is an agreement among improvisers "to engage in an 'empathic communication across time' and to employ an 'ethics of respect' for the performative journey with/in which they are about to engage" (Smith and Waterman, 2013, pp.84–85).

If good improvising depends on empathic communication, then it is clear that a failure of attentiveness constitutes a formidable barrier to success. Being wedded to ideology is one such failure. This is true even when the ideology consists of a number of positive ideas about improvisation: that everyone should have a voice, that no one person should dominate, and that defaulting to learned behaviors is a limitation to be overcome. "Empathic communication across time" includes being willing to follow someone down a road that looks uninviting or even dangerous according to our preconceptions. In musical or theatrical or dance improvisation, the stakes feel high, but the risk is, after all, relatively small. We may be taken somewhere that is unpleasant and we may not like the aesthetic outcome. In the end, improvisers may not reach agreement but, arguably, even a "failed" improvisation in that sense may be redeemed by its mindfulness. Improvisation models the social relations that both structure and animate our wider lives; "good improvisation" is conducted in "good faith." However, if we fail to empathise with others in the process of improvising, then we close ourselves off to the possibility of transformation, and that constitutes a considerable loss.

All improvisation is social. For some, the goal of improvisation is to tap into something larger than ourselves, to work in concert with others to achieve a harmonious, unified expression. For others, improvisation is a dynamic dance in which individuality is defined and affirmed within subtle shifts of power. Even solo improvisation entails being responsive both to immediate context and to memory.

The improvising composer Pauline Oliveros has a piece that exemplifies all of these approaches. *Tuning Meditation* (1990) is designed to allow people to improvise together across abilities: it is for musicians and non-musicians, skilled improvisers and neophytes. The guidelines form a simple algorithm. Imagine a tone, and after taking a deep breath exhale while singing it. Continue by making one of three choices: to copy a tone you hear someone else singing, to introduce a new tone into the mix, or to remain silent and listen. Everyone moves among these three choices throughout the improvisation, which lasts as long as people continue to sing. *Tuning Meditation* has been performed by as few as six and as many as 6000 people (using remote radio broadcasts as well as a concert hall audience). It is easy to lose yourself in the sonorous mass of harmonies emanating from all around the performance space, yet each person bears a singular responsibility. The object of the piece, Oliveros maintains, is to communicate purposefully with as many different people as possible during the improvisation. The imperative of empathic communication prevents participants from focusing on the sound mass as if it was something external to the individuals creating it.

In the end, trust is worth the risk. Improvisation is by nature a process of negotiation, of myriad small decisions taken responsively. Bringing herself fully to these negotiations is the improviser's principal task and main resource. What would it be like to make music, or dance, or theatre only with others who already think like you, have similar backgrounds, beliefs, and vocabularies? Safe, perhaps, but ultimately static. What would it be like to seek out fellow improvisers with sharply contrasting experiences, abilities, and ideas? Risky, to be sure, but far more adventurous! The goal of such improvisation would be to become open to the unexpected and the new, to expand mind, body, and senses. Such improvisation might even be personally and socially transformative.

Works Cited

Adams, D., 1979. *The Hitchhiker's Guide to the Galaxy.* New York: Harmony Books.

Napier, J., 2006. A Subtle Novelty: Repetition, transmission and the valorisation of innovation within North Indian Classical Music. *Critical Studies in Improvisation / Études critiques en improvisation*, 1(3). Available at: www.criticalimprov.com/article/view/55. [Accessed 28 August 2012].

Nooshin, L., 2003. Improvisation as "Other": Creativity, Knowledge and Power: The Case of Iranian Classical Music. *Journal of the Royal Musical Association*, 128(2), pp.242–96.

Oliveros, P., 1990. Tuning Meditation. In: P. Oliveros, 1990. *Deep Listening Pieces*. Kingston, N.Y.: Deep Listening Publications.

Smith, J. D. and Waterman, E., 2013. Listening Trust: The Everyday Politics of George Lewis's "Dream Team." In: A. Heble and R. Wallace, eds. 2013. *People Get Ready: The Future of Jazz is Now!*. Durham, NC: Duke University Press. pp.44–68.

9 Improvisation

Constantin Stanislavski

Translated by Elizabeth Reynolds Hapgood

Stanislavski (1863–1938) was born in Moscow as Constantin Sergeyevich Alexeyev. His wealthy manufacturing family shared his love of the performing arts, but when at the age of 25 Constantin formed his first theatre company, he took "Stanislavski" as a stage name to distance himself from the well-known Alexeyev name. Stanislavski co-founded the still-existing Moscow Art Theatre in 1898 as a protest against the old manner of acting including theatricality, affectation, and the star system. His ideas inspired the later development of method acting, in which actors adopt their characters' motivations as their own. His best-known legacy in North America is the Actors Studio, established in New York City in 1947, which to this day continues as a major force in method-based theatrical and film acting. Although his ideas remain influential, he essentially saw improvisation as a tool for training actors—an exercise of the imagination, which in turn would stimulate new interpretations when the actor came to interpret scripted work. Despite his bourgeois connections, Stanislavski was able to survive the upheaval of the Bolshevik Revolution largely because of his socially conscious reputation and collective methodology.

Key words: theatre; politics of improvisation; pedagogy

When teaching is oriented toward a practical and even interesting objective it is easier to convince and influence students. ... Our point of departure in training actors is to have them learn by acting [improvisations]. ... One cannot go on teaching for years in a classroom and only at the end ask a student to act. In that space of time he will have lost all creative faculty. ... Creativeness must never cease, the only question being the choice of material on which to base it. ... In our kind of acting we make frequent use of improvisations. ... This kind of creativeness gives a freshness and an immediacy to a performance.

In the beginning it is best to take subjects which are within your reach, and not too overburdened with complicated psychology ... but even the most primary kind of exercises must be carried to the point of mastery, of virtuosity in execution. It is not the job of teachers to give instruction in how to create, we should only push students in the right direction, while training their taste, requiring from them the observance of the laws of nature, and the execution of their simplest exercises carried to the point of art, which is to say absolute truthfulness and technical perfection.

Improvisations which they work out themselves are an excellent way to develop the imagination. ... Student actors who have been trained on improvisations later on find it easy to use their imaginative fancy on a play where this is needed.

In addition to the development of imagination improvisations ... have another asset: while working on one an actor naturally, without even perceiving it, learns the creative laws of organic nature and the methods of psycho-technique.

—Collected Works, Vol. III
—*Year Book of the Moscow Art Theatre, 1947*

10 Afterthoughts

Keith Johnstone

By his own account a poor student in his youth, Keith Johnstone has inspired generations of talented playwrights, directors, actors, and comedians with teaching methods that empower the imagination. In the late 1950s at the Royal Court Theatre in London, he worked at making spontaneity and improvisation dynamic forces in devised theatre, pioneering the use of masks and costumes as methods of liberating emotions that are themselves masked by the "performance" of everyday life. His idea of "status transactions"—in which performers try to pitch their status above, or below, those of their partners—has been adopted as a technique not only in improvised theatre, but in script writing and most famously, in comedy. At Canada's University of Calgary, he invented Theatresports, which has given rise to an entire genre of spontaneous, improvised comedy. He is the author of the books *Impro: Improvisation and the Theatre* and *Impro for Storytellers*. In the same way that Mattin works with the "fragile moments" of musical improvisation, Keith Johnstone, in theatrical improvisation, looks for ways that the actor can cause "havoc" even while remaining "safe." Johnstone's invaluable writings are imbued with the constant awareness of the power relationships that energise great theatrical moments.

Key words: theatre; dialogue; the body; pedagogy; safety

> To prepare fleas for the Flea Circus (as in the Cole Porter lyric, 'Bees do it, even educated fleas do it'), cover them with a sheet of glass so that it smashes them back each time they leap. Two days of this and they'll never jump again and are described as 'educated.'

The Body

Many of us 'keep a grip' on ourselves as if we might fly apart, or as if our eyes might drop out and get stepped on. Shoulders are held high, pelvises are locked, breathing is restricted, and weight that should be carried on our bones is supported by muscle (which is why we feel lighter if our posture improves).

I've heard it argued that this decline into adulthood is as inevitable as kittens turning into cats, but whoever saw an adult cat with tight eyes? Animals move wonderfully, because there's no way that we can give them advice. If we could tell them to 'Pick up those paws up!' and 'Stiffen those whiskers!' and 'Keep that tail up!' adult cats would clump about bumping into furniture.

Droop your head and look miserable (you can find the mood if you say things like 'I hate you, Daddy!' or 'Why can't I, Mummy?'). No one admires such a child, and the average adult will say, 'Chin up!'

Raise your chin but keep the misery (the slump). The back of your neck is now shorter, and instruction number two follows almost immediately: 'Shoulders back!'

If your head is forward the shoulders should also hang forward. Pulling them back adds more tension and emphasizes your caved-in chest: 'Chest out!'

Obey this and your pelvis tilts, allowing your abdomen to bulge: 'Stomach in!'

You feel heavier and everything admirable about your posture has now been trashed. Try to walk and what happens? Your feet drag: 'Pick your feet up!' say the adults, and then, in desperation, 'Stand up straight!'

Anyone obeying the previous instructions can't obey this one, but obedient children will try to experience 'straightness' by pressing their knees back, and this hyper-tension soon does irreparable damage.[1]

The Mind

If people are clamping their body together as if it might fall apart, perhaps the same is true of the mind. Could it be that our instructions on how to use our consciousness are as damaging as our advice about posture? Should we really be told to 'Think!' and 'Try to concentrate!' and 'Be original!' as if thought required effort, and as if originality lay somewhere outside of ourselves? Should we really think of ourselves as 'one consciousness' and force our imagination to confirm this?

It's not easy to kill the curiosity of an ape, but sitting it at a desk for year after year of organized boredom might do the trick. Our preoccupation with trivia suggests that the urge to learn is intact, but that learning anything of significance has become stressful. The Executive producer of the David Letterman show, Robert Morton, said, 'If you walk away from this show learning something, then we haven't done our job'.[2] If entertainment is designed to pass the time without teaching us anything, then I have to presume that it's a spin-off of our education system. Other cultures have feasts, celebrations and morality plays, and they may tear our hearts to ensure that the sun comes up, but I think that entertainment is peculiar to us, and many of us are entertained for most of our waking hours. [...]

Quality

If the process is good, I assume the end-product will be good. This stops me believing that an improvised scene has 'quality' if it resembles a written scene (as though improvisation were just a step on the road to improvisational theatre).

Players are working well when:

- They are enjoying the scenes they're in (this is not the same as enjoying being onstage)
- They're giving the audience the 'future' that it anticipates (while avoiding obscene and disgusting scenes)
- They're taking care of each other and being altered by each other
- They're daring, mischievous, humble and courageous
- The work feels 'natural', 'effortless' and 'obvious'
- No one is trying to be 'original' or to think up 'clever' ideas
- They're uniting the spectators into 'one creature'

- They're being themselves, rather than fleeing from self-revelation
- We care about the values expressed in the work
- The audience's yearnings, anxieties and fantasies are being made flesh

Players are probably working badly when they are:

- 'Shining'
- Being negative (e.g. killing ideas, presenting scenes about vomiting, and so on)
- Fighting each other for control (i.e. when they're afraid of being controlled)
- 'Planning' instead of 'attending'
- Wrecking stories for the sake of easy laughs (or for any other reason)
- Suppressing the kinetic dance
- Ignoring moral implications
- Wallowing in clichés (e.g. hunting for treasure, asking for 'household chores' to act out, and so forth)

Great Audiences

- Do not cheer uncritically
- Never sit with folded arms
- Are united with the players against the Judges
- Are benevolent (the players must do everything possible to create and sustain this benevolence)
- Laugh in huge unthinking waves, and, when silent, are absolutely silent
- Are reluctant to leave at the end of the show

Great Improvisers

A great improviser can make us laugh at any moment, and can give us moist eyes at any moment.

Great improvisers 'go with the flow', accepting that they're in the hands of God, or the Great Moose. Their attitude is the opposite of those 'beginners' for whom improvisation is very difficult and who find the demons on the stage just as threatening as those in life. When a great improviser is inspired, all limits seem to disappear. Sometimes it's as if there's extra light on the stage, and the players' outlines seem sharper. Competent improvisers give us flashes of this, but great improvisers can supply this demonic light (or heavenly radiance) for minutes at a time.

I'm describing something that all parents have seen (unless they were blinded by their intellects). Very young children can be so flooded, so pumped-up, so exploded with joy that it's as if they're streaming light into the universe. It's why some cultures regard them as gods who only gradually become human.

Great improvisers can sometimes come within spitting distance of that kind of power (as can great actors).

Getting Jaded

It's wonderful to be surfing on huge waves of laughter, but it begins to pall; you discover that your skills are no longer developing, and that most of the scenes are pointless, and that your contemporaries are drifting away to be replaced by young teenagers.

Maybe you give up, or maybe you give up only to get sucked back in again—after all, it's an interesting 'hobby'. With luck, you may eventually realize that very little of 'you' was ever present on the stage; and that verbal thinking kills spontaneity; and that the world is not six, or sixteen, or sixty seconds in the future; and that a good story is worth any amount of cheap laughs; and that the winning and losing are all ashes.

At this point, Theatresports becomes thrilling and dangerous all over again, and once more a great adventure.

Notes

1 There are other reasons why the muscles clamp up—for example, as a way to blot out suffering. Release muscles that are chronically tense and you're likely to be overwhelmed by long-forgotten pain and misery—this is commonplace.
2 Toronto *Globe and Mail*, 22 November 1993.

11 Thoughts on Improvisation: A Comparative Approach

Bruno Nettl

From an early age Bruno Nettl was fascinated with musical improvisation. Born in Prague in 1930, he was inspired early in his life by the discovery of unscored Indian classical music. Nettl and his family moved to the USA in 1939, and in 1964 he began teaching at the University of Illinois. Much of his most important work has been done with the music of indigenous peoples in North America, Iran, and South India. In 1983 Nettl published his seminal work *The Study of Ethnomusicology: Twenty-Nine Issues and Concepts* (revised and reissued in 2005). In 1998, with Melinda Russell, he edited *In the Course Of Performance: Studies in the World of Musical Improvisation*, and in 2009, with Gabriel Solis, he edited *Musical Improvisation: Art, Education, and Society*. Four decades after it appeared, "Thoughts on Improvisation" remains an invaluable introduction to the worldwide practice of musical improvisation, which in fact questions the ways in which we compartmentalise music-making: "Should we not then speak perhaps of rapid and slow composition rather than of composition juxtaposed to improvisation?"

Key words: world music; ethnomusicology; pedagogy

In 1938 Ernst Ferand published what continues to be the only large, scholarly book on the subject of musical improvisation.[1] A rather thorough search reveals that this book was but little reviewed and was received with only mild enthusiasm.[2] Although it develops many concepts with considerable sophistication, and gives much data as to the nature of improvisation in various periods of European music history, it seems not to have had great impact on its own time, despite the fact that, through his later encyclopedia articles and anthologies, Ferand has obviously remained the single outstanding authority in international musicology on this subject. Perhaps his work was taken lightly simply because the subject of improvisation was taken lightly by musicologists; it seems to have been regarded as something not having cardinal importance[3]—as not truly art, but craft, which results in such "microcosmic" alterations or elaborations of composed music as ornamentation *or* the realization of figured bass, or in such musical acrobatics as the ability of a few organists to extemporize fugues on themes suggested to them on the spur of the moment.

The concept of improvisation has become much more prominent in musicology since that time, largely because of the increased attention given to musics which appear to depend much more heavily on improvisation than does European art music. There are now many studies of jazz and of Indian, Indonesian, Middle Eastern and African music that deal explicitly or, more frequently, implicitly with improvisation. Courses, both practical and scholarly, are devoted to this subject, as are sessions at scholarly meetings.[4] But in the area of scholarly conceptualization Ferand is still the last word; and while he made admirable use of the information available to him on non-Western music, it is probably time to begin to rethink the idea of improvisation, to see whether it merits consideration as a single process, whether it has integrity as an idea separate from other, related ideas about creating of music, and whether all the things that we now call improvisation are indeed the same thing.

In studying the definitions found in music dictionaries and encyclopedias, we encounter two apparently conflicting views of improvisation. Some sources, such as *MGG* (in an article by Ferand),[5] indicate the relevance of the concept to non-Western, particularly tribal, musics, and state that, given the absence of notation, these are basically improvised. Others[6] confine the idea of improvisation only to music for which there is basically a notation system from which the improviser departs; in this view non-Western music, in which one cannot really distinguish between improvisation and composition, cannot be said to represent either concept. The *Harvard Dictionary*[7] implies this by entirely omitting non-European music from its article. Obviously the relationship of improvisation to composition and notation is a complex one, on which there is no general agreement.

Specifically or implicitly accepted in all the general discussions is the suddenness of the creative impulse. The improviser makes unpremeditated, spur-of-the-moment decisions, and because they are not thought out, their individual importance, if not of their collective significance, is sometimes denied. The above-mentioned encyclopedias are proportioned so as to spend far less space on improvisation and the kinds of music that result from it than on various kinds of composition; and, consonant with the general Western view of the process, they treat it as a minor art or craft of musicianship.

The general literature on improvisation deals largely with the phenomenon in Western music and attempts to gain a historical perspective on the role of the process in the performance practice of the past. Only briefly mentioned are the large number and variety of non-European musical systems which make sharp distinctions between improvisation and the performance of standardized pieces, or those in which the improvisatory element is a major component of all performance. Ferand was well aware of the existence of these systems and refers to them frequently, without making them a major substantive component of his work.[8] A new edition of his study, or a new, truly comprehensive book on the subject, would have to examine the various types of improvisation that are actually recognized, though perhaps not designated by a single specific term, in India. It would have to come to grips with the special nature of the *maqam* and *dastgah* systems (the modal structures of the Arabic world and Iran) and comment on the interrelationships of various performances of an epic, by one performer, in the Yugoslav heroic song tradition. It should deal with the kinds of group improvisation found in African drum ensembles and in the music of the Indonesian gamelans. It should, moreover, try to explore the notion that the improvisatory process is present to varying degrees in tribal music such as that of the American Indian; and it should explain the improvisatory side of communal recreation in European folk music.

The customary picture of improvisation, then, would and should be greatly expanded by an understanding of non-Western cultures. Unfortunately, the recent ethnomusicological literature contributes to this end in only a piecemeal fashion, providing specialized studies of systems and subsystems without giving much attention to the nature of the concept, and certainly making little attempt to be comparative. (Indeed, when it comes to providing a comparative view, Ferand is still the most insightful scholar.) The aim in these pages will be to present, very briefly, some thoughts of a comparative sort on the nature of improvisation as a concept and as a process, using material from a number of cultures, in an attempt, if not to clarify, then to pose some questions about, the meaning of this elusive idea. If the concept of improvisation can be said to be at all viable, it should be considered one of the few universals of music in which all cultures share in one way or another.

Improvisation and Composition

Improvisation and composition are opposed concepts, we are told[9]—the one spontaneous, the other calculated; the one primitive, the other sophisticated; the one natural, the other artificial. But, on the other hand, we are also given to believe that improvisation is a type of composition, the type that characterizes those cultures that have no notation, a type that releases the sudden impulse to music through the direct production of sound. We hear that improvisation ends where notation begins, yet at the same time we are told that certain non-Western cultures which do not use notation distinguish between the two processes, if not explicitly, then by the way they internally classify their musics. Thus, while we feel that we know intuitively what improvisation is, we find that there is confusion regarding its essence.

For example, let us take the idea of unprepared and sudden creation as the major criterion and examine it in the light of what we know about American Indian music, one of the best described non-Western musical cultures. It is known that the Plains Indians seek visions in order to learn songs, and that these songs come to them during periods of ecstasy sometimes brought on by fasting and self-torture. The sudden creation of a song is in line with statements from Plains Indians that songs can be and normally are learned in a single hearing.[10] Are these songs improvised when they are first sung? It would appear so. But we are told also that the visionary, upon learning a song, sings it to himself and, as it were, "works it out" when he walks back to his band or tribe. Once the song exists, it takes on the trappings of establishment, like a composition in the Western sense. The composer is known, remembered, and named, and the circumstances of composition are sometimes recounted before singing. Repeated recordings show that the song remains reasonably stable. Is this composition or improvisation?

For the Pima Indians of the southwestern United States, on the other hand, songs existed (in the supernatural world) but had to be "unraveled" by humans in order to be realized.[11] Here we find an idea which may approximate that of Western style composition in its resort to calculation. But there is no notation, and the style of Pima songs, generally speaking, is actually not very different from that of Plains music.

A third North American example comes from the Eskimo, who recognize two ways of making songs, a conventional one and an improvised one—the latter being the type of song represented by the famous song-duels wherein quarreling men settle disputes by mocking each other.[12] The use of a repertory of standard formulas is suspected,[13] but this is something shared with at least some other cultures which improvise. Again, the improvised songs show no basic dissimilarity of style when compared with the composed or traditional songs.

Is there, then, an essential difference between the composed and the improvised American Indian materials? Stylistic differences are negligible, notation is not present, and it is only the suddenness of inspiration in certain cases that allows us to make the distinction. But this kind of distinction can also be made in Western art music, by comparing, for example, the painstaking and often protracted method of Beethoven with Schubert's quick, spontaneous creation of lieder.[14] Again, broadly viewed, the styles are not substantially different. Should we not then speak perhaps of rapid and slow composition rather than of composition juxtaposed to improvisation? And would we not do well to think of composition and improvisation as opposite ends of a continuum, with a Schubert and a Beethoven at the extremes, likewise with the improvising Eskimo at one extreme, the Pima at the other, and the Plains Indians somewhere in the middle? [...]

Let us look briefly at another aspect of the composition-improvisation relationship. In those musics which are said to be improvised a number of compositional techniques and devices at the microcompositional level appear to be characteristic. Among them are repetition, simple variation of short phrases, melodic sequence, the tendency to start two successive sections with the same motive, the tendency to increase the length of sections as the performance progresses, and perhaps others. Now all of these techniques are also present in the "set" or "fixed" compositions of certain cultures. Is their distribution significant? The "fixed" compositions from some of the cultures that have systematic improvisation, such as India and Iran, exhibit features found in improvisation *Kritis,* the long, metric devotional songs that are central to the vocal and instrumental concert music of the South Indian tradition, and are likely to have repetition and minor variation of short lines just as do the improvisations upon musical themes taken from them. It is interesting, therefore, to find a given culture using essentially the same compositional techniques, whether the material is, by our standards, composed or improvised. This fact may eventually shed some light on the ultimate genesis of musical systems. Is it possible that those cultures which used certain compositional techniques were driven by the very nature of these techniques to develop systems of improvisation? Or did some cultures, perhaps millennia ago, begin their musical traditions by allowing performers great freedom in their renditions of a model, and then permit musicians, using the techniques developed in the "free rendition" period of their music history, to devise more stably fixed melodies? This is an area in which, even more than elsewhere in this paper, we can do little other than speculate.

A final observation concerns the use in Western music of the special techniques whose frequent occurrence in improvisatory styles is characteristic. It appears that some of these techniques are especially common in certain periods of music history, particularly the Baroque, and likewise in the works of certain composers (such as Mozart, Chopin, and Schubert) who were known to work rapidly and spontaneously, and whose output was great. It is thus conceivable that, *mutatis mutandis,* the musical thought processes of a Schubert are much more closely related to the improvisations of Indian and Middle Eastern musicians than are those of a Beethoven. The fact that Schubert wrote down certain of his works rapidly and, if we are to believe some descriptions,[15] without working and reworking them very much, could lead us to regard his musical thinking as basically improvisatory. Thus, rather than making the presence or absence of notation the major criterion for improvisation and composition, and dividing music into two spheres, that of improvisation-oral tradition and that of composition-notational, we could speculate upon the·division of the world's musical cultures and of their subsystems—genres, periods, composers—into two groups. One of these would be the music which is carefully thought out, perhaps even worked over with a conscious view to introducing innovation from piece to piece and even from phrase to phrase; the other, that which is spontaneous but model-bound, rapidly created, and simply conceived. The first gives up spontaneity for deliberation, while the second eschews a search for innovation in favor of giving way to sudden impulse. Neither need be considered improvisation, and neither is restricted to any particular level of musical or cultural complexity.

Improvisation and the Model

Having apparently done what we could to demolish the idea of improvisation as a concept separate from composition, we must now reinstate it for the purpose of examining certain aspects of performance wherein the musician is free to contribute materials of his own spontaneous making. The improviser, let us hypothesize, always has something given to work from—certain things that are at the base of the performance, that he uses as the ground on which he builds. We may call it his model. In some cultures specific theoretical terms are used to designate the model: *raga* and *tala* (the basic concepts of melodic and rhythmic organization in India), and other, basically modal configurations—*patel* in Javanese and Balinese gamelan music, *dastgah* in Iran, *maqam* in Arabic and Turkish music. In these cultures or others, names of musical performance-forms are used to designate the model: the blues sequence of chords in jazz, the nonmetric *taqsim* in Arabic music. On the other hand, the model may be a specific composition, and a culture may in effect designate the model by giving the names of tunes in jazz, of *kritis* in South India, of specific songs in the Yugoslav epic tradition. Or, again, styles indicating some specific pitch or rhythmic content (figured bass in Western music, or *abadja* and *kpanlogo*, rhythmically distinctive styles of West African drumming) can reveal the existence of an improvisatory model and its recognition as such by its culture. The same is true of such styles as *alap* and *gatt* (nonmetric or metric) in North India, and in South India *tanam, niraval,* and *svara kalpana* (three types of improvisation distinguished mainly by the treatment of text and the rhythm), each style here being defined by a certain type of sound. In the relatively rare instances of polyphonic improvisation the model may be a tune sung by one voice (against which the other is to improvise) and a set of allowable harmonic intervals as well as their characteristic sequences. There are, then, very diverse kinds of models used in the world of improvisation. These we would next like to examine comparatively, in accordance with their positions in the two continua of density and audibility.

There would appear to be a wide gulf between a show tune, which is basically a temporal event with beginning, middle, and end, and a *raga, maqam,* or *dastgah*, which is at first glance taken to be a theoretical construct, something a performer must think of as a unit, keeping all its elements more or less in mind all the time. But to these "theoretical" models of Asian music it turns out that musicians take a time-oriented approach, considering them objects that have beginnings and endings, and that consist somehow of sequences of thought. Thus we may take it that each model, be it a tune, a theoretical construct, or a mode with typical melodic turns, consists of a series of obligatory musical events which must be observed, either absolutely or with some sort of frequency, in order that the model remain intact. For example, in a jazz improvisation based on a series of eight chords, these chords must themselves appear in some acceptable form, and in order. In a performance of Persian *avaz,* the nonmetric improvisation that is central in a complete performance of Persian classical music, certain signposts or points of reference must appear;[16] these are certain central tones, opening and closing motifs, melodic indications signalling the coming of closing sections, etc. It is possible to make a list of these points of reference—a kind of table of contents of the mode. All of them need not appear in a performance, but some must be evident, in order for the performance to warrant credibility. Similar points of reference appear in the *taqasim* of Arabic music. These include not only beginning and cadential motifs but also the lengths of sections, signposts of a different kind, indeed, which are at least to a degree obligatory; thus, a long section must come at the end of a *taqsim,* and possibly about the middle of the whole piece as well.

The improviser and the listener use length of section as a way of gauging the progress of the piece. On the other hand, in the model of Indian *alap* (the nonmetric introductory exposition of a *raga*) as in Persian *avaz* and Arabic *taqsim*, the gradual introduction of higher tones functions as points of reference.

Diverse though these points of reference may be in nature, how close together or far apart they are may be measured, at least very roughly. We can refer to this measurement as density. In comparing various types of models, we find that those of jazz are relatively dense, those of Persian music, of medium density, and those of an Arabic *taqsim* or an Indian *alap*, relatively lacking in density. Figured bass, and Baroque music in which a soloist improvises ornamentation, are perhaps the densest models of all. Does the density of a model have an effect on a performer's freedom? It seems likely that a performer of improvisation using a dense model tends to vary less from performance to performance than one whose model lacks density, and that the kinds of improvisatory thinking that goes on in various musical cultures, different though they are in style and content, can therefore be compared.

A musical repertory, composed or improvised, may be viewed as the embodiment of a system, and one way of describing such a system is to divide it theoretically into its component units. These units are, as it were, the building blocks which tradition accumulates, and which musicians within the tradition make use of, choosing from among them, combining, recombining, and rearranging them. These building blocks are, even within a single repertory, of many different orders. They are the tones selected from a tone system; they are melodic motifs; they are harmonic intervals and interval sequences in improvised polyphony; they are types of sections (e.g., the exposition of sonata forms). These few examples show how greatly varied they are in extent and size.

Studying the building-block components of improvisatory styles is similar to studying density, since the "points of reference" that govern density are in some cases identical with the blocks, or with demarcations between them. Among the various improvisatory styles already mentioned, building blocks may be illustrated by the following: (1) In some West African drum ensembles each of several percussionists play a single short motif repeatedly, juxtaposing it to the others in a highly complex polyrhythmic texture. The master drummer uses these motifs, mixing them, combining them, drawing on them, one by one; they therefore are his building blocks, and they are of a relatively short duration or small size. (2) In the Yugoslav epic tradition short musical phrases that accompany the individual ten-syllable lines are the relevant units. A singer sings one line again and again, though with minor variations, until for a number of reasons a new but equally traditional melody is taken up. These themes are among the building blocks of the Yugoslav tradition. (3) In North Indian drumming a similar role is filled by the *theka*, the specific audible formula associated with a *tala*, the theoretical metric pattern. [...]

The point to be made is that in both folk and art music repertories composers use similar kinds of building blocks. A brief study of Czech folk songs, for instance, provided evidence that a small number of motifs appears over and over again, at various points in the songs; in fact, the entire repertory can be reduced to a limited set of short phrases from which composers seem to have drawn. And, on a large scale, composers of Western art music can be shown to have used similar procedures.

However, one certainly receives the impression that the supply of building blocks in an improvised style is much less extensive than in "composed" music, and that perhaps an improvisatory repertory can be developed only if the options are limited. Interestingly enough, the building blocks sometimes operate micro-cosmically in the manner of the entire model in macrocosm. What a Persian musician does in a single *gusheh* (a section of a *dastgah* with specific range and thematic content) is a good deal like what takes place in the entire performance; the relationship of the components of a *gusheh* very much resembles the relationship of the *gushehs* in the whole piece. In the Arabic *taqsim* and the Carnatic *alapana* the way in which a tone acts as the basis for embellishment and thereby acquires emphasis is similar to the way in which tone levels and ranges such as tetrachords are explored and established as focal points in the entire model. Large building blocks allow the performer considerable freedom for internal variation. Thus, the section type of the *taqsim* is subject to much more variation than, say, the ornamented note in a seventeenth-century piece. The degree to which the improviser actually makes decisions, with the sudden inspiration that some regard as the hallmark of improvisation, is partially dependent on the size of the building blocks. The larger the blocks, the greater the internal variability.

Points of reference and building blocks are definitive characteristics of the model on which improvisation may be based. With regard to both, improvisatory music shows itself to be different in degree, but not in essence, from the traditions on which "composed" music is based. The same is true where "audibility" of the model is involved. We are dealing with a wide range of model types: notes, cadential figures, section types identified by length, melodic phrases, or lines, rhythmic lines or formulas, entire tunes, chord sequences, and modal concepts to which are attached a large group of traits—scales, motifs, and typical sequences of focal points in range and tonality, as well as rhythmic tendencies.

This question directs us of course to the role of teaching. In each of the improvisatory styles that we have considered, the student must in some way learn the model before he can improvise upon it, though the formality of his instruction varies. In Indian and Persian classical music it is intense; in at least some Arabic music and in jazz it is mainly a matter of listening and trial-and-error participation; in Yugoslav epic-singing it is intermediate to these methods, for songs are learned from a specific teacher whose role is critical.[17] But more important for us here is the nature of the model itself. In some systems it is actual music that may also be performed without improvisation, in some it is basic sound material that the musician learns but does not execute in a true performance, and in still others it is largely theoretical subject matter, consisting of verbal instructions and exercises.

Models exhibiting more or less comprehensive audibility are exemplified by the show tune that becomes the basis for jazz improvisation and by the Yugoslav epic song that is learned *in toto* before it becomes subject to variation by the performer. Slightly less "audible," in the sense that it is rarely regarded as something to be actually performed, is the *radif* of Persian classical music, a long series of compositions that are in style not different from the improvisations that are developed by each teacher from the common tradition and taught to students who must memorize them before going on to improvise. Performances of Persian music can easily be classified according to how much they depart from the *radif*, or teaching version (and some performances depart very little from it).

Of medium audibility are the kinds of models that consist partly of theoretical concepts that are taught, and partly of short building blocks such as motifs. The improviser does not perform in his own way a piece that already exists, but uses materials that have been learned to some extent in isolation, or at least in a form which makes it impossible simply to reiterate them. Two examples of these practices are (1) some aspects of the classical music of India (whose models are incredibly complex, numerous, and multifaceted) in which exercises that provide insight into the characteristics of a raga are taught, and (2) certain facets of Arabic music, in which the practitioners may learn the theory of the *maqamat*, but focus, in their practical study, on musical motifs and other matters that are not by themselves performed as music.

"Inaudible" or "minimally audible" models exist in a number of cultures, but particularly in Western music. For example, while the pianist for a silent movie typically had at his disposal certain chords, chord progressions, and melodic materials, he did not use any traditional model of his "score" (his performance as a whole) or even of sections of any considerable length. Similarly, the organist who performs a fugue extempore on a theme given to him by the audience has, aside from the theme itself (and that new to him), no model more specific than whatever is generic to fugue. Some improvisers in avant-garde music of the 1960s wished to avoid the use of any model, and, paradoxically, if the innovation itself is to be the model, it can hardly be considered an audible one. Thus, while a model of some sort is a necessary condition of any improvisation, the audibility of the model, like its density, varies from culture to culture and from repertory to repertory.

Improvisation and the Performer

It is axiomatic that improvised music requires a greater creative effort on the part of the performer than does composed music, and, indeed, one way we may perhaps define improvisation is by measuring the degree to which the performer is creatively involved. Let us consider what is known about the way in which performers in repertory differ from each other in the performance of material based on one model, and to what extent the performances of an individual differ from each other.

A number of studies have been made investigating this problem. Among the most significant or relevant are those of: (1) Katz,[18] who compares two generations' performance practice in one genre, with particular regard to ornamentation; (2) Nettl and Riddle,[19] who explore the work of one performer and his range of practice in one Arabic *maqam;* (3) Nettl and Foltin,[20] who investigate the range of a number of performers of one Persian mode, including only the nonmetric improvisations; (4) Massoudieh,[21] whose task is similar but involves a different, smaller sample; (5) Wilkens,[22] who compares one amateur and one professional musician in the Persian tradition; (6) Touma,[23] who tries to comprehend the scope of performance of one Arabic *maqam,* Bayati, as used in several forms and by several musicians; (7) Zorana Ercegovac,[24] whose unpublished master's thesis deals with excerpts of performances of one song by three singers, on nine occasions, in the tradition of Yugoslav epic poetry; (8) Reichow,[25] who tries to comprehend the notion of a *maqam* on the basis of both composition and performance; (9) Gerson-Kiwi,[26] who explores the Persian *dastgah* system on the basis of one musician's work; and (10) Rycroft,[27] who studies the work of one East African guitarist. This is by no means a complete list, but it represents much of the work done thus far that focuses on the degree of variation in performance by one musician or one tightly knit group, or on the basis of one model. The majority of such studies have been based on Middle Eastern music; and curiously few dealing with Indian music or jazz have been produced. But perhaps the nature of model performance forms, theoretical system, or the soloistic quality of the Middle Eastern styles is the reason for this imbalance.

In any event, clearly ethnomusicologists are only at the beginnings of their study of improvisational technique. More information on individual performers and on performances based on one model, and then comparisons of these, are needed before much insight can be gained. But what we already have at hand indicates some trends for which future scholars may watch. First, performances by a given musician working with one model vary far less than those of different musicians. This is obviously what a reasonable guess would have been; it is apparent that an individual musician establishes a personal practice from which he does not depart very much. Cursory examinations of Indian music[28] show this. Second, most cultures have a rather specific set of expectations of the performer, including the requirement of sticking reasonably close to the model. The musician who is highly creative and tries to avoid using the points of reference and the building blocks of the model is chastised for his ignorance of the model; an identical performance each time is almost equally unacceptable, but perhaps not quite as culpable, and this point is of great import because it strengthens our view that the improviser is really simply the performer of a traditional piece, establishing his own way of rendering it. Third—and here the difficulty of generalizing becomes perhaps most evident—performers tend to feel that they are playing an extant piece, not improvising with mere reference to something extant. An exception seems to occur in certain improvisatory styles of Western music, which is music that has all along singled out improvisation as a separate, minor art, the sphere of the comparatively few musicians competent to engage in it.

We might close with the observation that the recent studies of non-Western music have indeed added enormously to our understanding of improvisation. But most of these studies—those listed above are the exceptions—concern themselves with the identification and explication of models, not with the ways in which musicians deal with a model and depart from it. Even those studies that are concerned with the latter topics take a prescriptive attitude, indicating what may be done; few examine, through a comparison of field records, what actually is, or has been, done.

But the conclusion which recurs again and again in our thoughts is that perhaps we must abandon the idea of improvisation as a process separate from composition and adopt the view that all performers improvise to some extent. What the pianist playing Bach and Beethoven does with his models—the scores and the accumulated tradition of performance practice—is only in degree, not in nature, different from what the Indian playing an *alap* in *Rag Yaman* and the Persian singing the *Dastgah* of *Shur* do with theirs.[29]

Notes

1 Ernst Ferand, *Die Improvisation in der Musik* (Zurich, 1938).
2 Reviews appeared in few journals, among them *Music and Letters*, XX/3 (July. 1939), pp. 337–39; and *Rivista musicale* italiana, XVII (1959), pp. 425–26.
3 For an illustration of this attitude, see the article "Extemporization," in the fifth edition of *Grove's Dictionary of Music and Musicians*.
4 Seminars on comparative approaches to improvisation have been held by the author, for example, at the University of Illinois. Meetings and symposia range from e. g., the large, six-lecture series, organized by Leonard Meyer and Ella Zonis at the University of Chicago in 1968–69, to shorter sessions at meetings of societies, e. g., the Society for Ethnomusicology annual meeting in 1973, at Urbana, Illinois.
5 Ferand, in an article in *Die Musik in Geschchte und Gegenwart,* which parallels his thinking in *Die Improvisation in der Musik,* says, "The division—taken for granted in Western musical life of today—that splits the original unity and simultaneity of creation and reproduction was and is foreign to the musical usage of the primitive and many other non-European cultures; the inventor and executor of a composition, the producing and reproducing musician, were originally in most cases one and the same person" (Vol. VI. col 1096).
6 For example, *Riemenns Musiklexikon, Sachtesl* (Malnz, 1967), in an unsigned article says, "Strictly speaking, only in the West, and even there only beginning at a rather late historical stage, can one speak of improvisation, since non-Western and older European music stands

outside the distinction between composition and performance which is essential to the concept of improvisation" (p. 390).

7 Willi Apel. *Harvard Dictionary of Music*, 2nd ed. (Cambridge, Mass, 1969), pp. 404–5.

8 About forty-five pages in *Die Improvisation in der Musik* are devoted to "primitive" and oriental musics.

9 This statement is based on Ferand and on other previously cited articles.

10 Bruno Nettl. "Studies in Blackfoot Indian Musical Culture, Part II," *Ethnomusicology,* XI/3 (September, 1967), p. 301.

11 George Herzog. "A Comparsion of Pueblo and Pima Musical Styles," *Journal of American Folklore*, XLIX (1936), p. 333, and his "Music in the Thinking of the American Indian," *Peabody Bulletin*, May, 1938, p. 2.

12 A number of sources on Eskimo composition are discussed and summarized in Alan P. Merriam, *The Anthropology of Music* (Evanston. Ill, 1964), pp. 175–77.

13 Several Eskimo song texts dealing with composition are given by Laura Boulton in the booklet accompanying the record album, *The Eskimos of Hudson Bay and Alaska* (New York, Folkways Record FE4444, 1954), pp. 4–5. Among the most interesting is this one: "All songs have been exhausted / He picks up some of all / And adds his own / And makes a new song."

14 Ferand is, of course, aware of the supposedly improvisatory nature of Schubert's compositional process, at least in certain instances. See *Die Improvisation in der Musik*, pp. 3–4, and the references therein.

15 See, for example, Alfred Einstein, *Schubert: A Musical Portrait* (New York, 1951), p. 92. Ferand, *Die Improvisation in der Musik*, p. 4, refers to the possibility that certain works by Liszt, Chopin, and Schubert may actually be "Fixierungen von Improvitation."

16 The best explanation of these signposts appear, *passim,* in Hormoz Farhat. "The Dastgah Concept in Persian Classical Music" (Ph. D, diss. UCLA, 1966). See also Bruno Nettl, with Bela Foltin, Jr. *Daramad of Chahergah: A Study in the Performance Practice of Persian Music* (Detroit, 1972), pp. 25–28, and the just published work by Ella Zonis, *Classical Persian Music: An Introduction* (Cambridge, Mass., 1973).

17 Albert B. Lord, *The Singer of Tales* (Cambridge, Mass, 1960), pp. 13–29.

18 Ruth Katz, "The Singing of Baqqashot by Aleppo Jews: A Study in Musical Acculturation," *Acts Musicologics,* XL (1968), pp. 65–85.

19 Bruno Nettl and Ronald Riddle. "Taqsim Nahawand, a Study of Sixteen Performances by Jihad Racy," unpublished paper.

20 Bruno Nettl and Bela Foltin, Jr., *Daramad of Chahargah.*

21 Mohammad Taghi Massoudieh, *Awaz-a-Sur* (Regensburg, 1968).

22 Eckart Wilkens, *Künstler and Amateurs im perstischen Santurspiel* (Regensburg, 1967).

23 Habib Touma, *Der Maqam Bayati im arabischen Taqsim* (Berlin, 1968).

24 Zorana Ercegovac, "The Song of Baghdad A Comparison of Nine Performances" (M.A thesis, University of Illinois, Urbana, 1975).

25 Jan Reichow. *Die Entfallung eines Melodiemodells im Genus Sukah* (Regensburg, 1971).

26 Edith Gerson-Kiwi. *The Persian Doctrine of Dastga Composition* (Tel-Aviv, 1963).

27 David Rycroft, "The Guitar Improvisations of Mwends Jean Bosco," *African Music,* III/1 (1962), pp. 86–102.

28 I am indebted to Daniel Neuman for information and discussion of the concept of improvisation in Northern Indian music. See, however, N A. Jairaubboy, *The Rags of North Indian Music* (Middletown, Conn, 1971), p. 31, which implies agreement with the point made here, but which also indicates that "when the musician is performing beyond his normal capacity the music becomes alive."

29 This study was carried out with the help of the University of Illinois Research Board, which provided research assistance. I am grateful to Doris Dyen Root for compiling the bibliography and abstracting literature which was in part used here. The paper was written while the author was an Associate of the University of Illinois Center for Advanced Study.

12 Theatre of the Oppressed

Augusto Boal

Translated by Charles A. McBride

Augusto Boal (1931–2009) was born in modest circumstances in Rio de Janeiro. Interested in theatre from an early age, he began, while studying chemical engineering at Columbia University, to attend New York's School of Dramatic Arts, where he discovered the work of Bertolt Brecht and Constantin Stanislavski. In 1956 he returned to Brazil to work with the Arena Theatre in São Paulo, where he created a Seminar in Dramaturgy to encourage young Brazilian playwrights. Several years after the 1964 military coup d'état, Boal was arrested, tortured, and exiled to Argentina, where he wrote and published *Torquemada* (1971), and, using ideas from his friend Paulo Freire, wrote *Theatre of the Oppressed* (1973). Returning to Brazil in 1986, he established a Centre for the Theatre of the Oppressed in Rio de Janeiro. In later years, as well as travelling extensively to workshop his theatrical concepts, Boal became a Rio de Janeiro city councilor, and the year before his death he was nominated for the Nobel Peace Prize. Boal's *Theatre of the Oppressed*, along with his other works, has deeply influenced improvisational political and social performance practices globally. It is used across disciplines to rehearse new social options and provide creative and political expression to those who have traditionally been denied a voice.

Key words: community theatre; politics and theatre; South America; forum theatre; revolution

[...]

Third Stage: The Theatre as Language

This stage is divided into three parts, each one representing a different degree of direct participation of the spectator in the performance. The spectator is encouraged to intervene in the action, abandoning his condition of object and assuming fully the role of subject. [...] This stage focuses on the theme to be discussed and furthers the transition from passivity to action.

First degree: *Simultaneous dramaturgy*: This is the first invitation made to the spectator to intervene without necessitating his physical presence on the "stage."

Here it is a question of performing a short scene, of ten to twenty minutes, proposed by a local resident, one who lives in the *barrio*. The actors may improvise with the aid of a script prepared beforehand, as they may also compose the scene directly. In any case, the performance gains in theatricality if the person who proposed the theme is present in the audience. Having begun the scene, the actors develop it to the point at which the main problem reaches a crisis and needs a solution. Then the actors stop the performance and ask the audience to offer solutions. They improvise immediately all the suggested solutions, and the audience has the right to intervene, to correct the actions or words of the actors, who are obligated to comply strictly with these instructions from the audience. Thus, while the audience "writes" the work the actors perform it simultaneously. The spectator's thoughts are discussed theatrically on stage with the help of the actors. All the solutions, suggestions, and opinions are revealed in theatrical form. The discussion itself need not simply take the form of words, but rather should be effected through all the other elements of theatrical expression as well.

Here's an example of how simultaneous dramaturgy works. In a *barrio* of San Hilariòn, in Lima, a woman proposed a controversial theme. Her husband, some years before, had told her to keep some "documents" which, according to him, were extremely important. The woman – who happened to be illiterate – put them away without suspicion. One day they had a fight for one reason or another and, remembering the documents, the woman decided to find out what they were all about, since she was afraid they had something to do with the ownership of their small house. Frustrated in her inability to read, she asked a neighbor to read the documents to her. The lady next door kindly made haste to read the documents, which to the surprise and amusement of the whole *barrio,* were not documents at all, but rather love letters written by the mistress of the poor woman's husband. Now this betrayed and illiterate woman wanted revenge. The actors improvised the scenes until the moment when the husband returns home at night, after his wife has uncovered the mystery of the letters. The woman wants revenge: how is she to get it? Here the action is interrupted and the participant who was interpreting the woman asked the others what should be her attitude in relation to her husband.

All the women of the audience entered into a lively exchange of views. The actors listened to the different suggestions and acted them out according to instructions given by the audience. All the possibilities were tried. Here are some of the suggested solutions in this particular case:

1) To cry a lot in order to make him feel guilty. One young woman suggested that the betrayed woman start to cry a lot so that the husband might feel bad about his own behavior. The actress carried out this suggestion: she cried a lot, the husband consoled her, and when the crying was over he asked her to serve his dinner; and everything remained as it was before. The husband assured her that he had already forgotten the mistress, that he loved only his wife, etc., etc. The audience did not accept this solution.

2) To abandon the house, leaving her husband alone as a punishment. The actress carried out this suggestion and, after reproaching her husband for his wicked behavior, grabbed her things, put them in a bag, and left him alone, very lonely, so that he would learn a lesson. But upon leaving the house (that is, her own house), she asked the public about what she should do next. In punishing her husband she ended up punishing herself. Where would she go now? Where could she live? This punishment positively was not good since it turned against the punisher, herself.

3) To lock the house so that the husband would have to go away. This variation was also rehearsed. The husband repeatedly begs to be let in, but the wife steadfastly refused. After insisting several times, the husband commented:

Very well, I'll go away. They paid me my salary today, so I'll take the money and go live with my mistress and you can just get by the best way you can." And he left. The actress commented that she did not like this solution, since the husband went to live with the other woman, and what about the wife? How is she going to live now? The poor woman does not make enough money to support herself and cannot get along without her husband.

4) The last solution was presented by a large, exuberant woman; it was the solution accepted unanimously by the entire audience, men and women. She said: "Do it like this: let him come in, get a really big stick, and hit him with all your might – give him a good beating. After you've beat him enough for him to feel repentant, put the stick away, serve him his dinner with affection, and forgive him. ... "

The actress performed this version, after overcoming the natural resistance of the actor who was playing the husband, and after a barrage of blows – to the amusement of the audience – the two of them sat at the table, ate, and discussed the latest measures taken by the government, which happened to be the nationalization of American companies.

This form of theater creates great excitement among the participants and starts to demolish the wall that separates actors from spectators. Some "write" and others act almost simultaneously. The spectators feel that they can intervene in the action. The action ceases to be presented in a deterministic manner, as something inevitable, as Fate. Man is Man's fate. Thus Man-the-spectator is the creator of Man-the-character. Everything is subject to criticism, to rectification. All can be changed, and at a moment's notice: the actors must always be ready to accept, without protest, any proposed action; they must simply act it out, to give a live view of its consequences and drawbacks. Any spectator, by virtue of being a spectator, has the right to try his version – without censorship. The actor does not change his main function: he goes on being the interpreter. What changes is the object of his interpretation. If formerly he interpreted the solitary author locked in his study, to whom divine inspiration dictated a finished text, here on the contrary, he must interpret the mass audience, assembled in their local committees, societies of "friends of the *barrio*," groups of neighbors, schools, unions, peasant leagues, or whatever; he must give expression to the collective thought of men and women. The actor ceases to interpret the individual and starts to interpret the group, which is much more difficult and at the same time much more creative.

Second degree: *Image theater*: Here the spectator has to participate more directly. He is asked to express his views on a certain theme of common interest that the participants wish to discuss. The theme can be far-reaching, abstract – as, for example, imperialism – or it can be a local problem such as the lack of water, a common occurrence in almost all the *barrios*. The participant is asked to express his opinion, but without speaking, using only the bodies of the other participants and "sculpting" with them a group of statues, in such a way that his opinions and feelings become evident. The participant is to use the bodies of the others as if he were a sculptor and the others were made of clay: he must determine the position of each body down to the most minute details of their facial expressions. He is not allowed to speak under any circumstances. The most that is permitted to him is to show with his own facial expressions what he wants the statue-spectator to do. After organizing this group of statues he is allowed to enter into a discussion with the other participants in order to determine if all agree with his "sculpted" opinion. Modifications can be rehearsed: the spectator has the right to modify the statues in their totality or in some detail. When finally an image is arrived at that is the most acceptable to all, then the spectator-sculptor is asked to show the way he would like the given theme to be; that is, in the first grouping the *actual image* is shown, in the second the *ideal image*. Finally he is asked to show a *transitional image,* to show how it would be possible to pass from one reality to the other. In other words, how to carry out the change, the transformation, the revolution, or whatever term one wishes to use. Thus, starting with a grouping of "statues" accepted by all as representative of a real situation, each one is asked to propose ways of changing it.

Once again, a concrete example can best clarify the matter. A young woman, a literacy agent who lived in the village of Otuzco, was asked to explain, through a grouping of live images, what her home town was like. In Otuzco, before the present Revolutionary Government,[1] there was a peasant rebellion; the landlords (that no longer exist in Peru), imprisoned the leader of the rebellion, took him to the main square, and, in front of everyone, castrated him. The young woman from Otuzco composed the image of the castration, placing one of the participants on the ground while another pretended to be castrating him and still another held him from behind. Then at one side she placed a woman praying, on her knees, and at the other side a group of five men and women, also on their knees, with hands tied behind their backs. Behind the man being castrated, the young woman placed another participant in a position obviously suggestive of power and violence and, behind him, two armed men pointing their guns at the prisoner.

This was the image that person had of her village. A terrible, pessimistic, defeatist image, but also a true reflection of something that had actually taken place. Then the young woman was asked to show what she would want her village to be like. She modified completely the "statues" of the group and regrouped them as people who worked in peace and loved each other – in short, a happy and contented, ideal Otuzco. Then came the third, and most important part, of this form of theater: how can one, starting with the actual image, arrive at the ideal image? How to bring about the change, the transformation, the revolution?

Here it was a question of giving an opinion, but without words. Each participant had the right to act as a "sculptor" and to show how the grouping, or organization, could be modified through a reorganization of forces for the purpose of arriving at an ideal image. Each one expressed his opinion through imagery. Lively discussions arose, but without words. When one would exclaim, "It's not possible like this; I think that … " he was immediately interrupted: "Don't say what you think; come and show it to us." The participant would go and demonstrate physically, visually, his thought, and the discussion would continue. In this particular case the following variations were observed:

1) When a young woman from the interior was asked to form the image of change, she would never change the image of the kneeling woman, signifying clearly that she did not see in that woman a potential force for revolutionary change. Naturally the young women identified themselves with that feminine figure and, since they could not perceive themselves as possible protagonists of the revolution, they left unmodified the image of the kneeling woman. On the other hand, when the same thing was asked of a girl from Lima, she, being more "liberated," would start off by changing precisely that image with which she identified herself. This experiment was repeated many times and always produced the same results, without variation. Undoubtedly the different patterns of action represent not chance occurrence but the sincere, visual expression of the ideology and psychology of the participants. The young women from Lima always modified the image: some would make the woman clasp the figure of the castrated man, others would prompt the woman to fight against the castrator, etc. Those from the interior did little more than allow the woman to lift her hands in prayer.

2) All the participants who believed in the Revolutionary Government would start by modifying the armed figures in the background: they changed the two men who were aiming their guns at the victim so that they would then aim at the powerful figure in the center or at the castrators themselves. On the other hand, when a participant did not have the same faith in his government, he would alter all figures except the armed ones.

3) The people who believed in magical solutions or in a "change of conscience" on the part of the exploiting classes, would start by modifying the castrators – viewing them in effect as changing of their own volition – as well as the powerful figure in the center, who would become regenerated. By contrast, those who did not believe in this form of social change would first alter the kneeling men, making them assume a fighting posture, attacking the oppressors.

4) One of the young women, besides showing the transformations to be the work of the kneeling men – who would free themselves, attack their torturers and imprison them – also had one of the figures representing the people address the other participants, clearly expressing her opinion that social changes are made by the people as a whole and not only by their vanguard.

5) Another young woman made all kinds of changes, leaving untouched only the five persons with their hands tied. This girl belonged to the upper middle class. When she showed signs of nervousness for not being able to imagine any further changes, someone suggested to her the possibility of changing the group of tied figures; the girl looked at them in surprise and exclaimed: "The truth is that those people didn't fit in! ... " It was the truth. The people did not fit into her view of the scheme of things, and she had never before been able to see it.

This form of image theater is without doubt one of the most stimulating, because it is so easy to practice and because of its extraordinary capacity for making thought *visible*. This happens because use of the language idiom is avoided. Each word has a denotation that is the same for all, but it also has a connotation that is unique for each individual. If I utter the word "revolution," obviously everyone will realize that I am talking about a radical change, but at the same time each person will think of his or her "own" revolution, a personal conception of revolution. But if I have to arrange a group of statues that will signify "my revolution," here there will be no denotation-connotation dichotomy. The image synthesizes the individual connotation and the collective denotation. In my arrangement signifying revolution, what are the statues doing? Do they have weapons in their hands or do they have ballots? Are the figures of the people united in a fighting posture against the figures representing the common enemies; or are the figures of the people dispersed, or showing disagreement among themselves? My conception of "revolution" will become clear if, instead of speaking, I show with images what I think.

I remember that in a session of psychodrama a girl spoke repeatedly of the problems she had with her boyfriend, and she always started with more or less the same phrase: "He came in, embraced me, and then. ... " Each time we heard this opening phrase we understood that they did in fact embrace; that is, we understood what the word *embrace* denotes. Then one day she showed by acting how their meetings were: he approached, she crossed her arms over her breasts as if protecting herself, he took hold of her and hugged her tightly, while she continued to keep her hands closed, defending herself. That was clearly a particular connotation for the word *embrace*. When we understood her "embrace" we were finally able to understand her problems with her boyfriend.

In image theater other techniques can be used:

1) Each participant transformed into a statue is allowed one movement or gesture, and only one, each time a signal (like a clap of hands) is given. In this case the arrangement of images will change according to the individual desire of each participant.
2) The participants are first asked to memorize the ideal image, then to return to the original, actual image, and finally to make the movements necessary to arrive again at the ideal image – thus showing the group of images in motion and allowing the analysis of the feasibility of the proposed transitions. One will then be able to see if change occurs by the grace of God or if it is brought about by the opposing forces operating within the very core of the group.
3) The sculptor-participant, once his work is finished, is asked to try to place himself in the group he has created. This sometimes helps the person to realize that his own vision of reality is a cosmic one, as if he were a part of that reality.

The game of images offers many other possibilities. The important thing is always to analyze the feasibility of the change.

Third degree: *Forum theater*: This is the last degree and here the participant has to intervene decisively in the dramatic action and change it. The procedure is as follows: First, the participants are asked to tell a story containing a political or social problem of difficult solution. Then a ten- or fifteen-minute skit portraying that problem and the solution intended for discussion is improvised or rehearsed, and subsequently presented. When the skit is over, the participants are asked if they agree with the solution presented. At least some will say no. At this point it is explained that the scene will be performed once more, exactly as it was the first time. But now any participant in the audience has the right to replace any actor and lead the action in the direction that seems to him most appropriate. The displaced actor steps aside, but remains ready to resume action the moment the participant considers his own intervention to be terminated. The other actors have to face the newly created situation, responding instantly to all the possibilities that it may present.

The participants who choose to intervene must continue the physical actions of the replaced actors; they are not allowed to come on the stage and talk, talk, talk: they must carry out the same type of work or activities performed by the actors who were in their place. The theatrical activity must go on in the same way, on the stage. Anyone may propose any solution, but it must be done on the stage, working, acting, doing things, and not from the comfort of his seat. Often a person is very revolutionary when in a public forum he envisages and advocates revolutionary and heroic acts; on the other hand, he often realizes that things are not so easy when he himself has to practice what he suggests.

An example: An eighteen-year-old man worked in the city of Chimbote, one of the world's most important fishing ports. There are in that city a great number of factories of fish meal, a principal export product of Peru. Some factories are very large, while others have only eight or nine employees. Our young man worked for one of the latter. The boss was a ruthless exploiter and forced his employees to work from eight o'clock in the morning to eight at night, or vice versa – twelve consecutive hours of work. Thus the problem was how to combat this inhuman exploitation. Each participant had a proposal: one of them was, for example, "operation turtle," which consists in working very slowly, especially when the boss is not looking. Our young man had a brilliant idea: to work faster and fill the machine with so much fish that it would break with the excessive weight, requiring two or three hours to fix it. During this time the workers could rest. There was the problem, the employer's exploitation; and there was one solution, invented by native ingenuity. But would that be the best solution?

The scene was performed in the presence of all the participants. Some actors represented the workers, another represented the boss, another the foreman, another a "stool pigeon." The stage was converted into a fish meal factory: one worker unloading the fish, another weighing the bags of fish, another carrying the bags to the machines, another tending the machine, while still others performed other pertinent tasks. While they worked, they kept up a dialogue, proposing solutions and discussing them until they came to accept the solution proposed by the young man and broke the machine; the boss came and the workers rested while the engineer repaired the machine. When the repair was done, they went back to work.

The scene was staged for the first time and the question was raised: Were all in agreement? No, definitely not. On the contrary, they disagreed. Each one had a different proposal: to start a strike, throw a bomb at the machine, start a union, etc.

Then the technique of forum theater was applied: the scene would be staged exactly as it had been the first time, but now each spectator-participant would have the right to intervene and change the action, trying out his proposal. The first to intervene was the one who suggested the use of a bomb. He got up, replaced the actor who was portraying the young man, and made his bomb-throwing proposal. Of course all the other actors argued against it since that would mean the destruction of the factory, and therefore the source of work. What would become of so many workers if the factory closed up? Disagreeing, the man decided to throw the bomb himself, but soon realized that he did not know how to manufacture a bomb nor even how to throw it. Many people who in theoretical discussions advocate throwing bombs would not know what to do in reality, and would probably be the first to perish in the explosion. After trying his bomb-solution, the man returned to his place and the actor replaced him until a second person came to try his solution, the strike. After much argument with the others he managed to convince them to stop working and walk out, leaving the factory abandoned. In this case, the owner, the foreman, and the "stool pigeon," who had remained in the factory, went to the town square (among the audience) to look for other workers who would replace the strikers (there is mass unemployment in Chimbote). This spectator-participant tried his solution, the strike, and realized its impracticability; with so much unemployment the bosses would always be able to find workers hungry enough and with little enough political consciousness to replace the strikers.

The third attempt was to form a small union for the purpose of negotiating the workers' demands, politicizing the employed workers, as well as the unemployed, setting up mutual funds, etc. In this particular session of forum theater, this was the solution judged to be the best by the participants. In the forum theater no idea is imposed: the audience, the people, have the opportunity to try out all their ideas, to rehearse all the possibilities, and to verify them in practice, that is, in theatrical practice. If the audience had come to the conclusion that it was necessary to dynamite all the fish meal factories in Chimbote, this would also be right from their point of view. It is not the place of the theater to show the correct path, but only to offer the means by which all possible paths may be examined.

Maybe the theater in itself is not revolutionary, but these theatrical forms are without a doubt a *rehearsal of revolution*. The truth of the matter is that the spectator-actor practices a real act even though he does it in a fictional manner. While he *rehearses* throwing a bomb on stage, he is concretely rehearsing the way a bomb is thrown; acting out his attempt to organize a strike, he is concretely organizing a strike. Within its fictitious limits, the experience is a concrete one.

Here the cathartical effect is entirely avoided. We are used to plays in which the characters make the revolution on stage and the spectators in their seats feel themselves to be triumphant revolutionaries. Why make a revolution in reality if we have already made it in the theater? But that does not happen here: the rehearsal stimulates the practice of the act in reality. Forum theater, as well as these other forms of a people's theater, instead of taking something away from the spectator, evoke in him a desire to practice in reality the act he has rehearsed in the theater. The practice of these theatrical forms creates a sort of uneasy sense of incompleteness that seeks fulfillment through real action. […]

Notes

1 The government established after the October 1968 revolution and headed by President Juan Velasco Alvarado (replaced in August 1975 by Francisco Morales Bermúdez). (Translator's note.)

13 Group Creativity

Musical Performance and Collaboration

Keith Sawyer

After receiving his computer science degree from MIT in 1982, R. Keith Sawyer began his professional career designing video games for Atari, and then as a management consultant on innovative technologies. At the University of Chicago, he studied creativity with Mihaly Csikszentmihalyi, and received his PhD in psychology in 1994. His research on creativity, collaboration, and learning has been enriched and informed by his long career as an improvising pianist, in jazz as well as improv theatre. Sawyer is the author of 14 books and many scientific articles. In 2012, Oxford University Press issued a new edition of his acclaimed *Explaining Creativity: The Science of Human Innovation*. Sawyer's personal signature as a teacher, writer, and speaker is his ability to extend creative models and improvisational concepts across disciplines. Whether discussing business, the arts, or the social sciences, he champions the concept of innovation as a collaborative venture rather than as the product of individual genius. As Sawyer writes, "musical collaboration can help us to understand all collaboration." Towards this end, "Group Creativity" extends Csikszentmihalyi's concepts of "flow" into a collaborative vision of "group flow," and advances a model of musical and theatrical pedagogy that, incorporating notions of emergence and intersubjectivity, provides important insights into the teaching process itself with insights into the work of key Chicago theatrical improvising groups.

Key words: dialogue; interdisciplinarity; jazz; flow; classical music; pedagogy

The conversations of jazz

[...] Ingrid Monson's 1996 book *Saying Something* analyzed many examples of musical collaboration in jazz, along with transcribed musical notation that demonstrated in wonderful detail how musicians converse in a jazz improvisation. Monson described an interview with drummer Ralph Peterson in which she played a tape of a live performance of Peterson's composition 'Princess' with pianist Geri Allen and bassist Essiet Okon Essiet. During Allen's solo, Peterson's drum accompaniment was very dense, and there were several instances in which Allen and Peterson traded ideas with each other. During the interview, Monson and Peterson sat together and listened closely to the tape. Monson recognized that one of the conversational exchanges seemed to be based on the distinctive, catchy pattern from Dizzy Gillespie's famous performance of 'Salt Peanuts' and noted this to Peterson. He replied:

> Yeah! 'Salt Peanuts' and 'Looney Tunes' – kind of a combination of the two. [Drummer] Art Blakey has a thing he plays. It's like: [he sings a rhythmic phrase from the song]. And [pianist] Geri played: [he sings Allen's standard response]. So I played the second half of the Art Blakey phrase: [he sings the second part of Blakey's drum pattern].
>
> (Monson, 1996: 77)

Geri Allen immediately recognized the musical quotation from her performances with Blakey and then responded with her usual response, indicating that she recognized and appreciated Peterson's communication (musical transcripts can be found in Monson, 1996: 78–79). As in this example, musical communication in jazz depends on all of the musicians knowing the 'language' extremely well – not only the notes of the songs, but even knowing how a certain performer typically plays a certain song with a specific other performer. Peterson then told Monson:

> But you see what happens is, a lot of times when you get into a musical conversation, one person in the group will state an idea or the beginning of an idea and another person will *complete* the idea or their interpretation of the same idea, how they hear it. So the conversation happens in fragments and comes from different parts, different voices.
>
> (Monson, 1996: 78)

Monson, herself a jazz drummer and trumpet player, concluded her example by writing 'There is a great deal of give and take in such improvisational interaction, and such moments are often cited by musicians as aesthetic high points of performances' (1996: 80).

Jazz musicians engage in this sort of conversational exchange in the improvised ensemble activity known as 'trading fours' or 'trading eights', the number referring to the number of measures that a soloist is allocated to play before the next soloist begins. Because the chorus form is 32 measures trading eights is a relatively rapid transition; each player has barely enough time for one or two phrases. Rather than develop their own musical ideas or starting a completely new idea, each musician continues in the spirit or mood established by the prior players, responding to, and building on, the prior musician's eight bars (Berliner, 1994: 369–70). Rufus Reid told Berliner how he tries to weave the prior soloist's ideas into his own solo, but not always in an obvious way, and not always by direct quotation; he said it was more interesting to elaborate on the prior idea. In their musical conversations, musicians constantly balance coherence and innovation, borrowing material from the previous phrase and then transforming it.

The dialogues of improvisational theater

In improvisational theater, an ensemble of actors creates a scene on stage, without any prearranged dialogue, no character assignments and no plot outline. Everything about the performance is collectively created by the actors, on stage in front of the audience. The following brief transcript of the first 30 seconds of an improvised theater sketch, which lasted a total of about 5 minutes, helps to demonstrate the collaborative, contingent, and emergent aspects of improvised dialogues.

Example 1

Four actors stand at the back of the stage. Actor A begins the scene.

(1)   (*Actor A walks to center stage, pulls up a chair and sits down, miming the action of driving by holding an imaginary steering wheel*)

(2)   (*Actor B walks to A, stands next to him, fishes in pocket for something*)

(3)   A: On or off?

(4)   B: I'm getting on, sir. (*Continues fishing in his pocket*)

(5)   A: In or out?

(6)   B: I'm getting in!
          I'm getting in!

(7)   A: Did I see you tryin' to get in the back door a couple of stops back?

(8)   B: Uh …

Actor A, taking the first turn, is able to act without creative constraints. His initial non-verbal act is to sit in a chair and mime the act of holding a steering wheel. This suggests that he is the driver and is sitting in a vehicle. However, this initial suggestion leaves many possible options for Actor B in turn (2). For example, B could have pulled up a second chair and sat down next to the 'driver', and he would have become a passenger in a car. A's initial act does not indicate whether the vehicle is moving or not; it does not indicate the type of vehicle: it does not indicate the role of his character, nor the relationship with any other character. B's act in (2) also leaves many options open for A in turn (3). In (3), for example, A could have addressed B as his friend, searching for theater tickets. The range of dramatic options available on stage are practically unlimited: for example, at (2), B could have addressed A as Captain Kirk of Star Trek, initiating a TV-show parody. A's utterance (3) begins to add more detail to the emerging dramatic frame. 'On or off' would not be an appropriate statement for a car driver. It suggests that A is a professional driver of a bus (but also, note, is compatible with A driving a plane, boat, or spaceship). (3) also implies a relationship: B is a paying customer of A.

A few minutes of examination of any improvisational transcript indicates many plausible, dramatically coherent utterances that the actors could have performed at each turn. A combinatorial explosion quickly results in hundreds of potential performances, branching out from each actor's utterance. This combinatorial unpredictability leads improvisational interaction to be highly contingent from moment to moment. In spite of this contingency, by (8) the actors have established a reasonably complex drama, a collectively created dramatic frame that will guide the subsequent dialogue. They know that A is a bus driver, and that B is a potential passenger. A is getting a little impatient, and B may be a little shifty, perhaps trying to sneak on. In the remainder of the sketch, the actors must retain dramatic coherence with this frame. Of course, each actor's turn will suggest additional details or plot twists; the dramatic frame is always changing, emerging from the acts of all actors.

Example 1 was the first eight turns of a 5-minute improvised scene. Some of the more ambitious Chicago groups perform a fully improvised 1-hour play: because these improvisations are so much longer than the more typical short scenes, this is called *long form* improvisation. For example, in 1993, I videotaped many performances of a group called Jazz Freddy (see Sawyer, 2003b). The actors chose this name to emphasize the similarities between their free-form style of improvisation and the musical interactions of a jazz ensemble. Each night, Jazz Freddy performed a fully improvised 1-hour play in two acts separated by an intermission. On 24 April 1993, just after the lights went up, two cast members stepped to the front of the stage and quieted the audience. The first asked the audience to suggest 'an event' and someone shouted, 'The Olympics'. The second actor asked the audience to provide 'a location' and someone shouted, 'A convent.'

The lights went down, as the 10 cast members walked to the sides of the stage to sit in chairs that had been placed there. One of the actors, John, pulled a chair to the center of the stage and sat in it, facing the audience, as the stage lights came up.

Example 2

Lights up. We see John carrying a chair to front stage right and he sits down facing the audience. He mimes working at a desk – takes a cap off a pen, opens a book, starts to make underlining motions as he studies the page. He stops to rub his eyes. He then turns the page, and underlines some more. The other actors watch intently from the sides of the stage: the audience is completely quiet. After about 20 seconds, Mary stands up from her position at the opposite side of the stage, and walks over to John, miming the act of carrying something in both hands, held in front of her:

(1)	Mary	Here are those papers.	*Puts down the 'papers'.*
(2)		(2 second pause.)	*She remains standing.*
(3)	John	Thanks.	*Looks up to face Mary.*
		(2 second pause.)	
(4)		I really appreciate your doing those copies for me.	
(5)			*Bill approaches from stage left, also carrying 'papers', and stops next to Mary.*
(6)	Bill	Here are those papers.	*Puts down the papers,*
(7)	John	Thanks a lot.	*Still facing the two.*
(8)		You guys have really been great.	
		(2 second pause.)	
(9)		I'm gonna stop booking for now.	*Closes book on desk.*
(10)	Mary	[OK]	
(11)	Bill	[Sure]	
		(1 second pause.)	
(12)		I'm gonna go get some more papers.	
(13)	John	Alright.	*He stands up.*
		(1 second pause.)	
(14)		Thanks a lot, I appreciate it.	
(15)	Bill	You're welcome.	
		(1 second pause.)	
(16)		We mean it.	*As he says this, Bill touches Mary's arm: Mary reaches up her other hand to grasp his hand: they stand holding hands.*
(17)	John	Thanks for being in my corner.	
(18)	Bill	We always will be.	

A few minutes further into this scene, the actors collectively decided that the scene would begin a plot associated with the 'Olympics' suggestion. After about 5 minutes and three distinct scenes, the group collectively transitioned to a new plot line, this one taking place in a convent.

In the beginning of this performance, the actors leave unusually long pauses between their turns of dialogue, because they are just getting into the flow of the evening's performance. As the basic elements of the plot begin to emerge, the actors develop a rhythm and the pace accelerates; as the performance progresses, they leave shorter pauses and the dialogue begins to sound more like a normal conversation. The dramatic frame gradually gathers steam; in the first 30-minute act, the group creates two distinct plots, one associated with the Olympics and one taking place in a convent. In the second act, the plots begin to weave together, as several of the female athletes decide to become nuns.

This Jazz Freddy dialogue demonstrates the key characteristics of group creativity. It is unpredictable, particularly in the timing and pacing of the interaction; the actors do not know who is going to speak next, nor when they will begin speaking. As a result, anyone can take the next conversational turn; it is impossible to know ahead of time who it will be. Even an offstage actor can walk on and take the next turn, as Bill does in turns (5) and (6). More so than Example 1, the dialogue turns each leave a wide range of potential future possibilities still open. The dialogue demonstrates the moment-to-moment contingency associated with group creativity. The creation of the dramatic frame is fundamentally collaborative; no single actor imposes an idea for the scene on the others. Instead, the elements of the drama collaboratively emerge from the collective actions of the group. The dramatic frame is an emergent group-level phenomenon, impossible to explain in terms of the individual actor's creative impulses or inspirations.

The centralized mindset

The key characteristics of group creativity are improvisation, collaboration, and emergence. But we tend to neglect these characteristics. Instead, we often try to attribute the group's creativity to a single person: the group leader, the soloist, the director or conductor. For example, famous jazz photographers like Herman Leonard or William Gottlieb are best known for their close-up portraits of famous musicians. The canonical portrait shows the soloist lost in thought, often with his eyes closed, oblivious to his surroundings. Such photos reinforce our instinctive tendency to attribute group creativity to a single person's genius, rather than to the group's emergent dynamic. For the cover of my 2003 book *Group Creativity*, I wanted to use a classic black and white jazz photograph of an entire group, visibly engaged in group interaction (Sawyer, 2003a). I had a hard time finding such a photo, even though I knew from my own playing experience that musical interaction is at the center of jazz. Ingrid Monson was the first to emphasize the importance of collaborative interaction in the rhythm section in her 1996 book *Saying Something*, and she, too, had a hard time finding the group photo that appeared on the cover of her book (personal communication).

If group communication is the essence of live jazz, then why do so many photos isolate a single musician away from the rest of the band? Because of what Resnick (1994) called our 'centralized mindset'. Most of us, when faced with an example of an emergent group phenomenon, almost subconsciously assume that there is a single leader or organizer. Resnick used the example of the flock of geese, migrating south in a 'V' shape. When you see a V-shaped flock of birds, you probably assume that the bird in front is leading, and that the other birds are following. In fact, this isn't the case – most bird flocks don't have leaders at all. Rather, the orderly 'V' shape that crosses the sky emerges from all of the birds acting together, each responding only to the ones nearby. Like group creative performances, the flock is organized without an organizer.

Resnick points out that our centralized mindset almost invariably leads us to assume that complex group behavior results from a central controller. It's the same mindset that makes improv theater audiences assume that the group secretly has a script, or that makes you assume that a traffic jam must have been caused by an accident or a broken down car, even though many traffic jams are emergent phenomena – collectively 'caused' by the interactional dynamics of many cars engaged in complex trafile patterns (Resnick, 1994).

Back to the script

Group creativity isn't all improvised anew in each performance; there are common elements that are repeated across many performances. There is always some structure in improvisational performance: we even use scripted lines in everyday conversation. Example 3 reproduces the dialogue from a Sunday newspaper 'Blondie' cartoon from 1996. The comic strip is about a stereotypical 1950s nuclear family, living an almost comically ordinary suburban lifestyle. Dagwood has just arrived at the barber shop, and is sitting down in the barber's chair, as the barber welcomes him from behind the chair. The dialogue goes as follows:

Example 3

Barber:	The usual?
Dagwood:	Yep.
Barber:	How's all the family?
Dagwood:	They're fine.
	(The next two frames show the barber silently snipping Dagwood's hair.)
Dagwood:	Usually your third comment is 'Think it's going to rain?' What happened?
Barber:	*(Burying his head in his hands in shame)* I knew this would happen some day ... I forgot my lines!

In everyday situations like getting a haircut, we often use lines that we've heard other people use – we don't always make up completely new things to say. When the barber says, 'How's all the family?' no one would claim that he's being creative. These aren't really his own words, since thousands of people have said exactly that line in exactly that situation before. Like the barber, we often use catchphrases in conversation – phrases like 'Could I talk to you for a minute?' or 'Give me a break.' Because a million people have said exactly the same sentence, we could think of these sentences as scripted lines. Linguists call these little bits of script *formulaic speech*. But using formulaic speech still requires improvisational creativity: a catchphrase can send many different implicit messages, depending on the situation.

Example 4 displays some catchphrases from a textbook teaching English as a Second Language (ESL). These bits of formulaic speech show that learning another language isn't just about vocabulary and grammar rules, it's about learning the catchphrases and the right way to use them creatively.

Example 4

How are you?
My name is ———.
I am ——— years old.

I like to eat fish and apple.
My favorite color is red.
Thank you!

You're not the creator of these catchphrases, and when you say them, you're not really speaking your own words. For example, when someone says, 'Go ahead, make my day,' you can't help but think of Clint Eastwood's character in the movie *Dirty Harry,* and you might also recall President Reagan's famous repetition of the line.

The idea that speakers often use language that they inherit from prior speakers was an important theme of the Russian literary theorist Mikhail Bakhtin (1981). Bakhtin argued that even though each speaker intends his or her words to have a novel, personal meaning, those words have unavoidable connotations associated with past situations of use. A catchphrase demonstrates this point particularly well, because it's so obvious that the line has been spoken by others before. When we use a catchphrase, or say something with a stereotypical inflection or accent, everyone can't help but think of all of the other occasions on which they've heard the same thing. These connotations are like unavoidable baggage that the words bring with them from past situations of use: they're built into the catchphrases, the price we pay for using them. Bakhtin coined the term *dialogic* to describe this two-leveled nature of language: the two levels are the speaker's own meaning, and everyone's memory of how these words have been used in the past.

The structures used in improvisation aren't always verbal. Actors assume that they share a lot of cultural knowledge with the audience; and actors wouldn't be able to communicate so quickly with each other unless they shared a large body of cultural knowledge and practices. Good improv actors are pop-culture experts, and improv actors assume that the audience will catch the references they make to popular TV shows or movies: bits and pieces of dialogue, familiar characters, or events from a famous sitcom episode or movie scene. Bernie Sahlins, a founder of The Second City theater in Chicago, explains that these pop culture references are a shorthand way of communicating quickly with your fellow actors and with the audience (see his interview in Sweet, 1978). Improv actors know that each social group has its own distinctive speech style and catchphrases; a well-chosen catchphrase or a distinctive accent can implicitly tell us a great deal about a character: ethnic background, profession (lawyer or doctor), family role (father or son), status (an authority figure such as a policemen or the boss), distinctive cultural stereotypes like cowboy, Southern redneck or gay male. When the first actor steps to the front of the stage and starts to enact a 'Mad German Scientist' character, a whole set of script possibilities is immediately suggested and other possibilities get closed off. Actors use these styles of talking to communicate characters and situations, quickly and implicitly communicating to each other about the emerging drama.

This kind of implicit communication is an example of what linguists call *indexicality,* from the Latin word for 'point to' or 'indicate'. Your words are indexical when they indicate something about the situation that isn't in the literal meaning of the words. Using a well-known catchphrase or speech style is indexical, because it implicitly communicates something about the situation: for example, if an actor starts talking in a southern US accent, he or she implicitly communicates to the audience that the setting for the scene is somewhere in southern USA without ever having to say, 'Here we are in Ole Mississippi'. Some linguists estimate that as much as 90 percent of all of our spoken language is at least partially indexical – in other words, very little of what we say is completely context-free (e.g. Bar-Hillel, 1954).

The structures of improvisation

> The freer the form, the greater must be the underpinnings of discipline.
>
> (Ted Flicker, quoted in Sweet, 1978:161)

Although improv ensembles improvise their dialogue, there are two forms of structure that guide their emergent improvisations: scenarios that guide the overall improvisation and formulaic speech that actors use in their individual lines. These structures are always in dialectic with improvisation.

These two kinds of improvisational structures have parallels in musical improvisation. Parallel to an overall scenario that guides an improvisation, most jazz improvisations are based on the structure of the chorus of the mid-American popular song. The chorus is 16 or 32 bars, with an AABA or ABAC structure. For example, the jazz standard 'How High the Moon' was one of Charlie Parker's favorites, with an ABAC structure. He liked it so much, he wrote another song using the same overall structure, known as 'Ornithology'. 'Ornithology' is 'by' Charlie Parker, but he didn't try to hide the fact that it had the same harmonic structure as 'How High the Moon'. Is it really a different song, or is it the same song? How different does it have to be?

These overall structures correspond to the ritualized conversational exchanges that fluent native speakers can jointly participate in, without even thinking hard about it: the greeting routines taught in ESL classes or the small-talk exchanges between Dagwood and the barber.

In musical improvisation, scholars have identified parallels with formulaic speech. These are usually known as 'motifs'; some improvisational traditions are referred to as 'motivic improvisation', meaning that the performer's creativity rests in choosing which one of a set of conventional musical phrases will be played next. Some jazz performers improvise in a partially motivic style: for example, Charlie Parker had a repertoire of over 100 personal licks that he used repeatedly, in many different solos (Owens, 1995). These correspond to scripted bits of conversation like 'How are you?' except that they are idiosyncratic, associated specifically with Parker.

The three characteristics of group creativity – improvisation, collaboration, and emergence – all take place within a background of structuring elements. Yet the existence of these structures does not detract from the emergent, collaborative nature of group creativity. In fact, improvisation could not take place at all without some shared conventions, because otherwise communication would be impossible.

Group flow

> Tonight, things are going well. Tonight, watching them improvise is like watching an expert surfer. The surfer's incredible balance keeping him constantly poised on the crest of a wave; the cast, working from instinct rooted in hours of workshops and past improv sets, riding the crest of the moment. When they are on top, it is a sight to see. There is a thrill in watching them, a thrill born of the precariousness of their position and the ever-present threat that a misjudgment may send them hurtling into a wipeout.
>
> (Sweet, 1978: xxxix)

There are many metaphors one can use to describe a talented ensemble when they are 'on', in interactional synchrony, performing well. One might say that they have a *good chemistry*, or that things are *clicking* or *in sync*. For example, Jimerson (1999) wrote about a pick-up basketball team, 'we played quietly and efficiently. We rarely spoke and played effortlessly and effectively. As teammates, we were "in sync" with each other' (p. 13). For just about any sports team, one can speak of the *group spirit,* the *team spirit,* or the *esprit de corps.* A commentator might say *they gelled as a unit* or that they displayed *good teamwork.* All of these metaphors focus on the entire group and on their performance together as an ensemble. Even if the individual performers are prepared and focused, a good ensemble performance doesn't always emerge.

When a group is performing at its peak, I refer to it as being in *group flow,* in the same way that an individual performing at his or her peak often experiences a subjective feeling of flow. The concept of group flow is related to Csikszentmihalyi's (1990) flow theory, but with a critical difference. Csikszentmihalyi intended flow to represent a state of consciousness within the individual performer, whereas group flow is a property of the entire group as a collective unit. Group flow has been neglected in studies of flow, which have focused on how individuals attain flow through their own actions (cf. Jimerson, 1999). In group flow, everything seems to come naturally; the performers are in interactional synchrony (Sawyer, 2003a). In this state, each of the group members can even feel as if they are able to anticipate what their fellow performers will do before they do it.

Group flow is an emergent property of the group. Group flow can inspire musicians to play things that they would not have been able to play alone, or that they would not have thought of without the inspiration of the group; 'the highest points of improvisation occur when group members strike a groove together' (Berliner, 1994: 588). In a study of pick-up basketball games, Jimerson (1999) wrote that flow is caused by groups when it is 'a result of their interaction with other people, [who] cooperatively maintain their flow, and respond to each other differently than they did before' (p. 35). Group flow helps the individual performers to attain their own flow state. When jazz musicians describe the subjective experience of performing in a group, they frequently refer to the important role played by the emergent group flow in propelling their own performance to ever higher levels: 'Sometimes, I really feel that I am just the vehicle, the body, and that something is really singing through me, like I am not controlling everything that I am singing' (Carmen Lundy, in Berliner, 1994: 392).

Like other emergent phenomena, group flow is hard to predict in advance, even knowing a great deal about the psychologies of the participating performers. Jazz musicians and improv theater ensembles alike have little idea how successful a performance will be: there are simply too many intangible factors that cannot be known until the performance begins. Franklin Gordon said: 'It doesn't happen every single night ... but at some point when the band is playing and everyone gets locked in together, it's special for the musicians and for the aware, conscientious listener. These are the magical moments, the best moments in jazz' (Berliner, 1994: 388).

Musicians use a wide variety of metaphors to describe group flow: riding a wave, gliding across a ballroom with a dance partner, or lovemaking (Berliner, 1994: 389). Jazz bassist Chuck Israels says: 'If it's working, it brings you very close. It's a kind of emotional empathy that you develop very quickly. The relationship is very intimate' (Berliner, 1994: 349–50). Curtis Fuller said: 'when that's really happening in a band, the cohesiveness is unbelievable. Those are the special, cherished moments. When those special moments occur, to me, it's like ecstasy. It's like a beautiful thing. It's like when things blossom' (Berliner, 1994: 389). There is an open communicative channel among the performers; each performer is open and listening to the others and each performer fully attends to what the others are doing, even as they are contributing to the performance themselves.

Melba Liston said: 'everybody can feel what each other is thinking and everything. You breathe together, you swell together, you just do everything together, and a different aura comes over the room' (Berliner, 1994: 392).

Many Chicago improvisers refer to group flow using the term *groupmind*. Groupmind is the entire troupe working intuitively together toward the same goals. The perfect working of groupmind is an intense experience: comedian Jim Belushi famously said that the high that comes from group flow was 'better than sex' (Seham, 2001: 64: compare Berliner on jazz, 1994: 389). Actor Alan Alda referred to this state, saying 'you're actually turned into something that's inside the actor's mind and there's a kind of mental music that's played and that everybody shares' (Sweet, 1978: 326). Improv actors often speak of group flow as 'a state of unselfconscious awareness in which every individual action seems to be the right one and the group works with apparent perfect synchronicity' (Seham, 2001: 64). Performers often talk about the groupmind in spiritual terms, and believe it channels 'a truth beyond their own conscious reasoning' (Seham, 2001: 64).

In musical ensembles, group flow requires a type of parallel processing: the musicians are playing non-stop, yet while they are playing they must simultaneously listen to their band members, hearing and immediately responding to what they are playing: 'You have to be able to divide your senses ... so you still have that one thought running through your head of saying something, playing something, at the same time you've got to be listening to what the drummer is doing' (Sawyer interview). You can't relax your attention or else you will fall behind. Bassist Chuck Israels said: 'From the very moment the performance begins, you plunge into that world of sounds ... and your whole consciousness changes' (Berliner, 1994: 348). Improvisational musicians often try to replicate this experience mentally as they practice alone. For example, a drummer might imagine a bass line as he plays (Berliner, 1994: 350).

In both jazz and improv, we find that groups performing at their peak are in a state of group flow akin to Csikszentmihalyi's (1990) flow. Group flow is an emergent group property and is not the same thing as the psychological state of flow. It depends on interaction among performers and it emerges from this process. The group can be in flow even when the members are not; or the group might not be in flow even when the members are. The study of group flow thus requires a fundamentally social psychology and must proceed by examining the interactional dynamics among members during performance.

Group creativity in scored music

> There is in principle no difference between the performance of a modern orchestra or chorus and people sitting around a campfire and singing to the strumming of a guitar or a congregation singing hymns under the leadership of the organ. And there is no difference in principle between the performance of a string quartet and the improvisations at a jam session of accomplished jazz players.
>
> (Schutz, 1964: 177)

Even in scored and conducted ensembles, group creativity is necessary to an effective performance, because a score under-determines performance. Otherwise, 'performing works would be akin to minting coins' (Godlovitch, 1998: 85); as orchestral musicians sometimes put it, 'you're either making music or just playing notes' (Faulkner, 1985: 74).

Several studies of orchestral interaction have been inspired by Schutz's classic 1964 paper 'Making Music Together', which emphasized the interactional processes in ensemble music. Schutz noted that many musical groups achieve synchrony and intersubjectivity without a conductor. Several studies of interaction in musical groups have been influenced by Schutz and his focus on intersubjectivity; for example, Malhotra (1981) studied the gestural communication that serves to coordinate an orchestral performance. She discovered that although the conductor plays an important role in organizing the performance, musicians do not always attend visually to the conductor, and 15 percent of them report *never* looking at the conductor. When not attending to the conductor, musicians hear and see those sitting near them, and much of the ensemble coordination occurs through gestures, facial expressions, and bodily movements. For example, 'the first violinist's raised eyebrow may indicate to a second violin that he or she is playing slightly flat and must raise his or her pitch. The nodding of the first bassoonist's head or raising of the right eyebrow can cue in the second bassoon' (1981: 105–6).

As Weeks (1996a) noted, much of the ensemble interaction among musicians is hidden from the audience during a performance and the intention of all involved is to give the audience the somewhat misleading impression that the musicians are reading 'the musical text as the composer intended it, under the direction of the conductor *then-and-there*' (p. 248). Weeks focused his research on rehearsals, analyzing the interactions of talk and gesture that serve to coordinate the performance and to help the musicians reach a common understanding of the piece. This coordinating talk is completely absent from public performance, and many of the non-verbal gestures are omitted as well. In Weeks's analyses, ensembles require the most interactional work to coordinate temporal features of the performance: the initial tempo of the piece; the rate to slow down the tempo in a ritardando – a passage in which the composer has indicated that the tempo should slow down; and the relative durations of the fermata, a mark on the score that indicates that a note should be held for an indeterminate length of time (1996b).

Improvisational coordination becomes salient when one of the performers makes a mistake, playing a wrong note or losing the tempo of the piece. Musicians refer to this as 'covering up' a mistake. Weeks (1990) analyzed the interactional processes that occurred during the rehearsal of a chamber group of seven musicians that had no conductor. He documented how a cellist and pianist executed a series of 'collaborative maneuvers' (p. 211) to recover from several mistakes made by the cellist, so that the performance could continue in such a way that the average listener would not notice the variation. The covering-up action involved a retrospective contextualization of the mistake, redefining it by modifying the scored performance that immediately followed so that it retroactively seemed to have been the correct note or tempo to have played (p. 216). The ensemble's modification resulted in dropping almost two beats from the scored performance. Weeks (1990) concluded that 'although the score has served as a guide, the determination of the specific place the group is at a given moment is thereby a complex *collaborative accomplishment*' (p. 219).

Educational implications

My focus on group creativity and collaborative improvisation treats music as a communicative activity. Music is a collaborative practice, and improvised group music results in an emergent, unpredictable performance. But many educators teach music as a solitary activity – practicing fingering and scales for hours, at home alone; studying to learn how to read notated music effortlessly; memorizing a solo piece for recital performance. But if music is a collaborative practice and if communication is central to musical creativity, then our educational methods should emphasize group interaction. There are many exciting projects designed to teach children by drawing on the power of group creativity and communication.

For example, the Toy Symphony Project was developed by the Hyper-instruments research group at the MIT Media Lab in Cambridge, MA, USA. Its goal is to introduce children to the creative music-making process by using specially designed 'music toys' that enable children to engage in sophisticated performing and composing – activities normally accessible only after years of study. Through the use of two specially designed music toys called Beatbugs and Music Shapers, children and adults alike can shape and modify musical lines with expressive gesture and delicate touch. The research group also developed a graphical composition tool, Hyperscore, that allows children to draw dots and lines that the computer then turns into musical compositions.

The Beatbug is an example of a music toy designed to encourage musical collaboration among students (Jennings, 2003; Weinberg et al., 2002). The Beatbug is a hand-held percussion instrument, about the size and shape of an Easter egg. Beatbugs are designed to be played in groups of eight and all eight are connected to the same Macintosh computer. The Beatbug is held in one hand and struck with the other, sending a signal to the computer to produce a percussion sound. The synthesized sound is played through speakers placed in the room and through a small speaker inside the Beatbug. Each of the eight Beatbugs produces its own distinctive timbre and light emitting diodes (LEDs), which flash to provide additional visual feedback.

In concert, the eight Beatbugs are placed in 'snake' mode, which is designed to encourage maximum group interaction and communication. The leader begins by making a short rhythmic motif, which is then sent (by the computer) to another member of the group. That player then has the option to embellish and manipulate the pattern before sending it on to a third player. After the pattern makes several cycles through the group, the pattern is assigned permanently to one of the Beatbugs. This pattern continues to play in the background as the 'snake' of interaction continues, with the other players interacting to develop yet another collaborative pattern.

As Pat Campbell argued in her studies of children's musical cultures (1998), all children learn musical practices by being informally socialized into a community of practice, their peer culture. The Beatbugs support a kind of musical education that is fundamentally collaborative and emergent. It taps into children's natural ability to improvise in social groups (Sawyer, 1997). Sociocultural approaches suggest that the goal of musical educators should be to create musical communities of practice, rather than to transmit musical knowledge. In this way, children are socialized into collective musical practices.

When teachers create these musical communities, they should keep in mind that learners need more structure than experts. These structures have been called *scaffolds* and the educational practice is known as *guided participation*. For example, when the Beatbugs are in 'snake' mode, the children's improvised interactions occur within a strictly specified structure, one that is enforced by the computer software. Unfortunately, many educators have the mistaken belief that scaffolding means that the teacher supports the child during their learning. It's not the teacher that scaffolds the child: it's the collective practice, the activity itself (the enactment of which must be skillfully facilitated by the teacher, of course).

Learning in musical communities of practice corresponds to the way that children naturally learn in family and peer settings. Children learn music through family musical practices, through informal playground games and rhymes. Jacques Dalcroze first had the insight that learning music should be like learning your native language, an idea also advocated by Suzuki. These educators shared the insight that musical learning works best when educators create musical communities of practice that allow children to learn by participating.

Effective group activities provide for different levels of participation, to accommodate different learning styles and different developmental levels. Each child appropriates the collective practice at his or her own pace, and to a different degree. And effective group activities provide for easy movement from peripheral participation to a more central role (Lave and Wenger, 1991). An effective group activity, from the community of practice perspective, allows all learners to participate meaningfully regardless of their level: and it is structured so that each level of participation naturally propels the child to increasing appropriation, mastery and central participation.

In such classrooms, students learn more than the mechanics of music. They learn interactional skills; they learn how to listen and to respond appropriately; they learn to collaborate; they learn to communicate in social contexts. In these collective improvisational activities, children may learn a deeper musical understanding than they would from structured activities. This sort of improvisational learning is even more important in the early years. In my studies of preschool play (1997) I found that between the ages of 3 and 5, children are learning to improvise through communication, negotiation and collaboration.

Children learn best in collaborative, creative classrooms (Sawyer, 2004a). Creative and improvisational teaching is an effective tool for collaborative and constructivist learning of any content (Sawyer, 2004a, 2004b). The teacher leads the classroom in group improvisations, rather than acting as a solo 'performer' in front of the class 'audience'. Students become socialized into classroom communities of practice, in which the whole class collaborates in each student's learning.

I started out talking about group creativity, and I ended up advocating a sociocultural approach to music education. The sociocultural approach requires a reconceptualization of the goals of music education. The classroom is no longer considered the site for the transmission of musical knowledge, but rather a place where children are socialized into musical communities of practice.

Conclusion

The study of musical collaboration can provide insights into the study of all group creativity. To make this case, I gave examples of both music and theater group improvisations and I identified the shared characteristics of both types of group creativity. These characteristics are found in all collaboration: in classroom group discussion, in creative domains including art and science and in creative work teams.

The study of other forms of group creativity can help us to understand musical interaction. Concepts that were developed to analyze improvised dialogues – such as formulaic speech and indexicality – can be applied to musical communication. We should be looking into studies of group creativity, in psychology and in sociology, for ideas, examples, insights and guiding frameworks.

Musical collaboration can help us to understand all collaboration. Other scholars who study group creativity can learn a lot from what we know about group creativity in musical groups. And education researchers who are interested in how children learn from participating in communities of practice could gain insights from our knowledge of how children become socialized into communities of musical practice.

Musical collaboration provides us with a way of better understanding the essence of group creativity.

References

Bakhtin, M.M. (1981) 'Discourse in the Novel', in M.M. Bakhtin, *The Dialogic Imagination,* pp. 259–422. Austin: University of Texas Press.

Bar-Hillel, Y. (1954) 'Indexical Expressions'. *Mind* 63(251): 359–79.

Berliner, P. (1994) *Thinking in Jazz: The Infinite Art of Improvisation.* Chicago: University of Chicago Press.

Campbell, P.S. (1998) *Songs in their Heads: Music and its Meaning in Children's Lives.* New York: Oxford.

Csikszentmihalyi, M. (1990) *Flow: The Psychology of Optimal Experience.* New York: HarperCollins.

Faulkner, R. (1983) 'Orchestra Interaction: Communication and Authority in an Artistic Organization', in J.B. Kamerman and R. Martorella (eds). *Performers and Performances: The Social Organization of Artistic Work,* pp. 71–83. New York: Praeger.

Godlovitch, S. (1998) *Musical Performance: A Philosophical Study.* New York: Routledge.

Jennings. K. (2003) '"Toy Symphony": An International Music Technology Project for Children'. *Music Education International* 2: 3–21.

Jimerson, J.B. (1999) 'Interpersonal Flow in Pickup Basketball', unpublished manuscript, Indiana University, Bloomington.

Lave, J. and Wenger, E. (1991) *Situated Learning: Legitimate Peripheral Participation.* New York: Cambridge University Press.

Malhotra, V.A. (1981) 'The Social Accomplishment of Music in a Symphony Orchestra: A Phenomenological Analysis', *Qualitative Sociology* 4(2): 102–25.

Monson, I. (1996) *Saying Something: Jazz Improvisation and Interaction.* Chicago: University of Chicago Press.

Owens, T. (1995) *Bebop; The Music and its Players.* New York: Oxford.

Resnick. M. (1994) *Turtles, Termites, and Traffic Jams: Explorations in Massively Parallel Microworlds.* Cambridge: MIT Press.

Sawyer, R.K. (1997) *Pretend Play as Improvisation: Conversation in the Preschool Classroom.* Mahwah, NJ: Erlbaum.

Sawyer. R.K. (2003a) *Group Creativity: Music, Theater, Collaboration.* Mahwah, NJ: Erlbaum.

Sawyer, R.K. (2003b) *Improvised Dialogues: Emergence and Creativity in Conversation.* Westport, CT: Greenwood.

——(2004a) 'Creative Teaching: Collaborative Discussion as Disciplined Improvisation. *Educational Researcher* 33(2): 12–20.

——(2004b) 'Improvised Lessons: Collaborative Discussion in the Constructivist Classroom', *Teaching Education* 15(2): 189–201.

Schutz, A. (1964) 'Making Music Together: A Study in Social Relationships', in A. Brodessen [ed.] *Collected Papers.* Vol. 2: *Studies in Social Theory,* pp. 159–78. The Hague: Martinus Nijhoff.

Seham, A.E. (2001) *Whose Improv is it Anyway? Beyond Second City.* Jackson: University Press of Mississippi.

Sweet, J. (1978) *Something Wonderful Right Away: An Oral History of the Second City and the Compass Players.* New York: Avon Books.

Weeks, P. (1990) 'Musical Time as a Practical Accomplishment: A Change in Tempo', *Human Studies* 13: 323–59.

——(1996a) 'A Rehearsal of a Beethoven Passage: An Analysis of Correction Talk', *Research on Language and Social Interaction* 29(3): 247–90.

——(1996b) 'Synchrony Lost, Synchrony Regained: The Achievement of Musical Coordination'. *Human Studies* 19: 199–228.

Weinberg, G., Aimi, R., and Jennings, K. (2002) 'The Beatbug Network: A Rhythmic System for Interdependent Group Collaboration', paper presented at the 2002 Conference on New Instruments for Musical Expression (NIME-02), 24–26 May, Dublin, Ireland.

14 Community Performance

Improvising Being-Together

Petra Kuppers

After obtaining a PhD in Feminist Theory/Performance Studies from the Falmouth College of Arts, Petra Kuppers worked in the Contemporary Arts Department at Manchester Metropolitan University on the integration of participatory arts theory with practice and education. She travels the world exploring international disability culture, using performance methods as a research methodology. Kuppers now teaches at the University of Michigan, where she holds joint appointments in the departments of English; Art and Design; Theatre, Music, and Dance; and Women's Studies. She also teaches on the low-residency MFA in Interdisciplinary Arts at Goddard College's Port Townsend Campus. Her books include *The Scar of Visibility: Medical Performances and Contemporary Art* (2007), *Cripple Poetics: A Love Story* (2008), and *Disability Culture and Community Performance: Find a Strange and Twisted Shape* (2011). In "Community Performance," Kuppers refers to the ideas of Jean-Luc Nancy and Michel de Certeau to point her experiences in a Welsh village towards a worldwide movement to empower those who are marginalised because of disabilities, economics, geography, nationality, or gender.

Key words: disabilities; community; theatre; the body; pedagogy

At the heart of this chapter are two art projects which articulate at-home-ness in myth stories: 'Earth Stories' and 'Sleeping Giants' – digital videos that emerged out of a two-year long workshop series with a group of mental health system survivors in Wales, in the United Kingdom. As a resident of a small Welsh village, and a fellow disabled person, I collaborated with people using the village's mental health self-help center, and we created communal poetry, dance, performance, traditional music, and video. In the following, I use 'we' when I speak about our practices and intents, and I use it advisedly – there is of course a tension between our art work and my academic writing about it, claiming a communal voice that cannot be anything but my own single one. But given both our experiences together and the theme of this chapter, I have chosen to stay with the precariously positioned 'we:' the (im) possibility of community in the cauldron of essentialized identities and notions of 'the nation.'

We used local legends and myths to find new ways of affirming our presences in our environment. With this, we found concrete ways of intervening in the negative representation of disabled people, and in particular mental health system survivors, in our locality and beyond. Acts of storytelling allow me to discuss our work as a meditation on how to approach community art work that wants to speak from a group, *and* from individuals, without canceling out experiences, showing the longing to 'belong' and yet the inability to completely merge with one another. As individuals, we exist in relation – we are neither fully separate, nor fully embraced within a group. So how can we both create and query 'community?'

Philosopher Jean-Luc Nancy provides theoretical tools to consider community beyond self/other relations. In *The Inoperative Community*, he configures community by thinking about the way that being-together can resist and deconstruct dominant power relations, which attempt to weld the process of being-together into a fixed state. Community exists in relationship and negotiation, and in openness:

> Community is what takes place always through others and for others. It is not the space of the egos—subjects and substances that are at bottom immortal—but of the I's, who are always others (or else are nothing).
>
> (Nancy, 1991: 15)

The Others of the I emerge because of the finite nature of the singular: for Nancy, singular beings lean towards others, searching 'contact of the skin (or the heart) of another singular being ... [another finite being] always other, always shared, always exposed' (1991: 28). This community is inoperative because the moment of sharedness, of an absolute connection, is sundered as it emerges: it is negated by the singularity of the I, just as the I leans and cannot help but lean towards the other. There are no egos that claim immortality, only I's that know of their limit and seek others who share this limit, too.

Storytelling and myth-making are important parts of Nancy's articulation of the inoperative community, a community that becomes inoperative at the same moment at which it offers relation:

> We know the scene: there is a gathering, and someone is telling a story. They were not assembled like this before the story; the recitation has gathered them together. In the speech of the narrator, their language for the first time serves no other purpose than that of presenting the narrative and of keeping it going. It is no longer the language of their exchanges, but of their reunion, the sacred language of a foundation and an oath. The teller shares it with them and among them.
>
> (Nancy, 1991: 43–44)

Storytelling, sharing language, and myth-making is the offering that allows the horizon of community to appear: 'That the work must be offered to communication means that it must in effect be offered, that is to say, presented, proposed, and abandoned on the common limit where [singularities] share one another' (73).

In storytelling (and Nancy uses the 'foundational scene' of a circle, and a male storyteller), singularities can experience the shared limit: foundational stories make community inoperative, as the distance between the story's ontological claim is thrown back onto the experience of the singularity's limit, and the possibility of the I's death. Wanting to listen, hear, and tell, we are abandoned to the distance between the story and our I, but we lean in, move our heads into the circle, hovering in the space between the I and the communal story.

To me, Nancy's account of community speaks of continuous flows – of a leaning movement, of responsibility, of meanings. These I's who are others – singularities constantly in negotiation, touching their limit – are provisional, temporal. Life flows – no point of standstill, definition, or grounding of identity in ontology is possible in this conception of improvisational community. In this chapter, this emphasis on the I's who are others informs the discussion of art-making as improvisational flow.

In the two art projects, everyday performance was the ground on which we built our communal art work: being unconsciously and consciously in spaces that we call home, but that have histories, dominant narratives, dominant ways of being seen. Our disabilities meant exclusion from some of the spaces we were investigating and inhabiting. The environment we chose was our Welsh village, surrounded by the green hills of a National Park. The exclusions we experienced worked on a variety of levels, from physical access to do with stairs, public transportation, or stamina, to imaginary access to do with patterns of usage, ownership of a locale's imagination, and the use it is put to. Through performance, and, importantly, through mediation of those performances in public environments, we inscribed our right of access to these spaces, making our presences felt. The performance act became the performative act: a conscious inscription of difference into sedimented patterns of naturalized 'law.' With this, our work is not located within art therapy, changing ourselves, but within political labor, changing ourselves and our world.

Our communal practice refused to be singularly authored, and this anti-romantic tactic links our work back to everyday practices of storytelling. Community, this impossible goal, is tactically erected as a place to momentarily speak from.[1] With this chapter, I am offering a contemplation not (only) of a community of minds, but of cohabitation, embodiment, and enworldedness as necessary aspects of thinking towards a coming community.

Local stories

To speak about 'community,' I find it important to establish the ecology of the specific example of an intervention into the formation and articulation of community as a process. 'Community' emerges as many things in the following: as a national ideal, a marketing tool, an experience, a hope, and a problem.

The village of Ystradgynlais, where all activities I am discussing here took place, is situated on the edges of the Brecon Beacons, a National Park in the middle of Wales. Ystradgynlais used to support itself through the mining industry, and the rolling hills surrounding it have been changed by Roman soldiers, Celtic inhabitants, sheep grazing, and now disused railway lines. The people supported by this land include a Welsh-speaking minority and a majority of English-speaking inhabitants. The language of Wales suffered under English imperialist policy, and has been rooted out by various historical practices, such as forbidding the language from being spoken in school and in public meetings. More recently, the language has been reintroduced into school curricula, and a culture war surrounds its problematic position in modern Wales.

Many people live in Wales whose family origins might lie in Ireland, Italy, India, France, or elsewhere, and who might have settled in Wales during the Industrial Revolution, when Welsh ironworks provided jobs for many. Other people might include more recent incomers who have entered Wales as part of the counter-culture movement or as down-shifters from the South of England. This last category of inhabitants is often and tellingly referred to as 'white settlers' by many Welsh who understand themselves as natives.[2]

Against an image of Wales as a country of anti-imperialistic segregationist politics stands the image of Wales perpetuated in tourist brochures. This image is the rural idyll, with bucolic pastoral characters such as sheep farmers, sheep dog owners, and craftspeople who make things with their hands out of wood and reed.

All of these images, though, do not capture the reality for many of the people living in Ystradgynlais, and in particular the experiences of people hidden on the economic margin, the unemployed and the disabled. Both the fiercely national and the bucolic

Figure 14.1 'Earth Stories' group at the old iron smelting works in Ystalyfera

image rely on segregationist and exclusionary concepts of community, on a single vision that references historical origin and continuity. This kind of mobilization of 'community' is deeply suspect to feminists and others who wish to consider social change in conjunction with collective action. Thus Iris Marion Young critiques 'community' ideals when they become a desire for social wholeness and identification – a form of politics that relies on sameness, and which in turn erects exclusionary zones and borders (1990). Benedict Anderson, in *Imagined Communities*, sees the problem of national community and its seductiveness in a different light: here, '[I]t is imagined as a community, because, regardless of the actual inequality and exploitation that may prevail in each, the nation is always conceived as a deep, horizontal comradeship' (1991: 5–7). But how can we mobilize a community politics that keeps alive openness, provisionality, and respect for difference?

In order to address this question, I collaborated with fellow disabled people in Wales. We realized that to create affective and effective arts for social change, we needed to find points of entry into the representational canon, into the images and stories of Wales.

If we wanted to affect images of mental health issues in our local rural environment, the terrain of landscape art was a good framework, since it is such a prevalent and legible genre in Welsh culture. It is for this reason that I first conceptualized the project under the name of *Landscaping Women*: I saw a structural affinity between art historical arguments that found women to be the mute ground of landscape art, where nude female bodies were equated with so-called virgin soil, and disability's invisible, yet structural relation to the labor-poor economy of Wales. Many disabled people in Wales became so due to their labor in coalmines: white finger vibration symptoms and lung diseases are common, as is arthritis. Depression and other mental health symptoms are also common in Wales, one of the poorest regions in Britain. Nationally and internationally, though, mental health issues in the countryside are marginalized – mental health has become increasingly focused upon as an urban problem, one associated with the rise of modernity's social arrangements and alienations.

Few of these realities of contemporary rural life find their way into the romanticized images of Wales. And, just as many people living in the village of Ystradgynlais do not recognize themselves in the images of their region presented on television, their presences and bodies are also invisible in the landscape of the National Park itself. In order to enter the Park you need capital: the main access is by car. But also, more subtly, access is regulated in other ways: taking to the outdoors, walking in the wild hills, is a middle-class leisure activity, requiring a certain cultural capital as well. It is framed by the literature of the walkers in the Lake District, of the romantic sublime, of solitude, and of communion with nature. TV images of the Brecon Beacons, for many the main access to their local landscape, emphasize a place set apart from the everyday, a place of Sunday TV programming and English voices, tweed and shepherds (a mythologized working-class occupation which seems far removed from the roots of mining activity that still pervades the stories of the village). Fishing, sheep husbandry, and farming form the mainstream images – and the visible reality of these occupations tends to be male-dominated. Many of the participants of the mental health self-help group were female, and they found their voices marginalized not only by disability and class, but also by gendered constructions.

For the people I worked with, other obstacles presented themselves in terms of access to the Park: social security welfare checks do not easily allow for the bus fare for public transport ventures into the Park; for some of the older participants of the workshops, mobility was a problem. Also, their circumscribed activity of everyday life doesn't lend itself to one-off outings. The self-help center is a place of routines, and therefore of safety: aspects of mental health issues that need to be taken into account in the design of any workshop. The answer to access was not to bring a bus onto the heath, but to find meaningful ways of structuring activity within the National Park and to find connections between the park and the everyday.

In the first meetings within the group, we agreed that one of our prime objectives for the creation of art works was to reimage ourselves, to speak for us and for others about our lived reality of mental health as people living where we did. Everybody in the group had had significant mental health experiences and encounters with the mental health system. Life experiences included voice-hearing, the diagnosis of schizophrenia, manic depression, anxiety disorders, and so on. Some had been hospitalized in their past, and knew first-hand the horror stories of some institutions. Many were on drug regimes. Some had prison experiences; others had been homeless. Amongst us were retired miners, factory workers, one teacher, and homemakers. For many of us, loneliness and the experience of the I as singular stood in tension with a way of life that romanticizes village life, communality, and community. As we began our work together, we had to assert to each other again and again 'you cannot know … you know,' that double bind of singular beings and community that Nancy offers.

In our initial meetings and discussions, over tea, we decided that we wanted to use the vocabulary that surrounded us in the media world, the vocabulary of land, myths, and history, both personal and national. These are the important, foundational stories of our environment, and we wanted to approach ownership of them – even though we were aware of their problematic nature. Our lives are not apart from these images, and the desire to be seen mixed uneasily with the desire to use the images and narratives that shape the mediation of our world to ourselves.

Figure 14.2 Ystradgynlais Mental Health User Group participant

The initial idea of working in the mental health self-help center was, then, to combine elements of disability politics and story telling. We wanted to break the silence sur-rounding mental health issues, in particular in rural areas, but we wanted to present our experiences in an ambivalent way; not merely to stress the negative experiences, but to retain our dignity and pride. Negotiating the tensions and opportunities between the individual voice and a communal myth-making became central elements of the poetics we built together.

Methods: the 'Lady of the Lake'

The focus of the first sets of workshops, in 2001, was the story of the 'Lady of the Lake.' This story is centered on a lake high up in the hills of the Brecon Beacons, in an area of moors and high fens. The story mirrors similar myths in various British and international locations: a female fairy steps out of the waters, leaves her kingdom to marry a mortal and not fit in, or to marry a mortal not worthy of her; and then to vanish again, having transformed aspects of human experience. A local fish-and-chip shop displays the following summary of the Brecon Beacon's 'Lady of the Lake' story, painted as part of a mural and written in flowery 'heritage' script on its walls:

> In the midst of beautiful mountain scenery, about 16 miles from here, is the lovely lake of Llyn y fan fach. Here, legend has it that a beautiful woman appeared to a poor shepherd boy who was so taken by her that he asked for her hand in marriage. She agreed, but only on condition that he wouldn't strike her 3 times. However, he

found cause to and she returned to the lake with her dowry of animals. Behind her were left 3 sons who became the famous doctors of Wales.

(Mural at the Bwyty West End Café, Llandovery)

In the imagination of local people, the story of the 'Lady of the Lake' has, naturally, many more facets, subsets, versions, and events than the bare-bones story narrated on this local wall. In the self-help group, we found in particular that stories that emphasized the reasons for the violence of the husband on his fairy wife were of interest in many of the versions that mainly the women in the group knew and had selected to remember.

In the workshops that followed, we used performance tableaux, rituals, creative writing methods, and spatial chorus work to create moments out of the legend's connection with our lives. Through this legend work, we accessed a realm of political practice similar to the kind of practices that de Certeau calls 'tactical,' which undermine the 'strategic' – the central force, inscribing its laws legitimately. The strategic is forceful, dominant; it can lay down rules, generalize these, and make them work. The tactical is the work of the minor, the non-dominant:

> A tactic insinuates itself into the other's place, fragmentarily, without taking it over in its entirety, without being able to keep it at a distance.
>
> (de Certeau, 1984: xix)

De Certeau offers the distinction between the strategy and the tactic as a way of understanding the nature of resistance within the field of discourse. Resistance is not conceptualized as fully there, conscious, strategic, an organized political practice. Instead, de Certeau sees everyday practices as tactical interventions: he likens walking, shopping, talking, and so on, to acts that momentarily, locally, impact on power structures. An embodied knowledge of the street allows a way of living that negotiates the dictates of street grids, and the vision of social planning, abstraction, or metaphorization of life: by walking the street, the 'soulless' plan becomes a lived experience that could, potentially, open up a moment of difference. People get away with things:

> [V]ictories of the 'weak' over the 'strong' (whether the strength be that of powerful people or the violence of things or of an imposed order, etc.), clever tricks, knowing how to get away with things, 'hunter's cunning,' maneuvers, polymorphic situations, joyful discoveries, poetic as well as warlike.
>
> (de Certeau, 1984: xix)

De Certeau's work on the politics and poetics of the everyday outlines how Foucault's resistances can function in practice. His work shows how life deals with rules and how these rules can only be bound by temporality given the force of life running through them, leavening their strength.

Legends and myths, the energies expended on 'story-telling' a location and thereby making it 'human,' play an important part in this interaction between strategies and tactics. The absolute rule of 'history' as a monolithic discourse, one that has naturalized itself into truth, is put into question by the power of the minor story, the legend. De Certeau writes: '[W]hereas historiography recounts in the past tense the strategies of instituted powers, these "fabulous" stories offer their audience a repertory of tactics for future use' (1984: 23).

De Certeau sees hollow places in the everyday, moments of layering that become accessible in the activity of the everyday, that make the everyday habitable by creating 'depth' and 'space,' spatial metaphors that create 'habitation' – a space where one can be, rather than having to be in one way only. Legends have an important function in this desire to make a space out of a place, making it human-shaped, habitable, weaving it into the practices of the everyday. They help to create a phenomenological, lived experience of a location:

> It is through the opportunity they offer to store rich silences and wordless stories, or rather through their capacity to create cellars and garrets everywhere, that local legends permit exits, ways of going out and coming back in, and thus habitable spaces.
>
> (de Certeau, 1984: 106)

Legends are seen here as 'exits:' as Spielraum, room to play, offering the potential to not be caught in an endless, dominant signification. They allow for a place to be seen differently. This ability of legends to open up spaces for difference was used in the process of 'Earth Stories': using the make-believe of the legend allowed our group to make-believe about our own situation, and therefore to allow our imagination to soar. Ultimately, this strategy allowed us to see ourselves not fixed *in* discourse, but to *experience* discourse as a Spielraum. And yet, this 'freedom' also highlighted again and again the distance between myth and the limited I, the inoperable nature of storytelling that haunts our gatherings.

De Certeau links this ability of stories and their historical, layered ghosting of a specific location to tactics evading the fixed knowledges of Foucault's *Panopticon*:

> There is no place that is not haunted by many different spirits hidden there in silence, spirits one can 'invoke' or not. Haunted places are the only ones people can live in, and this inverts the schema of the Panopticon.
>
> (1984: 108)

These local stories create forms of knowledge that are minor, local, momentarily evoked, in tension with the 'public': 'this is a sort of knowledge that remains silent. Only hints of what is known but unrevealed are passed on "just between you and me"' (de Certeau, 1984: 108). These links between knowledge and minor discourses and between practice and transformatory repetition became graspable in the workshops. Every time we joke about the woman's perception of the strikes her husband gives her, the perspective shifts momentarily from the 'inevitable' difference between human and fairy to gender issues: traditional tellings of the story use the point-of-view of the young man who wants to wed the lovely lady he saw in the lake while he was herding his sheep. Every time we transpose our local environment into the gothic genre, we see our world with different eyes, and the 'normal' loses its hold temporarily. Nancy's community of I's who are others, who journey together to see themselves shifting, becoming, and yet are part of a common place, emerges in this improvisatory play. Becoming other, stepping outside the rules of place and space, means being both more and more fully the I's we already are: our imagination and ways of being allow for more than one facet of subject position, but we are always bound back to the conditions of singularity, subjectivity, imagination, and context that we live in. We can recognize the strangenesses and familiarities in each other, the moment where the story and the I are cast asunder, where the experience of the limit exiles us from full presence in the myth we make. But instead of retreating to disappointed selves, we can see otherness within ourselves, and we can begin to build community that is both located in specific conditions and yet open to difference. The tactical uses of holding open the multiplicity of the I are not without serious discomfort, though: no place of rest and certainty is available.[3]

In our projects, all of us weld our identities in new provisional alignments: Welsh, English, German, farmer, miner, unemployed, academic, artist, writer, performer, family member, patient, victim, survivor, client, and many more. When we work together, paying careful heed to the multiple identities means that we strive to hold open the unknown: a sense of difference within the known, within the warm atmosphere of our meetings. Listening to the poetry we write, many of these singularities emerge as multiple, in new constellation, as we trust ourselves to share. The sharing is the core part of this relation: not the content of what is shared, or the reception of the shared content and its understanding. The act of leaning anchors our circle. Nancy's leaning towards community allows me to think of these differences and otherings, as well as those that swing among us unsaid, unwritten, and as yet unthought, as potentialities that feed our community, and question its boundaries and definitions.

De Certeau offers a phenomenology of resistance: of the embodiment of living within structures, opening up spaces for people to live in. The political hope I hold is that the accumulation of layers, distancing us from the 'dominant' story of our world and its relations, and from our story of our self, doesn't just alienate us, but opens up Nancy's I's as others. This offers up a reservoir of richness that binds us with different ties to one another and to our locality. I believe that a stronger grasp of the potential of group communication and a sense of pride in the 'deep' location surrounding us can awaken social processes and political consciousness. Art-making played a significant part in this transformatory process: the workshops were process-based, but over a period of time, we shaped aspects of our work together into a product that could leave the circle of the self-help center and travel into the wider social world. Early on in one workshop, we created a short performance piece about the 'Lady of the Lake,' consisting of a number of tableaux and transitions, and a narrative recited as a choral, with individual voices taking on different 'characters.' The group showed great pride in their creation after a number of run-throughs, and the moving together, creating spaces and openings for one another, set a new tone of intimacy and openness in the following workshops. As we talked about the experience, it became clear that, while we felt a desire to show our work, we acknowledged a multitude of problems in bringing the performance 'live' to local events. And thus, our version of the 'Lady of the Lake' traveled to the outside as a video, combining spoken poetry and visuals, recording us in the countryside we were talking about. This provided a very useful vehicle for allowing our imaginations to soar, and our writing and our stories became wilder, as we all realized that a different set of rules (strategies) governs the universe of video-making when compared with live art.

Embodiment as a reservoir and repetition of knowledge played an interesting part in the way that memories became retrievable, and entered from the private into the social: when we were exploring the connection between our childhood memories and the story, most of us pointed to moments of outside physical activity as a pivotal point in our memories: walking in a group of school children, standing by a gate in the garden, playing in a field. Meditating on the myth brought many of the participants to recall the feeling of grass under their fingers, or their emotions as they sat amongst rocks. We discussed how video would allow us to show intimate perspectives, including the touch of hand on

Figure 14.3 Still from 'Earth Stories' video

stone, in close-up.[4] Sensations usually characterized as 'minor' or 'private' took on a different charge as we gave ourselves permission to focus on our way of telling, and how it felt right to us. Soon our workshops moved outside, from the living room of the community center to the small garden. We collected sensations, feelings, stories, moments, images and scenes. I acted as facilitator and scribe: recording with whatever means possible what we hoarded, moderating discussions that edited our collection of everyday practices and local re-tellings down to manageable size. Our poems were all communal: we agreed on a theme to write about, and then we all produced four lines, with sometimes only single words in each line. Then we read them out to each other. And finally read them communally: in a circle, everybody reading their first line, then as the circle came round again the second one. In this way, a communal theme created a coherence in the poem, but one that was beyond the individual author. In these poetry rounds, the *I*'s do not share their singularity, but we lean in, from our own singularities into a rhythm, a round:

> Giant river boulders, round hollows ground into them, by the rushing river twirling into deep dark pools.
> Branches bent, fingers grip, fear flings me into the hole.
> Grass bends into the earth.
> In the craggy rocks, an opening to an underground tunnel.
> I am frightened of the darkness.
> The sense of not knowing where will it lead to, how long will it go on for.
> Suddenly there is light ahead – a cave in the mountainside.
> Deliver me from the fear of darkness, lady of the lake.
> The lady of the lake appears in the garden, and flies to the moon and the stars, and promises good times will appear once more.
>
> (from 'Earth Stories' videopoem)

Figure 14.4 Still from 'Earth Dance' video

Anxieties: Sleeping Giants

If 'Earth Stories' was our summer story, our celebration, and our engagement with mainstream aesthetics, the next video we created, 'Sleeping Giants,' was our winter work. It is harsher; its production is even further removed from 'the professional' as we took the camera with us all the time, with different videographers amongst us capturing the shots.

The videopoem deals with another local story: as you move towards Ystradgynlais and through it, you can see a hill above the village. The outline of the hill is like a lying man, and the formation is called the 'Sleeping Giant.'

> I wish I could lie still
> For a long long time like you do
> Is the sleeping giant going to wake up?
> Is the sleeping giant going to wake up?
> Head in the clouds
> Stone body
> tilting feet first
> down into the earth
>
> (From 'Sleeping Giants' videopoem)

This 'mountain man' is not visible from any static point – the best views can only be gained by traveling in a car. The route follows the closed and disused line of the canal that used to transport coal from the Beacons and Ystradgynlais to the iron works. And this connection between the giant and the coal, the hill and the mine workings, the cave, the weight of history, the lost grandeur of Welsh economic power, is the back-story of our second videopoem. In it, we search: our original idea was anchored in the detective genre, searching compulsively for the Giant. Compulsion disorders and anxiety is something many of us in the group share, and we saw here a way of again transforming individual mental habits into an artistic vision.

> Find a deep cave to the heart of the giant
> It is dark but my eyes adjust
> Two small points of light in the darkness
> I can see the light through the crevices of his fingers
> Heart beating faster, I could feel the warmth and the need to get closer to the giant's heart.
> The giant's heart is a cave of stalagmites, an unchartered country.

(from 'Sleeping Giants' videopoem)

By reading de Certeau, I help develop my sense of the communal importance of our art-making, I find companionship that helps to make sense of why I think there's juice here, in these twisted tales. I can make sense of the empowerment, the euphoria of re-imaging ourselves.

But, of course, the act of labor itself is always visible; the tactic remains momentary, minor, a forced insertion. Performance substitutes, cites, re-creates. However, performance does not offer an easy substitute; it offers a labored one. To quote Joseph Roach, 'a stand-in for an elusive entity that it is not but that it must vainly aspire both to embody and to replace' (1996: 3). This Sleeping Giant is not mythical, ritualistic, always-already-there, outside history. In our practice, the Giant becomes discursive, historically contingent, an oratorical procedure. By recounting when we saw him, we historicize him, binding his presence to the time of our lives – bridging distances between *I*'s and myths. With this, our Giant as myth, retold, offers us a process of community communication. By desta-bilizing the founding story, we fight for entry into the realm where new meaning can be founded at the same time as we continue to be suspicious of founding stories and their exclusionary effects. And it is our loss of certainty, our anxiety, that allows for new community to come into being, in being-together, and in joint exploration:

> Here the mythic hero – and the heroic myth – interrupts his pose and his epic. He tells the truth: that he is not a hero, not even, or especially not, the hero of writing or literature, and that there is no hero, there is no figure who alone assumes and presents the heroism of the life and death of commonly singular beings. He tells the truth of the interruption of his myth, the truth of the interruption of all founding speeches, of all creative and poietic speech, of speech that schematizes a world and that fictions an origin and an end. He says, therefore, that foundation, poiesis and scheme are always offered, endlessly, to each and all, to the community, to the absence of communion through which we communicate and through which we communicate to each other not the meaning of community, but an infinite reserve of common and singular meanings.

(Nancy, 1991: 79)

When we as a group engage our local myths, we do so with an agenda and a tactical sense. We substitute the dominant myth, but the act of substitution creates a new anxiety and liminality, new impossible desires for wholeness and plentitude: a traumatics of political art labor. The mythological fullness of mythology is not available to us. Our myth is a substitute myth, hewn out of dominant images as a response to them.

As I am writing this, the metaphor of the coal mine keeps inserting itself into my textual fantasy, but I have to resist: the bodily and mental trauma of the work deep in the mountain, finding dirt that fuels machines, doesn't map onto the kind of myth excavation that searches for material to reimagine mental health. But the origins of the fantasy are clear: an investment in the local, in the everyday, in repetition, are at the heart of both mining and our art-making. The cave of the heart becomes a space of doublings and hauntings.

Conclusion: community art

In 'Earth Stories' and 'Sleeping Giants' we translate, and call for community flexibility, multi-lingual, multi-embodied access. We transpose perceptual or cognitive difference into sources of artistic endeavor. Our communal practice that refuses to be singularly authored binds our work back to everyday practices of storytelling. And ultimately, our work also comes back to the traditional places of storytelling. Eventually, both 'Earth Stories' and 'Sleeping Giants' had very successful exhibition records, traveling to the British National Film Theatre (as part of different years of the National Disability Film Festival), and to many other international film festivals, conferences, and disability culture meetings. But these circuits were quite far removed from the realities of the Welsh village and the everyday funding and acceptance struggles of a mental health self-help organization in its own locality. More importantly, then, our videos played and continue to play locally. The Mental Health Self-Help Center uses the videos as part of its regular stand at the local markets, where the stand functions to raise awareness of the center and its function in the community. The videos have also helped the center to raise funds: they provide marketing material and give an insight into the abilities, depth, and creativity of the people using the center. In all of these marketplaces, where information is exchanged and public visibility tested, our re-visions of ourselves tactically undermine stereotypes of disability. In the video interviews that accompany the videopoem about the 'Lady of the Lake,' two participants say this about their experiences in the project:

> When we began this project, I was very apprehensive about starting it. I've always written, but it was always personal, private to me. But I never ever dreamed that anything like this could have come out of it. Because people with a mental health problem, there is such a stigma attached to it. It is like people with a mental health problem are non-achievers, but that's not true to all. Because what we achieve in doing this project is more that I could ever dreamed of doing!
>
> Being part of this project has been a revelation. I worked in a group, which wasn't something I was used to doing when I had my own mental distress, disability. I always had the feeling that something good could come out of something that at the time was so very bad and black and terrible. But I know that if we go really deep inside ourselves, we can reach a creative point and that is what working in this group has revealed to me.
>
> (video transcript)

In the processes of the project, its products and in the use we make of these products in the locality, the impossible goal of community emerges as a performance and as a provisional place from which to speak. Working and re-working the connections between the everyday, the artistic, the land and the people, the village and the mental health self-help group, images of mental health and conceptual or temporal difference, plentitude and desire, we again and again start to knit places to live in, and we do so in being-together. We lean, connecting *I*'s and others, singular story and myth. The last words of this chapter, then, come from our group rather than from one single voice:

> This is not a giant of despair,
> this is a giant of hope
> I saw him after the snowfall
> silent and frozen in time
> His cheek was wet
> He lay there like a monster,
> quiet and still
> I thought if he yawned,
> his arms would reach the sky

Notes

1 In 'history from below' framings and the ethical performance studies tradition associated with Dwight Conquergood (1989, 1991), I need to be clear and transparent about how power and capital flowed around the project. This work was initially funded by a MIND Millennium Award, a fund that allowed people to create work that strengthened their communities, without a salary or artist's fee component for the organizer. After the first year, additional funds from the University of Wales, Swansea, Adult Outreach Department, and, most significantly, from the National Endowment for Science, Technology and the Arts, allowed us to extend our work. During the project, I was a research fellow at Manchester Metropolitan University, Contemporary Arts Department, and, towards the end of our time together, I worked at Bryant University in the United States, from which I came back to visit. My academic appointments allow me to work in this open, collaborative, and research-focused manner, without the expectation of 'peer-reviewed' outcomes or significant venues for my art practice. It is important to stress, though, that while community arts are (relatively speaking) thriving in many countries, community artists often struggle to make a living.

  In the case of these projects in Wales, the fact that I do not necessarily get paid for projects I facilitate can be an important feature of building trust and working together. In other projects, and always depending on funding structures, this issue is dealt with differently: during other projects in Rhode Island, USA, every participant was paid for participation in every workshop, as a recognition of their creative labor, appropriate to the way that recognition is usually bestowed in the United States. For many of these participants, our artist collective, The Olimpias, was an important economic reality in their lives, an issue that again impacts our work in significant ways.

  Participants and collaborators in The Olimpias projects are aware that I am an academic, and I shared information about the ways that value and recognition flow within the academy. But they also know that I do not write about projects immediately, or after only short contact, and that I carefully guard privacy and confidences. When I do write about projects, it is with permission, with the trust of the community, and usually after a long period of reflection. In the main, collaborators know me as a fellow disabled woman, with many stories and issues that I share with them but are not for publication or public consumption, just like their own. They know me as a disability culture activist, and they know that my writing is in aid of a larger political project: the validation and celebration of disability culture and community arts.

2 As a 'white settler,' I was well aware of the packaging of the countryside where I had made my home at that time, and of the local stories and myths that were, in all manner of shape and form, presented for quick consumption for tourists, and that fed back into the imagination of children growing up in Wales. Over time, through working as a dance and creativity tutor in hospices, community halls, elder centers, and other places where older people would open up their story reservoirs to me, I had come to appreciate the depth and range of many of these

tales, which were only incompletely and in shortened form received by the mainstream marketing campaigns. At this time, I was working as a community dance leader, and created dance or participated in community dance events with local children and adults, where the Welsh stories of fairies, giants, Arthur's saga material, and Merlin stories were used as basis for dance themes: an effective and interesting way of socializing children and adults into their local story environment, but one that often relied on anodyne and 'cleaned-up' versions of the stories transmitted.

3 Art historian Miwon Kwon focuses on this aspect of community arts when she discusses the problems that face the community artist as member of a community:

[T]he artist engages in an ongoing process of describing and enacting his/her allegiance and commitment, constructing and maintaining a dual identity (as artist here, as community member/representative there), and of course, all subjects within this network are internally split or estranged as well, continuously negotiating a sense of identity and subjectivity through differential encounters with the other (2002: 136–37).

4 For a more in-depth discussion of the video methods we employed, see Kuppers (2001). Some of the specific exercises, session shapes, and arts methodologies used in the Sleeping Giants and Earth Stories projects appear in my *Community Performance: An Introduction* (2007). And for a recent study of The Olimpias performance as research methods and community performance work, see Kuppers (2011).

Works Cited

Anderson, Benedict (1991) *Imagined Communities: Reflections on the Origin and Spread of Nationalism*. London and New York: Verso.

Conquergood, Dwight. "Poetics, Play, Process and Power: The Performative Turn in Anthropology." *Text and Performance Quarterly*, 9 (1989): 82–88.

——. "Rethinking Ethnography: Towards a Critical Cultural Poetics." *Communication Monographs*, 58.2 (1991): 179–94.

de Certeau, Michel (1988) *The Practice of Everyday Life*. Berkeley, Los Angeles, London: University of California Press, 1988.

Kuppers, Petra (2001) "A New Landscapes: Community Art, Video Process and Fantasies of Disability." *Afterimage, The Journal of Media Arts and Cultural Criticism*, 29:3, Nov/Dec. 2001, 24–25.

——. (2007) *Community Performance: An Introduction*. London and New York: Routledge.

——. (2011) *Disability Culture and Community Performance: Find a Strange and Twisted Shape*. New York: Palgrave Macmillan.

Kwon, Miwon (2002) *One Place After Another: Site-Specific Art and Locational Identity*. Cambridge, London: The MIT Press.

Nancy, Jean-Luc (1991) *The Inoperative Community*. Trans. P. Connor, L. Garbus, M. Holland and S. Sawhney. Minneapolis: University of Minnesota Press.

Roach, Joseph (1996) *Cities of the Dead. Circumatlantic Performance*. New York: Columbia University Press.

Young, Iris Marion (1990) "The Ideal of Community and the Politics of Difference," in L. J. Nicholson (ed.), *Feminism/Postmodernism*. New York and London: Routledge.

15 "Paradise Now": Notes

Judith Malina and Julian Beck

The Living Theatre in New York City is the oldest experimental theatre group in the USA; when they founded it in 1947, actress Judith Malina and painter/poet Julian Beck were very influenced by Antonin Artaud's seminal anthology *The Theatre and its Double*. In the 1950s The Living Theatre became a major influence in the development of "off-Broadway" theatre; in 1959 it premiered Jack Gelber's drama of jazz music and drug addiction, *The Connection*. The Living Theatre has always worked, and played, with the "fourth wall" between actors and audience, and over the years it has built a unique reputation for being collective, experimental, anti-commercial, even confrontational; during the 1960s, its openness to nudity and transgressive language and concepts resulted in its members being arrested and imprisoned at various times in New York, Brazil, and throughout Europe. The sample of pre-rehearsal discussion for *Paradise Now,* a semi-improvisational performance inviting audience participation, is a kind of improvised performance in itself, introduced by Malina and Beck as other voices join to colour, diversify, and problematise the discussion topics. It is a celebration of artistic work as a collaborative process.

Key words: theatre; politics; jazz

The Living Theatre

During the course of the rehearsals for Paradise Now, *Judith and I and many other members of the company kept notebooks recording more or less what was said and tracing the development of the ideas of and for the play. The notebooks then served as a gathering place for these ideas, a storeroom which we visited repeatedly and from which we drew supplies in constructing the play. The following seven entries record the first two pre-rehearsal discussions between Judith and me, and the first five general discussions, what we call the first five rehearsals, with the entire company. The first five of about 100. Discussions such as these have become an integral part of our working method, and were the source material out of which* Mysteries, Frankenstein, Paradise Now, *and the* mise-en-scène *for* Antigone *were created.*

JULIAN BECK

TLT	The Living Theatre		SBI	Steven Ben Israel
JB	Julian Beck		JH	Jenny Hecht
JM	Judith Malina		ST	Steve Thompson
NH	Nona Howard		RH	Roy Harris
HH	Henry Howard		CB	Cal Barber
RC	Rufus Collins		GG	Gene Gordon
CE	Carl Einhorn		LT	Luke Theodore
WS	William Shari		JA	Jim Anderson
FH	Frank Hoogeboom		DS	Dorothy Shari
E	Echnaton		JT	Jim Tiroff
RB	Rod Beere		DVT	Diana Van Tosh

January 27, 1968: Arth-am-See, Switzerland

JM: To find a form: short scenes? developmental theme?

JB: What do we have to say—i.e., what do we know—that gives us the right to make this play?

I think the form could be anything. It could be the form of *Frankenstein*. Developmental but the subject stays on top of the narrative and the final effect is cumulative.

Glimpses of the post-revolutionary world. Does that include glimpses of how to get there?

JM: It would seem very unimportant to me if it didn't contain some suggestions of how to get there. For me it can't be political enough.

JB: It has to. Because Paradise Now is How To Get There.

Paradisial Events apart from the transitionary period. What is the object of the striving? Depiction of the state of being we imagine as desirable.

JM: We can't map out how to get there because we don't have the map. But we have to make a map. This is the paradox.

JB: Simplest answer: we don't have the map but we have some clues, hints, foretastes, intimations.

The Scientific Method:
> Induction
> Deduction
> The proclamation of principles

JM: Or like the prophet, he plunges into it and dances it out.

> The Philosophical Approach; no map but clues.
> The Rational: empirical.

The way of the prophetic artist who plunges into the abyss to fetch it out. This sounds very alluring. This is where it could all go. But I think this would be a mistake.

JB: The Form.
> The Acting Form as The Form.
> The Acting Form as The Mise-en-Scéne.
> State-of-Being Acting as opposed to Enactment Acting.

Games with Rules.

JM: I would like to see the whole thing as one big game with rules.
JB: Maybe. A free theatre form. Chance?
JM: Something between chance and free theatre. I think of a free theatre piece with
       chance type rules. But rules chosen for their appropriateness and not at random.
       The rules should have something paradisial about them, as the rules in *The Brig*
       have something hellish about them. Rules as the Principles. The discovery of the
       principle of gravity teaches you how to fly (to the degree that flying defies the rules
       of gravity). You can defy the law by understanding the principle. What the actors
       are doing shall always be paradisial. That is, it would always be a pleasure to do.
       They point out that everything in *Frankenstein* is horrible to do.

January 28, 1968: Vicinity of Lugarno

JB: Practical time. When to rehearse: what and how many hours? How to divide the
       time then: discussion, physical work, exercise, staging.
       What we know. Investigations of what we do not know.
       How to divide the time most usefully, the disposition of the company.
       The predilection for false leads into the Mysteries, the mysterious.
       What are we searching for? To get the apples to the city.
       Anything else? What else?
       How much time is there to ask questions?
JM: The method of TLT is to find something, an idea, so true that when you do it
       with your body, it gets expressed.
       The study of the uses of exercise: Grotowski, Joe Chaikin.
       Superficial exercises as deceptive, clouding the vision.
       Can one waste time in earnest endeavor?
       To sharpen the points of the tools.
       To spend time making tools that will function to a purpose.

JB: Is reality only what's edible? Is Paradise only the edible?
JM: Yes, because I equate the word edible with consumable. [...]

January 31, 1968: Rome

Rehearsal No. 1
NH: Is not a play but a state of being
       comes out of a state of being
       this will result in freedom
       freedom is honesty
       the means and ends are the same
       the means and ends are honesty
       will result in new forms of human behavior unknown to the present eye
       a new—a fully realized—self can realize a new world
       anything else is merely politicking
       in this being lies a source of being on the earth
       none of the "à bas l'état" can happen without the change in the individual

each person on this trip will discover things about himself
to have a play *about* something is some form of masturbation
looking down the wrong end of the tunnel
my burning desire to see people burning to achieve this
there is no need to talk about discipline when everyone is burning
I would like to see this form of behavior given form
there is a difference between the path to pleasure and the one leading to joy
if beauty is truth what is beautiful
it is a state of being and not a play about a play
every moment is a play
the level is your choice
I think it is time to do it

SBI: Step No. 1, to create ritual that redeems the earth, done with a perfection that makes man aware that there is a divine process on earth that he can dance with.
That man is fulfilled by this combination of work and magic that then becomes something else.
The train of thought that can create conditions that bring about Paradise now.
The places we have been are the labyrinths, the caves out of which our thought must bring us.
A thinking that brings about deep clarity so that the individual can work with himself.

GG: I see people now that Greece has taken on a fascist regime.
I see people as I walk through Italy, Switzerland, Germany.
I see them raise their hands in a fascist salute:
I see the rise of fascism again.
I find it difficult to work on a play about Paradise Now without working on the real problems of fascism—money war wages.
Paradise Now means a complete change in the world.
If we don't see what's happening in every country, even in the USSR …

HH: May I interrupt … *Mysteries* and *Antigone* treat this. We are planning a play that transcends it, to create a play that will change, pop the bag, the outlook.

GG: We have to be sure of what we do if we want to change the world and live for centuries: why do we still smoke cigarettes?

WS: I want the right to feed myself poison.

SBI: At this point in the theatre, we have to give the alternative. To give people the things they can do to transcend, to exist.

NH: Means to be able to include everything, not to exclude.

GG: The people in Germany were kept away from what was happening.

JH: To do a play called Paradise Now
in a world which is doing a play called Hell
is a revolutionary act.
To find an anarchy (of a sort) in our community
An example for loving the world
That may be the next exemplary step in getting the world to change

GG: We have to include the whole swamp. We didn't fulfill *Frankenstein*.

JH: What do we mean by After Completion
By Before Completion as an ending

	By we don't know what comes next, but we are going after it?
GG:	To change the world we have to get rid of money and governments but to get there we have to listen in the streets and to the sound of our own voices shouting in anger at the waiter and the garage mechanic. It takes an understanding and if we don't get that understanding we are in grave difficulty.
JM:	But I think it very important to realize that we are not there and that we find out how to get there. The moral issues: "I didn't teach my son to live a longer and less happy life."
HH:	What is the behavior in Paradise? This is the question. The theatre is a laboratory. *Man Is Man—Brig—Mysteries—Frankenstein* ... The next play is called *Paradise*. What puts us there, how do we get there? Those scenes are going down, and this is what we can do about it—The theatre is unsatisfactory.
JH:	I think this behavior must be a happening between people.
HH:	Someone is grooving and someone shatters him. We do that all the time.
LT:	Paradise forms come out of suppressed areas—jazz out of a suppressed people—they took instruments, they found a way in which imitation was unnecessary and they learned to play, and then the jazz musicians came together.
JB:	If what you say is true about jazz then the problem is how to use that method to get the apples to the city.
JH:	To establish a state of being 24 hours per day.
HH:	The theatre is a place of magic and the unknown. This is the highest unknown.
JM:	*The Connection* intellectually examined the meaning of jazz in the modern world as the redemptive element and everyone on and off stage was in the swamp.
HH:	Now jazz musicians are playing everything they know and everything they have. Everybody has to blow himself so totally that he goes all the way every night. Past the images in all the National Geographics and the art books.
JM:	To make a personal effort to do everything good for your body between now and then.
JH:	What can you do with your body to help the other bodies?
GG:	The capitalist system has found a number of things to give to the people to keep them working and gold flow running.
Michele:	Jenny is speaking of people helping each other to find tranquillity. That an artistic presence permeate his daily existence.
GG:	Each word that comes out of our mouths glorifies us, but does it?
HH:	We have to develop the technique for creating *Paradise Now*.
RC:	I thought that when we were going to create *Paradise Now* we were going to create a miracle that will create an implosion.
FH:	I would like the experiment: a play that is a place of no judgement.
RC:	Reiteration of miracle.
SBI:	A trip to create organics.
HH:	Grotowski: to remove the resistances, and resistances about himself, themselves. Cieslak: his mind, body, so clear that he can go ... [...]

February 1, 1968: Filmstudio, Rome

RH: That the physical work and the performance be therapeutic for the actor and the spectator.

Changing colors: without lights. The actors changing colors. Perhaps we can do our own light show without lights. Change the temperature of the playing area, whatever way the human being can affect his environment—singing, dancing, chanting—building structures with our bodies: our architecture for the age of Paradise. A geometry onstage, using the body in a different way of new sounds: 35 people moving new. This can change every performance.

GG: The natural realities that are hidden by our society, hidden by those who use the suppression to exploit and maneuver.

RC: There is a current trip which is bringing people backwards. People are going back to Tibet. These people are finding their Paradise Now.

JB: There is here a concern with metaphysical powers and their expression. Paradise Now as a Miracle Play.

SBI: A good word for miracle is work.

JH: What we are looking for is not
something which has never been
but something which has always been

RH: Wind: to create forces:
wind throughout the audience
high pressure lungs here
high pressure lungs there

SBI: Transformation of energies, ideas, concepts.
Processes: instinctive in nature.
After transformation to transmutation.
Two types of forces: each of which has its positive and negative elements.
Techniques for transformation and transmutation.

RC: The whole thing, the whole hippie thing is a search for—

JB: A concern with primitive and mystic rituals.

SBI: To make good more interesting than evil.

CB: Are we doing this play for people who are sitting in their seats or does the audience have the possibility of participation?

SBI: The recurring process: take it and put it on the stage and call it *Paradise Now*.

ST: Paradise Now would create an open atmosphere and clean air so that the audience can rise up and fill the space in the theatre, the temple.

CB: There must be the possibility of liberation in the space.

SBI: What do we want the audience to do?

RC: To drop out.

JB: To change. To start the Revolution.

SBI: I don't know what I want the audience to do. Stop the war ... but how?

LT: Yes. He *said* this but he didn't and couldn't see.

CE: To stop the war is one of the questions.

ST: Yes, if you're so smart, how do you do it?

HH: Where do we begin? We have to presuppose that the war is stopped. Not how to stop the war or feed the people in India. Getting back to the source—it's been known for ages (Check the Book of the Golden Flower). The inability to experience each other. This is a point we must clarify now: is this play about stop-the-war or something else?

Revolutions come and give the same bad answers.

CE: We have to be ready to answer the questions of the public. In the rigid structure of the theatre—rigid seats, tickets, money, time—what are the alternatives?

JH: Our experiencing it on the stage is the statement.

CE: Not to shy away from the word political. Sitting on a mountain is political.

GG: This Paradise Now has to be free. The people in Italy are not free. But neither do we show them everything of ourselves. I'm not playing a game, I'm giving my life. I'm ashamed that we have to live in an economic system.

JB: Yes, ashamed of my world.

JH: Showing them something so nice that they want it.

JB & JM: To inspire the audience. A celebration. But the inspiration, the state of glory cannot let go of the earth of fire air water and flesh.

What is sight without eyes.

What happens to the body and the mind when it turns the wheel which is making the bread.

To do something for them, we have to know what we're doing, to make everyone artists as daring as the artist. Artificers/creators.

GG: We must give and take.

JB: The work is to make everyone artists, into their rightful state as creative beings.

Creative eating working sleeping being.

As we, not only in our work but in our lives.

LT: To change the audience. I have experienced this with our audiences.

HH: When jazz musicians play today, they play until it happens. 1–2–3 hours until we make it.

CB: How do we want to affect the Audience? How do we initiate the Audience? What is the center of the play? What is the behavior in Paradise?

JM: To find a point at which stopping the war, zapping out, getting apples to the city, mystical relations, all these must be the combined life process.

The new paradisial life is how do I diaper the baby and how do I fly, and bring them out of their shattered condition into true existence.

HH: What is the behavior after the revolution? That's what we have to show.

CE: What is the relation of Paradise to Death?

JH: A peace play (David McReynolds: Declaration of Peace).

RC: A play that is never outmoded. The play doesn't age.

CE: What do the people do?

RC: The audience must change because the play makes them take the trip. The forms differ from city to city.

JH: We have to stop thinking of the audience as Argives, as people beneath us to be taught. They are with us, are us.

CB: If this play is the vehicle, we have to find out what the behavior of the vehicle is.

ST: Maybe we can't take them. Maybe we can only go ourselves.

RC: But we can assume that we can't go without oneness, not until we are together.

HH: I want the audience to see a new HH onstage. Tuning into another's trip is a knack, an experience.

GFM: I find it very difficult to talk about something without experiencing it. How can I drink boiling water? I am interested in that.

JH: The physical-mystical trips that can be done.
      These people are not living in Paradise.
      These people in the east and south and north.
      These things for us are only symbols of their trip.
      I don't see any connection between their tricks,
      the hocus pocus of other cultures,
      we have only the souvenirs of their cultures.
      We feel an affinity with the souvenirs, that's all.

HH: In 1968, images are hocus pocus. But states of being, of nature, are interesting. I can be this Tantric cross (pendant) or this ... or you can be that white screen: that's a point at which we begin theatre.

PC: Levels of freedom.

JB: Strobe lights and long stretches of silence are an attempt to change the concept of time.

HH: But it also changes perception and perhaps helps us to see the same blue. But I don't know how important that is.

JM: What's important is the form of communication. As with language, we can store and eternalize knowledge. Now we need another form of post-lingual communication.

JB: I think we have to think about the efficacy of our Paradise Now. We have to judge the Paradise that we create.

RC: Unification is Paradise.

JB: What is Paradise? (CE's question) Is it the mystical experience or is it making a shoe?

CE: The moment is always passing. Our visions of Paradise are only fleeting. You don't lose the vision but it isn't always available.

ST: I think it's always available.

CE: We're talking about changing the availability, maintaining the experience.

JH: Digging the scenery.

HH: As an exercise: I have the Tantric piece ... How we failed in *Frankenstein,* so that we succeed in this.
      Frankenstein lacks two continuities: it is the perfect example of space theatre, the changing from level to level. The pieces don't glide into each other. The lack of common purpose. *Frankenstein* is about the human mind.

ST: Norbert Wiener taught us that the human mind is a machine, and it must be studied to learn how it works. I am now doing an exercise seeing and hearing everything that is happening here, and everything begins to fade from a dream condition into a real condition. [...]

16 Chicanas' Experience in Collective Theatre

Ideology and Form

Yvonne Yarbro-Bejarano

Even as, with *The Improvisation Studies Reader: Spontaneous Acts,* we celebrate collective action, we must admit the difficulties and complexities of collectivity. As Yvonne Yarbro-Bejarano describes, Chicana theatrical artists face resistance not only from the hegemonic theatrical culture from which they are consistently marginalised, but even from within the culture they attempt to nurture and to celebrate. Dr Yarbro-Bejarano was the inaugural Director of the Chicana and Chicano Studies Program in Stanford's Center for Comparative Studies in Race and Ethnicity. For several decades now, she has been involved with the critique of dominant hetero-normative discourses in Chicana/o Studies, as well as the analysis of cultural representations of Chicana/o queer sexualities, subjectivities, bodies, and desires. Since 1994 she has been developing the digital archive *Chicana Art,* a database of images and information, featuring women artists, for research and teaching. Dr Yarbro-Bejarano is the author of the books *Feminism and the Honor Plays of Lope de Vega* (1994) and *The Wounded Heart: Writing on Cherríe Moraga* (2001). She was a crucial part of the organisation of the international conference Feminicide = Sanctioned Murder: Gender, Race and Violence in Global Context in May 2007, which examined the extreme gender violence that has assumed epidemic proportions in such countries as Mexico, Guatemala, El Salvador, and Argentina.

Key words: race; ethnicity; theatre; gender

[...]

I

Any discussion of working in collective versus commercial theatre must take into account certain economic and social factors specific to Chicanas. Because of their class, race and culture, Chicanas have historically been shut out of commercial theatre. The tracking prevalent in the educational system effectively discourages Chicanos in general from going into theatre. The percentage of Chicanas with sound professional training in acting, directing or playwriting is abysmally low and reflects the general economic exploitation and racial discrimination that characterises the experience of Chicanos as a group. The fact that now and then a particularly determined individual may 'make it' through the system does not alter the systematic exclusion of Chicanos as a whole from mainstream theatre.

Chicanos as a social group have been excluded not only from theatre, but from all middle-class forms of literary production. The reasons for this are historical, social and economic. Since 1848, the history of Chicanos in this country has been one of economic oppression and social inequality. The vast majority of Chicanos in the United States belong to the working class, and the absence of upward mobility together with linguistic discrimination have resulted in severely limited access to literacy and education. As a result, Chicano literary expression has been largely popular in form, and oral in transmission.

One of the projects of the Chicano movement in the late '60s and early '70s was to validate popular and oral forms of cultural expression, and to counter the lack of access to the mainstream literary establishment with the creation of a Chicano communications network. This network included community newspapers featuring local, grass-roots poets writing in Spanish or bilingually, as well as Chicano literary magazines and publishing houses. Dozens of Chicano theatre groups sprang up, inspired by the example of the Teatro Campesino.

This group, founded by Luis Valdez in 1965, was extremely important in providing a specifically Chicano alternative to mainstream theatre. Initially made up of and directed at farmworkers, the Teatro Campesino contributed to the struggle headed by César Chávez to form a farmworkers' union. It is difficult to overestimate the significance of this group's exuberant validation of bilingual Chicano speech and cultivation of a rough, funky and funny, extremely dynamic style, drawing on popular Chicano and Mexican culture.

The majority of Chicanas in theatre became involved during this period, working with collective theatre groups that saw both their function and structure as part of a political struggle. All of the women I talked to spoke of their experience in collectives in very positive terms. Many cited as a major plus of collective work the opportunity to develop themselves in different areas, including acting, writing, directing, administration and workshops. Although in practice, the experience may vary because of the definition and organisation of the particular collective, many remain committed to the idea of direct and equal participation as a member of a unified and supportive group in the creation and development of characters, scripts and mise-en-scènes, as well as the work's political statement and the general policies of the group.

In opposition to the hierarchical division of labour characteristic of commercial theatre, the collective gives Chicanas and Latinas the chance to share responsibility for decisions, to have input into the entire process, to spearhead projects and assume leadership positions. The collective lifestyle in itself is seen as part of a political process, providing the opportunity to work out in the daily practice of human relationships the ideology underlying the plays. Some women spoke of the importance of participating in progressive or liberal activities and organisations, and practising collectivism in workshops, classes and performances at festivals. As opposed to the individualism of commercial theatre, the subordination to decisions coming down from on high, the concentration on money and the star mentality, the collective provides a supportive structure for the personal needs of the individuals as well as a forum to air criticisms. These women also appreciated the goal of catering to a specific audience in the attempt to create a truly Chicano theatre, one that would address the problems and general reality of a specific community.

The commitment to the dreams and aspirations of Chicano theatre, in which not only the plays but also the group organisation attempted to oppose the dominant ideology of a capitalist, sexist and racist society, has helped women endure the economic sacrifices and heavy demands of extended collective work.

II

From 40 to 50 groups at its height, the number of Chicano theatre groups has dwindled to a mere handful. Of the surviving collectives, the San Francisco Mime Troupe and the Teatro de la Esperanza offer viable options for Chicanas and Latinas, though of course they are not without problems and contradictions. Besides incorporating a child care policy in their structure, Esperanza struggles to reconcile women's issues with a progressive analysis of the social and economic problems of the Chicano community.

The San Francisco Mime Troupe, which has a long history of political theatre work, is currently engaged in the struggle to maintain a progressive orientation in their plays given the varying levels of political consciousness of the different members of the company. The pressure of creating new shows for the free theatre in the parks during the summer, and the indoor performances and touring during the year has led to the unfortunate situation in which the play is often still being written while the actors are in rehearsal, seriously reducing the opportunity to research and discuss the politics of the piece as a collective. It is embarrassing for some that not all members of the group can field questions about the political issue dramatised by the play. The lack of ideological cohesiveness in the group has led to what some see as a softening of the politics in their work. The theme of factory shutdowns in their recent work, *Steeltown,* suggests a continuing commitment to exploring pressing political problems.

The San Francisco Mime Troupe is, nevertheless, one of the few multi-racial and multi-ethnic collectives, and has been so since the early '70s. An Asian-American has recently joined the black, Chicano and white members of the group as musician and actor. Wilma Bonet is the only Latina in the Mime Troupe, hired to replace the Chicana actress, María Acosta Colón, who decided to develop her skills in administrative work within the group.

As the only Latina, Bonet has the sense of representing her community in the group. She serves as a moderator for all Latin roles, making sure they are not stereotypes. With the Chicanos in the group, she has been instrumental in bringing about open discussions of racism within the collective, including problems in the area of casting and relationships between white and non-white members. These discussions have greatly helped in dealing with racism in the company, a problem confronted by the group as one of extreme importance since the 'Minstrel Show'. Although Bonet feels personal and economic pressures, she stays with the group because of the rewards of having equal input into the creative process, and augments her income with commercials, ads and any other work she can find in which she can use her acting skills. She is pleased with the roles she has played, including a character in their play, *Last Tango in Huahuatenango,* based on Nora Astorga, and her most recent work in *Steeltown,* in which she plays the wife of a laid-off steelworker who drinks and abuses her. The character is passive at the beginning, but undergoes a change within the play. Although she felt she had to prove herself first, Bonet has been successful in her struggle to play non-Latina roles, such as her hilarious robot in *Fact-Wino vs. the Moral Majority,* and her portrayal of Laurencia in *Fuenteovejuna.*

Some Chicanas and Latinas have formed collectives made up exclusively of women. Teatro Raíces, in San Diego, does popular political theatre in the *acto,* or Chicano agit-prop, tradition. Valentina Productions, composed of women in San José, performed a polished collage of poetry, dance, music and pantomime called *Voz de mujer* at the 11th Chicano/ Latino Theatre Festival in San Francisco in September 1981. Valentina's goal was to provide a support group for women in theatre and to explore women's issues through theatre.

Although the response to the show was very positive, the group disbanded shortly after the festival, succumbing to the major problems that beset all collectives – extreme shortage of time and money. Most of the members worked full time, many had children, and the demands became too great. An additional problem, which hastened their demise, was the lack of ideological cohesion within the group. Members were brought together around the idea of doing women's theatre, but they all had different perspectives on women's issues. Since they were at different levels, *Voz de la mujer* sought the lowest common denominator, treating 'safe' themes, for example the exaltation of motherhood and the analysis of male–female relationships, with an emphasis on solidarity with men and the desire not to offend or alienate them. Some women wanted to present more controversial issues, but the group as a whole was not ready.

Olivia Chumacero, of the Teatro Campesino, has been exploring other options. The Teatro Campesino has concentrated on a cultural nationalist analysis of the Chicano experience, blending *indigenismo* and religious elements in their post-political phase. Founder Luis Valdez' turn toward commercial theatre in *Zoot Suit* and the establishment of a new theatre in San Juan Bautista, has been accompanied by an emphasis on cultural identity at the expense of a materialist analysis of the concrete conditions that create the oppression and exploitation of Chicanos as a largely working-class group. The work of Luis Valdez with the Teatro Campesino can generally be characterised as male-oriented. The central characters are always men, while the women revolve around them on secondary levels. In the *actos*, their peripheral status is propagated through stereotyped gender roles. They are the mothers, sisters, girlfriends or wives of the main male characters. The *mitos* of their religious phase added the Virgin of Guadalupe to the roster of stereotyped role models. This tendency to relegate women to secondary levels of importance is seen clearly in *Zoot Suit*. Besides the usual polarisation of portraying Chicanas as either whores or virgins, the play establishes an opposition between Della, Henry's *pachuca* girlfriend, and Alice, a Jewish woman who played a crucial role in the defence committee. The politically unsophisticated Chicana stands in contrast to the progressive white woman, but in the long run, Alice fares no better than Della. Alice's politics – based on the radical commitment of a real person – could have helped in giving the play the ideological clarity it lacks; instead her politics are played for laughs. As the play progresses it becomes evident that the main function of the two women is to provide the male character with the romantic dilemma of whom to choose. This depiction of women is accompanied by the text's subtle message that the white lawyer is the saviour of the Chicano youths, an insinuation captured in the paternalistic scene in which the lawyer, raised a good few feet above the youths by the blocking, convinces them to have faith in the American system of justice.

Could the portrayal of women in the work of the group heavily dominated by Luis Valdez or in the work of Valdez himself have something to do with his declared assimilationist goals? According to Valdez, he is not doing 'Chicano' theatre, but rather 'New American' theatre, and he envisions the '80s as a new period of integration for minorities, who would nonetheless maintain a sense of cultural pride and dignity (*Mother Jones*, June 1979). More recently he declared that 'We're working on our reality and commitment as Americans. ... It took us a while to call ourselves Americans' (*San Francisco Examiner*, 9 August 1981). Is this 'New American' theatre just another way of talking about commercial theatre, as opposed to 'Chicano' theatre, which has long been understood to be part of a larger political struggle? *The Rose of the Rancho,* to cite but one example among the shows which have been produced since *Zoot Suit* at the new theatre in San

Juan Bautista, was performed July and August of 1981 at $7.50 top ticket to a predominantly Anglo, middle-class audience. The treatment of women in the play – the domineering mother, the submissive, childlike servant, the incredibly foolish and unappealingly flirtatious title character – is completely consistent with the assimilationist revision of the Mexican-American war that the play presents. Valdez' most recent commercial venture, *Corridos,* has come in for heavy criticism from women who object to the choice of ballads that depict women as victims of rape and murder. The section celebrating the role of women in the Mexican revolution concentrated on their duty to 'follow their men' and make them their coffee and tortillas. Once again, the notion of the white saviour appears: the character of John Reed is the only male who is depicted as having some sensitivity for the women's predicament.

The Teatro Campesino produced their last collective work, the *Carpa de los Rascuachi,* in '75–'76, although *Fin del Mundo,* which toured in 1980, was also somewhat collectively elaborated. The recent development toward commercial theatre has reduced the opportunities for some of the women members of the company, who have turned to other venues. Chumacera has been working on her own, depending on grants to develop community theatre workshops. She has maintained a social and political focus, and is currently involved with theatre workshops with battered women and youth involved with drugs.

Sylvia Wood, formerly of Teatro Liberted of Tucson, Arizona, is working part time at Pima Community College, writing and staging one original script a year. Although she is happy to be concentrating on her writing, she feels isolated, and misses the experience of working collectively. Working part time to develop her writing has not relieved the economic pressures of doing theatre.

After working with Valentina, Cara Hill de Castañón participated in *Tongues of Fire.* Although *Tongues of Fire* was not produced by a collective, it represents the range of experimental options for Chicanas and Latinas outside commercial theatre. The *teatropoesia* piece was created and performed as part of a conference on Chicanas in 1981 at Mills College in Oakland, with grant money available to bring together writer, director and actresses. *Tongues of Fire* broke ground in Chicano theatre for its depiction of Chicanas and its ideological analysis of their specific problems. The play centred on the Chicana writer, analysed in terms of sex, class, race and culture. Based on the collection of writings by radical women of colour *This Bridge Called My Back, Tongues of Fire* explored the personal and collective history of Chicanas, contradicting gender stereotyping through irony and humour.

De Castañón also recently worked with the Teatro de la Esperanza. The progressive orientation of the Teatro de la Esperanza throughout the 12 or 13 years they have been in existence has functioned as a kind of cement which holds the group together and allows for continuity in spite of turnover in personnel. Having a common ideological base enables the members of Esperanza to feel responsible for the political as well as the artistic dimensions of their work, and they screen for politics in auditioning for the collective. Besides offering consistent analyses of the relationship between the discrimination and exploitation of Chicanos in this country and the larger structures of imperialism and corporate capitalism, they have broken ground in the creation of female characters in Chicano theatre and in the area of gender stereotyping in general. It is not uncommon for women to play male or androgynous roles in Chicano theatre, as in the Teatro Campesino Socorro Valdez' portrayal of Death, the Devil, a lowrider, etc., or Ana Olivares' General Rata in *The Octopus.* But in their last two works, Esperanza has men playing female roles, for example, the spunky older woman character in their musical show, *La muerte viene cantado.*

The group experimented with a collective protagonist in their first play, *Guadalupe*. In their next three plays, *La víctima, Hijos* and *The Octopus,* a limited male protagonist is countered by a strong female character who functions as a catalyst transforming the consciousness of the male characters or bringing their contradictions to a point of maximum tension.

Although de Castañón values collective work in Chicano theatre, she pointed out the scarcity of available groups and her own geographical limitations. Since having a baby, she is forced to look for work exclusively in San José. Like Olivia Chumacero, she has partially resolved the problem by working on her own, performing and touring a one-woman show based on the life and writings of Sor Juana Inés la Cruz. She has also auditioned for the upcoming season in San Jose's repertory company.

III

It is within a context of crisis, then, that we must place the experience of Chicanas and Latinas – a crisis that is linked to the waning of the Chicano movement and the economic recession, accompanied by a swing to the right politically in the US. The few collectives that still exist face a daily struggle for survival, paying extremely low wages and becoming increasingly dependent on grants and touring. The rewards of doing popular political theatre have been drastically reduced by the lack of connectedness to a broad-based political or social movement and the failure to develop a working-class Chicano audience in their base communities, due largely to the necessity to tour in order to survive. While the rewards have dwindled, the demands have increased.

Many women have expressed a sense of frustration and exhaustion. Although people continue to validate the opportunity to participate in all aspects of theatre work, the shared responsibility of many different tasks demands enormous quantities of time and energy. Collectives such as the Teatro de la Esperanza are understaffed and overcommitted, simultaneously producing shows, touring, organising, attending festivals and building networks with the popular political theatre in Latin America. Members of collectives can hardly subsist on the extremely low wages paid by collectives, when wages are paid at all.

The collective structure often makes the decision process maddeningly slow. Equally slow is the artistic process of collective creation, which, in some cases, leads to artistic stagnation and makes the beginning of every tour extremely hectic as the group struggles to finish the show before they hit the road. Acutely aware of technical deficiencies, especially in the area of playwrighting, many have taken leaves to study and improve their skills. The necessity of regular touring has been very draining as well as a strain on personal relationships, and people at times find it difficult to balance the pros of a collective lifestyle and the need for privacy.

While these problems are common to both men and women working in collectives, there are others that are specific to women. In some mixed collectives, Chicanas and Latinas have struggled against contradictions between the supposed progressive orientation of the group and the perpetuation of social and cultural attitudes about gender roles. A sexist double standard exists within many groups, affecting everything from behaviour on tours to the existence of the 'double day' for women, who must bear the additional responsibilities of home and family. While calling themselves a collective, in some cases the real power has been exercised by one man, severely limiting the input of Chicanas into the decision-making process. Many women have dropped out of theatre work altogether because of the frustration of not having their insights and personal experience taken into real consideration. Many were critical of the kinds of roles they were asked to play, yet were unable to influence the development of female characters when they voiced their opinion that the group was seriously lacking in their theatrical representation of Chicanas.

For many social and cultural reasons, it has been harder for Chicanas and Latinas who have children – especially single mothers – to work in collectives. Women with children face pressure from spouses and lovers to stop doing theatre and attend to 'motherly duties', while most collectives do not provide for child care or see it as a political problem. Women have had to struggle, not always successfully, to make their collectives recognise the special problems of women with children, who restrict their time and energy and make it difficult for them to tour. Now the San Francisco Mime Troupe provides extra financial support for people with children, although because of their overall economic situation the extra $20 only amounts to a symbolic recognition of the problem. The difficulties of women with children become most acute when touring; the options are to leave the children behind or take them along, both of which are problematic. Sylvia Wood, formerly of Teatro Libertad, attempted to partially solve the problem by writing her children into the scripts, so at least they would learn something since they had to be at rehearsals anyway. The Teatro de la Esperanza is unique in incorporating child care into its policy. Anyone who joins the group, whether they have children or not, is required to do his or her share of child care.

Many women have become disillusioned with male dominance in mixed collectives and their unwillingness to develop strong female roles or address women's needs. Others have become dissatisfied with what they feel was an excessively rigid concept of collectivity, submitting everything to consensus while actually concentrating power in male hands and stifling the individual development of other members. In her research on women in theatre, Yolanda Broyles has found that in situations where men dominate as power holders, Chicanas and Latinas are not stagnating. They either struggle to influence the collective by staying in it or branch out to explore other options. Some women point out that in the past, they have been severely limited by youth, inexperience and lack of ideological and theoretical sophistication, factors that contributed to the predominance of male leadership. Some feel that by striking out on their own, they will gain strength and experience that will place them in a better position to increase women's voices in collectives.

IV

If Chicanas decide they are tired of working in a collective, what alternatives do they really have? Chicanas and Latinas are usually only hired for 'ethnic' parts, usually terrible stereotypes, reinforcing the image of the Latina as sex bomb, or relegating her to typecast roles such as maid or mother. In much commercial theatre, being brown is bad, and lighter-skinned Chicanas and Latinas will be chosen for parts over darker ones, except when the role calls for Indian features. Wood remarked that in casting for the few productions employing Chicanas or Latinas, Latinas are often chosen over Chicanas, because they tend to have more training. Even in commercial productions of Chicano theatre, such as Luis Valdez' *Corridos*, Chicanas and Latinas with collective experience auditioning for roles felt they were passed over because they were not the right 'type'.

Diane Rodríguez, veteran of the Teatro Campesino, has had experience both in regional and 'downtown' commercial theatre. She has been in three shows at the Old Globe Theatre and was recently in a commercial production in San Francisco, *Women Behind Bars*, by Tom Eyen (of *Dream Girls* fame). On the whole, Rodríguez has found this experience positive. She spoke of being stretched in her exposure to other directors and actors, which has enabled her to identify the areas she needs to work on as an actress and has encouraged her to take more risks with her art. She is making good money and enjoys working with a cast of mature women. At the same time, there are negative aspects to her experience in non-collective theatre. She must struggle with the added pressure of reviews and the producer's power – the producers can remove you from the show if they don't like your work. Rodríguez finds herself confronted by dilemmas expressed by many Latina and Chicana actresses: enjoying the luxury of confining her participation to performing her part and picking up her cheque, yet missing input into the creative process; wanting to express herself politically and socially in her theatre work, yet playing stereotypes of Latin women; wanting her own career, yet still being committed to the collective process.

Rose Cano is a Peruvian actress who has lived in Seattle since she was a child. She is a recent graduate of the Cornish Institute's Professional Training Programme. So far, commercial theatre has been a viable option for her. She recently performed a one-woman show in the Broadcloth series of The Women's Theatre in cooperation with the Women's Programmes of Seattle Central Community College, and plans to tour the show. Severely limited in the market by her colour, Cano is aware that directors will not cast Latinas for non-Latin roles, and is fighting against the perception that she 'can't do' Noel Coward and other theatre classics. There is no Chicano or Latino theatre in Seattle – although there is an Asian-American theatre company, and The Group, the resident company at the Ethnic Cultural Theatre of the University of Washington, is multiracial, and tries to do colour blind casting for plays that have some social and political content.

Still, Cano feels that if she wants good roles, she will have to write them herself. Her training at Cornish included playwrighting, and her one-woman show, *Self-Portrait*, is her latest attempt to fight the obstacles for Latinas in commercial theatre. In *Self Portrait*, Cano was inspired by her family to explore her self and her cultural roots. She creates five female characters who have most influenced her life: Angelita, the mentally challenged 11-year-old sister; Carmen, her older Americanised sister; Mrs Johnson, the Mexican-American cleaning woman; her mother, the rock of the family, and her 88-year-old grandmother. Each character speaks to Dolores, the character representing Cano, and at the end, she is pulled between the 'demands of family and cultural values and the need to establish her own life and separate self'.

It is interesting to see how Cano resolved the problem of dramatising a bilingual experience for a monolingual audience. The play is bilingual; some 30% of the text is Spanish. The grandmother speaks only Spanish, but Cano treats her character in a highly gestural fashion. The others mix Spanish and English, but anything important in Spanish is also said in English. The linguistic aspect of the work includes the recreation of Mrs Johnson's speech, which is neither English nor Spanish, but a creative hybrid of both. Cano is motivated by the desire to share her ethnic background with Seattle audiences, who are largely unfamiliar with other cultures. In her treatment of her Americanised older sister, Cano criticizes Latinas who accept the media's image of 'woman', which involves a rejection of who they really are. In the character of Mrs Johnson, the cleaning woman, Cano juxtaposes Peruvian and Mexican cultures, and although she shows their differences, she is aware of the common problems of being non-white in a white society and of maintaining a Latin cultural identity within the dominant culture.

V

Collective theatre certainly does not have a corner on formal experimentation. But the groups discussed display a spectrum of forms that respond to the goals of Chicano and/or popular political theatre through the miming of working-class culture. The San Francisco Mime Troupe has a long tradition of using popular forms, including the minstrel show, western, melodrama, spy thriller and recently the comic book in the Fact Person/Wino series. *Tongues of Fire* uses the *teatropoesía* form, which has some history in the Chicano theatre movement. But instead of presenting a collage of relatively unrelated poetic texts in a stage setting, Barbara Brinson-Pineda, who scripted the show, created a structure with five sections, grouping the poems around particular themes. The unifying thread that ties the sections together is the character of the Chicana writer.

The Teatro Campesino is responsible for the creation of forms and images that have influenced a whole theatre movement. Drawn loosely after the agit-prop model, the *acto* combined satire, bawdy humour and stock characters with a broad playing style characterised by its funky dynamism and expressive use of gesture and body movement. In their religious phase, the company created the *mito*, such as *Fin del mundo*, which served as a vehicle for the expression of universal truths of Catholicism and indigenous philosophies. At the same time, the group experimented with *corridos*, which entailed the simultaneous singing and dramatisation of the popular ballads of Mexican and Chicano oral tradition. The Teatro Campesino has created a whole repertory of characters that have given Chicano theatre a specific visual imagery all its own; the *calaveras*, or skeletons, based on Jose Guadalupe Posada's lithographs, represented an attempt to express certain indigenous attitudes toward life and death, but this ideological content is not necessarily tied to the form. Its link with Mexican popular art of a satirical nature makes it a perfect springboard for rapid character changes. Other characters are equally expressive of Chicano urban lifestyles, for example, the *pachuco*, or its contemporary equivalent, the *cholo*. Another form developed by the Teatro Campesino, which I call the historical procession, tracing the history of Chicanos back to pre-Colombian times, through the Conquest, Independence and Revolutionary Mexico to the United States, initiated a tradition within the Chicano movement as well, influencing the Mexican group Mascarones, now Teatro Zero, which participated in the Chicano theatre movement. Valentina also used the historical procession form to give shape to their selection of poetic texts, dance and mime.

After an initial phase of developing *actos,* the Teatro de la Esperanza created the docudrama form that they used in their first three plays. This form combines drama and documentation, framing the action with quotes and statistics, scene titles and musical commentaries in the attempt to demystify certain aspects of theatre. This form reflects their adaptation of Brechtian principles within a Chicano cultural context, and also reveals similarities with the Joker system developed by Brasilian post-Brechtian Augusto Boal, who has also worked closely with the Chicano theatre movement. Not content to rest on their laurels, the company abandoned the docudrama form in their fourth play, *The Octopus,* to experiment with political allegory enclosed by a cabaret/circus frame. For their latest two efforts, Esperanza works within a Chicano theatre tradition, using the same form and characters as the Teatro Campesino, but with political content and more sensitivity to women's issues. Their musical show, *La muerte viene contado,* uses the *corridos* form, but the choice of texts avoids the pitfalls of the Valdez production. Esperanza selected a *corrido* that tells the story of a woman who shoots a captain who has raped her and killed her brother. Other sections celebrated the role of women in the Nicaraguan revolution and dramatised Domitila's famous speech at the Women's Conference in Mexico City.

Esperanza's latest show, *Lotería,* works with another form of Mexican popular culture, the lottery, which is played like bingo but with figures instead of numbers: the sun, the little old lady, the drunk, the dandy, etc. The show's characters are built around the figures of the lotería, in the creative development of popular political theatre that works within a collective visual imagination. Esperanza has been working closely with the new theatre movement in Cuba and Latin America for several years now. The members remarked on the difference between the definition of collective that they have been trying to work with – where everything is done collectively, including writing and directing – and the kinds of collectives they have come in contact with in Latin America. The Cubans, for example, tend to delegate certain functions according to people's strengths. After collecting data *on* the chosen topic directly from their target community, one person will write the script, after the topic has been discussed and/or improvised by the collective. This text is then submitted to extensive collective improvisation and continually rescripted to accommodate audience reactions.

This ongoing interchange within a network of popular political theatre is bound to have an invigorating effect on the Chicano theatre movement. While this moment is a difficult one, I would agree with Yolanda Broyles that Chicanas and Latinas are not stagnating or dropping out. I have the impression that they continue to search for a theatrical practice that will reconcile individual and collective needs.

17 Spontaneous Combustion

Notes on Dance Improvisation from the Sixties to the Nineties

Sally Banes

In "Spontaneous Combustion," Sally Banes describes the attempts of dancers—in common, as we see throughout *The Improvisation Studies Reader: Spontaneous Acts,* with similar undertakings by filmmakers, actors, visual artists, and musicians—to rebirth their artform as "a place where anything could be imagined and tried out." While admitting that this concept had its own limitations, she relates how it nurtured many diverse offshoots inspired by "an explicitly stated politics of identity, in terms of gender, sexual preference, race, and ethnicity." In Chicago Banes founded the performance collectives MoMing and the Community Discount Players before moving, in 1976, to New York City, where she earned a PhD from New York University; her dissertation became the basis of her 1984 book, *Democracy's Body: Judson Dance Theater 1962–64.* In her dance works, Banes has deliberately blurred the borders between performance and everyday living. Her books include *Terpsichore in Sneakers: Post-Modern Dance* (1980), *Writing Dancing in the Age of Post-modernism* (1994), *Dancing Women: Female Bodies on Stage* (1998), *Subversive Expectations: Performance Art and Paratheater in New York 1976–85* (1998) and *Before, Between, and Beyond: Three Decades of Dance Writing* (2007). Banes is currently Marian Hannah Winter Professor of Theatre History and Dance Studies at the University of Wisconsin-Madison.

Key words: dance; interdisciplinarity; the body

Historically, improvisation in postmodern dance has served a variety of functions and signaled different meanings since the 1960s:

- spontaneity
- self-expression
- spiritual expression
- freedom
- accessibility
- choice
- community
- authenticity
- the natural
- presence
- resourcefulness
- risk

- political subversion
- a sense of the connectedness of playfulness, child's play, leisure, and sports.

Although improvisation can mean all of these things, different aspects/values/goals have emerged at disparate historical moments. And even when some of the same issues arise, they do so in a different key, given new historical circumstances. Dance improvisation in a culture of abundance in the 1960s had a different significance—both for doers and watchers—than dance improvisation did in a culture of scarcity in the early and mid-nineties.

The Sixties and Seventies

The sixties and seventies saw an emphasis in postmodern dance on freedom, abundance, and community; improvisation often served to embody these values, not only in dance, but in the other arts as well. These were political issues, although not always stated explicitly. In the 1960s, artists like Anna Halprin on the West Coast and Simone Forti on the East Coast were committed to improvisatory methods, what one might call either "indeterminate choreography" or "open choreography" (as opposed to determinate, "closed" choreography), "situation-response composition," or "in situ composition." Unlike chance procedures, which took the choice-making element out of the self, improvisation seemed to many during this period a way of engaging the deep, untapped creative resources of each person. Various improvisatory events were held, such as Concert #14 of the Judson Dance Theater in April 1964, which included seven dances created by individuals and one twenty-five-minute group piece. (Although critic Jill Johnston complained the evening "couldn't get ... off the ground," Yvonne Rainer's contribution to the event, *Some Thoughts on Improvisation,* included as a "soundtrack" a recording of Rainer reading an important theoretical essay she had recently written on the workings of the situation-response method.)[1] Also, groups devoted to open choreography emerged. An all-women's group, the Natural History of the American Dancer, organized in the early seventies by Barbara Dilley, has long since been forgotten. But there were two visible and memorable stimuli to dance improvisation during this period: the Contact Improvisation movement and the group Grand Union.

Contact Improvisation, a form that evolved out of explorations by Steve Paxton in the early seventies, began as a series of experiments for men in duets dancing together in ways that might avoid aggression and embrace tenderness.[2] But it soon became a gender-integrated form that allowed both men and women to investigate various means of moving in one-on-one or small group encounters: giving and taking weight, lifting, carrying, leading, following, wrestling, and partnering in myriad ways; finding movement templates in social dancing, sports, and martial arts, such as Aikido.[3] Since the 1970s, Contact Improvisation has become a worldwide practice. One finds communities of Contactors in the United States, Canada, Europe, Japan, Australia, and New Zealand. Probably the bulk of Contact Improvisation happens in nontheatrical settings, in "jams" where dancers and nondancers get together to work out. Contact Improvisation is thus not primarily a theatrical form but an ongoing practice. Occasionally, Contact Improvisers will show the work in a theatrical setting, but in a casual way in which the audience feels it is more or less observing the jamming behavior that would occur even without spectators. Besides its worldwide networks of practitioners meeting regularly to jam together, the movement spawned a journal, *Contact Quarterly,* that publishes articles on Contact experiences and related body therapies, as well as names and addresses of groups around the globe.

For Steve Paxton, Contact Improvisation both signified and helped create a set of interconnected values important to the artistic avant-garde in the sixties and seventies: playfulness, freedom, spontaneity, authenticity, and community. "I like it when bodies are free and when the emotional state is open and accepting and sensitive," Paxton has remarked. "When the psychology isn't hassled or political or tied in knots. I like it when people can do things that surprise themselves," Paxton continues. "Where it comes from is just human play, human exchange—and animal play. It's like horseplay or kitten play or child's play, as well." Comparing the mental state of the Contact Improviser with that of an alert, confident basketball player, he concludes, "I enjoy the sharings that have come out of it, with other dancers and with the people who have seen it. ... It seems a way of learning that I like a lot."[4]

As Contact Improvisation spread in the late seventies, it became associated with other countercultural or alternative culture trends, including gender issues of equality, of women's strength, and of men's sensitivity. In Contact Improvisation, men could lift men, women could lift women, and women could lift men. All-men's Contact groups in the United States and Britain, such as Mangrove and Men Working, created situations in which men could partner one another in gentle, nonmacho ways, harking back to the origins of the form. Women could find strength, and men could find support.[5]

Ramsay Burt stresses the surprising, spectacular elements of the form.[6] Yet for many improvisers of the eighties and nineties (some of whom were born in the sixties and had no firsthand knowledge of the origins of postmodern improvisation) Contact Improvisation gained a reputation as a perhaps too gentle, passive, even boring way of dancing. Instead of focusing on the occasional unexpected lift or handstand, younger artists saw only dancers tangled together, endlessly rolling around on the floor. Moreover, they felt that Contact did not function primarily for the viewer, but for the participant, and therefore it could not always deliver a satisfying theatrical product. For the younger generation, Contact became a negative foil against which to invent a new approach to situation-response composition.

Grand Union, an improvisatory group to which Paxton also belonged, was entirely a theatrical phenomenon. Lasting only from 1970 to 1976, the Grand Union grew out of experiments Rainer had initiated in her dance *Continuous Project—Altered Daily,* in which she gave the performers permission, as she put it, to improvise blocks of material. If Contact Improvisers saw situation-response composition as an ongoing process done outside the theater more often than inside, and only occasionally witnessed by spectators, Grand Union improvised solely for audiences. The group was so committed to open, in situ choreography as theatrical performance that once it was formed, its members (Paxton, Yvonne Rainer, David Gordon, Trisha Brown, Douglas Dunn, Barbara Dilley, Lincoln Scott, and Nancy Lewis) prided themselves on never meeting offstage to have rehearsals or practice sessions, but instead, coming into each performance "cold." Though there were occasional crashes, more often the Grand Union took off from that cold base like a collective rocket.

Still, the Grand Union was committed to process, in a way that was consonant both with other contemporary movements in the arts and with collectivist political movements of the early and mid-seventies. Part of its risk-taking was to lay both the process of improvisation and the process of group dynamics open at all times to public scrutiny in performance. The group explored movement interaction and social intercourse in various "keys" of reality: fictional, dramatic, metatheatrical, and everyday. Material might be learned, rehearsed, or performed in a finished state. Structures were invented, repeated, dropped, and remembered. And everything was commented upon, analyzed, mock-ritualized, and transformed in an ironic mode that made the group's antics resemble a surrealistic vaudeville. They danced, sang, played records, quoted movies, took care of one another, took star turns, argued, found partners, did solos, created images with objects and flamboyant costumes, and altogether created the feeling that the stage was a place where anything could be imagined and tried out.[7]

Trisha Brown's description of her earliest experience performing with the Grand Union conveys the group's style. Brown had never been part of Rainer's company, and she explains that as a Grand Union member she did not want to learn any material from *Continuous Project—Altered Daily,* because she believed in an "unpremeditated ... blank slate approach" to improvisation. Brown remembers:

> At Rutgers on November 6, 1970, my first performance with the Grand Union, I worked alone, unable and unwilling to participate in "known material." This self-imposed isolation caused extreme discomfort, there were so many of them throwing pillows in unison and so few of me looking awkward. Luckily, Steve stepped into my dilemma and asked, "Would you like to dance?" as he extended his arms in the traditional ballroom position of the male lead and we were off ... for about five years.[8]

She describes other key moments:

> Steve Paxton arriving with a burning candle installed on his hat symbolizes [the beginning stage of Grand Union] for me. That and the night we verbally reduced a foam-rubber mattress to a kitchen sponge. ... If you said "Drop a hat," everyone threw them in the air. Subversion was the norm. Everything was fair game except fair game. ... There were time lapses, empty moments, collusion with the audience, massive behavior displays, pop music, outlandish get-ups, eloquence, bone-bare confrontations, lack of concern, the women's dance, taking over, paying deference, exhilaration, poignancy, shooting one's wad, wadding up one's wad, making something out of nothing, melodramarooney, cheap shots, being oneself against all odds and dancing. Dancing and dancing and dancing.[9]

If Contact Improvisation, with its (not always exclusive) focus on the duo, stripped away everything but the bare bones of partnering, Grand Union maximized all sorts of group situations and dynamics, as well as metatheatrical commentary, to proliferate both texts and imagery in an open choreography of constant surprise.

Oddly enough, Contact Improvisation and the Grand Union—both in their different ways embodying an ethos of leisurely movement exploration, bodily richness, and collective or cooperative politics—flourished in the seventies, a time of economic recession and political quiescence (in terms of mass political movements). Perhaps this disjunction is not so strange as first appears, however. The initiators of these groups came to artistic maturity in the sixties, a time of political and artistic upheaval and economic abundance. While these forms of indeterminate choreography fiscally suited the seventies (in that they were inexpensive to produce), they remained rooted artistically and sociopolitically in the sixties. They carried forward into the seventies an oppositional sixties attitude toward bodily, imaginative, and political liberation.

The Eighties and Nineties

The eighties and nineties saw various changes in the postmodern dance world. For one thing, a new form of inter-art avant-garde collaboration flourished in the eighties, a unified *Gesamtkunstwerk* that—marketed now to attract larger audiences combining art, music, theater, and dance spectators and involving several artistic contributors from different artistic fields—could not always risk the uncertainties (both financial and artistic) that open choreography implies. Also, generational succession in an avant-garde always questing for the new meant that a fresh crop of choreographers and dancers emerged, a generation trained and inspired by the generation of the sixties and seventies, but in search of distinctive, dissimilar paths. By the nineties, a key area of difference between the two generations developed: the content of the dance tended toward an explicitly stated politics of identity, in terms of gender, sexual preference, race, and ethnicity.

The late eighties and nineties saw a reemergence of interest in improvisation, but diverging in both motivations and meanings from those of the earlier generation. If many dancers in the sixties saw situation-response composition as a way of accessing the "authentic" self, postmodern culture in the eighties and nineties declared that there is no singular, authentic self, but only a fragmented multiplicity of shifting identities. This stance was nicely exemplified in John Jasperse's improvisation (from a Hothouse event at P.S. 122 in New York, December 1993) in which his body was marked not as blurring boundaries between male and female, in the androgynous mode of the seventies, but rather, as simultaneously extremely masculine and extremely feminine. By the nineties, the debate about self and identity had become complicated. There is a contradiction between postmodernism/poststructuralism and identity politics in regard to the notion of subjectivity. While identity politics does not necessarily require essentialist notions of a group (either racial, ethnic, gendered, or sexual) still, it often reverts to essentialist rhetoric. And even the position that some have called "strategic essentialism" asserts that there is—if only contingently—a genuine "I" (whether gay, black, female, Latino, and so on), whereas postmodernism in the cultural/theoretical sphere denies it. So this debate about self, subjectivity, and affiliation has affected danced representations of identity, or questions thereof.

If dancers in the sixties saw open choreography as a way of expressing freedom and creating community, cultural critics in the eighties and nineties questioned the meaning of freedom and community—even the community that identity politics might promise. Several decades ago, improvisation was a leisurely means for exploration, participating in a culture of abundance. But the recession of the seventies seemed at the time only temporary; by the early nineties, the prospects of worldwide financial crises made abundance and leisure seem antique, nostalgic notions from the past.

Finally, while avant-garde dance improvisers in the sixties and seventies were predominantly white but influenced by an African American aesthetic (especially as practiced in the progressive jazz music of the period), in the eighties and nineties, many more people of color appeared in avant-garde venues. Groups such as Urban Bush Women brought African American improvisatory traditions directly into postmodern dance practice, sometimes using improvisation to create material and sometimes leaving room for open choreography in performance. Those traditions include an interweaving of music and dance and a view of the relationship of the individual to the collectivity as not only a political, but also a spiritual value. Jawole Willa Jo Zollar, artistic director of Urban Bush Women, declares that "improvisation is a spiritual philosophy as well as a movement tool. It includes the Marxist concept of collectivity, the African notion of cooperative tribal action, the Native American council."[10]

This is not to say that African American dance groups (for instance, that of Dianne McIntyre) were not using improvisation all along. But in the sixties and seventies, the

African American vanguard in dance took an entirely different direction from the predominantly white avant-garde, so that both venues and audiences for the two worlds separated. Postmodern dance was seen by many African American dancers as dry formalism, while African American dance was considered by some white postmodernists as too emotional and overexplicit politically. In the eighties, a wave of African American postmodern dancers emerged, while at the same time a heightened political sensibility—often focusing on identity politics—and a renewed taste for direct action led white postmoderns to prefer explicit content. For some, situation-response composition served as a metaphor for Realpolitik, in that it requires tactical thinking and acting in public, in response to issues of power and choice in the group. In contrast, closed or determinate choreography molds the world to a vision. Practical politicians have no such luxury.

Improvisation, of course, continues to be used in dance in a variety of ways, not only to generate material for performance that will later become permanent (this, of course, has been a compositional method used for untold ages), or as a shifting component of a set piece of choreography, but also as offstage daily practice or preparation. But in the early nineties, there was an efflorescence of improvisation as direct performance: not as preparation for the event, but as the material of the event itself. Festivals and series abounded, including Hothouse at P.S. 122, Bread to the Bone at the Knitting Factory (both in New York), the New York Improvisation Festival, and Engaging the Imagination in San Francisco.

If the improvisations of the sixties and seventies created the feeling that "we've got all the time in the world to play and explore," those of the nineties had a sense of urgency, a feeling of grabbing you by the lapels. Young dancers may turn to indeterminate choreography in each generation, but the nineties generation was one that felt frenetic—responding, as Jennifer Monson put it, to the violence and risky energy all around it, as well as to shorter attention spans. "Improvisation now is different from the seventies," she pointed out. "Contact Improvisation was slow and gentle; I needed to explode. There is a fierce physicality that may be an impact of the New York City environment [as opposed to Vermont, Steve Paxton's home for the past thirty years]. For me, improvisation has political overtones. What I do is related to the work of the Lesbian Avengers, a direct action group."[11]

The nineties generation inhabited a very different historical moment than did its predecessors. Freedom took on new meaning in a post-cold war world. And erotics have altered implications in a world with AIDS. Spontaneity, resourcefulness, attitudes toward time and bodies—all had added layers of significance in a world of urban homelessness and violence in the eighties and nineties.

Yet even in the nineties group, there were echoes of certain values of the previous generation. For Jasperse, seeing people think, make decisions, and act—all in real time— is part of the method's excitement, recalling Paxton's excitement about witnessing surprises. And Jasperse's sense of satisfaction that making improvisatory work increases the ephemeral nature of dance, leaving no product to purchase or to hang on a wall, harks back to the conceptual artists of the seventies. Still, his interest in finding "extreme physical states and unachievable scores," his use of heavy-metal music that assaults the ears, his cross-gendered images—all are pure nineties.[12]

I also see differences in approaches to improvisation on different coasts. In New York I see a search for extremes, for physical risks. This is a view of community that is different from the preceding generation: one not so much of harmony and health, but rather one that recognizes splits, differences, and pains, as well as pleasures. At the same time, the politics of New York improvisers seem less explicit, more a metaphoric function of onstage actions. In California, where Anna Halprin still teaches, there seems to be more of a holistic approach in several senses. Not only is open choreography connected to mind/body therapeutic modes, but dance improvisation also shares personnel and venues with theatrical improvisation and performance art. Generational relations, as well, are continuous, not oppositional. At the same time, however, perhaps because of the connection to theater and performance art, dancers such as Rachel Kaplan present more explicit, even confrontational political agendas in their work.

On another front, the enterprise growing out of Contact Improvisation known as DanceAbility, which joins able-bodied and disabled dancers in movement explorations based on a broad range of human movement, extends to its logical and radical implications the sixties' promise of democratic accessibility for *all* bodies in postmodern dance. It implies not just accessibility, but empowerment, because disabled dancers lead and teach able-bodied dancers, as well as vice versa. DanceAbility expands the egalitarian idea of the sixties in its attempt to create equality of *condition,* not just of opportunity. That is, it reconfigures the dance so everyone can be a dancer. The ordinary movements valorized by postmodern choreographers in the sixties were still the ordinary movements of able-bodied dancers. In the sixties, even in the avant-garde and even in the counterculture, to be all-inclusive was still (albeit unwittingly for many) to exclude those whose marginal status—whether due to color, race, ethnicity, or physical ability—made them invisible to the majority. Disability is the final frontier for dance, where DanceAbility has extended the egalitarian franchise. In this sense, DanceAbility becomes an important expression of identity politics.[13]

Conclusion

Although the younger generation of improvisers often positions itself as contesting the practices of an older generation, some familiar aspects of improvisation reemerged in the early nineties: a yearning to take chances, a delight in surprise, a desire to collectivize creation. Yet history never repeats itself exactly. What came in between the effervescence of the sixties and the riskiness of the nineties was the Reaganite eighties, a decade of bodily and political *control.* In dance, this fascination with control often took the form of physical virtuosity that flaunted a highly regimented body. In the nineties, although a fitness craze still obsessed our culture, there was a reaction formation in the avant-garde to fetishizing discipline. While younger improvisers looked for physical extremes (which can still be a virtuoso gesture), they also wanted—and needed—to let go, to let the body and the imagination overflow all boundaries.

This desire to let go was sharpened by a feeling of carpe diem, an urge to seize the moment and to live to one's utmost in the present. Especially in the age of AIDS, to overflow one's bodily boundaries can symbolize danger. But it can also stand for a refusal to cut off human contact, even in the face of danger. It can serve to criticize the sexual and other forms of bodily repression that have trailed the AIDS pandemic. And, in a larger sense, it attacks an increasingly puritanical view of the body by mainstream culture. Thus the nineties strain of improvisation combined two seemingly contradictory facets: open-endedness and urgency. Perhaps what fueled the nineties taste for improvisation (not only in dance, but also in comedy and theater) was a millennial sensibility that various ends were close at hand.

Notes

1 Jill Johnston. "Judson 1964: End of an Era: I," *Village Voice,* January 21. 1965, 12; reprinted in *Ballet Review* 1, no. 6 (1967): 8; Rainer's essay was published in her *Work, 1961–73* (Halifax, Nova Scotia: The Press of the Nova Scotia College of Art and Design: New York: New York University Press, 1974), 298–301.

2 See Sally Banes. *Terpsichore in Sneakers: Post-Modern Dance* (Middletown, Conn.: Wesleyan University Press. 1987; 1st ed. Boston: Houghton Mifflin, 1980), 64–65.

3 See Cynthia Novack, *Sharing the Dance: Contact Improvisation and American Culture* (Madison: University of Wisconsin Press, 1990) for an in-depth study of Contact Improvisation and its cultural meanings.

4 "Beyond the Mainstream," directed by Merrill Brockway, *Dance in America,* PBS, WNET, New York, 1980.

5 Issues of gender in Contact Improvisation have been discussed by both Novack and Ramsay Burt, *The Male Dancer: Bodies, Spectacle, Sexualities* (London: Routledge, 1995).

6 Ramsay Burt. *The Male Dancer: Bodies, Spectacle, Sexualities* (London: Routledge, 1995), 154–55.

7 For an in-depth study of the Grand Union, see Margaret Hupp Ramsay, *The Grand Union (1970–1976): An Improvisational Performance Group* (New York: Peter Lang, 1991).

8 "The Grand Union, Q & A," in Banes, *Terpsichore,* 225.

9 Ibid.

10 Quoted in Sally Banes, "Dancing in Leaner Times," *Dance Ink* 2, no. 3 (Winter 1991–92), repr. in Sally Banes, *Writing Dancing in the Age of Postmodernism* (Hanover, N.H.: Wesleyan University Press, 1994), 343.

11 Telephone interview with Jennifer Monson, June 5, 1994.

12 Interview with John Jasperse, New York City, May 28, 1994.

13 On DanceAbility and the identity politics of the disabled dancing body, see Ann Cooper Albright, *Choreographing Difference: The Body and Identity in Contemporary Dance* (Hanover, N.H.: Wesleyan University Press and the University Press of New England, 1997).

18 Luminous Axis – Blade-form Panel (Graphic Score)

Wadada Leo Smith

The vibrant promise of this "blade-form" panel, with its vivid colours and provocative angles and swirls, from a composition on the 2002 CD *Luminous Axis*, illustrates the philosophy that Wadada Leo Smith stated as early as 1973 in his book *Notes (8 Pieces) Source a New World Music: Creative Music*: "The method and symbols used by the improviser in retaining an improvisation have never been (and must never be) standardized." Smith's 2013 Pulitzer Prize nomination testified to the power of a body of work that the trumpeter/composer has been building since the 1960s, centred around his systemic music language, "Ankhrasmation." He has taught at the University of New Haven, the Creative Music Studio in Woodstock, NY, and Bard College, and since 1993, at the California Institute of the Arts, where he is currently the director of the African-American Improvisational Music programme at The Herb Alpert School of Music. A longtime member of the AACM, he is well-known for his collaborations with Anthony Braxton, Peter Kowald, Henry Kaiser, John Zorn, and others. Wadada Leo Smith's compositions have been performed by ensembles all over the world, and he has recorded almost 40 albums of his own work. *Notes (8 Pieces)* has been translated into Japanese and Italian.

Key words: graphic scores; AACM; creative music

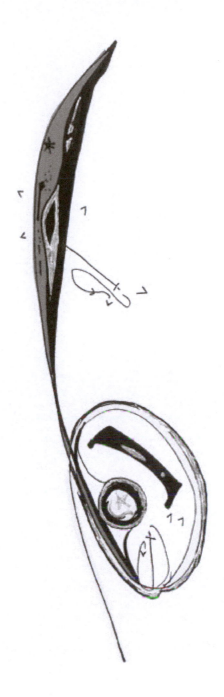

Figure 18.1 Blade-form Panel

Part 3
Flow

19 Improvised Flow: Opening Statements

Susan Leigh Foster

Early in her university studies, Susan Leigh Foster was informed by a senior academic that dance is a non-cognitive activity that has no place in the university curriculum. Years later, Foster concluded PhD studies at UC Santa Cruz with her dissertation, *Reading Dancing: Gestures Towards a Semiotics of Dance*, and at UC Riverside, developed and launched the USA's first PhD programme in dance history and theory. Her exceptional essay, "Taken by Surprise" (which appears in this volume along with her new piece on "Flow"), is itself a transcribed improvisation, based on a keynote address which, in keeping with the topic, Susan Leigh Foster deliberately improvised. It touches on subjects germane to any improviser who, in their art, "tacks back and forth between the known and the unknown, between the familiar/reliable and the unanticipated/unpredictable." Throughout her career she has dissolved the barriers between explorations of critical theory and the constructions, improvisations, and excitement of live performance. Foster has been presenting concerts of original work since 1977. She is the author of *Reading Dancing: Bodies and Subjects in Contemporary American Dance* (1986), *Choreography and Narrative: Ballet's Staging of Story and Desire* (1996), *Dances that Describe Themselves: the Improvised Choreography of Richard Bull* (2002), and *Choreographing Empathy: Kinesthesia in Performance* (2011). She is also the editor of the anthologies *Choreographing History* (1995) and *Corporealities* (1996) and co-editor of the journal *Discourses in Dance*.

Key words: dance; theatre; the body; spoken improvisation

Can I attain a state, arrive at a place, summon the energy, create the conditions such that this introduction flows out of me? so that my thoughts transform into phrases that can be typed, preferably without typos, into the document? so that the whole argument that I am making coheres without my anticipating in advance the direction it will take? so that the essay writes itself at the same time that I am writing it? I want it to happen like Tom Johnson's *Running out of Breath* (1976), where the dancer-runner recites the score for the piece perfectly coordinated to end at the moment she can no longer talk because she has quite literally run out of breath. Alas, it's probably not going to happen like that, but at least I've made a running start.

This section of *The Improvisation Studies Reader: Spontaneous Acts*, focusing on "flow," offers a wonderfully diverse array of essays, considering flow within the arts of acting, dancing, and composing music, as well as more generally across a large spectrum of activities such as prose writing, rock climbing, and chess playing. These essays also consider flow from very different perspectives. Mihaly Csikszentmihalyi examines flow as psychological state of mind, whereas Tricia Rose identifies it as an aesthetic principle that informs the practices of graffiti, breakdancing, and rapping. Rob Wallace looks for evidence of flow in the production of literary works both as an effect of the writing process and the stylistic structuring of the text. Michael Chekhov offers a primer for how to work towards achieving flow as an actor. Flow is thus an experience that can be located within the creation and production of an event, or it can be attributed to the experience of the witness of that event.

One idea about flow that arises from within this collection of essays is the fact of flow's elusiveness. Flow is not, as Csikszentmihalyi observes, accessible in "everyday life" (see his essay in this volume). An exceptional experience that involves a state of immersion within one's actions, it is distinct from the dispersed and fragmented mentality of quotidian existence. One can train to experience flow, as Chekhov proposes, by rigorously building up the skills that make flow more probable. One can also arrange for the conditions within which flow is most often experienced, such as the limiting of one's field of attention so that the mind is more likely to stay focused. However, as either participant in or observer of an event, flow is something one happens upon.

A second idea about flow that emerges across the essays is that it consists in moving spontaneously and continuously from one action or event to the next. For example, Guy Debord presents an overview of the dérive, a practice developed by the Situationists, calling upon participants to scramble and ramble for lengthy periods of time, exploring neighbourhoods and regions of city or countryside. Debord connects these spontaneous strolls to the psychoanalytic encounter wherein the patient is encouraged to describe without censorship or the demands of coherence the contents of his or her thoughts. Jack Kerouac, in identifying the "essentials of spontaneous prose," calls upon the author to follow "free deviation (association) of mind into limitless blow-on-subject seas of thought … " (see his contribution to this volume). Csikszentmihalyi describes the autotelic experience of flow as a sense of being completely involved with the activity one is performing, where each action follows smoothly upon the previous action.

Rose complicates this idea of flow as continuous by examining flow as one of three generating principles that, along with rupture and layering, work synergistically to create the aesthetic foundation upon which graffiti, breakdancing, and rapping are constructed. Flow provides a sinuous continuity, which is then broken through various strategies of rupture, only to be re-incorporated into the flow in order to produce a layering of materials. For Rose flow and rupture together recreate the social conditions in which inner city black youth were living when breakdancing and graffiti were forged as tools to assist in managing the affects of social dislocation. She describes breakdancing as creating sustaining narratives that can be accumulated, layered, embellished, and transformed. "However, be prepared for rupture, find pleasure in it, in fact, *plan on* social rupture" (see Rose, this volume).

While Rose looks at flow from the point of view of someone witnessing breakdancing, it is also possible to envision flow from within the performer's experience of the dance. From that perspective, the rupture and discontinuity in breakdancing might form part of the flow, as the dancing demands a continual absorption into itself of highly contrasting and diverse elements. Rupture becomes another in a series of choreographic options that can be selected as the dancer composes the dance in performance. Rupture might present itself seamlessly and without rupture, as it were, as the next obvious choice to make. In this sense flow stands for the possibility while composing that each next move, whether abrupt or continuous, could present itself without hesitation or interruption.

If flow can be associated with the sequence of choices someone is making while composing in performance, it can also define the actions of a performer who is executing material that has already been composed. Dancing in Merce Cunningham's work suggests that possibility. Cunningham's choreography often builds upon a set of decisions concerning how to move that were made using aleatoric procedures. The performer then learns these actions movement by movement and repeats the same sequences faithfully in each performance. In this context flow might be experienced as a feeling of immersion in the action, a loss of ego or self-consciousness, a oneness of purpose, and a sense of conviction about what is coming next. Chekhov's primer for how to achieve this kind of spontaneity and naturalness in acting sets forth a series of exercises that will assist the actor, not as a stand-up comedian who is formulating material in performance, but as a performer delivering lines from a play that has been written, directed, and rehearsed. His exercises help the actor learn to let each moment unfold from the previous one so as not to anticipate feelings, actions, or dialog. Flow can thus be experienced as one improvises the performance or as one executes material that is already sequenced and learned.

Anthony Braxton's notation symbols for various kinds and qualities of sound propose a third kind of experience of flow for a performer interacting with a pre-established score that also requires spontaneous decisions to be made. Not unlike a game of chess in which the overarching structure, as well as the rules of engagement, are pre-determined, artists in various media have often constructed scores that allow for improvised actions as part of their execution. Flow, in these performances, centres on the interactivity between the stipulated directions and the spontaneous solutions or responses to those directions that are enacted by the performers. Improvisers very often tack back and forth between previously established material and new discoveries. A breakdancer, for example, will incorporate familiar moves or reiterate or adapt moves made by someone else into new sequences. In such situations the parameters for how to shape the overall performance are more flexible or, in some cases, pre-determined but unstated. In contrast, the player responding to a score using symbols such as Braxton's knows with certainty the progression of events, just not the exact nature of the sounds he or she will produce.

All of these experiences of flow, while composing, performing, interacting with a score, are compounded and complicated when the event calls for multiple participants. In such situations, each individual is engaging with both pre-established rules and their own responses to those directives alongside the actions of others. Whether playing basketball or performing the score for a dance, participants must continually accommodate and incorporate the decisions made by others, recalibrating their own next movements to fit within the ever-changing milieu of the group. Here, flow can entail a sense that the group is like-minded and cohesive enough to collectively craft the performance. For the group of breakdancers, flow could be located in the abundance of circulating citations, the richness of the call and response, and the inventive ways that each dancer plays off the others. For the Cunningham dancer, flow occurs in that moment when one arrives to join another dancer in perfect unison. For the dancer responding to a Braxton-like score, flow is sensed in the congenial efforts of all members of the group to attune their responses one to another.

Is the experience of flow equivalent to "being in the zone"? being in a "groove"? Does it happen when it seems that the dance is making itself at the same time that I am making the dance? Why not all those things?

Work Cited

Johnson, T., 1976. *Running out of Breath*. Dance score.

20 A Theoretical Model for Enjoyment

Mihaly Csikszentmihalyi

Born of Hungarian parents in Fiume, Italy, in 1934, Mihaly Csikszentmihalyi left school at 16, but, bewildered by the behaviour he had witnessed during the Second World War, became interested in psychology. He emigrated to the United States at the age of 22, receiving his PhD in 1965 from the University of Chicago. Much of his career has been spent in the study of happiness and creativity and, as the reader may sample in "A Theoretical Model for Enjoyment," centres around the concept of "flow." Dr Csikszentmihalyi has described flow as deep involvement in an activity for its own sake with a lack of ego and no sense of time. In "A Theoretical Model," the author further describes flow as an autotelic experience—refuting more goal-oriented models in favour of an action done for its own sake. Since 1999 Mihaly Csikszentmihalyi has been a Distinguished Professor of Psychology and Management at Claremont Graduate University in California, where he established the Quality of Life Research Center. The best-known of his many books is *Flow: The Psychology of Optimal Experience* (1990).

Key words: flow; psychology; pedagogy

Interviews with participants in autotelic activities confirmed the questionnaire results. With near unanimity, respondents (even those who received extrinsic rewards for their activity: composers, chess champions, and surgeons) stated that they devoted time and effort to their activity because they gained a peculiar state of experience from it, an experience that is not accessible in "everyday life." In each case, intrinsic rewards appeared to overshadow extrinsic ones as the main incentives for pursuing the activity.

But what is this autotelic experience that motivates people to pattern their lives in ways so inimical to conventional wisdom? It is easier, at first, to say what the experience is not like. It is not boring, as life outside the activity often is. At the same time, it does not produce anxiety, which often intrudes itself on awareness in "normal" life. Poised between boredom and worry, the autotelic experience is one of complete involvement of the actor with his activity. The activity presents constant challenges. There is no time to get bored or to worry about what may or may not happen. A person in such a situation can make full use of whatever skills are required and receives clear feedback to his actions; hence, he belongs to a rational cause-and-effect system in which what he does has realistic and predictable consequences.

From here on, we shall refer to this peculiar dynamic state—the holistic sensation that people feel when they act with total involvement—as *flow*.[1] In the flow state, action follows upon action according to an internal logic that seems to need no conscious intervention by the actor. He experiences it as a unified flowing from one moment to the next, in which he is in control of his actions, and in which there is little distinction between self and environment, between stimulus and response, or between past, present, and future. Flow is what we have been calling "the autotelic experience." There are two reasons for our changing names in midcourse. The first is relatively trivial: flow is less awkward than the former label. The second is more substantive: in calling an experience "autotelic," we implicitly assume that it has no external goals or external rewards; such an assumption is not necessary for flow. Later we shall see that one of the main traits of flow experiences is that they usually are, to a lesser or greater extent, autotelic—that is, people seek flow primarily for itself, not for the incidental extrinsic rewards that may accrue from it. Yet one may experience flow in any activity, even in some activities that seem least designed to give enjoyment—on the battlefront, on a factory assembly line, or in a concentration camp.

Flow is most readily experienced, however, in certain kinds of activities. The pursuits we studied—climbing, chess, basketball—are *flow activities* that seem to provide the corresponding (flow) experience. Games are obvious flow activities, and play is the flow experience *par excellence*. Yet playing a game does not guarantee that one is experiencing flow, just as reciting the pledge of allegiance is no proof of patriotic feelings. Conversely, the flow experience can be found in activities other than games. One such activity is creativity in general, including art and science. The composers and dancers in our sample described their feelings in ways that did not differ substantially from the descriptions of climbers or chess players. Surgeons involved in medical research and mathematicians working on the frontiers of their field answered the interviews in terms that were almost interchangeable with those used by players. Almost any description of the creative experience (see, for example, Montmasson, 1932; Ghiselin, 1952; Dillon, 1972; Getzels and Csikszentmihalyi, 1975) includes experiential accounts that are in important respects analogous to those obtained from people at play.

Besides play and creativity, experiences analogous to flow have been reported in contexts usually called "transcendental" or "religious." Maslow's (1962, 1965, 1971) peak experiences and De Charms's (1968) "origin" state share many distinctive features with the flow process. The same is true of accounts of collective ritual (Deren, 1953; Worsley, 1968; Turner, 1969); of the practice of Zen, Yoga, and other forms of meditation (Herrigel, 1953, 1960; Eliade, 1969; Naranjo and Ornstein, 1971); or of practically any other form of religious experience (Laski, 1962; Rahner, 1967; Moltmann, 1972).

In a variety of human contexts, then, one finds a remarkably similar inner state, which is so enjoyable that people are sometimes willing to forsake a comfortable life for its sake. In many cases, the importance of this experience is blurred by what appear to be the external goals of the activity—the painting that the artist wants to create, the theory that the scientist strives to prove, or the grace of God that the mystic seeks to attain. On a closer look, these goals lose their substance and reveal themselves as mere tokens that justify the activity by giving it direction and determining rules of action. But the doing is the thing. We still have to hear of an artist who packed up his brushes after completing a painting, or even paid much attention to a canvas after it was finished; or of a scientist who felt rewarded enough by a discovery to cease his investigations. Achievement of a goal is important to mark one's performance but is not in itself satisfying. What keeps one going is the experience of acting outside the parameters of worry and boredom: the experience of flow.

Elements of Flow Experience

Perhaps the clearest sign of flow is the merging of action and awareness. A person in flow has no dualistic perspective: he is aware of his actions but not of the awareness itself. A tennis player pays undivided attention to the ball and the opponent, a chess master focuses on the strategy of the game, most states of religious ecstasy are reached through complex ritual steps; yet for flow to be maintained, one cannot reflect on the act of awareness itself. When awareness becomes split, so that one perceives the activity from "outside," flow is interrupted. Therefore, flow is difficult to maintain for any length of time without at least momentary interruptions. Typically, a person can maintain a merged awareness with his or her actions for only short periods, which are broken by interludes when he adopts an outside perspective. These interruptions occur when questions flash through the actor's mind: "Am I doing well?" "What am I doing here?" "Should I be doing this?" When one is in a flow episode (*in ludus* as opposed to *inter ludes*), these questions simply do not come to mind.

Steiner (1972, p. 94) gives an excellent account of how it feels to get out of the state of flow in chess, and then back into it again:

> The bright arcs of relation that weld the pieces into a phalanx, that make one's defense a poison-tipped porcupine shiver into vague filaments. The cords dissolve. The pawn in one's sweating hand withers to mere wood or plastic. A tunnel of inanity yawns, boring and bottomless. As from another world comes the appalling suggestion ... that this is, after all, "only a game." If one entertains that annihilating proposition even for an instant, one is done for. (It seemed to flash across Boris Spassky's drawn features for a fraction of a second before the sixty-ninth move of the thirteenth game.) Normally, the opponent makes his move and in that murderous moment addiction comes again. New lines of force light up in the clearing haze, the hunched intellect straightens up and takes in the sweep of the board, cacophony subsides, and the instruments mesh into unison.

For action to merge with awareness to such an extent, the activity must be feasible. Flow seems to occur only when tasks are within one's ability to perform. That is why one experiences flow most often in activities with clearly established rules for action, such as rituals, games, or participatory art forms like the dance.

Here are a few quotes from our interviews with people engaged in flow-producing activities. Their words illustrate what the merging of action and awareness means in different cases.

An outstanding chess player: "The game is a struggle, and the concentration is like breathing—you never think of it. The roof could fall in and, if it missed you, you would be unaware of it."

An expert rock climber: "You are so involved in what you are doing [that] you aren't thinking of yourself as separate from the immediate activity. ... You don't see yourself as separate from what you are doing."

A dancer describing how it feels when a performance is going well: "Your concentration is very complete. Your mind isn't wandering, you are not thinking of something else; you are totally involved in what you are doing. Your body feels good. You are not aware of any stiffness. Your body is awake all over. No area where you feel blocked or stiff. Your energy is flowing very smoothly. You feel relaxed, comfortable, and energetic."

A basketball player from a state-champion high school team: "The only thing that really goes through my mind is winning the game. I really don't have to think, though. When I am playing, it just comes to me. It's a good feeling. Everything is working out—working smooth." And one of his teammates: "When I get hot in a game ... like I said, you don't think about it at all. If you step back and think about why you are so hot, all of a sudden you get creamed."

In some activities, the concentration is sustained for incredible lengths of time. A woman world-champion marathon swimmer has this to say: "For example, I swam in a twenty-four-hour race last summer. You dive in at 3 P.M. on Saturday and you finish at 3 P.M. on Sunday, it's 49 degrees in the water, and you are not allowed to touch the boat or the shore. ... I just keep thinking about keeping my stroke efficient ... and, you know, thinking about the strategy of the race and picking up for a little while and then ease off, things like that. ... Every once in a while, just because of the long time, your mind wanders. Like I'll wake up and say, 'Oh, I haven't been thinking about it for a while!'"

This merging of action and awareness is made possible by a second characteristic of flow experiences: a centering of attention on a limited stimulus field. To ensure that people will concentrate on their actions, potentially intruding stimuli must be kept out of attention. Some writers have called this process a "narrowing of consciousness," a "giving up the past and the future" (Maslow, 1971, pp. 63–65). One respondent, a university professor in science who climbs rock, phrased it as follows: "When I start on a climb, it is as if my memory input has been cut off. All I can remember is the last thirty seconds, and all I can think ahead is the next five minutes."

This is what various chess experts say: "When the game is exciting, I don't seem to hear nothing—the world seems to be cut off from me and all there is to think about is my game." "I am less aware of myself and my problems ... at times, I see only the positions. I am aware of spectators only in the beginning, or if they annoy me." "If I am busting a much weaker player, I may just think about the events of the day. During a good game, I think over various alternatives to the game—nothing else." "Problems are suspended for the duration of the tournament except those that pertain to it. Other people and things seem to have less significance."

The same experience is reported by basketball players: "The court—that's all that matters. ... Sometimes on court I think of a problem, like fighting with my steady girl, and I think that's nothing compared to the game. You can think about a problem all day but as soon as you get in the game, the hell with it!" "Kids my age, they think a lot ... but when you are playing basketball, that's all there is on your mind—just basketball ... everything seems to follow right along."

A dancer describes this centering-of-attention experience in the following way: "I get a feeling that I don't get anywhere else ... I have more confidence in myself than at any other time. Maybe an effort to forget my problems. Dance is like therapy. If I am troubled about something, I leave it out the door as I go in [the dance studio]."

And a woman composer of modern music says virtually the same thing: "I am really quite oblivious to my surroundings after I really get going. I think that the phone could ring, and the doorbell could ring, or the house burn down, or something like that. ... When I start working, I really do shut out the world. Once I stop, I can let it back in again."

In games, rules define the relevant stimuli and exclude everything else as irrelevant. But rules alone are not always enough to get a person involved with the game. Hence, the structure of games provides motivational elements which will draw the player into play. Perhaps the simplest of these inducements is competition. The addition of a competitive element to a game usually ensures the undivided attention of a player who would not be motivated otherwise. When being "beaten" is one of the possible outcomes of an activity, the actor is pressured to attend to it more closely. Another inducement is the possibility of material gains. It is usually easier to sustain flow in simple games, such as poker, when gambling is added to the rules. But the payoff is rarely the goal of a gambler. As Dostoevsky (quoted in Freud, 1959) clearly observed about his own compulsion in a letter to A. M. Maikov (Aug. 16, 1867), "The main thing is the play itself, I swear that greed for money has nothing to do with it, although heaven knows I am sorely in need of money." Finally, certain play activities rely on physical danger to produce centering of attention, and hence flow. Such is rock climbing, where one is forced to ignore all distracting stimuli by the knowledge that survival is dependent on complete concentration.

The addition of spurious motivational elements to a flow activity (competition, gain, danger) makes it also more vulnerable to intrusions from "outside reality." Playing for money may increase concentration on the game, but paradoxically one can also be more easily distracted from play by the fear of losing. A Samurai swordsman concerned about winning will be beaten by an opponent who is not thus distracted. Ideally, flow is the result of pure involvement, without any consideration about results. In practice, however, most people need some inducement to participate in flow activities, at least at the beginning, before they learn to be sensitive to intrinsic rewards.

In occupations, as opposed to flow activities, extrinsic rewards are usually of the foremost importance. Most jobs would not be done unless people were paid for doing them. But occupations can be greatly enriched if the pattern of action they require provides flow experiences. The best example of such an occupation is surgery [...]. When a "job" has some of the characteristics of a flow activity, intrinsic motivation to perform it seems to become a powerful incentive added to that provided by extrinsic rewards.

A third characteristic of flow experiences has been variously described as "loss of ego," "self-forgetfulness," "loss of self-consciousness," and even "transcendence of individuality" and "fusion with the world" (Maslow, 1971, pp. 65, 70). When an activity involves the person completely with its demands for action, "self-ish" considerations become irrelevant. The self (Mead, 1934) or the ego (Freud, 1927) has traditionally been conceived of as an intrapsychic mechanism which mediates between the needs of the organism and the social demands placed upon it. A primary function of the self is to integrate one person's actions with that of others; hence, it is a prerequisite for social life (Berger and Luckmann, 1967). Activities which allow flow to occur (activities such as games, rituals, or art), however, usually do not require any negotiation. Since they are based on freely accepted rules, the player does not need to use a self to get along in the activity. As long as all the participants follow the same rules, there is no need to negotiate roles. The participants need no self to bargain with about what should or should not be done. As long as the rules are respected, a flow situation is a social system with no deviance (Csikszentmihalyi and Bennett, 1971).

Self-forgetfulness does *not* mean, however, that in flow a person loses touch with his own physical reality. In some flow activities, perhaps in most, one becomes more intensely aware of internal processes. This heightened awareness obviously occurs in Yoga and many religious rituals. Climbers report a great increase in kinesthetic sensations, a sudden increase in ordinarily unconscious muscular movements. Chess players are very aware of the working of their own minds during games. What is usually lost in flow is not the awareness of one's body or of one's functions, but only the self *construct,* the intermediary which one learns to interpose between stimulus and response.

Here are some quite different ways in which rock climbers describe this state:

> The task at hand is so demanding and rich in its complexity and pull that the conscious subject is really diminished in intensity. Corollary of that is that all the hangups that people have or that I have as an individual person are momentarily obliterated. ... It's one of the few ways I have found to ... live outside my head.
>
> One tends to get immersed in what is going on around him, in the rock, in the moves that are involved ... search for handholds ... proper position of body—so involved he might lose the consciousness of his own identity and melt into the rock.
>
> It's like when I was talking about things becoming "automatic" ... almost like an egoless thing in a way—somehow the right thing is done without ... thinking about it or doing anything at all. ... It just happens ... and yet you're more concentrated. It might be like meditation, like Zen is a concentration. One thing you are after is one-pointedness of mind, the ability to focus your mind to reach something.
>
> You become a robot—no, more like an animal. It's pleasant. There is a feeling of total involvement. ... You feel like a panther powering up the rock.

The same experience is reported by people involved in creative activities. An outstanding composer has this to say about how he feels when he is writing music: "You yourself are in an ecstatic state to such a point that you feel as though you almost don't exist. I've experienced this time and time again. My hand seems devoid of myself, and I have nothing to do with what is happening. I just sit there watching it in a state of awe and wonderment. And it just flows out by itself." And a chess player says: "Time passes a hundred times faster. In this sense, it resembles the dream state. A whole story can unfold in seconds, it seems. Your body is nonexistent—but actually your heart pumps like mad to supply the brain."

Still another characteristic of a person in flow is that he is in control of his actions and of the environment. He has no active awareness of control but is simply not worried by the possibility of lack of control. Later, in thinking back on the experience, he will usually conclude that, for the duration of the flow episode, his skills were adequate for meeting environmental demands; and this reflection might become an important component of a positive self-concept.

A dancer expresses well this paradoxical feeling of simultaneously being in control and being merged with the environment: "If I have enough space, I am in control. I feel I can radiate an energy into the atmosphere. It's not always necessary that another human being be there to catch that energy. I can dance for walls, I can dance for floors. ... I don't know if it's usually a control of the atmosphere. I become one with the atmosphere." Another dancer says: "A strong relaxation and calmness comes over me. I have no worries of failure. What a powerful and warm feeling it is! I want to expand, hug the world. I feel enormous power to effect something of grace and beauty."

In chess, basketball, and other competitive activities the feeling of control comes both from one's own performance and from the ability to outperform the opponent. Here are a few chess players: "I get a tyrannical sense of power. I feel immensely strong, as though I have the fate of another human in my grasp. I want to kill!" "I like getting lost in an external situation and forgetting about personal crap—I like being in control." "Although I am not aware of specific things, I have a general feeling of well-being, and that I am in complete control of my world."

In nonflow states, such a feeling of control is difficult to sustain for any length of time. There are too many imponderables. Personal relationships, career obstacles, health problems—not to mention death and taxes—are always to a certain extent beyond control.

Even when the sense of control comes from defeating another person, the player often sees it as a victory over his own limitations, rather than over the opponent. A basketball player says: "I feel in control. Sure. I've practiced and have a good feeling for the shots I can make. ... I don't feel in control of the other player—even if he's bad and I know where to beat him. It's me and not him that I'm working on." An ace handball player also stresses this notion of control over self: "Well, I have found myself at times when I have super concentration in a game whereby nothing else exists—nothing exists except the act of participating and swinging the ball. [The other player must] be there to play the game, but I'm not concerned with him. I'm not competing with him at that point. I'm attempting to place the ball in the perfect spot, and it has no bearing on winning or losing."

Flow experiences occur in activities where one can cope, at least theoretically, with all the demands for action. In a chess game, for instance, everything is potentially controllable. A player need not fear that the opponent's move will produce any threats except those allowed by the rules.

The feeling of control and the resulting absence of worry are present even in flow situations where "objectively" the dangers to the actor are quite real. The famous British rock climber Chris Bonington describes the experience very well: "At the start of any big climb I feel afraid, dread the discomfort and danger I shall have to undergo. It's like standing on the edge of a cold swimming pool trying to nerve yourself to take the plunge; yet once [you are] in, it's not nearly as bad as you have feared; *in fact, it's enjoyable. ... Once I start climbing, all my misgivings are forgotten.* The very harshness of the surroundings, the treacherous layer of verglas covering every hold, even the high-pitched whine of falling stones, all help build up the tension and excitement that are ingredients of mountaineering" (Quoted in Unsworth, 1969; italics added).

Although the dangers in rock climbing and similar activities are genuine, they are foreseeable and hence predictable and manageable; a person can work up to mastering them. Practically every climber says that driving a car is more dangerous than the incredible acrobatic feats on the rock, and in a sense it may be true: when one is driving a car, the elements outside his control are more numerous and dangerous than in climbing. In any case, a sense of control is definitely one of the most important components of the flow experience, whether or not an "objective" assessment justifies such feeling.

Another quality of the flow experience is that it usually contains coherent, non-contradictory demands for action and provides clear, unambiguous feedback to a person's actions. These components of flow, like the preceding ones, are made possible because one's awareness is limited to a restricted field of possibilities. In the artificially reduced reality of a flow episode, one clearly knows what is "good" and what is "bad." Goals and means are logically ordered. A person is not expected to do incompatible things, as he is in real life. He or she knows what the results of various possible actions will be. A climber describes it as follows: "I think it's one of the few sorts of activities in which you don't feel you have all sorts of different kinds of demands, often conflicting, upon you. ... You aren't really the master, but are moving with something else. That's part of where the really good feeling comes from. You are moving in harmony with something else, the piece of rock as well as the weather and scenery. You're part of it and thus lose some of the feeling of individual separation." In this description several elements of flow are combined: noncontradictory demands for the activity, the issue of control, and the feeling of egolessness.

But in flow, one does not stop to evaluate the feedback; action and reaction have become so well practiced as to be automatic. The person is too involved with the experience to reflect on it. Here is the clear account of a basketball player: "I play my best games almost by accident. I go out and play on the court and I can tell if I'm shooting O.K. or if I'm not—so I know if I'm playing good or like shit—but if I'm having a super game I can't tell until after the game. ... Guys make fun of me because I can lose track of the score and I'll ask Russell what the score is and he'll tell me and sometimes it breaks people up—they think 'That kid must be real dumb.'" In other words, the flow experience differs from awareness in everyday reality because it contains ordered rules which make action and the evaluation of action automatic and hence unproblematic. When contradictory actions are made possible (for instance, when cheating is introduced into a game), the self reappears to negotiate between the conflicting definitions of what needs to be done, and the flow is interrupted.

A final characteristic of the flow experience is its "autotelic" nature. In other words, it appears to need no goals or rewards external to itself. Practically every writer who has dealt with play (for instance, Huizinga [1939] 1950; Piaget, 1951, 1965; Callois, 1958) has remarked on the autotelic nature of this activity. In the *Bhagavad Gita,* Lord Krishna instructs Arjuna to live his whole life according to this principle: "Let the motive be in the deed and not in the event. Be not one whose motive for action is the hope of reward."

A young poet who is also a seasoned climber describes the autotelic experience in words that would be difficult to improve on. It is from this person's interview that we borrowed the word *flow* to describe the autotelic experience—a word which we noticed recurring spontaneously in other respondents' reports. "The mystique of rock climbing is climbing; you get to the top of a rock glad it's over but really wish it would go forever. The justification of climbing is climbing, like the justification of poetry is writing; you don't conquer anything except things in yourself. ... The act of writing justifies poetry. Climbing is the same: recognizing that you are a flow. The purpose of the flow is to keep on flowing, not looking for a peak or utopia but staying in the flow. It is not a moving up but a continuous flowing; you move up only to keep the flow going. There is no possible reason for climbing except the climbing itself; it is a self-communication."

A top woman chess player in the United States, although she receives a certain amount of fame and money, is still motivated primarily by the experience itself rather than by the extrinsic rewards: "The most rewarding thing is the competition, the satisfaction of pitting your mental prowess against someone else. ... I've won ... trophies and money ... but considering expenses of entry fees, chess associations, et cetera, I'm usually on the losing side financially."

A medical doctor who has participated in many expeditions to the highest mountains on earth reflects on the need for extrinsic rewards: "The world has to look for a star, the whole time. ... You don't look at the Milwaukee Bucks, you look at Jabbar, which is so wrong. It's so understandable, it's so childlike. It seems to me that an expedition should be totally beyond that. If I had my way, all expeditions would go secretly and come back secretly, and no one would ever know. Then that would have a sort of perfection about it, perhaps, or be more near to perfection."

A famous composer explains why he composes (after a long and hearty laugh at the "inanity of the question"): "One doesn't do it for money. One does it for, perhaps, the satisfaction it gives. I think the great composers, all the great artists, work for themselves, period. They don't give a damn for anybody else. They primarily satisfy themselves. ... If you get any fame out of it, it's when you are dead and buried, so what the hell's the good of it. ... This is what I tell my students. Don't expect to make money, don't expect fame or a pat on the back, don't expect a damn thing. Do it because you love it."

As the quoted statements show, the various elements of the flow experience are linked together and dependent on each other. By limiting the stimulus field, a flow activity allows people to concentrate their actions and ignore distractions. As a result, they feel in potential control of the environment. Because the flow activity has clear and non-contradictory rules, people who perform in it can temporarily forget their identity and its problems. The result of all these conditions is that one finds the process intrinsically rewarding.

Structure of Flow Activities

Some people can start a flow episode just by directing their awareness to conform with the requirements of flow, like limiting the stimulus field so as to allow the merging of action and awareness. But most people rely on external cues for getting into flow states, so we might speak of flow activities as those structured systems of action which usually help to produce flow experiences. Although one can enter flow while engaged in any activity, some situations (such as games, art, and rituals) appear to be designed almost exclusively to provide the experience of flow. It is therefore useful to begin a formal analysis that will answer the question: How do some activities make possible the experience of flow?

Despite vast differences among them, flow activities seem to share certain characteristics. More specifically, activities that reliably produce flow experiences are similar in that they provide opportunities for action which a person can act upon without being bored or worried. A more formal way of presenting this idea is illustrated in Figure 1. The model is based on the axiom that, at any given moment, people are aware of a finite number of opportunities which challenge them to act; at the same time, they are aware also of their skills—that is, of their capacity to cope with the demands imposed by the environment. When a person is bombarded with demands which he or she feels unable to meet, a state of anxiety ensues. When the demands for action are fewer, but still more than what the person feels capable of handling, the state of experience is one of

Figure 20.1 Model of the Flow State

worry. Flow is experienced when people perceive opportunities for action as being evenly matched by their capabilities. If, however, skills are greater than the opportunities for using them, boredom will follow. And finally, a person with great skills and few opportunities for applying them will pass from the state of boredom again into that of anxiety. It follows that a flow activity is one which provides optimal challenges in relation to the actor's skills.

From an empirical point of view, there are some clear limitations to the model. The problem is that a state of flow does not depend entirely on the objective nature of the challenges present or on the objective level of skills; in fact, whether one is in flow or not depends entirely on one's *perception* of what the challenges and skills are. With the same "objective" level of action opportunities, a person might feel anxious one moment, bored the next, and in a state of flow immediately afterward. In a given situation, therefore, it is impossible to predict with complete assurance whether a person will be bored or anxious or in a state of flow. Before the flow model can be empirically applied, then, we will have to identify those personality characteristics which make people underestimate or overestimate their own skills as well as the "objective" demands for action in the environment. In other words, we will have to acquire an understanding of the autotelic personality makeup, which we still lack. For a preliminary understanding of the flow experience, however, it is enough to consider the "objective" structure of the situation.

An example of one such situation is shown in Figure 2. In rock climbing, the challenge consists in the difficulties of the rock face—or pitch—which one is about to climb. Each climb, and each move in a climb, can be reliably rated in terms of the objective difficulties it presents. The generally adopted system of ratings ranges from F^1 (a scramble) to F^{11} (the limits of human potential). A climber's skills can also be rated on the same continuum, depending on the difficulty of the hardest climb he has completed. If the hardest climb a person ever did is rated F^6, skill level can also be expressed as F^6. In this case, we have fairly "objective" assessments of both coordinates. Figure 2 suggests some of the predictions

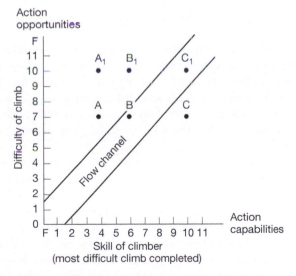

Figure 20.2 Example of Flow and Nonflow Situations in Rock Climbing

one might make about the experiential state of a climber if one knows the rating of both the rock and the climber.

It should be stressed again that the prediction will be accurate only if the individuals involved perceive the difficulties and their own capabilities "objectively." Although this is never completely the case, it is a useful assumption. For instance, as Figure 2 suggests, F^4 climbers on an F^7 pitch will tend to be worried; on an F^{10} pitch they will be anxious. Similarly, people with F^{10} skills will be bored climbing an F^7 pitch—unless they decide to raise its challenges by adopting some tacit rule such as using only one arm, doing the climb without protection, or focusing their attention on new action possibilities (for instance, teaching a novice how to climb).

Rock climbing is a good flow activity because no single individual can master all the F^{11} pitches in the world and because even the same climb can be rendered more challenging by weather conditions or self-imposed handicaps. Athletics in general have theoretically unreachable ceilings, although record-breaking performances are nearing the asymptote. Other flow activities—such as art, creativity, and religious ecstasy—also have infinite ceilings and thus allow an indefinite increase in the development of skills or in the ability to organize experience.

Another type of flow activity is the game of chess. The skill of chess players is objectively measured by the United States Chess Federation ratings which each person earns as a result of performing in tournaments and championships. Chess, unlike rock climbing, is a competitive activity. In a chess game, therefore, the challenges a person faces do not originate in some material obstacle, like the difficulty of a rock face, but mainly in the skill of the opponent. A player with a USCF rating of 2000 when matched against one rated 2150 will be confronted with action opportunities in excess of capabilities of the order of 7.5 percent. Whether such a discrepancy in the challenge/skill ratio is enough to make the weaker player worried and the stronger one bored is, of course, impossible to tell in advance. Since each individual undoubtedly has his own threshold for entering and leaving the state of flow, the bands that delimit the state of flow from those of boredom and worry, in Figures 1 and 2, are only illustrative. For certain activities and for certain persons the band might be much narrower or much wider. The diagrams show only the direction of relationships, not the precise limits. The transition points remain to be determined empirically.

People in a state of worry can return to flow through an almost infinite combination of two basic vector processes: decreasing challenges or increasing skills (see Figure 3). If they choose the latter, the resulting flow state will be more complex because it will involve more opportunities and a higher level of capabilities. Conversely, if one is bored one can return to flow either by finding a means to increase environmental challenges or by handicapping oneself and reducing the level of skills. The second choice is then less complex than the first.

It is to be stressed again that whether a person will experience flow at all and, if he does, whether it will be at a complex or at a simple level depends only in part on the objective conditions in the environment or the concrete structure of the activity. What counts even more is the person's ability to restructure the environment so that it will allow flow to occur. Artists, poets, religious visionaries, and scientists are among those who have learned to use cognitive techniques to order symbols so that they can "play" with them any time and anywhere, to a certain extent regardless of environmental conditions. Ideally, anyone could learn to carry inside himself the tools of enjoyment. But whether the structure is internal or external, the steps for experiencing flow are

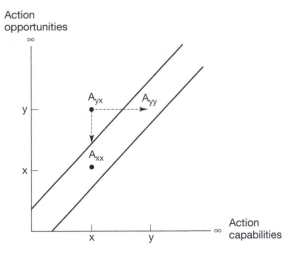

Figure 20.3 Two Ways of Experiencing Flow

presumably the same; they involve the same process of delimiting reality, controlling some aspect of it, and responding to the feedback with a concentration that excludes anything else as irrelevant.

Figure 3 also suggests the relationship between flow and what is ordinarily meant by "pleasure"; that is, the satisfaction of basic needs—hunger, sex, and so forth. In the present model, the experience of pleasure tends to be one of low complexity, since it does not require the use of complex skills. One can think of flow as a continuum, ranging from repetitive, almost automatic acts (like doodling or chewing gum) to complex activities which require the full use of a person's physical and intellectual potential. [...]

Notes

1 The term *flow* is what anthropologists call a native category—a word frequently used by the informants themselves to describe the experience.

Works Cited

Berger, P.L. and Luckmann, T. *The Social Construction of Reality*. Garden City, N.Y.: Doubleday, 1967.

Callois, R. *Les Jeux et les Hommes*. Paris: Gallimard, 1958.

Csiksentmihalyi, M. and Bennett, S. "An Exploratory Model of Play." *American Anthropologist*, 1971, 73 (1), 45–58.

De Charms, R. *Personal Causation*. New York: Academic Press, 1968.

Deren, M. *Divine Horsemen*. London: Thomas and Hudson, 1953.

Dillon, J.T. "Approaches to the Study of Problem-Finding Behaviour." Unpublished manuscript, University of Chicago, 1972.

Eliade, M. *Yoga: Immortality and Freedom*. Princeton, N.J.: Princeton University Press, 1969.

Freud, S. *The Ego and the Id*. London: Allen and Unwin, 1927.

——"Dostoevsky and Parricide." In E. Jones (Ed.), *Collected Papers of Sigmund Freud*, vol. 5. New York: Basic Books, 1959.

Getzels, J. W., and Csikszentmihalyi, M. "Creative Problem-Finding: A Longitudinal Study with Artists." Unpublished manuscript, University of Chicago, 1975.

Ghiselin, B. (Ed.) *The Creative Process*. New York: Mentor, 1952.

Herrigel, E. *Zen in the Art of Archery*. New York: Pantheon, 1953.

——*The Method of Zen*. New York: Pantheon, 1960.

Huizinga, J. *Homo Ludens*. Boston: Beacon Press, 1950. Originally published 1939.

Laski, M. *Ecstasy: A Study of Some Secular and Religious Experiences*. Bloomington: Indiana University Press, 1962.

Maslow, A. *Towards a Psychology of Being*. Princeton, N.J.: Van Nostrand, 1962.

——"Humanistic Science and Transcendent Experience." *Journal of Humanistic Psychology*, 1965, 5 (2), 219–27.

——*The Farther Reaches of Human Nature*. New York: Viking, 1971.

Mead, G. H. *Mind, Self, and Society*. Chicago, University of Chicago press, 1934.

Moltmann, J. *Theology of Play*. New York: Harper, 1972.

Montmasson, J. M. *Invention and the Unconscious*. New York: Harcourt, Brace, 1932.

Naranjo, C. and Ornstein, R. E. *On the Psychology of Meditation*. New York: Viking, 1971.

Piaget, J. *Play, Dreams and Imitation in Childhood*. New York: Norton, 1951.

——*The Moral Judgment of the Child*. New York: Free Press, 1965.

Rahner, H. *Man at Play*. New York: Herder and Herder, 1967.

Steiner, G. "Fields of Force." *New Yorker*, Oct. 28, 1972, pp. 42–117. Also published in book form: *Fields of Force*. New York: Viking, 1974.

Turner, V. *The Ritual Process*. Chicago: Aldine, 1969.

Unsworth, W. *North Face*. London: Hutchinson, 1969.

Worsley, P. *The Trumpet Shall Sound*. New York: Schocken, 1968.

21 Keynote Presentation (Guelph) 2007 (Graphic Score)

Anthony Braxton

Beginning in the 1960s, Anthony Braxton was part of a nucleus of young African American musicians such as Roscoe Mitchell, Henry Threadgill, and Wadada Leo Smith, who consolidated their talents in two very different musical environments: first military bands, and then Chicago's Association for the Advancement of Creative Musicians. The pioneering AACM became Braxton's first major support community for a long career of groundbreaking improvisation, composition, and musical/ philosophical conceptualisation. He has recorded with most of the major figures in American, and European, improvised music, and his compositional efforts incorporate specialised computer programming languages, experiments with large ensembles playing over large spaces, and his idiosyncratic compositional naming and notation. He is currently a professor of music at Wesleyan University in Middletown, Connecticut, teaching music composition, music history, and improvisation.

Key words: composition; African American culture; jazz; interdisciplinarity; pedagogy

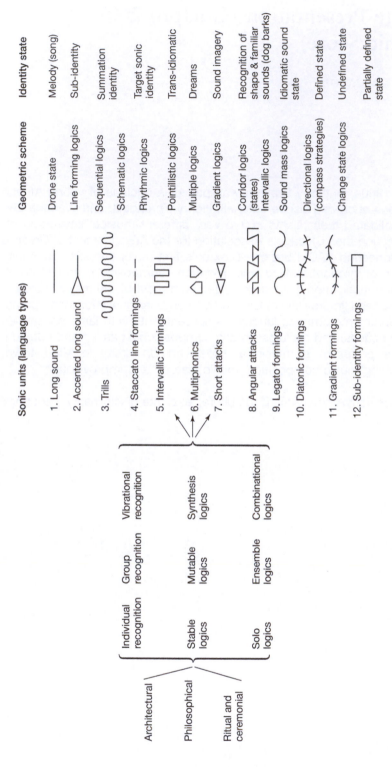

Figure 21.1 Keynote Presentation (Guelph) 2007 (Graphic Score)

22 The Impermanent Art

Merce Cunningham

Merce Cunningham (1919–2009) began his professional career at age 20 as a soloist in the Martha Graham Dance Company. A life partnership with composer John Cage (which began in the 1940s and ended only with the composer's death in 1992) spanned many groundbreaking collaborations, and in 1953 he founded the Merce Cunningham Dance Company as a forum for new concepts of dance. Cage and Cunningham agreed that although dance and music might occur at the same time in the same performance, they could be created independently of each other, enabling the audience to forge their own connections between the heard and the seen. They also eschewed conventional narratives, even the conventional logic, of dance performances, and for some works, such as *Suite by Chance* (1953), introduced "chance" procedures—although the fact that these procedures are decided by the composer has given them a controversial relationship to improvisation. Over his long career, Cunningham welcomed new technologies, working with dance on film, computer-programmed choreography, and even motion capture technology for the piece *Biped* (music by Gavin Bryars) in 1999.

Key words: dance; composition; interdisciplinarity; digital media

There has been a shift of emphasis in the practice of the arts of painting, music and dancing during the last few years. There are no labels yet but there are ideas. These ideas seem primarily concerned with something being exactly what it is in its time and place, and not in its having actual or symbolic reference to other things. A thing is just that thing. It is good that each thing be accorded this recognition and this love. Of course, the world being what it is—or the way we are coming to understand it now—we know that each thing is also every other thing, either actually or potentially. So we don't, it seems to me, have to worry ourselves about providing relationships and continuities and orders and structures—they cannot be avoided. They are the nature of things. They are ourselves and our materials and our environment. If a dancer dances—which is not the same as having theories about dancing or wishing to dance or trying to dance or remembering in his body someone else's dance—but if the dancer dances, everything is there. The meaning is there, if that's what you want. It's like this apartment where I live—I look around in the morning and ask myself, what does it all mean? It means: this is where I live. When I dance, it means: this is what I am doing. A thing is just that thing. In painting, now, we are beginning to see the painting, and not the painter nor the painted. We are beginning to see how a painted space is. In music, we are beginning to hear free of our well-tempered ears.

In dance, it is the simple fact of a jump being a jump, and the further fact of what shape the jump takes. This attention given the jump eliminates the necessity to feel that the meaning of dancing lies in everything but the dancing, and further eliminates cause-and-effect worry as to what movement should follow what movement, frees one's feelings about continuity, and makes it clear that each act of life can be its own history: past, present and future, and can be so regarded, which helps to break the chains that too often follow dancers' feet around.

There doesn't seem to me the need to expound any longer on the idea that dance is as much a part of life as anything else. Since it takes place in one form or another almost constantly, that is evidence enough. The play of bodies in space—and time. When I choreograph a piece by tossing pennies—by chance, that is—I am finding my resources in that play, which is not the product of my will, but which is an energy and a law which I too obey. Some people seem to think that it is inhuman and mechanistic to toss pennies in creating a dance instead of chewing the nails or beating the head against a wall or thumbing through old notebooks for ideas. But the feeling I have when I compose in this way is that I am in touch with a natural resource far greater than my own personal inventiveness could ever be, much more universally human than the particular habits of my own practice, and organically rising out of common pools of motor impulses.

Since dance as a part of life seems self-evident enough—a few words about what dance is not. "Not this, not that." Dance is not social relationships. Though it may influence them. Dance is not emoting, passion for her, anger against him. I think dance is more primal than that. In its essence, in the nakedness of its energy it is a source from which passion or anger may issue in a particular form, the source of energy out of which may be channeled the energy that goes into the various emotional behaviors. It is that blatant exhibiting of this energy, i.e., of energy geared to an intensity high enough to melt steel in some dancers, that gives the great excitement. This is not feeling about something, this is a whipping of the mind and body into an action that is so intense, that for the brief moment involved, the mind and body are one. The dancer knows how solidly he must be aware of this centering when he dances. And it is just this very fusion at a white heat that gives the look of objectivity and serenity that a fine dancer has.

Our ecstasy in dance comes from the possible gift of freedom, the exhilarating moment that this exposing of the bare energy can give us. What is meant is not license, but freedom, that is, a complete awareness of the world and at the same time a detachment from it.

In thinking about contemporary dance, I am concerned here with the concert dance, I find that it is the connection with the immediacy of the action, the single instant, that gives the feeling of man's freedom. The body shooting into space is not an idea of man's freedom, but is the body shooting into space. And that very action is all other actions, and is man's freedom, and at the same instant his non-freedom. You see how it is no trouble at all to get profound about dance. It seems to be a natural double for metaphysical paradox.

In reference to the current idea that dance must be expressive of something and that it must be involved with the images deep within our conscious and unconscious, it is my impression that there is no need to push for them. If these primordial, pagan or otherwise archetypical images lie deep within us, they will appear, regardless of our likes and dislikes, once the way is open. It is simply a matter of allowing it to happen. The dancer's discipline, his daily rite, can be looked at in this way: to make it possible for the spirit to move through his limbs and to extend its manifestations into space, with all its freedom and necessity. I am no more philosophical than my legs, but from them I sense this fact: that they are infused with energy that can be released in movement (to appear to be motionless is its own kind of intoxicating movement)—that the shape the movement takes is beyond the fathoming of my mind's analysis but clear to my eyes and rich to my imagination. In other words, a man is a two-legged creature—more basically and more intimately than he is anything else. And my legs speak more than they "know"—and so does all nature. So if you really dance—your body, that is, and not your mind's enforcement—the manifestations of the spirit through your torso and your limbs will inevitably take on the shape of life. We give ourselves away at every moment. We do not, therefore, have to try to do it. Our racial memory, our ids and egos, whatever it is, is there. If it is there, it is there; we do not need to pretend that we have to put it there. In one of my most recent solo works, called "Untitled Solo," I choreographed the piece with the use of "chance" methods. However, the dance as performed seems to have an unmistakable dramatic intensity in its bones, so to speak. It seems to me that it was simply a question of "allowing" this quality to happen rather than of "forcing" it. It is this "tranquility" of the actor or dancer which seems to me essential. A tranquility which allows him to detach himself and thereby to present freely and liberally. Making of himself such a kind of nature puppet that he is as if dancing on a string which is like an umbilical cord: mother-nature and father-spirit moving his limbs, without thought.

My use of chance methods in finding continuity for dances is not a position which I wish to establish and die defending. It is a present mode of freeing my imagination from its own clichés and it is a marvelous adventure in attention. Our attention is, normally, highly selective and highly editorial. But try looking at events another way and the whole world of gesture, the whole physical world in fact, is as if jabbed by an electric current.

It has been a growing interest in "each thing-ness" that has led me to the use of chance methods in finding dance continuity.[1] In my case, and for one particular work, this involved an elaborate use of charts from which came the particular movements, the rhythm (that is, the division and the duration of the time they were done in), and the space they appear in and how they divide it. There were separate charts for each of the three elements—movement, time, and space. Then I tossed pennies to select a movement from the movement chart, and this was followed by tossing pennies to find the duration of that particular movement, and following that the space and direction of the movement were tossed for. This method might lead one to suspect the result as being possibly geo-metric and "abstract," unreal and non-human. On the contrary, it is no more geometric than the lines of a mountain are, seen from an airplane; it is no more abstract than any human being is, and as for reality, it is just that, it is not abstracted from something else, but is the thing itself, and moreover allows each dancer to be just as human as he is.

One of the things that has interested me for a long time, is how our balance works, not the fact that we can balance in many different ways and so find out how many ways, but just that we do balance at all, and how. On two legs or one. Dancing has two things in it: balance of the weight, and shift of that weight in space and time, that is, in greater or smaller areas, and over longer or shorter lengths of time. It depends upon the flexibility of the architecture of the body. The variety of that flexibility is limited only by the imagination of the dancer and you can see where that has brought us already. I suppose there are actually relatively few movements that we do, and it's probably most pleasant for the dancer in his searching for movement if he lights upon one of these in a straightforward simple way. Lack of fullness in a particular movement, or exaggeration of a movement outside the particular limits of its own shape and rhythm produces mannerism, I should think. And, equally so, the fullest possible doing of a particular movement with the minimum necessity of visible energy and the clearest precision in each element of that movement might possibly produce style. But when this is allowed to go out the window for further effect, prolongation of pose for bravura or other such delights of the performer's ego, then the first thing lost is serenity, and in the rush to catch up, the dancer stumbles, expressively if not physically.

Buckminster Fuller, the architect, once spoke of his feeling that man had migrated around the globe via two means: with the wind, that is under sail and perhaps eastward generally; and against the wind, that is across the land. This image of movement and resistance somehow makes me think of how an idea of mobile and static could be witnessed in the ways a dancer can be trained. The prime motivation can either be made a static one, that is by letting the position of the torso come first within the possibilities of its flexibility, and then to that adding the activity of the legs, or the prime motivation can be put in the legs, making a mobile situation upon which the back and upper limbs rest. This all presumes that a relationship runs up and down the spine into the arms and legs, to begin with, and that the base of the torso where the legs join the back both stops the action of the limbs and allows it to continue. And the wondrousness of being free and clear with both of these bodily components at the same time!

But the pleasure of dance does not lie in its analysis, though one might sometimes be led to think otherwise. Dancing is a lively human activity which by its very nature is part of all of us, spectators and performers alike. It's not the discussion, it's the doing and seeing—of whatever kind. As an adolescent I took lessons in various forms of American popular stage dancing including tap and a land of exhibition ballroom. But my teacher insisted there was not such a thing as just "tap" there was "the waltz clog," "the southern soft shoe,'" "the buck and wing," and all were different, and she would proceed to show us how they were different. The rhythm in each case was the inflecting force that gave each particular dance its style and color. The tempo for a slower dance, for instance, allowed for a certain weight and swing and stopping of the arms that wasn't indicated in a faster dance. These lessons eventually led to performances in various halls as the entertainers for local events and finally a short and intoxicating "vaudeville tour." I remember one of these situations when we (there were four of us), stood huddled and cold in a sort of closet that was the lone dressing room, behind the tiny platform that was the stage this time, and our teacher was in the front of the hall making last minute preparations. Finally she hurried back, took one look at the four of us, and smiled and said, "All right, kids, we haven't any make-up, so bite your lips and pinch your cheeks, and you're on." It was a kind of theatre energy and devotion she radiated. This was a devotion to dancing as an instantaneous and agreeable act of life. All my subsequent involvements with dancers who were concerned with dance as a conveyor of social message or to be used as a testing ground for psychological types have not succeeded in destroying that feeling Mrs. J. W. Barrett gave me that dance is most deeply concerned with each single instant as it comes along, and its life and vigor and attraction lie in just that singleness. It is as accurate and impermanent as breathing.

Notes

1 The actual technique of "choreography by chance" is the subject of an article by Remy Charlip in the January 1954 issue of *Dance Magazine*.

23 Improvisation and Ensemble

Michael Chekhov

At one time Constantin Stanislavski would say that if anyone wanted to know what he was teaching, they should go and see what Michael Chekhov was doing. In fact, it could be said that Chekhov took Stanislavski's teachings a step further, his vision of improvisation as an end in itself anticipating the kind of work to be introduced by The Living Theatre, Keith Johnstone, and Viola Spolin. "The actor's … compelling desire and highest aim … " Chekhov writes, "can be achieved only by means of free improvisation." A nephew of playwright Anton Chekhov, Michael Chekhov (1891–1955) was considered Stanislavski's most brilliant student, but unlike his mentor, his work found little favour with Soviet authorities. In 1928 he left the USSR and in 1936 established the Chekhov Training Studio in England. In 1939 the school moved to Ridgefield, Connecticut, but in 1942 it lost all its young male members to the draft, so Chekhov's friend Sergei Rachmaninoff invited him to Hollywood, where he acted in many films (receiving an Academy Award nomination for his work in Alfred Hitchcock's *Spellbound*), coached stars such as Marilyn Monroe, Gregory Peck, and Patricia Neal, taught a group called The Drama Society, and two years before his death, published his book *To the Actor*.

Key words: theatre; Constantin Stanislavski; pedagogy

> Only artists united by true sympathy into an Improvising Ensemble can know the joy of unselfish, common creation.

[…] [T]he highest and final aim of every true artist, whatever his particular branch of art, may be defined as the desire to express himself freely and completely.

Each of us has his own convictions, his own world outlook, own ideals and ethical attitude toward life. These deeply rooted and often unconscious creeds constitute part of man's individuality and its great longing for free expression.

Profound thinkers impelled to express themselves create their own philosophical systems. Similarly, an artist who strives to express his inner convictions does so by improvising with his own tools, his particular form of art. The same, without exception, must be said for the actor's art: *his* compelling desire and highest aim also can be achieved only by means of free improvisation.

If an actor confines himself merely to speaking the lines provided by the author and executing the "business" ordered by the director, and seeks no opportunity to improvise independently, he makes himself a slave to the creations of others and his profession a borrowed one. He erroneously believes that both author and director have already improvised for him and that there is little room left for the free expression of his own creative individuality. This attitude, unfortunately, prevails among too many of our actors today.

Yet every role offers an actor the opportunity to improvise, to collaborate and truly co-create with the author and director. This suggestion, of course, does not imply improvising new lines or substituting business for that outlined by the director. On the contrary. The given lines and the business are the firm bases upon which the actor must and can develop his improvisations. *How* he speaks the lines and *how* he fulfills the business are the open gates to a vast field of improvisation. The "hows" of his lines and business are the ways in which he can express himself freely.

More than that, there are innumerable other moments between the lines and business when he can create wonderful psychological transitions and embroider his performance on his own, where he can display his true artistic ingenuity. His interpretation of the whole character down to its minutest features offers a wide range for his improvisations. He need only begin by refusing to play just himself or resorting to worn-out clichés. If he but stop considering all his parts as "straight" ones and will try to find some fine characterization for each—that, too, will be a rewarding step toward improvisation. The actor who has not felt the pure joy of transforming himself on the stage with each new part can scarcely know the real, creative meaning of improvisation.

Furthermore, as soon as an actor develops the ability to improvise, and discovers within himself this inexhaustible well from which every improvisation is drawn, he will enjoy a sense of freedom hitherto unknown to him, and will feel himself much richer inwardly.

The following exercises are designed to develop the ability to improvise. Try to keep them as simple as they are given here.

Exercise 12 (for individual work)

First decide which are the starting and concluding moments of your improvisation. They must be definite pieces of action. In the beginning, for instance, you may get up quickly from a chair and with firmness of tone or gesture say, "Yes," while in the concluding moment you may lie down, open a book and start reading quietly and leisurely. Or you may start with gaily and hastily putting on your overcoat, hat and gloves, as if intending to go out, and end by sitting down depressed and perhaps even in tears. Or you may begin by looking out the window with fear or great concern, trying to hide yourself behind the curtain and then, exclaiming, "Here he is again!" recoil from the window; and for the concluding moment you might play the piano (real or imaginary) in a very happy and even hilarious mood. And so on. The more contrasted the starting and concluding moments, the better.

Do not try to anticipate what you are going to do between the two chosen moments. Do not try to find any logical justification or motivation for either the starting and concluding moments themselves. Choose them at random. Choose any two things that first pop into your head, and not because they will suggest or bracket a good improvisation. Just a contrasting beginning and end.

Do not try to define the theme or plot. Define only the mood or feelings of that beginning and end. Then give yourself over to whatever momentary suggestions occur to you by pure intuition. Thus, when you get up and say, "Yes"—if that is your beginning—you will freely and with full confidence in yourself begin to "act," mainly following your feelings, emotions and moods.

And the middle part, the whole transition from starting to concluding points, is what you will improvise.

Let each successive moment of your improvisation be a psychological (not logical!) result of the moment preceding it. Thus without any previously thought-out theme, you will move from the starting to the concluding moment, improvising all the way. By doing so you will go through the whole gamut of different sensations, emotions, moods, desires, inner impulses and business, all of which will be found by you spontaneously, on the spot, as it were. Perhaps you will become indignant, then pensive, then irritated; perhaps you will go through the stages of indifference, humor, gaiety; or perhaps you will write a letter in great agitation, or go to the telephone and call someone, or anything else.

Any and every possibility is open to you according to your mood at the particular moment, or according to the accidental things you may encounter during the improvisation. All you have to do is listen to that "inner voice" which prompts all the changes of your psychology and all the business you resort to. Your subconscious will suggest things which cannot be foreseen by anyone, not even by yourself, if you will but yield freely and completely to the inspiration of your own improvising spirit. With the concluding moment present in your imagination, you will not flounder aimlessly and endlessly, but will constantly and inexplicably be drawn to it. It will loom before you as a magnetic guiding light.

Go on exercising this way, each time establishing a new beginning and a new end, until you have confidence in yourself, until you no longer have to stop and guess about things to do between the start and finish.

You may wonder why the beginning and end of this exercise, whatever they may prove to be, must be clearly defined at the outset. Why should what you are doing or the position of your body and mood be established at the start and finish, but the improvisation in between be permitted to flow spontaneously? Because real and true freedom in improvising must always be based upon necessity; otherwise it will soon degenerate into either arbitrariness or indecision. With no definite beginning to impel your actions and no definite end to complete them, you would only wander pointlessly. Your sense of freedom would be meaningless without a place to start or without direction or destination.

When rehearsing a play you naturally encounter a great number of "necessities" which demand your facile improvisational activity and ability. The plot, lines, tempo, the author's and director's suggestions, the acting of the others in the cast—all determine the necessities and the varying lengths between them to which you must accommodate yourself. Therefore, to prepare yourself for such professional conditions and to be able to adapt yourself to them, you develop your exercise by establishing similar necessities or limitations.

At first, in addition to the exact beginning and end, you will also define as one of the necessities the approximate duration of each exercise. For working alone, about five minutes is sufficient for each improvisation.

Next add to the same starting and concluding points one more point (necessity) somewhere in the middle of the improvisation. This must be just as definite a piece of action, with definite feeling, mood or emotion, as the start and finish.

Now go from the beginning to the middle point, and from there to the end, in the same way that you traversed the two points alone, but try not to spend more time on them than before.

After a while add one more point wherever you choose, and fulfill your improvisation by going through the four points in approximately the same amount of time that it took you to go through the two.

Continue to add more and more such points between start and finish. Choose them all at random and without attempt at coherence or logical selection; leave this task to your improvising psychology. But in this variation of the exercise do not take a new beginning and end each time.

Having thus accumulated a sufficient number of points and satisfactorily bridged them as so many steps, you may start to impose new necessities upon yourself in still another way: try to act the first part in a slow tempo and the last part in a fast tempo; or try to create a certain atmosphere around you and maintain it in either a chosen section or throughout the entire improvisation.

You can then heap further necessities into the improvisation by using different qualities, such as molding, floating, flying or radiating movements, separately or in any combinations you wish to set for yourself; or you may even try the improvisation with various characterizations.

Later on you can imagine a definite setting in which you have to improvise; then the location of the audience; then decide whether your improvisation is tragedy, drama, comedy or farce. Also try to improvise as though you were performing a period play, and in this case dress yourself in an imaginary costume of the chosen period. All these things will serve as additional necessities upon which to develop your free improvisation.

It is to be expected that, in spite of all the new and varying necessities you introduce, a certain pattern of plot will inevitably creep into your improvisation. In order to avoid this during your exercises you can, after a while, try transposing the beginning and the end; later you can change the order of the points in the middle section as well.

When you have exhausted this series of combinations, start the whole exercise afresh with a new beginning and end and all kinds of necessities; and, as before, without any premeditated plot.

The result of this exercise is that you develop the psychology of an improvising actor. You will retain this psychology while going over all the necessities you have chosen for your improvisation, regardless of their number. Later on, when rehearsing and performing on the stage, you will feel that the lines you have to speak, the business you have to do and all the circumstances imposed upon you by the writer and director, and even the plot of the play, will lead and direct you as did the necessities you found for your exercise. You will not notice any substantial difference between the exercise and your professional work. Thus you will eventually be confirmed in the belief that dramatic art is nothing more than a constant improvisation, and that there are no moments on the stage when an actor can be deprived of his right to improvise. You will be able to fulfill faithfully all the necessities imposed upon you and at the same time preserve your spirit of an improvising actor. A new and gratifying sensation of complete confidence in yourself, along with the sensation of freedom and inner richness, will be the reward of all your efforts.

The exercises on developing the ability to improvise also can, and should be, employed in ensembles of two, three and more partners. And although they are in principle the same as for the individual, there is nevertheless an essential difference which must be considered.

The dramatic art is a collective art and therefore, however talented the actor may be, he will not be able to make full use of his ability to improvise if he isolates himself from the ensemble, his partners.

Of course, there are many unifying impulses on the stage, such as the atmosphere of the play, its style, a well-executed performance, or exceptionally fine staging. And yet a true stage ensemble needs more than these ordinary consolidations. The actor must develop within himself a sensitivity to the creative impulses of others.

An improvising ensemble lives in a constant process of giving and taking. A small hint from a partner—a glance, a pause, a new or unexpected intonation, a movement, a sigh, or even a barely perceptible change of tempo—can become a creative impulse, an invitation to the other to improvise.

Therefore, before starting exercises on group improvisation it is recommended that the members concentrate for a while on a preparatory exercise designed to develop what we shall call the ensemble feeling.

Exercise 13 (for a group)

Each member of the group begins by making an effort to open himself inwardly, with the greatest possible sincerity, to every other member. He tries to be aware of the individual presence of each. He makes an effort, figuratively speaking, "to open his heart" and admit everyone present, as though he were among his dearest friends. This process is much the same as that of receiving, which was described in [my earlier work]. At the beginning of the exercise each member of the group should say to himself:

> The creative ensemble consists of individuals and must never be considered by me as an impersonal mass. I appreciate the individual existence of each and every one present in this room and in my mind they do not lose their identity. Therefore, being here among my colleagues, I deny the general concept of 'They' or 'We' and instead I say: 'He and She, and She and I.' I am ready to receive any impressions, even the subtlest, from each one taking part with me in this exercise and I am ready to react to these impressions harmoniously.

You will help yourself immeasurably by ignoring all shortcomings or unsympathetic features of the members of the group, but trying instead to find their attractive sides and the better qualities of their characters. To avoid unnecessary embarrassment and artificiality, do not overdo it with prolonged and overly sentimental stares into their eyes, too friendly smiles or other unnecessary devices.

It is quite natural that you may develop a warm attitude toward your partners, but this should not be misconstrued as an invitation to float around in the group or lose yourself in vague feelings. The exercise is intended, rather, to give you the psychological means for establishing a firm professional contact with your partners.

With the inner contact between themselves solidly established, the members of the group then go to the next step of the exercise. They outline a succession of simple actions to choose from. These might be walking quietly around the room, running, standing motionless, changing places, assuming positions against the walls or coming together in the center of the room. Three or four such definite actions will be sufficient.

No one must be told which of these movements will be the specific group action when the exercise begins. Each participant must divine, with his newly developed "openness," which of the agreed-upon actions the group as a whole desires to fulfill, then proceed to carry it out. Several false starts may be made by one or all, but eventually the common action will be arrived at in concert.

Still inherent in this guessing is the constant observation of the others by each member of the group. The closer and sharper the observation, the better the receptivity. The object is for all the members to select and perform the same action at the same time without prearrangement or hint of any kind. Whether they succeed or not is of no consequence, because the real value of the exercise lies in the effort to open one's self to the others and to intensify the actor's ability to observe his partners at all times, thus strengthening sensitivity toward the entire ensemble.

After a while, when the members of the group genuinely feel the sensation of being intimately united by the exercise, they should go to the exercise for group improvisation. This is different from the individual exercise. This time the *theme* must also be defined, but only in general or outline form. Will the group, to offer only a few suggestions, perform work in a factory of some kind, attend an elegant ballroom affair or house party, arrive or depart at a railway station or airport, be caught in a gambling raid, dine at a restaurant or make merry at a carnival? Whatever theme is chosen, the group next agrees on the setting. Here are the doors, tables, workbenches, orchestra, gates—whatever is called for by the particular locale which the chosen theme suggests.

The group then "distributes the parts." Neither premeditated plot nor any succession of events should be permitted. No more than the starting and concluding moments, with their initial business and corresponding moods, should be stated, as they were in the individual exercise. Also, the group should agree on the approximate duration of the improvisation.

Do not use too many words. Do not monopolize the dialogue, but speak only when it is natural and necessary to do so. Furthermore, the ability to improve or expand upon dialogue is not the actor's function, therefore you should not distract your attention from the improvisation with efforts to create the perfect lines for your part or the situation. The meaning of the exercise will not suffer if your words have no literary value and even sound awkward.

In all probability the first attempt at group improvisation will be chaotic despite everyone's sharpened sensitivity, openness and sense of unity. But everyone will receive a number of impressions from his partners. Each will recognize the others' intentions to create and develop the given situation, feel their moods and guess their conceptions of the scene imagined. He will also know his own unfulfilled intentions, his failure to conform to the plot, his partners, and so on. All these things, however, should not be discussed, but the members of the group should at once make another attempt to do the same improvisation, still relying upon their sense of unity and the contact they have established among themselves.

The second time the improvisation will undoubtedly assume a more definite shape, and many neglected intentions will find fulfillment. The group must repeat its efforts again and again until the improvisation reaches the point where it begins to look like a well-rehearsed little sketch. Meantime, in spite of inevitable repetitions of words, business and situations here and there, each member must maintain the psychology of an improvising artist.

Do not repeat yourself if you can help it, but instead try to find a new way of per-forming the same situation. Although you will have a natural inclination to retain and repeat the best achievements of the previous improvisations, do not hesitate to alter or discard them if your "inner voice" prompts you to hazard more expressive business or a more artistic interpretation of the moment, or even a new attitude toward the other participants. Your taste, your tact will tell you what can be altered and when, and what should be preserved for the sake of the ensemble and the plot in development. You will soon learn to be unselfish on one hand and still pursue your artistic freedom and desires on the other.

No matter how many times the group will want to repeat the same improvisation, its beginning and end should always remain clearly and exactly defined.

In group improvisation, it is well to remember, there is no need to establish any additional points between the start and the finish. They will gradually be found and crystallized as the improvisation progresses, the theme establishes itself and the plot grows and develops.

As soon as the improvisation assumes the appearance of a well-rehearsed sketch, the members of the group might decide to make it more interesting by adding a few necessities—atmospheres, characterizations, different tempos—all of which can be introduced one at a time.

When one theme is exhausted, the group can choose another and begin exercising it, again starting by establishing contact and unity as described in the beginning of this exercise.

Now the group is ready for the following experiment: Choose a scene from a play which none of the members has seen on the stage or screen, or perhaps acted in. Distribute the parts. Let one of you be made the "director" and asked to stage exactly the beginning and the end of the chosen scene. Then, knowing the content of the scene, start to improvise upon the whole middle part. Do not deviate too much from the psychology of the characters you are playing. Do not memorize the lines, except perhaps those of the beginning and the end. Let all the business and the mise-en-scène arise from your improvising initiative, as in previous exercises. You may speak a few lines here and there to approximate the author's, but if by chance you have retained some of them in your memory there is no need to mispronounce them deliberately in order to make them sound "improvised."

Do not as yet try to develop your characterization; otherwise your attention will be distracted from that "inner voice" which guides your improvisational activity. However, if the characteristic features of the role you are playing "insist" on coming to the fore and being incorporated, do not suppress them.

Having thus arrived at the end of the scene, ask your "director" to stage for you, again exactly, a little section of the scene somewhere in the middle. Then start your improvisation anew from the beginning to the "directed" middle point, and proceed from there to the end. In this way, filling in the gaps step by step, you will soon be able to play the entire scene as it is written by the author, maintaining throughout the *psychology of the improvising ensemble*. You will become more and more convinced that even while working upon an actual play, with all the director's and author's suggestions (necessities), you are still free to improvise creatively, and soon this conviction will become your new ability, your second nature, as it were.

Next the group can begin to develop the characterizations.

This exercise, as you undoubtedly see for yourself, is intended to familiarize you with the richness of your own actor's soul.

In concluding this chapter it is necessary to add a word of caution. If, while improvising, you begin to feel that you are becoming untrue or unnatural, you can be sure that it results either from the interference of your "logic" or from using too many unnecessary words. You must have the courage to rely completely on your improvising spirit. Follow the psychological succession of inner events (feelings, emotions, wishes and other impulses) that speak to you from the depths of your creative individuality and you will soon be convinced that this "inner voice" you possess never lies.

Simultaneously with the group exercises, it is highly advisable to continue the individual exercises, because both complement but do not substitute for each other.

24 Theory of the Dérive

Guy Debord

Translated by Ken Knabb

Born in Paris, Guy Debord (1931–94) joined the Letterist International at the age of 19, and along with many of his generation, demonstrated against the French war in Algeria. Throughout his life he decried the modern alienation he saw perpetuated by capitalism, government, and the ever-growing influence of mass media. In the 1960s he was a founding member of the Situationist International, the movement which introduced such concepts as *détournement* and *dérive*, "literally: 'drift' or 'drifting,'" the latter term explained here as a way of testing the relationships between the known and the new, the familiar and the unfamiliar. Debord's book *The Society of the Spectacle* (building upon a concept introduced by Roland Barthes) is credited as a major influence on the French student uprising of 1968. His films, which *Film Comment*'s Howard Hampton has referred to as a "cinema of annihilation," include *Hurlements en faveur de Sade* (*Howlings for Sade*), a film version of *The Society of the Spectacle*, and, unfinished at the time of his death by suicide in 1994, *Guy Debord, son art et son temps*. As well as "Spectacle," and *Comments on the Society of the Spectacle*, he wrote a number of autobiographical works including *Mémoires* (famous for being bound in sandpaper).

Key words: critical theory; France; politics; everyday life

One of the basic situationist practices is the *dérive*,[1] a technique of rapid passage through varied ambiences. Dérives involve playful-constructive behavior and awareness of psychogeographical effects, and are thus quite different from the classic notions of journey or stroll.

In a dérive one or more persons during a certain period drop their relations, their work and leisure activities, and all their other usual motives for movement and action, and let themselves be drawn by the attractions of the terrain and the encounters they find there. Chance is a less important factor in this activity than one might think: from a dérive point of view cities have psychogeographical contours, with constant currents, fixed points and vortexes that strongly discourage entry into or exit from certain zones.

But the dérive includes both this letting-go and its necessary contradiction: the domination of psychogeographical variations by the knowledge and calculation of their possibilities. In this latter regard, ecological science, despite the narrow social space to which it limits itself, provides psychogeography with abundant data.

The ecological analysis of the absolute or relative character of fissures in the urban network, of the role of microclimates, of distinct neighborhoods with no relation to administrative boundaries, and above all of the dominating action of centers of attraction, must be utilized and completed by psychogeographical methods. The objective passional terrain of the dérive must be defined in accordance both with its own logic and with its relations with social morphology.

In his study *Paris et l'agglomération parisienne* (Bibliothèque de Sociologie Contemporaine, P.U.F., 1952) Chombart de Lauwe notes that "an urban neighborhood is determined not only by geographical and economic factors, but also by the image that its inhabitants and those of other neighborhoods have of it." In the same work, in order to illustrate "the narrowness of the real Paris in which each individual lives ... within a geographical area whose radius is extremely small," he diagrams all the movements made in the space of one year by a student living in the 16th Arrondissement. Her itinerary forms a small triangle with no significant deviations, the three apexes of which are the School of Political Sciences, her residence and that of her piano teacher.

Such data – examples of a modern poetry capable of provoking sharp emotional reactions (in this particular case, outrage at the fact that anyone's life can be so pathetically limited) – or even Burgess's theory of Chicago's social activities as being distributed in distinct concentric zones, will undoubtedly prove useful in developing dérives.

If chance plays an important role in dérives this is because the methodology of psychogeographical observation is still in its infancy. But the action of chance is naturally conservative and in a new setting tends to reduce everything to habit or to an alternation between a limited number of variants. Progress means breaking through fields where chance holds sway by creating new conditions more favorable to our purposes. We can say, then, that the randomness of a dérive is fundamentally different from that of the stroll, but also that the first psychogeographical attractions discovered by dérivers may tend to fixate them around new habitual axes, to which they will constantly be drawn back.

An insufficient awareness of the limitations of chance, and of its inevitably reactionary effects, condemned to a dismal failure the famous aimless wandering attempted in 1923 by four surrealists, beginning from a town chosen by lot: Wandering in open country is naturally depressing, and the interventions of chance are poorer there than anywhere else. But this mindlessness is pushed much further by a certain Pierre Vendryes (in *Médium*, May 1954), who thinks he can relate this anecdote to various probability experiments, on the ground that they all supposedly involve the same sort of antideterminist liberation. He gives as an example the random distribution of tadpoles in a circular aquarium, adding, significantly, "It is necessary, of course, that such a population be subject to no external guiding influence." From that perspective, the tadpoles could be considered more spontaneously liberated than the surrealists, since they have the advantage of being "as stripped as possible of intelligence, sociability and sexuality," and are thus "truly independent from one another."

At the opposite pole from such imbecilities, the primarily urban character of the dérive, in its element in the great industrially transformed cities that are such rich centers of possibilities and meanings, could be expressed in Marx's phrase: "Men can see nothing around them that is not their own image; everything speaks to them of themselves. Their very landscape is alive."

One can dérive alone, but all indications are that the most fruitful numerical arrangement consists of several small groups of two or three people who have reached the same level of awareness, since cross-checking these different groups' impressions makes it possible to arrive at more objective conclusions. It is preferable for the composition of these groups to change from one dérive to another. With more than four or five participants, the specifically dérive character rapidly diminishes, and in any case it is impossible for there to be more than ten or twelve people without the dérive fragmenting into several simultaneous dérives. The practice of such subdivision is in fact of great interest, but the difficulties it entails have so far prevented it from being organized on a sufficient scale.

The average duration of a dérive is one day, considered as the time between two periods of sleep. The starting and ending times have no necessary relation to the solar day, but it should be noted that the last hours of the night are generally unsuitable for dérives.

But this duration is merely a statistical average. For one thing, a dérive rarely occurs in its pure form: it is difficult for the participants to avoid setting aside an hour or two at the beginning or end of the day for taking care of banal tasks; and toward the end of the day fatigue tends to encourage such an abandonment. But more importantly, a dérive often takes place within a deliberately limited period of a few hours, or even fortuitously during fairly brief moments; or it may last for several days without interruption. In spite of the cessations imposed by the need for sleep, certain dérives of a sufficient intensity have been sustained for three or four days, or even longer. It is true that in the case of a series of dérives over a rather long period of time it is almost impossible to determine precisely when the state of mind peculiar to one dérive gives way to that of another. One sequence of dérives was pursued without notable interruption for around two months. Such an experience gives rise to new objective conditions of behavior that bring about the disappearance of a good number of the old ones.[2]

The influence of weather on dérives, although real, is a significant factor only in the case of prolonged rains, which make them virtually impossible. But storms or other types of precipitation are rather favorable for dérives.

The spatial field of a dérive may be precisely delimited or vague, depending on whether the goal is to study a terrain or to emotionally disorient oneself. It should not be forgotten that these two aspects of dérives overlap in so many ways that it is impossible to isolate one of them in a pure state. But the use of taxis, for example, can provide a clear enough dividing line: If in the course of a dérive one takes a taxi, either to get to a specific destination or simply to move, say, twenty minutes to the west, one is concerned primarily with personal disorientation. If, on the other hand, one sticks to the direct exploration of a particular terrain, one is concentrating primarily on research for a psychogeographical urbanism.

In every case the spatial field depends first of all on the point of departure – the residence of the solo dériver or the meeting place selected by a group. The maximum area of this spatial field does not extend beyond the entirety of a large city and its suburbs. At its minimum it can be limited to a small self-contained ambience: a single neighborhood or even a single block of houses if it's interesting enough (the extreme case being a static-dérive of an entire day within the Saint-Lazare train station).

The exploration of a fixed spatial field entails establishing bases and calculating directions of penetration. It is here that the study of maps comes in – ordinary ones as well as ecological and psychogeographical ones – along with their correction and improvement. It should go without saying that we are not at all interested in any mere exoticism that may arise from the fact that one is exploring a neighborhood for the first time. Besides its unimportance, this aspect of the problem is completely subjective and soon fades away.

In the "possible rendezvous," on the other hand, the element of exploration is minimal in comparison with that of behavioral disorientation. The subject is invited to come alone to a certain place at a specified time. He is freed from the bothersome obligations of the ordinary rendezvous since there is no one to wait for. But since this "possible rendezvous" has brought him without warning to a place he may or may not know, he observes the surroundings. It may be that the same spot has been specified for a "possible rendezvous" for someone else whose identity he has no way of knowing. Since he may never even have seen the other person before, he will be encouraged to start up conversations with various passersby. He may meet no one, or he may even by chance meet the person who has arranged the "possible rendezvous." In any case, particularly if the time and place have been well chosen, his use of time will take an unexpected turn. He may even telephone someone else who doesn't know where the first "possible rendezvous" has taken him, in order to ask for another one to be specified. One can see the virtually unlimited resources of this pastime.

Our rather anarchic lifestyle and even certain amusements considered dubious that have always been enjoyed among our entourage – slipping by night into houses undergoing demolition, hitchhiking nonstop and without destination through Paris during a transportation strike in the name of adding to the confusion, wandering in subterranean catacombs forbidden to the public, etc. – are expressions of a more general sensibility which is no different from that of the dérive. Written descriptions can be no more than passwords to this great game.

The lessons drawn from dérives enable us to draft the first surveys of the psychogeographical articulations of a modern city. Beyond the discovery of unities of ambience, of their main components and their spatial localization, one comes to perceive their principal axes of passage, their exits and their defenses. One arrives at the central hypothesis of the existence of psychogeographical pivotal points. One measures the distances that actually separate two regions of a city, distances that may have little relation with the physical distance between them. With the aid of old maps, aerial photographs and experimental dérives, one can draw up hitherto lacking maps of influences, maps whose inevitable imprecision at this early stage is no worse than that of the earliest navigational charts. The only difference is that it is no longer a matter of precisely delineating stable continents, but of changing architecture and urbanism.

Today the different unities of atmosphere and of dwellings are not precisely marked off, but are surrounded by more or less extended bordering regions. The most general change that dérive experiences lead to proposing is the constant diminution of these border regions, up to the point of their complete suppression.

Within architecture itself, the taste for dériving tends to promote all sorts of new forms of labyrinths made possible by modern techniques of construction. Thus in March 1955 the press reported the construction in New York of a building in which one can see the first signs of an opportunity to dérive inside an apartment:

> The apartments of the helicoidal building will be shaped like slices of cake. One will be able to enlarge or reduce them by shifting movable partitions. The half-floor gradations avoid limiting the number of rooms, since the tenant can request the use of the adjacent section on either upper or lower levels. With this setup three four-room apartments can be transformed into one twelve-room apartment in less than six hours.

(To be continued.)

Notes

"Théorie de la dérive" was published in *Internationale Situationniste* #2 (Paris, December 1958). A slightly different version was first published in the Belgian surrealist journal *Les Lèvres Nues* #9

(November 1956) along with accounts of two dérives. This translation by Ken Knabb is from the *Situationist International Anthology* (Revised and Expanded Edition, 2006). No copyright.

1 *dérive*: literally "drift" or "drifting." Like *détournement*, this term has usually been anglicized as both a noun and a verb.

2 "The *dérive* (with its flow of acts, its gestures, its strolls, its encounters) was *to the totality* exactly what psychoanalysis (in the best sense) is to language. Let yourself go with the flow of words, says the psychoanalyst. He listens, until the moment when he rejects or modifies (one could say *detourns*) a word, an expression or a definition. The dérive is certainly a technique, almost a therapeutic one. But just as analysis unaccompanied with anything else is almost always *contraindicated,* so continual dériving is dangerous to the extent that the individual, having gone too far (not without bases, but …) without defenses, is threatened with explosion, dissolution, dissociation, disintegration. And thence the relapse into what is termed 'ordinary life,' that is to say, in reality, into 'petrified life.' In this regard I now repudiate my Formulary's propaganda for a *continuous dérive*. It could be continuous like the poker game in Las Vegas, but only for a certain period, limited to a weekend for some people, to a week as a good average; a month is really pushing it. In 1953–54 we dérived for three or four months straight. That's the extreme limit. It's a miracle it didn't kill us" (Ivan Chtcheglov, excerpt from a 1963 letter to Michèle Bernstein and Guy Debord, reprinted in *Internationale Situationniste* #9, p. 38).

25 "All Aboard the Night Train"

Flow, Layering, and Rupture in Postindustrial New York

Tricia Rose

Tricia Rose's 1995 book, *Black Noise: Rap Music and Black Culture in Contemporary America*, won an American Book Award from the Before Columbus Foundation, and the journal *Black Issues in Higher Education* named it one of the Top Books of the Twentieth Century. Her other books include *Longing To Tell: Black Women Talk About Sexuality and Intimacy* (2003) and *The Hip Hop Wars: What We Talk About When We Talk About Hip Hop—And Why It Matters* (2008). Born and raised in New York City, Dr Rose spent her childhood in Harlem and the Bronx. She received her BA in Sociology from Yale, and her PhD in American Studies from Brown University, where she is now Professor of Africana Studies. In its engagement with urban hip hop culture, "Flow, Layering, and Rupture" reveals improvising principles that are at work throughout many kinds of art-making.

Key words: African American culture; hip-hop

> Got a bum education, double-digit inflation
> Can't take the train to the job, there's a strike at the station
> Don't push me cause I'm close to the edge
> I'm tryin' not to lose my head
> It's like a jungle sometimes it makes me wonder
> How I keep from going under.
> > "The Message"[1]

[...]

Hip Hop

Hip hop culture emerged as a source for youth of alternative identity formation and social status in a community whose older local support institutions had been all but demolished along with large sectors of its built environment.

Alternative local identities were forged in fashions and language, street names, and most important, in establishing neighborhood crews or posses. Many hip hop fans, artists, musicians, and dancers continue to belong to an elaborate system of crews or posses. The crew, a local source of identity, group affiliation, and support system appears repeatedly in all of my interviews and virtually all rap lyrics and cassette dedications, music video performances, and media interviews with artists. Identity in hip hop is deeply rooted in the specific, the local experience, and one's attachment to and status in a local group or alternative family. These crews are new kinds of families forged with intercultural bonds that, like the social formation of gangs, provide insulation and support in a complex and unyielding environment and may serve as the basis for new social movements. The postindustrial city, which provided the context for creative development among hip hop's earliest innovators, shaped their cultural terrain, access to space, materials, and education. While graffiti artists' work was significantly aided by advances in spray paint technology, they used the urban transit system as their canvas. Rappers and DJs disseminated their work by copying it on tape-dubbing equipment and playing it on powerful, portable "ghetto blasters." At a time when budget cuts in school music programs drastically reduced access to traditional forms of instrumentation and composition, inner-city youths increasingly relied on recorded sound. Breakdancers used their bodies to mimic "transformers" and other futuristic robots in symbolic street battles. Early Puerto Rican, Afro-Caribbean, and black American hip hop artists transformed obsolete vocational skills from marginal occupations into the raw materials for creativity and resistance. Many of them were "trained" for jobs in fields that were shrinking or that no longer exist. Puerto Rican graffiti writer Futura graduated from a trade school specializing in the printing industry. However, as most of the jobs for which he was being trained had already been computerized, he found himself working at McDonald's after graduation. Similarly, African-American DJ Red Alert (who also has family from the Caribbean) reviewed blueprints for a drafting company until computer automation rendered his job obsolete. Jamaican DJ Kool Herc attended Alfred E. Smith auto mechanic trade school, and African-American Grandmaster Flash learned how to repair electronic equipment at Samuel Gompers vocational High School. (One could say Flash "fixed them alright.") Salt and Pepa (both with family roots in the West Indies) worked as phone telemarketing representatives at Sears while considering nursing school. Puerto Rican breakdancer Crazy Legs began breakdancing largely because his single mother couldn't afford Little League baseball fees.[2] All of these artists found themselves positioned with few resources in marginal economic circumstances, but each of them found ways to become famous as an entertainer by appropriating the most advanced technologies and emerging cultural forms. Hip hop artists used the tools of obsolete industrial technology to traverse contemporary crossroads of lack and desire in urban Afrodiasporic communities.

Stylistic continuities were sustained by internal cross-fertilization between rapping, breakdancing, and graffiti writing. Some graffiti writers, such as black American Phase 2, Haitian Jean-Michel Basquiat, Futura, and black American Fab Five Freddy produced rap records. Other writers drew murals that celebrated favorite rap songs (e.g., Futura's mural "The Breaks" was a whole car mural that paid homage to Kurtis Blow's rap of the same name). Breakdancers, DJs and rappers wore graffiti-painted jackets and tee-shirts. DJ Kool Herc was a graffiti writer and dancer first before he began playing records. Hip hop events featured breakdancers, rappers, and DJs as triple-bill entertainment. Graffiti writers drew murals for DJ's stage platforms and designed posters and flyers to advertise hip hop events. Breakdancer Crazy Legs, founding member of the Rock Steady Crew, describes the communal atmosphere between writers, rappers, and breakers in the formative years of hip hop: "Summing it up, basically going to a jam back then was (about) watching people drink, (break) dance, compare graffiti art in their black books. These jams were thrown by the (hip hop) DJ. ... it was about piecing while a jam was going on."[3] Of course, sharing ideas and styles is not always a peaceful process. Hip hop is very competitive and confrontational; these traits are both resistance to and preparation for a hostile world that denies and denigrates young people of color. Breakdancers often fought other breakdance crews out of jealousy; writers sometimes destroyed murals and rappers and DJ battles could break out in fights. Hip hop remains a never-ending battle for status, prestige, and group adoration, always in formation, always contested, and never fully achieved. Competitions among and cross-fertilization between breaking, graffiti writing, and rap music was fueled by shared local experiences and social position and similarities in approaches to sound, motion, communication, and style among hip hop's Afrodiasporic communities.

As in many African and Afrodiasporic cultural forms, hip hop's prolific self-naming is a form of reinvention and self-definition.[4] Rappers, DJs, graffiti artists, and breakdancers all take on hip hop names and identities that speak to their role, personal characteristics, expertise, or "claim to fame." DJ names often fuse technology with mastery and style: DJ Cut Creator, Jazzy Jeff, Spindarella, Terminator X Assault Technician, Wiz, and Grandmaster Flash. Many rappers have nicknames that suggest street smarts, coolness, power, and supremacy: L.L. Cool J. (Ladies Love Cool James), Kool Moe Dee, Queen Latifah, Dougie Fresh (and the Get Fresh Crew), D-Nice, Hurricane Gloria, Guru, MC Lyte, EPMD (Eric and Parrish Making Dollars), Ice-T, Ice Cube, Kid-N-Play, Boss, Eazy E, King Sun, and Sir Mix-a-Lot. Some names serve as self-mocking tags; others critique society, such as, Too Short, The Fat Boys, S_1W_S (Security of the First World), The Lench Mob, NWA (Niggas with Attitude), and Special Ed. The hip hop identities for such breakdancers as Crazy Legs, Wiggles, Frosty Freeze, Boogaloo Shrimp, and Headspin highlight their status as experts known for special moves. Taking on new names and identities offers "prestige from below" in the face of limited access to legitimate forms of status attainment.

In addition to the centrality of naming, identity, and group affiliation, rappers, DJs, graffiti writers, and breakdancers claim turf and gain local status by developing new styles. As Hebdige's study on punk illustrates, style can be used as a gesture of refusal or as a form of oblique challenge to structures of domination.[5] Hip hop artists use style as a form of identity formation that plays on class distinctions and hierarchies by using commodities to claim the cultural terrain. Clothing and consumption rituals testify to the power of consumption as a means of cultural expression. Hip hop fashion is an especially rich example of this sort of appropriation and critique via style. Exceptionally large "chunk" gold and diamond jewelry (usually fake) mocks, yet affirms, the gold fetish in Western trade; fake Gucci and other designer emblems cup up and patch-stitched to jackets, pants, hats, wallets, and sneakers in custom shops, work as a form of sartorial warfare (especially when fake Gucci-covered b-boys and b-girls brush past Fifth Avenue ladies adorned by the "real thing"). Hip hop's late 1980s fashion rage—the large plastic (alarm?) clock worn around the neck over leisure/sweat suits—suggested a number of contradictory tensions between work, time, and leisure.[6] Early 1990s trends—super-oversized pants and urban warrior outer apparel, "hoodies," "snooties," "tims," and "triple fat" goose down coats, make clear the severity of the urban storms to be weathered and the saturation of disposable goods in the crafting of cultural expressions.[7] As an alternative means of status formation, hip hop style forges local identities for teenagers who understand their limited access to traditional avenues of social status attainment. Fab Five Freddy, an early rapper and graffiti writer, explains the link between style and identity in hip hop and its significance for gaining local status: "You make a new style. That's what life on the street is all about. What's at stake is honor and position on the street. That's what makes it so important, that's what makes it feel so good—that pressure on you to be the best. Or to try to be the best. To develop a new style nobody can deal with."[8] Styles' "nobody can deal with" in graffiti, breaking, and rap music not only boost status, but also they articulate several shared approaches to sound and motion found in the Afrodiaspora. As

Arthur Jafa has pointed out, stylistic continuities between breaking, graffiti style, rapping, and musical construction seem to center around three concepts: *flow, layering,* and *ruptures in line*.[9] In hip hop, visual, physical, musical, and lyrical lines are set in motion, broken abruptly with sharp angular breaks, yet they sustain motion and energy through fluidity and flow. In graffiti, long-winding, sweeping, and curving letters are broken and camouflaged by sudden breaks in line. Sharp, angular, broken letters are written in extreme italics, suggesting forward or backward motion. Letters are double and triple shadowed in such a way as to illustrate energy forces radiating from the center—suggesting circular motion—yet, the scripted words move horizontally.

Breakdancing moves highlight flow, layering, and ruptures in line. Popping and locking are moves in which the joints are snapped abruptly into angular positions. And, yet, these snapping movements take place one joint after the previous one—creating a semiliquid effect that moves the energy toward the fingertip or toe. In fact, two dancers may pass the popping energy force back and forth between each other via finger to finger contact, setting off a new wave. In this pattern, the line is both a series of angular breaks and yet sustains energy and motion through flow. Breakers double each other's moves, like line shadowing or layering in graffiti, intertwine their bodies into elaborate shape, transforming the body into a new entity (like camouflage in graffiti's wild style), and then, one body part at a time reverts to a relaxed state. Abrupt, fractured yet graceful footwork leaves the eye one step behind the motion, creating a time-lapse effect that not only mimics graffiti's use of line shadowing but also creates spatial links between the moves that gives the foot series flow and fluidity.[10]

The music and vocal rapping in rap music also privileges flow, layering, and ruptures in line. Rappers speak of flow explicitly in lyrics, referring to an ability to move easily and powerfully through complex lyrics as well as of the flow in the music.[11] The flow and motion of the initial bass or drum line in rap music is abruptly ruptured by scratching (a process that highlights as it breaks the flow of the base rhythm), or the rhythmic flow is interrupted by other musical passages. Rappers stutter and alternatively race through passages, always moving within the beat or in response to it, often using the music as a partner in rhyme. These verbal moves highlight lyrical flow and points of rupture. Rappers layer meaning by using the same word to signify a variety of actions and objects: they call out to the DJ to "lay down a beat," which is expected to be interrupted, ruptured. DJs layer sounds literally one on top of the other, creating a dialogue between sampled sounds and words.

What is the significance of flow, layering, and rupture as demonstrated on the body and in hip hop's lyrical, musical, and visual works? Interpreting these concepts theoretically, one can argue that they create and sustain rhythmic motion, continuity, and circularity via flow: accumulate, reinforce, and embellish this continuity through layering; and manage threats to these narratives by building in ruptures that highlight the continuity as it momentarily challenges it. These effects at the level of style and aesthetics suggest affirmative ways in which profound social dislocation and rupture can be managed and perhaps contested in the cultural arena. Let us imagine these hip hop principles as a blueprint for social resistance and affirmation; create sustaining narratives, accumulate them, layer, embellish, and transform them. However, be also prepared for rupture, find pleasure in it, in fact, *plan on* social rupture. When these ruptures occur, use them in creative ways that will prepare you for a future in which survival will demand a sudden shift in ground tactics.

Although accumulation, flow, circularity, and planned ruptures exist across a wide range of Afrodiasporic cultural forms, they do not take place outside of capitalist commercial constraints. Hip hop's explicit focus on consumption has frequently been mischaracterized as a movement *into* the commodity market (e.g., hip hop is no longer "authentically" black, if it is for sale). Instead, hip hop's moment(s) of incorporation are a shift in the already existing relationship hip hop has always had to the commodity system. For example, the hip hop DJ produces, amplifies, and revises already recorded sounds, rappers use high-end microphones, and it would be naive to think that breakers, rappers, DJs and writers were never interested in monetary compensation for their work. Graffiti murals, breakdancing moves, and rap lyrics often appropriated and sometimes critiqued verbal and visual elements and physical movements from popular commercial culture, especially television, comic books, and karate movies. If anything, black style through hip hop has contributed to the continued Afro-Americanization of contemporary commercial culture. The contexts for creation in hip hop were never fully outside or in opposition to commodities; they involved struggles over public space and access to commodified materials, equipment, and products of economic viability. It is a common misperception among hip hop artists and cultural critics that during the early days, hip hop was motivated by pleasure rather than profit, as if the two were incompatible. The problem was not that they were uniformly uninterested in profit; rather, many of the earliest practitioners were unaware that they could profit from their pleasure. Once this link was made, hip hop artists began marketing themselves wholeheartedly. Just as graffiti writers hitched a ride on the subways and used its power to distribute their tags, rappers "hijacked" the market for their own purposes, riding the currents that were already out there, not just for wealth but for empowerment, and to assert their own identities. During the late 1970s and early 1980s, the market for hip hop was still based inside New York's black and Hispanic communities. So, although there is an element of truth to this common perception, what is more important about the shift in hip hop's orientation is not its movement from precommodity to commodity but the shift in control over the scope and direction of the profit making process, out of the hands of local black and Hispanic entrepreneurs and into the hands of larger white-owned, multinational businesses.

Hebdige's work on the British punk movement identifies this shift as the moment of incorporation or recuperation by dominant culture and perceives it to be a critical element in the dynamics of the struggle over the meaning(s) of popular expression. "The process of recuperation," Hebdige argues, "takes two characteristic forms ... one of conversion of subcultural signs (dress, music, etc.) into mass produced objects and the 'labelling' and redefinition of deviant behavior by dominant groups—the police, media and judiciary." Hebdige astutely points out, however, that communication in a subordinate cultural form, even prior to the point of recuperation, usually takes place via commodities, "even if the meanings attached to those commodities are purposefully distorted or overthrown." And so, he concludes, "it is very difficult to sustain any absolute distinction between commercial exploitation on the one hand and creativity and originality on the other."[12]

Hebdige's observations regarding the process of incorporation and the tension between commercial exploitation and creativity as articulated in British punk is quite relevant to hip hop. Hip hop has always been articulated via commodities and engaged in the revision of meanings attached to them. Clearly, hip hop signs and meanings are converted, and behaviors are relabeled by dominant institutions. As the relatively brief history of hip hop that follows illustrates, graffiti, rap, and breakdancing were fundamentally transformed as they moved into new relations with dominant cultural institutions.[13] In 1994, rap music is one of the most heavily traded popular commodities in the market, yet it still defies total corporate control over the music, its local use and incorporation at the level of stable or exposed meanings.

Expanding on the formulation advanced by Lipsitz and others [...] in the brief history of hip hop that follows [in *Black Noise: Rap Music and Black Culture in Contemporary America* (1994)] I attempt to demonstrate the necessary tension between the historical specificity of hip hop's emergence and the points of continuity between hip hop and several black forms and practices. It is also an overview of the early stages of hip hop and its relationship to popular cultural symbols and products and its revisions of black cultural practices. This necessarily includes hip hop's direct and sustained contact with dominant cultural institutions in the early to mid-1980s and the ways in which these practices emerge in relation to larger social conditions and relationships, including the systematic marginalization of women cultural producers. In each practice, gender power relations problematized and constrained the role of women hip hop artists and dominant cultural institutions shaped hip hop's transformations. [...]

Notes

1 Grand Master Flash and the Furious Five, "The Message" (Sugar Hill Records, 1982).

2 Rose interviews with all artists named except Futura, whose printing trade school experience was cited in Steve Hager, *Hip Hop: The Illustrated History of Breakdancing, Rap Music, and Graffiti* (New York: St. Martin's Press, 1984).

3 Rose interview with Crazy Legs, 6 November, 1991. *Piecing* means drawing a mural or masterpiece.

4 See Henry Louis Gates, Jr., *The Signifying Monkey: A Theory of African-American Literary Criticism* (New York: Oxford University Press, 1988), pp. 55, 87. Gates's suggestion that naming be "drawn upon as a metaphor for black intertextuality" is especially useful in hip hop, where naming and intertextuality are critical strategies for creative production.

5 Dick Hebdige, *Subculture: The Meaning of Style* (London: Routledge, 1979), see, especially pp. 17–19, 84–89.

6 For an interesting discussion of time, the clock, and nationalism in hip hop, see Jeffrey L. Decker, "The State of Rap: Time and Place in Hip Hop Nationalism," *Social Text*, no. 34, 53–84, 1993.

7 *Hoodies* are hooded jackets or shirts, *snooties* are skull caps, and *tims* are short for Timberland brand boots.

8 Cited in Nelson George et al., eds., *Fresh: Hip Hop Don't Stop* (New York: Random House, 1985), 111.

9 Although I had isolated some general points of aesthetic continuity between hip hop's forms, I did not identify these three crucial organizing terms. I am grateful to Arthur Jafa, black filmmaker, artist, and cultural critic, who shared and discussed the logic of these defining characteristics with me in conversation. He is not, of course, responsible for any inadequacies in my use of them here.

10 For a brilliant example of these moves among recent hip hop dances, see "Reckin' Shop in Brooklyn," directed by Diane Martel (Epoch Films, 1992). Thanks to A. J. for bringing this documentary film to my attention.

11 Some examples of explicit attention to flow are exhibited in Queen Latifah's *Ladies First:* "Some think that we can't flow, stereotypes they got to go"; Big Daddy Kane's *Raw:* "Intro I start to go, my rhymes will flow so"; in Digital Underground's *Sons of the P (Son's of the Flow):* "Release your mind and let your instincts flow, release your mind and let the funk flow."

12 Hebdige, *Subculture*, pp. 94–95.

13 Ibid. Published in 1979, *Subculture* concludes at the point of dominant British culture's initial attempts at incorporating punk. [...]

26 Writing Improvisation into Modernism

Rob Wallace

Writer, musician, and teacher Rob Wallace holds a PhD in English Literature from the University of California, Santa Barbara. His research focuses on poetry, improvisation, popular and "world" musics, and the intersections between literature and music. Along with teaching literature, music, and writing, Wallace is an active percussionist in a number of genres ranging from Hindustani classical music to free improvisation. He has performed and recorded with a wide variety of musicians, and his recordings can be found on the pfMENTUM and Ambiances Magnétiques record labels. In the following excerpt, from his 2010 book *Improvisation and the Making of American Literary Modernism,* he introduces and elucidates a complex discourse on the relationship of improvisation to Western culture's most consecrated and authoritative medium, the written word. Are a writer's improvisational skills only apparent when they "perform" in public readings, or can we apprehend and appreciate them on the printed page?

Key words: jazz; poetry; modernism

[...]

Improvisations

To discuss improvisation in a literary context we must define what it is, what it involves, and what is at stake when improvising. To answer these questions we have to look at the relationship between music, writing, orality, and performance. I should emphasize that my own definitions, like my subject matter, must be provisional. While I do argue that all of the poets under discussion here are engaged in similar kinds of improvisation, I also want to assert that each artist and each creative act implies a situational definition of improvisation; each kind of improvisation, while sharing certain features, will be different because each instance of the creative process is itself bound by time—the clock cannot be turned backwards. From moment to moment things change, and improvisation implies a heightened attention to this fact.

That being said, improvisation is a notoriously difficult word to accurately define.[1] One of the most recent significant studies of jazz improvisation, ethnomusicologist Paul Berliner's *Thinking in Jazz: The Infinite Art of Improvisation,* includes almost 900 pages of musical examples and text in an attempt to explain what improvisation consists of. By the end, Berliner settles on an essentially two-part definition: 1) Jazz (and by extension, improvisation) is a way of life, and 2) Improvisation is like speaking a language. He states:

It is not surprising, therefore, that improvisers use metaphors of language in discussing their art form. The same complex mix of elements and processes coexists for improvisers as for skilled language practitioners; the learning, the absorption, and utilization of linguistic conventions conspire in the mind of the writer or speaker—or, in the case of the jazz improvisation, the player—to create a living work.[2]

While the "music-as-language"/"musician-as-speaker-and-writer" metaphors have their limits, the way in which jazz and language so conveniently and frequently mix in the minds of musicians and commentators is part of the origin of my research into the connections between improvisation and literary modernism. As I will detail later, the linguistic features which writers both use and transgress, as well as the cognitive space they often attempt to represent, are strikingly analogous to improvisational practice precisely because they are examples of the same kinds of work that happens during an improvisation. Just how far the analogy can be pushed is not only a matter for critical insight, but a procedure that the poets themselves were often engaged in.

Improvisation, as I use it, is best understood in relation to a constellation of terms: spontaneity, metaphor (in the Greek sense of "carrying over")—hence, metamorphosis— risk-taking, recreating, theme and variation, the ability to change within a structure of rules which is itself constantly changing; bricolage.[3] In its most *basic* form, improvisation involves the reshuffling, revising, and recreation of information, using pre-existing materials to make something new. Improvisation is *not*, as it is sometimes perceived, completely free, or "doing whatever you feel like," although it strives for new and less restricted avenues of expression than the current set of rules can accommodate—a process often involving intuitive and even rash decisions. It requires skill and training, it can be learned, and it can fail horribly, precisely *because* there are tacit rules within the community of improvisers.

Since the structures and rules within which improvisation is enacted are *themselves* constantly changing, the best improvisers are often those who can break the rules in a way that makes everyone else want to follow them into new territory. In this way, even in the collective improvisation of a jazz group, the individual voice always remains important, as does the relationship between an improviser and an audience (a feature further emphasized by the "conversation" metaphor which Berliner and other scholars have focused on). Improvisation is action that occurs as the result of planning and memorization but does not depend on these plans, and it demands some sort of novelty and uniqueness every time. It has aesthetic and practical advantages and disadvantages: it can surprise but can also alienate; it can "work" in the sense that it allows the improviser to accomplish a given task, or it can fail and be a bad improvisation.

While a particular instance of improvisation can be judged aesthetically as bad or good, depending on the rules governing the improvisational situation, improvisation as a practice is not inherently "good" or "bad." Yet it has acquired variously pejorative or positive connotations depending on who is defining it. One of the most interesting perspectives on improvisation from a literary perspective is Stephen Greenblatt's "Improvisation and Power." Interestingly, Greenblatt's example of improvisation involves a role reversal regarding the usual agents of "negative" improvisation. The history of American race-relations has typically resulted in labeling improvisation as a characteristic of primitive, non-cerebral, animalistic behavior, due to the fact that the most prevalent American improvisers were black jazz musicians. Greenblatt, on the other hand, focusing on Iago's use of improvisational techniques in *Othello,* connects improvisation with the figure of the con man, the liar, and implies that improvisation served as the principal tool of European imperialism.[4]

This connection between improvisation and trickery is also a deeply American archetype, summed up best by P. T. Barnum's maxim, "there's a sucker born every minute." The ability to outwit someone without their knowing you're outwitting them requires skillful improvisation. But there is another variation to the con-man trickster figure in American culture, ranging from various Native American incarnations of Coyote to the West-African-derived "signifyin(g) monkey."[5] The trickster in African-American culture, while retaining the ambiguous nature of potential thief or con-artist, also embodies a survival technique in the face of oppression. Thus Ralph Ellison would connect the con-artist with the storyteller in his preface to *Invisible Man:*

> I knew that I was composing a work of fiction, a work of literary art and one that would allow me to take advantage of the novel's capacity for telling the truth while actually telling a "lie," which is the Afro-American folk term for an improvised story. Having worked in barbershops where that form of oral art flourished, I knew that I could draw upon the rich culture of the folk tale as well as that of the novel, and that being uncertain of my skill I would have to improvise upon my materials in the manner of a jazz musician.[6]

This concept of a trickster storyteller, capable of jiving his or her audience while at the same time delivering some kind of moral lesson underlies one version of "positive" improvisation. Such a trickster is tricky because life has been unfair, and the only way in which to deal with fate is to test one's luck by audaciously facing it down.[7]

Another version of the potential ethical benefits of improvisation has been developed recently in the work of critical improvisation studies scholars. Daniel Fischlin and Ajay Heble, for example, point out that while many kinds of improvisation are not necessarily radical or anti-hegemonic, "we could argue there to be an identifiable and radical form of improvisational practices in which concepts of alternative community formation, social activism, rehistoricization of minority cultures, and critical modes of resistance and dialogue are in evidence and worthy of the kind of attention they get in this book."[8]

The book referred to here, riffing on a phrase by jazz luminary Sun Ra, is titled *The Other Side of Nowhere: Jazz, Improvisation, and Communities in Dialogue.* This book represents both a continuation of an older tradition privileging improvisation as an ethical practice as well as a revision of the tradition. Whereas writers in the line of Ralph Ellison, Albert Murray, Stanley Crouch, and others have mapped out important areas of improvisational activity in American culture and how that activity has helped oppressed peoples survive, the newer generation of critical improvisation scholars in general are even more open to the potential benefits of improvisational practice, even as they view cultural practice in general from a cautious viewpoint informed by post-structuralism, ethnic studies, gender and sexuality studies, and leftist political theory.[9]

Among Fischlin and Heble's claims for the potential ethical and political use of improvisation are the notions that "improvisation, in some profound sense, intensifies humanity ... by intensifying acts of communication, by demanding that the choices that go into building communities be confronted" and that "improvised music making offers a resonant model for the marriage of theory and practice."[10]

The utopian themes developed here are analogous to the utopian goals dispersed throughout modernism, including the dreams of revising American idealism into

American reality. In this way jazz and improvisation become important to a specifically American context. Whether or not improvisation can actually accomplish the laudable goals of community building, stimulating critical practice and social transformation, or otherwise "intensifying humanity" is open for debate, and the authors discussed in [my] book [*Improvisation and the Making of American Literary Modernism*] display a variety of attitudes towards the potential ethical dimensions of improvisation. As in W. H. Auden's ambivalent maxim that "poetry makes nothing happen," the political and social effects of artistic improvisation are hard to detect, depending on what's being looked for. But generally speaking, as should be evident in this excursus on the problems of defining improvisation, to improvise is an act not limited to the realm of artistic production, and therefore it can be viewed, as theorist and improviser George Lewis has stated, as "an everyday practice."[11]

This blossoming out of improvisation as a totalizing process, an activity that can encompass not only the nightclub stage but a walk in the park or the negotiations between lovers could possibly lead us to a critical dead end. That is, if *everything* involves improvisation, what is particularly useful about talking about improvisation in the arts?[12] Haven't we lost the specificity of its utility? I think that we instead begin to see that improvisation, and what we will—again, provisionally—call, its opposite, composition, are two sides of a continuous spectrum of possibilities in any action in time.[13] The implications of this are that some amount of composition and some amount of improvisation occur in most activities, including writing, reading, and thinking. Yet for the purposes of this study, the specificity and importance of improvisation as a practice lies—beyond its usefulness in a given day-to-day situation—in the fact that it still maintains a deep historical connection to cultures of opposition.

As Fischlin and Heble recount, some of the earliest dictionary definitions of improvisation link the word to the histories of oppression that it remains associated with to this day:

> one of the earliest recorded uses of the word "improvisation" in English in 1811 ... associates it with "the flexibility of Italian and Spanish languages ... [which] renders these countries distinguished for the talent of improvisation" ... A slightly earlier use of the term "improvisator" (for improviser) occurs in 1795 and explicitly links extemporaneous verbal dexterity with music: "The Italian improvisator never attempts a ballad without striking his mandolino" ... Curiously, these early usages of improvisation cognates enact their own ethnic othering in which the consistent association between improvisatory discourse and Latin/Mediterranean cultures are implicitly opposed to Anglo-Saxon culture.[14]

If Fischlin and Heble here seem to be reading a dastardly design into what appear to be innocuous statements about Italian and Spanish improvising poets (they also take aim at Greenblatt's article discussed above) then consider that they are reading these definitions against the wider context of improvisation. Set against the European Enlightenment ideals of logic, structure, and reason, the possible benefits of improvisation seem to ring hollow. As Philip Pastras recounts in his survey of improvisation, the Southern European *improvissatore* was often viewed skeptically, like a negative version of the con-man. The improviser's skill with words and music was merely a mask for his deviousness and transient nature.[15]

What started as a cautious commentary on the spontaneous nature of Southern European poet-singers turned into at best a dismissal of African-American cultural forms, and at worst, outright racism as improvisation became connected with jazz. Jazz historiography reveals many striking examples of these two poles of opinion. For example, a 1917 *New York Sun* article by a commentator named Walter Kingsley states that "The highly gifted jazz artist can get away with five beats where there were but two before. Of course, beside the thirty-seconds scored for the tympani in some of the modern Russian music, this doesn't seem so intricate … "[16] Note how Kingsley opines that jazz music doesn't sound complicated compared to "modern Russian music," by which he most likely means Stravinsky's *Le Sacre Du Printemps,* famous for its rhythmic complexity (ironically, Stravinsky was significantly inspired by jazz). A 1918 editorial in *The New Orleans Times Picayune*—the paper of record from the city often cited as the birthplace of jazz—proclaims:

> Prominently, in the basement hall of rhythm, is found rag-time, and of those most devoted to the cult of the displaced accent there has developed a brotherhood of those who, devoid of harmonic and even of melodic instinct, love to fairly wallow in noise. On certain natures, sound loud and meaningless has an exciting, almost intoxicating effect, like crude colors and strong perfumes, the sight of flesh or the sadic pleasure in blood.[17]

Jazz on the one hand represents an analogous, if not as "intricate" a version of modern Western Art Music, and on the other hand, jazz is a sexualized expression of pure rhythm. The racial connotations here connect to a long history of African-American stereotyping: blacks as unsophisticated, instinctual, crude, violent, and sexual. While *jazz* might have become more disconnected from such early critiques, these two poles of expression—that jazz is musical (as opposed to noise), but not as sophisticated as European art music, or that it is imbued with negative sexual and violent impulses—are essentially where African-American musical expression still stands today in relation to Euro-American music, as contemporary debates surrounding hip-hop demonstrate.[18]

Afrological and Eurological Improvisations

Despite the racist attitudes towards jazz and other forms of African-American-derived improvisational practice, jazz has had a widespread impact and influence on American and global culture. As the poets [discussed in my book, *Improvisation and the Making of American Literary Modernism*] themselves demonstrate, black cultural forms were too ubiquitous to ignore and often provided very attractive alternatives to Anglo-European aesthetics. Yet the widespread racist connotations of *improvisation,* via its connection to jazz, have led to a lingering and sometimes subconscious negative view of the word improvisation itself. Composer, theorist, and improvising trombonist George Lewis has traced the development of two different traditions in American musical practice, which he dubs "Afrological" and "Eurological."[19]

Each of these traditions represents important aesthetic achievements, and Lewis is careful not to racially essentialize: "My constructions make no attempt," he says, "to delineate ethnicity or race, although they are designed to ensure that the reality of the ethnic or racial component of a historically emergent sociomusical group must be faced squarely and honestly."[20] In other words, as Lewis states, "African-American music, like any music, can be performed by a person of any 'race' without losing its character as historically Afrological."[21] Yet what Lewis shows in his account of these two traditions is that Eurological musicians and composers have often tried to discount or disavow the validity—and in some cases their direct relationships to—Afrological improvisation and to improvisation as a term. Instead of defining their musical practices as "improvisation," Eurological composers, most notably John Cage, used words like "experimental," "indeterminacy," "aleatory," or "chance." Lewis quotes fellow composer and improviser Anthony Braxton, who presents the argument in stronger terms: "Both aleatory and indeterminism are words which have been coined ... to bypass the word improvisation and as such the influence of non-white sensibility [on American music]."[22]

Despite Cage's claims regarding the relationship between his work and Zen, the *I Ching,* and other "Eastern" influences, Lewis asserts that the historical predominance of jazz is directly related to Cage's own procedures of indeterminacy. Lewis points out that bebop in particular, a major turning point in jazz history (and a significant influence on jazz in literature) was created several years prior to Cage's more radical techniques.[23] Lewis is not suggesting that jazz is the sole influence on Cage, but he is arguing that Cage's caginess regarding improvisational techniques originating in African-American cultural forms is indicative of a wider trend of discounting black improvisation and privileging so-called avant-garde or experimental practices, as if those practices were created in a vacuum of Eurological trial-and-error.

The problem that Lewis and other critics have located then, is not that there are different kinds of improvisation or different trends in musical practice, some of which are more associated with white culture and some more with black culture; the problem is that those very separations are set up from the beginning to be antagonistic towards one another because of the longer histories of racism related to improvisation. This also creates, as Lewis and other black composers have noted, a double-bind for African-American musicians who are interested in creating Eurological music: they are simultaneously viewed with suspicion by their black jazz peers and the white-dominated world of "composed" music. This dilemma reminds us of a central misunderstanding about improvisation: that it contains no elements of composition, forethought, or logic. It also overshadows the historical connections between black composers and jazz; most notably Scott Joplin.

It must be noted that neither Braxton nor Lewis is criticizing Cage's *music* per se; they are both extremely catholic composers and musicians.[24] They are merely calling for a more historically accurate account of the "experimental" music of the twentieth-century, with the recognition that many "experimental" and "avant-garde" concepts are matched by, if not synonymous with, developments in music that get denied high art status; i.e., jazz. The point is that *there is no pure improvisation any more than there is pure composition,* and furthermore that the "experimental" practices of Eurological composers are more closely related to *improvisation* than their own terminology would suggest.

John Cage's ambivalent relationship to black music echoes the same kinds of resistance to black aesthetic forms that we find throughout (white) literary modernism. On the one hand, white artists saw the uniqueness of black art, but because of their own racist attitudes, imbibed through centuries of structural prejudice, they remained hesitant to fully acknowledge the importance, much less the influence of black culture on their own thinking. Cage's comments below provide a relevant example:

> Methods of writing percussion music have as their goal the rhythmic structure of a composition. As soon as these methods are crystallized into one of several widely accepted methods, the means will exist for group improvisations of unwritten but culturally important music. This has already taken place in Oriental cultures and in hot jazz.[25]

This passage comes from a text written in 1937 called "The Future of Music: Credo." Here we can see the tension of Cage's attitudes towards improvisation: not only does he cite the importance of percussion—the instrument family responsible for some of the most important developments in jazz, via the invention of the drumset—he also acknowledges that "culturally important" music already exists, in the form of "group improvisations" in "Oriental" and "hot jazz" styles. Cage had what he was looking (and listening) for right in front of him but refused to fully credit the direct influence of these improvisational musics on his *own* work.

Is this being unfair to Cage? Can't an artist, after all, acknowledge the similarities of their work to what has come before without relinquishing their own creative talent? And is it inaccurate in the long run to call Cage's wide body of work "improvisational"? I think what is at stake here is not the degree to which Cage's music is improvisational—and I would argue that much of it is—but rather the degree to which his discourse about improvisation, connected as it inevitably is to issues of race, falls into a long tradition of ambivalence and distrust of African-American-derived improvisational music. Like Pound, Stein, and Stevens, Cage presents a frustrating but common example of the white artist who cannot fully admit the connections between their work and African-American cultural forms. Explicating Cage and his compositions/improvisations is beyond the scope of [my work here]. But within the work of the poets under analysis I hope to more clearly illuminate the connections between their artistic procedures and the contemporaneous African-American culture.

Braxton and Lewis's argument has much wider implications. Even though they are specifically referring to events related to post-1950 American music, a similar terminological smokescreen often serves to disconnect the various modernist avant-garde movements from the underlying African and African-American cultural forms that have significantly influenced them. As Jed Rasula has suggested in his essay "Jazz as Decal for the European Avant-Garde," the European wing of the various avant-garde movements were often more amenable than their American counterparts to embracing jazz.[26] But even when the artists themselves fessed up to their sometimes admittedly primitivistic jazz fetish, the critical discourse surrounding the avant-garde—especially in literature—has tended to ignore the significance of jazz on modernism.

Rasula rightly critiques Alfred Appel's 2002 book *Jazz Modernism: From Ellington and Armstrong to Matisse and Joyce* in its discounting of "the extent to which something called 'jazz' was absorbed into the modernist avant-garde."[27]

Similarly, Marjorie Perloff's lucid account of new kinds of modernist experimentation, *The Poetics of Indeterminacy,* nevertheless adopts the Cagian terminology in its title, and thereby deflects the issue of improvisation.[28] Ironically, in her chapter on Pound, Perloff cites a review by W. B. Yeats of Pound's *Cantos* that uses the word "improvisatore" to chastise Pound's writing.[29] Perloff rightly states that, Yeats's criticism notwithstanding: "Interruptions and twists, 'unbridged transitions,' and 'unexplained ejaculations,' the poetic act as 'brilliant improvisa[tion]'—these are accepted as a matter of course by contemporary poets and their readers."[30]

Is improvisation a better fit than indeterminacy? I'm not arguing here that terms like indeterminacy, aleatory, automatic, or even avant-garde itself *should* be replaced by improvisation, any more than I would say that we should take away Cage's term indeterminacy when he uses it to describe his own work. I am arguing, however, that improvisation should become more commonplace in the list of words that comprise the critical catalogue of modernist techniques. I am curious as to why a link between Dada,

Surrealism, and many other isms—even futurism, with its focus on novelty and newness, and as I argue later, Imagism and Vorticism—could not be said to be improvisation, as much as indeterminacy.

The heart of the matter is that racism, as well as a related belief that improvisation connotes a lack of sophistication or planning, made the use of the term improvisation less desirable to describe Anglo- and Euro-American artistic procedures which are themselves examples of improvisation: from automatic writing, oral poetic performance, early Dada "happenings" in the Cabaret Voltaire, or the writing of [some modernist] poets [...] to cite a few examples. At issue, then, is something beyond the evidence of the "influence" of improvisation. While there are clear connections between white and black cultural production, as critics like Ann Douglas have begun to more fully account for, the larger issue for this study is the relevance of improvisation as a concept in discussions of modernism. While jazz and African-American cultural forms are important avatars of improvisation, the word and the technique in a larger sense demand a more serious evaluation.

Jazz itself, as a word, still retains too many of the negative stereotypes and levity associated with its early days. This is one reason why many jazz musicians are uncomfortable labeling their music as "jazz" in the first place. As drummer Max Roach recounted in 1972: "The term 'jazz' has come to mean the abuse and exploitation of black musicians; it has come to mean cultural prejudice and condescension. It has come to mean all of these things, and that is why I am presently writing a book, *I Hate Jazz*. It's not my name and it means my oppression as a man and musician."[31]

Improvisation unfortunately retains these same kinds of connections—look no farther than headlines about the wars in Iraq and Afghanistan for descriptions of "Improvised Explosive Devices"—and thus lacks the critical and cultural value that other terms have warranted. In the course of [my work] I hope to prove the relevance of improvisation per se—not only Afrological-derived improvisation—and encourage a re-evaluation of the term's validity to critical discourse in modernist studies.

The negative connotations of improvisation aside, another obstacle in viewing improvisation as a *literary technique* and thus using it as a critical term, is the fact that improvisation is thought of primarily as a performance practice. Improvisation, in other words, seems distant from the seemingly fixed domain of writing, even in our post-Derridean world. I will now turn to this issue, and map out my procedures for reading improvisation in modernist writing.

Literary Improvisation, Jazz, and Modernism

Is it possible to improvise on paper, to use improvisation in writing? We can see the paradox of speaking of a piece of writing as improvised if we are focused on a performance-based model of improvisation. If a performance is fixed, how can it be an improvisation? Given the nature of writing, and the process of revision, editing, revision, editing, printing/publishing, reprinting, and so on, we *could* say that the entire writing process is an extended improvisation, where a set of materials (words, a poem, a novel, etc.) is developed over time and achieves a final form (i.e., the published work—but this itself takes multiple and mutable forms). Such is also the case for a jazz improvisation, which might actually begin in conception as a musician learns a tune by practicing at home, rehearsing with musicians, and then performing it in public. Of course the major difference here is the ephemeral nature of the "final" jazz improvisation; unlike a book, unless it is recorded there is no documentation of a performance.

Yet even recordings of jazz music are less fixed than one might expect; both in terms of the improvised nature of the music itself, but also in the technical manipulation used to alter the "original" (which was already a mutable, improvised "product") through over-dubbing, remastering, etc. Paradoxically, such manipulations can cause jazz to become reified in a manner similar to other "fixed" artwork. Nevertheless, the dynamic between live performance, recordings of live performance, studio trickery, and further revisions of those recordings and trickery (in the form of reissues of "jazz classics") forms a constantly changing stream of performances within the capitalist commodification of the music.[32]

It is this ephemeral nature, the notion that what you are hearing has never happened before and will never happen again, that makes musical improvisation particularly captivating for musician and listener. Most of the writers that I focus on—Ezra Pound, Langston Hughes, Gertrude Stein—were deeply invested in the aural and performance aspect of literature, and this is one way in which we can see the influence of improvisational practice in their work. The concept of "jazz poetry" via the Beats is by now a familiar concept, to the point where the poet accompanied by jazz combo is a nostalgic footnote to the counterculture of the 1950s.

The poet performing his or her work with musical accompaniment seems to be the most obvious example of an interaction between text and improvisation. Even if the text is fixed, a performance of a given piece will change, just as classical music or other genres of composition change, from performance to performance. This kind of aural improvisation can be found in the careers of Pound and Hughes in particular, who both read to musical accompaniment—in Pound's case, his own amateur drumming—and participated in various other recorded and live performance situations: radio plays, operas, etc. In fact, it is a focus on the *aural* nature of language that plays a significant part in my reading of Hughes, Pound, and Stein's work as improvisational. But this still doesn't get us past the issue of the poem on the printed page. How are these texts improvisational?

Let me step back for a moment and reassert a point that bears continued emphasis: an improvisation can never be "pure" anymore than a fixed composition can be "pure." There are structured and less-structured varieties of improvisation. In his study of literary improvisation Philip Pastras details the historical precedents for modernist improvised writing. Among these earlier examples, he lists "the Gothic romance, the idea of poetry as fantasia, the emphasis on spontaneity, [and] the incantational enumeration of the catalogue."[33] He states that "The kinds of writing that can be described as improvisation are many and varied: from the Homeric poems (in fact, all oral epic traditions) to Samuel Johnson's *Rambler* essays, to Henry James's *The Turn of the Screw*, to surrealist automatism—the list is long and presents a variety of genres, authors, languages and historical periods."[34] In order to explain how these disparate examples of writing can be considered improvisatory, Pastras develops a taxonomy of literary improvisation, encompassing three distinct but related kinds of improvisation:

> (1) as a *mode* of composition, when the writing becomes spontaneous on its own, without regard to the intentions or to the working habits of the writer (in other words, what most writers and critics call "inspiration"); (2) as a *method of* composition, when an author improvises in order to create the raw material out of which he refines his poems or stories; (3) as a *discipline* when a writer trains himself to improvise with such skill that he can give form to an emotion as he feels it, and give shape to an impulse as it arises.[35]

Pastras goes on to assert that "The arts of drama and music certainly require the discipline of improvisation, even if the actors or musicians are performing 'set' pieces: performance allows no room for revision, and improvisation is a means of training an artist's concentration."[36]

For Pastras, the "discipline" of improvisation is most important, and he therefore focuses primarily on two poets who explicitly state that they are improvising in this manner: William Carlos Williams and Yannis Ritsos.[37] But Pastras also points out that it is often hard to determine whether or not a work is *intentionally* improvised, creating an interesting relationship between a reader's perception and a writer's technique: "the difference between improvisation as method and as discipline has more to do with the intentions of the writer than with the extent of his revisions."[38] For example, Pastras argues that Byron was interested in "creating the *effect* of improvisation" in a poem like *Don Juan* and hence he is using improvisation as *method,* rather than *discipline.*[39] On the other hand, Samuel Johnson's *Rambler* essays do not appear to be improvised, even though they were composed under the *discipline* of improvisation—in other words, the essays' highly-polished form belies their quick composition.[40]

Both of these situations have analogies in jazz improvisation. In the former case, a musician can construct a solo, for example, based on the harmonic, rhythmic, and melodic rules of a given structure (i.e., a popular song on which the musician will improvise). This preparation can be accomplished in the practice room, over a series of hours, days, weeks, or years, until the ultimate performance of this material becomes second nature to the musician, and hence paradoxically feels spontaneous. The latter case is a related phenomenon, facilitated by a highly sophisticated ability to improvise also due to long hours of practice. Many jazz improvisers—John Coltrane and Keith Jarrett, for example—have been noted for their remarkable ability to "spontaneously compose" highly coherent, logical musical statements of great length. Both of the above situations complicate the conventional view of a "pure improvisation." A solo performance in jazz, then, is a balance between spontaneity and planning, based on the particular improviser's technical skill on their instrument and previous discipline in learning their craft.

Because of the ambiguity in the "planned" vs. "unplanned" structure of improvisation, Pastras's framework implies that even if an author does not *intend* to make an improvisational work, from the viewpoint of the reader we can describe a given work as improvised in the following ways, slightly modifying Pastras's taxonomy:

1. By investigating the author's compositional technique and determining whether or not it is improvisational; in other words, showing that the work was done in one sitting, in a rush of inspiration—the *discipline* of improvisation—*regardless of how structured or unstructured it appears.* Often the most spontaneous improvisations constitute sophisticated structures.
2. By locating and naming the *improvisational effects* in a text—the *method* of improvisation, even if the author doesn't name it as such—and again, this might mean interpreting terms like "indeterminacy," "aleatory," "imagistic," or other such tags as analogues to improvisation. Here we might define various formal features such as: fragments; free-verse poetic structures which expand and contract to fit an author's themes; excessive wordplay and attention to the aural dimensions of language (thereby bringing the language closer to the realm of music).
3. By developing a theory of improvisation—close to what Pastras calls a "mode"— exhibiting the metaphysical and philosophical ideas inherent in improvisation itself,

and by tracing this theory within a given text. I believe this is what Pastras means when he states, "Because a sense of time is so crucial to even a simple dictionary-definition of improvisation, the subject itself moves with astonishing rapidity into the swamps of the metaphysical, aesthetic and ontological speculation."[41]

Rather than getting "swamped" by the idea of time, however, modernist writing often attempts to express what it feels like to be in time. Existing in time, and expressing what it feels like to be in time, is perhaps what makes improvisation such a powerful aesthetic technique as well as a potentially useful life-practice. As Porter Abbott has noted of the "wisdom" which we can possibly extract from "reader-resistant" modernist texts, improvisation also implies an openness to "knowing what it feels like not to know."[42] [...]

[...] All of the authors discussed use some amount of improvisational *discipline:* Pound with his typewriter carriage banging away as an odd prefiguration of Kerouac, Hughes writing blues and jazz-influenced verse in the moment, Stein transcribing her thoughts onto the blank page, and Stevens composing poems to the rhythms of his walking and breathing. The work of all of these poets also exhibits the *method* of improvisation: in Pound and Hughes, for example, we find a system of recombinant fragments that provides the source material for longer "open works."

This latter phrase, coined by Umberto Eco, is another analogue for improvisation. Significantly, Eco discusses jazz and improvisation sympathetically, as in the following passage where he ponders the relevance of improvisation as a narrative device in television montage: "This should in itself be enough to make us reconsider certain aesthetic concepts, or at least to lend them greater flexibility, in particular those concerning the productive process and the personality of the author, the distinction between process and result, and the relationship between a finished work and its antecedents (or, more broadly, what led to it)."[43]

In his articulation of improvisation, Eco outlines the shift in focus that a discussion of improvisation requires; even as I analyze given works by each poet, what might be more important than the works themselves is the *process* in which the works take part. This requires, therefore, an attention to my third perspective outlined above, the development of a theory of improvisation that can be seen both in a given artist's work and in the life of that artist. [...] I negotiate the complex relationships between improvisation and its origins in African-American culture on my group of poets, while also connecting their work to other improvisational arenas.

[...]

Notes

1 I use jazz definitions and analogies from the jazz world not only because they are relevant to my writers, but also because jazz theory/criticism is one of the main and only places where improvisation has been theorized. Other disciplines with some degree of theorization of improvisation are drama and dance. Thanks to Daniel Fischlin for reminding me of these issues.

2 *Thinking in Jazz*, 492. For another view of the linguistic connections between jazz improvisation and narrative/speech, see a relatively recent work on jazz improvisation by ethnomusicologist Ingrid Monson entitled, not coincidentally, *Saying Something: Jazz Improvisation and Interaction* (Chicago: University of Chicago Press, 1996).

3 Thanks to Dick Hebdige for informing me of the Greek sense of "metaphor."

4 Stephen Greenblatt, "Improvisation and Power," in *Literature and Society*, ed. Edward Said (Baltimore: Johns Hopkins University Press, 1980), 57–99. Greenblatt's definition of improvisation is instructive:

I shall call that mode improvisation, by which I mean the ability to both capitalize on the unforeseen and transform given materials into one's own scenario. The 'spur of the moment' quality of improvisation is not as critical here as the opportunistic grasp of that which seems fixed and established. Indeed, as Castiglione and others in the Renaissance well understood, the impromptu character of an improvisation is itself often a calculated mask, the product of careful preparation. What is essential is the Europeans' ability again and again to insinuate themselves into the preexisting political, religious, even psychic, structures of the natives and to turn those structures to their advantage. (60)

5 See Henry Louis Gates Jr., *The Signifyin(g) Monkey: A Theory of African-American Literary Criticism* (Oxford: Oxford University Press, 1988).

6 "Preface," *Invisible Man*, xxii-xxiii.

7 For an elaboration of this theme, see Jackson Lears, *Something for Nothing: Luck in America*.

8 Daniel Fischlin and Ajay Heble, eds., *The Other Side of Nowhere: Jazz, Improvisation, and Communities in Dialogue* (Middletown, CT: Wesleyan University Press, 2004).

9 A refreshing mix of both these traditions can be found in the two monumental volumes co-edited by Robert G. O'Meally, *The Jazz Cadence of American Culture* and *Uptown Conversation: The New Jazz Studies*.

10 *The Other Side of Nowhere*, 3, 25.

11 Lewis noted this in conversation during his lecture, "Living with Creative Machines." The text of some of this lecture has been printed as "Living with Creative Machines: An Improviser Reflects," in *Afrogeeks: Beyond the Digital Divide*, Anna Everett and Amber J. Wallace, eds. (Santa Barbara: Center for Black Studies Research, University of California, Santa Barbara, 2007), 83–99.

12 Vijay Iyer noted this in a discussion with DJ Spooky from the 2008 Guelph Jazz Festival and Colloquium; "Improvising Digital Cultures," (panel discussion, University of Guelph, Guelph, ON, September 3, 2008). Charles O. Hartman reminds us of the difficulties of clearly discussing the "improvisational" aspects of a piece of writing in *Jazz Text: Voice and Improvisation in Poetry, Jazz, and Song* (Princeton: Princeton University Press, 1991), 38.

13 "Composition" is paradoxically used by Jacques Attali to denote a liberatory music based in improvisation. See chapter five of *Noise: The Political Economy of Music*. Derek Bailey comments on the difficulties of defining the differences between composition vs. improvisation; see *Improvisation*, 140. One of Bailey's sometime collaborators, drummer Eddie Prévost, argues that there must be some difference worth talking about between the two forms, however, indicating an ethical dimension to the improviser's ability to adapt. See his book *No Sound is Innocent* (Matching Tye, near Harlow, England: Copula, 1995). Thanks to Sydney Levy, Jocelyn Holland, and the participants of their course "Improvisation: Baroque to Digital" for helping to clarify these ideas on the continuum between improvisation and composition.

14 *The Other Side of Nowhere*, 16. For two other interesting explications of various definitions of improvisation, see Philip Pastras's chapter entitled "Definitions" (*A Clear Field*, 1–34) and Dick Hebdige's "Even unto Death: Improvisation, Edging and Enframement."

15 Pastras, *A Clear Field*, 9.

16 Walser, *Keeping Time*, 7. Both this and the following quotation are from Robert Walser's incredible anthology of primary source documents spanning the whole range of jazz history, *Keeping Time: Readings in Jazz History*.

17 Ibid., 8.

18 For views on hip hop's reception see Tricia Rose's *Black Noise: Rap Music and Black Culture in America* (Middletown, CT: Wesleyan University Press, 1994). Ironically, now that jazz is somewhat institutionalized in the halls of cultural power—most notably, Jazz at Lincoln Center, directed by Wynton Marsalis—more recent black improvised music like hip hop continues to undergo the same kinds of primitivizing, racist treatment that jazz has historically encountered. Even more ironically, some of the condemnation of hip hop comes from within the jazz community itself, where an on-going identity crisis about what kinds of sounds and cultural aesthetics should truly define jazz still rages.

19 Lewis, "Improvisation after 1950."

20 Ibid., 133.

21 Ibid.

22 Ibid., 139.

23 Ibid.
24 In his remarks at the 2007 Guelph Jazz Festival Colloquium, Braxton expressed his admirable eclecticism, noting of his teaching schedule that "Next semester I have a class: Karlheinz Stockhausen and Sun Ra. And this semester I have a class: Max Roach, Lennie Tristano and Miles Davis. I am trying to combine masters. I am working on my Hildegard von Bingen [and] Wagner class." This lecture is available online as both a transcript and streaming video; see Anthony Braxton, "Keynote Address at the Guelph Jazz Festival, 2007, Macdonald Stewart Art Centre, Guelph, Ontario, Canada," *Critical Studies in Improvisation / Études critiques en improvisation,* Vol. 4, No, 1 (2008), *http://journal.lib.uoguelph.ca/index.php/csieci/article/view/ 520/1009.*
25 Cage, *Silence,* 5.
26 Rasula's article also indicates the possibilities for much further study of the trans-Atlantic and, indeed, global, connections between Afrodiasporic aesthetics and non-Afrodiasporic cultures.
27 "Jazz as a Decal for the European Avant-Garde," 13. For an even more trenchant critique of Appel's book, see Eric Lewis's review, "Appel, Ellington, and the Modernist Canon," in *Critical Studies in Improvisation / Études critiques en improvisation,* Vol. 1, No, 2 (2005), *http://journal. lib.uoguelph.ca/index.php/csieci/article/view/21/55*
28 I should note that Perloff is nevertheless open to some of the arguments presented here, and I have benefited from her comments on portions of earlier drafts of this book.
29 Perloff, *The Poetics of Indeterminancy,* 156.
30 Ibid. Charles O. Hartman, echoing Perloff's assessment of a radical poetics operating via indeterminacy, suggests that T. S. Eliot's more conservative poetics temporarily eclipsed the improvisatory dynamic of William Carlos Williams and other modernists; see Hartman, *Jazz Text: Voice and Improvisation in poetry, Jazz and Song* (Princeton, Princeton University Press, 1991), 45.
31 Roach, "Beyond Categories," in Walser, 307. Roach never published this book, unfortunately.
32 Whether or not such commodification can be resisted by improvised music is still up for debate. Nevertheless, it is shocking to many listeners when they discover that recordings they thought were "live" have in fact been manipulated in the studio: examples include Thelonious Monk's "Brilliant Corners" and Duke Ellington's Newport Jazz Festival Performance of "Crescendo and Diminuendo in Blue," among others. Thanks to Karl Coulthard for pointing out this complex circuit of "live" and "simulated" sounds; see his essay "Looking for the Band: Walter Benjamin and the Mechanical Reproduction of Jazz," in *Critical Studies in Improvisation / Études critiques en improvisation,* Vol. 3, No. 1 (2007), *http://journal.lib.uoguelph.ca/index.php/csieci/ article/view/82/426.*
33 Pastras, *A Clear Field,* iii.
34 Ibid., vi-vii.
35 Ibid., 14.
36 Ibid., 14–15.
37 Ibid., 15.
38 Ibid.
39 Ibid., 16.
40 Ibid.
41 Ibid., 4.
42 Abbott, "Garden Paths," 2.
43 Umberto Eco, *The Open Work,* 109.

Works Cited

Abbott, Porter H. "Garden Paths and Ineffable Effects: Abandoning Representation in Literature and Film." (Forthcoming article, 2008.)

Attali, Jacques. *Noise: The Political Economy of Music.* Translated by Brian Massumi. Minneapolis: University of Minnesota Press, 1989.

Bailey, Derek. *Improvisation: Its Nature and Practice in Music.* New York: Da Capo, 1992.

Berliner, Paul F. *Thinking in Jazz: The Infinite Art of Improvisation.* Chicago: University of Chicago Press, 1994.

Cage, John. *Silence.* Cambridge, MA: M.I.T. Press, 1966.

Eco, Umberto. *The Open Work*. Translated by Anna Cancogni. Cambridge: Harvard University Press, 1989.

Ellison, Ralph. *Invisible Man*. New York: Vintage International, 1995.

Fischlin, Daniel and Ajay Heble, eds. *The Other Side of Nowhere: Jazz, Improvisation, and Communities in Dialogue*. Middletown, CT: Wesleyan University Press, 2004.

Greenblatt, Stephen. "Improvisation and Power." *Literature and Society*. Edited by Edward Said. Baltimore: Johns Hopkins University Press, 1980, 57–99.

Lears, Jackson. *Something for Nothing: Luck in America*. New York: Penguin Books, 2003.

Lewis, George. "Improvisation after 1950: Afrological and Eurological Perspectives." Fischlin and Heble, 2004, 131–62.

O'Meally, Robert G., ed. *The Jazz Cadence of American Culture*. New York: Columbia University Press, 1998.

Pastras, Philip James. *A Clear Field: The Idea of Improvisation in Modern Poetry*. Diss. Graduate School of New Brunswick, Rutgers, State University of New Jersey. New Brunswick, NJ, 1981.

Perloff, Marjorie. *The Poetics of Indeterminacy: Rimbaud to Cage*. Evanston, IL: Northwestern UP, 1981.

Rasula, Jed. "Jazz as Decal for the European Avant-Garde." *Blackening Europe: The African American Presence*. Edited by Heike Raphael-Hernandez. New York: Routledge, 2004, 13–34.

Walser, Robert ed. *Keeping Time: Readings in Jazz History*. New York: Oxford University Press, 1999.

27 Stone Sketch (Graphic Score)

Germaine Liu

with Nicholas Loess

Germaine Liu is a Toronto-based visual artist, performer/composer, and improviser. As a percussionist, she has worked with Anne Bourne, Matt Brubeck, Peggy Lee, John Oswald, Joe Sorbara, Scott Thomson, and many others. She studied percussion with John Goddard and Jesse Stewart during her undergraduate degree at the University of Guelph, and composition with David Mott while completing an MA in Music Composition at York University. Since 2008, Liu and video artist Nicholas Loess have been collaborating on multi-media projects; for *Stone Sketch*, Loess utilised his photographs and video to document Liu's process and performance, while simultaneously attempting to provide a quotation (rather than a translation) of what was occurring musically and gesturally between Liu and the stones. Liu and Loess use their collaboration to explore the relationship between time, movement, music, and gestural relationship, and to have the images document and speak about the process, rather than position them as ends in themselves. These images were first displayed as part of a graphic score exhibition called Hearing-Visions-Sonores at the University of Guelph in 2009.

Key words: graphic score; environment; gesture; percussion

STONE SKETCH1

©GERMAINE LIU 2009

About 2 to 3 years ago, I met two stones at Gros Cap, Ontario on the shore of Lake Superior.

DESCRIPTION OF THE TWO STONES:

Head-End

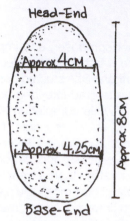

Approx 4CM.

Approx. 4.25CM

Approx. 8CM

Base-End

- Russet stone with small black pits covering the surface area.
- Texture of the surface is in between smooth and rough, but closer to smooth
- The shape of the russet stone resembles an ellipse with one end slightly wider than the other

- Black stone with grey and brown wavy lines sparsely dispersed over the surface
- Texture of the surface is smooth
- The shape of the black stone resembles a bird's head and its beak, or a rounded spear head.

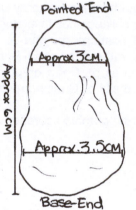

Pointed End

Approx 3CM.

Approx. 3.5CM

Approx 6 CM

Base-End

Figure 27.1 Stone Sketch 1

STONE SKETCH

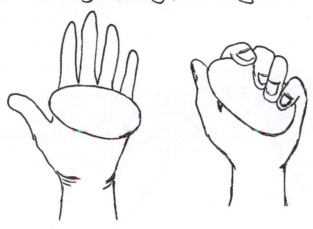

HOW TO HOLD THE STONES:

I hold one stone in each hand.
The russet stone rests in the palm of my left hand, its longer side lined up with the joints of my fingers so that I am able to close my hand over it. The head-end of the stone faces my thumb and the base-end lies on the right-fleshy part of my palm.

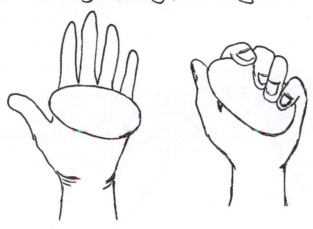

Figure 27.2 Stone Sketch 2

STONE SKETCH

The black stone is held in my right hand, gripped in between my thumb and middle finger. The length of my index finger matches the length of the thinnest edge of the stone. My finger is pressed against this edge to secure the stone in between my thumb and middle finger. The three fingers together look like an eagles claw. The base-end of the stone is pressed against my palm, the pointed end faces outward, away from it.

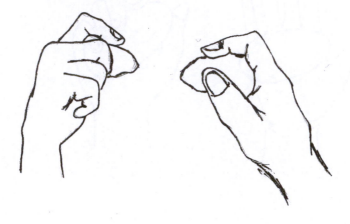

Figure 27.3 Stone Sketch 3

STONE SKETCH

4

HOW TO PLAY THE PIECE:

① I begin the piece by drawing and retracing an imaginary line with the black stone in a continuous back and forth motion, hovering over the russet stone at a close distance (about an inch above) making a small wind.

② While in motion, a magnetic-like attraction starts to occur between the stones and my hands. Gradually, I let the stones come in and out of contact with each other, making aperiodic clicking sounds. As I explore these sounds, the tension of my grasp on the russet stone changes from time to time, and the angles at which the stones meet also varies.

③ After some time, I bring the stones in full contact, cross-fading from clicking to scraping sounds. As I scrape the black stone against the russet stone, I am continuously shifting the degrees of friction in addition to the angles of contact between the two stones as well as the tension of my grasp on the russet stone.

Figure 27.4 Stone Sketch 4

STONE SKETCH

④ The movement of my right hand gradually accelerates until I reach my highest speed, pushing to my full range of motion. Once I have reached my highest speed, I shift immediately to a slow speed that corresponds to the rhythm of my breathing where the direction of the back and forth motion changes each time an inhalation or exhalation is complete.

⑤ While continuously retracing the line on the russet stone in this speed, I open my left hand to relax the tension on the russet stone when I exhale, and close the hand to tighten my grip against the stone as I inhale.

⑥ I gradually lighten the touch of the black stone against the russet stone until they are no longer in contact. Once the stones are no longer touching, the piece ends.

THERE IS NO PARTICULAR TIME LIMIT FOR THE PIECE. THE SCORE IS MEMORIZED PRIOR TO PERFORMANCE.

Figure 27.5 Stone Sketch 5

28 Essentials of Spontaneous Prose

Jack Kerouac

Along with Allen Ginsberg, Jack Kerouac (1922–69) is the leading name among the American postwar writers who became known as "the Beats." Like Ginsberg, he frequently cited jazz music as an influence, and attempted to make his own writing into a kind of spontaneous music, at the same time—as shown, however idiosyncratically, in these "Essentials"—taking a systematic and analytical approach to his own work. Born Jean-Louis Kerouac to French-Canadian parents in Massachusetts, Kerouac dropped out of university to join the Merchant Marine, spending his shore leaves in New York City with his new friends Ginsberg, William Burroughs, and Neal Cassady. Influenced by the many cross-country road trips he and Cassady made together, Kerouac tried to write a novel about life on the road that would be as spontaneous as the life itself, typing and submitting the manuscript on a single unbroken roll of paper. When *On the Road* was finally published in 1957, Kerouac found instant fame, but all the attention was a shock to his fragile self-esteem. Although he continued to write, he resisted the embrace of the emerging counter-culture, adopting conservative politics, drinking heavily, and eventually dying at home twelve years after the publication of his most famous novel.

Key words: literature; beat literature; jazz; flow

SET-UP The object is set before the mind, either in reality, as in sketching (before a landscape or teacup or old face) or is set in the memory wherein it becomes the sketching from memory of a definite image-object.

PROCEDURE Time being of the essence in the purity of speech, sketching language is undisturbed flow from the mind of personal secret idea-words, *blowing* (as per jazz musician) on subject of image.

METHOD No periods separating sentence-structures already arbitrarily riddled by false colons and timid usually needless commas—but the vigorous space dash separating rhetorical breathing (as jazz musician drawing breath between outblown phrases)—"measured pauses which are the essentials of our speech"—"divisions of the *sounds* we hear"—"time and how to note it down." (William Carlos Williams)

SCOPING Not "selectivity" of expression but following free deviation (association) of mind into limitless blow-on-subject seas of thought, swimming in sea of English with no discipline other than rhythms of rhetorical exhalation and expostulated statement, like a fist coming down on a table with each complete utterance, bang! (the space dash)—Blow as deep as you want—write as deeply, fish as far down as you want, satisfy yourself first, then reader cannot fail to receive telepathic shock and meaning-excitement by same laws operating in his own human mind.

LAG IN PROCEDURE No pause to think of proper word but the infantile pileup of scatological buildup words till satisfaction is gained, which will turn out to be a great appending rhythm to a thought and be in accordance with Great Law of timing.

TIMING Nothing is muddy that *runs in time* and to laws of time—Shakespearian stress of dramatic need to speak now in own unalterable way or forever hold tongue—*no revisions* (except obvious rational mistakes, such as names or *calculated* insertions in act of not writing but *inserting*).

CENTER OF INTEREST Begin not from preconceived idea of what to say about image but from jewel center of interest in subject of image at *moment* of writing, and write outwards swimming in sea of language to peripheral release and exhaustion—Do not afterthink except for poetic or P. S. reasons. Never afterthink to "improve" or defray impressions, as, the best writing is always the most painful personal wrungout tossed from cradle warm protective mind—tap from yourself the song of yourself, *blow!*—*now!*—*your* way is your only way—"good"—or "bad"—always honest, ("ludicrous"), spontaneous, "confessional" interesting, because not "crafted." Craft is craft.

STRUCTURE OF WORK Modern bizarre structures (science fiction, etc.) arise from language being dead, "different" themes give illusion of "new" life. Follow roughly outlines in outfanning movement over subject, as river rock, so mindflow over jewel-center need (run your mind over it, *once*) arriving at pivot, where what was dim-formed "beginning" becomes sharp-necessitating "ending" and language shortens in race to wire of time-race of work, following laws of Deep Form, to conclusion, last words, last trickle—Night is The End.

MENTAL STATE If possible write "without consciousness" in semitrance (as Yeats' later "trance writing") allowing subconscious to admit in own uninhibited interesting necessary and so "modern" language what conscious art would censor, and write excitedly, swiftly, with writing-or-typing-cramps, in accordance (as from center to periphery) with laws of orgasm, Reich's "beclouding of consciousness." *Come* from within, out—to relaxed and said.

Belief & Technique For Modern Prose

List Of Essentials

1. Scribbled secret notebooks, and wild typewritten pages, for yr own joy
2. Submissive to everything, open, listening
3. Try never get drunk outside yr own house
4. Be in love with yr life
5. Something that you feel will find its own form
6. Be crazy dumbsaint of the mind
7. Blow as deep as you want to blow
8. Write what you want bottomless from bottom of the mind
9. The unspeakable visions of the individual
10. No time for poetry but exactly what is
11. Visionary tics shivering in the chest
12. In tranced fixation dreaming upon object before you

13. Remove literary, grammatical and syntactical inhibition
14. Like Proust be an old teahead of time
15. Telling the true story of the world in interior monolog
16. The jewel center of interest is the eye within the eye
17. Write in recollection and amazement for yourself
18. Work from pithy middle eye out, swimming in language sea
19. Accept loss forever
20. Believe in the holy contour of life
21. Struggle to sketch the flow that already exists intact in mind
22. Dont think of words when you stop but to see picture better
23. Keep track of every day the date emblazoned in yr morning
24. No fear or shame in the dignity of yr experience, language & knowledge
25. Write for the world to read and see yr exact pictures of it
26. Bookmovie is the movie in words, the visual American form
27. In praise of Character in the Bleak inhuman Loneliness
28. Composing wild, undisciplined, pure, coming in from under, crazier the better
29. You're a Genius all the time
30. Writer-Director of Earthly movies Sponsored & Angeled in Heaven

Part 4
Dissonance

29 Improvised Dissonance: Opening Statements

Jesse Stewart

"All improvised music alternates between improvised consonances and improvised dissonances," writes Jesse Stewart. His essay, "Improvised Dissonance," theorizes the concept of dissonance in relation to improvised music, questioning both its musical and social implications. After majoring in both music and visual art as an undergraduate student, Stewart completed two Master degrees, in ethnomusicology and composition, at York University. In 2008, he received his PhD in Literary and Theatre Studies at the University of Guelph. As a percussionist, he has performed and/or recorded with musicians including William Parker, Hamid Drake, Pauline Oliveros, David Mott, and many others. He has been widely commissioned as a composer and his music has been performed at festivals throughout Canada, the United States and Europe. Among Stewart's most recent recordings, the self-titled debut recording by Stretch Orchestra (with Kevin Breit and Matt Brubeck) was honored with the 2012 Juno Award for Instrumental Album of the Year. Stewart has published widely on the subjects of music and art in journals including *American Music, Black Music Research Journal, Contemporary Music Review, Intermedialities,* and *Interdisciplinary Humanities*. He is an Associate Professor of music composition in Carleton University's School for Studies in Art and Culture.

Key words: music; jazz; Canada; consonance

The history of dissonance—as well as its corollary, consonance—can be thought of as a long improvisation full of different voices, shifting definitions, and changing attitudes. A detailed history of the concept of dissonance is well beyond the scope of this short essay,[1] which instead theorises dissonance in relation to musical improvisation, focusing in particular on one performance of improvised music that was widely perceived to be highly dissonant. But first, I will provide a brief gloss on the concept of dissonance itself.

"Dissonant" literally means "apart sounding." Thus, in its most general musical sense, the term refers to a lack of agreement between sounds. Within Western art music, the concepts of consonance and dissonance have historically been applied primarily to pitch, perhaps not surprisingly given the primacy of melody and harmony within Western musical discourse. Both natural and cultural factors shape our perceptions of the level of agreement—or lack thereof—between pitched sounds. Natural factors include the physiology and neurology of auditory perception such as the so-called "critical band"—the range of audio frequencies within which a tone will interfere with the perception of another tone, creating a sense of auditory "roughness." Certain physical properties of sound also shape our perceptions of dissonance, most notably the harmonic series: intervals that occur for the first time lower in the harmonic series, and therefore have simpler frequency ratios, are generally perceived to be more consonant than more complex frequency ratios occurring higher in the series. This is due to the greater degree of overlap between the partials involved in lower number harmonics. Another acoustic phenomenon that shapes our perception of dissonance is "beating," wherein two sounds of slightly different frequency produce wave interference that is perceived as fluctuations in volume at a rate proportional to the difference between the two frequencies. Beating is generally perceived to be highly dissonant (and "out of tune") in most Western art music traditions. However, in other contexts—Balinese gamelan music for example—such beating is integral to the music and highly valued. This discrepancy illustrates the importance of cultural factors in shaping our perceptions of dissonance.

Repeated exposure to a particular system of musical logic—and to the cultural codes embedded therein—also contributes significantly to our perceptions of dissonance. For example, twelve-tone equal tempered tuning, in which octaves are divided into twelve equally spaced pitches, has become so omnipresent in music of the Western world over the past century that intervals that lie outside this framework often sound dissonant to many people's ears. For instance, when I play music in just intonation—that is, music in which the tuning system is based on whole-number frequency ratios derived from the harmonic series—in my university composition classes, students often state that the music sounds out of tune, even though the musical intervals involved are considerably *more* in tune (given the greater degree of overlap between their upper partials) than most of the musical intervals we hear in equal tempered tuning. The fact that we have come to accept tempered thirds (which give rather poor approximations of their justly tuned counterparts) as consonances further attests to the powerful effect that repeated exposure to equal temperament has had on our perceptions of consonance and dissonance. Indeed, a strong case could be made to suggest that equal temperament has come to assume a place of hegemony within Western music in the Gramscian sense of being taken for granted, but nonetheless ideologically coded.

In addition to culturally conditioned tuning frameworks, genre-specific musical conventions affect our perceptions of dissonance. Triad-based Western art music of the eighteenth and nineteenth centuries—music that continues to exert considerable influence over contemporary modes of musical and cultural production—tended to treat certain intervals (namely thirds, fourths, perfect fifths, and sixths) as consonances, while seconds, sevenths, and tritones were treated as unstable dissonances in need of immediate resolution to a harmonically stable consonance. If we accept, as I do, the proposition that systems of musical logic are never neutral or natural, but rather always carry traces of the social values and ideologies that led to their construction, we might regard the system of tonal harmony that has underpinned—and continues to underpin—the vast majority of Western music as a symbolic expression of a social order from which there is no escape: dissonance only exists as a temporary aberration that ultimately serves to reaffirm and strengthen the prevailing musical/social order.

However, not all modes of music making—even those that are based on tonal harmonic frameworks and equal temperament—treat dissonances in the same way. As James McGowan (2008) notes in his essay "'Consonance' in Tonal Jazz: A Critical Survey of Its Semantic History," jazz musicians routinely use "upper structures"—chord tones beyond the triad—that are dissonant and in need of resolution from the perspective of Western music theory, but are nonetheless treated as contextually stable consonances in jazz performance. Read in social terms, the jazz practice of allowing dissonant chords to sound without resolution to a consonance might be seen as a symbolic challenge to the prevailing musical and social order. This line of thinking has been explored most fully in Ajay Heble's book *Landing On the Wrong Note: Jazz, Dissonance, and Critical Practice*, which examines political dissidence vis-à-vis musical dissonance, exploring the roles that "dissonant jazz [has] played for subordinated social groups struggling to achieve control over the ways in which their identities have been constructed, framed, and interpreted" (2000, p.9). Building on Heble's pioneering work, I'd now like to examine dissonance in relation to musical free improvisation. If perceptions of dissonance are, at least in part, a function of genre-specific musical conventions, how can the concept be fruitfully applied to a mode of music-making that is often defined by the very absence of any prescribed musical rules or constraints?

The idea of dissonance as a lack of agreement between sounds can be usefully brought to bear on a musical analysis of free improvisation. In general, performances of improvised music convey a sense of musical agreement and stability when all of the performers seem to share some sort of common musical ground or collective musical space that they explore in tandem with one another. Regardless of pitch content, such passages might be thought of as consonant in the sense that the musicians *sound together*. However, in most performances of improvised music, performers will eventually stray from the stability of a shared musical space, initiating a new musical idea that may or may not be taken up by their co-performers. This venture into new sonic territory can be accomplished through the introduction of new pitch material, a new rhythmic concept, a new sonority or timbre, or even a new volume level—anything that initiates a departure from the musical status quo. The processes of musical negotiation that such changes initiate often feel musically unstable and transitory. As such, they might be thought of as a form of improvised dissonance in that they bring about a lack of agreement in sound with the aim of opening new sonic pathways for the musicians and audience to explore. All improvised music alternates between improvised consonances and improvised dissonances, so defined. However, the ratio between the two can vary substantially. In my experience as both a listener and performer of improvised music, the negotiation of musical differences/dissonances often yields the musical moments that I find most compelling. Dissonant musical interactions can be highly productive in that they can have the effect of forcing improvisers to play outside of their "musical comfort zone," where they can no longer rely on pre-formed musical ideas and habitual techniques. For me, these are often the most compelling moments in musical improvisation.

However, improvised dissonances are not inherently positive, nor are they always musically productive. Indeed, when taken to the extreme, they can have a negative impact on the music and on the experience of other musicians and the audience. I have witnessed numerous performances, for example, in which an improviser or group of improvisers consistently undermines the musical contributions of their co-performers by interrupting their musical contributions or ignoring those contributions altogether. Very often, such dissonant musical actions seem to take place along lines of difference: musicians in a minoritised position within an improvising ensemble seem to be the most frequent targets of such dissonant silencing tactics. In my experience, this is particularly true when it comes to women improvisers performing in male-dominated ensembles. Such musical dissonances expose the power dynamics that are always involved in musical performance, but often operate under the guise of musical freedom in supposedly "free" improvisation. With these issues in mind, I would like to conclude this essay by examining one performance of free improvisation that was widely perceived to be highly dissonant.

On Friday September 10, 2004, Tuvan-born vocalist Sainkho Namtchylak performed with veteran improvisers William Parker and Hamid Drake at the Guelph Jazz Festival, a festival dedicated to "presenting innovative jazz and creative improvised music in a community setting" (Guelph Jazz Festival, n.d.). The performance, which took place in the sanctuary of a United Church, began with Parker and Drake launching into an intense bass-drum rhythmic dialogue atop of which Namtchylak sang a three or four-note melodic motif. A few seconds later, she repeated the same motif. Then again. And again. She continued to repeat the same melodic fragment for over twenty minutes, offering a clear reminder that the words "ostinato" and "obstinate" come from the same Latin root.

Namtchylak's performance has spawned a considerable amount of written commentary, much of which is summarised in Fischlin, Heble, and Lipsitz' 2013 book *The Fierce Urgency of Now*, which examines the performance in the context of a discussion "of whether it's possible for things to go 'wrong' in an improvised performance" (p.206).[2] "Something did go 'wrong' that evening," the authors conclude. "But what went wrong, in [their] estimation wasn't so much about the music. ... any judgements that we make about this event, as indeed about any act of improvised music-making, need to be understood as being not just about the music, but perhaps, more suggestively, about broader social matters" (Fischlin, Heble, and Lipsitz, 2013, p.213). It seems to me that the concept of improvised dissonance can be usefully brought to bear on *both* the musical and social dimensions of the events that transpired that night. Therefore, I would like to critically examine that same performance, not as an example of improvisation gone wrong, but rather as a powerful example of improvised dissonance that continues to stir discussion and debate nearly a decade after it took place.

To my mind, and that of many in attendance, Namtchylak's vocals seemed highly dissonant, not because of their pitch content, but rather because of their relentless repetition. She seemed to make a point of deliberately sounding apart from her band mates—of ensuring that there could be no agreement in the sounds they made together—by choosing to not engage with, or respond to, anything that they played. Her body language during the performance also communicated a sense of dissonance: between repetitions of her vocal line, she frequently looked at her wristwatch, folded her arms, or placed her hands on her hips—gestures that all projected a sense of disinterest and discontent.

In contrast, Parker and Drake's duo performance wended its way through different meters, rhythmic feels, and tempos—seemingly all in an unsuccessful effort to dislodge the needle from the skipping record vocals. Given the almost telepathic level of musical communication between Drake and Parker—and the fact that they chose to continue to support their co-performer musically despite obvious challenges—their performance might be regarded as a model of extreme musical consonance in response to the dissonance being voiced by Namtchylak. This reading is consistent with Tracey Nicholls' (2010, n.p.) view of Parker and Drake's performance as an example of what she terms "an ethos of improvisation": " ... a commitment to work together to build something even in circumstances that may be much less than ideal."

As Namtchylak's performance went on, the tension in the room grew increasingly palpable. By the thirty-minute mark, a sizeable portion of the audience had left the concert at which point the festival organisers decided to intervene. The emcee for the evening approached the stage and waved his arms to get Namtchylak's attention. She stopped singing and signalled Parker and Drake to stop as well. "Please come with me," the emcee asked. "A car is waiting for you." The intervention was applauded by some and abhorred by others who voiced their support of Namtchylak and asked her to continue the performance. Parker and Drake remained quietly on stage during the exchange. In a mixture of Tuvan and English, Namtchylak publicly vented her anger over the interruption and aired a list of grievances, many of which were unintelligible to me. One thing I remember her commenting on was her displeasure about performing in a Christian church: "I have never been baptised!" she screamed. This statement suggests that for her, there was a cognitive dissonance between her Tuvan and Shamanic cultural heritage and the overtly Christian setting in which the concert took place, something that may have influenced her performance. After several uncomfortable minutes, William Parker began playing a Tibetan prayer bowl, its steady single tone building in intensity and exerting a calming effect on the room. Before long, all three musicians began performing once again, this time Namtchylak's vocals ranging from Tuvan-style overtone singing to ear-piercing screams. She still conveyed a strong sense of dissonance and anger, but it was tempered to some extent by the musical dialogue and interaction that took place between all three musicians.

As dissonant as Namtchylak's performance was, I found the festival's decision to interrupt the performance to be far more dissonant and disconcerting. For one thing, I had been enjoying the performance up until that point. To my ears, the dissonance and tension between the musical brick wall of the repeated vocal line and the shifting rhythmic counterpoint supplied by Drake and Parker was very interesting musically. Although I may have been in the minority in this regard, surveying the range of critical reactions to the performance suggests that I was not alone.[3] I also liked the fact that her performance deliberately pushed buttons and boundaries, eliciting an intense, visceral reaction from many members of the audience who became active participants in the collective improvised dissonance that ensued. To my mind, the history of creative improvised music has always been about pushing musical boundaries. Namtchylak's performance reminded me that there are still boundaries to push, that improvised dissonance still has the capacity to challenge complacency and provoke debate.

Notes

1 See Tenney (1988) for a discussion of the history of consonance and dissonance in Western art music.
2 See also Borgo (2005), Nicholls (2010), and Wilson (2004a; 2004b; and 2004c) for additional discussions of the Namtchylak/Parker/Drake performance.
3 See the responses to Carl Wilson's (2004a; 2004b; and 2004c) blog posts about the event for a cross-section of critical reactions to the performance.

Works cited

Borgo, D., 2005. *Sync or Swarm: Improvising Music in a Complex Age.* New York and London: Continuum.

Fischlin, D., Heble, A. and Lipsitz, G., 2013. *The Fierce Urgency of Now: Improvisation, Rights, and the Ethics of Cocreation.* Durham, NC: Duke University Press.

Guelph Jazz Festival, n.d. *About.* [online] Available at: http://guelphjazzfestival.com/about_us. [Accessed 13 August 2013].

Heble, A., 2000. *Landing On the Wrong Note: Jazz, Dissonance, and Critical Practice.* New York: Routledge.

McGowan, J., 2008. "Consonance" in Tonal Jazz: A Critical Survey of Its Semantic History. *Jazz Perspectives* 2(1), pp.69–102.

Nicholls, T., 2010. Speaking Justice, Performing Reconciliation: Twin Challenges for a Postcolonial Ethics. *Critical Studies in Improvisation / Études critiques en improvisation*, 6(1), [online]. Available at: www.criticalimprov.com/article/view/1082/1704. [Accessed 10 September 2013].

Tenney, J., 1988. *A History of "Consonance" and "Dissonance."* New York: Excelsior Music Publishing.

Wilson, C., 2004a. Guelph Fest's Fantastic Fiasco. *Zoilus*, 13 September. Available at: www.zoilus.com/documents/live_notes/2004/000208.php. [Accessed 12 August 2013].

——, 2004b. Guelph Revisited: Royal City Standoff. *Zoilus*, 15 September. Available at: www.zoilus.com/documents/live_notes/2004/000210.php. [Accessed 12 August 2013].

——, 2004c. Guelphgate, Part III. *Zoilus*, 16 September. Available at: www.zoilus.com/documents/general/2004/000212.php. [Accessed 12 August 2013].

30 Phantoms of the Other

Fragments of the Communal Unconscious

Rustom Bharucha

Rustom Bharucha is a writer, theatre director, dramaturge, and cultural critic based in Kolkata, India, whose work casts new light on India's cultural traditions in the face of globalisation. He has conducted workshops throughout the world on land and memory, the politics of touch, and migration. His books include *Theatre and the World: Performance and the Politics of Culture* (1993), *In the Name of the Secular* (1998), *The Question of Faith* (1993), *Rajasthan: an Oral History* (2003), and *Another Asia: Rabindranath Tagore and Okakura Tenshin* (2009). "Phantoms of the Other" is from one of his best-known books, *The Politics of Cultural Practice: Thinking through Theatre in an Age of Globalization* (2000). Here, Bharucha describes improvisation as the enactment of power relationships, which can be used didactically or exploited for comedic, dramatic, or shock value. Elsewhere, he has protested at the ways in which Indian theatre has been grossly mythologised and taken out of context by Western directors and critics. In Bharucha's concern for turning globalisation towards more fair and equitable practices, he provides an alternative vision that he feels could embrace true cultural pluralism. Bharucha is also founding director of the innovative project, Arna Jharna: The Desert Museum of Rajasthan, in the village of Moklawas, Jodhpur, Rajasthan.

Key words: theatre; performance art; cross-culture

In this chapter, I will focus on a few manifestations of the Other within the larger communalization of politics and culture in India today. Without assuming the clarity of an evolved theory of communalism, I choose to speak through what Edward Said once described as 'disorientations of direct encounters with the human' (Said 1979: 93). It is through these disorientations, these violent shifts in space and time, that I would like to problematize how the Other gets internalized, questioned, and performed in contemporary theatre practice in India, along with its more glaring (and inexplicable) manifestations in public culture. Inevitably, I will seek refuge in fragments, because what I have to offer is no master narrative, but an assemblage of aberrations, enigmas, and moments of violence that I have encountered in a range of seemingly indiscriminate representations: improvisations in theatre; 'defences of the fragment' in the historiography of communalism; police reports on caste violence; excerpts from interviews by the survivors of Partition – in short, articulations of the communal unconscious at different levels of critical reflexivity and accountability.

While the fragment has been valorized in recent subaltern historiography, its vulnerabilities have yet to be fully encountered. More often than not, the fragment becomes a strategic compensation for not being able to deal with the enormity of any event, or else it is simply a theoretical catch-word for dealing with 'minor', relatively undiscovered or marginalized resources in any field. At times, fragments are no different from the component parts of a missing narrative, but the implication is that these disconnected parts can always be reconfigured to form another whole, yet another narrative. I am not free from this tension to link a fragment to a narrative, as will become evident in my description of certain improvisations in theatre that have been sparked by preexisting narratives. But I am also aware that the most disturbing fragments are those that resist the hegemony of any clearly articulated text. Resolutely, they will defy assimilation into any cognitive framework. Without seeking a point of return to any state of coherence, the fragment remains unconstituted and seemingly detached from any referent.

Somebody's Other

I will begin my exposure of the communal unconscious with the somewhat provocative conjecture that it is linked to the construction of Somebody's Other. Containing two unknowns – a 'somebody' and an 'other' – these components seem to be linked through a relationship, bound by a possessive clause. Locating myself in relation to this construction, I am compelled to ask if I am an absence or some kind of recalcitrant element, another 'unknown' hovering around its periphery. As I confront the hidden agenda of its dynamics, I realize that I have no other option but to view myself as a 'third' element and that I am obliged to intervene.

But how does one intervene? As I problematize Somebody's Other, its enigma yields to the immediate pressures of the *realpolitik,* as the Other acquires a face, a name, a history. Theoretically loaded, politically charged, it becomes inextricably linked to the spectre of communalism by which entire communities are being differentiated, ostensibly on the grounds of religion, which has become a pretext for unleashing all kinds of violence in an increasingly fascist mode. As this 'banality of evil' enters our everyday lives, the mechanisms by which entire communities are othered are becoming increasingly more explicit. No longer enigmatic, somebody's other has become disturbingly real.

Almost as a survival instinct, one could qualify at the very outset that somebody's other need not be mine. But there is also a small, taunting voice that reminds me of another, more grim possibility that *I* could be somebody's other. Therefore, it becomes expedient not merely to negate the construction of somebody's other on politically correct grounds. One may have to oppose it for one's own survival and for the protection of a secular sense of history and identity.

Is there a way out, however, in which one does not have to problematize being othered in such an embattled context? Can the construction of somebody's other be dismantled through a blurring, if not dissolution, of its polarities? I would like to believe that this is not just desirable but necessary. Quite simply, if we had to constantly define ourselves in opposition to the constructs of otherness thrust on us, then this would be the surest way of othering ourselves. The moment we allow ourselves to be subsumed within predetermined categories of otherness, we automatically empower what we are set against, and in the process we fail to call attention to the differences in our own history and culture and to alternative paradigms of defining cultural identity.

The Communal Unconscious

Within the conceptual framework of 'Somebody's Other' as outlined above, I would now like to complicate the reading by describing in some detail this chapter's first fragment: an improvisation on violence conducted at the Ninasam Theatre Institute in Heggodu, Karnataka. Improvisations are perhaps even more fragmented than rehearsals. Indeed, they cannot be determined prior to enactment. More often than not, improvisations disintegrate or scatter into random images that do not add up to anything. The more 'successful' ones however, are sustained invisibly by an inner chemistry of energies, out of which a provisional grammar unfolds that holds the improvisation together. Tellingly, I find the less 'successful' improvisations more potentially illuminating not least because their vulnerabilities are more intense. Unlike rehearsals, which develop a certain pattern through the ritual of repetition, improvisations offer a psychoanalytic site in which the most evanescent glimmers of an actor's unconscious can be revealed, if not painfully exposed.

Inevitably, these improvisations (which I associate specifically with the state of pre-acting) are 'private' interactions between the actors and the director. Even more so than rehearsals, they are rarely 'open' to public viewing, which makes any description of their happening a necessarily partial and incomplete representation. I should emphasize at this point that what I am about to describe – the communal unconscious – is very much my reading of what I was privileged to see. I can claim no criterion of authentication or verifiability beyond what I describe in words of what was essentially a non-verbal experience.

While the duration or modalities of improvisations can almost never be determined, it would be illusory to imagine that they are entirely 'free' of directorial intervention. There are sections in an improvisation wherein one can enter a state of 'flow', where the very momentum and volition of the actors' interactions seem to merge of their own accord, rather like a soccer match in its final moments when you can no longer see who is passing the ball to whom. During such durations of 'flow', a director becomes an observer of an improvisatory process that totally circumvents what may have been intended through an exercise or a warm-up or an exploration of a motif. Thus, there is no apparent link between the stimulus of an improvisation and its execution.

In one particular improvisation with the Ninasam actors, I set the rules of a particular 'game': one actor in the group had to invent a non-verbal language, while the other actors had to attempt a dialogue with him in their mother-tongue (Kannada). Somewhat self-consciously, I had explored this exercise during an earlier work-process on *The Tempest* in Heggodu, where I had wanted the actors to explore a process of colonization through language. In the second improvisation, I had no such intention in mind. In fact, if I have to be frank, it was a 'filler' in a workshop session, an almost unconscious slippage on my part in which I had merely wanted to see how the improvisation would work out its own logic.

To my horror, what I saw emerging before my eyes was unprecedented in its eruption of violence. More clearly than in any of the histories of communalism that I had been reading in the febrile political atmosphere that had anticipated the demolition of the Babri Masjid, and more vividly than any of the images of communal atrocity that I had seen on television, I was made to confront a construction of the communalized Other. In this scenario, the non-speaking actor was differentiated as he was ridiculed, teased, humiliated, animalized, made to perform like an animal, poked, prodded, stamped on, violated, othered.

Concretized in the psycho-physical language of theatre, this process of othering was made all the more painful through the eyes, the gaze as it were of another actor, who did not participate in the improvisation but who chose to remain on its periphery. Almost quizzically, he watched the action with a slight smile as if he were recognizing something very familiar to him. Was it a coincidence that this actor happened to be the only person in the entire neighbourhood who belonged to what we in India euphemistically describe as 'the minority community' (i.e. Muslims)? In retrospect, it took time for me to accept that I was the other member from 'a minority community' (Parsees) – a community that has had the privilege of not having to think of itself in minoritarian terms, but perhaps for not too long. As I saw my otherness unconsciously mirrored in the eyes of this actor, whose own condition seemed to be shaped in front of – and between – us, I was deeply moved by the intimacy of the moment. I was seeing the other in my self.

But this is not all. As I was watching this communal scenario unfold through its own volition as it were, I also began to see the 'unconscious' of another narrative from a different history, culture, and time. In very emphatic terms, I began to encounter the archetypes of a primal play from which practically every movement in 'modern drama' has emerged, a radical text whose playwright had the genius and the courage to place an ordinary man at the very centre of his vision: Georg Büchner's *Woyzeck*. From this intensely fragmented play, we know how this most simple and downtrodden of protagonists is ruthlessly peripheralized, as he is made to stand outside of the enlightened norms of Reason, Civilization, Morality, and the Law, which are assumed by the other characters in the play. At no point in time was the reality of Büchner's common man more painful for me, his otherness acquiring a strange intelligibility in the communal context of contemporary India.

This is not the place for me to describe how the production evolved. What concerns me is the convergence of two constructions of otherness from different points in history, from two seemingly incommensurable cultural contexts, within the structure of an improvisation. Through the cracks in these intersecting narratives, which I could see in my mind's eye, I was also coming to terms with the mirroring of my unacknowledged otherness in the actor who was unable to participate in the improvisation, and who continued to hover around its periphery.

In retrospect, the consciousness of this moment alerted me yet again to the enigma of fluctuating times in theatre, whereby different languages, histories and cultures can meet at unconscious levels. It also made me confront, not unlike *Gundegowdana charitre* described in an earlier work, how the archetypes of a 'foreign' text can actually accentuate the immediacies of the historical moment in another cultural context. In this sense, the inter/intracultural possibilities of theatrical intervention need not be regarded as necessarily exclusive or antagonistic activities so long as they find a common ground within the 'political unconscious' of a particular group of actors in a specific context.

And yet, there are some deceptions in such formulations that should not be allowed to pass without critical qualification. For a start, it would be reductive to assume that there is a direct link between 'violence' in everyday life and a particular 'structure of action' in theatre. If the archetypes of *Woyzeck* surfaced for me in the pattern of actions played out by the actors in the course of the improvisation, it would be necessary to emphasize that this was my *interpretation* of a particular criss-crossing of images and memories in theatre at a particular point in time. It is necessary, I believe, not to essentialize such connections, but to submit their archetypal illumination to the scrutiny of particular facts in history. In the process, the archetype can be disturbed, if not obliterated, by the sheer intransigence of a moment of violence in real life that defies representation [...]

Works Cited

Said, Edward. *Orientalism*. New York: Vintage Books, 1979.

31 Bebop as Cultural Alternative

Daniel Belgrad

After undergraduate work at Princeton, Daniel Belgrad pursued graduate studies at Yale University, and in 1994 received his PhD in American Studies. He now teaches at the University of South Florida in Tampa, specialising in cultural and literary theory, as well as courses on nineteenth- and twentieth-century American cultural and intellectual history, and graduate courses specialising in U.S.-Mexico cultural interaction and the cultures of the American west and southwest. Dr Belgrad has presented talks and papers throughout the USA, as well as in Mexico, Croatia, and Ukraine. In 2002 he won the Oscar O. Winther Award from the Western Historical Association for his article "Power's Larger Meaning," which explores the use of ecology as a historiographical paradigm. "Bebop" is a chapter from his book *The Culture of Spontaneity: Improvisation and the Arts in Postwar America*. It serves as a refreshing reminder of the impact that the music called *bebop* had on a generation of musicians who came of age around World War II. Although it is now often referred to as a fixed and stale form, in its day bebop was welcomed as a music of freedom: " ... a more radical cultural stance than European modernist music ... a more democratic and participatory form of musical expression."

Key words: jazz; African American culture; postwar American culture

> There then came down in the ugly streets of us
> inside the head & tongue
> of us
> a man
> black blower of the now
> The vectors from all sources—slavery, renaissance.
> bop charlie parker.
> nigger absolute super-sane screams against reality
> course through him
> AS SOUND!
>
> Amiri Baraka, "Am/Trak" (1968)

In the 1930s, when Lester Young began to experiment with new tone qualities in his saxophone playing, a fellow member of Count Basie's swing band taunted him. Young retorted by tapping his forehead, saying: "There are things going on up there, man—some of you guys are all belly."[1] His words attest to the bebop impulse to reinvent jazz as an intellectual pursuit.

Bebop shared the disposition of other spontaneous art movements at midcentury to develop an alternative to corporate-liberal culture rooted in intersubjectivity and body-mind holism. Bebop embodied these principles in formal attributes emphasizing the African American musical idiom: polyrhythm, timbre, and a structure of call-and-response. Compared to the swing jazz from which it grew, bebop was a conversational music, played best in small ensembles rather than in big bands. Intersubjective reality was manifested in the way the music emerged, as each player maintained a spontaneous awareness of voices within and without. Bebop innovators also worked to integrate mind and body by exploring the realm of prosody: that boundary between ideas and feelings where music becomes an utterance, and words become pure sound.[2]

The Emergence of Bebop

The swing jazz of the "big band" era, dating roughly from the mid-1930s to the mid-1940s, had adapted the racy legacy of New Orleans jazz to the high-culture format of the concert orchestra, as epitomized in Norman Granz's popular "Jazz at the Philharmonic." Swing became a crossover phenomenon of unprecedented size in American music. Large swing dance bands became the defining feature of a musical era, playing for both white and black audiences and for U.S. servicemen overseas.[3]

By contrast, bebop jazz, emerging at the beginning of World War II, turned away from the European orchestral model and expanded on characteristically African American musical elements. In his book *Blues People,* LeRoi Jones identified these elements as antiphony (or call-and-response), polyrhythm, and prosodic tone. Jones, an African American intellectual and a prominent poet, wrote of bebop that it represented a healthy separatism and autonomy on the part of black culture, after the commercialized assimilationism of swing.[4]

Bebop developed between 1939 and 1941, during after-hours jam sessions at nightclubs in black Harlem: Monroe's Uptown House and, particularly, Minton's Playhouse, on 118th Street between 7th Avenue and Saint Nicholas. Musicians who played as "sidemen" in the swing bands—that is, among the orchestral sections devoted to reeds, brass, strings, or percussion—would congregate to play together after their night's work had ended.[5] Jam sessions brought back some of the fun of being a musician, which could be lost in the workaday playing culture of the big bands.

Jam sessions offered professional camaraderie and the opportunity to learn new techniques or to hear a new melodic sequence (or "lick"). They also gave musicians a chance to hone their skills through the competitive give-and-take of "cutting," a kind of musical dueling related to the verbal sparring of "playing the dozens."[6] Cutting had been a part of black musical culture at least since the days of ragtime; but in the swing era it took place almost wholly at the aggregate level of band against band, as in the "Battles of the Bands" at the Savoy Ballroom. Cutting as a test of skill and creativity between individual musicians had been for the most part eliminated from the performance culture of swing, in which only a few musicians got the chance to solo, while the rest played background harmonies or "riffs" in unison.

Most importantly, jam sessions offered a forum in which to practice improvisation. The fact that improvisation must be practiced need not be taken as a paradox. Improvising jazz solos does not consist mainly in inventing new licks, but in stringing together learned licks and references in new and appropriate combinations—just as new usages and phrasings are a greater part of the poet's work than coining neologisms is. [...]

Although the beboppers made use of their knowledge of modern music theory, they approached music from a very different social ground than the high-modern avant-garde did. As Henry Pleasants has observed, most European experimental music represented cultural conservatism "masked by a fulsome profession of modernism."[7] These modernists, despite their formal innovations, were wholly invested in revitalizing and preserving the institutional apparatus of nineteenth-century European musical culture: the symphony orchestra.

The circumstances of orchestral performance reinforced established social hierarchies and social virtues. Symphony hall architecture symbolically separated the physical spaces occupied by listeners of different social classes: upper-class listeners in the box seats, burghers in the orchestra, and plebeians in the balcony. Concert hall decorum equated listening with an attitude of deference.[8] Moreover, the performance technology of the symphony orchestra was text-based; precision and accuracy in following the printed score were among the key virtues of a symphonic musician. Self-expression was subordinated to a joint expression of the conception of the composer. The conductor was a manager charged with "orchestrating" the musicians in this task.

By contrast, the performance culture of bebop emphasized immediacy and spatial intimacy and encouraged expressions of appreciation at any point in the performance; this was its legacy from jazz, as a popular-culture form. In addition, the "given" text in bebop was minimal. Unlike most European concert music, most jazz was learned by ear from live performances or recordings. Such aural transmission was especially central to bebop, because its nuances of rhythm, tone, and timbre could not be captured in musical notation.[9] Finally, bebop performers "spoke" for themselves, not for the composer. The fixed authority of the conductor was replaced by a format in which the musicians passed authority among themselves according to flexible but reliable patterns. Ultimately, bebop embodied a more radical cultural stance than European modernist music, because it provided for a more democratic and participatory form of musical expression.

A Formal Contrast of Bebop and Swing

Methodologically, one of the best means of identifying the social content of any music is to compare it to the music from which it immediately derives.[10] In the case of bebop, this is swing. A rejection of the Western cultural norms encoded in the symphony orchestra was implicit in the emergence of bebop as a reaction against big-band swing; for swing had succeeded by assimilating jazz to orchestral techniques. In the narrower historical context, the formal differences between swing and bebop embodied spontaneity's challenge to America's wartime corporate-liberal culture.

The differences that generally distinguish bebop from swing jazz can be deduced from the specific differences distinguishing two versions of the same tune. In 1939, Charlie Barnet's big band recorded a popular rendition of the standard "Cherokee."[11] "Cherokee" is built on a basic 64-bar structure of four 16-bar phrases in an AABA sequence (the first phrase is played three times, twice before the "bridge" and once after). Late in 1945, Charlie Parker's Reboppers recorded a bebop version of "Cherokee" that they renamed "KoKo."[12] "KoKo" was created from "Cherokee" in two phases: first, modern chord changes were substituted for the conventional harmonies of the standard; then a completely new melody was improvised to accompany the new changes. Therefore it is possible to hum the melody of "Cherokee"—at a faster tempo—over the harmonic changes of "KoKo," though the original melody is nowhere in evidence.

Charlie Barnet, like all band leaders in orchestral jazz, aimed to provide his audience with music that they could dance to. The tempo and the conceptual simplicity of his "Cherokee" are suited to this aim. As the big-band equivalent of the orchestra conductor, Barnet worked to achieve a pleasing blend of sound, to which the voices of individual musicians were subordinated. For the most part, in Barnet's "Cherokee" the melody and countermelody are carried by whole sections of the band playing in unison. One soloist introduces the melody in the first two 16-bar phrases and returns in the second phrase of the second chorus to provide a countermelody, but these solos follow the rules of harmonic tonality blending easily into the sound of the whole.[13] There is, moreover, an orderliness or deference in the way the band showcases the soloist—who is, not incidentally, Charlie Barnet himself.

Like most band leaders, Barnet worked with "arrangers" who developed orchestrations tailored to the style and resources of his band. Arrangers provided the band members with written scores, which were then carefully rehearsed. The orchestral quality of Barnet's "Cherokee" is especially featured in an eight-bar transitional phrase between the two choruses, during which the sections work together like a fine precision drill team.

The success of big band performances depended on a well-drilled unity, supported by practices like those described above. The organizational features audible in the music were present in the performance culture of big band swing as well. Band uniforms emphasized visual unity. Band leaders fined musicians for lateness or infractions of neatness or comportment. Individual section players could be replaced easily and often were. As Sonny Criss observed, "You're part of the establishment in big bands. Part of an assembly line and they restrict you."[14]

The corporate image cultivated by the big bands was not just for show; it was a mechanism of survival. The business side of the swing music industry was dominated by corporate booking agents who provided the band leaders with live gigs and radio spots. The fate of a band was intimately linked to its fortune with a few large entertainment empires, like those of Moe Gale (the owner of the Savoy Ballroom), MCA, and the General Artists Corporation.[15] Composer-arrangers who wrote big band music also worked in other forms of corporate middlebrow media, writing Broadway musicals, movie scores, and serials and commercials for television.[16]

For the individual sideman, playing for most big bands was an unhappy compromise between creative urges and financial necessities. Big bands systematically showcased leading soloists and offered little opportunity to other band members for artistic or professional advancement. Trumpeter Tony Frusella, for instance, compared the musical culture of Charlie Barnet's big band to the regimentation of army life. "When I got out of the army ... I got this hot-shit gig with Charlie Barnet. It was a big band and I was in the trumpet section. But like it was bull shit because all you'd do was get up and blow the same notes with a bunch of other guys. It was just like the army."[17]

By contrast, the bebop adaptation of "Cherokee" into "KoKo" foregrounds improvisational solos. What is immediately obvious in the piece by Charlie Parker's Reboppers is the greater range and freedom of the soloists. After a 32-bar introduction shared by Parker and Dizzy Gillespie, Parker improvises across two 64-bar choruses, mixing in dissonant notes and quotations from other pieces, all at approximately twice the tempo of Barnet's "Cherokee."

The polyrhythmic complexity and irregular phrasings that characterize bebop jazz are signals that it is a music meant for listening and not for dancing. Miles Templar made this point in defending bebop to the readers of the *Partisan Review* in 1948. "One need not go 'trucking on down' the aisle of Town Hall at a jazz concert to show appreciation for the music," Templar wrote. "The bopper's enthusiasm is a quiet thing. He wants to dig everything that's being done and he knows that distractions will cause him to miss the thread of whatever the musician is building. You see this enthusiasm on all hands and on all faces during a bop concert or session."[18]

Listeners trying to track the "thread" of the solos in "KoKo" had to pitch their attention at a high level of nervous excitement. This was definitely not the easygoing sound of Barnet's "Cherokee." The fast tempo and high energy level of bebop restricted it to a skilled coterie of musicians and encouraged those musicians to take creative risks. In bebop, the spontaneous articulation of new musical ideas was valued above precision or accuracy. As Bud Johnson stated: "I'd like to hear a guy go after something and make a mistake sometimes. That's excitement too. Not just be too perfect."[19]

Bebop was a style in which control of the music belonged not to the conductor or the arranger but to whoever was soloing. Because of this, some reviewers criticized bebop as solipsistic. As important as the virtuoso soloist was to bebop, however, the dynamics of the small ensemble were more so. "KoKo" begins and ends with 32-bar segments (AA) of conversational give-and-take between Parker and Gillespie. Each of these segments is divided into 4 eight-bar phrases; the first and last are rehearsed duets, but in between are sixteen bars in which the two engage in an improvisational antiphony, or call-and-response. Each has eight bars in which to make a musical statement; this was known as "trading eights."

The relations among the musical voices in bebop music are quite different from those in swing. The riffs of the players in the background "carry" the soloist less deferentially. In "KoKo," the drummer, Max Roach, "drops bombs," punctuating Parker's horn playing with comments and encouragement. Dizzy Gillespie on the piano does the same. Parker responds to these comments in passing. The close coordination of listening and voicing involved in playing bebop was called "picking up on" the other musicians.

Beboppers defended the intersubjective quality of their music against critics who heard only the soloist. When the *Partisan Review* characterized bebop as insincere, detached, and solipsistic, Miles Templar wrote in rebuttal:

> The back-up is not a subordinate thing in bop. Bop back-ups are essential to the solo. It's those sustained chords behind Diz that make his solos wistful. Those saxes are analogous to the chorus in a Greek tragedy. They raise their voices, questioning the protagonist, agreeing with him on certain points, wondering about others.[20]

Miles Davis emphasized the intersubjective dynamic among a group he assembled late in 1957:

> One voice can change the entire way a band hears itself, can change the whole rhythm, the whole timing of a band, even if everyone else had been playing together forever. It's a whole new thing when you add or take away a voice. ...
>
> Because of the chemistry and the way people were playing off each other, everybody started playing above what they knew almost from the beginning. Trane [John Coltrane] would play some weird, great shit, and Cannonball [Adderley] would take it in the other direction, and I would put my sound right down the middle or float over it, or whatever. And then I might play real fast, or buzzzzz, like Freddie Webster. This would take Trane someplace else, and he would come back with other different shit and so would Cannonball.[21]

In its emphasis on solos within a small ensemble, bebop marked a return to the pre-swing jazz of New Orleans, rooted in the African American cultural heritage. Some modern jazz musicians saw the interdependence of group improvisation as a more "African" alternative to the Western orchestral tradition. Archie Shepp, for instance, has written of "a certain communal intelligence expressed in the music ... deeply rooted in ... [Afro American] tradition."[22] Miles Davis similarly contrasted the Western method of orchestral arrangement to the group improvisation that characterized Charlie Parker's creativity: "He didn't conform to Western ways of musical group interplay by organizing everything. Bird was a great improviser and that's where he thought great music came from and what great musicians were about ... just the opposite of the Western concept of notated music."[23]

On the whole, bebop musicians preferred this attitude in the band leaders they worked with. Lennie Tristano remarked that he would rather work with Parker than with Gillespie (who formed a bebop big band) or with Thelonious Monk. Those two insisted on having more personal control over the music. Charlie Parker, said Tristano, "based his approach on having you learn to improvise and how to express feeling spontaneously."[24] The ideal bebop number was like a musical conversation among the musicians.

Once a conversational dynamic is understood to be the structural model for bebop, it becomes clear that other bebop innovations developed to enhance the conversation. The asymmetrical phrasing of bebop soloists that replaced the "square" four-bar phrasing of swing allowed a greater range of musical utterances, much as if we had all suddenly decided to stop talking in rhyming couplets. Thus Miles Templar wrote in the *Partisan Review*: "The most important thing in bop is the phrasing."[25] And Miles Davis, making the same point, remarked that the model for bebop phrasing was the cadences of speech.[26] Davis recalled hearing Dizzy Gillespie and Charlie Parker play in Billy Eckstine's band in 1944, with Sarah Vaughan singing. It was a revelation to him how the three voices entwined, collapsing the distance between the horn solos and the human voice.[27]

Bebop musicians further increased the expressiveness of their solo utterances by developing a larger vocabulary of rhythms, tones, and timbres. As Henry Pleasants described this aspect of the music:

> Trumpets were played higher than they had ever before been played, saxophones were made to yield a thousand or so notes a measure, along with uncouth grunts and squeals at the extremes of the range. Double-bass players developed a dexterity beyond the wildest imagining of any symphony orchestra bassist, and drummers opened up an entirely new world of rhythmic and percussive variety.[28]

Bebop's return to African-based polyrhythms was pioneered by drummer Kenny Clarke, who played with Dizzy Gillespie in Teddy Hill's big band between 1938 and 1942. Around 1940, Clarke experimented with keeping the basic rhythm on the top cymbal rather than, as was traditional, on the bass drum. This innovation made the rhythm more subtle and at the same time easier to complicate with half-beats or even quarter-beats. It simultaneously freed the bass drum from its role as a metronome, so that it could be used to complement the soloists with the accents that came to be called "bombs."

Kenny Clarke led the way for Max Roach. By playing the sock cymbal with the right hand rather than the left, Roach and the bebop drummers after him freed the left hand in turn from the need to keep the beat, leaving it independent to drum out polyrhythms. In this way, the drum became a solo instrument. In "KoKo," Max Roach takes a drum solo after Parker's two choruses and before the 32-bar conclusion. In the combination of

Roach's asymmetrical phrasing and polyrhythmic drumming, the basic meter of the piece seems to disappear entirely.

In the dynamic of the ensemble, the modern style of drumming emphasized the need for the other musicians to keep their attention poised in order to pick up on the beat. With Clarke's drumming style, the horn players could no longer rely on a loud marking of the time by the bass drum; they had to keep the meter in their heads.[29] At the same time, the drum became a significant voice encouraging the other soloists. As Bud Johnson recalled:

> The drums played a great part in creating. … If a cat is saying [imitates drummer], you're liable to say [imitates horn]. You'll fall behind it and fit with him, actually you're really creating together … But if a drummer's just sayin' [imitates another drumming style, just keeping the time], then … it's very difficult for a guy to play. So anyway this transition all came through, I would say, the drums.[30]

To encourage the conversational dynamic, bebop not only expanded the expressive range of each instrument, but also provided for each instrument to have its own register in the overall arrangement of sound. The drummer, by keeping time with the cymbals instead of the bass drum, complemented the bass fiddle rather than drumming over it. Bebop piano, pioneered by Bud Powell and Thelonious Monk, also moved up into midrange, so that the bass, left alone in the lower register, could be heard as a solo voice. When the pianists moved to midrange, they simultaneously freed their left hands, which before had kept rhythm, for use in improvisation.[31] Leaving the midrange to the piano, the horns explored extended harmonics high up on the tonal register.

With its conversational dynamics and emphasis on the cadences of speech, bebop can be understood as a music in which the instruments are the "voices" of musicians speaking through prosody alone. Bebop's aspiration to pure prosody is reflected in the scat singing that often accompanied it.[32] Beboppers recorded numbers with titles like "Bu-Dee-Daht"; "Oop-Bop-She-Bam" (Kenny Clarke with Fats Navarro, Sonny Stitt, and Bud Powell, 1946); and "Oop-Pop-a-Da" (Dizzy Gillespie and Orchestra, 1947).

The pure prosody of bebop was in many respects the musical equivalent of the "ideograph" in painting. It was a nonverbal communication grounded in sensual perceptions and intended to appeal to unconscious emotions rather than to the intellect. Its challenge to corporate liberalism and to the "Western" mode of thinking was implicit in this alternative "bias of attention," connoting the value system of a minority culture (in this case, the African American subculture).[33] In *Blues People*, published in 1963, LeRoi Jones contrasted the culture of jazz to that of "Western man and his highly industrialized civilization," arguing that jazz encoded "the opposing *Weltanschauung* of the African."[34]

Bebop as a Cultural Alternative

The "Africanisms" that LeRoi Jones identified in African American music—antiphony, polyrhythm, and prosodic tone—embodied the values of intersubjectivity and body-mind holism that were central to the postwar avant-garde. As a vision of sociality, the antiphonal structure of bebop suggests an intersubjective dynamic, one in which the individual and the community empower one another. Each presence enlivens the others, creating a whole that is animated by a collective energy without which the individual expression would not itself exist.[35] There is no dichotomy pitting the individual against the group; to have a voice among other voices entails no fundamental conflict. Nor is unity of purpose enforced by a hierarchical authority structure. Intersubjectivity implies that participatory democracy is the form of political economy with the greatest vitality and the most potential power. According to anthropologist John Szwed:

> Jazz requires that musicians be able to merge their unique voices in the totalizing, collective improvisations of polyphony and heterophony. The implications of this esthetic are profound and more than vaguely threatening, for no political system has yet been devised with social principles which reward maximal individualism within the framework of spontaneous egalitarian interaction.[36]

As a bias of attention [...] intersubjectivity prioritizes face-to-face, personal interactions. One "situates" oneself through these interactions rather than in relation to some abstract social scaffolding.[37] This was the cultural politics that Dwight Macdonald called for in his essay "The Root Is Man," and that the culture of spontaneity pursued through a variety of artistic media. The participatory ethic of bebop radically opposed the attitude of passive spectatorship encouraged by corporate-liberal culture in the 1940s.[38]

The second of Jones's "Africanisms," polyrhythm, emphasizes the intersubjective nature of time. Time is a perception that has to do with what phenomenologists have called *mitwelt:* the coordination of our internal, subjective reality with external processes. Phenomenologically, time is a sense of how our internal rhythms or paces jibe with those of the things and people around us. Clock time is an abstraction (a social construct) that facilitates the efficient conduct of *mitwelt* transactions—enabling us, for example, to be on time for appointments, or to sell our time on an hourly basis.[39] Clock time is the psychological state of *mitwelt,* reified and given objective status in the culture. As the corporate industrial economy has grown more complex and totalizing, time in American society has become increasingly abstract: standard time zones were established to facilitate rail transportation in 1883; daylight saving time was introduced during World War I, and then permanently reinstituted during World War II.[40]

Rhythm, by contrast, preserves the sense of *mitwelt* time as relational and intersubjective. George Lipsitz has asserted that the polyrhythms of African American music encourage the listener "to think of time as a flexible human creation rather than as an immutable outside force."[41] Bebop reemphasized the polyrhythmic aspects of jazz, in reaction against the orchestrated *mitwelt* of swing. Charlie Parker was renowned for blowing phrases that began on the eleventh bar of a twelve-bar blues, thus inverting the rhythm (which emphasizes every second measure).[42] The other soloists had to maintain an awareness of how Parker's solo related to the structure of the whole, or they would enter the piece a measure too late or too early. This is a specific instance of a quality of attention that Charles Keil has observed in African American culture generally: being "on time" is less important than being "in time." Proper timing "requires that individuals coming in keep 'careful track of the pulse.'"[43] Thus LeRoi Jones wrote in a letter to Charles Olson in 1958 that he was sending Olson a poem "about *time*, the phenomenological concept of time, from *my* birth till my death, time consisting not of any foolishness like minutes or hours or any abstract (as external, imposed) thoughts, but the time that is *event*."[44]

An intersubjective worldview is the necessary correlative of an attitude of body-mind holism. (For once the mind and the body are conceived as a unity, how can the "objective" be separated out from subjective experience?) Jones in his letter to Olson referred to time as a phenomenon of the integrated body-mind.[45] And rhythm is exactly that: time as experienced through the body. Indeed, Miles Davis wrote that good jazz music was always "up in the body" of the musician.[46]

Ethnolinguists have linked the primacy of rhythmic perception to other cultural qualities associated with body-mind holism; particularly, the "subordination ... of representation to action [and] of concept to attitude." This complex of associations, which ethnolinguists have dubbed "oral" culture, is characteristic of the culture of spontaneity, as well.[47] By contrast, musicologist John Shepherd has described Western industrial societies as dominated by the opposite biases:

> The emphasis placed by industrial societies on rational, verbal objectivity has led these societies to relegate to insignificance the realizations of any symbolic mode which implicitly challenge their dominant world sense. The unspoken—or, more appositely, unwritten—assumption is that everything that is real can be expressed in objective, rational language and its extensions, and that reality as embodied in the rational word is somehow higher than, or ontologically prior to any other evidence of reality accruing from other sources.[48]

Bebop, by emphasizing and extending the realm of prosody, offered a model of "oral" values in the midst of industrial America. LeRoi Jones asserted in *Blues People* that African American music maintained the "psychological correlative" of an oppositional "socio-economic psychological disposition," through its attention to the prosodic qualities of rhythm, tone, and timbre.[49] He traced African American musical prosody to the "talking drums" of Africa and the ideophones of African languages, which similarly cultivated a sensitivity to nuanced sound.[50]

The complex vocalizations of bebop offered a model of "secondary orality" or post-literacy: the possibility of asserting the values of an oral culture within a culture already conditioned by writing. In his novel *On the Road*, Jack Kerouac described a Slim Gaillard performance in which Gaillard used spontaneous scat syllables and drumming in an avant-garde strategy of defamiliarization:

> He does and says anything that comes into his head. He'll sing "Cement Mixer, Put-ti-Put-ti" and suddenly slow down the beat and brood over his bongos with fingertips barely tapping the skin as everybody leans forward breathlessly to hear; you think he'll do this for a minute or so, but he goes right on, for as long as an hour, making an imperceptible little noise with the tips of his fingernails, smaller and smaller all the time till you can't hear it any more and sounds of traffic come in the open door.[51]

In reestablishing the values of orality in the United States, the beboppers were engaging in a cultural project that was the complementary inverse of the "modernization" of African societies in their contact with the industrialized West. The jazz clubs were their "middle ground," as Richard White has named the geographical and social zone in which a cross-cultural dialogue takes place and the dominance of no single culture is established.[52]

The bebop "revolution" in jazz assumed different guises between 1940 and 1960, as its recovery of orality intersected with the racial politics of the times. Around 1949, cool jazz developed as an offshoot of bebop, heralded by the Miles Davis album *Birth of the Cool*. Cool was an elaboration of the tone and phrasing of Lester Young; its slower rhythms did not evoke the same high levels of nervous excitement that bebop did. But the distinction between bebop and cool jazz was not a definite one. Many musicians moved easily between the more frenetic sound of bebop and the more "laid back" style of cool.

As the 1950s progressed, however, it became clear that the more relaxed or reserved mood of cool jazz made it more appealing to white musicians and audiences. In the mid-1950s, black musicians including Art Blakey, Horace Silver, J. J. Johnson, and Sonny Rollins initiated a reaction against the more mellifluous aspects of cool jazz, returning to the driving rhythms of bebop. Their style came to be known as "hard bop." The advent of hard bop coincided with new developments bringing race relations to the forefront of American domestic politics: the Supreme Court decision barring Jim Crow segregation in *Brown v. Board of Education;* the rise of the Southern Christian Leadership Conference in the Montgomery, Alabama, bus boycott; and the murder of fourteen-year-old Emmett Till in Mississippi, for allegedly flirting with a white woman. In the smaller world of jazz musicians, increasing competition for employment among "cool" jazz musicians had begun to take on racial overtones. The year 1955 also marked the death of Charlie Parker from heroin addiction, attesting to the difficult life of the black musician in a racist society.[53]

Hard bop reasserted the African and Afro-Caribbean connections of bebop, as in Cannonball Adderley's "Jive Samba."[54] Horace Silver's father had immigrated from the Cape Verde islands; Art Blakey had lived in West Africa between 1947 and 1949. Hard bop's strong downbeats also attest to an influence from rhythm-and-blues: the popularity of cool jazz favored white musicians in the competition for jazz gigs, so more black musicians had begun to play R&B.[55]

The experimental harmonies and meters of bop were extended even further in modal and "free jazz," explored by Miles Davis and John Coltrane in *Milestones* (1958) and by Ornette Coleman in *Free Jazz* (1960).[56] Free jazz added atonality to the polytonality of the bebop repertoire, and distanced its prosodic utterances even farther from the regimen of time signatures, metronomes, and measures. Ornette Coleman, born in 1930, had come to jazz through R&B. In the early 1950s, in Los Angeles, he had begun playing experimental atonal melodies on a toy plastic alto sax, with Don Cherry accompanying him on a miniature trumpet.

Painters and poets who were actively pursuing the aesthetic of spontaneity in their own media congregated at the Five Spot, the Cafe Bohemia, Arthur's Tavern, and the Village Vanguard in New York City, to hear the jazz experiments of Charlie Parker, Thelonious Monk, Charles Mingus, Sonny Rollins, Cecil Taylor, Ornette Coleman, and many others. Modern jazz aficionados in abstract expressionist circles included Jack Tworkov, Grace Hartigan, Alfred Leslie, Willem de Kooning, Mike Goldberg, Norman Bluhm, Joan Mitchell, Franz Kline, and Frank O'Hara. Larry Rivers was himself a bebop saxophonist. Peter Voulkos taught himself jazz guitar. Lee Krasner has asserted the profound influence of bebop on Jackson Pollock's painting during the crucial year, 1946, when he developed his gesture-field style of painting: "He would get into grooves of listening to his jazz records—not just for days—day and night, day and night for three days running. ... He thought it was the only other really creative thing happening in this country."[57] The beat poets, especially, took bop prosody as the basis of their spontaneous poetics.

Notes

1 Quoted in Grover Sales, *Jazz: America's Classical Music* (New York: Prentice-Hall, 1984), 117. See also Don Heckman, "Pres and Hawk: Saxophone Fountainheads," *Down Beat* (Jan. 3,

1963): 20–22; reprinted in Lewis Porter, ed., *Lester Young: A Reader* (Washington: Smithsonian Institution Press, 1991), 258.

2 Linguistically, prosody refers to those elements of a verbal utterance that are not contained in the symbolic sign that is the word, but communicated through other means: rhythm, accent, tone, timbre—the musical elements of speech made by the body and, as Paul Zumthor has written in his study of oral poetry, "otherwise untranslatable into language." Paul Zumthor, *Oral Poetry: An Introduction*, Kathryn Murphy-Judy, trans. (Minneapolis: University of Minnesota Press, 1990), 131, 138.

3 See LeRoi Jones, *Blues People: The Negro Experience in White America and the Music that Developed from It* (New York: William Morrow, 1963), 176. See also David Stowe, *Swing Changes: Big Band Jazz in New Deal America* (Cambridge, MA: Harvard University Press, 1994).

4 Jones, *Blues People*, 26–27 and 175–76.

5 Ira Gitler, *Swing to Bop: An Oral History of the Transition in Jazz in the 1940s* (New York: Oxford University Press, 1985), 4. See also Acklyn Lynch, "Black Culture in the Early Forties," in *Nightmare Overhanging Darkly: Essays on African American Culture and Resistance* (Chicago: Third World Press, 1993), 65.

6 See Thomas Kochman, "Fighting Words," in *Black and White Styles in Conflict* (Chicago: University of Chicago Press, 1981), 52–58; and Roger D. Abrahams, "Rapping and Capping: Black Talk as Art," in John F. Szwed, ed., *Black America* (New York: Basic Books, 1970), 134–35.

7 Henry Pleasants, *Serious Music—and All That Jazz!* (New York: Simon and Schuster, 1969), 104.

8 See Lawrence Levine, *Highbrow/Lowbrow: The Emergence of Cultural Hierarchy in America* (Cambridge, MA: Harvard University Press, 1988), 59–60, 104–46, 178–82, and 188–93.

9 As John Szwed and Morton Marks have observed, "Everything we know about Afro-American musical performance style tells us that this music was played with greater flexibility and rhythmic subtlety than the notation of sheet music can suggest." John F. Szwed and Morton Marks, "The Afro-American Transformation of European Set Dances and Dance Suites," *Dance Research Journal* 20:1 (Summer 1988): 31–32. The term "bebop" itself is said to have originated from Gillespie's practice of scat singing his musical ideas to his sidemen because all the sixteenth and thirty-second notes made them too difficult to write down and to read. Gitler, *Swing to Bop*, 199.

10 I am applying to musical genres the method of cultural morphology explicated by Fredric Jameson in his essay "On Interpretation," in *The Political Unconscious: Narrative as a Socially Symbolic Act* (Ithaca: Cornell University Press, 1981), 35, 57, 63, and 81. Social conditions precipitate psychological and cultural responses, which register as modifications in existing discursive forms.

11 The song was by Ray Noble. Barnet's rendition can be found on RCA Victor, *Great Dance Bands of the Thirties and Forties* (LPM-2081); and on RCA Victor, *Golden Anniversary Album* (PR-111).

12 "KoKo," recorded Nov. 26, 1945, Charlie Parker, alto sax: Dizzy Gillespie, trumpet, piano; Curley Russell, bass; Max Roach, drums; included in *The Smithsonian Collection of Classic Jazz* R033/P7–19477 (CBS, 1987).

13 See Barney Kessel, quoted in Gitler, *Swing to Bop*, 158.

14 Quoted in ibid., 170.

15 See George Simon, *The Big Bands* (New York: Macmillan, 1971), 40–69.

16 Pleasants, *Serious Music*, 134.

17 Quoted in Ronald Sukenick, *Down and In: Life in the Underground* (New York: Beech Tree Books, 1987), 11–12.

18 Miles Templar, Reply to Anatole Broyard, *Partisan Review* 15:9 (Sept. 1948): 1054.

19 Quoted in Gitler, *Swing to Bop*, 52.

20 Templar, Reply to Anatole Broyard, 1054. For the original criticism, see Anatole Broyard, "A Portrait of the Hipster," *Partisan Review* 15:6 (June 1948): 721–27.

21 Davis, Miles. *Miles: The Autobiography* (New York: Simon and Schuster, 1989), 221–22. Without give-and-take among the soloists, the bebop sound would not come out right. In 1949, Miles Davis played with Oscar Pettiford's band, and later lamented: "That band wasn't into playing as a group. Everybody was playing these long solos and shit, trying to outdo the next guy. It was all fucked up and it was a shame, because it could have been something else." Davis, *Miles*, 125.

234   *Daniel Belgrad*

22 Archie Shepp, foreword to John Clellon Holmes, *The Horn* ([1958] New York: Thunder's Mouth Press, 1987), iii.
23 Davis, *Miles*, 89.
24 Quoted in Gitler, *Swing to Bop*, 302.
25 Templar, Reply to Anatole Broyard, 1054.
26 Davis, *Miles*, 70.
27 Ibid., 9.
28 Pleasants, *Serious Music*, 145.
29 Kenny Clarke, quoted in Gitler, *Swing to Bop*, 55.
30 Quoted in ibid., 52–54.
31 Ibid., 101, 106.
32 Among the most famous scat singers of the bebop era were Sarah Vaughan, Ella Fitzgerald, Betty Carter, Leo Watson, Mel Torme, Slim Gaillard, Babs Gonzales, Jackie Cain, Roy Kral, Dave Lambert, and Buddy Stewart. See Gitler, *Swing to Bop*, 232–33. See also Roy Carr, Brian Case, and Fred Dellar, *The Hip: Hipsters, Jazz, and the Beat Generation* (Boston: Faber and Faber, 1986), 22–25.
33 George Lipsitz has observed that the exclusion of African Americans from full participation in white society has meant that their subculture is not completely permeated by the values of the dominant culture. Lipsitz points out the ways in which black music (particularly rock and roll) has remained outside the particular discipline imposed by corporate industrialism, which valorizes predictability, reproducibility, impersonality, and delayed gratification. (George Lipsitz, "Dialogic Aspects of Rock and Roll," *Time Passages: Collective Memory and American Popular Culture* [Minneapolis: University of Minnesota Press, 1990], 111.) It seems necessary to add to Lipsitz's analysis that African American culture has preserved alternative values not only as the passive result of white exclusion. Historically, blacks have asserted grounds for rejecting assimilation to the dominant culture even when it seemed available as an option. See, for instance, James Baldwin, *The Fire Next Time* (New York: Vintage, 1963), 40–44. African American culture is not defined by the absence of dominant culture, but by the transplantation and hybridization of African cultures in America. See, for instance, William A. Stewart, "Understanding Black Language," in Szwed, ed., *Black America*, 123–26.
34 Jones, *Blues People*, 1, 6, and 142.
35 Thomas Kochman has traced this intersubjective dynamic through several aspects of African American secular and religious culture. See Thomas Kochman, "The Force Field," in *Black and White Styles in Conflict*, 109–10.
36 John Szwed, "Josef Skvorecky and the Tradition of Jazz Literature," *World Literature Today* 54:4 (Autumn 1980): 588.
37 See John Shepherd, *Music as Social Text* (Cambridge: Polity Press, 1991), 20. See also Thomas Kochman, "Information as Property," in *Black and White Styles in Conflict*, 97–98.
38 As Thomas Kochman has written, "about the only *incorrect* thing you can do is not to respond at all." Kochman, "Force Field," 111.
39 Rollo May and I. Yalom, "Existential Psychotherapy," in Raymond J. Corsini, ed., *Current Psychotherapies*, 3rd ed. (Itasca, Il: F. E. Peacock, 1984), 358. See also Michael O'Malley, *Keeping Watch: A History of American Time* (New York: Viking, 1990).
40 Alan Trachtenberg, *The Incorporation of America* (New York: Hill and Wang, 1982), 60. Van English, "Daylight Saving Time," in *Encyclopedia Americana*, International ed. (Danbury, CT: Grolier, 1996), vol. 8, 548.
41 Lipsitz, *Time Passages*, 112.
42 Davis, *Miles*, 101.
43 Charles Keil, "Motion and Feeling in Music," *Journal of Aesthetics and Art Criticism* 24:3 (1966): 345. Cited in Kochman, "Force Field," 111.
44 LeRoi Jones to Charles Olson, Dec. 9, 1958, Olson Papers, Archives and Special Collections Department, Thomas J. Dodd Research Center, University of Connecticut Libraries; used with permission. Olson himself had written in 1951: "All that TIME IS, is RHYTHM and there is no way of knowing any rhythm OTHER THAN YOUR OWN, than by your own." Olson, *Letters for Origin, 1950–1956*, Albert Glover, ed. (London: Cape Goliard Press, 1969), 83.
45 "[T]ime the physical event (or spiritual, emotional, psychological, psychical &c. for that matter) but time the phenomenon." Jones to Olson, Dec. 9, 1958.

46 Davis, *Miles*, 100.

47 Zumthor, *Oral Poetry*, 24. See also Walter Ong, *The Presence of the Word* (New Haven: Yale University Press, 1967); and Ong, *Orality and Literacy: The Technologizing of the Word* (New York: Methuen, 1982), 11 and 36–57.

The distinction between oral and literate cultures is not dichotomous. The exact extent to which cultures can be characterized along a continuum from orality to literacy has been hotly debated by scholars.

Those thinkers supporting a distinction between the worldviews of cultures on the basis of literacy versus orality include Walter Ong, Jack Goody, Paul Zumthor, Franz Bauml, Brian Stock, Paul Saenger, Marshall McLuhan, and Albert Lord. See Lord, *The Singer of Tales* ([1960] Cambridge, MA: Harvard University Press, 1964); Goody, *The Domestication of the Savage Mind* (New York: Cambridge University Press, 1977); and Edmund Carpenter and Marshall McLuhan, "Acoustic Space," in Carpenter and McLuhan, eds., *Explorations in Communication: An Anthology* (Boston: Beacon Press, 1960), 68. Eric Havelock's *Preface to Plato* (Cambridge, MA: Belknap Press, 1963) argued that it was the development of phonetics in particular that constituted a revolution in culture.

Negative responses to this distinction arose on the grounds that the characterization of "oral" cultures relied too heavily on primitivist discourses. See the critique by Ruth Finnegan, "Literacy versus Non-Literacy: The Great Divide?" in Robin Horton and Ruth Finnegan, eds., *Modes of Thought: Essays on Thinking in Western and Non-Western Societies* (London: Faber, 1973). Finnegan argued that so-called oral cultures must not be thought of as incapable of self-awareness, individualism, irony, or fictionality. See also Deborah Tannen, "The Myth of Orality and Literacy," in William Frawley, ed., *Linguistics and Literacy* (New York: Plenum Press, 1982).

A mutually satisfactory understanding seems possible. See Goody, *The Logic of Writing and the Organization of Society* (New York: Cambridge University Press, 1986), xv; and Finnegan, *Literacy and Orality: Studies in the Technology of Communication* (New York: Blackwell, 1988), 146 and 160. As the cultural determinism of Goody's earlier studies of oral culture had been tempered by a neo-Marxist argument that recognized economic and cultural interpenetration, Finnegan has conceded that the distinction between literacy and orality does identify cultural orientations facilitating different forms of cognitive development.

48 Shepherd, *Music as Social Text*, 79.

49 Jones, *Blues People*, 28, 142, and 6.

50 Ibid., 26. For more on African languages having a class of words called "ideophones," or sound ideas, see Zumthor, *Oral Poetry*, 102.

51 Jack Kerouac, *On the Road* (New York: Viking Penguin, 1957), 146.

52 Richard White, *The Middle Ground: Indians, Empires, and Republics in the Great Lakes Region, 1650–1815* (New York: Cambridge University Press, 1991), x, 50–53. Paul Zumthor has written: "In other parts of the world, [our technological] civilization—being spread over terrain less suited to its rapid implementation—lets us perceive a reality that it condemns in the long run but with which it now colludes. African societies offer the perfect example of this." Zumthor, *Oral Poetry*, 46.

53 For a fictional treatment of this theme, see James Baldwin, "Sonny's Blues," reprinted in Marcela Breton, ed., *Hot and Cool: Jazz Short Stories* (New York: Penguin, 1990), 92–130. Baldwin offers an excellent description of the intersubjectivity of bebop as an alternative to alienation.

54 David Rosenthal, *Hard Bop: Jazz and Black Music, 1955–1965* (New York: Oxford University Press, 1992), 37–40 and 48. The late forties had witnessed an infusion of Afro-Cuban music into bebop. In 1948 and 1949, Charlie Parker recorded with Machito's Afro-Cuban orchestra. Cuban conga-drum player Chano Pozo brought Dizzy Gillespie's big band its distinctive Afro-Cuban rhythms, the basis of recordings like "Cubana Be, Cubana Bop." See Gitler, *Swing to Bop*, 292.

55 Rosenthal, *Hard Bop*, 21–22.

56 Other pioneers of free jazz in the 1950s included Cecil Taylor and Albert Ayler.

57 Rosenthal, *Hard Bop*, 75. David Amram, *Vibrations* (New York: Viking Press, 1968), 261–62. Larry Rivers, *What Did I Do? The Unauthorized Autobiography of Larry Rivers* (New York: HarperCollins, 1992). Rose Slivka, *Peter Voulkos: A Dialogue with Clay* (Boston: new York Graphic Society, 1978), 40. Lee Krasner, quoted in B. H. Friedman, *Jackson Pollock: Energy Made Visible* (New York: McGraw Hill, 1972), 88–89.

32   Happenings in the New York Scene

Allan Kaprow

After spending his early years in Arizona, Allan Kaprow (1927–2006) went to New York City where, after attending New York University, Columbia University, and the Hans Hofman School of Fine Arts, he spent many years teaching, painting, and writing. In the late 1950s he began collaborating with others in devising a "concrete art" made of everyday materials—his suggestions included paint, chairs, food, electric and neon lights, smoke, water, old socks, a dog, and movies. This demand for indeterminacy and messiness is echoed in this 1961 essay "Happenings in the New York Scene." He and the other members of the Fluxus group looked to infuse a spirit of improvisation and of surprise into what they saw as a complacent art scene. As with other contributors to this volume, Kaprow sees audience participation as crucial, and although he seeks to liberate the arts, and its practitioners, through performance, he already predicts that the process will have to be renewed and reinvented by subsequent generations. "These are our greenest days," he writes. "Some of us will become famous, and we will have proven once again that the only success occurred when there was a lack of it."

Key words: New York City; visual art; Fluxus; interdisciplinarity

If you haven't been to the Happenings, let me give you a kaleidoscope sampling of some of their great moments.

Everybody is crowded into a downtown loft, milling about, like at an opening. It's hot. There are lots of big cartons sitting all over the place. One by one they start to move, sliding and careening drunkenly in every direction, lunging into one another, accompanied by loud breathing sounds over four loudspeakers. Now it's winter and cold and it's dark, and all around little blue lights go on and off at their own speed while three large brown gunnysack constructions drag an enormous pile of ice and stones over bumps, losing most of it, and blankets keep falling over everything from the ceiling. A hundred iron barrels and gallon wine jugs hanging on ropes swing back and forth, crashing like church bells, spewing glass all over. Suddenly, mushy shapes pop up from the floor and painters slash at curtains dripping with action. A wall of trees tied with colored rags advances on the crowd, scattering everybody, forcing them to leave. There are muslin telephone booths for all with a record player or microphone that tunes you in to everybody else. Coughing, you breathe in noxious fumes, or the smell of hospitals and lemon juice. A nude girl runs after the racing pool of a searchlight, throwing spinach greens into it. Slides and movies, projected over walls and people, depict hamburgers; big ones, huge ones, red ones, skinny ones, flat ones, etc. You come in as a spectator and maybe you discover you're caught in it after all, as you push things around like so much furniture. Words rumble past, whispering, deedaaa, baroom, love me, love me; shadows joggle on screens; power saws and lawn mowers screech just like the I.R.T. at Union Square. Tin cans rattle and you stand up to see or change your seat or answer questions shouted at you by shoeshine boys and old ladies. Long silences when nothing happens, and you're sore because you paid $1.50 contribution, when bang! there you are facing yourself in a mirror jammed at you. Listen. A cough from the alley. You giggle because you're afraid, suffer claustrophobia, talk to someone nonchalantly, but all the time you're *there,* getting into the act ... Electric fans start, gently wafting breezes of New-Car smell past your nose as leaves bury piles of a whining, burping, foul, pinky mess.

So much for the flavor. Now I would like to describe the nature of Happenings in a different manner, more analytically—their purpose and place in art.

Although widespread opinion has been expressed about these events, usually by those who have never seen them, they are actually little known beyond a small group of interested persons. This small following is aware of several different kinds of Happenings. There are the sophisticated, witty works put on by the theater people; the very sparsely abstract, almost Zen-like rituals given by another group (mostly writers and musicians); and those in which I am most involved, crude, lyrical, and very spontaneous. This kind grew out of the advanced American painting of the last decade, and those of us involved were all painters (or still are). There is some beneficial exchange among the three, however.

In addition, outside New York there is the Gutai group in Osaka: reported activity in San Francisco, Chicago, Cologne, Paris, and Milan; and a history that goes back through Surrealism, Dada, Mime, the circus, carnivals, the traveling saltimbanques, all the way to medieval mystery plays and processions. Of most of this we know very little; only the spirit has been sensed. Of what *I* know, I find that I have decided philosophical reservations. Therefore, the points I make are intended to represent, not the views of all those who create works that might be generically related, or even of all those whose work I admire, but of those whose works I feel to be the most adventuresome, fruitfully open to applications, and the most challenging of any art in the air at present.

Happenings are events that, put simply, happen. Though the best of them have a decided impact—that is, we feel, "here is something important"—they appear to go nowhere and do not make any particular literary point. In contrast to the arts of the past, they have no structured beginning, middle, or end. Their form is open-ended and fluid; nothing obvious is sought and therefore nothing is won, except the certainty of a number of occurrences to which we are more than normally attentive. They exist for a single performance, or only a few, and are gone forever as new ones take their place.

These events are essentially theater pieces, however unconventional. That they are still largely rejected by devotees of the theater may be due to their uncommon power and primitive energy, and to their derivation from the rites of American Action Painting. But by widening the concept "theater" to include them (like widening the concept "painting" to include collage), we can see them against this basic background and understand them better.

To my way of thinking, Happenings possess some crucial qualities that distinguish them from the usual theatrical works, even the experimental ones of today. First, there is the *context,* the place of conception and enactment. The most intense and essential Happenings have been spawned in old lofts, basements, vacant stores, natural surroundings, and the street, where very small audiences, or groups of visitors, are commingled in some way with the event, flowing in and among its parts. There is thus no separation of audience and play (as there is even in round or pit theaters); the elevated picture-window view of most playhouses is gone, as are the expectations of curtain openings and *tableaux vivants* and curtain closings ...

The sheer rawness of the out-of-doors or the closeness of dingy city quarters in which the radical Happenings flourish is more appropriate, I believe, in temperament and un-artiness, to the materials and directness of these works. The place where anything grows up (a certain kind of art in this case), that is, its "habitat," gives to it not only a space, a set of relationships to the various things around it, and a range of values, but an overall atmosphere as well, which penetrates it and whoever experiences it. Habitats have always had this effect, but it is especially important now, when our advanced art approaches a fragile but marvelous life, one that maintains itself by a mere thread, melting the surroundings, the artist, the work, and everyone who comes to it into an elusive, changeable configuration.

If I may digress a moment to bring this point into focus, it may reveal why the "better" galleries and homes (whose decor is still a by-now-antiseptic neoclassicism of the twenties) desiccate and prettify modern paintings and sculpture that had looked so natural in their studio birthplace. It may also explain why artists' studios do not look like galleries and why when an artist's studio does, everyone is suspicious. I think that today this organic connection between art and its environment is so meaningful and necessary that removing one from the other results in abortion. Yet the artists who have made us aware of this lifeline deny it; for the flattery of being "on show" blinds them to every insensitivity heaped upon their suddenly weakened offerings. There seems no end to the white walls, the tasteful aluminum frames, the lovely lighting, fawn gray rugs, cocktails, polite conversation. The attitude, I mean the worldview, conveyed by such a fluorescent reception is in itself not "bad." It is unaware. And being unaware, it can hardly be responsive to the art it promotes and professes to admire.

Happenings invite us to cast aside for a moment these proper manners and partake wholly in the real nature of the art and (one hopes) life. Thus a Happening is rough and sudden and often feels "dirty." Dirt, we might begin to realize, is also organic and fertile, and everything, including the visitors, can grow a little in such circumstances.

To return to the contrast between Happenings and plays, the second important difference is that a Happening has no plot, no obvious "philosophy," and is materialized in an improvisatory fashion, like jazz, and like much contemporary painting, where we do not know exactly what is going to happen next. The action leads itself any way it wishes, and the artist controls it only to the degree that it keeps on "shaking" right. A modern play rarely has such an impromptu basis, for plays are still *first written*. A Happening is *generated* in action by a headful of ideas or a flimsily jotted-down score of "root" directions.

A play assumes that words are the almost absolute medium. A Happening frequently has words, but they may or may not make literal sense. If they do, their sense is not part of the fabric of "sense" that other nonverbal elements (noise, visual stuff, action) convey. Hence, they have a brief, emergent, and sometimes detached quality. If they do not make sense, then they are heard as the *sound* of words instead of the meaning conveyed by them. Words, however, need not be used at all: a Happening might consist of a swarm of locusts being dropped in and around the performance space. This element of chance with respect to the medium itself is not to be expected from the ordinary theater.

Indeed, the involvement in chance, which is the third and most problematical quality found in Happenings, rarely occurs in the conventional theater. When it does, it is usually a marginal benefit of interpretation. In the present work, chance (in conjunction with improvisation) is a deliberately employed mode of operating that penetrates the whole composition and its character. It is the vehicle of the spontaneous. And it is the clue to understanding how control (the setting up of chance techniques) can effectively produce the opposite quality of the unplanned and apparently uncontrolled. I think it can be demonstrated that much contemporary art, which counts upon inspiration to yield that admittedly desirable verve or sense of the unselfconscious, is by now getting results that appear planned and academic. A loaded brush and a mighty swing always seem to hit the ball to the same spot.

Chance then, rather than spontaneity, is a key term, for it implies risk and fear (thus reestablishing that fine nervousness so pleasant when something is about to occur). It also better names a method that becomes manifestly unmethodical if one considers the pudding more a proof than the recipe.

Traditional art has always tried to make it good every time, believing that this was a truer truth than life. Artists who directly utilize chance hazard failure, the "failure" of being less artistic and more lifelike. The "Art" they produce might surprisingly turn out to be an affair that has all the inevitability of a well-ordered middle-class Thanksgiving dinner (I have seen a few remarkable Happenings that were "bores" in this sense). But it could be like slipping on a banana peel, or going to heaven.

If a flexible framework with the barest limits is established by selecting, for example, only five elements out of an infinity of possibilities, almost anything can happen. And something always does, even things that are unpleasant. Visitors to a Happening are now and then not sure what has taken place, when it has ended, even when things have gone "wrong." For when something goes "wrong," something far more "right," more revelatory, has many times emerged. This sort of sudden near-miracle presently seems to be made more likely by chance procedures.

If artists grasp the import of that word *chance* and accept it (no easy achievement in our culture), then its methods needn't invariably cause their work to reduce to either chaos or a bland indifference, lacking in concreteness and intensity, as in a table of random numbers. On the contrary, the identities of those artists who employ such techniques are very clear. It is odd that when artists give up certain hitherto privileged aspects of the self, so that they cannot always "correct" something according to their taste, the work and the artist frequently come out on top. And when they come out on the bottom, it is a very concrete bottom!

The final point I should like to make about Happenings as against plays is implicit in all the discussion—their impermanence. Composed so that a premium is placed on the unforeseen, a Happening cannot be reproduced. The few performances given of each work differ considerably from one another; and the work is over before habits begin to set in. The physical materials used to create the environment of Happenings are the most perishable kind: newspapers, junk, rags, old wooden crates knocked together, cardboard cartons cut up, real trees, food, borrowed machines, etc. They cannot last for long in whatever arrangement they are put. A Happening is thus fresh, while it lasts, for better or worse.

Here we need not go into the considerable history behind such values embodied in the Happenings. Suffice it to say that the passing, the changing, the natural, even the willingness to fail are familiar. They reveal a spirit that is at once passive in its acceptance of what may be and affirmative in its disregard of security. One is also left exposed to the quite marvelous experience of being surprised. This is, in essence, a continuation of the tradition of Realism.

The significance of the Happening is not to be found simply in the fresh creative wind now blowing. Happenings are not just another new style. Instead, like American art of the late 1940s, they are a moral act, a human stand of great urgency, whose professional status as art is less a criterion than their certainty as an ultimate existential commitment.

It has always seemed to me that American creative energy only becomes charged by such a sense of crisis. The real weakness of much vanguard art since 1951 is its complacent assumption that art exists and can be recognized and practiced. I am not so sure whether what we do now is art or something not quite art. If I call it art, it is because I wish to avoid the endless arguments some other name would bring forth. Paradoxically, if it turns out to be art after all, it will be so in spite of (or because of) this larger question.

But this explosive atmosphere has been absent from our arts for ten years, and one by one our major figures have dropped by the wayside, laden with glory. If tense excitement has returned with the Happenings, one can only suspect that the pattern will be repeated. These are our greenest days. Some of us will become famous, and we will have proven once again that the only success occurred when there was a lack of it.

Such worries have been voiced before in more discouraging times, but today is hardly such a time, when so many are rich and desire a befitting culture. I may seem therefore to throw water on a kindly spark when I touch on this note, for we customarily prefer to celebrate victories without ever questioning whether they are victories indeed. But I think it is necessary to question the whole state of American success, because to do so is not only to touch on what is characteristically American and what is crucial about Happenings but also partly to explain America's special strength. And this strength has nothing to do with success.

Particularly in New York, where success is most evident, we have not yet looked clearly at it and what it may imply—something that, until recently, a European who had earned it did quite naturally. We are unable to accept rewards for being artists, because it has been sensed deeply that to be one means to live and work in isolation and pride. Now that a new haut monde is demanding of us art and more art, we find ourselves running away or running to it, shocked and guilty, either way. I must be emphatic: the glaring truth, to anyone who cares to examine it calmly, is that nearly all artists, working in any medium from words to paint, who have made their mark as innovators, as radicals in the best sense of that word, have, once they have been recognized and paid handsomely, capitulated to the interests of good taste. There is no overt pressure anywhere. The patrons of art are the nicest people in the world. They neither wish to corrupt nor actually do so. The whole situation is corrosive, for neither patrons nor artists comprehend their role; both are always a little edgy, however abundantly smiles are exchanged. Out of this hidden discomfort there comes a stillborn art, tight or merely repetitive at best and at worst, chic. The old daring and the charged atmosphere of precarious discovery that marked every hour of the lives of modern artists, even when they were not working at art, vanishes. Strangely, no one seems to know this except, perhaps, the "unsuccessful" artists waiting for their day ...

To us, who are already answering the increasing telephone calls from entrepreneurs, this is more than disturbing. We are, at this writing, still free to do what we wish, and are watching ourselves as we become caught up in an irreversible process. Our Happenings, like all the other art produced in the last decade and a half by those who, for a few brief moments, were also free, are in no small part the expression of this liberty. In our beginning some of us, reading the signs all too clearly, are facing our end.

If this is close to the truth, it is surely melodrama as well, and I intend the tone of my words to suggest that quality. Anyone moved by the spirit of tough-guyism would answer that all of this is a pseudo-problem of the artists' own making. They have the alternative of rejecting fame if they do not want its responsibilities. Artists have made their sauce; now they must stew in it. It is not the patrons' and the publicists' moral obligation to protect the artists' freedom.

But such an objection, while sounding healthy and realistic, is in fact European and old-fashioned; it sees the creator as an indomitable hero who exists on a plane above any living context. It fails to appreciate the special character of our mores in America, and this matrix, I would maintain, is the only reality within which any question about the arts may be asked.

The tough answer fails to appreciate our taste for fads and "movements," each one increasingly equivalent to the last in value and complexion, making far that vast ennui, that anxiety lying so close to the surface of our comfortable existence. It does not account for our need to "love" everybody (our democracy) that must give every dog his bone and compels everyone known by no one to want to be addressed by a nickname. This relentless craving loves everything destructively, for it actually hates love. What can anyone's interest in this kind of art or that marvelous painter possibly mean then? Is it a meaning lost on the artist?

Where else can we see the unbelievable but frequent phenomenon of successful radicals becoming "fast friends" with successful academicians, united only by a common success and deliberately insensitive to the fundamental issues their different values imply? I wonder where else but here can be found that shutting of the eyes to the question of purpose. Perhaps in the United States such a question could not ever before exist, so pervasive has been the amoral mush.

This everyday world affects the way art is created as much as it conditions its response—a response the critic articulates for the patron, who in turn acts upon it. Melodrama, I think, is central to all of this.

Apart from those in our recent history who have achieved something primarily in the spirit of European art, much of the positive character of America can be understood by the word *melodrama:* the saga of the Pioneer is true melodrama, the Cowboy and the Indian: the Rent Collector, Stella Dallas, Charlie Chaplin, the Organization Man, Mike Todd are melodrama. And now the American Artist is a melodramatic figure. Probably without trying, we have been able to see profoundly what we are all about through these archetypal personages. This is the quality of our temperament that a classically trained mind would invariably mistake for sentimentality.

But I do not want to suggest that avant-garde artists produce even remotely sentimental works; I am referring more to the hard and silly melodrama of their lives and almost farcical social position, known as well as the story of George Washington and the Cherry Tree, which infuses what they do with a powerful yet fragile fever. The idea is partly that they will be famous only after they die, a myth we have taken to heart far more than the Europeans, and far more than we care to admit. Half-consciously, though, there is the more indigenous dream that the adventure is everything; the tangible goal is not important. The Pacific coast is farther away than we thought, Ponce de Leon's Fountain of Youth lies beyond the next everglade, and the next, and the next … meanwhile let's battle the alligators.

What is not melodramatic, in the sense I am using the word, but is disappointing and tragic, is that today vanguard artists are given their prizes very quickly instead of being left to their adventure. Furthermore, they are led to believe, by no one in particular, that this was the thing they wanted all the while. But in some obscure recess of their mind, they assume they must now die, at least spiritually, to keep the myth intact. Hence, the creative aspect of their art ceases. To all intents and purposes, they are dead and they are famous.

In this context of achievement-and-death, artists who make Happenings are living out the purest melodrama. Their activity embodies the myth of nonsuccess, for Happenings cannot be sold and taken home; they can only be supported. And because of their intimate and fleeting nature, only a few people can experience them. They remain isolated and proud. The creators of such events are adventurers too, because much of what they do is unforeseen. They stack the deck that way.

By some reasonable but unplanned process, Happenings, we may suspect, have emerged as an art that can function precisely as long as the mechanics of our present rush for cultural maturity continue. This situation will no doubt change eventually and thus will change the issues I address here.

But for now there is this to consider, the point I raised earlier: some of us will probably become famous. It will be an ironic fame fashioned largely by those who have never seen our work. The attention and pressure of such a position will probably destroy most of us, as they have nearly all the others. We know no better than anyone else how to handle the metaphysics and practice of worldly power. We know even less, since we have not been in the slightest involved with it. That I feel it necessary, in the interests of the truth, to write this article, which may hasten the conclusion, is even more fatefully ironic. But this is the chance we take; it is part of the picture ...

Yet I cannot help wondering if there isn't a positive side, too, a side also subject to the throw of the dice. To the extent that a Happening is not a commodity but a brief event, from the standpoint of any publicity it may receive, it may become a state of mind. Who will have been there at that event? It may become like the sea monsters of the past or the flying saucers of yesterday. I shouldn't really mind, for as the new myth grows on its own, without reference to anything in particular, the artist may achieve a beautiful privacy, famed for something purely imaginary while free to explore something nobody will notice.

33 Other: From Noun to Verb

Nathaniel Mackey

Among Nathaniel Mackey's many works is the fiction series "From a Broken Bottle Traces of Perfume Still Emanate," which spans the books *Bedouin Hornbook* (1986) until, to date, *Brass Cathedral* (2008). In 2006 he won the National Book Award for his poetry book *Splay Anthem*, and his critical works include *Discrepant Engagement: Dissonance, Cross-Culturality, Experimental Writing* (1993) and *Para-critical Hinge: Essays, Talks, Notes, Interviews* (2005). Dr Mackey is the editor of *American Poetry: The Twentieth Century* (2000, with Carolyn Kizer, John Hollander, Robert Hass, and Marjorie Perloff) and *Moment's Notice: Jazz in Poetry and Prose* (1993, with Art Lange), and since 1982 he has edited the magazine *Hambone*. After many years at U of C Santa Cruz, he recently became the Reynolds Price Professor of Creative Writing at Duke University. "Other: From Noun to Verb" first appeared in 1992 in the University of California journal *Representations*. This insightful essay makes clear how African Americans, "othered" within their own society, in turn othered the prevailing culture in their speech, in their writing, and in their music. Improvisation, particularly that of the jazz musician, occupies a special place within this process: "In matters of artistic othering," Mackey writes, "individual expression both reflects and redefines the collective, realigns, refracts it."

Key words: jazz; African American culture; popular music; poetry

I

Cultural diversity has become a much-discussed topic. I would like to emphasize that cultural diversity *is* cultural, that it is a consequence of actions and assumptions which are socially—rather than naturally, genetically—instituted and reinforced. The inequities the recent attention to cultural diversity is meant to redress are in part the outcome of confounding the social with the genetic; so we need to make it clear that when we speak of otherness we are not positing static, intrinsic attributes or characteristics. We need instead to highlight the dynamics of agency and attribution by way of which otherness is brought about and maintained, the fact that *other* is something people do, more importantly a verb than an adjective or a noun. Thus, I would like to look at some instances of and ways of thinking about othering—primarily othering within artistic media, but also othering within the medium of society, touching upon relation-ships between the two. Artistic othering has to do with innovation, invention, and change, upon which cultural health and diversity depend and thrive. Social othering has to do with power, exclusion, and privilege, the centralizing of a norm against which otherness is measured, meted out, marginalized. My focus is the practice of the former by people subjected to the latter.

The title "Other: From Noun to Verb" is meant to recall Amiri Baraka's way of describing white appropriation of black music in chapter 10 of *Blues People* [reprinted in this volume]. In that chapter he discusses the development of big-band jazz during the twenties and thirties by Fletcher Henderson, Duke Ellington, Jimmie Lunceford, and others and the imitation and commoditization of it by white musicians like Jimmy and Tommy Dorsey, Artie Shaw, Charlie Barnet, and Benny Goodman (who became known as the "King of Swing"). He calls the chapter "Swing—From Verb to Noun." Typical of the way he uses the verb/noun distinction is this remark: "But for most of America by the twenties, jazz (or *jass,* the noun, not the verb) meant the Original Dixieland Jazz Band (to the hip) and Paul Whiteman (to the square)."[1] Or this one:

> *Swing,* the verb, meant a simple reaction to the music (and as it developed in verb usage, a way of reacting to anything in life). As it was formalized, and the term and the music taken further out of context, *swing* became a noun that meant a commercial popular music in cheap imitation of a kind of Afro-American music.
>
> (212–13)

"From verb to noun" means the erasure of black inventiveness by white appropriation. As in Georg Lukács's notion of phantom objectivity, the "noun," white commodification, obscures or "disappears" the "verb" it rips off, black agency, black authority, black invention. Benny Goodman bought arrangements from black musicians, later hired Fletcher Henderson as his band's chief arranger, and later still brought black musicians Teddy Wilson, Lionel Hampton, Charlie Christian, and Cootie Williams into his band, but for the most part black musicians were locked out of the enormous commercial success made of the music they'd invented. The most popular and best-paid bands were white, and the well-paying studio jobs created by the emergence of radio as the preeminent medium for disseminating the music were almost completely restricted to white musicians.

"From verb to noun" means, on the aesthetic level, a less dynamic, less improvisatory, less blues-inflected music and, on the political level, a containment of black mobility, a containment of the economic and social advances that might accrue to black artistic innovation. The domain of action and the ability to act suggested by *verb* is closed off by the hypostasis, paralysis, and arrest suggested by *noun,* the confinement to a pre-determined status Baraka has in mind when he writes: "There should be no cause for wonder that the trumpets of Bix Beiderbecke and Louis Armstrong were so dissimilar. The white middle-class boy from Iowa was the product of a culture which could *place* Louis Armstrong, but could never understand him" (153–54). This confinement to a predetermined status (predetermined stasis), the keeping of black people "in their place," gives rise to the countering, contestatory tendencies I'll be talking about as a movement from noun to verb.

My topic, then, is not so much otherness as othering, black linguistic and musical practices that accent variance, variability—what reggae musicians call "versioning." As Dick Hebdige notes: "'Versioning' is at the heart not only of reggae but of *all* Afro-American and Caribbean musics: jazz, blues, rap, r&b, reggae, calypso, soca, salsa, Afro-Cuban and so on."[2] When Baraka writes of John Coltrane's recording of Billy Eckstine's "I Want to Talk About You," he emphasizes what could be called Trane's versioning of the tune, what I would call his othering of it:

Instead of the simplistic though touching note-for-note replay of the ballad's line, on this performance each note is tested, given a slight tremolo or emotional vibrato (note to chord to scale reference) which makes it seem as if each one of the notes is given the possibility of "infinite" qualification ... proving that the ballad as it was written was only the beginning of the story.[3]

Trane himself spoke of his desire to work out a kind of writing that would allow for "more plasticity, more viability, more room for improvisation in the statement of the melody itself."[4] His lengthy solos caused some listeners to accuse him of practicing in public, which, in a sense that is not at all derogatory, he was—the sense in which Wilson Harris calls one of his recent novels *The Infinite Rehearsal*.

Such othering practices implicitly react against and reflect critically upon the different sort of othering to which their practitioners, denied agency in a society by which they're designated other, have been subjected. The black speaker, writer, or musician whose practice privileges variation subjects the fixed equations which underwrite that denial (including the idea of fixity itself) to an alternative. Zora Neale Hurston writes of the gossipers and storytellers in *Their Eyes Were Watching God*:

It was the time for sitting on porches beside the road. It was the time to hear things and talk. These sitters had been tongueless, earless, eyeless conveniences all day long. Mules and other brutes had occupied their skins. But now, the sun and the bossman were gone, so the skins felt powerful and human. They became lords of sounds and lesser things. They passed nations through their mouths.[5]

Hurston is one of the pioneer expositor-practitioners of a resistant othering found in black vernacular culture. In her essay "Characteristics of Negro Expression," published in the thirties, she writes: "What we really mean by originality is the modification of ideas. ... So if we look at it squarely, the Negro is a very original being. While he lives and moves in the midst of a white civilization, everything he touches is re-interpreted for his own use."[6] Baraka's valorization of the verb recalls a similar move on Hurston's part thirty years earlier, her discussion of "verbal nouns" as one of black America's contributions to American English. She emphasizes action, dynamism, and kinetics, arguing that black vernacular culture does the same: "Frequently the Negro, even with detached words in his vocabulary—not evolved in him but transplanted on his tongue by contact—must add action to it to make it do. So we have 'chop-axe,' 'sitting-chair,' 'cook-pot' and the like because the speaker has in his mind the picture of the object in use. Action." She goes on to list a number of "verbal nouns," nouns and adjectives made to function as verbs, and "nouns from verbs," verbs masquerading as nouns, *Funeralize, I wouldn't friend with her,* and *uglying away* are among her examples of the former, *won't stand a broke* and *She won't take a listen* among those of the latter.

The privileging of the verb, the movement from noun to verb, linguistically accentuates action among a people whose ability to act is curtailed by racist constraints. I prefer to see a connection between such privileging and such curtailment than to attribute the former, as Hurston occasionally does, to black primitivity. Language is symbolic action, frequently compensatory action, addressing deprivations it helps its users overcome. The privileging of the verb, the black vernacular investment in what Hurston calls "action words," makes this all the more evident. The sort of analysis found in the passage from *Their Eyes Were Watching God* that I quoted is brought to bear on the movement from noun to verb in a piece which Hurston published in the early forties, "High John de Conquer."[7] The High John the Conqueror root that plays so prominent a role in African-American hoodoo is here personified and figured as a key to black endurance and resilience, "the secret of black song and laughter." In the title and throughout the piece, Hurston elides the last syllable of *conqueror,* as is frequently done in black speech. In doing so, honoring the vernacular in more senses than one, she changes *conqueror* to *conquer,* noun to verb, practicing what she expounds upon in "Characteristics of Negro Expression."

Hurston presents High John de Conquer as an inner divergence from outward adversity, the ability of enslaved Africans to hold themselves apart from circumstance. "An inside thing to live by," she calls it. She relates High John de Conquer to a propensity for laughter, story, and song, to black liberties taken with music and language. He embodies mastery of sound and mastery through sound, "making a way out of no-way." High John de Conquer moves quickly, as mercurial as he is musical: "His footsteps sounded across the world in a low but musical rhythm as if the world he walked on was a singing-drum. ... He had come from Africa. He came walking on the waves of sound." He embodies music, storytelling, and laughter as a kind of mobility, a fugitivity that others the slaves' condition:

> He walked on the winds and moved fast. Maybe he was in Texas when the lash fell on a slave in Alabama, but before the blood was dry on the back he was there. A faint pulsing of a drum like a goat-skin stretched over a heart, that came nearer and closer, then somebody in the saddened quarters would feel like laughing and say, "Now, High John de Conquer, Old Massa couldn't get the best of *him.* ... "

Hurston writes of the song High John de Conquer helps the slaves find: "It had no words. It was a tune that you could bend and shape in most any way you wanted to fit the words and feelings that you had."

The bending and shaping of sound, black liberties taken with music and language, caused Lucy McKim Garrison, one of the editors of *Slave Songs in the United States,* to write in 1862:

> It is difficult to express the entire character of these negro ballads by mere musical notes and signs. The odd turns made in the throat, and the curious rhythmic effect produced by single voices chiming in at different irregular intervals, seem almost as impossible to place on the score as the singing of birds or the tones of an Aeolian Harp.

Another of its editors, William Allen, likewise wrote:

> What makes it all the harder to unravel a thread of melody out of this strange network is that, like birds, they seem not infrequently to strike sounds that cannot be precisely represented by the gamut, and abound in "slides from one note to another and turns and cadences not in articulated notes. ... " There are also apparent irregularities in the time, which it is no less difficult to express accurately.

Henry G. Spaulding wrote in 1863: "The most striking of their barbaric airs it would be impossible to write out." The compilers of the Hampton spirituals, M. F. Armstrong and Helen W. Ludlow, wrote similarly a decade later: "Tones are frequently employed which we have no musical characters to represent. ... The tones are variable in pitch, ranging through an entire octave on different occasions, according to the inspiration of the singer."[8] One could go on and on with similar statements. Western musical notation's inability to capture the tonal and rhythmic mobility and variability such quotes remark upon confirms the fugitive spirit Hurston identifies with High John de Conquer. "It is no accident that High John de Conquer has evaded the ears of white people," she writes, punning on while poking fun at the use of accidentals by Garrison, Smith, and others to approximate the flatted or bent notes of the African American's altered scale.

Fugitive spirit has had its impact upon African-American literary practices as well. As fact, as metaphor, and as formal disposition, the alliance of writing with fugitivity recurs throughout the tradition. One recalls that in 1829 George Moses Horton hoped to buy his freedom with money made from sales of his book of poems, *Hope of Liberty*. One thinks of the role played by literacy in Frederick Douglass's escape, of Harriet Jacobs's denunciations of the Fugitive Slave Law, of the importance of the slave narratives to the antislavery movement. W.E.B. DuBois referred to the essays in *The Souls of Black Folk* as "fugitive pieces," and the impact of fugitive spirit can also be found in the work of William Melvin Kelley (the mass exodus in *A Different Drummer,* the bending and reshaping of language in *Dunfords Travels Everywheres*), Ishmael Reed (Quickskill in *Flight to Canada*), Toni Morrison (the flying African in *Song of Solomon,* the "lickety-split, lickety-split" at the end of *Tar Baby*, Sethe's escape in *Beloved*) and others. Ed Roberson, for example, in a recent poem called "Taking the Print":

See night in the sunlight's starry reflection
off the water darkening the water
by contrast.
                    The dark hiding in the water
also hid us in the river at night
Our crossing guided by the internal sight
on our darkness
                          the ancient graphis
and from this passage of abductions and escapes–
this newer imprimatur of the river
cut deep in the plate.
                              see in the river the ripples'
picture on the surface of the wind the lifting of the
image
has taken at the deeper face
                                    the starry freedom
written in the milky rivery line that pours
the brilliance of that image from a depth only black
night fleeing across this land
                              has to voice.[9]

An especially good example of the movement from noun to verb's identification or alliance with fugitive spirit is Aimé Césaire's 1955 poem "The Verb 'Marroner' / for René Depestre, Haitian Poet."[10] Written in response to Louis Aragon and the French Communist Party's call for a return to traditional poetic meters and forms, which Depestre supported in the journal *Présence africaine,* the poem insists upon openness, experimentation, and formal innovation:

Comrade Depestre
It is undoubtedly a very serious problem
the relation between poetry and Revolution
the content determines the form

and what about keeping in mind as well the dialectical
backlash by which the form taking its revenge
chokes the poems like an accursed fig tree

The poem announces and enacts its poetics under the sign of a neologistic verb. Césaire
invokes the history of fugitive slaves in the Caribbean, the runaway Africans known as
maroons who escaped the plantations and set up societies of their own. The French noun for
this phenomenon, *marronage,* is the basis for the word, the verb *marroner,* Césaire invents,
an act of invention exemplifying the independence for which the poem calls. The coinage has
no English equivalent. Clayton Eshleman and Annette Smith translate it "escape like slaves":

Is it true this season that they're polishing up sonnets
for us to do so would remind me too much of the sugary
juice drooled over there by the distilleries on the mornes
when slow skinny oxen make their rounds to the whine
of mosquitoes

Bah! Depestre the poem is not a mill for
grinding sugar cane absolutely not
and if the rhymes are flies on ponds
                              without rhymes
          for a whole season
away from ponds
                                        under my persuasion
let's laugh drink and escape like slaves

Such invention in Césaire's work, such othering of and taking of liberties with French,
has been referred to as "a politics of neologism."[11] A similar practice can be found in the
work of another Caribbean poet, Edward Kamau Brathwaite, who writes of Césaire:
"His fabulous long poem *Cahier d'un retour au pays natal* (1939) evolved the concept of
negritude: that there is a black Caliban Maroon world with its own aesthetics (*sycorax*),
contributing to world and Third World consciousness."[12] Brathwaite's recently completed
second trilogy, comprised of *Mother Poem, Sun Poem,* and *X/Self,* is characterized by a
versioning of English he calls "calibanization," a creolization "which comes into conflict
with the cultural imperial authority of Prospero."[13] One of the remarkable features of the
work, one of the features any reader will come away from it unable to forget, is its
linguistic texture—not only what's done with words but what's done to them. Brathwaite
makes greater use of West Indian nation-language (the term he puts in place of "dialect"
or "patois") than in the first trilogy, *The Arrivants,* but what he's doing goes farther than
that. In his use of "standard" English as well he takes his cue from the vernacular, subjecting
words to bends, breaks, deformation, reformation—othering.

Brathwaite concludes the next-to-last poem in *The Arrivants* with the lines "So on this
ground, / write; / ... on this ground / on this broken ground."[14] Nation-language, what
some would call broken English, partakes of that ground. "Calibanization" insists that in

West Indian folk speech English isn't so much broken as broken into, that a struggle for turf is taking place in language. "It was in language," Brathwaite has written, "that the slave was perhaps most successfully imprisoned by his master; and it was in his (mis-)use of it that he perhaps most effectively rebelled. Within the folk tradition, language was (and is) a creative act in itself."[15] This tradition of black liberties taken with language informs *Mother Poem, Sun Poem,* and *X/Self* with the weight of a history of anti-imperial struggle, a weight felt in so small a thing as the word. As in the anagrammatic "derangement" Shakespeare had recourse to in fashioning *Caliban* from *cannibal,* the puns, malapropisms, odd spellings, neologisms, and strained meanings Brathwaite resorts to speak of disturbances outside as well as inside the language, social disruptions the word is thus made to register.

Changing *militia* to *malitia* is one small instance of this.[16] As in this instance, most of Brathwaite's "calibanisms" underscore senses of malice and malaise, emphasize the hurt put on the land and on the people by slavery, the plantation system, colonialism, capitalism. The words partake of that hurt. It shows in the language both as referent and as a telling misuse inflicted on English, an abuse which brings that referent more emphatically to light. *The panes of his eyes* becomes *the pains of his eyes, the games we played* becomes *the games we paid, landscape* becomes *landscrape, the future* becomes *the few-/ ture.*[17] *Huts* becomes *hurts* and *hillsides* turn into *hillslides:*

> but those that drone their lorries all day up the sweating
>   hill to the factory of mister massa midas
> those mindless arch
>
> itects that cut the cane
> that built their own hurts on the hillslide[18]

Brathwaite avails himself of and takes part in a revolution of the word that has long been a part of Caribbean folk culture, a reinvention of English of the sort one hears in Rastafarian speech, where *oppressor* gets replaced by *downpressor, livicate* takes the place of *dedicate* and so forth.

But a revolution of the word can only be a beginning. It initiates a break while remaining overshadowed by the conditions it seeks to go beyond. The shadow such conditions cast makes for a brooding humor that straddles laughter and lament, allows no easy, unequivocal foothold in either. Oppositional speech is only partly oppositional. Cramp and obstruction have to do with it as well. In Brathwaite's recent trilogy we not only get the sorts of pointed, transparent wordplay I just quoted, but something more opaque and more disconcerting, not resolved as to its tone or intent. Brathwaite revels in a sometimes dizzying mix of parody and pathos, embrace complicated by a sense of the bizarre and even bordering on embarrassment here and there. His otherings accent fugitive spirit and impediment as well, the predicaments that bring fugitive spirit into being:

> but is like we still start
> where we start/in out start/in out start/in out start/in
>
> out since menelek was a bwoy & why
> is dat & what is de bess weh to seh so/so it doan sounn
>   like

brigg
flatts nor hervokitz

nor de pisan cantos nor de souf sea
bible

nor like ink. le & de anglo saxon
chronicles

&

a fine
a cyaan get nutten

write

a cyaan get nutten really
rite
while a stannin up here in me years & like i inside a me
   shadow
like de man still mekkin i walk up de slope dat e slide
in black down de whole long curve a de arch

i

pell

ago[19]

Brathwaite helps impeded speech find its voice, the way Thelonious Monk makes hesitation eloquent or the way a scat singer makes inarticulacy speak. This places his work in the New World African tradition of troubled eloquence, othered eloquence, I'm here sketching. Here, that is, trouble acts as a threshold. It registers a need for a new world and a new language to go along with it, discontent with the world and the ways of speaking we already have. A revolution of the word can only be a new beginning, "beating," as Brathwaite puts it, "its genesis genesis genesis genesis / out of the stammering world."[20]

My reference to Monk, as Hurston would say, is no accident. Indeed, had Hurston written "Characteristics of Negro Expression" later, she might have included "Rhythm-a-ning" and "Jackie-ing," two Monk titles, in her list of "verbal nouns." In her section on asymmetry ("Asymmetry," she begins it by saying, "is a definite feature of Negro art"), she might have quoted Chico O'Farrill's comments on the advent of bebop in the forties:

It was such a new thing, because here we were confronted for the first time with phrases that wouldn't be symmetrical in the sense that string-music phrasing was symmetrical. Here we were confronted with phrases that were asymmetrical. They would come in into any part of the phrase they felt like, and, at first, also the changes threw us off completely because it was a complete new harmonic—not new, but we'll say unusual harmonic concept that was so alien to what we had been doing. To us it was such a drastic change that I think anything that came afterwards wasn't as drastic as that particular first step from swing to bop. I think in a sense bop probably marks the real cut-off point of the old concept of swinging. I don't mean in the sense of swinging—we were still swinging—but the concept of the square structure of the music as to this new particular way of playing and writing.[21]

The bebop revolution of which Monk was a part—Ellington called it "the Marcus Garvey extension"—was a movement, in its reaction to swing, from noun to verb. It was a revolution that influenced a great number of writers, Brathwaite included, as can be seen, among other places, in his early poem "Blues."[22] Its impact upon Baraka's work and thought can be seen not only in *Blues People* but also in the poetics, the valorization of the verb, in the 1964 essay "Hunting Is Not Those Heads on the Wall."[23] There he espouses a poetics of process, arguing: "The clearest description of now is the present participle. ... Worship the verb, if you need something." Halfway through the essay he mentions Charlie Parker, having earlier remarked: "I speak of the *verb process,* the doing, the coming into being, the at-the-time-of. Which is why we think there is particular value in live music, contemplating the artifact as it arrives, listening to it emerge." The sense he advances that "this verb value" is an impulse to "make words surprise themselves" recalls the popular description of jazz as "the sound of surprise."

The white appropriation and commercialization of swing resulted in a music that was less improvisatory, less dependent upon the inventiveness of soloists. The increased reliance upon arrangements in the Fletcher Henderson mold led to a sameness of sound and style among the various bands. In *Blues People* Baraka quotes Hsio Wen Shih's comments regarding the anthology album *The Great Swing Bands*, a record Shih refers to as "terrifying" due to the indistinguishability of one band from another. It was against this uniformity that bebop revolted. "Benny Goodman," Howard McGhee recalls, "had been named the 'King of Swing.' ... We figured, what the hell, we can't do no more than what's been done with it, we gotta do somethin' else. We gotta do some other kind of thing."[24] ("Some other stuff," a common expression among black musicians, would become the title of an album by Grachan Moncur III in the sixties.) Mary Lou Williams said of her first meeting with Monk in the thirties: "He told me that he was sick of hearing musicians play the same thing the same way all the time."[25] Monk himself summed up his music by saying: "How to use notes differently. That's it. Just how to use notes differently."[26] It is no accident that bebop was typically performed by small combos rather than big bands, as was the case with swing. It accentuated individual expression, bringing the soloist and improvisation once more to the fore.

Baraka emphasizes nonconformity in his treatment of bebop in *Blues People,* stressing what he terms its "willfully harsh, *anti-assimilationist* sound" (181). The cultivation of a unique, individual style black music encourages, informs, and inspires his attitudes toward writing. In his statement on poetics for the anthology *The New American Poetry, 1945–1960* Baraka echoes Louis Armstrong's ad-libbed line on a 1949 recording with Billie Holiday,[27] calling it "How You Sound?" The emphasis on self-expression in his work is also an emphasis on self-transformation, an othering or, as Brathwaite has it, an X-ing of the self, the self not as noun but as verb. Of the post-bop innovations of such musicians as Albert Ayler and Sun Ra, he writes: "New Black Music is this: Find the self, then kill it."[28] To kill the self is to show it to be fractured, unfixed. The dismantling of the unified subject found in recent critical theory is old news when it comes to black music. I've seen Bukka White break off singing to exhort himself: "Sing it, Bukka!" Charles Mingus's autobiography begins: "In other words, I am three."[29] A recent composition by Muhal Richard Abrams has the title "Conversation with the Three of Me." Craig Harris remarks of the polyrhythmicity of one of his pieces: "It's about cutting yourself in half."[30]

Our interest in cultural diversity—diversity within a culture as well as the diversity of cultures—should lead us to be wary of hypostasis, the risk we take with nouns, a deadend that will get in the way of change unless "other," "self," and such are "given the possibility of 'infinite' qualification."[31] Wilson Harris, whose novel *The Infinite Rehearsal* I referred to earlier, has written of "qualitative and infinite variations of substance clothed in nouns," arguing that "nouns may reveal paradoxically when qualified, that their emphasis on reality and their inner meaning can change as they are inhabited by variable psychic projections."[32] In his new novel, *The Four Banks of the River of Space,* he speaks of "the instructive bite of music" on the way to suggesting that "breaking a formula of complacency" consists of "becoming a stranger to oneself."[33] As Monk's tune "Jackie-ing" tells us, even a so-called proper noun is a verb in disguise—present-participial, provisional, subject to change. John Gilmore, tenor saxophonist with Sun Ra's band for some thirty years, tells a story about the time he spent with Art Blakey's Jazz Messengers in 1965. After about a month, he says, the music was at so inventive a level that one night in Los Angeles, following one of his solos, trumpeter Lee Morgan looked over at him and asked: "Is that you, Gilmore?" Morgan then took a solo that caused Gilmore to ask the same thing of him: "Lee, is that you?"[34]

II

The "nounization" of swing furthered and partook in a commoditization of music that, as Jacques Attali points out, had been developing in the West since the 1700s. "Until the eighteenth century," he writes in *Noise: The Political Economy of Music,* "music was of the order of the 'active'; it then entered the order of the 'exchanged.'"[35] The process was completed in the twentieth century, he argues, with the birth of the recording industry and its exploitation of black musicians: "Music did not really become a commodity until a broad market for popular music was created. Such a market did not exist when Edison invented the phonograph; it was produced by the colonization of black music by the American industrial apparatus" (103). The transition from "active" to "exchanged," verb to noun, reflects the channeling of power through music it is the point of the book to insist upon:

> Listening to music is … realizing that its appropriation and control is a reflection of power, that it is essentially political. … With music is born power and its opposite: subversion. … Music, the quintessential mass activity, like the crowd, is simultaneously a threat and a necessary source of legitimacy; trying to channel it is a risk that every system of power must run. … Thus music localizes and specifies power, because it marks and regiments the rare noises that cultures, in their normalization of behavior, see fit to authorize.

> (6, 14, 19–20)

Attali is at all points alive to the shamanic roots of music, its magico-prophetic role, no matter how obscured those roots and that role tend to be by the legal, technological, and social developments he goes to great lengths to analyze and describe.

The idea of music as a conduit of power, a channeler of violence, a regulator of society, is particularly visible—unobscured—among the Carib-speaking Kalapalo of the Upper Xingu Basin in Brazil. Ellen B. Basso, in her study *A Musical View of the Universe: Kalapalo Myth and Ritual Performances,* deals with their ideas regarding sound and what she terms "orders of animacy," a hierarchic taxonomy at the top of which the Kalapalo place entities known as "powerful beings." These beings are nonhuman, though they sometimes appear in human form, and, Basso points out, "they are preeminently and essentially musical":

> Powerful beings are different from concrete historical figures because they and their acts are "always" and everywhere. ... This multiplicity of essence or "hyperanimacy" is coupled on the one hand with a multiplicity of feeling and consequent unpredictability and on the other with a monstrous intensity of some feeling or trait; hence powerful beings are dangerous beings. ... Their hyperanimacy and multiplicity of essence are perhaps what is deeply metaphorized by their association with musical invention.[36]

Music represents the highest degree or level of animacy, hyperanimacy, and in their musical performances the Kalapalo model themselves upon their images of powerful beings, aspiring to the condition of powerful beings. They seek both to endow themselves with and to domesticate hyperanimate power. Basso writes:

> Music (or more exactly, musical performance) is identified by the Kalapalo as having controlling force over aggressive, transformative, and wandering power; it is also a manifestation of that power. The ability of music to control and channel aggression, to limit hyperanimacy in ways that are helpful to people, has further consequences for understanding its importance within ritual contexts. This is because in such contexts of use, political life—the relations of control that some people effect over others—achieves its most concrete and elaborate expression.
>
> (246)

I would like to highlight two features of Kalapalo thought and practice concerning music and bring them to bear, by way of analogy, upon the minstrel show, a form of theatrical performance unique to the United States that emerged during the 1820s and reached its apex between 1850 and 1870. An appropriation of the slave's music and dance by white men who blackened their faces with burnt cork, going on stage to sing "Negro songs," perform dances derived from those of the slaves, and tell jokes based on plantation life, the minstrel show is an early instance of the cannibalization of black music to which we saw Attali refer. "Minstrelsy," Robert C. Toll observes in *Blacking Up: The Minstrel Show in Nineteenth-Century America,* "was the first example of the way American popular culture would exploit and manipulate Afro-Americans and their culture to please and benefit white Americans."[37] The first of the two aspects of Kalapalo thought and practice I would like to highlight is the fact that powerful beings are associated with darkness and with the color black, that for ritual performances the Kalapalo shaman darkens himself with pot black as a way of becoming, Basso explains, "less visibly human and appearing more like a powerful being" (248). Blacking up, the white minstrel practice of donning blackface makeup, amounts to a pseudo-shamanic performance in which the power of black musicality is complimented yet simultaneously channeled, caricatured, and contained. As is not the case for the Kalapalo shaman, for the white minstrel "less visibly human" means less than human, even as the appeal and the power of the music are being exploited.

Minstrelsy reveals the ambivalent, duplicitous relationship of nineteenth-century white Americans not only to black people but to music and language as well. The second aspect of Kalapalo thought and practice I would like to highlight relates to this, having to do with the distinctions the Kalapalo make among calls, speech, and music and among degrees of animacy. Human beings share with entities of lesser animacy the ability to emit calls and with entities of greater animacy, powerful beings, the ability to speak and to make music, but it is speech that is regarded as quintessentially human. Speech is the form of sound by which humans are characterized and symbolized in the taxonomic order, music the form with which powerful beings are identified. Interestingly, calls as well as music are considered more truthful, more trustworthy than speech:

> Human beings can express truthful and empirically motivated feelings best through *itsu* [calls]. Pain of varying degrees of intensity, deep sadness, shame, joy, sexual passion, frustration with oneself, indeed, the entire range of human emotion is expressed most succinctly (and by implication as truthful feeling) this way.
>
> Human beings are distinguished from other *ago* [living things], however, by their ability to speak, and it is through language that they are most commonly symbolized and distinguished from other categories of entities. … But language allows people to do something very different from animals. Human beings were created by a trickster, whose name "Taugi" means "speaks deceptively about himself." … Hence human beings are in essence deceitful beings because of their ability to speak. Therefore, people are capable not only of truthfully expressing their feelings, but—and this is the unmarked understanding of human speech for the Kalapalo—of creating an illusory screen of words that conceals their true thoughts.
>
> (67–68)

Music, the Kalapalo believe, is more to be trusted than speech because, rather than masking the mental, powerful beings "in J.L. Austin's sense … are performative beings, capable of reaching the limits of awareness of meaning by constructing action through a process that is simultaneously mental and physical" (71).

Calls and music both put sound in the service of sentience. In this they differ from speech, which valorizes the sentence, the humanly constructed realm of meaning, grammaticality, predication. The minstrel show, in its recourse to music (the slave's music, moreover, in which calls, cries, and hollers played a prominent part) and in its "translation" of that music into songs of sentiment (Stephen Foster's "Old Folks at Home," "Massa's in de Cold, Cold Ground," and so forth), critiqued even as it exemplified the deceptiveness of language. The implicit critique, the recourse to music and to sentimentality, to songs that advertised themselves as innocent of ambiguity, insincerity, or circumlocution, was accompanied by an explicit critique. This took the form of the stump speech and its malapropisms, the heavy reliance upon word play and puns in minstrel humor and such routines as the following, called "Modern Language":

BONES: How things have changed of late. A man can't depend on anything. A man must discount his expectations by at least 80 percent.

MIDMAN: In other words, "never count your chickens before they are hatched."

BONES: That sort of language is not up to the four hundred. You should say that this way: Never enumerate your feathered progeny before the process of incubation has been thoroughly realized.

MIDMAN: That does take the rag off the bush.

BONES: Wrong again. You should not say that. You should say: That removes the dilapidated linen from off the shrubbery.[38]

While the stump speech poked fun at black people's alleged insecure hold on language, such humor as this poked fun at language itself, at language's—especially elevated language's—insecure hold on the world. Minstrelsy, under cover of blackface, was able to vent apprehensions regarding the tenuousness of language, even as it ridiculed its target of choice for a supposed lack of linguistic competence. In regard to language as in other matters, the minstrel show allowed its audience to have it both ways.

One of the reasons for minstrelsy's popularity was what Alexander Saxton terms "the flexibility of standards which flourished behind the fake façade of blackface presentation."[39] That façade made it permissible to refer to such topics as homosexuality and masturbation, which were taboo on the legitimate stage, in the press, and elsewhere. Sentimental songs and female impersonation, as did the blackface façade, allowed performers and audience alike access to a world of emotion that was otherwise held to be off limits. Minstrelsy's wide appeal had largely to do with the illusion of escape from conventional strictures it afforded, the degree to which it spoke to a white, predominantly male imaginary. Minstrel star George Thatcher's description of his feelings after seeing his first minstrel show as a boy alerts us to the deep psychic forces at work (and also, incidentally, sheds light on the title of John Berryman's *Dream Songs,* which, dedicated to Thomas D. Rice, the "father" of blackface minstrelsy, makes use of the minstrel figure Bones): "I found myself dreaming of minstrels; I would awake with an imaginary tambourine in my hand, and rub my face with my hands to see if I was blacked up. ... The dream of my life was to see or speak to a performer."[40]

The influence of blackface minstrelsy extended well into the present century, having an impact upon vaudeville, musical comedy, radio, movies, television, and other forms of popular culture. It tells us a great deal regarding the obstacles in the way of a genuine multiculturality or cross-culturality, a genuine, nonexploitative cultural exchange. Toll recounts that in 1877 Bret Harte and Mark Twain wrote a minstrel play based on a poem of Harte's about the "heathen chinee." On opening night, Twain explained to the audience: "The Chinaman is getting to be a pretty frequent figure in the United States and is going to be a great political problem and we thought it well for you to see him on the stage before you had to deal with the problem." Toll goes on to remark that Twain's is a clear and accurate statement of one of minstrelsy's functions: "Although on the surface they just sang songs and told jokes about peculiar people, minstrels actually provided their audiences with one of the only bases that many of them had for understanding America's increasing ethnic diversity" (169). This base, however, was an impediment rather than an aid to cultural diversity, a strategy of containment through caricature designed to consolidate white privilege and power. The minstrel made use of music to channel power in the service of "orders of animacy" in which whites came out on top, to uphold unequally distributed orders of agency in which violence, albeit under control, was never out of the picture. Saxton remarks of a minstrel song: "This 'comic-banjo' piece, as it was described, appeared in a songster published in New York in 1863. Geographically and emotionally, it was only a block or two from a song such as this to the maiming and lynching of blacks on the sidewalks of New York during the draft riots of the same year" (23).

The subject of cultural diversity and the goal of a healthy cross-culturality are haunted by the specter of such appropriation as the minstrel legacy represents. We should not be surprised that not only pop-cultural but also high-cultural and avant-garde venues number among its haunts. I'm thinking, for example, of Gertrude Stein's early piece "Melanctha," described by her in "Composition as Explanation" as "a negro story." Katherine Mansfield, reviewing the book in which "Melanctha" appears, *Three Lives,* heard sentences overwhelmed by sound and sentience, much to her alarm. Moreover, she heard it as a minstrel band, a channeling of black musicality into prose:

Let the reader go warily, warily with *Melanctha*. We confess we read a good page or two before we realised what was happening. Then the dreadful fact dawned. We discovered ourselves reading in *syncopated time*. Gradually we heard in the distance and then coming uncomfortably near, the sound of banjos, drums, bones, cymbals and voices. The page began to rock. To our horror we found ourselves silently singing "Was it true what Melanctha said that night to him" etc. Those who have heard the Syncopated Orchestra sing "It's me—it's me—it's me" or "I got a robe" will understand what we mean. *Melanctha* is negro music with all its maddening monotony done into prose; it is writing in real ragtime. Heaven forbid Miss Stein should become a fashion.[41]

The analogue to what Mansfield misapprehends as black-musical monotony, Stein's notorious use of repetition advances a critique of language that is not unrelated to the one we see in the minstrel show. Under cover of blackness, she issues an avant-garde caveat regarding the trustworthiness of the linguistic sign and of the discursive, ratiocinative order it promotes. The search for and the nature of "understanding" are pointedly at issue in the story, especially in the relationship between impulsive, sensation-seeking Melanctha and reflective, respectability-minded Jeff:

"Yes I certainly do understand you when you talk so Dr. Campbell. I certainly do understand now what you mean by what you was always saying to me. I certainly do understand Dr. Campbell that you mean you don't believe it's right to love anybody." "Why sure no, yes I do Miss Melanctha, I certainly do believe strong in loving, and in being good to everybody, and trying to understand what they all need, to help them." "Oh I know all about that way of doing Dr. Campbell, but that certainly ain't the kind of love I mean when I am talking. I mean real, strong, hot love Dr. Campbell, that makes you do anything for somebody that loves you." "I don't know much about that kind of love yet Miss Melanctha. You see it's this way with me always Miss Melanctha. I am always so busy with my thinking about my work I am doing and so I don't have time for just fooling, and then too, you see Miss Melanctha, I really certainly don't ever like to get excited, and that kind of loving hard does seem always to mean just getting all the time excited. That certainly is what I always think from what I see of them that have it bad Miss Melanctha, and that certainly would never suit a man like me."[42]

On a typical page of dialogue between the two, the word *certainly* occurs as often as twenty times. Such repetition undermines the word, underscoring the uncertainty in which the two of them are immersed. Words are treated as though, rather than sticking to the real, as Jack Spicer put it, they were continually slipping from it. Repetition compulsively moves to make up for that slippage, accenting all the more the words' insecure grip on the world. Not unlike the Kalapalo, Jeff at one point complains that "the ordinary kind of holler" would offer "much more game," much more forthright expression (127). The story strongly suggests that the order of what the Kalapalo term *itsu* is where "understanding" most unproblematically resides:

And now the pain came hard and harder in Jeff Campbell, he groaned, and it hurt him so, he could not bear it. And the tears came, and his heart beat, and he was hot and worn and bitter in him.

Now Jeff knew very well what it was to love Melanctha. Now Jeff Campbell knew he was really understanding.

(145)

"Melanctha" recalls minstrelsy in that Stein uses one form of marginality, blackness, to mask another, to mask two others in fact—the avant-garde linguistic experimentation that we just noted (experimental writing being relegated to the fringes by middle-brow, if not outright philistine American predilections) and, albeit much less evident, lesbianism. Janice Doane and Carolyn Copeland argue that "Melanctha," as the latter puts it, "is not really a story about the ethnic reality of Negroes,"[43] that the story reworks material from the earlier novel *Q.E.D.* "Melanctha" can be said to be *Q.E.D.* done in blackface. Doane writes that "the lesbian affair *of Q.E.D.* is converted into the heterosexual affair of the 'Melanctha' story."[44] Copeland says the same at greater length:

> It will be recalled that *Q.E.D.*, written in 1903, concerned three homosexual women involved in a triangle. When one considers the trouble Theodore Dreiser had with *Sister Carrie* during that same period, it is not surprising that Gertrude Stein dropped the homosexual elements from her story before using the material again. Some very important elements of *Q.E.D.*, however, would have become problematic in a simple shift from homosexual to heterosexual in the story, and these elements must be discussed briefly.
>
> In *Q.E.D.* Adele and Helen together undergo a full and complete series of sexual experiences, and obviously they are not married when they experience them. It is important to Adele's full realization of how completely "out of rhythm" she and Helen are that they not be married. Adele must be able to walk away from the experience with no ties such as marriage to complicate it. At the turn of this century in America the only background against which a writer could portray premarital sexual relationships without having an outraged white, middle-class public to contend with was one dealing with Negroes. It was part of the white man's view of the black man that they were sexually promiscuous. If Gertrude Stein wished to drop the homosexual elements and make them heterosexual, her choice of Negroes instead of whites allowed her to retain as much as possible of the important extramarital elements involved. And this is exactly what she did.

(24–25)

Orders of marginality contend with one another here. It is instructive that blackness is the noun-mask under whose camouflage two other forms of marginality gain an otherwise blocked order of animacy or agency, an otherwise unavailable "verbness." We are at the sacrificial roots of the social order, the ritual murder of which music, Attali argues, is the simulacrum. Under cover of scapegoat blackness, the otherwise marginal cozies up to the center.[45]

I say this not to encourage turf wars among marginalized groups or individuals, but to raise a question. Wilson Harris writes of marginality in a way that is as promising as it is challenging. "Extremity or marginality, in my view," he writes, "lifts the medium or diverse experience to a new angle of possibility. ... It involves us in a curiously tilted field in which spatial pre-possessions and our prepossessions are dislodged. ... Marginality is a raised contour or frontier of habit in the topography of the heart and mind."[46] I think of this tilt as arising to contend with another form of tilt—that of unevenly allotted orders of agency, the unfair playing field, as it's commonly put.[47] I think of the tilt of Edgar Pool's tenor saxophone in John Clellon Holmes's novel *The Horn:*

> Edgar Pool blew methodically, eyes beady and open, and he held his tenor saxophone almost horizontally extended from his mouth. This unusual posture gave it the look of some metallic albatross caught insecurely in his two hands, struggling to resume flight. In those early days he never brought it down to earth, but followed after its isolated passage over all manner of American cities, snaring it nightly, fastening his drooping, stony lips to its cruel beak, and tapping the song.[48]

The idiosyncratic tilt of "isolated originality," modeled on Lester Young:

> It was only one of many bands he worked those years, the tireless jumping colored bands that flourished like a backwash after the initial wave of swing. But already he was blowing strange long lines, rising out of the section, indrawn and resolute, to stand before the circling dancers, tilt the big horn roofward from his body, and play his weightless, sharply veering phrases over the chunking of unsubtle drums. In those days, no one heard.

(89)

I also, however, think of another tilt we see in the novel, that of a whisky bottle "tilted into the coffee as he [Pool] spiked it generously" (194) during the last night of an alcoholic binge, the last night of his life. The tilt of entropy, exhaustion, disillusionment. Hence, my question: Which tilt will it be? In order that the latter not prevail, the discourse on cultural diversity will have to acknowledge both.

By this I mean that we need more than content analyses based on assumptions of representationality. The dislocating tilt of artistic othering, especially as practiced by African-American artists, deserves a great deal more attention than it's been given. While the regressive racial views of white writers like Stein and Ezra Pound tend to be regarded (if they're regarded at all) as secondary to their artistic innovations, black writers tend to be read racially, primarily at the content level, the noun level, as responding to racism, representing "the black experience." That black writers have been experimentally and innovatively engaged with the medium, addressing issues of form as well as issues of content, tends to be ignored. The ability to impact upon and to influence the course of the medium, to *move* the medium, entails an order of animacy granted only to whites when it comes to writing. The situation with regard to music is a bit better, black musicians having been acknowledged to be innovators, even though their white imitators enjoy commercial success and critical acclaim greatly disproportionate to their musical contributions. The nonrecognition of black artistic othering is symptomatic of the social othering to which black people are subjected, particularly in light of the celebration accorded artistic othering practiced by whites. This is a disparity the discussion of cultural diversity should be addressing.

Perhaps we can increase not only the quantity but also the quality of attention given to African-American art and cultural practices. Perhaps we can make it possible for the music of Henry Threadgill or David S. Ware to be as widely known as that of Wynton Marsalis; Ed Roberson's *Lucid Interval as Integral Music* or Will Alexander's *The Black Speech of the Angel* to win the sort of acclaim accorded Rita Dove's *Thomas and Beulah;* Amiri Baraka to be as well known for *The Dead Lecturer* as for *Dutchman*. If we are to do so, we must, à la Césaire, confront the neotraditionalism that has taken hold of late with a counter-tradition of marronage, divergence, flight, fugitive tilt. Henry Dumas put it well in "Black Trumpeter": "The wing praises the root by taking to the limbs."[49]

Notes

This essay was first presented as a lecture as part of "Otherness: A Symposium on Cultural Diversity" at the Detroit Institute of Arts, March 1991.

1 LeRoi Jones, *Blues People: Negro Music in White America* (New York, 1963), 143.
2 Dick Hebdige, *Cut 'n' Mix: Culture, Identity, and Caribbean Music* (London, 1987), 12.
3 LeRoi Jones, *Black Music* (New York, 1967), 66.
4 Liner notes, *Coltrane Live at the Village Vanguard Again!* (Impulse! AS–9124).
5 Zora Neale Hurston, *Their Eyes Were Watching God* (Urbana, Ill., 1978), 9–10.
6 Zora Neale Hurston, "Characteristics of Negro Expression," in *The Sanctified Church* (Berkeley, 1981), 49–68.
7 Ibid., 69–78,
8 Lucy McKim Garrison, William Allen, Henry G. Spaulding, M. F. Armstrong, and Helen W. Ludlow, quoted in Eileen Southern, *The Musk of Black Americans: A History* (New York, 1983), 191–94.
9 Ed Roberson, "Taking the Print," *Hambone* 9 (Winter 1991): 2.
10 Aimé Césaire, *The Collected Poetry,* trans. Clayton Eshleman and Annette Smith (Berkeley, 1983), 368–71.
11 James Clifford, *The Predicament of Culture: Twentieth-Century Ethnography, Literature, and Art* (Cambridge, Mass., 1988), 175–81.
12 Edward Kamau Brathwaite, *X/Self* (Oxford, 1987), 129–30.
13 Edward Kamau Brathwaite, *Mother Poem* (Oxford, 1977), 121.
14 Edward Brathwaite, *The Arrivants: A New World Trilogy* (Oxford, 1973), 265–66.
15 Edward Brathwaite, *The Development of Creole Society in Jamaica, 1770–1820* (Oxford, 1971), 237.
16 Edward Kamau Brathwaite, *Sun Poem* (Oxford, 1982), 56.
17 Ibid., 6, 19, 55, 87.
18 Ibid., 61.
19 Brathwaite, *X/Self,* 85–86.
20 Brathwaite, *Sun Poem,* 97.
21 Ira Gitler, *Swing to Bop: An Oral History of the Transition in Jazz in the 1940s* (New York, 1985), 153.
22 Edward Brathwaite, *Other Exiles* (London, 1975), 12–16.
23 LeRoi Jones, *Home: Social Essays* (New York, 1966), 173–78.
24 Gitler, *Swing to Bop,* 314.
25 Liner notes, *The Complete Blue Note Recordings of Thelonious Monk* (Mosaic MR4–101).
26 Liner notes, *Thelonious Monk Live at the It Club* (Columbia C2–38030).
27 "My Sweet Hunk O' Trash."
28 Jones, *Black Music,* 176.
29 Charles Mingus, *Beneath the Underdog* (New York, 1980), 7.
30 Liner notes, *Black Bone* (Soul Note SN 10550).
31 Artistic othering pertains to intracultural as well as intercultural dialectics. The will to change whereby African-American culture reflects critically upon the dominant white culture is intertwined with its impulse to reflect critically upon itself, the will to change whereby it redefines, reinvents, and diversifies itself. Bebop, for example, was a reaction to the datedness of the music played by black swing musicians as well as to its appropriation by white musicians. No last word, no seal of prophecy, bebop in turn became dated, subject to the changes initiated by Ornette Coleman, Cecil Taylor, Albert Ayler, and others during the late fifties and early sixties. An aspect of intracultural dialectics that we should not overlook is the role of eccentric individuals whose contributions come to be identified with the very culture which may have initially rejected them. Think of Ornette Coleman being beaten up outside a Baton Rouge dancehall in 1949 for

interjecting "modern" runs into an R&B solo; A. B. Spellman, *Black Music: Four Lives* (New York, 1970), 101. The recent ascendancy of cultural studies in academia tends to privilege collectivity and group definition over individual agency and self-expression, to see the latter as a reflection of the former. In relating the two, however, we should remember that in matters of artistic othering individual expression both reflects and redefines the collective, realigns, refracts it. Thus it is that Lester Young was in the habit of calling his saxophone's keys his people. Bill Crow reports that when the keys on his horn got bent during a Jazz at the Philharmonic tour Young went to Flip Phillips for help. "Flip," he said, "my people won't play!"; *Jazz Anecdotes* (New York, 1990), 272.

32 Wilson Harris, *Explorations: A Selection of Talks and Articles, 1966–1981* (Mundelstrup, Den., 1981), 139.
33 Wilson Harris, *The Four Banks of the River of Space* (London, 1990), 140–41.
34 Art Sato, "Interview with John Gilmore," *Be-Bop and Beyond* 4, no. 2 (March–April 1986): 21.
35 Jacques Attali, *Noise: The Political Economy of Music* (Minneapolis, 1985), 57.
36 Ellen B. Basso, *A Musical View of the Universe: Kalapalo Myth and Ritual Performances* (Philadelphia, 1985), 69–70.
37 Robert C. Toll, *Blacking Up: The Minstrel Show in Nineteenth-Century America* (New York, 1974), 51,
38 *Complete Minstrel Guide* (Chicago, n.d.), 49–50.
39 Alexander Saxton, "Blackface Minstrelsy and Jacksonian Ideology," *American Quarterly* 27, no. 1 (March 1975): 12.
40 Toll, *Blacking Up,* 33.
41 Quoted in Elizabeth Sprigge, *Gertrude Stein: Her Life and Work* (New York, 1957), 124–25.
42 Gertrude Stein, *Three Lives* (New York, 1990), 85–86.
43 Carolyn Copeland, *Language and Time and Gertrude Stein* (Iowa City, Ia., 1975), 24.
44 Janice Doane, *Silence and Narrative: The Early Novels of Gertrude Stein* (Westport, Conn., 1986), 52.
45 For a discussion of Stein's racist view of black people and of "Melanctha" as "the signpost of modernism's discourse on the nonwhite," see Aldon Lynn Nielsen, *Reading Race: White American Poets and the Racial Discourse in the Twentieth Century* (Athens, Ga., 1988), 21–28.
46 Wilson Harris, "In the Name of Liberty," *Third Text* 11 (Summer 1990): 15.
47 Hurston, in "Characteristics of Negro Expression": "After adornment the next most striking manifestation of the Negro is Angularity. Everything that he touches becomes angular."
48 John Clellon Holmes, *The Horn* (New York, 1988), 8.
49 Henry Dumas, *Play Ebony Play Ivory* (New York, 1974), 52.

34 Playing Like a Girl

The Queer Laughter of the Feminist Improvising Group[1]

Julie Dawn Smith

In "Playing Like a Girl" (2004), Julie Dawn Smith examines the history of the Feminist Improvising Group, formed in 1977 when Maggie Nicols and Lindsay Horner invited a small circle of women musicians to join them. In doing so, their engagement with music, humour, theatre, and gayness gave them a special place in the European improvising scene, but was not always welcomed by a loudly political, but often stolidly masculinist musicians' community. During her tenure with Coastal Jazz in Vancouver, BC, Julie Dawn Smith developed the High School Jazz Intensive, the Vancouver Creative Music Institute, the Creative Music Think Tank and the oral history project JazzStreet Vancouver. A former executive director of the Jazz Institute of Chicago, she served on the programming committee for the Chicago Jazz Festival, and co-produced/co-curated the "Women of the New Jazz" festivals and the "Face the Music" new music series. She has studied classical music, experimental and electronic composition, and South Asian music, and holds an honours BA in music from York University, a diploma in jazz and music studies from Humber College, an MA in interdisciplinary arts from Chicago's Columbia College, and a PhD in interdisciplinary studies from the University of British Columbia. She is currently Executive Director of the Guelph Jazz Festival.

Key words: music; women's studies; England

> Culturally speaking, women have wept a great deal, but once the tears are shed, there will be endless laughter instead. Laughter that breaks out, overflows, a humor no one would expect to find in women – which is nonetheless surely their greatest strength because it's a humor that sees man much further away than he has ever been seen.
>
> Hélène Cixous

In Greek mythology there is a story of an old woman named Baubo who, in an effort to help Demeter momentarily forget her grief over the loss of her daughter Persephone, pulled her dress up over her head, exposed her genitals and shouted obscene remarks and dirty jokes.[2] Apparently the distraction worked; accounts of the incident indicate Baubo's indecent gestures and lewd comments caused Demeter to laugh.

Scholars speculate that this obscene spectacle is replicated in a number of terra-cotta statues dated roughly from the fourth century B.C.E. Depicting a collapsed female body that consists of virtually nothing but two orifices, the statues reflect the Greek belief that women possess not one, but two mouths (Carson, "Gender," 72). One mouth is of course the opening to the oral cavity; the other leads to the cavernous depths of the female sex.

The anatomical deformity is strangely accentuated by the reversal of the mouths on the figures; that is, the "upper" mouth is situated in the statue's abdomen, the "lower" positioned on the top of her head. As poet and scholar Anne Carson suggests, the representation of Baubo's aural and visual gesture reflects the general confusion surrounding the representation of the female body in a masculinist culture: "This Baubo presents us with one simple chaotic diagram of an outrageously manipulable female identity. The doubling and interchangeability of mouth engenders a creature in whom sex is cancelled out by sound and sound is cancelled out by sex" ("Gender," 76). According to the legend, however, Baubo is in control of the erasure. Her spontaneous and excessive performance strategically utilizes the confusion and mutability associated with the female body in order to disrupt the representation of woman as passive and silent spectacle. Baubo's gesture obscures her upper mouth to make it appear as though her lower mouth is doing all the talking, enacting a strange ventriloquism that throws the voice produced by her vocal folds into the folds of her labia. The shock of Baubo's aural/visual play ruptures the moment of viewing with an unexpected interval—a stutter—that creates a "zone of disruption and de-stabilization" (Buckley, 60). Laughter and the stutter are sonic twins in this respect, disruptions that linger at the threshold of sense and non-sense. The stutter shatters the silent repetition of the female body, resists fetishization, penetrates the ear with the noise of resistance while it utters profanities that trouble patriarchal space. Perhaps this is why public soundings by women produce a great deal of anxiety: the female body breaks the silent repetition of representation with its stuttering laughter.

Julia Kristeva writes that laughter is a signifying practice, a lifting of inhibitions that is transgressive, transformational, pleasurable, and productive: "Every practice which produces something new (a new device) is a practice of laughter: it obeys laughter's logic and provides the subject of laughter's advantages" (*Revolution*, 225). The practice of laughter destabilizes the boundaries separating the conscious from the unconscious, jumbles the parameters of interior and exterior space, ridicules the isolation of body from mind, and defies the gravitational pull of predictability and repetition. It is a sonic borderline state, a space of psychic excess that generates a "constant calling into question of the psyche and the world" (Kristeva, *Sense*, 19). In other words, laughter is an improvisation.

Baubo's improvisational laugh engenders a sonic and somatic outpouring, an extemporaneous reversal that turns the body inside/out. Her actions exceed specularity; her sounds confound vision and defy anatomical expectations. When Baubo laughs, sound becomes flesh, corporeal play becomes aural display and sexuality is intoned. Baubo's laughter challenges the threshold of intelligibility and normalcy; she utters the limit, the place where the subject is both articulated and annihilated: inside/womb/life merges with outside/abjection/death. Perhaps this is why Demeter doubled over in laughter. She got the joke.

Some might interpret this allegory as a warning: women who improvise in public are in danger of surrendering to the visibility of their sexual difference by making a spectacle of themselves. Was it appropriate for Demeter to laugh given the circumstances? This is a rhetorical question of course; there is always a risk involved anytime a woman opens her mouth(s). Baubo's action suggests—as does Demeter's (re)action—that if the female body is always already spectacle by virtue of her difference, then making a spectacle of oneself by improvising that difference is a crucial performance of agency. As a critical reflection on the social order and a pleasurable "interval of potentiality" (Buckley, 60), the laughter of Baubo and Demeter confounds representation, reconfigures spectacle, regenerates, subjectivity, and improvises woman.

In his discussion of Baubo, Maurice Olender identifies three aspects associated with spectacle: gesture, desire, and gaze (89). Where and with whom desire is located is key to interpreting the spectacle, as desire mediates the network of power relations that circulate across the positions of spectacle and spectator. It is Baubo's desire to make herself a spectacle that disrupts the one-way gaze of the spectator, a refusal to mirror the "specular logic of the same" that defines the heterosexual voyeur (Moi, 133). In turn Baubo's distraction attracts Demeter—it reminds her of a knowledge that exists in excess of death, forgotten in her moment of grief—and her desire to respond is aroused.

The sonic exchange of desire between Baubo and Demeter underscores the possibility of an insurgent and noisy female improvisation. It points to the pleasure and the power of transgressive sounding, challenges the silence of repetition and questions the anxiety associated with female "noise." Baubo's perverse voice and Demeter's spontaneous laughter are simultaneously embodied and disembodied: "Sounds that are interstitial, defiant, peculiar at times ... *queer,* in the most musical sense of the term" (Mockus, 53). As one woman exposes her flesh/voice to the other, a flesh/voice is echoed back. The laughter quells the pain of death and the ache of abjection while it celebrates the sharp tongue, the promise of mutability, the flux of sound. This is an antiphonal exchange—an excessive gesture, a queer laughter—that breaks Demeter's silence, reciprocates Baubo's laugh, and resonates with/in both women. The story of Baubo is an improvisational sounding of body politics that as Mary Russo suggests, transforms the spectacle of the female body into active "multivalent, oppositional play" (62).

Fast forward to the 1970s: the legacy of Baubo and Demeter resonates with/in women improvisers, women who choose to make spectacles of themselves by sounding body, sexuality, knowledge, difference, freedom, and experience: "to smash everything, to shatter the framework of institutions, to blow up the law, to break up the 'truth' with laughter" (Cixous, "Castration," 258). Beginning in 1977 this revolution was sounded with particular energy in the queer laughter of the Feminist Improvising Group (FIG).

Improvising Freedom

Within the European music community interest in improvisational experimentation had developed more than a decade earlier in the 1960s, piqued by the presence of American expatriate free jazz musicians in Europe, the desire of local improvisers to stretch beyond the structures of idiomatic improvisation toward greater aesthetic freedom, and the dis-illusionment of improvisers with the growing commodification of music (Bailey, xi–xii; Prévost, 10). Percussionist Eddie Prévost suggests that although for some European improvisers jazz was viewed as a "major artistic and ideological force within the deve-lopment of a wider-ranging creative improvised music" that continually struggled to "escape the confinement of a white-dominated capitalist culture," it too had begun to solidify "into conventions that became as hard to escape as the unfreedoms of classical or popular musics" (10).

The appeal of freedom in improvisational practices resonated with/in the emerging political climate of the 1960s as improvisers began to discard codified procedures, including those found in jazz improvisation, in favor of experimental practices. These practices were not only concerned with aesthetics but with political, economic, and social matters as well. Irène Schweizer recounts that this politically charged time influenced her decision to stop playing "the changes" and to leave improvisational structures and systems behind: "For me, it was a natural development. We had always played the music of the time. In 1968 a lot of things were happening in Europe. There were student revolutions. Barriers were falling. It seemed natural to want to free yourself" (Hale, 15).

Nathaniel Mackey observes a similar impulse in black music, particularly free jazz, that challenged the dominant culture while striving toward aesthetic, individual, and collective freedom:

> During the sixties, assertions were often made to the effect that jazz groups provided glimpses into the future. What was meant by this was that black music—especially that of the sixties, with its heavy emphasis on individual freedom within a collectively improvised context—proposed a model social order, an ideal, even utopic balance between personal impulse and group demands.
>
> (34)

The parallel development of free jazz in the United States and free improvisation in Europe speaks of the ability of freely improvised music to cut across aesthetic boundaries of containment and categorization. James Snead describes this common aesthetic impulse:

> The extension of "free jazz," starting in the 1960s, into the technical practice of using the "material" qualities of sound—on the horns, for instance, using overtones, harmonics and subtones—became almost mandatory for the serious jazz musician and paralleled a similar movement on the part of European musicians branching out of the classical tradition.
>
> (222)

Although the simultaneous development of a congruent sonic aesthetic linked the practices of free jazz and free improvisation together, it has sometimes obscured the fact that the two were distinct (albeit interrelated) practices grounded in different traditions and communities. Joëlle Léandre explains the differences from a European perspective:

> We received free jazz in Europe at the time when Ornette Coleman and all the other players were creating, but free jazz is not free music, free jazz is a Black music too. Free music is, I think, definitely a European music. We have a long history of the music, we have Monteverdi, we have Bartok, we have Stockhausen, it's a long line. … I think that this kind of music, free music, is very much a European music, and where different people come from they bring their own ways to it. You know, we have very wonderful jazz musicians in France, but they play the American music, they don't play the European music (laughs) but what I like is all this mixture.
>
> (quoted in Vickery, 18)

The suggestion here is that neither free jazz nor free improvisation existed in a vacuum; neither, however, were they completely interchangeable. It is important to recognize that the hybridity and mixing of the practices did not obscure the differences, especially in regard to the intersection of aesthetic freedom with race and class.

For example, in free improvisation—exercised within a predominately white, male improvising community existing on the margins of avant-garde and mainstream music— the move toward aesthetic freedom was a critique of class structures and power networks embedded in European music and society. Renewed interest in improvisation challenges the marginalization of improvisational practices in European art music that culminated in the nineteenth century, by destabilizing the "dominant procedures through which music is made and consumed, especially in challenging established roles for composers, musicians, and audiences" (Durant, 276). Free improvisation questions how music functions in society, especially in relation to power, to become "a point of counter-identification against systems of control, hierarchy and subordination" (Durant, 270).

African-American explorations of freedom in free jazz similarly critiqued the function of music in relation to power, but did so in the context of racial oppression. Free jazz actively critiqued and resisted racial oppression of the dominant culture within a historical continuum that connected black music to the resistance of slavery and traced its musical roots to Africa:

> The music itself describes the political position of Blacks in America just as their position dictates their day-to-day life, the instruments they play and the places where their music can be heard. In the case of African-American music, the fact that the creators are the colonised in a colonialist society, has a vital bearing on the way the music has evolved, how it is regarded by the world at large, and the way in which the artists are treated.
>
> (Wilmer, *As Serious*, 14)

Neither free improvisation nor free jazz, however, extended their critiques to include the aesthetic, economic, or political liberation of women. For the most part, a practice of freedom that resisted gender oppression and oppression on the basis of sexual difference was excluded from the liberatory impulses of male-dominated improvising communities. The opportunity for freedom in relation to sexual difference, gender, and sexuality for women improvisers was strangely absent from the discourses and practices of both free jazz and free improvisation.

Thus, it is difficult to describe accurately just how integral women's contributions to the development of free improvisation and free jazz were in the early days, as women's participation was limited and remains underdocumented. Chronicles of free improvisation and free jazz from a variety of sources—including Derek Bailey's *Improvisation: Its Nature and Practice in Music*,[3] John Litweiler's classic book on free jazz, *The Freedom Principle: Jazz After 1958*; the more recent work of Kevin Whitehead in *New Dutch Swing*, documenting the scene in Holland; as well as John Corbett's provocative article, "Ephemera Underscored: Writing Around Free Improvisation" pay little or no attention to the music's female constituents. Perhaps because improvisationally based music struggled from the beginning for recognition, its practices and documents have not always been liberatory, often reduplicating the marginalization and exclusion women face(d) in more mainstream musical structures and in patriarchal society at large.

The particular challenges encountered by women improvisers due to the effects of gender and sex oppression, including the gendering of women's performances and audiences as feminine and/or lacking, are rarely acknowledged. In *Swing Shift: "All-Girl" Bands of the 1940s*, Sherrie Tucker discusses how "stories of devaluation and absence are woven into the familiar rhythms of the popular history books about the Swing Era" (3). As with the majority of women musicians in a variety of genres throughout history, all-women swing bands were either omitted from historical accounts, treated as novelties, or considered unauthentic because they were assumed to lack ability by virtue of their sexual difference. Angela Davis notes a similar masculinist bias in historical and critical accounts of the blues that fail "to take seriously the efforts of women blues musicians and the female reception of their work. As a consequence, the central part played by women both in the blues and in the history of African-American cultural consciousness is often ignored" (44–45).

In relation to free improvisation Irène Schweizer often acknowledges that although she was the only female instrumentalist on the European scene throughout the 1960s and the early 1970s her contributions are conspicuously absent from historical accounts:

> I had been taking part in the FMP festival during its development in the '60s and '70s, being the only woman on every festival. … There was a photo exhibition about all the jazz musicians from FMP festivals from 1968 to 1978, and not one single photo of me even though I took part every second year.
>
> (Les Diaboliques)

In contrast, Val Wilmer's classic book *As Serious as Your Life*—as one of the first documents of women's experiences in and around the "new jazz" in African-American communities—is an exception to the masculinist rule of exclusion. Wilmer's approach is twofold: she writes of women's experiences as support systems for their male musician partners and of their struggles as players trying to cope with a male-dominated scene. She pays particular attention to the intersections of race and class with gender and sexual difference, unearthing differences in the experiences and attitudes of both white and black women. Although the focus on women is not the core of Wilmer's project, it is extensive enough to paint an accurate, yet somewhat bleak portrait of women's position in relation to men and improvisation. Wilmer reports that many women gave up their own artistic ambitions to support their men. When they did venture out to play in clubs the reception was often lukewarm, and as Wilmer points out, the skepticism that scrutinized and devalued women's playing is summed up in the comment, "You sound good—for a woman!" (204).

By raising the issue of sexual politics in free jazz, Wilmer also unearthed the sexual politics of music criticism. She recounts that after writing these passages on women in her book, male critics criticized her for being insufficiently "feminist." She describes her dilemma:

> It was true that I had dwelt on women's supportive role rather than participatory contribution, but as someone pointed out, jazz wasn't exactly a feminist area of endeavor. Many's the time I have wished that I could rewrite that particular part of the book with a more thorough analysis of women's position. It was an intervention, though, and by and large, the response to *As Serious* was positive.
>
> (*Mama*, 287–88)

This reflection appears in Wilmer's subsequent book *Mama Said There'd Be Days Like This: My Life in the Jazz World,* a personal history centering on a young girl's passion for jazz that develops into a lifelong commitment to the music. Written from her perspective as a white, lesbian, working-class photojournalist, Wilmer details the complex negotiations required of her to navigate the world of jazz. The result is a superb descriptive journey that moves the reader through a number of seemingly incommensurable communities simultaneously. The exploration of her complex, shifting selves consistently questions white, heterosexual, middle-class notions of identity, community, and music and demonstrates alternative possibilities of community and care. Similar to Minnie Bruce Pratt's "Identity: Skin Blood Heart," Wilmer rewrites herself "in relation to shifting interpersonal and political contexts" that enable her to construct "a notion of community as inherently unstable and contextual, not based on sameness or essential connections, but offering agency instead of passivity" (de Lauretis, 12–13). This is the vision and possibility of community when the struggle toward freedom recognizes the intersections of sexual difference, gender, and sexuality in addition to race and class, as the basis for improvisational practices.

Playing the Personal Is Political

The impetus to gather a group of women improvisers together into a collective was galvanized by the glaring absence of women improvisers en masse in performance situations. At a musician's union meeting in London, vocalist Maggie Nicols expressed to multi-instrumentalist/composer Lindsay Cooper (Nicols) her desire to explore improvisation with other women. Even with the emergence of a burgeoning "women's music" scene, Cooper and Nicols recognized the glaring absence of women improvisers. As Cooper recounts: "We got talking and we agreed that improvisation had become very important and no women were doing it. And suddenly we thought, well, let's do it! Let's get women together and do it ourselves!" (personal interview).

Involvement in the feminist movement coupled with a strong commitment to class politics and lesbian activism encouraged Nicols and Cooper to commingle the personal and the political within an improvisational context. Although both women performed extensively with men, their experience playing with other women was very limited. Nicols wondered out loud what the experience of playing with women would be like:

> We recognized that women were being excluded and we wanted to just experience what it was like to play with other women. One of the strongest things for me that came out of the Women's Liberation Movement was the recognition of the connection between the personal and the political. So to say for me that it was a personal thing was also political. I wanted to feel the intimacy musically that I felt with women. You know when you hang out with women, that quality of shared experience. How would that translate artistically?
>
> (personal interview)

Already an accomplished player by the late 1970s, Lindsay Cooper continues to look back on her choice to play with other women as a crucial move that gave her confidence in her ability as an artist:

> It's hard to admit it but it's only now that I realise there were *years* when I felt intimidated by men and the assumptions concerning their abilities. It's actually fantastically liberating to realise I've been through all of that and recovered. This is not to say that one's internal oppression is the only thing to be faced because men can be difficult to work with, but what working with women has done for me is to give me a much stronger sense of myself as a musician. This means that now when I work with men I feel much more *centred*.
>
> (Wilmer, "Half," 4)

It was Nicols's approach to improvisation—an openness to inclusivity inspired by the philosophy and practice of her mentor and friend, drummer John Stevens—that initially shaped the Feminist Improvising Group. Nicols envisioned an open and changing pool of women musicians that would bring a wide range of approaches to improvisation, varied experience to technical facility, and stylistic diversity to spontaneous performances. The initial pool of musicians consisted of Cooper, Nicols, Corine Liensol, Georgie Born, and Cathy Williams. Irène Schweizer and Sally Potter joined the feminist Improvising Group in the spring of 1978, and Annemarie Roelofs, Frankie Armstrong, Angèle Veltmeijer, and Françoise Dupety participated intermittently to form a variety of combinations of up to eight women improvising together in any given performance.[4]

Nicols arranged the first public performance of an entirely female group of improvisers during a Music for Socialism concert at the *Almost Free* in London (Wilmer, *Mama*, 284). When the leaflet advertising the concert appeared, the name of the group was listed as the Feminist Improvising Group, a name neither Nicols nor Cooper had chosen:

> We didn't call ourselves the Feminist Improvising Group. We were going to call ourselves the Women's Improvising Group but the promoters of the Music for Socialism event gave us that name! So we grew into it. We actually took it on board. It was very strange that men gave us the name.
>
> (Les Diaboliques)

Nicols's suspicion of the feminist label was well founded as in the early days of the movement feminism was, in the words of Teresa de Lauretis, "anchored to the single axis of gender as sexual difference" (10). Second-wave feminism tended to present a singular, unified view of "woman" that ignored the differences that existed *between* women on the basis of sexuality, race, and class. As Nicols suggests: "I was skeptical in regard to the feminist label. Not that I don't consider myself a feminist, but more because of the association with dogmas" (Meier and Landolt, 17).

The feminist label had the potential to polarize the sexual politics already embedded in improvisation and to stigmatize women improvisers even further. Claiming a space for women in improvised music was contentious enough, but how much more contentious would it be for women to claim a feminist space within improvised music? Still, the term "feminist" had its charm. It was a subversive and powerful moniker that was, as Nicols slyly recounts, eventually adopted by the group: "We took on the challenge and we thought okay, so be it. You want feminism, we'll give you feminism. And we certainly did, scissors and all!" (Les Diaboliques).

Improvising Consciousness

The first performance of FIG was preceded by a sort of consciousness-raising rehearsal/workshop in which the players discussed among themselves their feelings and experiences as women. The discussion was a catalyst for the pastiche of sounds and images that found their way into the improvisation:

> I spoke about being a mother, Corine spoke about being treated like a child because of her disability, so already we had a mother-child scenario which we started the gig with. The others spoke of their particular personal/political issues as women— appearance, image, etc. We brought kitchen props. It was a sort of prepared spontaneity that was a very powerful, anarchic, humorous beginning.
>
> (Nicols)[5]

On stage the women appeared in drag, engaged in role-playing, performed domestic chores, peeled onions, and sprayed perfume. It was a performance Nicols describes as "absolute anarchy":

> The people were shocked, because they felt the power that was emerging from the women. We did not do that on purpose. We didn't even realize ourselves what was happening. We improvised, but we improvised our own lives and our biographies. We parodied our situation, perverted our dependencies and threw everything high into the air.
>
> (Meier and Landolt, 17–18)

Throwing everything high into the air was, for the Feminist Improvising Group, the improvisation of a "critical method." To use a common cliché of the early feminist movement, it was a way of making their voices heard. On this level FIG approached improvisation as a practice of self-discovery and a process of collective negotiation, politically motivated practices linked to the consciousness-raising groups of the 1970s that endeavored to express women's lived experiences. Although now debunked as ineffectual and essentialist (a marker of white, middle-class, radical feminism) the prioritization of gender issues in feminist consciousness-raising groups was both productive—

> Consciousness-raising groups affirmed the most dramatic insight of the early women's liberation movement: the personal is political. Individual women shared personal experiences with the aim of rendering explicit the underlying politics shaping women's lives.
>
> (Davis, 55)

—and exclusionary:

> Because of the complicated racial politics of the 1960s, which defined the women's movement as white, and because of its emphasis on personal micropolitics (often seen as a retreat from the macropolitics of race), black women generally found it difficult to identify with the strategy of consciousness-raising.
>
> (Davis, 55)

Teresa de Lauretis points to the substantive contributions of women of color and lesbians to consciousness raising that shifted the emphasis away from the narrowness of "personal micropolitics" toward a transformation of feminism as a "pursuit of consciousness and political practice" (5). This approach to consciousness raising required the recognition of and struggle with multiple dimensions of difference, a struggle that moved beyond the notion of writing the self toward a *re*writing of the self: "a process of struggle and interpretation ... in relation to a new understanding of community, of history, of culture" (de Lauretis, 18). Consciousness-raising groups could create a space for women to unearth knowledge that was subjugated as a result of oppression on the basis of gender and sexual difference. Practicing improvisation as a form of consciousness raising enabled women to experiment with a variety of power-sharing arrangements, to negotiate leadership, and to reimagine a political practice in which women controlled their own artistic destinies by drawing directly from their lived experiences.[6]

Although FIG's members were predominantly white, so too were they lesbian and working-class, thus the intersections of gender with race, class, and sexuality were important aspects of its improvisations. For Nicols a comprehensive knowledge of these intersections has always informed her improvisations:

> I see my music in connection to my political attitude. I am a woman and I identify myself with the worker's movement. That is my social background. In addition I have learned about social privileges and recognize I have privileges as a white woman in our society. I think I wanted to cross boundaries in many ways: social, emotional and in music. That is difficult to convey openly to an audience. That's why you have to be committed to the social environment you are a part of. I mean the political environment as well. You need to know what's going on around you, which political discussions are taking place.
>
> (Meier and Landolt, 18)

Being aware of the political environment also meant that the straight members of FIG, if uninitiated in the politics of lesbian sexuality, were soon politicized by their lesbian comrades:

> I was not so politically involved in Holland—besides making modern music—but I wasn't lesbian and I think that makes a difference. Talking to Lindsay and Maggie helped me a lot in forming my thinking at that time. And of course that is what was happening when we were touring and doing concerts, they were telling me what was happening, or they were talking over things in London. In that case it was much more political than any men's group who were just interested in playing music.
>
> (Roelofs)

FIG performances staged numerous parodies that commented on the aesthetic, political, economic, and social position of women on a number of levels. The mother/child scenario staged between Nicols (a white woman) and Liensol (a black woman) in the inaugural FIG performance (described by Nicols above)—"I was an insane mother while Corine behaved like a child"—can be read not only as a parody of the infantilization of a woman with a disability, but as an indictment of the racial politics of the early feminist movement performed as the oppression of a black woman by an authoritative white woman.[7]

FIG also critiqued whiteness in humorous parodies of middle-class domesticity. The incorporation of everyday domestic "found" objects such as vacuum cleaners, brooms, dustpans, pots and pans, and egg slicers—in Lindsay Cooper's words transforming "the sounds of women's work into a work of women's sounds"—highlighted women's work in the private sphere as well as the subordination of working-class women as domestics (Wilmer, *Mama*, 285). Throughout the performances one or more players could be found sweeping the stage, while others gathered in small ensembles to explore the sonic possibilities of household items.

FIG used drag to critique and parody the institution of compulsory heterosexuality that existed in society and in various forms of music as well: "To concentrate while singing [Nicols] usually puts her hands over her broken fly. ... Sally is "sweet" and "demure" in a well-known hetero love song" (Jankowski). This set the stage for role-playing and interactions between members of the group that challenged heteronormative roles causing one reviewer to comment: "On stage, they often touch each other. A lot of 'acts,' 'fights' and hugs ended up on the stage floor tonight" (Jankowski). By violating taboos of musical propriety and masculinist competition that prohibited musicians from touching one another, FIG more than hinted at the possibility of sensuous and sexual relationships between women. The integration of lesbian sexuality into the improvisational text enabled the Feminist Improvising Group to ask, "what gets *lost* when [a woman] and her music are studied in the 'company of men,' and what is recuperated when [a woman] joins 'the company of women?'" (Mockus, 52).

Following this trajectory Irène Schweizer continues to question the assumptions that constructed the world of jazz and improvised music as heterosexual:

> Why are so few jazz musicians gay? This question has never been asked. The jazz musician has a totally different image. He has to act macho: to read the notes with one eye and to peek around in the audience for nice women. With improvised music the consciousness of musicians has changed a little bit. There are some emancipated men: George Lewis, Maarten Altena, Lol Coxhill, but gay musicians? Even if they were gay, they wouldn't be showing it. With some exceptions like Cecil Taylor, but there are not many.
>
> (Meier and Landolt, 17)

The decentering of heterosexual interactions that are assumed to exist in and around musical performances and a refusal to "pass" as straight opened possibilities for the improvisation of female sexuality. In effect FIG queered space of improvisational practice. As Nicols explains, "We are not lesbians [on the music scene] by chance. That has something to do with autonomy. ... The lesbians were pioneers and had to be lesbian" (Meier and Landolt, 18).

Improvising Antiphony

Improvisation served as a site for the negotiation of individuality and collectivity through the multiplicitous interactions of improviser to improviser, improviser to audience, as well as audiences to one another. FIG performances improvised self and community as a feminist consciousness "attained through practices of political and personal displacement across boundaries between sociosexual identities and communities, between bodies and discourses" (de Lauretis, 18). Part of FIG's political and aesthetic program was to institute opportunities for antiphonal exchange between performers and audiences by consciously dismantling the divisions that separated them, a power-sharing tactic that extended well beyond the stage. For FIG member Sally Potter, breaking down the division between the audience and the performer was a political strategy that emerged from an awareness of feminist and class politics:

> Both the specialness ascribed to individual performers and the performer/audience divide itself are seen as unhealthy symptoms of a class divided society, the performer taking an honorary position of power. The strategy then becomes to break down the divide and emphasize participation as a way of saying anyone can do it.
>
> (291)

The idea that "anyone can do it" was often unpalatable to improvisers and audience members who valued the display of technical virtuosity as the marker of improvisational competence above all else. Improvising percussionist Eddie Prévost cautions against the tendency he calls "technological elitism," insisting that improvisation requires "dexterity of all kinds (social as well as technical)" (5). For Nicols the ability to integrate dexterity of all kinds into improvisation requires a skill she calls "social virtuosity":

> For me social virtuosity—social skills really—is part of [what it takes] to communicate with an audience and with other musicians. It also involves the social skills used to live your life. How you are in the community and those sorts of things. Being able to have that kind of creative spontaneity in every aspect of your life. (telephone interview)

For Irène Schweizer, reading technical virtuosity through social virtuosity provided an opportunity to redefine improvisation and (re)invent standards:

> It is very important that we all got the chance to play together. But there are also problems: Which musicians are you going to invite? Which are the standards you demand? Technical brilliance? Professionalism? Enthusiasm? Invention? Imagination? I would prefer a mixture of all. That's an important gain of FIG. It defined new standards. Until then these were defined by men.
>
> (Meier and Landolt, 18)

In part, inventing new standards meant dispensing with the notion that "men are destined to be the keepers of the musical flame." Val Wilmer describes this reinvention as "moving from total immersion in the lives of men who structured the music" toward an awareness of the "prejudices" women have internalized about their own abilities in an effort "to support women's right to an equal share of the bandstand" (Wilmer, "Half," 4).

Nicols remembers that FIG's challenge to "technological elitism" and fixed notions of "musical competency" was often dismissed by male musicians: "Whether it was the jazz community that said to Irene and me, 'you and Irene are really great but everybody else is crap' or the more progressive rock 'Henry Cow' people [who] would like what Lindsay and Georgie were doing and all that. So, divide and rule." Schweizer came up against similar sentiments:

> Some people asked me: "Why do you play with those women? They can't play and they're no good and you don't have to do that. Why do you play with those women?" It was always difficult for me to explain why, because for me it was just important to play like this in a group of women and to support them.

For Roelofs, the lack of support from men was disheartening but also suspect:

> We were eight people, some of whom were good players and some of whom weren't so experienced but were politically very right and in terms of improvising picked up nice things. [FIG] was more like a sort of workshop where people of all different kinds of levels attended. That could certainly be heard but, I don't know, maybe we could have hoped for more support from the men's side. [They could have said] well, just keep on going. But mostly the men said it's no good. I definitely think it's not only the musical level they were talking about. I think it was felt as a threat for a lot of men to just see so many women on stage.

Nicols, Schweizer, and Roelofs agree that the criticism received from men (often communicated indirectly) was frequently imbalanced and rarely constructive:

The critics were never medium, it was always high calling our work very interesting stuff or it was absolutely low, the deepest saying, how can a festival have these women? ... I think Lindsay and Maggie would certainly agree that the feeling we sometimes felt when the critics were criticizing us was very denigrating. They would say, these *women,* not these musicians, these *women,* argh, eight women on stage, oh god what's happening, get some men out there!

(Roelofs)

One incident that stands out in the minds of all of the FIG members I interviewed was their performance at the Total Music Meeting in Berlin in 1979 and the response of the well-known avant-garde musician Alexander von Schlippenbach. Nicols describes what happened as she remembers it:

He came up to us before the gig and he was kissing our hands. Now, we did a phenomenal gig there. I mean it was phenomenal. It was mad, it was anarchic. It was a mixture of grace and clumsiness—the audience loved it. Then we found out from [the organizer's partner] that Alex had gone to him and complained about us being there, saying that he could have found loads of men that would have played a lot better, that we couldn't play our instruments. I mean this included Irene and Annemarie and Lindsay and myself! And it was the hypocrisy of that. [Later] Lindsay and I went to a women's festival in the same place and we went into the gents toilets and wrote graffiti all over the gents toilets: "Watch out Alex von Schlippenbach, we've got our scissors ready." You know, we graffitied the gents toilets [laughs]. And it was only just recently that I started speaking to him again because I thought I've got to let it go. He probably doesn't even realize this.

The extent to which readings of FIG performances were effected by gender and sexual difference is difficult to assess or dissect. Was there a masculinist musical gaze/ear operative here? Did the disavowed gender anxiety—related to the spectacle of so many unsupervised and unpredictable women on the stage—(re)surface in the accusations of technical incompetence, lack of speed, and fluency? Guitarist Eugene Chadbourne, who also played at the 1979 Total Music Meeting, speculates that gendered style as well as sexual difference factored into the critical assessment of FIG's performances, although these were not the sole criteria:

My impression at the time was that the cool, in-crowd clique at the Total Music Meeting in Berlin wasn't into anything that was outside of what they were doing. ... This was my main experience with FIG because the festival went on over four nights and I think each group played three or four times. I was playing with the Japanese trumpeter Toshinori Kondo and our music was not well liked by either this in-crowd of older players or the audience. The lack of support for FIG must obviously extend beyond the boundaries of that group into the entire area of women musicians. ... I am sure the lack of men on stage made some men feel excluded. Then I guess the next step is they listen to the music or watch what is going on with an attitude, like let's see them prove themselves.[8]

At the most fundamental level, male improvisers regularly excluded women from their groups, and even if the exclusion was inadvertent, it was also blatant. This meant that the mere presence of FIG as an exclusively female group stirred controversy in the improvising community. The extreme reactions to FIG performances raised questions about the level of anxiety attached to the "exclusion" of men from FIG, the general lack of support for women improvisers, the heteronormative reading of improvisation, and the severity of critical response. The spectacle of women improvising without men tended to overshadow the improvisations themselves and obscure how the performances were received:

> It's amazing the number of men that were saying, "Why are there no men?" And yet nobody had ever dreamed to think of asking why there were men only [in groups]. They'd say, well, there are just no women around. There's a kind of weird, twisted logic whereby men think it's not deliberate, we haven't deliberately excluded women. And that's even more insidious because they just haven't thought about it. At least we thought about it.
> (Nicols, personal interview)

FIG demonstrated that free improvisation was not free of masculinist tendencies, heterosexual expectations, or immune to gender anxieties. Although not all practices in improvisation reinforced the normative performance of gender, sexual difference, and sexuality it is clear that the position and participation of queer and straight women in the development and deployment of improvisational practices and codes was, and to a great extent still is, tentative at best.

Nor was FIG immune to criticisms from feminist audiences purportedly supportive of "women's music."[9] The dogmatic feminist gaze that criticized FIG for being too virtuosic and abstract—interpreted as macho posturing and elitism—at times plagued them. Val Wilmer recalls one of several frustrating incidents when the collective was performing at Drill Hall in London as part of a newly organized Women's Festival:

> The Drill Hall concert left many women at a loss. It was a freewheeling, improvised piece, played by forthright musicians who obviously knew their instruments. But the "free music" idiom was unknown to most of the audience, and the unease and uncertainty were expressed about whether, being so "inaccessible," theirs was an elitist concept. It was bitterly frustrating for the musicians involved to be rejected in this way. Most of them had a history of struggle against male refusal to allow them a place on the bandstand. Now, having shown that not only could they play their instruments but were equipped to handle the most demanding of concepts, they were under attack from the quarter where they most needed friends.
> (*Mama*, 285)

There were, of course, many favorable reactions to FIG improvisations by both women and men that attended the concerts. FIG was able to introduce feminist politics to a largely uninitiated group of men as well as introduce free improvisation to a largely uninitiated group of women. Nicols cites FIG as an influence on the improvisational group "Alterations," while Cooper recalls reactions from a woman artist working in another medium: "I remember one gig FIG did and a friend of mine that I was working on a film with said: 'I don't know what on earth you're doing but I like it.' And I thought well, that really is all you need to say."

Overall, the Feminist Improvising Group did play in a number of women's festivals—the Stockholm Women's Music Festival, the Copenhagen International Women's Music Festival—and to a majority of all-women audiences:

Women, who did come because we were women, trusted us because we were women, and through that started listening to the music. I know that because of that experience a lot of women went on to listen to the whole spectrum of improvised music, not just women's music. So in a way we were ambassadors for the music as well. And I love the way—I'm being ironic here—women are not seen as an important audience.

(Nicols, personal interview)

In these performances FIG applied their skills of social and technical virtuosity, improvising issues particular to women from complex sociopolitical, economic, and aesthetic perspectives: "By treating improvisation not as an isolated artifact but as something springing directly from women's experience, the musicians drew women into their music who might not otherwise be concerned with the concept of free improvisation" (Wilmer, "Feminist").

The opportunity to play for women audiences became an opportunity to reconfigure the relationship between spectacle and spectator apart from the typical scenario of masculine desire that constructed improvised music as heterosexual, positioned women musicians as spectacles for the masculine gaze and/or assumed that women on and off the bandstand were either wives, girlfriends, or groupies. Instead, improvising on their own terms was a chance for women to foreground *their* bodies and *their* sounds for the pleasure of other women. If women in the audience were not particularly fluent in deciphering the codes of free improvisation, their fluency with the all-too-familiar tropes of the female body and women's precarious position to sound and spectacle was indeed proficient. FIG's improvisations were attuned to the facility of the audience to play with and against the political codes of race, gender, sexuality, and class as well as their facility to play with the aesthetic codes of improvisation. For FIG playing was a sonic negotiation of eroticism, resistance, liberation, joy, pleasure, power, and agency, a multilayered call and response between individual improvisers and a community of listeners.

FIG was instrumental in encouraging listeners/interpreters to negotiate the work from a queer perspective, opening a space for the listener who responds to the laughter of women with her own improvised laughter. In other words, the spectacle of the Feminist Improvising Group was a queer sounding that demanded queer listening, an antiphonal and erotic playing by ear that heard pleasure and desire in the strange resonances and sonic exchanges of women's embodied, lived experience. There is a moment during a FIG performance recorded live at the Stockholm Women's Music Festival in which the audience spontaneously responds to the screams, wails, and instrumental flurries of the players on stage with their own shrieks and ululations. The players pay attention to this response and reciprocate with/in a cacophony of sound: the flesh/voice of Baubo echoed in Demeter's laugh. The pleasure and pain heard in the disruptive stutters of Baubo and Demeter are heard again in the performances of the Feminist Improvising Group. The insurgent, noisy, female spectacle performed in ancient Greece is (re)played in the queer laughter of women improvisers, the improvised laughter of queer women.

Notes

1 See Young and Poynton.
2 For a comprehensive discussion of Baubo that includes the dating and significance of the statues attributed to this story, see Olender, "Aspects of Baubo" and accompanying plates.

3 A number of women I interviewed were bewildered by Bailey's omission of women improvisers from this project.

4 Instrumentation was as follows: Lindsay Cooper (bassoon, oboe, soprano sax); Maggie Nicols (voice, piano); Corine Liensol (trumpet); Georgie Born (bass, cello); Cathy Williams (voice); Irène Schweizer (piano); Sally Potter (voice, alto sax); Annemarie Roelofs (trombone, violin); Frankie Armstrong (voice); Angele Veltmeijer (flute, tenor, soprano and alto sax); Françoise Dupety (guitar).

5 The source of this excerpt is an informal written correspondence with Nicols that was not part of the formal interviews: used with permission.

6 Thanks to Becki Ross for this insight and for providing a perspective on the heterosexism and racism that pervaded many consciousness-raising groups of the time.

7 The scenario described to me by Nicols also appears in Meier and Landolt: "I was a mother and on stage there was a gap between me as a mother and as a performer. Corine was in a peculiar situation, she wanted to work on her music—she had played the piano and the violin since she was four years old—but she lost the function of her arm in a car accident. So she started to play the trumpet. She changed so much and threw everything she knew about composed music overboard. In addition she went through constant pain. ... All of this was raw material for our show" (18).

8 Elsewhere in the interview Chadbourne refers to the prevailing FMP style as "old-school macho."

9 See Tucker for a discussion of the differences between the political and aesthetic attitudes of women who played in the "all-girl" swing bands of the 1940s and second-wave feminists who discovered their music in the late 1970s.

Works Cited

Bailey, Derek. *Improvisation: Its Nature and Practice in Music.* New York: Da Capo Press, 1992.

Buckley, Sandra L. "An Aesthetic of the Stutter." In *Cassandra: Voices From the Inside,* edited by Freda Guttman, 58–61. Montreal: Oboro, 1998.

Carson, Anne. "The Gender of Sound." In *Cassandra: Voices From the Inside,* edited by Freda Guttman, 62–81. Montreal: Oboro, 1998. Originally printed in *Glass, Irony and God.* New York: New Directions, 1995.

——. "Putting Her in Her Place: Woman, Dirt, and Desire." In *Before Sexuality: Construction of Erotic Experience in the Ancient Greek World,* edited by David M. Halperin, John J. Winkler, and Froma I Zeitlin, 135–69. New Jersey: Princeton University Press, 1990.

Chadboune, Eugene. Email interview. 1 November 1999.

Chenard, Marc. "FM? and Beyond: A Conversation with Irène Schweizer." *Coda* (October-November 1998): 11–13.

Cixous, Hélène. "Castration or Decapitation?" In *Out 'There: Marginalization and Contemporary Cultures,* edited by Russell Ferguson, Martha Gever, Trinh T. Minh-ha, and Cornel West, 345–56. The New Museum of Contemporary Art and MIT' Press, 1990.

——. "Laugh of the Medusa." In *New French Feminisms,* edited by Elaine Marks and Isabelle de Courtivron, 245–64. Translated by Keith Cohen and Paula Cohen. Amherst: University of Massachsetts Press, 1980.

Cooper, Lindsay. Personal interview. 5 August 1999.

Corbett, John. "Ephemera Underscored: Writing Around Free Improvisation." In *Jazz Among the Discourses,* edited by Krin Gabbard, 217–40. Durham: Duke University Press, 1995.

Davis, Angela. *Blues Legacies and Black Feminism.* New York: Pantheon Books, 1998.

de Lauretis, Teresa. "Eccentric Subjects: Feminist Theory and Historical Consciousness." *Feminist Studies* 16, no. 1 (1990): 115–51.

Durant, Alan. "Improvisation in the Political Economy of Music." In *Music and the Politics of Culture,* edited by Christopher Norris, 252–82. London: Lawrence and Wishart, 1989.

Hale, James. "Irène Schweizer: Many and One Direction." *Coda* 276 (November-December 1997): 14–15.

Jankowski, Angely Thomas. "FIG: Feminist Improvising Group." N. pag. Zurich: N.p., 9 March 1979.

Kristeva, Julia. *The Sense and Non-sense of Revolt: The Powers and Limits of Psychoanalysis.* Translated by Jeanine Herman. New York: Columbia University Press, 2000.

——. *Revolution in Poetic Language.* Translated by Margaret Waller. New York: Columbia University Press, 1984.

Les Diaboliques. Personal interview. 5 November 1999.

Litweiler, John. *The Freedom Principle: Jazz After 1958.* New York: William Morrow, 1984.

Mackey, Nathaniel. *Discrepant Engagement: Dissonance, Cross-Culturality, and Experimental Writing.* New York: Cambridge University Press, 1993.

Meier, Rosmarie, and Patrick Landolt. Interview with Maggie Nicols and Irène Schweizer. "Wir Sind Nicht Zufallig Lesben. Das Hat Mit Autonomie Zu Tun." Translated by Suzanna Desinger and Berndt Desinger. 17–18 October 1986.

Mockus, Martha. "Lesbian Skin and Musical Fascination." In *Audible Traces: Gender. Identity, and Music,* edited by Elaine Barkin and Lydia Hamessley, 50–69. Zurich: Carciofoli, 1999.

Moi, "Toril. *Sexual Textual Politics: Feminist Literary Theory.* New York: Routledge, 1988.

Nicols Maggie. Personal interview. 4 November 1999.

——. Telephone interview. 4 March 2000.

Olender, Maurice. "Aspects of Baubo: Ancient Texts and Contexts." In *Before Sexuality: Construction of Erotic Experience in the Ancient Greek World,* edited by David M. Halperin, John J. Winkler, and Froma I Zeitlin, 83–113. New Jersey: Princeton University Press, 1990.

Potter, Sally. "On Shows." In *Framing Feminism,* edited by Rozsika Parker and Griselda Pollock, 290–92. London: Pandora, 1987.

Poynton, Cate. "Talking Like a Girl." In *Musics and Feminisms,* edited by Cate Poynton and Sally Macarthur, 119–27. Sydney: Australian Music Centre, 1999.

Prévost, Eddie. *No Sound Is Innocent.* Essex: Copula, 1995.

Roelofs, Annemarie. Personal interview. 11 August 1999.

Russo, Mary. *The Female Grotesque: Risk, Excess and Modernity.* New York: Routledge, 1994.

Schweizer, Irène. Personal interview. 5 November 1999.

Snead, James. "Repetition as a Figure of Black Culture." In *Out There: Marginalization and Contemporary Cultures,* edited by Russell Ferguson, et al., 213–30. The New Museum of Contemporary Art and MIT Press, 1990.

Tucker, Sherrie. *Swing Shift: "All-Girl" Bands of the 1940s.* Durham: Duke University Press, 2000.

Vickery, Steve. "Joëlle Léandre: Music Actuelle." *Coda* 243 (May-June 1992): 16–19.

Whitehead, Kevin. *New Dutch Swing: jazz+classical music+absurdism.* New York: Billboard Books, 1998.

Wilmer, Val. *As Serious As Your Life: The Story of the New Jazz.* Westport, Conn.: Lawrence Hill, 1980.

——. "Feminist Improvisers at Music for Socialism Festival." N.p. (1978?): n.pag.

——. "Half the Bandstand." *City Limits* (30 April—6 May 1982): 4.

——. *Mama Said There'd Be Days Like This: My Life in the jazz World.* London: The Women's Press, 1989.

Young, Iris Marion. *Throwing Like a Girl and Other Essays in Feminist Philosophy and Social Theory.* Bloomington: Indiana University Press, 1990.

35 Frozen Grand Central

Charlie Todd

Born in Columbia, South Carolina, Charlie Todd graduated from UNC Chapel Hill with a BA in Dramatic Art. In New York City in August 2001, Todd, on his way to a West Village bar, arranged with two college friends that, entering separately, they would approach him as strangers, pretending to recognise him as singer/songwriter Ben Folds. "It worked," Todd blogs. "I spent three hours in the bar as 'Ben Folds,' signing autographs, posing for photos, and drinking on the house. At the end of the night, I left the bar without revealing it had been a hoax … this experience got me excited about the potential of staging creative pranks in public places. As a comedian and actor new to the city, I discovered I could create my own perfor-mances rather than waiting around for someone to give me an opportunity." Improv Everywhere was born. Producing, directing, performing, and documenting the group's work, including pranks and flash mobs since 2001, Todd is the author, with Alex Scordelis, of *Causing a Scene: Extraordinary Pranks in Ordinary Places with Improv Everywhere*. Based in New York, Improv Everywhere "causes scenes of chaos and joy in public places and has executed over 100 missions involving thousands of undercover agents."

Key words: theatre; performance art; comedy; flash mob

From the Statue of Liberty to the Empire State Building, from Times Square to Central Park, New York City has no shortage of iconic landmarks. But if you're visiting the Big Apple and looking for a dose of that trademark New York hustle and bustle, you're not going to find a busier tourist attraction than Grand Central Terminal (popularly referred to as Grand Central Station). On any given day, more than 700,000 people visit or travel through Grand Central. Tourists flock to see the famous four-sided clock atop the main information booth (which is valued at $10 to $20 million), the vast mural of the constellations on the ceiling, or the forty-eight-foot-high sculpture of the Roman gods Minerva, Hermes, and Mercury gracing the building's façade. Even though the train station is chock full of famous sites to see, most tourists simply come to witness the mad dash of commuters scurrying through Grand Central like mice on a kitchen floor. More than 120,000 commuters dart across the main concourse every day, rushing to or from one of the station's forty-four train platforms (more platforms than any other train station in the world). Grand Central is so famous for the breakneck speed at which travelers hustle across its concourse that the words "Grand Central Station" are often used as a metaphor for anything that moves at a frenzied pace. This got me to thinking, *What would happen if Improv Everywhere visited the world's busiest train station, the building that is the heartbeat of New York City, and made it freeze in place?*

On a bitter cold Saturday afternoon, more than two hundred Improv Everywhere agents did just that—they made Grand Central come to a sudden and complete halt. By freezing in place at the exact same second for five minutes on the Main Concourse, our agents made everyone around them—commuters and tourists alike—stop in their tracks and observe the surreal sight of a train station frozen in time. Before most people could figure out why two hundred people were frozen in place, the agents unfroze and dispersed without acknowledging the fact they hadn't moved for five minutes.

When I posted the video of this mission online, Frozen Grand Central became an Internet sensation and a global phenomenon. Here's what inspired the Improv Everywhere freeze, a behind-the-scenes look at the infamous mission, and how the freeze craze spread like wildfire around the globe.

I. the plan

Most true Improv Everywhere fans know that Frozen Grand Central was not the first time I orchestrated a freeze; the original freeze took place during a mission called Slo-Mo Home Depot about one year prior to Frozen Grand Central. For Slo-Mo Home Depot, I planned to have a large group of agents shop in slow motion for five minutes in a Home Depot. I had wanted to try a mission that either slowed down or stopped time just because it seemed like an absurd thing to do. I picked Home Depot because they had just opened their first store in Manhattan, and I figured, *Why not have some fun in this ridiculously huge store on our tiny island?* Also, I just liked the way Slo-Mo Home Depot sounded.

I had a hunch that a big group of agents might turn up to do some slow-motion shopping, so I wanted to think of one more fun thing for the agents to do. The first thing that popped into my head was, *Why not have everybody just freeze in place for five minutes?* It seemed like a pretty simple idea, and it would be sure to get a reaction from Home Depot's employees and shoppers.

On the day of Slo-Mo Home Depot, 225 agents assembled outside the huge store in midtown Manhattan to help pull off the mission. Everyone synchronized his or her watch so they would know when exactly to start shopping in slow motion and when to begin freezing in place for five minutes. Our plan was to shop in slow motion for five minutes, then walk around at a normal pace for five minutes—tricking everyone into thinking that our little stunt was over—and then, bang!—we'd surprise them with the five-minute freeze.

We entered the home improvement superstore, and soon after, the agents began the slow-motion shopping segment of the mission. As I had hoped, it looked surreal to see our agents skulk around the store at a snail's pace. After five minutes of slo-mo shopping and five minutes of regular-speed browsing ended, everybody froze in place as planned. Shoppers laughed and gawked at the spectacle of a Home Depot populated with human statues. Shortly after the agents froze, by some freaky coincidence, Home Depot's sound system began playing the soft-rock song "Standing Still" by Jewel. Other than the Jewel song piping through the store's speakers, Home Depot became deathly quiet during the freeze. I never stopped to think that 225 people frozen in place are *a lot* quieter than 225 people moving around and talking. Seeing the mess of frozen agents was far more impressive than I anticipated.

After the mission ended, dozens of agents approached me and gushed about how much fun they had during the freeze and wanted to know if I had hacked into the store's sound system and played that Jewel song. I assured everyone that I had no part in playing "Standing Still" during the freeze—that was just serendipity—and that I also thought freezing in place was really fun—so much so that I wanted to do it again.

I scoured New York City looking for a location to do another freeze. Times Square seemed like it might work for a mass freeze—it is extremely recognizable and the hordes of tourists who hang out there would surely be startled by our stunt. Ultimately, I ruled it out because the taxi traffic that rips through Times Square would make the mission too hazardous. Then I thought about having our follow-up freeze at Rockefeller Center, but the plaza outside 30 Rock didn't seem big enough for what I wanted to pull off. The third location I considered was Grand Central Terminal. Envisioning two hundred or so frozen agents on the main concourse of the world's most famous train station seemed like it would be impressive enough to stop any tourist or commuter in their tracks.

One of the best parts of hosting a freeze mission is that it doesn't require any elaborate planning. Once our location was secure, I sent out an e-mail to all of my New York agents:

> Agents,
>
> Our next mission will take place this Saturday at 2 p.m. You must bring a watch with a second hand (or a digital watch that displays seconds). We are going to synchronize our watches for the mission, and it's important that we sync up to the exact second.
>
> Do not bring any type of camera. This mission, as all IE missions, should be participatory. We do not need any photographers, videographers, or members of the media. Only show up if you are ready to participate and have fun!
>
> This transmission is intended for IE Agents only. Feel free to bring friends. Please do not forward this message or blog about this event before it occurs. This should be tons of fun. Everything will be explained at Bryant Park, our meeting point.
>
> Thanks!
>
> Agent Todd

Bryant Park is located behind the Public Library on Forty-Second Street, just a couple blocks west from Grand Central. It was an extremely cold Saturday afternoon, but thankfully a little more than two hundred agents showed up to participate—about the same number as for Slo-Mo Home Depot. As soon as everyone had arrived, I hopped up on the edge of a fountain and addressed the crowd with a megaphone.

"All right, thanks for coming out, everybody," I said. "I'm really excited that you all are here because we're got a really cool mission to do today. We're going to be freezing in place for five minutes down the street at Grand Central. We need time to set up hidden cameras, so we're going to start the freeze at two thirty. At two thirty-five, I want everyone to unfreeze and move around for five minutes. Then at two forty, I want everyone to freeze again for another five minutes. After that, simply unfreeze and do not acknowledge other agents. If onlookers ask you what you were doing, just say, 'I don't know what you are talking about.' Then just leave the station."

I had all 207 agents synchronize their watches, and then they dispersed and left Bryant Park. I wouldn't see them again until the freeze was under way. After my briefing, I hurried over to Grand Central with my camera crew. By two P.M., all of the hidden cameras were in place—some of the photographers were stationed on the balcony and others would roam the concourse with hidden cameras peeking out of holes in rolling suit-cases. During the freeze, I wanted to walk around and solicit reactions from onlookers. About fifteen minutes before the freeze was scheduled to begin, I noticed agents trickling into the station. A mass of familiar Improv Everywhere faces were milling around the main concourse, but none of them were acknowledging each other. Some agents were looking at a newspaper, others were asking for directions to a particular track, a few were strolling around the station with their significant other, and some were in the middle of eating a snack. The throng of commuters was moving at its usual lightning-quick pace across the concourse. I kept my eye on the great gold clock in the middle of the concourse, and when the minute hand struck two-thirty, the blur of people whizzing through the station came to a sudden stop.

II. the mission

Even after all of the planning that went into the Grand Central freeze, seeing it actually happen was remarkable. It must have been shocking for tourists and commuters to see hundreds of people hustling across the concourse one second and then, in a flash, see time stop for more than two hundred of them. When I saw the freeze happen, it looked like somebody hit the pause button on a DVD player. Not only did our agents completely freeze, but everyone else around them stopped and tried to figure out what was going on. The eeriness of the situation was magnified by the dramatic silence that fell over the train station. It was amazing to see the massive, noisy main concourse enveloped by absolute quiet.

Much of the humor in Frozen Grand Central came from what the agents chose to do as they froze. One agent dropped a stack of papers and bent over to pick them up as he froze. Two agents froze during a kiss for the entire five minutes. Many agents were checking train schedules. Others were looking at their cell phones. Eating was probably the most popular activity to do while freezing; one agent froze while munching on a hot dog, another while eating a cookie, and another while eating yogurt. After the mission, Agent Jesse Good regretted his decision to freeze midbite while eating an apple. "I thought it would look funny, which it did," he said, "but I didn't anticipate the juice from the apple running down my chin and my arm for five minutes. I even noticed that my apple starting browning by the end of the freeze. It was pretty gross."

As I walked around poking and prodding at frozen agents, the reactions I solicited from random passersby ranged from amusement to shock at the still-life scene they were witnessing. "The onlookers in Frozen Grand Central were fairly similar to spectators in other Improv Everywhere missions," Agent Todd Simmons observed. "They couldn't decide whether we were crazy or if they had gone crazy."

Agent Simmons helped cause one of the most chaotic moments in the freeze by coming to a halt directly in the path of a motorized maintenance cart that was trying to cross the concourse. "I had a train schedule in my hands and I was frozen while staring at it," Agent Simmons remembered. "I didn't mean to do it, but I froze in the path of that maintenance cart. The guy driving the cart kept beeping his horn at me, trying to get me to move, but I wasn't budging. He must have thought I was the most self-absorbed commuter in the world. That cart driver was clearly exasperated with me just standing there in front of him." Fortunately, the cart driver was stopped by Agent Simmons and other agents with only about half a minute left to go in the mission, so we unfroze and were out of his way before he got too frustrated.

As the freeze kept going and going, visitors to Grand Central were clearly having just as much fun with the prank as we were. Total strangers started talking to each other, trying to figure out what was going on. Some hypothesized that we were a drama class; others thought it was a protest. Several tourists took out cameras and snapped photographs of the frozen agents. These onlookers didn't seem to realize that when you take a picture of a frozen person, nothing will seem out of the ordinary in the picture. With hidden microphones tucked into our shirts, several agents joined me as we walked around and struck up conversations with witnesses to our stunt. I spotted one man staring at an agent who was frozen while checking a text message on her cell phone.

"This is crazy, isn't it?" I said.

"You're tellin' me! I've never seen anything like this. They're just frozen!" he said.

"Look at that lady with her cell phone. I bet you could just walk up and take it out of her hand," I said.

"You know, I bet I could," the man said and laughed.

"Go for it," I said. "She's not moving. Just see if you can pick it up and put it back in her hand. I'll bet you she won't move."

The man tiptoed over to the agent and slowly took the cell phone out of her hand and then put it back. The agent never batted an eyelash. The man walked back over to me and started laughing uncontrollably.

"That was insane!" he said. "I can't believe she didn't move!"

As the freeze was nearing its conclusion, I noticed a few police officers stationed at an NYPD recruitment booth harassing Agent Good (who still had that half-eaten apple in his hand). They were shouting at him and waving their hands in his face, trying to get him to move.

"I'm gonna crack apple guy! He's gonna break!" one of the cops shouted.

Then, without notice, the freeze ended and Agent Good abruptly walked away. This startled the cops.

"Whoa!" the cop shouted. "Oh my God, he's moving!"

I approached these police officers at the recruitment booth to get their reaction.

"Do you know what that just was?" I asked.

"I have no idea! That is the craziest shit I have ever seen ... *and I'm a cop!*"

Our video of Frozen Grand Central has been viewed on the Internet by millions of people around the world, but one part of the mission isn't included in the video. As I mentioned earlier, I wanted to do two freezes back-to-back at Grand Central. In the Internet video, you only see the first freeze. When the first freeze ended, all of the onlookers erupted with thunderous applause and cheers. Many of them accosted our agents, asking, "Why were you frozen? Tell us!" The agents never broke character and simply responded by saying, "I have no idea what you are talking about." After five minutes of this chaos and confusion on the concourse, without notice, the agents froze again. The spectators on the concourse let out a collective groan; before they could figure out what was going on it had happened again. After another frozen five minutes, the 207 agents unfroze and received an even louder ovation from the hundreds of spectators. As the applause died down, the agents walked out of Grand Central Station without acknowledging each other or anyone else.

III. the aftermath

Frozen Grand Central was an exhilarating mission, but I definitely wasn't prepared for the overwhelmingly positive reaction the prank received when I posted the video online in

January of 2008. Within days of putting the video on YouTube, I was inundated with requests to re-create Frozen Grand Central around the world. Many people who watched the video thought our mission was some sort of political commentary or a statement on the human condition (it's not—it's just a scene of chaos and joy like all of our other missions). The number of views the video received online rocketed far past all of our other missions. Only two weeks after I posted the video, a thousand Londoners gathered in Trafalgar Square to re-create the freeze (without our help). It was flattering to receive so much attention for what I consider to be our simplest mission.

Soon after the Frozen Grand Central video started getting millions of hits on the Internet, the producers of the *Today* show on NBC contacted me. They wanted Improv Everywhere to conduct another freeze on air outside their studio, in the plaza of Rockefeller Center (one of the sites where I originally wanted to do the freeze). I hemmed and hawed over whether to accept their offer; I almost always turn down media requests for Improv Everywhere to re-create missions (usually it's because some reporter will want to interview me about our No Pants! Subway Ride while I'm in my boxers). I was about to say no, but then I thought, *What if we pulled a prank while we were on the* Today *show?*

On YouTube, dozens of people noted in the comments section of the Frozen Grand Central video that if they were present during the mission, they would have robbed one of our agents. It was funny to see how many people had that reaction after watching the video, though I doubt any anonymous commenter would actually have the guts to commit robbery. It also seemed like something I could incorporate into the *Today* show freeze to turn the tables and prank the popular morning show. After coming up with a plan for an auxiliary prank involving a heist, I called the *Today* show producers and said that Improv Everywhere would be delighted to do a freeze on the air.

On the morning of our *Today* show appearance, the producers told me that I was going to be interviewed inside the studio while our twenty-five agents froze outside on the plaza. Without telling anyone who worked at the *Today* show, I instructed Agent Jamey Shafer to stand outside and pretend to be a spectator watching the frozen agents. During the freeze, while cameras would be rolling live on national television, Agent Shafer was going to run up to a frozen Agent Ken Keech, rifle through his pockets, and run off with his wallet. Who knew what would happen next? Maybe NBC's security guards would chase Agent Shafer around the plaza? Maybe seeing a crime committed on live television would stir up a ruckus in the studio? It seemed like the perfect plan to cause a scene of chaos.

With twenty-five agents frozen in place outside the studio, my interview on the *Today* show began. The interview was going swimmingly, but I was waiting on pins and needles to see if my segment would be interrupted because one of our agents was robbed while frozen. The interview flew by quickly, and soon enough I was being thanked for coming on and then ushered out of the studio. As I stood in the *Today* show's greenroom post-interview, I was left to wonder, *Did Shafer and Keech not pull off the prank?*

It turned out that Agents Shafer and Keech executed the prank perfectly. Agent Shafer crept up behind Agent Keech, snatched his wallet, held it up for all to see, and bolted off the plaza in plain view of NBC security, the producers, and the cameramen. Unfortunately, the prank was not captured on camera, and the security guards and other NBC staff didn't seem to mind that one of our agents had just been pickpocketed. Even though Agent Shafer's robbery wasn't broadcast from coast to coast, having a group of agents appear on the *Today* show was fun, and we still got a pretty good laugh out of our pickpocket prank.

A few months after Frozen Grand Central exploded on the Web, I was invited to host a freeze at the Futuresonic Festival in Manchester, England. I was concerned that I might start getting known as "the freeze guy," but so long as the freeze guy gets to travel to cool places around the world to organize freezes, I'll always be happy to make the trip. One night while I was in Manchester, I started getting flooded with e-mails and text messages. Most of them said something to the effect of *You're on Law & Order!!!* These messages struck me as strange, because I didn't recall ever appearing on an episode of *Law & Order,* which is something that I'd probably be able to recall.

As it turned out, I wasn't actually on the long-running crime drama, but that week's episode of *Law & Order: Special Victims Unit* featured a fictional group of New Yorkers that staged massive public events very similar to the ones staged by Improv Everywhere. The leader of the group, played by Robin Williams (*the* Robin Williams, of *Dead Poets Society* and *Good Will Hunting* fame), committed a murder and was loosely based on me (except for the murder part). In the climactic scene of the episode, Robin Williams is arrested in the middle of a freeze at Grand Central. *Law & Order* re-created several shots from our video: they depicted a frozen woman eating a cup of yogurt and a frozen man bending over to tie his shoe. The one difference between their Frozen Grand Central and ours is that they had Mo Rocca (formerly of *The Daily Show*) standing on a stepladder and shouting "No sheep!" at everyone on the concourse; I can personally guarantee that we will never have anyone yelling "No sheep!" at our agents during a mission. The producers of *Law & Order* never contacted us before or after this episode aired, but it was flattering that they used one of our missions in a plotline, even if the leader of the prank group was a killer. When the Emmy committee nominated Robin Williams for his performance as the deranged leader of the prank group, I was rooting for him to win, but I was also kind of relieved when he lost. The last thing I want Improv Everywhere to be associated with is homicide.

The response to Frozen Grand Central has been truly unbelievable. The video has been viewed more than sixteen million times on YouTube, and in addition to the *Today* show, the prank has also been covered on *Good Morning America* and numerous news outlets around the world. But the most remarkable impact of Frozen Grand Central is that it has inspired people in nearly 200 other cities in dozens of countries to stage their own freeze missions. Thousands of global agents worldwide in places like Romania, Poland, Italy, China, Sweden, South Africa, and New Zealand have come together to make time stop for five short minutes. Here is a list of every city where a Frozen Grand Central-style freeze was re-created in the first six months after I posted our video on the Internet:

Afton, Wyoming
Arcadia, California
Arhus, Denmark
Atlanta, Georgia
Barcelona, Spain
Beijing, China
Beirut, Lebanon
Berlin, Germany
Berne, Switzerland
Bielefeld, Germany
Blacksburg, Virginia
Bloomington, Minnesota
Bogotá, Colombia
Boston, Massachusetts

Bratislava, Slovakia
Brisbane, Australia
Brno, Czech Republic
Brussels, Belgium
Calgary, Canada
Chicago, Illinois
Coimbra, Portugal
Constanta, Romania
Copenhagen, Denmark
Dublin, Ireland
Durham City, UK
Edina, Minnesota
Edinburgh, UK
Erlangen, Germany

Florence, Italy
Helsinki, Finland
Hong Kong, China
Kuala Lumpur, Malaysia
Lausanne, Switzerland
Leszczynski, Poland
London, UK
Los Angeles, California
Luxembourg, Luxembourg
Madrid, Spain
Malmö, Sweden
Manchester, UK
Manila, Philippines
Mexico City, Mexico
Minneapolis, Minnesota
Montreal, Canada
Newcastle-upon-Tyne, UK
Nuremburg, Germany
Orlando, Florida
Oxford, Ohio
Paris, France
Petrozavodsk, Russia
Portland, Oregon
Prague, Czech Republic
Pretoria, South Africa
Quebec City, Canada
Raleigh, North Carolina
Riga, Latvia
Rome, Italy
San Diego, California
San Francisco, California
Santa Barbara, California
Seattle, Washington
Shanghai, China
Shreveport, Louisiana
St. Andrews, Scotland
Stockholm, Sweden
Sydney, Australia
Tel Aviv, Israel
Tokyo, Japan
Toronto, Canada
Utrecht, Netherlands
Vancouver, Canada
Vienna, Austria
Wellington, New Zealand
Zurich, Switzerland

Part of the global success of this mission is due to the lack of language involved—freezing in place in public is funny no matter what your native tongue happens to be. It's remarkable that freezes have taken place in both Tel Aviv, Israel, and Beirut, Lebanon—two regions that have been warring for decades. And if you take a close look at that list of cities, you'll note that freezes have taken place in North America, South America, Asia, Europe, Africa, and Australia. Only Antarctica, the *frozen continent,* has yet to host a freeze. Get to it, arctic explorers!

It's crazy to think that a harmless mission in a Home Depot has grown into a worldwide prank with thousands of people of all ages and races, from Beijing to Bogotá, participating in the fun.

Part 5

Responsibility

36 Improvised Responsibility: Opening Statements

(Call and) Responsibility: Improvisation, Ethics, Co-creation

Daniel Fischlin

In improvisation, Daniel Fischlin believes, one encounters the other, and has a responsibility to this encounter. His essay reframes what is known as "jazz" as "an embodiment of hope— … a musical and social practice of hope and responsibility that has profoundly changed the world." Dr Fischlin is a composer and instrumentalist (guitar, lute) and a scholar specialising in early music, improvisational studies, human rights, and Shakespeare. In the latter field alone he has produced the book *Adaptations of Shakespeare* (2000), co-edited with Mark Fortier, and launched, at the University of Guelph, the SSHRC-funded Canadian Adaptations of Shakespeare Project (CASP), the Shakespeare Learning Commons, *'Speare* (an online 3D video game) and The Romeo and Juliet iPhone/iPad/iPod App. With Ajay Heble, Dr Fischlin has edited two books on the socio-political implications of improvised creative musics: *The Other Side of Nowhere* (2004) and *Rebel Musics* (2003). Dr Fischlin has a BFA in Music Performance and an MA in Interdisciplinary Studies from Concordia University, and a PhD in English literature from York University. His most recent books are *The Fierce Urgency of Now: Improvisation, Rights, and the Ethics of Cocreation*, co-authored with Ajay Heble and George Lipsitz (2013), and *Community of Rights – Rights of Community*, co-authored with Martha Nandorfy (2011).

Key words: human rights; interdisciplinary studies; Canada

I

Improvisation does not occur in a sonic, or for that matter, social vacuum. Its cries and calls, hoots and hollers, invocations and incantations address fellow musicians, audience members, and the protean self of the person making the sound. But improvisation also includes among its addressees, histories, memories, feelings, unspoken and unthought imaginaries barely hinted at, spectral – or that see the light of day only because a *particular* improvisation made it so, made it thinkable, feel-able, articulable as the sound of that precise moment of address.

Every scene of improvisation is haunted by these multiple addressees – is *composed* of these hauntings.

Speaking or sounding in an improvisation carries with it the responsibility of these multiple, synchronic, and diachronic audiences. How to address these audiences in good faith? How to reflect in the aesthetics of the improvisation the wider social contexts out of which any given improvisation arises? How to be beautiful, dissonant, unpredictable, emancipatory, and playful out of respect for what it means to be fully human, fully expressive of creation as a necessary response to being?

Improvisation is *apostrophe* in the old rhetorical sense of an address to an absence, a personification of something that is called into being by *apostrophe*. It is expressive of a co-dependent relation between creative iteration (call) and the response of others to that invitation to speak and sound together.

Co-dependent relations entail responsibilities: the need to consider what the other has to say; to respond constructively; to disagree; to remain silent *until* one has something to say; to add consonance or dissonance; to change the topic of conversation; even to critique ossified notions of what being responsible might mean in order to provide means of achieving new creative outcomes (think bebop in relation to big-band swing; or free playing in response to bebop). Moreover, improvisation entails vulnerability – a responsibility to the self and other, their interdependent relations, and their commitment to engage in co-creative acts of listening and sounding as a function of what it means to make oneself vulnerable to the other, to address the vulnerability of the self.

Improvisation is simultaneously autonomous in the moment of its creation (anything can potentially happen) and dependent in that same moment on all the contingencies that have produced that moment. Improvisation can:

> emphasize the responsibility of the improviser for every aspect of the work, not just the moment of performance but also the tradition of which it is a part and the originary mimetic impulse that this tradition struggles to preserve. What this entails is a responsibility for the alterity that interrupts the familiar situation … such that the distance between improviser and improvisation is not mystified but recognized for what it is as an integral part of the continuation of the work beyond the instant of its beginning.
>
> (Peters 108)

Improvisation embodies alterity and the conditions that not only produce alterity but that allow us to encounter it creatively, ethically. The other is always a token of co-dependency, co-creation. Being in creative, sustainable relation to one's own contingency requires responsibility to the other. Improvisation is the practice of that relation: a living embodiment of multiple ways of addressing the ethical relation to alterity.

Improvisation is also an invocation of the event horizon of what is thinkable, doable in the moment in which it occurs. It embodies both the finality of the moment and what occurs in that moment and the ineluctable potential that any moment releases as a veering toward that event horizon of possibility. Its quandary is that it embodies both presence and absence. Both the moment itself as it is created and the "what-could-have-been" buried in every moment, the alternative potential that improvisation artfully explores.

Being "in time" necessitates a response to time, expresses a relationship to time that is at once intensely ludic in the moment but also a memorialisation of all past times, and a salute to times that could be. Histories flow from these improvisatory acts in time. Improvisation responds to time, is responsible to the potential always found in time.

Improvisation, then, is *always already* a response to something.

That something is the call, the invocation to speak in sound.

From the call – from all precedent calls, all antecedents to the possibility of the call – comes the moment in the now in which improvisatory iteration occurs.

That moment is the response, but also the responsibility to speak – to enter into the warp and weft of past iterations, past addressees, past improvisatory articulations that respond to the call, that enter into dialogue with the history of the call, that share the responsibility of responding to the call, that make sound the response to an ethical interrelation provoked by dialogue, community, dissonance, consonance and the striving to communicate.

II

There is no improvisation without a response that is also a responsibility to the underlying questions that ground all improvisation: What do *you* have to say? Here and now? Whom will you address? What will you add to the ineluctable, unavoidable dialogue that improvisatory music emblematises?

Though every improvisatory call-out may not have an adequate response, if a response is even necessary, nonetheless the call-out bears with it a responsibility to ask the right question, to give a timely response, to engage in the potential for dialogue that improvisation makes possible.

Evan Parker, in a 2006 talk on Coltrane, tells the following story:

> I found out also that when [Frank] Kofsky was a student at Berkeley University, he asked Coltrane to play a concert to raise money for an organization for improving the situation for Black students in the University system there. Coltrane was agreeable to that idea but the University then forbade the organization to exist. This is as recently as 1961, so it's important to remember and to keep our eye on what people are telling us we can't have today. Two million people on the streets of London saying they didn't want a war, but one man [Tony Blair] and his friend in America [George W. Bush] decided it was a good idea, and now we have to live with the consequences of that for the rest of our lives. Coltrane spoke to the Vietnam War in the same interview [with Frank Kofsky]: "This music is an expression of higher ideals to me, so therefore, brotherhood is there. I believe with brotherhood there would be no poverty, and with brotherhood there would be no war." So Coltrane is no longer a jobbing musician at this point, he's feeling the weight of responsibility that comes with his position, his new position as being considered one of the leading voices in the music and he's using that situation to speak up.
>
> The weight of responsibility Coltrane felt in large part stemmed from his spirituality, which was awakened after Miles Davis sacked him because he was drunk and drug addicted and unreliable. For Coltrane, being fired by Davis must have come as a very profound shock, as well as he was playing, because he always played very well. But clearly he felt something had to be done about this and so the famous story of him going to a room in his auntie's house and shutting the door and staying there until he had broken his addiction to heroin. I suppose that's what he's referring to when he said: "During the year 1957, I experienced, by the grace of God, a spiritual awakening which was to lead me to a richer, fuller, more productive life." At this point Coltrane was clearly moving towards a sense of his own destiny and perhaps even a sub-conscious intimation that his life would not be a long one. An urgent sense of purpose begins to motivate all of his playing. And I think at this point we also hear that he's moving away from the conventions of the day.

The responsibility to exercise one's freedom of speech, to one's own sense of purpose, to testing and overturning conventions, to non-violence, to brotherhood and sisterhood – all are explicit in Parker's anecdote about Coltrane struggling into his own improvisatory voice, a sense of the responsibility that voice carried with it, both politically and aesthetically.

Coltrane's epiphany, as Parker puts it, echoes one of the key tenets of Sufi master and Northern Indian classical musician Hazrat Inayat Khan, who states, "The value of man [sic] is as great as his responsibility, for what mountains cannot bear mankind has carried through life; and that is why a responsible man [sic] naturally shows a spiritual quality in all connections, in all relationships."

Improvisation is the embodiment of this spiritual quality that makes connections and relationships worthy of being called such. Connections require links forged out of dialogue, listening, responding – being responsible to what makes it possible to be together with others.

In *The Mysticism of Music, Sound and Word*, Khan took pains to explain that "Music loses its freedom by being subject to the laws of technique, but mystics in their sacred music … free both their composition and improvisations from the limitations of technicality." Coltrane's struggles with addiction coincide with his struggle to free himself from the technical considerations of the tenor saxophone. He took on the responsibility of addressing what it might mean to free himself from both in order to achieve purpose in his life via aesthetic freedom of speech.

Improvisation embodies the spirit of this self-transformation that arises from a response to conditions that limit freedom.

American jazz guitarist Sonny Sharrock, renowned for his forays into free jazz in the 60s, had this to say about free improvisation:

> Finally, there is freedom – the most misunderstood and the most misused of all these elements [of improvisation]. Freedom grows out of improvisation. It is both your emotional peak and your deeper self. It is the cry of jazz. The one rule for playing free is that you can play anything you want. A critic once remarked to me that it takes a great amount of taste to play free. He was wrong. Artists cannot be hampered by the restriction of taste. What playing free does take is imagination and confidence. In free playing, there is nothing else to stand on; it's like walking in space. If you're confident, you will not fall. The road forms beneath your feet as your imagination takes you places arrived at by no other means. My confidence in the beauty of the music carries me through. Coltrane's *Ascension* [MCA, 29020] is the best example of freedom. Jugglers, tinkers, and fools try to play free; however, they will never succeed. It is reserved only for the masters.
>
> (Sharrock, 2002)

The key line in Sharrock's comments is that "Freedom grows out of improvisation." Freedom, as an event horizon of the possible, is what improvisation as a musical and social practice invokes, leads toward, produces as a potential outcome. In all improvisation there is a fundamental responsibility to making manifest this key principle, however difficult it is to attain. It is the responsibility of the improviser to strive toward freedom of the imagination, of expression, of iteration, of technique in ways that expand what it means to be human in unexpected form.

If music is "entangled in a prison of expectations,"[1] improvisation provides a potential antidote to the prison-house of expectation. Freedom in improvisation comes with the responsibility to break with expectation – to find new meaning outside of imposed conventions; new tools for saying things differently, apart, outside of orthodoxies that are creative constraints.

III

In the 1590s, in its earliest English uses, the word "responsible" was used to mean "answerable (to another, for something)," from the Latin word *respondere*, "to respond" or to "offer something in return." By the nineteenth century the meaning had shifted to include the sense of being "morally accountable for one's actions," while retaining the sense of "obligation" in the Latin root.

The etymology of the word sets forth an array of principles that describe dialogue, interchange, listening, being answerable to someone for something, being ethically obligated. These meanings are at work in any improvisation where similar ethical frames are evident. In listening one prepares to answer. In playing one calls out for an answer. There is an ethical charge to these basic structures of improvisation that carries over into the social practice of responsibility, the social practice of improvisation. Observing these principles allows for right, mindful action to occur.

And, in some cases, the responsible thing to do in an improvisation is to test what it means to be irresponsible. Improvisation always allows for contention, for being with dissonance and tension, for outbreaks that test the limits of a collective sounding even when obligation is present.

Sometimes disavowal of an imposed obligation is the only way forward, as was the case with the oppressive conditions defining slavery. Being non-compliant, in the etymological sense of "irresponsible," in this situation led to resistant forms of musical expression, led to the civil rights movement, led to redefining exploitative relations and systemic racism. This example teaches us that one group in oppressive relations of power to another cannot arbitrarily define responsibility. Responsibility is co-created out of group dynamics and consensus, where tension and dissonance are key factors in establishing a mutually acceptable, dynamic, processual form of being in community. Improvisation acts out this form of social practice in musical terms.

Creative spontaneity, spontaneous acts of creativity enact hope. They beckon toward what might come of the moment – a hope for what creative interaction brings. Hope is an avatar of freedom – it is the imagination of freedom, the imagination of what the world might be like. Improvisation is a form of responsible hope.

Hope is also intimate liberation. It lives on under oppression in ways that ally it with intimate, sometimes unknowable acts of the imagination, flourishing even as it is constrained or deprived of enactment. It cannot be dissociated from spirit, conscience, creative being.

Frederick Douglass, speaking against slavery, said "The first work of slavery is to mar and deface those characteristics of its victims which distinguish *men* from *things*, and *persons* from *property*. Its first aim is to destroy all sense of high moral and religious responsibility" (167). Spirit entails responsibility, conscience – the recognition, in this case, that people are not property.

The oppression located firmly in the African diaspora and enslavement that produced the conditions for one of the greatest improvising musical traditions ever also gave rise to the spirit of the civil rights movement. The latter is the expression of ethical commitment to a deep underlying spiritual recognition of the underlying integrity and equality of all humans. The *telos* of slavery may have been to destroy the responsibility of ethical conduct. Instead it produced a musical and social practice of hope and responsibility that has profoundly changed the world. Hope will not be denied. Improvisation is a constant reminder that it is possible to hope – and to do so in response to conditions that seek to limit human potential and creativity. Again, hope as intimate liberation.

And improvisation as an embodiment of hope – a social practice, practising hope through creation. But also a musical practice with wider applications to other social forms in which hope and responsibility are ineluctably linked.

These aspects of what it means to hope imply corresponding responsibilities. What to do with that freedom? How to map the imaginary onto the real in ways that enhance the quality of life, the right to create, the need for community, the mindful adaptation to the environment that makes life possible.

Improvisation is creative activity oriented toward hope: both a response and a responsibility to the question of what to make of freedom in a contingent world. Like one of the underlying principles associated with civil rights – the need to begin all encounter out of a fundamental respect for difference and the need to encounter difference creatively, non-violently, with integrity – improvisation embodies in practice a similar principle.

Improvisation is, in its most achieved forms of expression, fundamentally opposed to univocal discourse and drawn to pluralist practices. With the hope for creative means of expressing freedom, encountering difference, and exploring pluralist, contingent relations to the world, improvisation takes on the responsibility of performing that hope publicly, enacting it in ways that demonstrate the principle in practice:

> Successful improvisations ... are those which build tensions through a process of inventive performance strategies and soundings offered up by individual performers in order that these contributions might be considered and contested by others in the group. The group has the responsibility of listening, and the freedom to reinterpret individual offerings, so that they might creatively resolve the "problem situation" in such a way that, ideally, a rich, coherent musical experience issues forth ...
>
> (Nicholls 98)

Embedded in that hope, in that call toward hope, is also a response. The response that is a responsibility to take on hope, make it real in the moment, seize hold of what is *there* in *that* moment and transmute it into something new, compelling, transformative, active.

Engaging in spontaneous acts of creation embodies the hope that these acts will produce something meaningful. In that meaning that is created, whether as a sign of community, as a marker of what I have called earlier the event horizon of the possible, or as a critical intervention, there is a responsibility in the making of spontaneity towards the meaning generated out of it.

This is so because the so-called freedom implicit in spontaneous acts of creation is heavily mediated by histories, disciplines, affective memories, technical and environ-mental contingencies, economics, power, identity, and so forth. The moment may be free or an expression of the search for a tangible freedom but it carries forward with it the contexts that make any given moment possible. These contexts are a form of call. The specific histories of diasporic Africans responding to slavery and oppression are one such call. So, too, is the network of community affiliations, dissonances, and creative outputs that precede any response. There is a responsibility to those contexts in every improvised act, if only to provide an adequate response to these calls that precede the moment of making.

Improvisation requires deep listening. It requires the intimacy that comes of listening to the other soundings calling out for response. Listening in that creative register is an ethical act – an act that embodies responsibility, an expression of contingent encounter, a co-dependent and co-creative ethical relation. It arises from self as a function of otherness.

What might it mean to take the musical practice of improvisation – its rich models of call and responsibility – into the embodied social practice of being in community, being in biotic relation to the earth, being an ethical expression of the idea, "you are therefore I am"?

In the improvised, potential answers to that question is the beginning of what it might mean to be response-ible.

Notes

1 I'm indebted to my fifteen-year old daughter Esmé Nandorfy-Fischlin for this phrase from a very frank poem she wrote ("A Silent Tune") about her complicated relationship to the piano and to music in general.

Works Cited

Douglass, F. 1999. Lecture on Slavery, No. 1, delivered in Corinthian Hall, Rochester, New York, December 1, 1850. In: P. S. Foner, ed. 1999. Abridged and adapted by Y. Taylor. *Frederick Douglass: Selected Speeches and Writings*. The Library of Black America. Chicago: Lawrence Hill Books. pp. 163–69.

Khan, H. I., n.d. *"Music."* In *Volume II – The Mysticism of Music, Sound and Word*. [online] Available at: http://wahiduddin.net/mv2/II/II_7.htm. Accessed 2 January 2014.

——., n.d. *"Responsibility.* In *Volume VI, The Alchemy of Happiness*. [online] Available at: http://wah"iduddin.net/mv2/VI/VI_39.htm. Accessed 2 January 2014.

Nicholls, T., 2012. *An Ethics of Improvisation: Aesthetic Possibilities for a Political Future*. Plymouth, U.K.: Lexington Books.

Parker, E., 2006. Coltrane: A Talk by Evan Parker. *Jazz Em Agosto*. Lisbon, Portugal, 5 August 2006. Transcript available at: www.pointofdeparture.org/PoD9/PoD9EvanParker.html. Accessed 21 May 2012.

Peters, G., 2009. *The Philosophy of Improvisation*. Chicago: University of Chicago Press.

Sharrock, Sonny, 2002. Sonny Sharrock: On Improvisation. As told to Dannette Hill. [online] Available at: www.jazzguitar.com/features/sharrock.html. Accessed 20 May 2012.

37 Gittin' To Know Y'all

Improvised Music, Interculturalism, and the Racial Imagination

George E. Lewis

In the mid-1970s George Lewis, a young member of Chicago's Association for the Advancement of Creative Musicians, began garnering acclaim as a virtuoso trombonist who could negotiate equally well the horizons of free improvisation and the traditions of the jazz song form. But already suspicious of easy definitions, Lewis took the "great trombonist" moniker and rolled it, along with subsequent others, into an expansive and still-expanding body of interdisciplinary work. He designed the improvising software "Voyager," and began a career distinguished by collaborative encounters not only with artists in other media but also, according to mutual design, with the media themselves. In 2009 he won an American Book Award for *A Power Stronger Than Itself: The AACM and American Experimental Music*, and he is editor of the forthcoming *Oxford Handbook of Critical Improvisation Studies*. In "Gittin' to Know Y'all" (2002) one can read the fruits not only of Lewis' fastidious research into scholarly and critical documentation, but of his years of musical collaboration the world over, as he examines the political implications of European improvisers who declare themselves "emancipated" from American jazz influences, and the ongoing marginalisation of the AACM in the history of experimental music. Currently Lewis is Edwin H. Case Professor of American Music at Columbia University.

Key words: African American culture; European improvisation; new music; collaboration

Introduction

Turning the face of music historiography toward a relatively frank engagement with issues of race, ethnicity and class has rarely proceeded without discontents. While popular music studies, including jazz history and criticism, have addressed race matters for quite some time, studies that deal specifically with these issues in the self-described "experimental" musics, including improvised music, are rather few in number, evincing a rather stunted discourse. In the foreword to their book, *Music and the Racial Imagination,* editors Ronald Radano and Philip Bohlman use the term "silence" to describe the historical aporias that accompany this discursive lack (37).

Among the vanishingly small number of texts that explicitly address constructions of race in experimental music, those produced by improvisors stand out, including work by Malcolm Goldstein (1988) and Wadada Leo Smith (1973), and Anthony Braxton's massive three-volume *Tri-Axium Writings* (1985), an effort which, while in dialogue with such texts as LeRoi Jones' *Blues People* (1963), John Cage's *Silence* (1961) and Karlheinz Stockhausen's *Texte* (1971), extends considerably beyond these texts, both in length and in range of inquiry.

This general erasure of race seems at variance with experimental music's presumed openness, its emphasis upon resistance, and its excavations of subaltern and marginalized histories of sound. The primary direction of my analysis, then, concerns the ways in which not only music scholars, but also musicians themselves, have either confronted or avoided engagement with issues of race in experimental music. I seek to identify some uninterrogated tropes concerning process, history and methodology that, when brought to light, do seem to embody coded assumptions about race, ethnicity, class, and about the possibilities for artists to move across, transgress and possibly erase borders.

As critical tools in advancing my theorizing, I wish to return to the terms "Eurological" and "Afrological," which I used in a previous essay ("Improvised Music") to historicize the particularity of perspectives developed in culturally divergent environments. These terms refer metaphorically to musical belief systems and behavior that, in my view, exemplify particular kinds of musical "logic." The terms refer to social and cultural location, rather than phenotype (skin color); they are theorized here as historically emergent, and must not be used to essentialize musical direction in terms of ethnicity or race.

As I maintain in "Improvised Music after 1950: Afrological and Eurological Perspectives," these constructions make no attempt to delineate ethnicity or race, although they are designed to ensure that the reality of the ethnic or racial component of a historically emergent socio-musical group must be faced squarely and honestly. In fact, the term "race" here is viewed as a historical construct whose borders are consanguineous with those of class and place. The fluidity that marks this intersection produces complex, mobile identities that do not respect traditionally monolithic taxonomies that assume race as a necessary precondition of musical method, infrastructure and materials.

The Two Avant-gardes

As a prime site for this examination, I will consider aspects of the histories, musical directions, methodologies and historical reception of two experimental music communities which emerged at around the same moment in time: the European "free jazz" or "free improvisation" movement, an international development that spanned the continent, and the Association for the Advancement of Creative Musicians (AACM), which emerged from Chicago's racially segregated, all-black South Side. Both of these movements are framed in music histories as key representatives of a second generation of the "free jazz" movement spearheaded by Ornette Coleman, Albert Ayler, Cecil Taylor, and John Coltrane, among many others. At the same time, the goals, methods, materials, geographical base, historical outlook, cultural stances and critical reception of the two avant-gardes problematize simplistically linear generational readings of the sort too often advanced in jazz historiography.

By 1965, these two distinct musical avant-gardes, based on different continents and unaware of each other, yet sharing important characteristics, goals and acknowledged musical antecedents, were in the process of crystallization. It is good to remind younger people who are used to the idea of improvised music as a rather large international field that in 1965, these two vanguards were by some accounts extremely small. In a 1969 interview, Lester Bowie estimates Chicago AACM membership at about twenty-five

(Caux 19). Peter Brötzmann, when asked in 1968 about the size of the pool of European free jazz players with whom he could feel compatible, responded, perhaps only partially tongue-in-cheek, "I think I could get a good group going with 15 people" (Schmidt-Joos 129).[1]

Perhaps the first extensively documented musical collaboration between members of these two avant-gardes took place in December of 1969, at the "Free Jazz Treffen" in Baden-Baden, a small town nestled in the German Schwarzwald, known since Roman times for the curative powers of its *Bäder*. The "meeting" was supported by the state-owned Südwestfunk radio network, and organized by the important critic and radio producer, Joachim Ernst Berendt. A recording of several pieces that were created for the meeting survives; the recording was released in 1970 under the name of Lester Bowie, with a pointedly ironic title, *Gittin' to know y'all*.

Through the prism of this event, and using the recording of the Bowie work, I wish to highlight aspects of the histories and methodologies of these two socio-musical complexes. Along the way, I try to provide some answers to the question of why these two avant-gardes, despite their evident similarities, remain relatively distanced from each other in terms of certain kinds of collaborations.

The European Emancipation

There is a general agreement among scholars working on European improvised music that at the end of the 1950s, European jazz was in the throes of an identity crisis. Music historian Ekkehard Jost describes the European jazz of this era as "an exotic plant on barren soil ... that must have seemed as bizarre as British flamenco" (Jost, *Europas Jazz* 11).[2] In thrall to what Wolfram Knauer calls an "epigonal Americanism" (156), European jazz musicians were said to inhabit a landscape in which aesthetic, methodological and stylistic direction flowed for the overwhelming part from the metropole of America to the tributaries in their own lands. In a sense, the notion of "European jazz" itself was an expression of American cultural hegemony that conflated all of the combined histories, languages, and styles of the continent into a single monolith.

The situation would eventually lead to a kind of declaration of independence from that hegemony. Beginning roughly in the mid-1960s, this move toward aesthetic self-determination took musical form as musicians combined extensions, ironic revisions and outright rejections of American jazz styles with a self-conscious articulation of historical and cultural difference. The critically important first generation of musicians who confronted these issues of identity included Willem Breuker, Misha Mengelberg, and Han Bennink in the Netherlands; Fred van Hove in Belgium; Irene Schweizer and Pierre Favre in Switzerland; Albert Mangelsdorff, Manfred Schoof, Alexander von Schlippenbach, Peter Brötzmann, Karl Hans Berger and Gunter Hampel in Germany; and Maggie Nicols, John Stevens, Trevor Watts, Paul Rutherford, Derek Bailey, Tony Oxley, Barry Guy, Kenny Wheeler, and Evan Parker in England.

The work of these and many other musicians would soon result in the emergence of a panoply of approaches that, taken together, constitute one of the critically important developments within a composite notion of late twentieth-century musical experimentalism. Historical accounts represent this new breed of Europeans as having first promulgated a new, specifically European style of "free jazz" that built upon the innovations in form, sound, method, and expression advanced by Ornette Coleman, Albert Ayler, Cecil Taylor, John Coltrane, and other African-American musicians of the early 1960s. Later, the new European musicians were widely credited with the development of a more open conception of "free improvisation" that was generally acknowledged in Europe to have broken away from American stylistic directions and jazz signifiers.

Borrowing from a critically important event in nineteenth-century American history, the end of chattel slavery, Berendt, in a 1977 essay, called this declaration of difference and independence "The Emancipation" (Berendt, "Ein Fenster" 222), a term that has entered the general lexicon of German jazz historiography. There is little question that this term, with its explicit recall of the nineteenth-century freeing of American slaves, references notions of blackness. What is new here is the ironic use of the reference to simultaneously unify Europe under the banner of whiteness, and to portray as subaltern the culture that, until recently, had dominated the planet.

If "American models" of jazz were effectively African-American models, then in Berendt's re-presentation of the emancipation narrative, Europeans became Spivak's voiceless subalterns, with African-American musical culture cast as a symbolically putative slave-master. Indeed, as Berendt maintains, "the creative European musician has ceased to imitate American musicians. He has ceased to compete with him in areas – above all in swing and in the field of black traditions – in which he cannot catch him" (*Das Jazzbuch* 374).[3]

Knauer's account of the historical working-out of the Emancipation challenges the notion that the process happened in one short, sharp shock. Knauer identifies a phase of becoming and a phase of being, which allows him to examine the Emancipation as a gradual process. For Knauer, the trombonist Albert Mangelsdorff, one of the first German jazz musicians to become well known in the United States, is seen as representing a new consciousness in German jazz. Maintaining that art is an expression of its time and place, Mangelsdorff concluded in 1963 that "For that reason, a jazz musician in Europe should not demand of himself to play like a colored musician in New York or Chicago; he should not try it and one should not expect it of him, because his problems are different and his surroundings are subject to other circumstances" (qtd. in Knauer 147–48).[4]

There is little question, however, that the first generation of European free jazz improvisors were heavily influenced by now-canonical African-American figures from the jazz tradition. Confounding simplistically linear and rigid notions of "roots" and "influence," as well as bombastic accusations of appropriation and perhaps even "theft," it is clear that at this early stage in the development of European free improvisation, the musicians made no attempt to deny the Afrological influence upon their work. Indeed, both critics and musicians have generally overlooked the crucial, ongoing investment by the current field of European free improvisation as a whole in fundamental notions of sonic personality that are based primarily in Afrological models.

In the context of improvised musics that exhibit strong influences from Afrological ways of music-making, musical sound – or rather, "one's own sound" – becomes a carrier for history and cultural identity. "Sound" becomes identifiable, not with timbre alone, but with the expression of personality, the assertion of agency, the assumption of responsibility, and an encounter with history, memory and identity. Yusef Lateef maintains that "The sound of the improvisation seems to tell us what kind of person is improvising. We feel that we can hear character or personality in the way the musician improvises" (Lateef 44). Essentially the same notion was advanced in the 1940s by Charlie Parker, who declared that "Music is your own experience, your thoughts, your wisdom. If you don't live it, it won't come out of your horn" (qtd. in Levin and Wilson 24).

Therefore, what Knauer describes as a coming to a consciousness of difference, an acknowledgment of "European-ness," can arguably be viewed as a direct expression of the Afrological notion of improvisation as a process of finding one's own sound. On this point, Erroll Garner is at one with Albert Mangelsdorff. Garner counsels that "If you take up an instrument, I don't care how much you love somebody, how much you would like to pattern yourself after them, you should still give yourself a chance to find out what you've got and let that out" (Taylor 97). Similarly, exemplifying Knauer's notion of *Selbstbewußtwerdung,* or becoming-conscious-of-self, Mangelsdorff felt that even as one admires American musicians, "one should not forget, in the midst of all admiration, that first of all, one should express musically one's own personality, one's own conception of jazz" (qtd. in Knauer 150).[5]

Form, Sound and Difference

For Berendt, the trenchancy and vitality of the "New Thing," the innovations of Ayler, Coleman, Taylor, Coltrane, and others, was based upon an assertion of freedom from "the tyranny of regularly accented meter, functional harmony, symmetrical cycles and phrase endings."[6] Berendt asserted that these new developments were more exciting to European jazz musicians and their audiences than they were in the United States, not least because of the greater acceptance by European concert music audiences of "atonality" (Berendt, *Das Jazzbuch* 370).

Extending Berendt's analysis, I would place certain preconditions for the acceptance of European free improvisation somewhat earlier. By the early 1950s, bebop had already problematized, on an international basis, the high-art/low-art divide (Belgrad 182–83). Indeed, for some later historians, such as Daniel Belgrad, "bebop embodied a more radical cultural stance than European modernist music, because it provided for a more democratic and participatory form of musical expression" (Belgrad 185).

On both sides of the Atlantic, the grudging acceptance as high art of a music in which black perspectives and cultural markers dominated made the emergence of a European-based, post-Emancipation high art based on improvisation (as well as concomitant state support for such work) a thinkable proposition. Even more radical, as Jost saw it, was how the Emancipation operated as "a powerful psychomusical act of validation that not only placed the established rules of jazz improvisation on tenterhooks, but in the end, also placed the identity of jazz music itself in question" (*Europas Jazz* 12).[7] In other words, if jazz is American, then who are we as Europeans?

Knauer sees the late 1960s as the watershed year in which responses to this question would begin to take shape. With the 1966 declaration by Alexander von Schlippenbach that "We don't call it New Thing, but Own Thing" ("Own Thing" 69),[8] "European jazz" moves from *Selbstbewußtwerdung,* becoming self-aware, to *Selbstbewußtsein,* being self-conscious of its own power and possibility. By 1967, the earliest recordings of Peter Brötzmann, Gunter Hampel, Peter Kowald, Irene Schweizer, John Stevens, Manfred Schoof, Willem Breuker, Misha Mengelberg, Han Bennink, Fred van Hove, Wolfgang Dauner, and the Globe Unity Orchestra had been released, and European "free jazz" was receiving substantial notoriety, albeit mainly in Europe itself.

According to Knauer, this initial period of *Selbstbewußtsein* also included extensive engagement by some of these musicians, such as Schlippenbach, with European contemporary music (151). Commentators such as Berendt and Bert Noglik have observed that European improvisors were much closer than Americans to the geographical and cultural roots of the postwar European musical modernism of Stockhausen, Boulez, and others. Berendt asserted that the European improvisor "knows his Stockhausen and his Ligeti more closely that any of his American colleagues."[9] Moreover, a link would soon be forged in Europe between the composition-centered and improvisation-based avant-gardes, involving such composers as Vinko Globokar, Hans Werner Henze, and Alexander von Schlippenbach's composition teacher, Bernd Alois Zimmermann.

The long history of engagement with European musical modernism by African-American modernists such as Charlie Parker and Duke Ellington doubtlessly provided strong precedent for even more extensive involvement by later generations, including formal academic study, as with AACM composers such as Roscoe Mitchell, Joseph Jarman, and Anthony Braxton. For Noglik, however, even in the absence of overt influence from Euromodernist methods, a kind of unconscious engagement – perhaps a metaphor for genetic/cultural memory – is available to European improvisors in a way that Americans could never experience: "In terms of inclination, for example, by way of comparison, the encounter (consciously or instinctively) with advanced composed music – as regards a certain breadth and differentiation of aspiration – affected the creative work of European improvising musicians" (Noglik 214).[10]

For Berendt, the end of functional harmony in both jazz and contemporary Western music also heralded the recrudescence of collective improvisation, which the critic saw as a hallmark of the new European jazz. It is certain that the need for a collective orientation was deeply felt among the new musicians. For instance, Manfred Schoof, in a 1965 interview, critiques an Albert Ayler recording on the grounds that "you feel no 'with each other' and no 'for each other.' There are three individual actions that don't lead to a real collective" ("Hie Logan" 174).[11] Writing in 1973, Berendt maintained that "European jazz is – also in its emphasis – a collective jazz, in which the individual proceeds from the ensemble."[12] Berendt points to the example of the Globe Unity Orchestra, in which Alexander von Schlippenbach's hybrid mediation between improvisative and compositional methods emerges "from a particular relationship to collectivity and to the European tradition" (*Das Jazzbuch* 371).[13]

By 1968, as Europe was in turmoil and the cozy, American-dominated postwar political arrangements were under wide-ranging attack from a new generation of young Europeans, this notion of collectivity would provide an important symbol for the eventual political and economic unification of Germany (and Europe) as well. At this time, cross-border collaborations between Europeans from different states were complicated not only by formidable borders in Western Europe, but by the intractability of the East-West divide, symbolized most potently by the division of Germany. With the Cold War still producing a divided Germany and a Balkanized Europe, as well as the first effects of the postcolonial condition, the new European free music could be read as asserting the desirability of a borderless Europe – if not the decline of the notion of the unitary European nation-state itself.

Following Knauer, the first fruits of *Selbstbewußtsein* manifested themselves as a kind of "rebellion" (152) in which the younger generation of European musicians sought to discover a new, even revolutionary freedom. In 1966, Peter Brötzmann, among the most radical of the younger generation of musicians, located his own construction of personal narrative, not in the Afrological notion of sound as personality, but in pure personal expression as taught in the wake of Abstract Expressionism: "From painting I learned to utilize the freedom of personal expression. One should not recognize any restraint in simply knocking over the traditional" (qtd. in Knauer 152).[14] Nonetheless, in the period between 1965 and 1970, Brötzmann, like most European improvisors, saw himself as extending the jazz tradition, both personally and as a representative of a specifically original European variant: "I'm drawing throughout on the stuff that King Oliver did 50 years ago" (qtd. in Schmidt-Joos 129).[15]

The extended aesthetic reflections that took place in conversations printed in the pages of *Jazz Podium* included many of the key players of the period, such as Buschi Niebergall,

Wolfgang Dauner, Irene Schweizer, Peter Kowald, Manfred Schoof, Pierre Courbois, Gunter Hampel, Pierre Favre, and Alexander von Schlippenbach. For the most part, the musicians' discourse in these early years concerned the aesthetics and practice of jazz, and their role in that field. Similarly, in a 1973 interview, Evan Parker asserted, "I still use the word 'jazz.' For me, I'm playing jazz" (Carr 66).

The Crucible of Chicago

In May of 1965, a number of Chicago musicians, diverse in age, gender, and musical direction, received a postcard from four of their mid-career colleagues – pianists Jodie Christian and Richard Abrams, drummer Steve McCall and trumpeter Philip Cohran – calling for a general meeting, and specifying fourteen issues to be discussed in relation to forming a new organization for musicians. This and subsequent meetings, held on Chicago's South Side, led to the formation of the Association for the Advancement of Creative Musicians, whose composite musical directions comprised one of the critically important developments in late twentieth-century experimental music.

The wide-ranging discussions in these early meetings, in which musicians are speaking frankly among themselves, rather than to any outside media, evince nothing so much as an awakening of the subaltern to the power of speech. Already on display was the radical collective democracy and solidarity that later became a central aspect of AACM ideology, and which would at times prove baffling to outsiders, as we will see in examining press reports of the *Gittin' to know y'all* session. The meeting participants included bassist Malachi Favors, saxophonists Maurice McIntyre, Joseph Jarman, and Roscoe Mitchell, pianist Claudine Myers (later Amina), and trombonist Julian Priester (Abrams et al.). The proceedings were conducted using more or less standard parliamentary procedure, and were recorded on audiotape. Each participant stated his or her name for identification purposes before speaking.

The taped evidence does not support the notion advanced overwhelmingly by most critical reception that the AACM was formed in order to promote or revise "new jazz," "the avant-garde," or "free music." Rather, with the very first order of business, the desire of its membership to create and perform a generalized notion of what they called "original music" was centered:

Richard Abrams:	First of all, number one, there's original music, *only*. This will have to be voted and decided upon. I think it was agreed with Steve and Phil that what we meant is original music proceeding from the members in the organization.
Philip Cohran:	I think the reason original music was put there first was because of all of our purposes of being here, this is the primary one. Because why else would we form an association? By us forming an association and promoting and taking over playing our own music, or playing music period, it's going to involve a great deal of sacrifice on each and every one of us. And I personally don't want to sacrifice, make any sacrifice for any standard music.
Steve McCall:	We've all been talking about it among ourselves for a long time in general terms. We'll embellish as much as we can, but get to what you really feel because we're laying a foundation for something that will be permanent.

(Abrams et al., Vol.1)

The name "Association for the Advancement of Creative Musicians" and the acronym "AACM" were adopted unanimously at a subsequent general meeting, and by August of that year the organization was chartered by the state of Illinois as a non-profit, tax-exempt corporation. The documents submitted as part of the charter request included a set of nine purposes, to which the membership continues to subscribe in 2002:

- To cultivate young musicians and to create music of a high artistic level for the general public through the presentation of programs designed to magnify the importance of creative music
- To create an atmosphere conducive to artistic endeavors for the artistically inclined by maintaining a workshop for the express purpose of bringing talented musicians together
- To conduct a free training program for young aspirant musicians
- To contribute financially to charitable organizations
- To provide a source of employment for worthy creative musicians
- To set an example of high moral standards for musicians and to uplift the public image of creative musicians
- To increase mutual respect between creative artists and musical tradesmen (booking agents, managers, promotors, and instrument manufacturers, etc)
- To uphold the tradition of cultured musicians handed down from the past
- To stimulate spiritual growth in creative artists through recitals, concerts, etc, through participation in programs.

(Association for the Advancement of Creative Musicians 1–2)

In early August of 1965, an "open letter to the public" introducing the new organization and announcing its first concerts appeared in the *Chicago Defender*, the important African-American newspaper of record. Written by Richard Abrams and Ken Chaney, the letter declared that, "The ultimate goal is to provide an atmosphere that is conducive to serious music and performing new unrecorded compositions [...] The aim is universal in appeal and is necessary for the advancement, development, and understanding of new music" ("Creative Musicians"; Abrams and Chaney). The language used in the nine purposes, as well as the language of this announcement, which uses terms reminiscent of high-culture, pan-European music – "new music," "serious music" – already distances the organization from jazz-oriented signifiers.

The first US articles on the AACM began to appear as early as 1966. International attention was not long in coming; between October of 1966 and December of 1968, a series of ten detailed and highly enthusiastic reports on "The New Music," by the young Chicago-based producer-critics Chuck Nessa, John Litweiler, and University of Chicago microbiologist Terry Martin, appeared in the Canadian journal *Coda*. In 1968, Martin published the first major European article on the AACM, in the English journal *Jazz Monthly*. In 1966, the first commercial recording by an AACM composer, Roscoe Mitchell's *Sound*, was released by an independent Chicago-based firm, Delmark Records, and in May of 1967, Philip Cohran released two seven-inch recordings of his music on his own Zulu Records label.

In a 1973 article, two early AACM members, trumpeter John Shenoy Jackson and co-founder and pianist/composer Abrams asserted that "The AACM intends to show how the disadvantaged and the disenfranchised can come together and determine their own strategies for political and economic freedom, thereby determining their own destinies"

(Abrams and Jackson 72). This optimistic declaration, based in notions of self-help as fundamental to racial uplift, cultural preservation and spiritual rebirth, was in accord with many other challenges to traditional notions of order and authority that emerged in the wake of the Black Power movement.

AACM musicians emerged from a musical tradition that had already played a major world role in problematizing the border between popular and high culture. At the same time, these artists, like many others, were experiencing at first hand the breakdown of genre definitions and the mobility of practice and method that was starting to inform the emerging postmodern musical landscape. Thus, rather than simply extending the definition of jazz, AACM musicians articulated the more radical project of emancipation from any and all fixed definitions, particularly boundaries of race and place – two of the particular circumstances within which their ideas emerged.

This notion of emancipation could be seen as parallel to the European historical dynamic, albeit in reaction to a different set of circumstances. AACM musicians challenged the use of jazz-related images to police and limit the scope of black cultural expression and economic advancement. Through their music and in interviews, AACM musicians constantly challenged racialized hierarchies of aesthetics, method, place, infrastructure, and economics that sought to limit their mobility of genre, method, and cultural reference.

Not only did this project constitute an understandable reaction from musicians who grew up in working-class homes in one of the most segregated ghettoes in the United States, but it was also in keeping with the overall project of African-Americans with respect to politics, economics, and culture. By articulating notions of genre mobility and by actively seeking dialogue with a variety of traditions, these musicians had placed themselves in an excellent position to recursively intensify and extend Charlie Parker's emancipatory assertion: "Man, there's no boundary line to art."

Nonetheless, the activities of the early AACM have generally been framed as crucial to the emergence of a "second generation" of "free jazz" or "New Thing" music that revised many of the standard methods and musical tropes that had marked the first generation.[16] The European free jazz musicians, however, were at once both a first and a second generation. To the extent that the pioneers of the European movement drew heavily upon the methods, materials, and histories of American jazz, acknowledging progenitors such as Coleman, Ayler, Taylor, and Coltrane, the work of the new Europeans constituted part of a second generation within a gradually globalized notion of jazz. At the same time, in a local sense the new European musicians also constituted a first generation of European free improvisors, who by the mid-1970s gradually began to align themselves with an emerging pan-European nationalism.

Paris: The Catalyst

Between 1967 and 1968, these two avant-gardes began to become aware of each other. During this time, the now-landmark series of Delmark and Nessa recordings of AACM music by Abrams, Jarman, Braxton, Mitchell, Bowie, and their colleagues were becoming known in Europe. Steve McCall, the first AACM member to visit Europe, provided a personal link between the AACM and the first wave of European free jazz musicians, collaborating as early as 1967 with German vibraphonist Gunter Hampel and Dutch saxophonist-clarinetist Willem Breuker. Perhaps in response to McCall's reports from the field, by 1969 a number of AACM members literally flew over New York City, the traditional Mecca for jazz musicians, taking the AACM message to Paris, the undisputed center of black American expatriate cultural production in Europe, and arguably the most accommodating city in the world to the new black American music.

Within days of their arrival in Paris in June of 1969, the Art Ensemble of Chicago – Roscoe Mitchell, Joseph Jarman, Malachi Favors, and Lester Bowie – caused something of an immediate sensation with the first of their regular performances at the Theatre du Lucernaire in the Montparnasse district. The group's unusual hybrid of energy, multi-instrumentalism, humor, silence, found sounds, and homemade instruments – and most crucially, extended collective improvisation instead of heroic individual solos – proved revelatory to European audiences. Following closely on the heels of the Art Ensemble were Leroy Jenkins, Leo Smith, and Anthony Braxton, who arrived in Paris that same month and quickly garnered important notice for their work as well.

For the most widely published American cultural historians working on blacks in Paris (Stovall), the Paris-based black musical experimentalists of the 1960s, 1970s, and 1980s are all but invisible. In the contemporaneous French media, however, black musicians were extensively and consistently chronicled, not only in jazz magazines, but also in the French newspaper of record, *Le Monde*. Multi-issue articles appeared in the pages of *Jazz Magazine* and its cousin, *Jazz Hot,* with intricate poststructuralist disquisitions detailing the thoughts, political theories, and compositional processes of Braxton, Jarman, Bill Dixon, Archie Shepp, and Clifford Thornton.

Within a few months of their arrival in Paris, the AACM musicians received their first major interview in a European publication. Rather than submit to individual interviews, Lester Bowie, Joseph Jarman, Malachi Favors, Leroy Jenkins, Leo Smith, and Roscoe Mitchell were interviewed as a group, introducing the AACM to French readers with a hopeful, expansive vision of their future. In response to a question about the AACM's future plans, Lester Bowie was enthusiastic in his stated intention to "install the AACM everywhere, on every corner of the universe" (Caux 17).[17]

Philippe Carles and Jean-Louis Comolli's classic 1971 *Free Jazz/Black Power* can be said to have articulated a sociopolitical analysis of the AACM and other black musicians that was far more heavily influenced by LeRoi Jones' ideas than many of the AACM musicians themselves were. But besides having had little or no direct contact with Jones/Baraka up to that point in time, the early AACM musicians tended to subordinate politics to musical expression. For instance, in response to a question about the group's connection with the Black Panthers, Jarman replied that affiliation with political organizations was "outside the aims of the AACM"[18] and that the original nine purposes were sufficient to explain their political position. Ultimately, through an encounter with the AACM's music, listeners "in turn can become more active and responsible" (Caux 17).[19]

AACM musicians advanced ongoing critiques of media discourses, with trenchant analyses of how language was used to place borders around black expression. At the conclusion of the interview, Bowie explicitly asserts, in his own way, the need to develop new discourses around music, with the clear implication that jazz discourses in particular were in need of revision and expansion: "In fact, the jazz press has to reevaluate what's going on right now in the music, going further in looking at everything Joseph [Jarman] was talking about, and what our message is about. Now, you have to invent a new way of talking about things" (Caux 18).[20]

Besides a critical stance toward media, the trademark AACM solidarity is also on display in this interview. Leo Smith's reply to a question concerning the meaning of "the tradition – the blues, for example,"[21] by asserting that "We want to integrate all forms of music [...]. Everything and anything is valid. Why differentiate what is tradition from what isn't? That separation serves no purpose."[22] When Mitchell is asked for his opinion about Smith's comment, he replies, laughing, "Leo just said what I could have said [...] Why repeat it?"[23] This exchange in turn prompts Jarman to reassert the full mobility of the AACM project of "original music": "We play blues, rock, Spanish music, gypsy, African, classical music, European contemporary music, voodoo [...] anything you want [...] because, in the end, it's 'music' that we play: we create sounds, period" (Caux 18).[24]

This exchange illustrates the extent to which the early AACM notion of "original music" was unbound by strict adherence to free improvisation, notated composition, constructed notions of blackness, or any other fixed notion of method or tradition. Rather, as Lester Bowie asserted not long after the dawn of postmodernism, "We're free to express ourselves in any so-called idiom, to draw from any source, to deny any limitation. We weren't restricted to bebop, free jazz, Dixieland, theater or poetry. We could put it all together. We could sequence it any way we felt like it. It was entirely up to us" (qtd. in Beauchamp 46).

The Meeting: Collectivity and its Discontents

The Baden-Baden Free Jazz Meetings of the late 1960s and early 1970s revised the standard jazz festival model in a number of respects. First, rather than featuring fixed groups or compositions, the "meetings" were, in a sense, musician-centered events, assuming a diplomatic model in presenting opportunities for intercultural unity in the wake of the Emancipation, while framing improvisation itself as a site for musical and cultural exchange. Moreover, the meetings could also be read as performing an analogous function for improvisors to what the Darmstadt *Ferienkurse* represented for composers. As with the later work of Company, the brainchild of English guitarist and first-generation European improvisor Derek Bailey (*Company 5*), the Baden-Baden meetings exemplified the core conception of placing musicians in a space with few or no externally imposed preconditions – or rather, the histories and personalities of the musicians themselves constituted the primary preconditions.

Steve McCall provided entrée for the newcomers into the expatriate and itinerant musicians' community in Paris (Beauchamp 74). Given his knowledge of the European music scene, McCall could well have been in a position to suggest to festival organizers that the Chicagoans be invited to the 1969 edition of the *Free Jazz Treffen*. Besides McCall, three other members of the "Chicago avant-garde" who were living in Paris – Lester Bowie, Joseph Jarman, and Roscoe Mitchell – came to Baden-Baden for the event, along with the pianist Dave Burrell. Ensconsced in the Schwarzwald, they met sixteen European musicians, including Albert Mangelsdorff, Eje Thelin, Alan Skidmore, Heinz Sauer, Gerd Dudek, John Surman, Willem Breuker, Terje Rypdal, Leo Cuypers, Tony Oxley, and Karin Krog.

In hindsight, the Baden-Baden event could be viewed as an early example of an intercultural event between the two emerging musical vanguards. As Bowie himself affirmed, shortly before his untimely passing, "I called it *Gittin' to Know Y'all* because that's what it was – being acquainted with them, getting to know each other" (Interview). The *Gittin'* session held out the promise of the formulation of what ethnomusicologist Mark Slobin calls an "affinity interculture," a "transnational performer-audience interest group" in which audiences and musicians cross various borders, continually reorganizing themselves into fluid, shifting, diverse communities with fluid definitions, "even when they are not part of a heritage or a commodified, disembodied network – and particularly when the transmission is of the old-fashioned variety – face to face, mouth to ear" (Slobin 68).

Following Jason Stanyek, what is critical here is precisely this kind of "intercorporeality" ("Transmissions" 90) – a body-based, face-to-face exchange of ideas and sounds where, to gloss Judith Butler, improvising bodies themselves are precisely what matter. In Stanyek's formulation, this kind of intercultural music-making "serves to reinforce difference and to rupture contiguities. Interculturalism thrives on both proximity and distance" ("Articulating" 44). In this way, in the affinity interculture, race can be a factor in parsing musical utterance, alongside methodology, materials, class, and subject position.

This basis in notions of difference and intercorporeality allows a contemporary listener to hear the performance of *Gittin' to know y'all* as the working-out of a transnational, intercultural exchange of sonically-based cultural artifacts in terms of historical positionality, including constructions of race and class. At this time, however, intercultural music-making was framed primarily in terms of what Stanyek terms a "music-as-universal-language trope" that was "about the transcending (and effacing) of difference" ("Articulating" 44). Given such an understanding, it must have come as a shock to many of the attendees to find that the 1969 meeting exposed a vast aesthetic, methodological, social, cultural, and sonic gulf separating the two avant-gardes.

This gap was expressed first in Bowie's title, where the term "y'all" appears to instantiate an ironic demarcation between Us and Them. Moreover, the title seems to fix the Europeans within the focus of the black American gaze; otherwise, the piece could have been called *Gittin' to Know Us'n*. In terms of the formal syntax of Ebonics grammar, the directional sense of "y'all" can certainly be reversed, since the European musicians were also "gittin' to know" this new generation of black American improvisors. Unlike a name such as "Globe Unity," however, the use of the word "y'all" itself constitutes a marker of difference.

Bowie and his AACM cohorts had been living in Europe just eight months, invited by drummer and organizer Claude Delcloo, who also came to Baden-Baden and participated in the sessions (Beauchamp 28). Mitchell had come into contact with Mangelsdorff from his Army days in 1958, when he was stationed in Heidelberg, while Bowie and Jarman were newcomers to Europe, "gittin' to know" its peoples, cultures, and musics. Thus, rather than promoting aspirations of unity, the title of Bowie's piece seems designed to signal his intent to present a symbolically autobiographical experience of nomadism that, in part inadvertently, placed himself and his AACM colleagues on the one hand, and the European free music community on the other.

Perhaps this attempt to foreground African-American experience, and to examine differences that were already present, was at variance with at least one reviewer's notion of the proper articulation of collectivity. According to one reviewer, several other Chicago musicians, including Leo Smith, Anthony Braxton and Leroy Jenkins, turned up in Baden-Baden without a real invitation to the meeting, and were both surprised and upset that they were not allowed to take part in the performance – although who it was that barred their participation is not mentioned in the review. The reviewer complains that during the course of the meeting, the six Chicagoans "separated themselves, formed a clique whose unapproachability stood in contrast to Bowie's certainly honorably intended work of contact, and somewhat disturbed the otherwise refreshingly familial character that distinguished the meeting" ("Das bietet" 56).[25] For this reviewer, the "one-big-happy-family" of musicians was destroyed by the "unzertrennliche Bruderschaft" – inseparable brotherhood – exhibited by the Chicagoans.

The review cited racism as the cause of the problems, and the clear implication was that the Chicago "clique" was to blame: "The black-white problem spread itself like a shadow over the event" ("Das bietet" 56).[26] Certainly, jazz has been obliged to deal with race throughout its history, as difficult as this has been at times, and any music as heavily influenced by jazz as European improvised music would have to deal with race as well, particularly in a situation of intercultural and interracial collaboration. But this simplistic reproach, directed exclusively at the black musicians, effectively "e-raced" not only obvious creative differences, but the asymmetrical class differences, both personally and in terms of socioeconomic systems – the children of the underdeveloped Chicago ghetto suddenly face-to face with the relatively privileged descendants and beneficiaries of the *Wirtschaftswunder*[27] and the Marshall Plan.

In the course of the recorded performance of *Gittin' to know y'all,* both the American and the European improvisors seem to alternately embrace and reject blues and jazz-based sonic signifiers. Listening to the piece with the ears of a third-generation improvisor, Bowie's piece may be heard as a kind of negotiated settlement between two very different ideologies and methodologies of music-making. The music appears to mediate between two different subject positions, oscillating between the ferocious intensity of "heroic" individual solos of the sort Coltrane was noted for, and what by 1970 had become standard AACM practice of partial perspectives and unstable silences.

Even given these various sources of ambivalence and instability, the *Jazz Podium* critic found that the 1969 performance of the Bowie work "led to an ideal collective playing, to a real unity. An abundance of individual voices sensed the same soul" ("Das bietet" 56).[28] For this critic, the work was in step with the growing ideological understanding that what was different about post-Emancipation European jazz was its articulation of collectivity as the path to a new unity – an intercultural transcendence of difference on the European continent itself. This affirmation of the importance of collectivity was seen as part of the European transition away from an American-centered "free jazz" that, for Berendt in 1976, exemplified a preoccupation with singular heroic figures: "Whoever reflects upon the high points in European jazz in recent years always thinks of the collective. Whoever thinks about high points in American jazz of the 1960s, then as now, thinks of great individuals: Cecil Taylor, Pharoah Sanders, Ornette Coleman" (Berendt, *Das Jazzbuch* 371).[29]

Of course, the AACM, which Berendt does not mention, constitutes the other radically collective grouping that emerges at more or less the same moment as the European musicians Berendt cites. Without the AACM, Berendt's argument stands on its own two feet; to have cited the AACM would have complicated and weakened a seemingly stable binary. In fact, for both the AACM and the European improvisors, musical articulations of collectivity could be seen as challenging the ongoing American fascination with individualistic social Darwinism.

By the early 1970s, the European musicians were entering the period of the *Grossen Orchester* and the so-called *Kaputtspielphase*. In a 1972 interview, first-generation European free improvisor Peter Kowald described the approach this way: "It was mainly about breaking down the old values; that means, letting everything about harmony and melody fall away" (qtd. in Jost, *Europas Jazz* 113). According to Jost, *Kaputtspielen* took musical form in tendencies toward restlessness, very fast non-tempi and collective "powerplay" (Jost, *Europas Jazz* 116–17). Perhaps more crucially, *kaputtspielen* helped to further crystallize the rejection of US musical hegemony. As Kowald declared, "Today it is evident for the first time that as musical influence, most Americans of our generation don't interest us in the slightest" (qtd. in Jost, *Europas Jazz* 113).[30]

The *Gittin' to Know Y'All* performance engages this notion of powerplay, with moments of collective intensity that recall late Coltrane, particularly *Om*. The musical practices of the Art Ensemble of Chicago, though inclusive of this kind of method, also included extreme articulations of silence along the lines of Bowie's 1967 *Numbers 1&2*, recorded just two years earlier in Chicago. Moreover, contemporaneous accounts and recordings of AEC performances from the Paris period indicate that Bowie and his AACM cohorts had not suddenly abandoned their silences, irony and humor. In *Gittin' to Know Y'all,* however, these kinds of approaches are as conspicuously absent as in much European improvised music of the period – excepting, of course, the sophisticated wit and whimsy of the Dutch school of Mengelberg, Bennink, and Breuker.

With Lester Bowie as soloist and leader, the piece starts with a drone on A. Then as now, slow, meditative, repetitive textures were very uncommon in European improvised music, but often used in AACM music, such as Joseph Jarman's "Song to Make the Sun Come Up" (*As if*) and Richard Abrams's "The Bird Song" (*Levels*). Drones were commonly used as transitional devices in the live performances of the Art Ensemble; moreover, one function of drone textures in many cultures is to evoke the spiritual, a trope that is relatively absent from the European improvisors' discourses. As Steve Lake observes, the musicians on *Machine Gun* were unlikely to be found chanting *Om*.

In contrast, the AACM purposes explicitly include a desire "to stimulate spiritual growth in creative artists." Joseph Jarman wrote in a 1967 edition of the AACM's short-lived newsletter: "Man need not destroy himself or his GODS (anti-western rationalism) simply because he has become so advanced intellectually; this music means NOTHING more than the act of it, the human giving that it entails, the homage to the source of all life, the spirit that is man in the universe" ("On Questions"). Directly realizing a negative aesthetics of modernism, the paradox of *Kaputtspielen*, from the standpoint of Emancipation discourse, emerged in the similarity of many such performances to the spirit of late Coltrane – as with the opening salvo of Peter Brötzmann's *Machine Gun*, which despite the assertion of English critic Steve Lake that the music "sounds nothing like American models," is easily heard as a gloss on the first movement of Coltrane's *Meditations*. Thus, after the opening drone, a kind of hectic restlessness sets in, eventually evoking Coltrane's *Ascension*, even to the extent of a nearly direct quote by one saxophonist from a particular passage played by Coltrane in that work.

Further differences between the two camps would emerge, prefigured by the Baden-Baden meeting. Jost notes that in the music of European improvisors, "compositional plans remained, in general, limited to a minimum" (*Europas Jazz* 113).[31] Bert Noglik's recounting of the well-known story of Paul Rutherford's freely improvised "performance" of the Luciano Berio "Sequenza V" for trombone solo (Noglik 263) serves as a salient example of how the European improvisors' critique of European high-culture composition often embodied an ideology of binary opposition between free improvisation and extended notated composition. Indeed, the notion that compositional devices should be either kept to a minimum or entirely avoided is an ideology to which many European musicians continue to adhere, as in Evan Parker's assertion that "if anyone in the production of a musical event is dispensable, it is the score-maker, or the 'composer,' as he is often called" (Bailey, *Improvisation* 81).

The AACM musicians, on the other hand, were emphasizing a hybrid compositional-improvisative discourse that incorporated insights, sounds, techniques, and methods from a variety of areas, including European high musical modernism. Unlike free improvisors, or either modernist or postmodernist pan-European composers, the composition/

improvisation binary lacked any real force in AACM practice. Rather, AACM composers were often drawn to postmodern collage and interpenetration strategies that blended, opposed or ironically juxtaposed the two disciplines. The AACM critique of high-culture composition, in contrast to the European improvisors, was not centered on the Eurologically-based binary of notation versus freedom, but upon an opposition to the silencing of black perspectives – an ideology that privileged fluidity, mobility, and hybridity. AACM musicians were headed away from, not toward, an exclusive preoccupation with free improvisation, as befits their status as a second generation rather than a first. For these musicians, in the wake of the volcanisms of Coltrane, Taylor, Murray, Shepp, and Ayler, this more delicate, nuanced approach was as revolutionary and anti-hegemonic as the previous "free jazz" claimed to be, not just in its challenge to notions of what American free music should sound like, but to notions of the "proper" processes by which working-class black musicians should produce music.

In fact, the focus in standard histories on the role of improvisor as constitutive of the AACM's activity follows a trope that has become standard in the historiography and criticism of black American music. In examining the activity of the first wave of the AACM, the limits of that trope in accounting for the diversity of black musical subjectivity quickly become disclosed. As we can see from the following meeting excerpt, the dominant focus of the AACM as strongly *composer-centered* was fostered right from the start, eventually leading to the extensive engagement with notation that we see in so many AACM members' works. Thus, there was no rhetoric of refusal of composition, but an engagement where composition itself became an act of resistance.

Richard Abrams:	Now, for the benefit of those who were not here last week, we decided that we in this organization will play only our own music – original compositions or material originating from the members within the group.
Julian Priester:	It would seem to be that if you put too many restrictions on the activities at this point, you're going to put a lot of obstacles in your way. For instance, to me, everyone in here is not a composer, so right there you exclude them.
Richard Abrams:	No, no one's excluded, you see. You may not be Duke Ellington, but you got some kind of ideas, and now is the time to put 'em in. Wake yourself up. This is an awakening we're trying to bring about.

(Abrams et al., Vol. 2)

In the context of the 1970s, Abrams' reference to bringing about "an awakening" through composition recognizes that this simple assertion by Afro-Americans – defining oneself as a composer – was a challenge to the social and indeed the economic order of both the music business and the aesthetics business. Moreover, the reference to Ellington is quite understandable on a number of levels, given the fact that throughout his career, Ellington's image of himself as a composer working with and through African-American forms was constantly challenged, stigmatized, and stereotyped. Thus, Ellington could be viewed as a symbol, not only of excellence and innovation, but also of optimistic perseverance; again, as with Ellington, the dissonance between the AACM composers' catholicity of methods and materials and the immobility of their genre classification as jazz was seen by AACM members as largely race-based.

Finally, vacillating between relative calm and full-out intensity, the Bowie work seems to be providing a way for the AACM musicians to "blend in," as immigrants must do, while being unable to completely suppress their difference even if they wanted to. Thus, while *Gittin' to know y'all* constitutes something of an anomaly in AACM practice, it can be heard as a reflection of an uneasy attempt at musical hybridity.

Complementary Cultural Nationalisms

In citing the "strategically essentialist" character of 1970s black cultural nationalism – certainly an influence on some individual AACM members – Stuart Hall (citing Gayatri Spivak) claims that "historically, nothing could have been done to intervene in the dominated field of mainstream popular culture, to try to win some space there, without the strategies through which those dimensions were condensed onto the signifier 'black'" (29). In the paragraphs to follow, I suggest that in an environment dominated by epigonal Americanisms, a similar strategic essentialism was at work in preparing the next stage of the evolution of European free music – the 1970s drive to distance the new tradition from its jazz roots by asserting a purely European character for it.

The English critic Steve Lake, an early leader in the drive to create a critical space for a European improvised music, cites Brötzmann's 1968 *Machine Gun* as "the first jazz album you could call 'European'," in that the musicians came from five different European countries. But by the mid-1970s, the political stance of the new European musicians had moved well beyond the notion of "European jazz." An emerging pan-European political nationalism was certainly an influence on the emergence, reception, and production of European free improvisation, at a time when there were patrolled borders between France and Belgium, Holland and Germany, and West Germany and East Germany.

By the mid 1970s, this cultural nationalism was being strongly asserted by the first-generation, post-Emancipation European free musicians. As Misha Mengelberg saw it in 1974, an essential aspect of the new consciousness was aimed at bringing the new music into the European cultural consensus – which would include the kind of government support for cultural production that had become an integral part of European social democracy. To make the case for inclusion, the new musicians conceived a nativist politics that identified African-American music and musicians as foreign competitors.

Thus, as with generations of black musicians before them – as with Charlie Parker's 1949 assertion that bebop was not jazz (Levin and Wilson 24) – by the mid-1970s many European musicians began to deny that they had anything to do with jazz (Jost, *Europas Jazz* 14). As Mengelberg declared, "the music we play, we and the other European musicians, even those who invoke 'free jazz,' has no longer anything to do with Afro-American music. But we are inspired, it must be acknowledged, by this music in order to create our own" (Brötzmann, Bennink, and Mengelberg 20).[32] In the same series of interviews, Alexander von Schlippenbach, in response to a question about Sun Ra, observes that "I think that what they are doing is inseparable from the situation of black Americans, and the problems that we have in Europe are different" (Schlippenbach 18).[33]

In the light of such statements, it seems odd that the black cultural nationalist aspect of the Art Ensemble's term, "Great Black Music," is often roundly criticized, while the pan-European cultural nationalism of the European free improvisors often remains uninterrogated. For some, such as Mengelberg, the redefinition of their work as "nouvelle musique improvisée européenne" – new European improvised music – had immense political significance: "Our improvised music is political […] the fact that we defined our political position made our music more powerful that it ever had been, and at least as powerful as that of the Afro-American musicians" (Brötzmann, Bennink, and Mengelberg 20).[34] Ironically, the strategy outlined by Mengelberg strongly resembles theoretical and historical antecedents in Pan-Africanist worldviews that were routinely attributed to black American musicians active in this same period, such as Archie Shepp and Clifford Thornton.

Both the European improvisors and the AACM pursued projects of collectivity, politically and musically. The challenge for the Europeans was to unify musicians from a variety of nations, languages and histories – a multicultural project of recognizing unity within diversity. The AACM project of collectivity aimed at the reverse – the maintenance of diversity within unity in the face of a massive, corporate-driven appropriation and flattening of black culture generally. Black music in its various forms was both admired and feared as arguably the most widely influential music of the twentieth century. At the same time, black music had become the most commodified art in history, and the space of positions for alternative black musical expression was becoming vanishingly small.

The need to move beyond the dependent conception of "European jazz" to a putatively indigenous concept of free music seemed a logical outgrowth of the same kind of drive for self-realization that the AACM pursued for different reasons, and to recall Mangelsdorff's phrase, under "other circumstances." For European improvisors, the term "jazz" had become first and foremost a marker of the link to epigonality; the very word "jazz" pointed to Americanized musical norms. Accordingly, discourses of distance appeared as they had among the black musicians, including borrowings of terms such as "zeitgenössische Musik" [contemporary music], "folklore imaginaire," and the currently preferred, if somewhat bland, "improvised music."

No longer bound by the externally imposed hegemony of "European jazz," the musicians sought to bring themselves together, reasserting a pan-European culture. This revised strategy of unification, moreover, would no longer be based in the older notions of liberation from American hegemony generally, but rather in a need for the musicians to distance themselves from historical and aesthetic responsibility to specifically African-American cultural tropes. In Nietzschean terms, the new European free music was emancipating itself by breaking the cycle of *ressentiment* that made the debt of Europe to African-American tradition impossible to pay. Perhaps inevitably, this project would be interpreted by subsequent generations in a way that conflated ethnicity and race.

The Way Ahead?

Bowie's highly-charged attempt at *Gittin' to know y'all* seems to have set a certain tone; up to the present day, collaborations between European improvisors and AACM improvisors have been very limited. Tellingly, these collaborations have centered on free improvisation events; in the case of the late-1970s hybrids of composition and improvisation promulgated by AACM composers, such as Anthony Braxton, Roscoe Mitchell, and Leo Smith, the presence of European musicians is all but nonexistent. These extended works were realized in performance by ensembles comprised largely of AACM members and other American musicians.[35]

One might have thought that a strong case for an ongoing, vital exchange between the two avant-gardes could be made on the basis of the overlap of interests and methodologies. However, if, as Renato Poggioli asserts, an avant-garde needs a metropole to assert difference, the two avant-gardes were each working in reaction to a different construction of the metropole. In any event, the point here is that the absence of collaboration can express a complex mix of aesthetic, historical, and methodological positions. Just as in 1969, resorting to simplistic explanations based on accusations of individual racism between members of the two vanguards obscures far more than it reveals.

More to the point is the fact that these two generationally similar avant-gardes (the major exponents in both vanguards were born between 1930 and 1950), employing methodologies that overlapped to a considerable extent, were both seeking to obtain footholds for their music in Europe, a fact which inevitably placed them in competition for resources. Complicating the position of the Americans in the race were the problems of being foreigners in an increasingly nativist European political and cultural landscape. Another problem lay closer to home – the perception of the United States cultural situation expressed by Muhal Richard Abrams in 1982: "Look, this country here was never focused, in whatever area, to tolerate a black image" (qtd. in Jost, *Jazzmusiker* 198).[36] Making the Europeans' position more complex was the *ressentiment*-based perception by some musicians of the desires of the home, European audience, broached in 1974 by Brötzmann: "In general, the public prefers the black musicians and Americans" (Brötzmann, Bennink, and Mengelberg 21).[37]

The critiques of jazz advanced by first-generation European improvisors evolved from a rejection of African-American cultural hegemony in jazz to an eventual asserted severance of the link to the jazz tradition itself. A newer generation of critics, along with many musicians, moved beyond this relatively benign position to frame free improvisation in a way that erased African-American agency and influence altogether. This movement sought to fold the practice and history of free improvisation into a composite construction of a whiteness-based, transnational, pan-European experimental aesthetic that would frame as axiomatic the permanent marginalization of African-American agency.

Thus, composer and improvisor Anne LeBaron, writing almost forty years after the Emancipation, makes a claim that would have astonished first-generation European free musicians. After citing the "modernist origins of free jazz" in the work of Coltrane, Taylor, and others, the writer proceeds to claim that "With the exception of maverick composer-improviser Anthony Braxton, the Americans maintained closer relationships with conventions associated with traditional jazz (such as repetitive harmonic structures and fixed rhythmic pulses) while 'free jazz' in Europe tended to demolish anything smacking of the formulaic [...] The abandonment of clichéd conventions in American jazz in the 1960s was more gradual, less radical than in the European free jazz movement" (LeBaron 39).

As we have seen already in this essay, however, the passing of the era of strict tempo had already become a given by the mid-1960s. Moreover, the early European free musicians explicitly regarded this and other new frontiers of form, materials, and method as having originated with American free jazz, not from their own work. In fact, as we have already heard from Berendt, first-generation European free musicians, who had heard John Coltrane, Albert Ayler, Roswell Rudd, John Tchicai, Milford Graves, and others at first hand, were influenced by their work precisely *because* of the absence of "repetitive harmonic structures and fixed rhythmic pulses" (*Das Jazzbuch* 370).

LeBaron's account, however spurious in its attempted revisionism, draws (perhaps unwittingly) upon a particularly complex stereotype of African-American music-making that treats "jazz" not as a fluid, contested, dynamic genre with porous borders, but as a body of received, unchanging methods, with hermetically sealed histories, and most crucially, an always-already supply of blacks who, regardless of background, interests or affinities, are genetically bound to the embodiment of the stereotype. The work of the postcolonial theorist Homi Bhabha can help us to unpack this particular version of what is, after all, a common discursive strategy – practically a cliché (see, for instance, Toop).

For Bhabha, the stereotype is "a form of knowledge and identification that vacillates between what is always 'in place,' already known, and something that must be anxiously repeated […]. It is the force of [this] ambivalence that gives the colonial stereotype its currency: ensures its repeatability in changing historical and discursive conjunctures; informs its strategies of individuation and marginalization; produces that effect of probabilistic truth and predictability which, for the stereotype, must always be in excess of what can be empirically proved or logically construed" (Bhabha 66). Bhabha's articulation (in Stuart Hall's sense of the term) of the notion of "stereotype" with the concept of "ambivalence" allows us to uncover the extent to which LeBaron's analysis rests upon what George Lipsitz has called a "possessive investment in whiteness" (see Lipsitz) and concomitant appeals to networks of power and pan-ethnic particularism. In this way we are able to see how the critique of jazz can become a springboard for a more fundamental erasure of black culture, and finally, of the black people who create it.

For commentators such as Tom Nunn (14–16) and LeBaron (39) free improvisation can be distinguished from free jazz in terms of a well-specified set of musical characteristics. However, the exact nature of the difference appears to be difficult for the proponents of this theory to identify – already a source of ambivalence. LeBaron appears to take a cue from John Cage (Kostelanetz 162–64) in looking askance upon fixed tempi and recurrent harmonic structures. The underlying claim is that the absence of these elements counts as a mark of "progress," or in LeBaron's case, a boundary marker between modernism and post-modernism.

Here, we see Bhabha's colonial stereotype at work. As we have seen in examining the experience of the European improvisors, the "truth" of the "fixed pulse" stereotype is "far in excess of what can be logically construed" by people who were familiar with mid-1960s African-American experimentalism – such as the first-generation European free jazz improvisors. Thus, the constant, anxious repetition of the canard that jazz is somehow intrinsically doomed to endless recycling of "clichéd conventions" becomes essential to the marginalization and subsequent erasure of African-Americans as experimental music-makers. On this view, anxiety and ambivalence on the part of the critic must necessarily result from the divergence between what is historically known and what is being asserted.

Since the notion that free improvisation and free jazz differ in the articulation of regular pulse and repetitive harmony cannot be taken seriously once its cycle of stereo-typic repetition has been interrupted, one influential version of the free jazz/free improvisation dialectic, advanced by the improvisor Derek Bailey, redeploys the stereotype at a higher level of abstraction. Bailey's formulation of "idiomatic" and "non-idiomatic" genres or traditions of improvisation is still based on the notion that some musics rely for their identity on the articulation of fixed forms and received wisdoms: "Idiomatic improvisation […] is mainly concerned with the expression of an idiom – such as jazz, flamenco or baroque – and takes its identity and motivation from that idiom" (*Improvisation* xi-xii).

In contrast, Bailey asserts that "'Non-idiomatic' improvisation has other concerns and is most usually found in so-called 'free' improvisation and, while it can be highly stylised, is not usually tied to representing an idiomatic identity" (*Improvisation* xi-xii). From this vague definition, however, it may be difficult to see how free improvisation avoids becoming an idiom like all the others out there. The most historically consistent answer to this would frame non-idiomatic improvisation as drawing primary sustenance from modernism's negative aesthetic.

Thus, "non-idiomatic" improvisation and free improvisation prove to be one and the same, expressing the tautology A = A. On this view, the very being of "non-idiomatic" improvisation must become parasitic upon the existence of an "idiomatic" genre of improvisation – a fixed star, if you will. Among the many supposedly idiomatic improvised musics in the world, there are many from which to choose for that honor, but it has traditionally been jazz, the most influential improvisative music of the twentieth century, which has "served to animate many projects in the formation and exploration of a particularly Eurological improvisative sensibility" (Lewis, "Improvised" 144).

Even as free jazz becomes a handy second (fixed) term in the binary equation, in the context of the improvisative musics that emerged from the mid-1960s, the explanatory power of both the free jazz/free improvisation and the idiomatic/non-idiomatic dialectics rests in large measure upon an erasure from the history of improvisation of the very group whose work problematizes both dialectics – the AACM. Thus, we find an aporia in the Bailey, Nunn, and LeBaron texts (and many others) with respect to the AACM as a group, although individual AACM artists may well be included as footnotes – such as the AACM musician Anthony Braxton, who is often exceptionalized (i.e. tokenized) in texts on "new music."

Whether Braxton is admitted to the pantheon – allowed to "transcend race," in the colorblindness language of the American political right wing – or simply "e-raced," like the AACM colleagues of his generation – the Art Ensemble of Chicago, Muhal Richard Abrams, or many others – the racialized character of the inclusion decision itself reveals an asymmetry of power where historical erasure itself becomes a tactic in the competition. Thus, the supposed difference between free jazz and free improvisation becomes disclosed as resting not upon methodological or sonic difference, but upon ethnic and racial identifiers that become mapped onto method in a way that not only advances a whiteness-based version of the relationship between African-American improvisative culture and postmodernism, but revokes the genre mobility of the African-American improvisor.

This dynamic, if successful, would import similar discourses to those now active in historical constructions of the "American experimental music" tradition, which was actively ethnicized and racialized by its most ardent proponents, who saw themselves as part of a unitary European heritage and timeline (Lewis, "Improvised" 138). Viewed historically, this "American" tradition proved to be no different from its predecessors in finding African-American musical traditions quite indigestible. The effect was to ground the very identity of American experimentalism upon a radical absence of African-Americans, or – empaneling Cage himself as a hostile witness – a form of "silence," to follow Radano and Bohlman.

So far, the American experimental tradition has been unable to break free from its singularly anxious preoccupation with this kind of pan-European identity politics, which threatens to transform a vital tradition into a marginalized microworld that appropriates freely, yet furtively, from other ethnic traditions, yet has no place to recognize any histories as its own other than those based in a racialized construction of pan-Europeanism. The danger for that tradition seems clear enough in a globalized world with fluid borders of practice and transcultural exchanges that are no respecters of race, tradition, or genre. As the dynamics of globalization oblige both the United States and Europe to make the transition to the construction of multicultural societies, the single-minded pursuance of cultural identity politics inevitably appears as an increasingly shrill, yet futile set of exhortations to hold back the night.

Moreover, in a discursive environment where African-American histories – and yes, leadership – will forever be proscribed, intercultural rupture of the kind we have seen between these two avant-gardes is inevitable, making collaboration between them difficult, unlikely, even impossible. Abrams frames the process in this way: "For generations, what it comes to is that they imitate black music, sever it from its roots, and in that way, obscure its origins. And this has grown into a habit with those people. They do it quasi-automatically. Even in this time they do it. And they don't even notice that they are insulting us" (qtd. in Jost, *Jazzmusiker* 197).[38] In this case, the hurt can be not only general, but deeply personal.

For a history of free improvisation, of all things, to adopt such a path, to pursue such a massive erasure, would be precisely the wrong kind of emancipation – an ultimately fatal enactment of "ambivalence." In contrast, an inclusive, nonracialized historical account of late twentieth-century and twenty-first-century free improvisation, based on a fluid notion of tradition, could recognize adherents to the form coming from all over the world, articulating a multicultural, multi-ethnic base for histories of experiment in improvised music. This would interrupt the repetition of the jazz stereotype, since by definition African-American experimental musical agency could not be bracketed off into a separate category based on racialized signifiers such as "free jazz."

Finally, as Radano and Bohlman attest, "music resists silence, and music has the power to undo the historical aporia of silence" (37). What I am hoping is that some responsible individual will stand up and write the history I am calling for, and break the circle of ambivalence once and for all. I am pleased to believe that such a history will not be long in coming.

Acknowledgements

This article originally appeared in German as Lewis 2002. I would like to thank Wolfram Knauer, Arndt Weidler, and the Jazzinstitut Darmstadt, which published the original essay, for encouraging the English-language publication of this essay, and also for their tremendous support in allowing me to create an extensive photocopy library of contemporaneous reviews from German and French journals. This work, which took place in 1998 and 1999, made the writing of this and many other recent papers much easier. I am also grateful to my student Jason Robinson for his presentation of Bhabha's notion of ambivalence. Finally, I am indebted to a recent lecture at the University of California, San Diego, by my former student, Prof. Jason Stanyek of the University of Richmond, who showed me what I was actually trying to do with this paper by doing it better than I had.

Notes

All translations by the author.

1 "Ich glaube, ich könnte eine gute Gruppe mit 15 Leuten auf die Beine stellen" (Schmidt-Joos 129).

2 "eine exotische Pflanze auf kargem Boden […] die ebenso bizarre erscheinen mußte wie britischer Flamenco" (Jost, *Europas Jazz* 11).

3 "der schöpferische europäische Jazzmusiker hat aufgehört, amerikanische Musiker zu imitieren. Er hat aufgehört, auf Gebieten mit ihm zu konkurrieren – vor allem in swing und im Bereich schwarzer Traditions – in denen er ihm doch nie erreichen kann" (Berendt, *Das Jazzbuch* 374).

4 "Deshalb sollte ein Jazzmusiker in Europa nicht von sich verlangen, so zu spielen wie ein farbiger Musiker in New York oder Chicago, er sollte es nicht versuchen und man sollte es nicht von ihm erwarten, weil seine Probleme andere sind und sein Lebenskreis anderen Bedingungen unterworfen ist" (qtd. in Knauer 147–48). Rendering the racial marker "farbige" as "colored" (meaning African-American) respects the idiom for the period in Germany.

5 "man sollte bei aller Bewunderung nicht vergessen, daß man in erster Linie seine eigene Persönlichkeit, seine eigene Konzeption des Jazz musikalisch ausdrücken sollte" (qtd. in Knauer 150).

6 "der Diktatur des gleichmäßig durchgeschlagenes Metrums, der herkömmlichen Funktionalharmonik, der symmetrischen Perioden und Phrasenabläufe" (Berendt, *Das Jazzbuch* 370).

7 "ein gewaltiger psychomusikalischer Kraftakt, der nicht nur das altgewohnte Regelsystem der Jazzimprovisation aud den Angeln hob, sondern in dessen Folge schließlich auch die jazzmusikalische Identität selbst ins Frage gestellt wurde" (Jost, *Europas Jazz* 12).

8 "Wir sagen dazu nicht New Thing, sondern Own Thing" ("Own Thing" 69).

9 "seinen Stockhausen und seinen Ligeti genauer kennt als irgendeiner seiner amerikanischen Kollegen" (Berendt, *Das Jazzbuch* 374).

10 "Tendenziell hat sich beispielsweise die Begegnung mit avancierter komponierter Musik (bewußt oder unbewußt) auf das Schaffen europäischer Improvisationsmusiker vergleichsweise eher und – was eine gewisse Breite und Differenziertheit der Bestrebungen anbelangt – stärker ausgewirkt" (Noglik 214).

11 "man spurt kein Miteinander und kein Füreinander. Es sind drei Einzelaktionen, die sich nicht zu einem wirklichen Kollektiv führen" ("Hie Logan" 174).

12 "Der europäische Jazz ist – ebenfalls schwergewichtig – ein kollektiver Jazz, in dem der einzelne in dem Ensemble ausgeht" (Berendt, *Das Jazzbuch* 371).

13 "aus einem besonderem Verhältnis zum Kollektiv und zur europäischen Tradition" (Berendt, *Das Jazzbuch* 371).

14 "Ich habe in der Malerei gelernt, die Freiheit des persönlichen Ausdrucks zu gebrauchen [...] Man sollte keine Hemmungen kennen, das Althergebrachte einfach umzustoßen" (qtd. in Knauer 152).

15 "Ich beziehe mich durchaus auf die Dinge, die King Oliver vor 50 Jahren gemacht hat" (qtd. in Schmidt-Joos 129).

16 See Litweiler for a discussion of "generations" in free jazz.

17 "installer I' partout, à tous les coins de l'univers" (Caux 17).

18 "étranger aux desseins de l'AACM" (Caux 17).

19 "peuvent devenir à leur tour plus actifs et plus responsables" (Caux 17).

20 "Il faut, en effet, que la presse spécialisée dans le jazz réévalue ce qui se passe actuellement dans la musique, aille plus loin dans l'examen de tout ce dont Joseph parlait et qui constitue notre message [...] Il faut, maintenant, inventer une nouvelle façon de parler des choses" (Caux 18).

21 "la tradition-le blues, par example" (Caux 18).

22 "Nous voulons intégrer toutes les formes de musique [...] Tout et n'importe quoi sont valables. Pourquoi séparer la tradition et ce qui ne l'est pas? Cette separation ne sert à rien" (Caux 18).

23 "Leo vient de dire ce que je pourrais dire [...] pourquoi alors le répéter?" (Caux 18).

24 "Nous jouons le blues, nous jouons le jazz, le rock, la musique espagnole, gitane, africaine, la musique classique, la musique européenne contemporaine, vaudou [...] tout ce que vous voudrez [...] parce que, finalement, c'est 'la musique' que nous jouons: nous créons des sons, un point c'est tout" (Caux 18).

25 "sonderten sich ab, bildeten eine Clique, deren Unzugänglichkeit in Kontrast zu Bowies sicher ehrlich gemeintem Kontaktstück stand und den sonst so erfrischend familiären Charakter, der diese Treffen auszeichnet, etwas störte" ("Das bietet" 56).

26 "Das Schwarz-Weiß Problem breitete sich wie ein Schatten über das Geschehen" ("Das bietet" 56).

27 The term, literally "economic miracle," is generally used to refer to West Germany's rapid post-World War II economic recovery.

28 "führte zu einem idealen Zusammenspiel, zu einer wirklichen Einheit Eine Fülle individueller Stimmen spürte den gemeinsamen Kern" ("Das bietet" 56).

29 "Wer an die Höhepunkte im europäischen Jazz der letzten Jahre denkt, denkt immer an Kollektive [...] Wer an die Höhepunkte im amerikanischen Jazz der sechziger Jahre denkt, denkt nach wie vor an große Einzelne: Cecil Taylor, Pharoah Sanders, Ornette Coleman" (Berendt, *Das Jazzbuch* 371).

318   *George E. Lewis*

30 "Da ging es hauptsächlich darum, die alten Werte wirklich kaputtzubrechen, das heißt, alles an Harmonie und Melodie wegfallen zu lassen [...] Heute ist zum ersten Mal klar, daß die meisten Amerikaner unserer Generation als musikalischer Einfluß gestohlen bleiben können" (Jost, *Europas Jazz* 113).
31 "Kompositorische Maßnahmen bleiben im allgemeinen auf ein Minimum beschränkt" (Jost, *Europas Jazz* 113).
32 "la musique que nous jouons, nous et d'autres musiciens européens, même ceux qui se réclament du "free jazz," n'a plus rien à voir avec la musique afro-américaine. Mais nous nous sommes inspirés, il faut le reconnaître, de cette musique pour créer la nôtre" (Brötzmann, Bennink, and Mengelberg 20).
33 "Je pense que ce qu'ils font est indissociable de la situation des Noirs américains, et les problèmes que nous avons en Europe sont différents" (Schlippenbach 18).
34 "Notre musique improvisée est politique [...] le fait que nous ayons défini notre position politique a rendu notre musique plus puissante qu'elle ne l'était, et au moins aussi puissante que celle des musiciens afro-américains" (Brötzmann, Bennink, and Mengelberg 20).
35 One can enumerate the AACM musicians who have collaborated the most extensively with European improvisors literally on the fingers of one hand: Anthony Braxton, Leo Smith, Steve McCall, and this author. Others who have done so to a limited extent include Fred Anderson, who toured with pianist Dieter Glawischnig in 1976, Leroy Jenkins (Paris 1969–70), and the participants in the 1969 Baden-Baden event. Since the late-1990s, Hamid Drake, a close associate of many AACM musicians, has been active with a variety of first-generation Euroimprovisors. In the main, however, most of the better-known AACM musicians – Anderson, Muhal Richard Abrams, Roscoe Mitchell, Joseph Jarman, Lester Bowie, Malachi Favors, Famoudou Don Moye, Henry Threadgill, Amina Claudine Myers, Kalaparush Ahrah Difda, Adegoke Steve Colson, Iqua Colson, Ernest Khabeer Dawkins, Kahil El-Zabar, Douglas Ewart, Chico Freeman, and Edward Wilkerson – have rarely or never collaborated with European improvisors, or have not done so since the early 1970s. As of the early twenty-first century, one observes that the latest generation of AACM artists, such as Nicole Mitchell and Jeff Parker, are becoming more involved in these collaborations.
36 "Siehst du, dieses Land hier war niemals darauf eingestellt, in irgendeinem Bereich ein Schwarzes Image zu tolerieren" (qtd. in Jost, *Jazzmusiker* 198).
37 "En général, le public préfère les musiciens noirs et américains" (Brötzmann, Bennink, and Mengelberg 21).
38 "Seit Generationen läuft es darauf hinaus, daß sie die Schwarze Musik imitieren, sie von ihren Wurzeln trennen und dadurch ihre Herkunft verdunkeln. Und das ist bei den Leuten zur Gewohnheit geworden. Sie tun es quasi automatisch. Genau in dieser Zeit tun sie auch das. Und sie merken nicht einmal, daß sie uns beleidigen" (qtd. in Jost, *Jazzmusiker* 197).

Works Cited

Association for the Advancement of Creative Musicians. Charter Documents. Chicago, Illinois: State of Illinois Charter, 1965. Copy in Collection of George E. Lewis.
Abrams, Muhal Richard. Interview with the author. 26 Dec. 1997. Chicago, Illinois.
——. *Levels and Degrees of Light.* Vinyl LP. Delmark DS-413, 1967.
Abrams, Richard, and Ken Chaney. Press release. August 1965. Chicago, Illinois. Archives of the AACM.
Abrams, Muhal Richard, and John Shenoy Jackson. "Association for the Advancement of Creative Musicians." *Black World* 23.1 (1973): 72–74.
Abrams, Richard, et al. AACM Meeting. Vol. 1. Rec. 8 May 1965. Audiotape. Chicago, Illinois, Collection of Muhal Richard Abrams.
——. AACM Meeting. Vol. 2. Rec. 15 May 1965. Audiotape. Chicago, Illinois, Collection of Muhal Richard Abrams.
——. AACM Meeting. Vol. 3. Rec. 27 May 1965. Audiotape. Chicago, Illinois, Collection of Muhal Richard Abrams.
Bailey, Derek. *Company* 5. Rec. 1977. Incus CD41, 2001.

——. *Improvisation: Its Nature and Practice in Music*. London: British Library National Sound Archive, 1992.

Beauchamp, Lincoln T., Jr., ed. Art *Ensemble of Chicago: Great Black Music – Ancient to the Future*. Chicago: Art Ensemble of Chicago, 1998.

Belgrad, Daniel. *The Culture of Spontaneity: Improvisation and the Arts in Postwar America*. Chicago: U of Chicago P, 1998.

Berendt, Joachim Ernst. *Das Jazzbuch: Von Rag bis Rock*. Frankfurt am Main: Fischer Taschenbuch Verlag, 1976.

——. *Ein Fenster aus Jazz: Essays, Portraits, Reflexionen*. Frankfurt am Main: S. Fischer Verlag, 1977.

Bhabha, Homi K. *The Location of Culture*. New York: Routledge, 1994.

Bowie, Lester. *Gittin' to know y'all*. Vinyl LP. MPS 15269,15038, 1970.

——. Interview with the author. Rec. 22 July 1999. Audiotape. Brooklyn, New York.

——. *Numbers 1 & 2*. Nessa N-1 (vinyl disc), 1968.

Braxton, Anthony. *Tri-Axium Writings*. 3 vols. Dartmouth: Synthesis, 1985.

Brötzmann, Peter. *Machine Gun*. FMP CD24, 1968.

Brötzmann, Peter, Han Bennink, and Misha Mengelberg. "Onze Européens parlent de leur musique." Interview with Didier Pennequin. *Jazz Magazine* 220 (1974): 19–21.

Cage, John. *Silence*. Middletown: Wesleyan UP, 1961.

Carles, Philippe, and Jean-Louis Comolli. *Free Jazz/Black Power*. 1971. Paris: Gallimard, 2000.

Carr, Ian. *Music Outside: Contemporary Jazz in Britain*. London: Latimer, 1973.

Caux, Daniel. "AACM de Chicago." *Jazz Hot* 254 (October 1969): 16–19.

"Creative Musicians Sponsor Artists Concert Showcase." *Chicago Defender* 7–13 August 1965.

"Das bietet Baden-Baden im Winter: Das Free Jazz Treffen des SWF," *Jazz Podium* 2/XIX(1970):56.

"Das Pierre Favre Trio." *Jazz Podium* 11/XVII (1968): 344–45.

Fabre, Michel, and John A. Williams. *A Street Guide to African-Americans in Paris*. Paris: Cercle d'Etudes Afro-Americaines, 1996.

Floyd, Samuel A. Jr. *The Power of Black Music: Interpreting Its History from Africa to the United States*. New York: Oxford UP, 1995.

Goldstein, Malcolm. *Sounding the Full Circle*. Sheffield: Goldstein/Frog Peak, 1988.

Hall, Stuart. "What is This 'Black' in Black Popular Culture?" *Black Popular Culture: A Project by Michele Wallace*. Ed. Gina Dent. Seattle: Bay, 1992. 21–33.

"Hie Logan – Da Ayler." *Jazz Podium*, 7/XIV (1965): 172–74.

Jarman. Joseph. *As If It Were the Seasons*. Delmark 417, 1968.

——. "On Questions Asked of Me by Jerry Figi on Our Music." *AACM Newsletter*. AACM, 1967, n.p.

Jones, Le Roi. *Black Music*. New York: William Morrow, 1968.

——. *Blues People*. New York: William Morrow, 1963.

Jost, Ekkehard. *Europas Jazz, 1960–80*. Frankfurt am Main: Fischer Taschenbuch Verlag, 1987.

——. *Free Jazz*. Vienna: Universal, 1975.

——. *Jazzmusiker: Materialen zur Soziologie der afro-amerikanischen Musik*. Frankfurt am Main: Ullstein Materialen, 1982.

Knauer, Wolfram. "Emanzipation wovon? Zum Verhältnis des amerikanischen und des deutschen Jazz in den 50er und 60er Jahren." *Jazz in Deutschland: Darmstädter Beiträge zur Jazzforschung, Band 4*. Ed. Wolfram Knauer. Hofheim: Wolke Verlag Hofheim, 1996.

Kostelanetz, Richard, ed. *John Cage: An Anthology*. 1970. New York: Da Capo, 1991.

Lake, Steve. Liner notes. *Machine Gun*. Peter Brötzmann Octet. Rec. 1968. FMP CD24, 1990.

Lateef, Yusef A. "The pleasures of voice in improvised music." *Views on Black American Music. Selected Proceedings from the Fourteenth, Fifteenth, Sixteenth and Seventeenth Annual Black Musicians' Conferences, University of Massachusetts at Amherst. No 3,1985–1988*. Ed. Roberta Thelwell. Amherst: 1988.43–46.

LeBaron, Anne. "Reflections of Surrealism in Postmodern Musics." *Postmodern Music, Postmodern Thought*. Eds. Judy Lochhead and Joseph Auner. New York: Routledge, 2002. 27–73.

Levin, Michael, and John S. Wilson. "No Bop Roots in Jazz: Parker." *Down Beat* 9 Sept. 1949. Rpt. *Down Beat* 61.2 (1994): 24–26.

Lewis, George. Afterword. "Improvised Music After 1950: Afrological and Eurological Perspectives." *The Other Side of Nowhere: Jazz, Improvisation, and Communities in Dialogue.* Eds. Daniel Fischlin and Ajay Heble. Middletown: Wesleyan UP, 2004. 163–72.

——. *"Gittin' to know y'all:* Von improvisierter Musik, vom Treffen der Kulturen und von der 'racial imagination.'" *Jazz und Gesellschaft: Sozialgeschichtliche Aspekte des Jazz.* Ed. Wolfram Knauer. Hofheim: Wolke-Verlag, 2002. 213–47.

——. "Improvised Music After 1950: Afrological and Eurological Perspectives." *The Other Side of Nowhere: Jazz, Improvisation, and Communities in Dialogue.* Eds. Daniel Fischlin and Ajay Heble. Middletown: Wesleyan UP, 2004. 131–62.

——. "Singing Omar's Song: A (Re)construction of Great Black Music." *Lenox Avenue,* 4 (1998): 69–92.

Lipsitz, George. *The Possessive Investment in Whiteness: How White People Profit from Identity Politics.* Philadelphia: Temple UP, 1998.

Litweiler, John. *The Freedom Principle: Jazz after 1958.* New York: Da Capo, 1984.

Noglik, Bert. *Klangspuren: Wege improviserter Musik.* Frankfurt am Main: Fischer Taschenbuch Verlag, 1992.

Nunn, Tom. *Wisdom of the Impulse: On the Nature of Musical Free Improvisation.* San Francisco: Self-published, 1998.

"Own Thing: Drei vom Manfred Schoof Quintett in einem JP Gespräch." *Jazz Podium* 3/XV (1966): 66–69.

Poggioli, Renato. *The Theory of the Avant-Garde.* Trans. Gerald Fitzgerald. Cambridge, MA: Belknap, 1968.

Radano, Ronald M. "Jazzin' the Classics: the AACM's Challenge to Mainstream Aesthetics." *Black Music Research Journal* 12.1 (1992): 79–95.

——. *New Musical Figurations: Anthony Braxton's Cultural Critique.* Chicago: U of Chicago P, 1993.

Radano, Ronald, and Philip V. Bohlman, eds. *Music and the Racial Imagination.* Chicago: U of Chicago P, 2000.

Schlippenbach, Alexander von. "Onze Européens parlent de leur musique." Interview with Didier Pennequin. *Jazz Magazine* 220 (1974): 18.

Schmidt-Joos, Siegfried. "Weil viele Dinge geändert werden müssen: Ein Gespräch mit Peter Brötzmann." *Jazz Podium* 4/XVII (1968): 128–29.

Slobin, Mark. *Subcultural Sounds: Micromusics of the West.* Hanover (NH): Wesleyan UP, 1993.

Smith, Leo. *Notes (8 pieces); source – a new world music: creative music.* Connecticut: Self-published, 1973.

Spivak, Gayatri Chakravorty. "Can the subaltern speak?" *Marxism and the Interpretation of Culture.* Eds. Cary Nelson and Lawrence Grossberg. Urbana: U of Illinois P, 1988. 271–313.

Stanyek, Jason. "Articulating Intercultural Free Improvisation: Evan Parker's Synergetics Project." *Resonance* 7.2 (1999): 44–47.

——. "Transmissions of an Interculture: Pan-African Jazz and Intercultural Improvisation." *The Other Side of Nowhere: Jazz, Improvisation, and Communities in Dialogue.* Eds. Daniel Fischlin and Ajay Heble. Middletown: Wesleyan UP, 2004. 87–130.

Stockhausen, Karlheinz. *Texte zur Musik 1963–1970.* Köln: DuMont Schauberg, 1971.

Stovall, Tyler. *Paris Noir: African Americans in the City of Light.* New York: Houghton Mifflin, 1996.

Taylor, Arthur. *Notes and Tones: Musician-to-Musician Interviews.* 1977. New York: Da Capo, 1993.

Toop, David. "A New Style of Improvisation That Spurns All Constraints." *New York Times* 13 May 2001. B19.

Yogananda, Paramahansa. *Autobiography of a Yogi.* 1946. Los Angeles: Self-realization Fellowship, 1981.

38 Kinship, Intelligence, and Memory as Improvisation

Culture and Performance in New Orleans

Joseph Roach

Joseph Roach is an experienced stage director as well as theatre historian and scholar of performance studies. His publications include *Cities of the Dead: Circum-Atlantic Performance*, *The Player's Passion: Studies in the Science of Acting*, and essays published in a wide range of scholarly journals. He is the editor (with Janelle Reinelt) of *Critical Theory and Performance* and *Changing the Subject: Marvin Carlson and Theatre Studies, 1959–2009*. Roach is the recipient of a Lifetime Distinguished Scholar Award from the American Society for Theatre Research, and a Distinguished Achievement Award from the Andrew W. Mellon Foundation. In 2009, he was awarded an honorary Doctor of Letters from the University of Warwick (UK) and the Fletcher Jones Distinguished Fellowship from the Huntington Library. He is currently Sterling Professor of Theater and English at Yale. "Kinship, Intelligence, and Memory as Improvisation" contrasts famous New Orleans performance traditions with the controversy around the city's Liberty Place Monument to offer keen insights about English literature as a colonising force, about the famous Mardi Gras as political theatre, and about "the doublings and inversions" of performance as precursor to political overthrow.

Key words: theatre; social change; memory; Richard Schechner; Margaret Thompson Drewal; racial politics

On 14 September 1874, an armed force under the direction of an organization called the Crescent City White League carried out a bloody *coup d'état* against Louisiana Governor William Pitt Kellogg and his racially integrated administration. The authors of the blueprint for the event, the "Platform of the Crescent City White League," included Fred Nash Ogden, the former Confederate officer who would lead over 8,000 paramilitary volunteers against the state government's Metropolitan Police and Negro Militia. The "Platform" proclaimed in advance the victory of what its authors called "that just and legitimate superiority in the administration of our State affairs to which we are entitled by superior responsibility, superior numbers and superior intelligence." Although Governor Kellogg survived to be reinstated by Federal troops several days later, Reconstruction in Louisiana was soon effectively aborted, and the era of Southern Redemption begun.

Phrased in the past tense, this account disguises a continuous reenactment of a deep cultural performance that many New Orleanians call the present. Over the past several years, as the city has contended with the legalities of integrating the "Old Line" Mardi Gras organizations, which date from the nineteenth century, another, closely related issue has festered in city council chambers, on editorial pages, and in the streets: the disposition of the "Liberty Monument," an obelisk erected to honor the perpetrators of the terrorist *coup* of 1874. On this stage of contested but collective memory, intensified by the political rise of former Klansman David Duke, the city of New Orleans has made a national spectacle of its cultural politics, going over some of the same ground it covered 100 years ago when *Plessy v. Ferguson,* the Louisiana public accommodations lawsuit that challenged Jim Crow, provided the United States Supreme Court with the occasion to establish "separate but equal" as the law of the land.

In writing this essay about a particularly volatile form of local knowledge – the rites and secular rituals of a performance-saturated interculture – I have two, more general goals.

First, without in any way diminishing the importance of any one of the more familiar categories of difference and exclusion that cultural studies surveys, I want to apply current trends in the emerging field of performance studies to suggest how categories of race, class, gender, and sexuality may be produced by (and remain imbedded in) complex networks of other measures of human difference. Based on my research into the local conditions of cultural performance in New Orleans, I have chosen kinship, intelligence, and memory to represent these other measures. They are no more or less constructed, no more or less essential, no more or less naturalized than other rubrics within human taxonomies, but they have remained far less prominent in discussions of alterity. Like other culturally encoded categories of difference, tradition insists on the rootedness of kinship, intelligence, and memory in "Nature," even – or perhaps especially – when the facts of their constructedness within cultural and social norms may be explicitly demonstrated. The secret history of Mardi Gras in New Orleans documents this process of naturalization by exposing putatively timeless annual rituals as contingent improvisations.

Second, I preface my account of this historical instance of culture as performance with a version of the development of performance studies as an interdisciplinary (or post-disciplinary) methodology. Not entirely by coincidence, this history also involves New Orleans. As a framework for my account, I am adopting Richard Schechner's definition of performance, set forth most comprehensively in *Between Theater and Anthropology* (1985), as "restored behavior" or "twice-behaved behavior" – (re)presentations that can be rehearsed, repeated, and, above all, recreated (35–116). The concept of restored behavior emerges from the cusp of the arts and human sciences as the process wherein cultures understand themselves reflexively and whereby they explain themselves to others. Theater, as a high-culture form, remains important in this formulation as a genre with a rich theoretical lexicon, in light of which the cultural significance of other performance modes may be interpreted (Beeman, Balme). The concept of the restoration of behavior extends performance to include what Brooks McNamara terms "invisible theater" and Michel de Certeau calls the "practice of everyday life." Looked at in this light, literature itself (and not just dramatic literature) may be understood as the historic archive of restored behavior, the repository and the medium of transmission of performative tropes like Mary Poovey's proper lady, say, or Karen Halttunen's confidence man.

I want further to limit my definition of performance, however, by adopting John J. MacAloon's restriction, proposed in the preface to *Rite, Drama, Festival, Spectacle: Rehearsals Toward a Theory of Cultural Performance* (1984). MacAloon argues that performance is a particular class or subset of restored behavior "in which one or more persons assume responsibility to an audience and to tradition as they understand it." This qualifier adds not only an element of self-consciousness (or "reflexivity") as an intensifying precondition for the raising of restored behavior to the level of cultural performance, but it also introduces an element of risk and risk-taking. "Performances are anything but routine," MacAloon continues: "By acknowledging responsibility to one another and to the traditions condensed and objectified in the 'scripts,' agents and audiences acknowledge a risk that things might not go well. To agree to perform is to agree to take a chance" (9). Performance thus entails a compact between actors and audience (even when their roles are rapidly handed back and forth, as in carnival), a compact that promises the production of certain mutually anticipated effects, but the stipulations of the compact are often subject to negotiation, adjustment, and even transformation. The range of human interactions defined within these limits delineates the field of performance studies, to which institutional history I now turn.

I

Theoretically speaking, performance studies, like jazz, can claim its status as an American invention. The formation of the field in the 1960s – including its predilection for the comparative juxtaposition of matrixed and nonmatrixed performances, its interest in street theater and non-scripted events, its valorization of popular entertainment and oral performance, and its methodological engagement with ethnographic, folkloric, and anthropological approaches – owes more than it has perhaps fully acknowledged to the Afro-Caribbean retentions and adaptations of New Orleans. My version of the disciplinary history of performance studies begins with the early years of *The Tulane Drama Review* (*TDR*), which, under Richard Schechner's editorship, "served as a sort of clearing-house of the new ideas, seeking out and encouraging new theoreticians and practitioners in America and spreading news of work in Europe and elsewhere" (Carlson 254). Among those new ideas was an expanded notion of what constituted a performance event, including non-scripted Happenings and ritual practices from many cultural traditions.

Quite apart from *TDR*, however, theater and drama had maintained from its disciplinary inception a receptiveness to cultural anthropology, largely stemming from the influence of Sir James Frazer on the Cambridge Ritualists – Jane Harrison, Gilbert Murray, and F. M. Cornford – who stressed the origin of drama in rites of death and renewal. Although these Hellenists worked with the texts of Attic tragedy and comedy, they imagined between the lines a world of forgotten gestures, intonations, practices, and meanings that "evolved" from the primordial rituals of vegetation worship, regicide, and sympathetic magic. They carried into the study of pre-history their version of the old anthropological distinction between civilized and savage on the basis of literacy. Because many of Frazer's key examples in *The Golden Bough* come from Africa, inscribed by the Cambridge Ritualists as "primitive" analogues to the origins of Greek theater, an interesting ligature developed in anticipation of Martin Bernal's *Black Athena: The Afroasiatic Roots of Classical Civilization* (1987), whereby the ritual fragments of African oral traditions re-oriented the received meaning of the most hallowed texts of the Eurocentric canon.

The Ritualist emphasis on the stasis and sacrificial conservatism of rites and rituals continued to inform the reigning teleology of theater history, which traced the evolutionary progress of drama in the West from "the sympathetic magic of 'primitive peoples' before the beginning of history to the Pisgah sights of European modernism at its end" (Reinelt and Roach 293). Most histories of the theater prefaced their accounts of the origins of the ancient theater with photographs of "tribal" rituals from around the world. These tribes presumably occupied a place in cultural evolution equivalent to that of the pre-history of Greece, or more precisely, they existed outside of time altogether as political nullities in a disconnected realm, untroubled by progress or even by history itself. Theater thus derived from anthropology one of the latter field's most troubling (and troubled) issues, what Johannes Fabian in *Time and the Other* calls the "denial of coevalness" between the anthropologist and his or her human "object" of study (31). Such chronopolitics of difference denied the cultural performances of traditional societies' participation in history, while at the same time they accepted the products of the anthropologists' or historians' own tradition as the aesthetic consummation of a most satisfactory evolution. In theater studies, this ethnocentric mind-set segregated the study of canonical forms, such as Greek or Elizabethan drama, for instance, from many of the world's most prolific performance genres.

In New Orleans, however, the elitist bias and Eurocentrism of these influences encountered a uniquely countervailing alternative in the popular culture of carnival, especially in the simultaneous interpenetration of European and African-American festive traditions. The topical presentness of these forms in the streets of an American city disrupted the denial of coevalness. The ethnographic "field" was not on another continent but in the next block, a block likely to be peopled by the creolized descendants of most European, African, and American extractions, but still divided by segregationist violence in law and custom. Given its role as a polyglot entrepôt on the circum-Caribbean rim, the historic collision of cultures in New Orleans has customarily been marked by public performances. The eye-popping juxtaposition of these events has the surrealistic effect of defamiliarizing the forms of one culture (making the familiar strange) in the very process whereby it increases understanding of others (making the strange familiar). In *The Future of Ritual* (1993), Richard Schechner looks back on those "seething public processions," such as the famous African-American "Zulu" parade, which, when he last saw it in the 1960s, translated the turbulence of the Civil Rights era into "black and gold painted coconuts [hurled] like cannonballs at white spectators" (74–75). The real show is clearly in the streets, and the participants annually enact therein a local version of intercultural co-production, which insists that their histories and identities, though distinctive in their own ways, do in fact overlap in many others.

Memory and history do not always or even often agree (Le Goff), for differing conventions and technologies of retention shape the contents as well as the form of remembrance. In a passage that has great resonance for the performance culture of New Orleans, Kwame Anthony Appiah's *In My Father's House: Africa in the Philosophy of Culture* (1992) describes the contested terrain of literacy at the modern juncture of African and European languages, and he concludes: "On the other side [orality], there are many devices for supporting the transmission of a complex and nuanced body of practice and belief without writing" (132). Performance studies attempts to find not only a way of writing about these "devices" but also a way of researching them by participating in them. Performance offers itself as an alternative or a supplement to textual mediation. A shared belief in the possibility of such participation links a variety of otherwise autonomous practitioners, though they may differ widely over methodological particulars (Hymes, Bauman and Briggs, Conquergood).

To this configuration of the field of performance studies, the work of Victor Turner remains generative. Turner's formative experience in the field was with the Ndembu people of Africa, among whom he developed his idea of "social dramas," the stagings and resolutions of conflicts within a society, which afford "a limited area of transparency in the otherwise opaque surface of regular, uneventful social life" (*Schism and Continuity* 93). As performances of and by the community, they are "at once the distillation and typification of its corporate identity" (*Celebration* 16). Perhaps most important of all, Turner's development of the Van Gennepian concept of liminality, the "threshold" stage of "becoming" in rites of passage, theorized an entire area for performance research. In an oft-cited and oft-critiqued experiment at New York University, Richard Schechner and Turner adapted Ndembu initiation rituals for use in a co-led workshop on liminal experience (*From Ritual to Theatre* 89–101). I do not accept the dismissive characterization of such intercultural experiments as "naive and unexamined ethnocentricity" (Bharucha 14), but neither do I view them as unproblematic. Nor did Schechner and Turner. In such a transfer of ritual practices from their source, and in the particular cultural appropriation of African "corporate identity" that such an experiment performs, the anthropologist-directors re-enacted the secret history of the field that they were engaged in inventing: performance studies as the restoration of borrowed African behaviors in the radically redefined contexts of the postmodern global interculture. They attempted the cross-cultural transfer of memory without writing, and in the proposed reflexivity of their embodiment, the Ndembu appeared only to disappear in the project of improvising somebody new.

That is one reason why the question of improvisation remains one of the pressing issues on the interdisciplinary agenda of performance studies today. The idea of improvisation adds the element of reflexive self-invention to the matrix of repetition described by the concept of restored behavior. It troubles the inherent conservatism attributed to ritual by Turner's concept of the "social drama." The importance of improvisation in ritual is elaborated by Margaret Thompson Drewal in her important book on West African performance, *Yoruba Ritual: Performers, Play, Agency* (1992, with video supplement). Drawing upon Linda Hutcheon's theory of parody as repetition with a critical distance (and difference) and Henry Louis Gates, Jr.'s analysis of Jelly Roll Morton's riff on Scott Joplin ("Maple Leaf Rag [A Transformation]"), Drewal examines the importance of transformational improvisation in Yoruba ritual praxis "as *repetition with revision*" (2–6, her emphasis). Improvisation introduces a space for play within memory itself and, as Drewal's title suggests, for agency within the performative compact of traditions and conventions of restored behavior.

Outside of Afrocentric traditions of "signifying" – which foreground the signifier to dramatize both the presence and the adaptability of remembered affiliations (Gates; cf. Berliner 257) – the most intriguing point about the ubiquity of improvisation in performance, especially Eurocentric performance, is that its memory is so often erased by its very success. The present stabilizes the past by representing itself as the inevitable consummation of deliberate steps, but to do this it must smooth over the unbidden eruptions necessary to its own creation. Not only are African forms forgotten, but also effaced are the traces of the process whereby improvisation celebrates (not negates) memory. This retroactive solemnification of the marriage between ritual and amnesia is elegantly summarized in Franz Kafka's miniature parable: "Leopards break into the temple and drink the sacrificial chalices dry; this occurs repeatedly, again and again: finally it can be reckoned on beforehand and becomes part of the ceremony" (qtd. States 40). Improvisation and its erasure figure prominently in the struggle between the intertwined performance traditions of New Orleans, as I hope to demonstrate. In so doing, I offer the disclosure of suppressed improvisations as a method of cultural critique.

II

The carnival krewes originated among English-speaking New Orleanians in the mid-nineteenth century in order to establish a more socially regulated alternative to promiscuous masking of Creole Mardi Gras (Young). Formed along with exclusive men's clubs, such ostensibly festive organizations as the Mistick Krewe of Comus and the sub-sequent krewes of Momus, Proteus, and Rex have set the social tone for New Orleans since the post-Reconstruction era (Kinser, Mitchell, O'Brien). Their rites of passage offer a rich array of ethnographic and historical materials that highlight performance as the principal mode whereby elite cultures produce themselves by contrast with the excluded.

One informative document is a privately printed, first-person account by William J. Behan, wholesale grocer and sugar factor, later mayor of the city of New Orleans, of his 1871 initiation into the original and most exclusive krewe, the Mistick Krewe of Comus, whose membership was and is secret, and its co-extensive social arm, the Pickwick Club. Behan recalls:

> At that time, when a duly elected member was presented to the Pickwick Club, he was met by the Sergeant-at-Arms, booted and spurred, and equipped with the largest and fiercest-looking saber which could be found. The position of Sergeant-at-Arms was filled by the most robust member of' the Krewe, and one whom nature had endowed with the most sonorous basso-profundo voice to be heard on the operatic stage. He was an awe-inspiring figure, and the spirit of the new-comer quailed within him, as he was led blindfolded, into the darkened and mysterious chamber where the ceremony of initiation was to take place. The room was draped with sable curtains, and ornamented (if such a word can apply) with owls, deaths heads, cross-bones and similar blood-curdling devices. Behind the curtains, the merry Krewe of Comus was concealed, but never was this reassuring fact suspected until having administered the oath to the aspirant, the President asked in a loud and solemn voice: "Are you willing that this stranger be admitted," and then a mighty and unanimous roar burst forth from behind the curtains: "We are," and the curtains were drawn back, disclosing the merrymakers. Now, the room was flooded with light, solemnity yielded to hilarity, and the evening waxed merrier and merrier, for the "Big Mug" had been discovered, filled with the wine of the gods, for Comus and his Krewe.
>
> (2)

It is perhaps challenging to keep in mind that the performers in this social drama are not boys, in possession of a tree house, but grown men – social, commercial, and civic leaders of a city that was then reconstituting itself as an Anglo-American version of a Latin-Caribbean capital. By Behan's account, the Comus initiation follows the classic pattern of rites of passage – separation, liminality, and reincorporation – and his hearty effort to take the whole affair lightly conceals neither the serious purposes of homosocial affiliation that the rite reaffirms, nor the oligarchical entitlements afforded by membership in the community that it secretly and selectively enlarges.

The Pickwick Club and the Krewe of Comus exerted social discipline over the families of the New Orleans elite by a system of rigorous black-balling in which fathers controlled the marriageability of one another's daughters – and hence the uppercrust's densely endogamous kinship networks – by minutely regulating both club membership and the annual invitations to the coming-out balls of the Mardi Gras social season (Ryan). In the useful *Hand-Book of Carnival*, furnished by J. Curtis Waldo in 1873, the secret rites of social selection of the Mistick Krewe of Comus are explained in relationship to its public parades at Mardi Gras:

> Not only have the gorgeous and fantastic processions been the occasion of an out-door demonstration on the part of almost the entire population, but the tableaux and ball

which terminate the evening's festivities have ever been a subject of the deepest anxiety with a certain class of our population. The beautiful and costly cards of invitation and the mysterious manner of their distribution, combine with the social position of those selected, to invest this part of the entertainment with a still deeper interest. It has grown to be a recognized evidence of caste to be the recipient of one of these mysterious biddings, and here is the sole clue we have to the character of the organization.

(6–7)

Waldo's choice of the word *ever* to describe a practice that had been instituted fourteen years earlier (and had been interrupted by the Civil War) shows how by 1873 the intruding leopards had established themselves in the memory of some as eternal consumers at the ritual chalices of Mardi Gras.

William J. Behan's initiation to the Krewe of Comus and the Club of Pickwick in 1871 and Waldo's sycophantic *Hand-Book* of 1873 offer revelatory insights into the self-creation (out of little more than their supposed intelligence, really) of a dominant social elite. As fictive kin, they invented themselves through restored behavior – repetition with revision – the improvisatory quality of which has since receded from the living memory of their descendants, but not from their family memoirs. In the mid-nineteenth century, their records disclose, they underwent a kind of collective puberty, a self-dramatizing and even violent quest for identity and position. Victor Turner's elaboration of Van Gennep's classic study of tribal rites of passage led him to the crucial concept of liminality, a "betwixt and betweenness," the vulnerable state that precedes (yet is indispensable to) full acceptance by the group. The word *liminal* well describes many of the Anglo-American New Orleanians of mid-century, as they invented their own traditions of social selection amidst the failing memories of the creolized interculture they appropriated and then replaced (Hirsch and Logsdon).

William J. Behan, the vulnerable "new-comer" whose spirit "quailed" before the awe-inspiring paraphernalia of the threshold between inclusion and exclusion, stands in symbolically for many others. I have found the names and addresses of twenty-seven of the original Comus members of 1857, their homes and offices, and all are representative of an ill-defined assortment of American opportunists, a number from Mobile, Alabama, drawn to New Orleans between the Louisiana Purchase and the Civil War, to seek their fortunes. A memorandum from the daughter of the first president of the Pickwick Club records the addresses as well as the professions of the founders – steamboat agents, accountants, lawyers, produce wholesalers, and a "cotton pickery" – in all eighteen merchants, four professionals, three bankers, and two unknowns (Werlein Memorandum, Churchill Family Papers). Most have distinctly English-sounding names (there is an Addison, a Pope, and a Newton among the founders), but others, like Behan, who joined after the Civil War, are Irish or Scottish.

In antebellum New Orleans, such American fortune-hunters, once contemptuously sneered at as "Kaintucks" and "Riverboatmen," countered the old lineage and established caste system of the francophone Creoles by advertising frequently and shrilly their intrinsic merit based on intelligence. They contrasted Yankee ingenuity – in manufacturing and marketing goods, in draining swamps and digging canals, in building houses and laying down trolley lines – with what they took to be Creole decadence, sloth, and stupidity. The self-inventing, improvisatory rhetoric of the period still resonates in a privately printed history of the Mistick Krewe of Comus, compiled to celebrate its centenary year: "The people of

New Orleans are under three influences – the French, the Spanish, and the Anglo-Saxon. The Spanish influence is especially shown in the early architecture of the city, the French influence by the manner and customs of the people, the Anglo-Saxon by aggressiveness in developing the commercial and business growth of the city" (Herndon 6). The strong signifier of superior aggression and superior industry sets apart the category pompously labeled Anglo-Saxon, concealing its rag-tag origins, the teeming refuse of several distant shores.

The collective rite of passage for this ill-defined group – and the demonstration of its supposed intelligence – was an improvisation on a borrowed theme. In the 1850s, the Anglo-Americans reinvented "Mardi Gras": Comus began the tradition (unbroken except by war and police-strikes until 1992) of elaborate float parades and tableau balls, which resembled royal entries and masques of Renaissance princes, to supplant the willy-nilly bacchanal of Latin carnival. Early on, this was a very fluid kind of association of fictive kin – mostly young men, mostly wholesalers, who met regularly "Uptown" at John Pope's drug store on the corner of Jackson and Prytania streets – as yet neither a class nor a caste, but rather an imagined kinship network founded upon mutual appreciation for one another's industry, invention, and powers of organization. The founding president's daughter sets the scene:

> New Orleans in 1857 was but a comparatively small place spread over a very considerable area and divided into a number of small districts, each of the latter being either under separate administrations or were recently become a part of the City. It was not an unusual thing then, as it is now in small cities, for the better element of young business and professional men to gather of an evening at the leading drug store and to sit or stand around, smoke a cigar and pass a few words with one another before returning to their work or going elsewhere. ... At that time this neighborhood was the centre of the then new residential district; there resided the well-to-do American (as opposed to the French) residents of the City. ... [At John Pope's drug store] the early affairs of the Mystic Krewe of Comus were doubtless frequently discussed; and it was here that the inception of the Pickwick Club was made.
>
> (Werlein Memorandum 2–3)

Reinventing Creole carnival prior to and immediately following the Civil War was an improvisation, a repetition with revision, a space for play, in which the homosocial kin, hanging out together at the local drug store, decided to transform their world by building a club house and conspicuously over-spending on party hats and *papier-mâché*.

One strong proof for this assertion resides, I believe, in the privileged role of English literature in the krewe's early attempts to accumulate cultural capital to assert anglophone pre-eminence. The name "Comus" derives from the stately masque of the same name by John Milton. The first procession of the Mistick Krewe of Comus in 1857 impersonated "The Demon Actors in Milton's *Paradise Lost*." Another early Comus parade took up Spenser's *Faerie Queene,* and, according to J. Curtis Waldo, in his later *History of the Carnival in New Orleans* (1882), "illustrated in appropriate groupings the principal episode of that delicate and fanciful creation, which, in the centuries that have elapsed since its birth, has lost no beauty or splendor by comparison" (12). Without completely ruling out the possibility that Spenser's epic romance spoke urgently to the hearts of New Orleans dry-goods merchants, the more likely explanation is that they were claiming kin, performing their intelligence with learned citations. The "Pickwick Club," of course, quoted Charles Dickens, suggesting its generous openness to the good-hearted members of a motley krewe. The by-laws of the club explain that it was formed by Comus members "to give continuity to comradeship born under the mask" and to "conceal the secrets of their other identity" (*The Pickwick Club* 3).

That "other identity," like the ritual staging of Behan's initiation, mixes menace with mirth. Underneath the veneer of boyish self-invention seethed a deep capacity for violence, soon to be tested: "Most of the membership exchanged billiard cue for the musket and offered their lives for the Southern Cause" (*The Pickwick Club* 4). They returned in bitter defeat to find the city of New Orleans occupied by Federal troops, with blacks and creoles of color soon thereafter seeking important public offices and the reconstructionist Republicans able to remain at least nominally in charge. The response of the club and krewe membership to this state of affairs was a campaign of armed terrorism, culminating in the *coup* of 1874. My research has confirmed in detail what many native New Orleanians generally know as a commonplace: that the officer corps of the White League (and a not insignificant number of its rank and file) formed an interlocking directorship with the secret membership of the exclusive Mardi Gras krewes and men's clubs, especially Comus-Pickwick. Like the Ku Klux Klan elsewhere in the South, the carnival krewes took advantage of their "comradeship under the mask" to assert the entitlements of their group, most obviously against blacks, but eventually against others with whom they made temporary alliances of convenience: the Crescent City White League had a separate regiment into which Italians were segregated, for instance, and another for the Irish. Unlike the Klan, the krewes have ever since maintained a strict standard of exclusion by caste. By confirming the roster of White Leaguers in Augusto Miceli's *The Pickwick Club of New Orleans,* privately printed in 1964, with *The Roll of Honor: Roster of the Citizen Soldiery Who Saved Louisiana*, compiled in 1877 by carnival historian J. Curtis Waldo, I have confirmed a list of over 120 names of Comus-Pickwickians who took up arms to fight "The Battle of Liberty Place" in 1874.

First on Waldo's *Roll of Honor* is Major General Fred Nash Ogden, the hemp merchant and member of the Pickwick Club (Miceli Appendix "J"). Ogden was a Confederate veteran, cited for valor at Vicksburg, and the coauthor of the "Platform of the Crescent City White League," which denounced the "stupid Africanization" of Reconstruction, whereby "the negro has proved himself as destitute of common gratitude as of common sense." Next on the list of heroes is Brigadier General William J. Behan, the wholesale grocer, also a wounded veteran of Gettysburg, whose brother was killed at Antietam on his eighteenth birthday, and whose Van Gennepian rite of passage into Comus and the Pickwick Club has already been cited. Most ominously, however, in terms of the history of American race relations in the twentieth century, was the armed service of a young lawyer in Company E of the Second Regiment, "Louisiana's Own" (*Roll of Honor* 24): Edward Douglass White, later Justice and ultimately Chief Justice of the Supreme Court of the United States, who joined the majority opinion in *Plessy v. Ferguson*. Justice White was also a member of the Pickwick Club and perforce the Mistick Krewe (Miceli Appendix "J").

To historians of cultural performance, the most fascinating phenomenon to emerge from this juncture of *coup* and carnival is the way in which Comus rehearsed the former by improvising the latter. At Mardi Gras in 1873, eighteen months prior to the "The Battle of Liberty Place," the theme for the Krewe of Comus parade and ball was "The Missing Links to Darwin's *Origin of Species*." It presented animal-like caricatures of hated public figures from Reconstruction, such as Ulysses S. Grant as a verminous potato bug or the

"Radical" J. R. Pitkin as "The Cunning Fox [carrying a carpetbag] which joins the Coon." This taxonomy, arranged by phyla in a parodic version of "survival of the fittest," culminated in the mock crowning of the "The Gorilla," a caricature of the Negro Lt. Governor of Louisiana, strumming a banjo with hairy paws, as the "Missing Link of Darwin's Eden." In the tradition of carnivalesque inversion, the lowest changed places with the highest, but this "topsy-turvydom" mocked the regime that supposedly had created its own Lords of Misrule by placing black people in positions of power over whites in the first place. The White League's "Platform" denounced Reconstruction as "the most absurd inversion of the relations of race," and its members volunteered to set the State of Louisiana right-side up again by turning it up-side down.

The sense of doubleness provoked by this inversion, however, played itself out in the form of a weird kind of identification through disguise. White carnival during Reconstruction took on the mask of blackness to protest what it saw as the injustice of its postwar abjection and exclusion from power. The Krewe of Momus, for instance, representing a mounted battalion of Moors in blackface, performed such a drama of protest in their street parade for Mardi Gras of 1873: "Trooping down the streets of an American City, between rows of stately modern edifices, came the dusky battalions of the race who could not be conquered, and who fought with blind savagery for things they only prized because the hated Christians desired it. Their swarthy faces and barbaric splendour of their trappings recalled the vanished centuries" (Waldo, *Hand-Book* 60). In the collective memory of both blacks and whites under slavery, the historic license of carnival had provided a locus in which rebellions in the name of Liberty could at least be imagined, if not implemented. In Martin Delany's abolitionist novel, *Blake; or, the Huts of America* (1859), the threat of a slave revolt flickers amidst the "games, shows, exhibitions, theatrical performances, festivals, masquerade balls, and numerous entertainments and gatherings" on the eve of Mardi Gras in New Orleans: "It was on this account that the Negroes had been allowed such unlimited privileges this evening. Nor were they remiss to the utmost extent of its advantages" (98–99). Delany evokes the memory of the best-organized slave revolt in North American history, the Louisiana rising of 1811, when, during carnival season, a force of over 500 freedom fighters marched on New Orleans under Haitian officers with flags unfurled and drums beating (Hofstadter and Wallace 190). The restoration of behavior that such an adventure inspires reappears through the doublings and inversions of white carnival: the face of the "fittest" behind the black mask of the gorilla representing Darwin's "Missing Link" certainly belonged to a member of the Mistick Krewe of Comus, perhaps to Brigadier General Behan himself, who was known to have taken a masked role in the parade (Miceli Appendix "H").

There is no question that the insanity of American racial politics dominated this event, but there also flourished at its heart an invented and symbolic kinship, performed in the rites of fraternal initiation of New Orleanian krewes, performed again in the streets as Mardi Gras parades, rehearsed as acts of homosocial bonding in carnival disguise, and then restored as behavior in storming the gates of the statehouse. In their own words, they forged their bond on the strength of their "superior intelligence." In their own imagery, they took the risks implicit in the compact of performance, the rite of passage, the admission behind the curtains into social power. In their own lethal festival, they enacted the rites of kinship through violence. Back from Gettysburg and Vicksburg, but still playing war, these boy-men and their sons and younger brothers occupied New Orleans, reinvented it, and reenacted it annually. In the expansion of restored behavior to the level of reflexive cultural performance, in the mystifying production of social identity and difference, one initiation ceremony may inquire for thousands, "Are you willing that this stranger be admitted?" – to which an invisible chorus may or may not then answer, "We are."

III

On 15 June 1993, the Advisory Committee on Human Relations, which reports to the New Orleans City Council, held a hearing on the disposition of the "Liberty Place Monument." Erected at the height of Jim Crow and Southern Redemption in the 1890s, the monument lionized the White League and elevated to martyrdom the handful who lost their lives in its cause. In connection with street improvements in 1989, the monument had been removed and placed in storage, where it remained until a lawsuit by "historic pre-servationists" forced the city reluctantly to re-erect it (Eggler B–1). Contemplating its removal for the second time on the grounds that it represented a "nuisance" and that it honored those who had shot dead a number of city and state policemen, the New Orleans City Council asked its Advisory Committee on Human Relations to render an opinion on memories evoked by the monument and their impact on the city's "great cosmopolitan population consisting of large numbers of people of every race, color, creed, religion, age, physical condition, national origin and ancestry" ("Scope of the HRC Hearings"). As carnival itself was the subject of a heated integration controversy, the monument became the scene of a number of demonstrations, counter-demonstrations, and confrontations.

As a study in the performance of memory, the hearing of 15 June, which was chaired by Rabbi Edward P. Cohn, provided moments of breath-taking improvisation that coagulated, before the eyes of the onlookers, into law and history. Speaking in support of the preservationist Friends of the Liberty Monument was David Duke, former Klansman and Nazi enthusiast, who celebrated Adolph Hitler's birthday as recently as 1988 and whose run for the U.S. Senate and then the Louisiana Governorship attracted a majority of the white votes cast in both elections. Duke's testimony touched only indirectly on the White League and not at all on the carnival krewes, whose members, in any case, have despised white-trash opportunists since the days of John Pope's drug store. Speaking of what he called "the true meaning of the monument," Duke cited the battles of Lexington and Concord as the real precedents invoked by the Battle of Liberty Place and its cenotaph: there the patriotic "Minutemen" fought and died for their freedom against the occupying forces of "tyranny." Removing the Liberty Monument would be tantamount to desecrating statues of Washington and Jefferson, he continued, which would be defacing public property symbolizing "Liberty" itself, an act with dire consequences. To remove the Monument would be to rewrite history, argued Duke, who denies the Holocaust: "Then we don't have a civilization any more. We have a jungle."

The slippage that conjured the "Founding Fathers" out of the self-congratulatory erection honoring silk-stockinged rioters starkly illustrates the convenience of Eurocentric memory, which serves to erase the troubling evidence of intervening improvisations by direct appeal to origins. To Duke this distinction suggested a choice between the alternatives of "civilization" and "jungle." Carried away by his defense of American civilization against a rising tide of barbarism, he likened the opponents of the monument to "book-burning Nazis." Rabbi Cohn interrupted the testimony at this point to ask with perfect chairmanly decorum, as if clarifying an obscure phrase for the record, "Nazis, Mr. Duke? Pardon me, but did I hear you say 'Nazis'?" Duke nodded affirmatively but with apparent confusion; then he continued his eulogy, paraphrasing, without attribution and perhaps accidentally, the "mystic chords of memory" passage from Lincoln's First Inaugural Address.

A silent witness to the 15 June hearing was city council member-at-large Dorothy Mae Taylor, who was instrumental in framing and passing the 1991 civil rights ordinance that prompted Comus, Momus, and Proteus to end their Mardi Gras parades, even though the intent of council's legislation was to end segregation, not celebration. Her silence was eloquent. Taylor's leadership, which was visited by more denunciations and ridicule than support, even from some of the other council members who had voted for the ordinance (Vennman, "Boundary Face-Off" 89–104), was forged in the crucible in New Orleans racial politics in the 1960s (Hirsch and Logsdon 262–319). Taylor's record in this regard seemed to fall prey to collective amnesia. The 1991 ordinance developed logically from the civil rights legislation of the 1960s, and indeed from the historic argument of fair and equal access to public accommodations. Even before the final and softened version of the ordinance had been made law, however, the krewes of Comus, Momus, and Proteus cancelled their 1992 parades, and many New Orleanians blamed Taylor for trashing carnival tradition. The Mardi Gras festivities of the three krewes continue now only in private as debutante balls behind closed doors (and here and there in the form of some guerrilla-style street parading, lampooning city council members and others).

The society pages of the local paper report on the symbolism and iconography of these festivities, however. In the 1993–94 season, the Harlequins, a youth Mardi Gras affiliate of the Old-Line krewes, staged a most pointed pageant. On the surface, the film *Jurassic Park* seemed to provide a theme for the preliminary training-debut of the Harlequin Queen and the Maids of her Court. Underneath the surface, an explicit restoration of behavior evoked the local creation myths of race and caste:

> As the tableau began, several Jurassic species, including the Comusaurus, the Proteadactyl and Momusraptor, were seen meandering through the primeval forests. They were being watched by "modern man," who was confident that his science, his culture, his civilization, were superior to that of these ancient beasts. Man's confidence led him to believe that times were changing, that ancient species should die off and be replaced, and that the dinosaurs must go. Darwin's ghost looked down upon the scene with a wry grin, and the end of the reign of the dinosaurs was proclaimed. But then something went awry. The dinosaurs refused to accept their fate and rose up in rebellion, proclaiming that they too had rights. Modern man was unable to dominate them and in the end, the dinosaurs were left to themselves.
>
> ("Primeval partying" E–3)

On the liminal occasion of a rite of passage that serves to mark acceptance of its initiates into society and announce their availability for exchange within its patriarchal kinship network, the soon-to-be marriageable daughters of the krewes performed a most precise embodiment of selective cultural memory. The Darwinian anxiety about being replaced by another "species" directly quotes the Mistick Krewe of Comus 1873 parade and grand tableau: "The Missing Links to Darwin's *Origin of Species*." The "rebellion" of the dinosaurs, justified by a proclamation of their "rights," makes a clear reference to the coup of 1874 and its enactment of "the survival of the fittest" at the expense of the racially mixed Kellogg government.

There are no trivial rituals. In the service of memory, or in its betrayal, performances have powerful, if often unpredictable consequences. Knowing nothing of the Mistick Krewe of Comus Mardi Gras parade and ball of 1873, historians of constitutional law stress the importance of the almost magical sway of "Social Darwinism" over the Supreme Court of the United States at the turn of the century (Highshaw 64–65), particularly in the opinions rendered by Justice Edward Douglass White, Pickwickian, formerly Private White, Company E, Crescent City White League. Many other influences, no doubt, shaped the Justice White's reasoning in *Plessy v. Ferguson*, but probably none more exhilarating to one who regarded himself as speaking for the "fittest" than the overthrow of Reconstruction in Louisiana by Carnival in New Orleans.

Of the persistence of memory about "The Battle of Liberty Place" among the descendants of the White Leaguers, historian Lawrence N. Powell has written: "For decades to come, their sons and grandsons – even granddaughters – felt compelled to measure themselves against the legend born that humid September afternoon" (Powell B-7). From the intense dialogue between the illusion of rote repetition, which erases the memory of improvisation, and repetition with revision, which foregrounds it, performance studies gets a critical edge. The future of ritual, however, remains uncertain and deeply contested. As of this writing, the Liberty Monument still stands in New Orleans, a shrine not only to the Pyrrhic re-enactment of "comradeship born under the mask," but also to the implacable erasure of improvisation that occurs when memory turns to stone.

References and Select Bibliography

Primary Sources

Behan, William J., "Pickwick Club Reminiscences," New Orleans: privately printed, 1912. Louisiana Collection, Tulane University Library.

Delany, Martin R., *Blake: or, The Huts of America* (1859–61), Boston: Beacon Press, 1970.

Eggler, Bruce, "Barthelemy: Monument will be re-erected," New Orleans *Time-Picayune*, 22 Sept 1992, B-1\-\2.

Herndon, Thomas C., "One Hundred Years of Comus: Report of the Historical Committee of the M. K. C," 1956–57, Rogers Family Papers, Manuscripts Division, Tulane University Library.

Miceli, Augusto P., *The Pickwick Club of New Orleans*, New Orleans: The Pickwick Press, 1964. Historic New Orleans Collection.

The Pickwick Club: Historical Summary, Act of Incorporation, By-Laws and Roster of Membership, New Orleans: privately printed, 1929. Churchill Family Papers, Manuscripts Division, Tulane University Library.

"Platform of the Crescent City White League of New Orleans," New Orleans, 27 June 1874. Fred Nash Ogden Papers, Manuscripts Division, Tulane University Library.

"Primeval partying for Harlequins," New Orleans *Times-Picayune*, 29 Dec. 1993, E-3.

"Scope of the HRC 'Liberty Monument' Hearings," Human Relations Commission, Advisory Committee on Human Relations, City of New Orleans, 15 June 1993.

Waldo, J. Curtis, *Hand-Book of Carnival, containing Mardi Gras, its Ancient and Modern Observance. History of the Mistick Krewe of Comus, Twelfth Night Revelers and Knights of Momus, With Annals of the Reign of His Majesty the King of Carnival in New Orleans*, New Orleans: W. E. Seebold, 1873. Historic New Orleans Collection.

——*History of the Carnival in New Orleans, 1857–1882*, New Orleans: L. Graham & Son, 1882. Louisiana Collection, Tulane University Library.

——*The Roll of Honor of the Citizen Soldiery Who Saved Louisiana*, revised and complete, New Orleans: privately printed, 1877. Louisiana Collection, Tulane University Library.

Werlein Memorandum. Letter dated 18 June 1915 to Philip Werlein, President, Pickwick Club (unsigned) from the daughter of Charles H. Churchill, founding president. Churchill Family Papers, Manuscripts Division, Tulane University Library.

Secondary Sources

Appiah, Kwame Anthony, *In My Father's House: Africa in the Philosophy of Culture*, New York and Oxford: Oxford University Press, 1992.

Balme, Christopher B., "Cultural Anthropology and Theatre Historiography: Notes on a Methodological Rapprochement," *Theatre Survey* 35 (1994): 33–52.

Bauman, Richard and Charles Briggs, "Poetics and Performance as Critical Perspectives on Language and Social Life," *Annual Review of Anthropology* 19 (1990): 59–88.

Beeman, William O., "The Anthropology of Theater and Spectacle," *Annual Review of Anthropology* 22 (1993): 369–93.

Berliner, Paul, *Thinking in Jazz: The Infinite Art of Improvisation*, Chicago and London: University of Chicago Press, 1994.

Bernal, Martin, *Black Athena: The Afroasiatic Roots of Classical Civilization*, 2 vols., New Brunswick, NJ: Rutgers University Press, 1987–91.

Bharucha, Rustom, *Theatre and the World: Performance and the Politics of Culture*, London and New York: Routledge, 1993.

Carlson, Marvin, *'Theories of the Theatre: A Historical and Critical Survey, from the Greeks to the Present*, expanded edn. Ithaca, NY and London: Cornell University Press, 1993.

Conquergood, Dwight, "Rethinking Ethnography: Towards a Critical Cultural Politics," *Communication Monographs* 58 (1991): 179–94.

de Certeau, Michel, *The Practice of Everyday Life*, trans. Stephen F. Rendall. Berkeley and Los Angeles: University of California Press, 1984.

Drewal, Margaret Thompson, *Yoruba Ritual: Performers, Play, Agency*, Bloomington and Indianapolis: Indiana University Press, 1992.

Fabian, Johannes, *Time and the Other: How Anthropology Makes Its Object*, New York: Columbia University Press, 1983.

Gates, Henry Louis, Jr., *The Signifying Monkey: A Theory of Afro-American Literary Criticism*, New York: Oxford University Press, 1988.

Halttunen, Karen, *Confidence Men and Painted Women: A Study of Middle-class Culture in America, 1830–1870*, New Haven and London: Yale University Press, 1982.

Highshaw, Robert B., *Edward Douglass White: Defender of the Conservative Faith*, Baton Rouge and London: Louisiana State University Press, 1981.

Hirsch, Arnold and Joseph Logsdon, *Creole New Orleans: Race and Americanization*, Baton Rouge and London: Louisiana State University Press, 1992.

Hofstadter, Richard and Michael Wallace (eds), *American Violence: A Documentary History*, New York: Alfred Knopf, 1970.

Hymes, Dell, *Foundations in Sociolinguistics: An Ethnographic Perspective*, Philadelphia: University of Pennsylvania Press, 1975.

Kinser, Samuel, *Carnival, American Style: Mardi Gras at New Orleans and Mobile*, Chicago and London: University of Chicago Press, 1990.

Le Goff, Jacques, *History and Memory*, trans. Steven Rendall and Elizabeth Claman, New York: Columbia University Press, 1992.

MacAloon, John J., *Rite, Drama, Festival, Spectacle: Rehearsals Toward a Theory of Cultural Performance*, Philadelphia: Institute for the Study of the Human Issues, 1984.

McNamara, Brooks, "Invisible Theatre: Folk and Festival Tradition in America," in *Theatre Byways: Essays in Honor of Claude L. Shaver*, eds C.J. Stevens and Joseph Aurbach, New Orleans: Polyanthos, 1978, pp. 6–16.

Mitchell, Reid, *All on a Mardi Gras Day: Episodes in the History of New Orleans Carnival*, Cambridge, Mass. and London: Harvard University Press, 1995.

Myerhoff, Barbara, "The Transformation of Consciousness in Ritual Performance: Some Thoughts and Questions," in *By Means of Performance: Intercultural Studies of Theatre and Ritual,* eds

Richard Scheduler and Willa Appel, Cambridge and New York: Cambridge University Press, 1990, pp. 245–49.

O'Brien, Rosary Hartel, "The New Orleans Carnival Organizations: Theatre of Prestige," dissertation: UCLA, 1973.

Powell, Lawrence N., "Put Liberty Monument in proper setting: a museum," New Orleans *Times Picayune,* 17 March 1993, B–7.

Poovey, Mary, *The Proper Lady and the Woman Writer: Ideology as Style in the Works of Mary Wollstoncraft, Mary Shelley, and Jane Austen*, Chicago: University of Chicago Press, 1984.

Reinelt, Janelle and Joseph Roach (eds), *Critical Theory and Performance*, Ann Arbor: University of Michigan Press, 1992.

Roach, Joseph R., "Carnival and the Law in New Orleans," *The Drama Review: A journal of Performance Studies* 37 (1993): 42–75.

Ryan, Mary, *Women in Public: Between Banners and Ballots, 1825–1880*, Baltimore and London: Johns Hopkins University Press, 1990.

Schechner, Richard, *Between Theater and Anthropology*, Philadelphia: University of Pennsylvania Press, 1985.

——*The Future of Ritual: Writings on Culture and Performance*. London and New York: Routledge, 1993.

States, Bert O., *Great Reckonings in Little Rooms: On the Phenomenology of Theater*, Berkeley and Los Angeles: University of California Press, 1985.

Turner, Victor, ed., *Celebration: Studies in Festivity and Ritual*, Washington, DC: Smithsonian Institution Press, 1982.

——*From Ritual to Theatre: The Human Seriousness of Play*, New York: PAJ Publications, 1982.

——*Schism and Continuity: A Study of Ndembu Village Life*, Manchester: Manchester University Press, 1957.

Vennman, Barbara, "Boundary Face Off: New Orleans Civil Rights Law and Carnival Tradition," *The Drama Review: A Journal of Performance Studies* 37 (1993): 76–109.

——"New Orleans 1993 Carnival: Tradition at Play in *Papier-Mâché* and Stone," *Theatre Insight* 5 (1993): 5–14.

Young, Perry, The *Mistick Krewe: Chronicles of Comus and his Kin*, 1931. Rpt. New Orleans: Louisiana Heritage Press, 1969.

39 Swing: From Verb to Noun

Amiri Baraka (LeRoi Jones)

Born in Newark in 1934, Amiri Baraka has written over 40 books of essays, poems, drama, and music history and criticism. Under his birth name LeRoi Jones, he made an impact as a provocative and insightful jazz critic who championed the new movements sweeping through jazz at the end of the 1950s. Already controversial as a critic, Baraka continued to make waves when his first books of poetry appeared in the early 1960s, along with his plays *Dutchman* and *The Slave* (both 1964). Through the years when controversies raged around the musics of Ornette Coleman, John Coltrane, Archie Shepp, Albert Ayler, and Cecil Taylor, Baraka remained a champion of their status as artists and of their music as an embodied philosophy and politics. In this piece, Baraka is at his best, offering genuinely unique insight into how the spontaneity of jazz as performed by black musicians gets turned into a static form when appropriated by white musicians. He has lectured and given readings of his work throughout the USA, the Caribbean, Africa, and Europe. His awards and honours include an Obie Award for drama, the American Academy of Arts & Letters award, the James Weldon Johnson Medal for contributions to the arts, and grants from the Rockefeller Foundation and National Endowment for the Arts. The following piece appeared in *Blues People* (1963).

Key words: jazz; African American culture; literature

The blues was conceived of by freedmen and ex-slaves—if not as a result of a personal or intellectual experience, at least as an emotional confirmation of, and reaction to, the way in which most Negroes were still forced to exist in the United States. The blues impulse was a psychological correlative that obscured the most extreme ideas of *assimilation* for most Negroes, and made any notion of the complete abandonment of the traditional black culture an unrealizable possibility. In a sense, the middle-class spirit could not take root among most Negroes because they sensed the final fantasy involved. Besides the pay check, which was the aspect of American society that created a modern black middle class, was [...] also available to what some of my mother's friends would refer to as "low-type coons." And these "coons" would always be unavailable both socially and culturally to any talk of assimilation from white man or black. The Negro middle class, always an exaggeration of its white model, could include the professional men and educators, but after the move north it also included men who worked in factories and as an added dig, "sportsmen," *i.e.*, gamblers and numbers people. The idea of Negro "society," as E. Franklin Frazier pointed out, is based only on acquisition, which, as it turns out, makes the formation of a completely parochial meta-society impossible. Numbers bankers often make as much money as doctors and thereby are part of the Negro "society." And even if the more formal ("socially responsible") Negro middle class wanted to become simply white Americans, they were during the late twenties and thirties a swelling minority.

The two secularities I spoke of are simply the ways in which the blues was beginning to be redistributed in black America through these years. The people who were beginning to move toward what they could think of as citizenship also moved away from the older blues. The unregenerate Northerners already had a music, the thin-willed "society" bands of Jim Europe, and the circus as well as white rag had influenced the "non-blues" bands of Will Marion Cook and Wilbur Sweatman that existed before the migration. But the huge impact the Southerners made upon the North changed that. When the city blues began to be powerful, the larger Negro dance bands hired some of the emigrants as soloists, and to some degree the blues began to be heard in most of the black cabarets, "dance schools," and theaters. The true jazz sound had moved north, and even the blackest blues could be heard in the house parties of Chicago and New York. But for most of America by the twenties, jazz (or *jass*, the noun, not the verb) meant the Original Dixieland Jazz Band (to the hip) and Paul Whiteman (to the square). Whiteman got rich, the O.D.J.B. never did.

The O.D.J.B. was a group of young white men who had been deeply influenced by the King Oliver band in New Orleans; they moved north, and became the first jazz band to record. They had a profound influence upon America, and because they, rather than the actual black innovators, were heard by the great majority of Americans *first*, the cultural lag had won again.

A Negro jazz band, Freddie Keppard's Original Creoles, turned down an invitation to record a few months before the O.D.J.B.; Keppard (myth says) didn't accept the offer because he thought such a project would merely invite imitation of his style! That is probably true, but it is doubtful that Keppard's band would have caught as much national attention as the smoother O.D.J.B. anyway, for the same reason the O.D.J.B. could never have made as much money as Whiteman.

It is significant that by 1924, when Bessie Smith was still causing riots in Chicago and when young Louis Armstrong was on his way to New York to join the Fletcher Henderson band—and by so doing, to create the first really swinging *big* jazz band, the biggest names in "jazz" were Whiteman and the Mound City Blue Blowers, another white group. Radio had come into its own by 1920, and the irony is that most Negroes probably thought of jazz, based on what they had heard, as being a white dilution of older blues forms! It was only after there had been a few recordings sufficiently distributed through the black Northern and urban Southern neighborhoods, made by Negro bands like King Oliver's (Oliver was then in Chicago with his historic Creole Jazz Band, which featured Louis Armstrong, second cornet), Fletcher Henderson's, and two Kansas City bands—Bennie Moten's and Clarence Williams', that the masses of Negroes became familiar with jazz. At Chicago's Lincoln Gardens Café, Oliver first set the Northern Negro neighborhoods on fire, and then bands like Moten's and Williams' in the various clubs around Kansas City; but Henderson reached his Negro audience mostly via records because even when he got his best band together (with Coleman Hawkins, Louis Armstrong, Don Redman, etc.), he was still playing at Roseland, which was a white club.

The earliest jazz bands, like Buddy Bolden's, were usually small groups. Bolden's instrumentation was supposed to have been cornet, clarinet, trombone, violin, guitar, bass (which was one of the first instrumental innovations for that particular group since most bands of that period and well after used the tuba) and drums. These groups were usually made up of musicians who had other jobs (like pre-classic blues singers) since there was really no steady work for them. And they played most of the music of the time: quadrilles, schottisches, polkas, ragtime tunes, like many of the other "cleaner" groups around New Orleans. But the difference with the Bolden band was the blues quality, the Uptown flavor, of all their music. But this music still had the flavor of the brass marching bands. Most of the musicians of that period had come through those bands; in fact, probably still marched with them when there was a significant funeral. Another quality that must have distinguished the Bolden band was the improvisational character of a good deal of their music. Charles Edward Smith remarks that "the art of group improvisation—like the blues, the blood of jazz—was associated with this uptown section of New Orleans in particular. As in folk music, two creative forces were involved, that of the group and that of the gifted individual."[1]

Most of the uptown bands were noted for their "sloppy ensemble styles." The Bolden band and the other early jazz groups must have sounded even sloppier. The music was a raw mixture of march, dance, blues, and early rag rhythm, with all the players improvising simultaneously. It is a wonderful concept, taking the unison tradition of European march music, but infesting it with teeming improvisations, catcalls, hollers, and the murky rhythms of the ex-slaves. The Creoles must have hated that music more than anything in life.

But by the time the music came upriver along with the fleeing masses, it had changed a great deal. Oliver's Creole Band, the first really influential Negro jazz band in the North, had a much smoother ensemble style than the Bolden band: the guitar and violin had disappeared, and a piano had been added. In New Orleans, pianists had been largely soloists in the various bawdy houses and brothels of Storyville. In fact, pianists were the only Negro musicians who worked steadily and needed no other jobs. But the early New Orleans jazz groups usually did not have pianos. Jelly Roll Morton, one of the first jazz pianists, was heavily influenced by the ragtime style, though his own rags were even more heavily influenced by blues and that rougher rag style called "barrelhouse." As Bunk Johnson is quoted as saying, Jelly played music "the whores liked." And played in a whorehouse, it is easy to understand how functional that music must have been. But the piano as part of a jazz ensemble was something not indigenous to earlier New Orleans music. The smoother and more clearly polyphonic style of Oliver's band, as opposed to what must have been a veritable heterophony of earlier bands like Bolden's—Kid Ory's Sunshine Orchestra, the first black jazz band to record (Los Angeles, 1921), gives us some indication—showed a discipline and formality that must certainly have been imposed to a large degree by ragtime and the more precise pianistic techniques that went with it.

Oliver's band caused a sensation with audiences and musicians alike and brought the authentic accent of jazz into the North. Garvin Bushell remembers: "We went on the road with Mamie Smith in 1921. When we got to Chicago, Bubber Miley and I went to hearing Oliver at the Dreamland every night. [This was before Armstrong joined the band and they moved to Lincoln Gardens.] It was the first time I'd heard New Orleans jazz to any advantage and I studied them every night for the entire week we were in town. I was very much impressed with their blues and their sound. The trumpets and clarinets in the East had a better 'legitimate' quality, but their [Oliver's band's] sound touched you more. It was less cultivated but more expressive of how people felt. Bubber and I sat there with our mouths open."[2]

Louis Armstrong's arrival at twenty-two with Oliver's band had an even more electrifying effect on these northern audiences, which many times included white jazz musicians. Hoagy Carmichael went to the Lincoln Gardens with Bix Beiderbecke in 1923 to hear that band:

"The King featured two trumpets, a piano, a bass fiddle and a clarinet ... a big black fellow ... slashed into *Bugle Call Rag.*

"I dropped my cigarette and gulped my drink. Bix was on his feet, his eyes popping. For taking the first chorus was that second trumpet, Louis Armstrong."

"Louis was taking it fast. Bob Gillette slid off his chair and under the table ... Every note Louis hit was perfection."[3]

This might seem amusing if it is noted that the first and deepest influences of most white Northern and Midwestern jazz musicians were necessarily the recordings of the O.D.J.B., who were imitating the earlier New Orleans styles, and Oliver, who had brought this style to its apex. Thus, this first hearing of the genuine article by these white musicians must have been much like tasting real eggs after having been brought up on the powdered variety. (Though, to be sure, there's no certainty that a person will like the original if he has developed a taste for the other. So it is that Carmichael can write that he still preferred Beiderbecke to Armstrong, saying, "Bix's breaks were not as wild as Armstrong's but they were hot and he selected each note with musical care."[4])

Blues as an autonomous music had been in a sense inviolable. There was no clear way into it, *i.e.*, its production, not its appreciation, except as concomitant with what seems to me to be the peculiar social, cultural, economic, and emotional experience of a black man in America. The idea of a white blues singer seems an even more violent contradiction of terms than the idea of a middle-class blues singer. The materials of blues were not available to the white American, even though some strange circumstance might prompt him to look for them. It was as if these materials were secret and obscure, and blues a kind of ethno-historic rite as basic as blood.

The classic singers brought this music as close to white America as it could ever get and still survive. W. C. Handy, with the publication of his various "blues compositions," *invented* it for a great many Americans and also showed that there was some money to be made from it. Whiteman, Wilbur Sweatman, Jim Europe, all played Handy's compositions with success. There was even what could be called a "blues craze" (of which Handy's compositions were an important part) just after the ragtime craze went on the skids. But the music that resulted from craze had little, if anything, to do with legitimate blues. That could not be got to, except as the casual expression of a whole culture. And for this reason, blues remained, and remains in its most moving manifestations, obscure to the mainstream of American culture.

Jazz made it possible for the first time for something of the legitimate feeling of Afro-American music to be imitated successfully. (Ragtime had moved so quickly away from any pure reflection of Negro life that by the time it became popular, there was no more original source to imitate. It was, in a sense, a premature attempt at the socio-cultural merger that later produced jazz.) Or rather, jazz enabled separate and *valid* emotional expressions to be made that were based on older traditions of Afro-American music that were clearly not a part of it. The Negro middle class would not have a music if it were not for jazz. The white man would have no access to blues. It was a music capable of reflecting not only the Negro and a black America but a white America as well.

During the twenties, serious young white musicians were quick to pick up more or less authentic jazz accents as soon as they had some contact with the music. The O.D.J.B., who came out of a parallel tradition of white New Orleans marching bands, whizzed off to Chicago and stunned white musicians everywhere as well as many Negro musicians in the North who had not heard the new music before. Young white boys, like Beiderbecke, in the North and Midwest were already forming styles of their own based on the O.D.J. B.'s records and the playing of another white group, the New Orleans Rhythm Kings, before Joe Oliver's band got to Chicago. And the music these boys were making, or trying to make, had very little to do with Paul Whiteman. They had caught the accent, understood the more generalized emotional statements, and genuinely moved, set out to involve themselves in this music as completely as possible. They hung around the Negro clubs, listening to the newly employed New Orleans musicians, and went home and tried to play their tunes.

The result of this cultural "breakdown" was not always more imitation. As I have said, jazz had a broadness of emotional meaning that allowed of many separate ways into it, not all of them dependent on the "blood ritual" of blues. Bix Beiderbecke, as a mature musician, was even an innovator. But the real point of this breakdown was that it reflected not so much the white American's increased understanding of the Negro, but rather the fact that the Negro had created a music that offered such a profound reflection of America that it could attract white Americans to want to play it or listen to it for exactly that reason. The white jazz musician was even a new *class* of white American. Unlike the earlier blackface acts and the minstrels who sought to burlesque certain facets of Negro life (and, superficially, the music associated with it), there were now growing ranks of white jazz musicians who wanted to play the music because they thought it emotionally and intellectually fulfilling. It made a common cultural ground where black and white America seemed only day and night in the same city and at their most disparate, proved only to result in different *styles*, a phenomenon I have always taken to be the whole point (and value) of divergent cultures.

It is interesting that most of these young white musicians who emerged during the early twenties were from the middle class and from the Middle West. Beiderbecke was born in Davenport, Iowa; that town, however, at the turn of the century was a river port, and many of the riverboats docked there—riverboats whose staffs sometimes included bands like Fate Marable's, Dewey Jackson's, and Albert Wynn's, and musicians like Jelly Roll Morton and Louis Armstrong. Beiderbecke's first group, the Wolverines, played almost exclusively at roadhouses and colleges in the Midwest, most notably at Indiana University.

A few years after the Wolverines had made their reputation as what George Hoefer calls "the first white band to play the genuine Negro style of jazz," another group of young white musicians began to play jazz "their own way." They were also from the Midwest, but from Chicago. Eddie Condon, Jimmy McPartland, Bud Freeman, PeeWee Russell, Dave Tough, and some others, all went to Austin High School and became associated with its style of playing known as "Chicago jazz," which took its impetus from the records of the O.D.J.B. and the New Orleans Rhythm Kings dates on the North Side of Chicago.

Chicago and nearby parts of the Midwest were logically the first places where jazz could take root in the North (although there were some parallel developments in New York). In a sense Chicago was, and to a certain extent is now, a kind of frontier town. It sits at the end of the riverboat runs, and it was the kind of industrial city that the first black emigrants were drawn to. It had many of the heavy industries that would employ Negroes, whereas New York's heaviest industry is paperwork. And in Chicago, during what was called the "Jazz Age," there was an easiness of communication on some levels between black and white that was not duplicated in New York until some time later. Chicago at this time was something like the musical capital of America, encompassing within it black emigrants, white emigrants, country blues people, classic stylists, city house-party grinders, New Orleans musicians, and young Negro musicians and younger white musicians listening and reacting to this crush of cultures that so clearly typified America's rush into the twentieth century.

The reaction of young white musicians to jazz was not always connected directly to any "*understanding* of the Negro." In many cases, the most profound influence on young white musicians was the music of other white musicians. Certainly this is true with people like Beiderbecke and most of the Chicago-style players. But the entrance of the white man into jazz at this level of sincerity and emotional legitimacy did at least bring him, by implication, much closer to the Negro; that is, even if a white trumpet player were to learn to play "jazz" by listening to Nick LaRocca and had his style set (as was Beiderbecke's case) *before* he ever heard black musicians, surely the musical debt to Negro music (and to the black culture from which it issued) had to be understood. As in the case of LaRocca's style, it is certainly an appropriation of black New Orleans brass style, most notably King Oliver's; though the legitimacy of its deviation can in no way be questioned, the fact that it is a deviation must be acknowledged. The serious white musician was in a position to do this. And this acknowledgment, whether overt or tacit, served to place the Negro's culture and Negro society in a position of intelligent regard it had never enjoyed before.

This acknowledgment of a developed and empirical profundity to the Negro's culture (and as the result of its separation from the mainstream of American culture) also caused the people who had to make it to be separated from this mainstream themselves. Any blackness admitted within the mainstream existed only as it could be shaped by the grimness of American sociological (and political) thought. There was no life to Negroes in America that could be understood by America, except negatively or with the hopeless idealism of impossible causes. During the Black Renaissance the white liberal and sensual dilettante "understood" the Negro. During the depression, so did the Communist Party. The young white jazz musicians at least had to face the black American head-on and with only a very literal drum to beat. And they could not help but do this with some sense of rebellion or separateness from the rest of white America, since white America could have no understanding of what they were doing, except perhaps in the terms that Whiteman and the others succeeded in doing it, which was not at all—that is, explaining a bird by comparing it with an airplane.

"Unlike New Orleans style, the style of these musicians—often and confusingly labeled 'Chicago'—sacrificed ease and relaxation for tension and drive, perhaps because they were mastering a new idiom in a more hectic environment. They had read some of the literature of the 20s—drummer Dave Tough loved Mencken and the *American Mercury*—and their revolt against their own middle class background tended to be conscious. The role of the improvising—and usually non-reading—musician became almost heroic."[5]

Music, as paradoxical as it might seem, is the result of thought. It is the result of thought perfected at its most empirical, *i.e.*, as *attitude*, or *stance*. Thought is largely conditioned by reference; it is the result of consideration or speculation against reference, which is largely arbitrary. There is no *one* way of thinking, since reference (hence value) is as scattered and dissimilar as men themselves. If Negro music can be seen to be the result of certain attitudes, certain specific ways of thinking about the world (and only ultimately about the *ways* in which music can be made), then the basic hypothesis [...] is understood. The Negro's music changed as he changed, reflecting shifting attitudes or (and this is equally important) *consistent attitudes within changed contexts*. And it is *why* the music changed that seems most important to me.

When jazz first began to appear during the twenties on the American scene, in one form or another, it was introduced in a great many instances into that scene by white Americans. Jazz as it was originally conceived and in most instances of its most vital development was the result of certain attitudes, or empirical ideas, attributable to the Afro-American culture. Jazz as played by white musicians was not the same as that played by black musicians, nor was there any reason for it to be. The music of the white jazz musician did not issue from the same cultural circumstance; it was, at its most profound instance, a learned art. The blues, for example, which I take to be an autonomous black music, had very little weight at all in pre-jazz white American culture. But blues is an extremely important part of jazz. However, the way in which jazz utilizes the blues "attitude" provided a musical analogy the white musician could understand and thus utilize in his music to arrive at a style of jazz music. The white musician understood the blues first as music, but seldom as an attitude, since the attitude, or world-view, the white musician was responsible to was necessarily quite a different one. And in many cases, this attitude, or world-view, was one that was not consistent with the making of jazz.

There should be no cause for wonder that the trumpets of Bix Beiderbecke and Louis Armstrong were so dissimilar. The white middle-class boy from Iowa was the product of a culture which could *place* Louis Armstrong, but could never understand him. Beiderbecke was also the product of a subculture that most nearly emulates the "official" or formal culture of North America. He was an instinctive intellectual who had a musical taste that included Stravinsky, Schoenberg, and Debussy, and had an emotional life that, as it turned out, was based on his conscious or unconscious disapproval of most of the sacraments of his culture. On the other hand, Armstrong was, in terms of emotional archetypes, an honored priest of his culture—one of the most impressive products of his society. Armstrong was not *rebelling* against anything with his music. In fact, his music was one of the most beautiful refinements of Afro-American musical tradition, and it was immediately recognized as such by those Negroes who were not busy trying to pretend that they had issued from Beiderbecke's culture. The incredible irony of the situation was that both stood in similar places in the superstructure of American society: Beiderbecke, because of the isolation any deviation from mass culture imposed upon its bearer; and Armstrong, because of the socio-historical estrangement of the Negro from the rest of America. Nevertheless, the music the two made was as dissimilar as is possible within jazz. Beiderbecke's slight, reflective tone and impressionistic lyricism was the most impressive example of "the artifact given expression" in jazz. He played "white jazz" in the sense that I am trying to convey, that is, as a music that is the product of attitudes expressive of a peculiar culture. Armstrong, of course, played jazz that was securely within the traditions of Afro-American music. His tone was brassy, broad, and aggressively dramatic. He also relied heavily on the vocal blues tradition in his playing to amplify the expressiveness of his instrumental technique.

I am using these two men as examples because they were two early masters of a developing *American* music, though they expressed almost antithetical versions of it. The point is that Afro-American music did not become a completely American expression until the white man could play it! Bix Beiderbecke, more than any of the early white jazzmen, signified this development because he was the first white jazz musician, the first white musician who brought to the jazz he created any of the *ultimate concern* Negro musicians brought to it as a casual attitude of their culture. This development signified also that jazz would someday have to contend with the idea of its being an art (since that *was* the white man's only way into it). The emergence of the white player meant that Afro-American culture had already become the expression of a particular kind of American experience, and what is most important, that this experience was available intellectually, that it could be learned.

Louis Armstrong's departure from the Oliver Creole Jazz Band is more than an historical event; given further consideration, it may be seen as a musical and socio-cultural event of the highest significance. First, Armstrong's departure from Chicago (as well as Beiderbecke's three years later, in 1927, to join the Goldkette band and then Paul Whiteman's enterprise) was, in a sense, symbolic of the fact that the most fertile period for jazz in Chicago was finished and that the jazz capital was moving to New York. It also meant that Louis felt mature enough musically to venture out on his own without the presence of his mentor Joe Oliver. But most important, Armstrong in his tenure with Fletcher Henderson's Roseland band was not only responsible to a great degree for giving impetus to the first big jazz band, but in his capacity as one of the hot soloists in a big dance (later, jazz) band, he moved jazz into another era: the ascendancy of the soloist began.

Primitive jazz, like most Afro-American music that preceded it, was a communal, collective music. The famous primitive ensemble styles of earlier jazz allowed only of "breaks," or small solo-like statements by individual players, but the form and intent of these breaks were still dominated by the form and intent of the ensemble. They were usually just quasi-melodic punctuations at the end of the ensemble chorus. Jazz, even at the time of Oliver's Creole Band, was still a matter of *collective improvisation*, though the Creole Band did bring a smoother and more complex polyphonic technique to the ensemble style. As Larry Gushee remarked in a review of a recent LP of the Creole Band (Riverside 12–122) "the Creole jazz Band ... sets the standard (possibly, who knows, only because of an historical accident) for all kinds of jazz that do not base their excellence on individual expressiveness, but on form and *shape* achieved through control and balance."[6]

The emergence of this "individual expressiveness" in jazz was signaled impressively by Armstrong's recordings with a small group known as the Hot Five. The musicians on these recordings, made in 1925 and 1926, were Kid Ory, trombone; Johnny Dodds, clarinet and *alto saxophone*; Lil Hardin, now Mrs. Armstrong, piano; and Johnny St. Cyr, banjo. On these sides, Armstrong clearly dominates the group, not so much because he is the superior instrumentalist, but because rhythmically and harmonically the rest of the musicians followed where Louis led, sometimes without a really clear knowledge of where that would be. The music made by the Hot Five is Louis Armstrong music: it has little to do with collective improvisation.

"The 1926 Hot Five's playing is much less purely collective than King Oliver's. In a sense, the improvised ensembles are cornet solos accompanied by *impromptu countermelodies* [my italics], rather than true collective improvisation. This judgment is based on the very essence of the works, and not merely on the cornet's closeness to the microphone. Listen to them carefully. Isn't it obvious that Armstrong's personality absorbs the others. Isn't your attention spontaneously concentrated on Louis? With King Oliver, you listen to the band, here, you listen first to *Louis*."[7]

The development of the soloist is probably connected to the fact that about this time in the development of jazz, many of the "hot" musicians had to seek employment with larger dance bands of usually dubious quality. The communal, collective improvisatory style of early jazz was impossible in this context, though later the important big jazz bands and big "blues bands" of the Southwest solved this problem by "uniting on a higher level the individual contribution with the entire group."[8]

The isolation that had nurtured Afro-American musical tradition before the coming of jazz had largely disappeared by the mid-twenties, and many foreign, even debilitating, elements drifted into this broader instrumental music. The instrumentation of the Henderson Roseland band was not chosen initially for its jazz possibilities, but in order to imitate the popular white dance bands of the day. The Henderson band became a jazz band because of the collective personality of the individual instrumentalists in the band, who were stronger than any superficial forms that might be imposed upon them. The saxophone trio, which was a clichéed novelty in the large white dance bands, became something of remarkable beauty when transformed by Henderson's three reeds, Buster Bailey, Don Redman, and Coleman Hawkins. And just as earlier those singular hollers must have pierced lonely Southern nights after the communal aspect of the slave society had broken down and had been replaced by a pseudoautonomous existence on many tiny Southern plots (which represented, however absurd it might seem, the widest breadth of this country for those Negroes, and their most exalted position in it), so the changed society in which the large Negro dance bands existed represented, in a sense, another post-communal black society. The move north, for instance, had broken down the old communities (the house parties were one manifestation of a regrouping of the newer communities: the Harlems and South Chicagos). Classic blues, the public face of a changed Afro-American culture, was the solo. The blues that developed at the house parties was the collective, communal music. So the jam sessions of the late twenties and thirties became the musicians' collective communal expression, and the solo in the large dance bands, that expression as it had to exist to remain vital outside its communal origins. The dance bands or society orchestras of the North replaced the plot of land, for they were the musician's only means of existence, and the solo, like the holler, was the only link with an earlier, more intense sense of the self in its most vital relationship to the world. The solo spoke singly of a collective music, and because of the emergence of the great soloists (Armstrong, Hawkins, Hines, Harrison), even forced the great bands (Henderson's, Ellington's, and later Basie's) into wonderfully extended versions of that communal expression.

The transformation of the large dance bands into jazz bands was in good measure the work of the Fletcher Henderson orchestra, aided largely by the arrangements of Don Redman, especially his writing for the reed section which gave the saxophones in the Henderson band a fluency that was never heard before. The reeds became the fiery harmonic and melodic imagination of the big jazz bands. And it was the growing prominence of the saxophone in the big band and the later elevation of that instrument to its fullest expressiveness by Coleman Hawkins that planted the seed for the kind of jazz that is played even today. However, it was not until the emergence of Lester Young that jazz became a saxophone or reed music, as opposed to the brass music it had been since the early half-march, half-blues bands of New Orleans.

Louis Armstrong had brought *brass jazz* to its fullest flowering and influenced every major innovation in jazz right up until the forties, and bebop. Earl Hines, whose innovations as a pianist began a new, single-note line approach to the jazz piano, was merely utilizing Armstrong's trumpet style on a different instrument, thereby breaking out of the ragtime-boogie-stride approach to piano that had been predominant since that instrument was first used in jazz bands. Coleman Hawkins' saxophone style is still close to the Armstrong-perfected brass style, and of course, all Hawkins' imitators reflect that style as well. Jimmy Harrison, the greatest innovator on the trombone, was also profoundly influenced by Armstrong's brass style.

With the emergence of many good "hot" musicians from all over the country during the mid-twenties, the big jazz bands continued to develop. By the late twenties there were quite a few very good jazz bands all over the country. And competent musicians "appeared from everywhere, from 1920 on: by 1930 every city outside the Deep South with a Negro population (1920 census) above sixty thousand except Philadelphia had produced an important band: Washington, Duke Ellington; Baltimore, Chick Webb; Memphis, Jimmie Lunceford; St. Louis, the Missourians; Chicago, Luis Russell and Armstrong; New York, Henderson, Charlie Johnson, and half a dozen more."[9]

So an important evolution in Afro-American musical form had occurred again and in much the same manner that characterized the many other changes within the tradition of Negro music. The form can be called basically a Euro-American one—the large (sweet) dance band, changed by the contact with Afro-American musical tradition into another vehicle for that tradition. Just as the Euro-American religious song and ballad had been used, so with the transformation of the large dance band into the jazz band and the adaptation of the thirty-two-bar popular song to jazz purposes, the music itself was broadened and extended even further, and even more complex expressions of older musical traditions were made possible.

By the late twenties a great many more Negroes were going to high school and college, and the experience of an American "liberal" education was bound to leave traces. The most expressive big bands of the late twenties and thirties were largely middle-class Negro enterprises. The world of the professional man had opened up, and many scions of the new Negro middle class who had not gotten through professional school went into jazz "to make money." Men like Fletcher Henderson (who had a chemistry degree), Benny Carter, Duke Ellington, Coleman Hawkins, Jimmie Lunceford, Sy Oliver, and Don Redman, for example, all went to college: "They were a remarkable group of men. Between 1925 and 1935 they created, in competition, a musical tradition that required fine technique and musicianship (several of them were among the earliest virtuosi in jazz); they began to change the basis of the jazz repertory from blues to the wider harmonic possibilities of the thirty-two-bar popular song; they created and perfected the new ensemble-style big-band jazz; they kept their groups together for years, working until they achieved a real unity. They showed that jazz could absorb new, foreign elements without losing its identity, that it was in fact capable of evolution."[10]

These men were all "citizens," and they had all, to a great extent, moved away from the older *lowdown* forms of blues. Blues was not so *direct* to them, it had to be utilized in other contexts. Big show-band jazz was a music of their own, a music that still relied on older Afro-American musical tradition, but one that had begun to utilize still greater amounts of popular American music as well as certain formal European traditions. Also, the concept of making music as a means of making a living that had developed with the coming of classic blues singers was now thoroughly a part of the constantly evolving Afro-American culture. One did not expect to hear Bessie Smith at a rent party, one went to the theater to hear her. She was, at all levels, a *performer*. The young middle-class Negroes who came into jazz during the development of the show bands and dance bands all thought of themselves as performers as well. No matter how deeply the music they played was felt, they still thought of it as a public expression.

"If so many musicians came to jazz after training in one of the professions, it was because jazz was both more profitable and safer for a Negro in the 1920s; it was a survival of this attitude that decided Ellington to keep his son out of M.I.T. and aeronautical engineering in the 1930s."[11]

Just as Bessie Smith perfected vocal blues style almost as a Western artifact, and Louis Armstrong perfected the blues-influenced brass style in jazz (which was a great influence on all kinds of instrumental jazz for more than two decades), so Duke Ellington perfected the big jazz band, transforming it into a highly expressive instrument. Ellington, after the Depression had killed off the big theater-band "show-biz" style of the large jazz bands, began to create a personal style of jazz expression as impressive as Armstrong's innovation as a soloist (if not more so). Ellington replaced a "spontaneous collective music by a worked-out orchestral language."[12]

Ellington's music (even the "jungle" bits of his twenties show-band period, which were utilized in those uptown "black and tan" clubs that catered largely to sensual white liberals) was a thoroughly American music. It was the product of a native American mind, but more than that, it was a music that *could* for the first time exist within the formal boundaries of American culture. A freedman could not have created it, just as Duke could never have played like Peatie Wheatstraw. Ellington began in much the same way as a great many of the significant Northern Negro musicians of the era had begun, by playing in the ragtime, show-business style that was so prevalent. But under the influence of the Southern styles of jazz and with the growth of Duke as an orchestra leader, composer, and musician, the music he came to make was as "moving" in terms of the older Afro-American musical tradition as it was a completely American expression. Duke's sophistication was to a great extent the very quality that enabled him to integrate so perfectly the older blues traditions with the "whiter" styles of big-band music. But Ellington was a "citizen," and his music, as Vic Bellerby has suggested, was "the detached impressionism of a sophisticated Negro city dweller."

Even though many of Ellington's compositions were "hailed as uninhibited jungle music," the very fact that the music was so much an American music made it cause the stir it did: "Ellington used musical materials that were familiar to concert-trained ears, making jazz music more listenable to them. These, however, do not account for his real quality. ... In his work all the elements of the old music may be found, but each completely changed because it had to be changed. ... Ellington's accomplishment was to solve the problem of form and content for the large band. He did it not by trying to play pure New Orleans blues and stomp music rearranged for large bands, as Henderson did, but by re-creating all the elements of New Orleans music in new instrumental and harmonic terms. What emerged was a music that could be traced back to the old roots and yet sounded fresh and new."[13]

For these reasons, by the thirties the "race" category could be dropped from Ellington's records. Though he would quite often go into his jungle things, faking the resurrection of "African music," the extreme irony here is that Ellington was making "African sounds," but as a sophisticated American. The "African" music he made had much less to do with Africa than his best music, which [...] can be seen as a truly Afro-American music, though understandable only in the context of a completely American experience. This music could, and did, find a place within the main culture. Jazz became more "popular" than ever. The big colored dance bands of the thirties were a national entertainment and played in many white night clubs as well as the black clubs that had been set up especially for white Americans. These bands were also the strongest influence on American popular music and entertainment for twenty years.

The path of jazz and the further development of the Afro-American musical tradition paradoxically had been taken over at this level to a remarkable degree by elements of the Negro middle class. Jazz was their remaining connection with blues; a connection they could make, at many points, within the mainstream of American life.

The music had moved so far into the mainstream, that soon white "swing" bands developed that could play with some of the authentic accent of the great Negro bands, though the deciding factor here was the fact that there were never enough good white jazz musicians to go around in those big bands, and most of the bands then were packed with a great many studio and section men, and perhaps one or two "hot" soloists. By the thirties quite a few white bands had mastered the swing idiom of big-band jazz with varying degrees of authenticity. One of the most successful of these bands, the Benny Goodman orchestra, even began to buy arrangements from Negro arrangers so that it would have more of an authentic tone. The arranger became one of the most important men in big-band jazz, demonstrating how far jazz had gotten from earlier Afro-American musical tradition. (Fletcher Henderson, however, was paid only $37.50 per arrangement by Goodman before Goodman actually hired him as the band's chief arranger.)

The prominence of radio had also created a new medium for this new music, and the growing numbers of white swing bands automatically qualified for these fairly well-paying jobs: "The studio work was monopolized by a small group of musicians who turn up on hundreds of records by orchestras of every kind. One of the least admirable characteristics of the entire arrangement was that it was almost completely restricted to white musicians and it was the men from the white orchestras who were getting the work. The Negro musicians complained bitterly about the discrimination, but the white musicians never attempted to help them, and the contractors hired the men they wanted. At the Nest Club, or the Lenox Club the musicians were on close terms, but the relationship ended when the white musicians went back to their Times Square hotels. A few of them, notably Goodman, were to use a few of the Harlem musicians, but in the first Depression years the studio orchestras were white."[14]

So the widespread development of the swing style produced yet another irony—when the "obscurity" of the Negro's music was lessened with the coming of arranged big-band jazz, and the music, in effect, did pass into the mainstream of American culture, in fact, could be seen as an integral part of that culture, it not only ceased to have meaning for a great many Negroes but also those Negroes who were most closely involved with the music were not even allowed to play it at the highest salaries that could be gotten. The spectacle of Benny Goodman hiring Teddy Wilson and later Lionel Hampton, Charlie Christian, and Cootie Williams into his outrageously popular bands and thereby making them "big names" in the swing world seems to me as fantastically amusing as the fact that in the jazz polls during the late thirties and early forties run by popular jazz magazines, almost no Negro musicians won. Swing music, which was the result of arranged big-band jazz, as it developed to a music that had almost nothing to do with blues, had very little to do with black America, though that is certainly where it had come from. But there were now more and more Negroes like that, too.

Notes

1 "New Orleans and Traditions in Jazz," in *Jazz*, p. 39.
2 "Garvin Bushell and New York Jazz in the 1920s," *Jazz Review* (February 1959), p. 9.
3 Henry Carmichael, *The Stardust Road* (New York, Rinehart, 1946), p. 53.
4 As quoted in Marshall Stearns, *The Story of Jazz* (New York, Oxford University Press, 1956) p. 128.
5 *The Story of Jazz*, p. 129.
6 *Jazz Review* (November 1958), p. 37.
7 André Hodeir, *Jazz: Its Evolution and Essence* (New York, Grove Press, 1956), pp. 50–51.
8 Sidney Finkelstein, *Jazz: A People's Music* (New York, Citadel, 1948), p. 206.

348 Amiri Baraka (LeRoi Jones)

 9 Hsio Wen Shih, "The Spread of Jazz and the Big Bands," in *Jazz*, p. 161.
10 *Ibid.*, p. 164.
11 *Ibid.*, p. 164.
12 *Jazz: Its Evolution and Essence*, p. 33.
13 *Jazz: A People's Music*, p. 192.
14 Samuel Charters and Leonard Kunstadt, *Jazz: A History of the New York Scene* (New York, Doubleday, 1962), p. 262.

40 OAAU Founding Rally

Malcolm X

"You've got to get some power before you can be yourself." In one of his most famous speeches, an address at the founding rally of the Organization of Afro-American Unity (in June 1964), Malcolm X (1925–65) ingeniously links the talent of the black jazz improviser to the potential for African Americans to reinvent themselves in American society. Born Malcolm Little in Omaha, Nebraska, and after losing his father to an accident and his mother to mental illness, Malcolm, at age 16, moved to Boston, where he listened and danced to Duke Ellington and other Swing era artists at the Roseland Ballroom, but also succumbed to the street life of drugs, pimping, and theft. While in prison for burglary, Malcolm re-educated himself, discovered Elijah Muhammad's Nation of Islam, and changed his name. After his release in 1952, as a close disciple of Muhammad, Malcolm X became a major African American spokesman during the height of the Civil Rights era, but he eventually left the Nation of Islam, and broadened his views on race relations after visiting Africa and the Middle East. On February 21, 1965, three gunmen assassinated Malcolm X as he addressed a meeting of his newly formed Organization of Afro-American Unity at a Harlem ballroom. Later that year, his *Autobiography* was published; it has become one of the most influential books of the twentieth century.

Key words: African American culture; jazz; politics

[…] We will also have a cultural department. The task or duty of the cultural department will be to do research into the culture, into the ancient and current culture of our people, the cultural contributions and achievements of our people. And also all of the entertainment groups that exist on the African continent that can come here and ours who are here that can go there. Set up some kind of cultural program that will really emphasize the dormant talent of black people.

When I was in Ghana I was speaking with, I think his name is Nana Nketsia, I think he's the minister of culture or he's head of the culture institute. I went to his house, he had a—he had a nice, beautiful place; I started to say he had a sharp pad. He had a fine place in Accra. He had gone to Oxford, and one of the things that he said impressed me no end. He said that as an African his concept of freedom is a situation or a condition in which he, as an African, feels completely free to give vent to his own likes and dislikes and thereby develop his own African personality. Not a condition in which he is copying some European cultural pattern or some European cultural standard, but an atmosphere of complete freedom where he has the right, the leeway, to bring out of himself all of that dormant, hidden talent that has been there for so long.

And in that atmosphere, brothers and sisters, you'd be surprised what will come out of the bosom of this black man. I've seen it happen. I've seen black musicians when they'd be jamming at a jam session with white musicians—a whole lot of difference. The white musician can jam if he's got some sheet music in front of him. He can jam on something that he's heard jammed before. If he's heard it, then he can duplicate it or he can imitate it or he can read it. But that black musician, he picks up his horn and starts blowing some sounds that he never thought of before. He improvises, he creates, it comes from within. It's his soul, it's that soul music. It's the only area on the American scene where the black man has been free to create. And he has mastered it. He has shown that he can come up with something that nobody ever thought of on his horn.

Well, likewise he can do the same thing if given intellectual independence. He can come up with a new philosophy. He can come up with a philosophy that nobody has heard of yet. He can invent a society, a social system, an economic system, a political system, that is different from anything that exists or has ever existed anywhere on this earth. He will improvise; he'll bring it from within himself. And this is what you and I want.

You and I want to create an organization that will give us so much power we can sit down and do as we please. Once we can sit down and think as we please, speak as we please, and do as we please, we will show people what pleases us. And what pleases us won't always please them. So you've got to get some power before you can be yourself. Do you understand that? You've got to get some power before you can be yourself. Once you get power and you be yourself, why, you're gone, you've got it and gone. You create a new society and make some heaven right here on this earth.

And we're going to start right here tonight when we open up our membership books into the Organization of Afro-American Unity. I'm going to buy the first memberships myself—one for me, my wife, Attillah, Qubilah, these are my daughters, Ilyasah, and something else I expect to get either this week or next week. As I told you before, if it's a boy I'm going to name him Lumumba, the greatest black man who ever walked the African continent.

He didn't fear anybody. He had those people so scared they had to kill him. They couldn't buy him, they couldn't frighten him, they couldn't reach him. Why, he told the king of Belgium, "Man, you may let us free, you may have given us our independence, but we can never forget these scars." The greatest speech—you should take that speech and tack it up over your door. [...]

Part 6

Liveness

41   Improvised Liveness: Opening Statements

Improvisation and the "Live": Playing with the Audience

Clare Grant

In "Improvisation and the 'Live,'" Clare Grant discusses the very immediate problems of performances that truly embrace both audience and performer, so that "both parties pass through a liminal phase and into a new understanding of a public exchange." After two years of performing with the KISS Theatre Group in Europe, Grant returned to Australia, and in 1987 co-founded The Sydney Front, a collective of performers responding to the lack of an experimental edge in the city's mainstream theatre scene. She has been an important figure in the creation of new Australian works for theatre, radio, and film, including her own solo performance *Woman in the Wall.* Other performance works include *Burn Sonata* (1998), *Inland Sea* (2000, with Nikki Heywood), *Laquiem* (1999, with Andree Greenwell from writing by Kathleen Mary Fallon), and the film *The Mary Stuart Tapes* (2000, with John Gillies). Lecturer in Performance at the University of New South Wales since 1998, she has made a number of original, research-based performance works with students, as well as continuing to perform and act as freelance dramaturge. In 2012 she published *Staging the Audience: The Sydney Front*, an eight-pack collection of DVDs and archival documents.

Key words: theatre; Australia; interdisciplinarity

The paradox at the heart of all improvisation (as I learnt over 30 years ago in a Commedia Dell'Arte, workshop in Auckland, NZ, with Lecoq-trained Heather Rob) is that the greatest of freedoms as a performer is created in the most highly structured of situations. In Commedia it is the so-called "string of pearls," the series of pre-determined, narrative landing spots, that create the conditions in which the performer can conjure her riffs of action "live"; that is, in a moment of action created in the company of an audience. The more refined those pearls, the wilder the flights of the unexpected.

In a more contemporary context, performance may well be back "out on the streets," but, unlike Commedia, might well be in a petrol station, an art gallery or in a private home; it may be mediated through a range of ever-more sophisticated interactive media or it may be down with the performers, on the floor of a shared performance space. Audiences now often find themselves an integral part of the same event as the performers. No lazzi (sequence of plot points, or story) here, but a transaction that takes place, around parameters designed by the makers, between the audience and the performers, usually without the familiarity and comfort of a story-line to follow. These performances tend to be less representative and more presentational or even performative, in the sense that a new action is taking place and the audience is part of the making of that action. Here I'm taking "performative" to be an event in which something occurs that includes both audience and performer. A transaction takes place in which, if the infrastructure of the exchange has been thoroughly imagined and then established, both parties pass through a liminal phase and into a new understanding of a public exchange.

In the sense that neither party can fully know what will take place in the interaction, it is live, expanding but including the notion of the live that is shaped by the virtual presence of interactive media. That live moment is a moment of improvisation that must be prepared for with the same rigour, though with different structural parameters and arguably with many more variables, as that of the ancient street performers, safe up on their stage, still in a separate fictional world from their spectators.

> The drive to the live has long been the critical concern of performance and Live Art where the embodied event has been employed as a generative force to shock, to destroy pretence, to break apart traditions of representation, to foreground the experiential, to open different kinds of engagement with meaning, to activate audiences.
>
> (Heathfield, 2004)

With the recent advent of this activated audience creating spontaneous action, albeit within the parameters created by – and sometimes with – the performance-makers, the live and immersive performance becomes that much more unpredictable. Thus, whether the situation is vast or intimate, whether on a street or in theatre, whether mediated by technology or not, the success of the performance becomes so much more dependent on the rigorous preparations of those landing spots where an audience joins the improvisation.

The audience member (the audient) is alone in this open world of the performance floor, or more aware of her alone-ness even in the company of others. The performers "step off the stage" as invoked by Tim Etchells (2008) to do, hence the work diverges from the illusory world, and she is hungry for any locating detail that tells her: "Who, what, where, when, why am I in this?" The brain moves as lightning-fast as the Commedia performer, but with immense scepticism and a strong need for self-protection.

The audient must know where she stands, literally, in the instant, no matter how hypothetical or propositional the worlds she is led into might be, so she can let the larger story build into her body and release her from her scepticism, to join the game.

As audient, I must somehow come to understand each of those steppingstones, though not what the final outcome will be; be made to feel safe before I can feel the full thrill of being unsafe, and unpinned, and to find the limit of where I can go in this constructed world, perhaps with some new technological tools of engagement to learn as I go, or some new configuration of personal engagement to navigate. As an audience member, in a well-constructed event, I can fly as free as I can within the web of the Commedia structure, knowing my experience is being attended to by those who have gone before.

Performance is most live when we are in a space humming with immanence, but with a clear tangible and simple task to perform; it might be an open street space, or we might be standing on an empty, unmarked floor or maybe in a tiny booth with a silent other. In that vastness of potential meaning-making, we want clear, simple, pragmatic instructions to bounce away from; there's no time for interpretation or illustration, representation, symbolism or obscure expression in the immediacy of the moment-by-moment accumulating experience.

This is the place of the performative, the enacted "real." Something is happening here and, as audient, I am making what seem to be life-saving decisions; I have to be as sharp as the warrior in Suzuki training, ready for anything and wide open to everything presented to me. Illustration, representation, and interpretation *might* re-enter, as part of the world-logic-building, as another tool, just as much part of the givens as a piece of technological equipment, but just like those machines, they can't be the matter; in the live they are just a means to an end. There is no time for fiction, unless we're handed one, perhaps, as part of a specific task, and no time for a construction that doesn't announce itself as one.

Some time ago, I found myself trapped in a helmet suspended from the ceiling of the performance space at a work-in-progress performance (*Thrashing Without Looking*, 2010). The helmet moved within a certain range, but it projected only a fixed point of view, created by a camera over which I had no control. In the otherwise open performance area, I could move my body within the range of the helmet's cable but I had no power to select what I could look at. What I experienced was an extreme (and potentially fascinating) disjunction between my eyes and my body. There were immense areas of the large open space I couldn't see. With several others, I was exposed, in the centre of this expanse, to the second, non-helmeted half of the audience, while I blindly undertook a task: eating what turned out to be a delicious cake. It had been wheeled in front of me on a trolley, only sensed at the moment it bumped into my legs. The humiliating task was only manageable by negotiating some nauseatingly conflicting sensations from my seemingly dislocated eye and hand and my awareness of the presence of unknown others. I have since wondered how it might have been made possible for me to enter a larger game in which I could engage, to play, to have a sense of the *raison-d'être* of the performance, perhaps even to a point where I might have been thrilled to feel the humiliation, more fully engaged in its larger purpose.

If we know, as audience, where we are, what it is that we are in, and what we have to do, but still with the thrill of not knowing what it will add up to, there is the potential for mastery and agency and the expansion of our own sense of our daily experience. I'm remembering the moment of discovering that I was good at tracking virtual action while standing on a movable footpad in Blast Theory's *Desert Rain*. I still surprise myself years later to recall I was good at that.

Somehow, the audient needs to come to know that the "hosts"—the full system of front of house personnel, the publicity material, the physical arrangement of the space—will guide her through whatever rules govern the mise-en-scène that have been prepared for her, that these hosts have thought into all the parameters of what she might experience; that they have worked out every potential variant, either by creating some kind of role-modelling in the performance itself, or through dreaming up and playing out all the possibilities in their own improvisations in rehearsal – not just asking what this show is about, but what it is that is going to happen in the space: what will take place in the company of the audience, within the course of the work? The question is "What's going on here?" rather than "What is the story here?"

But that is the difficult bit as a maker, of course, to create a work that is so fully live for an audience, to devise action that is so fully imagined it is full of the unexpected for both audience and performer/makers; to imagine a space of agency and change in which every participant can experience a new twist in a situation that at first touch seems simple and to create the exhilaration of playing in the unknown.

A memory: I am performing. I am seated on a raised seating bank with my six colleagues, all in our largely synthetic bridal dresses, making notes in little black books while we scan the audience assembled in front of us on the performance floor, and I smell smoke. A rapid check determines it is coming from behind me and it takes only a few nanoseconds to realise that it must be John, burning the pages of his book. There was no prior planning for this and I don't believe we ever spoke about it, but I knew the pages would be shut on the flames and the book safely in its place well in time for the next action. In a tightly inscribed narrative, we would have had to have created an explanation, a rationalisation for the action in terms of the character. Instead, the music came to an end, and we all leapt up and swept into the next action, towards the next pearl.

Works Cited

Don Juan. 1992. On tour with The Sydney Front.

Etchells, T., 2008. Step Off The Stage. In D. Brine, ed. 2008. *The Live Art Almanac*. London: Live Art Development Agency.

Heathfield, A., 2004. Alive. In A. Heathfield, ed. 2004. *Live: Art and Performance*. London: Tate Publishing. pp. 6–15.

Thrashing Without Looking. 2010. M. Coutts, T. Meecham, L. Thoms, W. S. Wieland. Liveworks, Performance Space, Sydney.

42 Liveness

Philip Auslander

Just as the dynamic between composition and improvisation is often a power dynamic, so Philip Auslander describes the relationship between live and mediatised images in multimedia performance. Dr Auslander suggests that despite the immediacy and spontaneity of live performances, they can become merely "pale reflections" in the dominant landscape of new media. Philip Auslander is a professor at the Georgia Institute of Technology, teaching in the School of Literature, Communication, and Culture since 1999. His most recent books are a new edition of *Liveness: Performance in a Mediatized Culture* (2008/1999), which received the Callaway Prize for the Best Book in Theatre or Drama, *Performing Glam Rock: Gender and Theatricality in Popular Music* (2006), and as editor with Carrie Sandahl, *Bodies in Commotion: Performance and Disability* (2005; winner of the Association for Theatre in Higher Education's Research Award for Outstanding Book). He is also the editor of the four-volume reference collection *Performance: Critical Concepts* (2003). With a PhD in Theatre from Cornell University, Dr Auslander has written on aesthetic and cultural performances as diverse as theatre, performance art, music, stand-up comedy, robotic performance, and courtroom procedures. With his wife, the visual artist Deanna Sirlin, he edits *The Art Section: An Online Journal of Art and Cultural Commentary*. The following section is the Conclusion to his book *Liveness: Performance in a Mediatized Culture*.

key words; theatre; interdisciplinarity; new media; dance

My project here—analyzing the situation of live performance in a mediatized culture—has entailed documenting many of the ways in which mediatization impinges upon live events. Almost all live performances now incorporate the technology of reproduction, at the very least in the use of electric amplification and sometimes to the point where they are hardly live at all. But the influence of mediatization on live events is not simply a matter of equipment. Some live performances, such as certain Broadway plays and many sports events, are now literally made for television; the live event itself is shaped to the demands of mediatization. Others, like Madonna's concerts and Disney's *Beauty and the Beast*, recreate mediatized performances in a live setting.

In many instances, the incursion of the mediatized into the live has followed a particular historical pattern. Initially, the mediatized form is modeled on the live form but it eventually usurps the live form's position in the cultural economy. The live form then starts to replicate the mediatized form. This pattern is apparent in the historical relationship of theatre and television. Those involved in early television production first took the replication of the theatre spectator's visual experience as their objective. And the cultural discourse sur-rounding television successfully defined the new medium as delivering the same experience as the theatre only under conditions better suited to postwar suburban culture. This understanding of television contributed to its ability to displace the theatre within the cultural economy of the postwar period. I have argued here that, since the late 1940s, live theatre has become more and more like television and other mediatized cultural forms. To the extent that live performances now emulate mediatized representations, they have become second-hand recreations of themselves as retracted through mediatization.

This historical dynamic does not occur in a vacuum, of course. It is bound up with the audience's perception and expectations, which shape and are shaped by technological change and the uses of technology influenced by capital investment. As Jacques Attali (1985) shows, an economy based in repetition and the mass reproduction of cultural objects emerged when the production of unique cultural objects was no longer profitable. Analyzing audience desires when mediatized culture was in its infancy, Walter Benjamin (1986 [1936]) concluded that audiences were responding to the perceptual possibilities offered by the film medium. What this new mass audience wanted, in Benjamin's view, was a relationship to cultural objects defined by proximity and intimacy. He saw the desire for reproducible cultural objects as symptomatic of these needs. Building on Benjamin's analysis, I have suggested that our current concepts of proximity and intimacy derive from television. The incursion of mediatization into live events can be understood as a means of making those events respond to the need for televisual intimacy, thus fulfilling desires and expectations shaped by mediatized representations.

At various points, I have described the relationship between the live and the mediatized as competitive, conflictual, and agonistic. I must stress, however, that I consider this relation of opposition to exist only at the level of a cultural economy that responds to changing historical and technological circumstances. It is not an opposition rooted in essential differences between the live and the mediatized. Some contemporary performance practitioners and theorists like Eric Bogosian and Peggy Phelan derive a notion of live performance as a socially and politically oppositional discourse from ostensible ontological differences between live and mediatized representations. I have argued here that the qualities performance theorists frequently cite to demonstrate that live performance forms are ontologically different from mediatized forms turn out, upon close examination, to provide little basis for convincing distinctions. Mediatized forms like film and video can be shown to have the same ontological characteristics as live performance, and live performance can be used in ways indistinguishable from the uses generally associated with mediatized forms. Therefore, ontological analysis does not provide a basis for privileging live performance as an oppositional discourse.

In rejecting the argument for ontological differences between live and mediatized cultural forms, I suggested that the best way of thinking about that relationship is to look at the meanings and uses of live performance in specific cultural contexts. To that end, I offered a detailed analysis of the relationship between live and recorded performances in the culture of rock music. The historical narrative of the relationship between theatre and television applies as well to the general relationship between popular music and sound recording. Live performance ceased long ago to be the primary experience of popular music with the result that most live performances of popular music now seek to replicate the music on the recordings. Even in the case of a musical genre like jazz, where the artist is expected to produce a performance different from the recorded one, the recording is the standard according to which the live performance is judged.

The particular relationship of live and recorded performances in rock culture revolved around a complex articulation of the concept of authenticity that was central to the rock ideology of the 1960s and 1970s. I have argued here that rock authenticity is a concept that depends on a specific interaction of recordings and live performances rather than the nomination of one or the other as authentic. The primary experience of the music is as a recording; the function of live performance is to authenticate the sound on the recording. In rock culture, live performance is a secondary experience of the music but is nevertheless indispensable, since the primary experience cannot be validated without it. Although some rock fans do insist that live music is authentic in a way that recorded music is not, the relationship of live and mediatized performances in rock culture was never actually a relation of opposition in which the live was seen as authentic and the recorded as inauthentic. Rather, authenticity was produced through a dialectical or symbiotic relationship between live and mediatized representations of the music, in which neither the recording nor the live concert could be perceived as authentic in and of itself.

Arguably, as mediatization furthered its incursion into rock with the advent of music video, rock's ideology of authenticity lost its sway. In yet another iteration of the historical narrative I have proposed, music video displaced live performance in its relationship to sound recordings by taking over live performance's authenticating function. A relationship that had previously centered on a couple became a threesome: live performance of rock did not cease to exist, but was reduced to replicating and, thus, authenticating the *video* rather than the music itself. The importance of both live performance and the authenticity it certified have diminished considerably in rock culture. Rock ideology exists now only as a simulation deployed by the music industry. Through *MTV Unplugged*—with its emphasis on liveness and acoustic musicianship—and the strategic awarding of Grammys, the industry simulates the ideological distinctions on which rock culture is based (e.g. the distinction between the authentic and the inauthentic), thus maintaining its power as the arbiter of those distinctions.

After devoting most of this work to examining the status of live performance in cultural realms over which mediatization has achieved dominion, I turned to one social realm that has offered significant resistance to the incursion of mediatization: the legal arena. By discussing the failure of the prerecorded videotape trial to take root, I showed that the assumption that a trial is an ontologically live event is embedded so deeply in the discourse of American law that the mediatized trial simply could not become the dominant form. To demonstrate the centrality of live performance to legal procedure, I discussed both the system's strong preference for live testimony and the ways in which testimony is defined as a live performance of memory-retrieval in the present moment of the trial.

It is ironic that the legal system may be the one place in a mediatized culture in which live performance retains its traditional functions and values, since some performance theorists claim that live performance's ontology of disappearance and its persistence only in memory allow it to escape the reach of regulation and, thus, make it a site of resistance to the law. In examining intellectual property law, we can see that this is true to a limited degree. Although the law has increasingly approached the idea of making performance "ownable" as a cultural commodity through the development of the right of publicity, that area of law governs performance only if it is seen as a part of the performer's self. Live performance's temporal evanescence does remove it from the purview of copyright law. Even where performances are recorded, the underlying text is copyrighted but not the *performance* of the text. Therefore, it is fair to say that performance *qua* performance has so far escaped legal definition as a cultural commodity and is unregulated to that extent.

However, the notion that performance's disappearance into memory exempts it from regulation is untenable. As I showed, memory is both a site policed by the law and a central mechanism of law enforcement. The workings of memory themselves can be the objects of legal discipline, as George Harrison learned from the lawsuit over "My Sweet Lord." Far from providing a safe haven from regulation, spectatorial memory can be brought into legal discourse to determine whether a performance has infringed a copyright. Most significant of all, live performance and memory both enter the service of the law in the form of testimony, the live performance of memory retrieval. Given all the ways in which the legal system subjects memory to surveillance, adjudicates its operation, and presses it into service as an agent of legal procedure, the suggestion that memory is a realm exempt from regulation is clearly erroneous.

A colleague told me recently that my historical narrative describing the relationship between the live and the mediatized brought to her mind an image of two mirrors facing each other and bouncing an image back and forth between them. If the relationship between the live and the mediatized could be understood as the infinite regress this image suggests, then one would expect that after live performances had become more like mediatized ones, mediatized performances would start to resemble live performances that had internalized mediatization. Subsequent live performances would mirror those mediatized representations, and so on. To think about the relationship between the live and the mediatized in this way is implicitly to assume that each category has comparable cultural standing, that each has an equally strong interest in reflecting the other. But my view of cultural economy holds that at any given historical moment, there are dominant forms that enjoy much greater cultural presence, prestige, and power than other forms. Non-dominant forms will tend to become more like the dominant ones but not the other way around. At present, television is the dominant cultural form. Since television usurped the theatre's position in the cultural economy, theatre has become more like television. But has television gone on to become more like theatre-as-television? That Chapters 2 and 3 [in *Liveness: Performance in a Mediatized Culture*] both end with the suggestion that the way live performance is perceived and the cultural prestige accorded to it are generational issues indicates that the relationship between the live and the mediatized is a volatile question subject to significant change over time. If the cultural prestige of live performance were to increase in the future, a kind of back-and-forth exchange among different cultural forms might well occur. That seems unlikely, however. Currently, mediatized forms enjoy far more cultural presence and prestige—and profitability—than live forms. In many instances, live performances are produced either as replications of mediatized representations or as raw materials for subsequent mediatization. As I have argued here, any change in the near future is likely to be toward a further diminution of the symbolic capital associated with live events.

Bibliography

Attali, Jacques (1985) *Noise: The Political Economy of Music*, Brian Massumi (trans.), Minneapolis: University of Minnesota Press.
Benjamin, Walter (1986 [1936]) "The work of art in the age of mechanical reproduction," Harry Zohn (trans.), in *Video Culture: A Critical Investigation*, John G. Hanhardt (ed.), Layton, UT: Peregrine Smith Books, pp. 27–52.

Bogosian, Eric (1994) *Pounding Nails in the Floor With My Forehead*, New York: Theatre Communications Group.

Phelan, Peggy (1993a) *Unmarked: The Politics of Performance*, London, New York: Routledge.

——(1993b) "Preface: Arresting performances of sexual and racial difference: toward a theory of performative film," *Women & Performance: A Journal of Feminist Theory*, 6, 2:5–10.

43 The Revolution Will Not Be Televised

Gil Scott-Heron

Like Philip Auslander, Gil Scott-Heron (1949–2011) questions the relationship between history and its mediatisation and, like Malcolm X, he calls for change that will "put you in the driver's seat." In the years since its composition, Scott-Heron's most famous performance piece (1970) may be seen to have gained resonance in the way that, although the power of its famous names have faded, its call for action and empowerment is stronger than ever. Composed when Scott-Heron was only 21, it appeared on his first album *Small Talk at 125th and Lenox*, beginning a career dedicated to spreading messages of social justice, civil rights, and environmental responsibility. In 1978 his hit R&B single "Angel Dust" decried the ravages of PCP, and the next year, following the Three Mile Island nuclear accident, he released "We Almost Lost Detroit," about a less publicised near-disaster in Michigan. In his book *The Last Holiday*, Scott-Heron writes proudly about his efforts, with Stevie Wonder, to establish Martin Luther King Day as a US national holiday. His work was a clear influence on hip-hop and rap artists—although he resisted his received moniker "the godfather of rap." Rather he called himself a "bluesologist—a scientist who is concerned with the origin of the blues."

Key words: jazz; poetry; African American culture; new media

> You will not be able to stay home, brother.
> You will not be able to plug in, turn on and cop out.
> You will not be able to lose yourself on scag and
> skip out for beer during commercials because
> The revolution will not be televised.
>
> The revolution will not be televised.
> The revolution will not be brought to you by Xerox
> in four parts without commercial interruption.
> The revolution will not show you pictures of Nixon
> blowing a bugle and leading a charge by John
> Mitchell, General Abrams and Spiro Agnew to eat
> hog maws confiscated from a Harlem sanctuary.
> The revolution will not be televised.
>
> The revolution will not be brought to you by
> The Schaeffer Award Theatre and will not star Natalie
> Wood and Steve McQueen or Bullwinkle and Julia.

The revolution will not give your mouth sex appeal.
The revolution will not get rid of the nubs.
The revolution will not make you look five pounds thinner.
The revolution will not be televised, brother.

There will be no pictures of you and Willie Mae
pushing that shopping cart down the block on the dead run
or trying to slide that color t.v. in a stolen ambulance.
NBC will not be able to predict the winner at 8:32
on reports from twenty-nine districts.
The revolution will not be televised.

There will be no pictures of pigs shooting down
brothers on the instant replay.
There will be no pictures of pigs shooting down
brothers on the instant replay.
There will be no pictures of Whitney Young being
run out of Harlem on a rail with a brand new process.
There will be no slow motion or still lifes of Roy
Wilkins strolling through Watts in a red, black and
green liberation jumpsuit that he has been saving
for just the proper occasion.

Green Acres, Beverly Hillbillies and Hooterville
Junction will no longer be so damned relevant and
women will not care if Dick finally got down with
Jane on Search for Tomorrow because black people
will be in the streets looking for A Brighter Day.
The revolution will not be televised.

There will be no highlights on the Eleven O'Clock
News and no pictures of hairy armed women
liberationists and Jackie Onassis blowing her nose.
The theme song will not be written by Jim Webb or
Francis Scott Key nor sung by Glen Campbell, Tom
Jones, Johnny Cash, Englebert Humperdink or Rare Earth.
The revolution will not be televised.

The revolution will not be right back after a message
about a white tornado, white lightning or white people.
You will not have to worry about a dove in your
bedroom, the tiger in your tank or the giant in your toilet bowl.
The revolution will not go better with coke.
The revolution will not fight germs that may cause bad breath.
The revolution *will* put you in the driver's seat.

The revolution will not be televised will not be televised
not be televised be televised
The revolution will be no re-run, brothers.
The revolution will be LIVE.

44   The Present of Performance

Hans-Thies Lehmann

Translated by Karen Jürs-Munby

Hans-Thies Lehmann argues that drama is characterised by narrative, and defines postdramatic theatre, in his eponymous book, which includes "The Present of Performance," as theatre in which the progression of a story with its internal logic no longer forms the centre. It is a definition that shares common ground with Tim Etchells, The Living Theater, and other contributors to this volume. Dr Lehmann first undertook general and comparative literary studies in Berlin, where he received his PhD. At Johann-Wolfgang-Goethe University, Frankfurt/Main, he became Professor of Theatre Studies in 1988, founding a post-graduate program in Dramaturgy as well as the Frankfurt International Summer Academy. He has been active in theatre himself, creating his own projects as well as working with directors such as Peter Palitzsch, Jossi Wieler, Christof Nel, and Theodoros Terzopoulos. Dr Lehmann is president of the International Brecht Society and is widely recognised for his studies of the work of Brecht's disciple Heiner Müller. His books include *Bertolt Brechts, Hauspostille: Text und kollektives Lesen* (1978, with Helmut Lethen), *Theater und Mythos* (1991), and his best-known work, the much-translated *Postdramatic Theater* (1999).

Key words: Postdramatic Theatre, Europe, postmodernism/Jean-Luc Nancy, Tim Etchells, The Living Theater, Augusto Boal

Hans Ulrich Gumbrecht has demonstrated the extent to which the 'elementary gesture' of a 'production of presence' that 'seems to have taken away a lot of space from the forms, genres and rituals of representation'[1] is responsible for our fascination with sport (as a real event). According to this argument it is a matter of 'moving things within reach so that they can be touched'.[2] This is a rewording of Benjamin's thesis that the indomitable desire of the masses to move things closer was the basis for the de-auratization of the arts. For the hermeneutics of the production of presence, Gumbrecht draws on nothing short of the Eucharist, in which bread and wine are not the signifiers for Christ's body and blood but real presence in the act of communion, not something designated but substance: the model of a 'presence' that refers to itself and joins the gathered congregation in a ritual ceremony. In this sense, Gumbrecht compares the sports event to the medieval stage: here as there, it is not a hermeneutic attitude that is demanded. Unlike in modern theatre (according to Gumbrecht), the players on stage do not pretend that they do not notice the audience but instead interact with it.

The thesis that in sports we are dealing with the phenomenon of a performance (*Performanz*) symptomatic for the cultural development trend, and which does not function according to the registers of representation and hermeneutic interpretation, makes good sense. It indeed seems to be the case 'that the increasing importance of sports events is possibly part of a larger shift within contemporary culture',[3] in which the cultural phenomenon of the 'production of presence' (*not* mimesis or representation) is gaining in importance. It is another question, however, whether especially in sports the 'realistic' dimension of victory and defeat, (monetary) gain and loss, does not repress the epiphany of presence, so that in the end sport is still entirely dissimilar to theatrical rituals – a question that cannot be further discussed here. In any case, the combination of a naïve or blasphemous execution of a magic ceremony, interactive performance, and production of presence is an illuminating motif for post-dramatic theatre. It explains the latter's insistence on presence, the ceremonial and ritual tendencies, and the tendency to put it on a footing with rituals prevalent in many cultures. Gumbrecht does not ignore that such a presence can never be completely 'there' or 'fulfilled', in the full sense of the word, that it always retains the character of the 'longed for' and the 'alluded to', and always disappears when it enters into the reflected experience. He goes back to Schiller's idea of a reference which is not naïve but merely 'sentimental' in order to think of it as the 'birth of a presence' (Nancy), as a coming, an advent, a simply *imaginable* presence.[4]

Meanwhile, what is important for the theatre is not only the insight into the merely virtual mode of being of presence but also its ethically overdetermined quality of *co-presence*, i.e the mutual challenge. If there is a paradox of the actor (Diderot), then there is all the more a paradox of his presence. There is the gesture, the sound that he gives to us – but not simply as an emanation from this actor there, from the plenitude of his reality, but as an element produced by the complex situation of the theatre as whole, as a situation, which in turn cannot be summed up in its totality. What we encounter is an obvious presence but it is of a different kind than the presence of a picture, a sound, a piece of architecture. It is objectively – even if not intentionally – a co-presence referring to ourselves. Hence it is no longer clear whether the presence is given to us or whether we, the spectators produce it in the first place. The presence of the actor is not an ob-ject, an objectifiable present but a co-presence in the sense of an unavoidable implication of the spectator. The aesthetic experience of theatre – and the presence of the actor is the paradigmatic case here because as the presence of a living human being it contains all the confusions and ambiguities related to the limit of the aesthetic as such – this aesthetic experience is only in a secondary manner reflection. The latter rather takes place *ex post* and would not even have a motivation had it not been for the prior experience of an event that cannot be 'thought' or 'reflected' and which, in this sense, has the character of a shock. All aesthetic experience knows this bipolarity: first the confrontation with a presence, sudden and in principle this side of or beyond the rupturing, doubling reflection: then the processing of this experience by an act of retroactive remembering, contemplating and reflecting.

The aesthetics of fright *Ästhetik des Schreckens* of Karl Heinz Bohrer proves helpful in analysing the presence we are dealing with in performance and in those forms of theatre that abandon the paradigm of dramatic theatre. Aesthetic time is not metaphorically translated historical time. The "event" situated within aesthetic time does not refer to the events of real time.[5] What we consider the specific temporality of performance itself – as distinguished from the represented time – for Bohrer is an aspect of shock and fright. Inversely, we are exploring the question of fright as an element of the theatre aesthetic. Here it is worthwhile to look at Bohrer's elucidations on fright. Considering Caravaggio's *Medusa* as an example, he explains that aesthetic fright is distinguished from real fright through a stylization that turns the frightening into an ornamental form. Hence, only an 'imaginary identification' takes place.[6] The second quality is even more important: 'The face of this Medusa is not actually instilling fright itself but she herself seems to be seeing something frightening her own mythic destiny, so to speak.'[7] Trembling in itself, the aesthetic appearance is situated beyond the representation of empirical fright. It does not represent something actually frightening. As aesthetic reality, the present 'appearance', therefore, does not invite the explanation, investigation or for example, 'tragic' interpretation of the frightening but only the 'mimetic' experience of getting frightened. The viewer of the painting goes through the realization of getting frightened that is 'posed' in the picture. Bohrer deduces from this model the qualities of *intensity* and of the *enigma*, which he rightly regards as constitutive elements of 'aesthetic experience', which on its part can be described with the equivalent formulas 'sudden appearance' and 'self-referential epiphany'.[8] It is beyond our present consideration to what extent the aesthetic temporality of this epiphany exclusively or overridingly defines modernity. Bohrer states the existence of a 'Greek and modern "aesthetics of fright"'[9] and considers the epiphany of fright as an 'aesthetic structure ... that recurs in different phases of European literature and art history'; he regards fifth-century Athens, the late Renaissance and the time around 1900 as especially favourable 'breeding grounds' for the phenomenality of fright (which in itself is not founded historically but aesthetically).

At this point it is fitting, however, to relate Bohrer's reflection to theatre and to vary it. We could say it is perhaps not her own destiny that the head of the Medusa sees. Instead her fright relates to a frightening reality which cannot be named at all. Precisely for this reason, according to the logic of the painting, the object of the fright has to remain *outside of* the represented (representable) world. It is formless. The painted gaze of the severed head does not 'look' but in the logic of the painted picture expresses precisely the gaze of the dead Medusa, i.e. a 'not-seeing'. It is the death of the gaze, its emptiness, its failure that is frightening. Thus, a fundamental motif within contemporary theories of art and theatre enters our context: the idea of the 'shock' (Benjamin), of 'suddenness' (Bohrer), of 'being assailed' (Adorno), of 'being horrified' (*Erschrecken*) that is 'necessary for cognition' (Brecht), the idea of fright (*Schrecken*) as the 'first appearance of the new' (Müller), the 'threat that nothing happens' (Lyotard). Both the de-dramatized forms of theatre, which communicate a kind of empty contemplation, and the immediately terrorizing and uncanny forms of radical pain-performance demonstrate this: a psychological interpretation of the fright which constitutes the experience of presence cannot suffice (and rightly does not interest Bohrer, either). There we would always have to think of fright as triggered by a representable object or circumstance. In the dimension of theatre aesthetics, however, we must recognize the structure of a shock whose arousal is independent of an object – not a fright occasioned by a story or an event but a fright about fright itself, so to speak. It can be illustrated by the experience of being *startled* when we suddenly realize we are missing something or cannot remember something – we cannot say what – and this not-having or not-knowing 'suddenly' enters our consciousness as an experience of emptiness – a signal we cannot interpret but that nevertheless affects us. The present, which in this way is an experience that is not suspended or suspendable, is the experience of a lack or of having missed something. This experience of lack takes place at the seam of time. Contrary to the suspicion of aestheticism, such an *aesthetic of startling* in theatre would be another name for an aesthetic of responsibility. The performance addresses itself fundamentally to my involvement: my personal responsibility to realize the mental synthesis of the event; my attention having to remain open to what does not become an object of understanding; my sense of participation in what is happening around me; my awareness of the problematic act of spectating itself.

Postdramatic theatre is a *theatre of the present*. Reformulating presence as present, in allusion to Bohrer's concept of the 'absolute present tense' ('das absolute Präsens'), means, above all, to conceive of it as a process, as a verb. It can be neither object, nor substance, nor the object of cognition in the sense of a synthesis effected by the imagination and the understanding. We make do with understanding this presence as something *that happens,* i.e. drawing on an epistemological – and even ethical – category as distinguishing for the aesthetic realm. Bohrer's formula of the 'absolute present' is incommensurate with all conceptions that regard the aesthetic as an intermediary, a medium, a metaphor, or a representative of an other reality. Art is not an intermediary either of the real or the human, or the divine or the absolute. Art is not 'real presence' in the sense of George Steiner. Instead the 'other' that is strictly without content is 'created in this moment, not as an aesthetic Pentecost but as an epiphany *sui generis'* in the presence of the work of art.[10] The variants of such 'epiphanies' can be systematically deduced but can only be analysed and dissected in their respective concrete forms. This present is not a reified point of time but, as a perpetual disappearing of this point, it is already a transition and simultaneously a caesura between the past and the future. *The present is necessarily the erosion and slippage of presence.* It denotes an event that empties the now and in this emptiness itself lets memory and anticipation flash up. The present cannot be grasped conceptually but only as a perpetual self-division of the now into ever new splinters of 'just now' and 'in an instant'. It has more to do with death than with the often evoked 'life' of theatre. As Heiner Müller states: 'And the specificity of theatre is precisely not the presence of the live actor but the presence of the one who is potentially dying.'[11] In postdramatic theatre, the present in this sense of a floating, fading presence – which at the same time enters experience as 'gone' (*fort*), as an absence, as an 'already leaving' – crosses out dramatic representation.

Perhaps in the end postdramatic theatre will only have been a moment in which the exploration of a 'beyond representation' could take place on all levels. Perhaps postdramatic theatre is going to open out onto a new theatre in which dramatic figurations will come together again, after drama and theatre have drifted apart so far. A bridge could be the narrative forms, the simple, even trivial appropriation of old stories, and (not least of all) the need for a return of conscious and artificial stylization in order to escape the Naturalist glut of images. Something new is going to come, and to use Brecht's words:

> This superficial rabble, crazy for novelties
> Which never wears its bootsoles out
> Never reads its books to the end
> Keeps forgetting its thoughts
> This is the world's
> Natural hope.
> And even if it isn't
> Everything new
> Is better than everything old.[12]

Notes

1 H. U. Gumbrecht, 'Die Schönheit des Mannschafssports: American Football – im Stadion und im Fernschen', in G. Vatimo and W. Welsch (eds), *Medien-Welten-Wirklichkeiten*, Munich: Fink Verlag, 1998, p. 208. See also H. U. Gumbrecht's recent book, *Production of Presence. What Meaning Cannot Convey*, Stanford, CA: Stanford University Press, 2004.

2 Ibid.

3 Ibid., p. 211.

4 Ibid., p. 214.

5 K. H. Bohrer, *Das absolute Präsens*, Frankfurt am Main: Suhrkamp, 1994, p. 7. See also the translated essay collection K. H. Bohrer, *Suddenness: On the Moment of Aesthetic Appearance*, trans. by R. Crowley, New York: Columbia University Press, 1994.

6 Ibid., p.40ff.

7 Ibid., p. 41.

8 Ibid.

9 Ibid., p. 62.

10 Ibid., p. 181.

11 A. Kluge and H. Müller, *Ich bin ein Landvermesser: Gespräche, Neue Folge*, Hamburg: Rotbuch, 1996, p. 95.

12 B. Brecht, 'Everything New is Better than Everything Old', trans. by C. Middleton, in B. Brecht, *Poems 1913–1956*, ed. by J. Willet and R. Manheim with the co-operation of E. Fried, London: Methuen, 2000, p. 160.

Bibliography

Adorno, T. W., *Minima Moralia: Reflections from a Damaged Life*, trans. by E. F. N. Jephcott, London: New Left Books, 1974.

——, *Aesthetic Theory*, trans. by C. Lenhardt, ed. by G. Adorno and R. Tiedemann, London: Routledge and Kegan Paul, 1984.

Benjamin, W., *Illuminations*, trans. by H. Zohn (ed.) and with an introduction by H. Arendt, New York: Schocken Books, 1968.

Bohrer, K. H., *Das absolute Präsens*, Frankfurt am Main: Suhrkamp, 1994.

——, *Suddenness: On the Moment of Aesthetic Appearance*, trans. by R. Crowley, New York: Columbia University Press, 1994.

Brecht, B., *Brecht on Theatre: Development of an Aesthetic*, ed. and trans. by J. Willet, London: Methuen, 1974 [1964].

——, *Werke, Berliner und Frankfurter Ausgabe*, ed. by W. Hecht, J. Knopf, W. Mittenzwei and K.D. Müller, Frankfurt am Main: Suhrkamp, 1989 onwards.

——, *Poems 1913–1956*, ed. by J. Willet and R. Manheim with the cooperation of E. Fried, London: Methuen, 2000.

Gumbrecht, H. U., 'Die Schönheit des Mannschafssports: American Football – im Stadion und im Fernschen', in G. Vatimo and W. Welsch (eds), *Medien-Welten-Wirklichkeiten*, Munich: Fink Verlag, 1998.

——, *Production of Presence. What Meaning Cannot Convey*, Stanford, CA: Stanford University Press, 2004.

Kluge, A. and Müller, H., *Ich bin ein Landvermesser: Gespräche, Neue Folge*, Hamburg: Rotbuch, 1996, p. 95.

Lyotard, J-F., 'The Tooth, the Palm', in T. Murray (ed.), *Mimesis, Masochism and Mime: Politics of Theatricality in Contemporary French Thought*, Ann Arbor: University of Michigan Press, 1977, pp. 282–88.

——, *Essays zu einer affirmativen Ästhetik*, Berlin: Merve, 1982.

——, *The Postmodern Condition: A Report on Knowledge*, trans. by G. Bennington and B. Massumi, foreword by F. Jameson, Minneapolis: University of Minnesota Press, 1984.

——, *The Postmodern Explained: Correspondence 1982–1985*, trans. by D. Barry *et al.*, afterword by W. Godzich, Minneapolis: University of Minnesota Press, 1993.

Müller, H., *Gesammelte Irrtümer*, Frankfurt am Main: Verlag der Autoren, 1986.

——, *Heiner Müller Material*, ed. by F. Hörnigk, Göttingen: Steidl Verlag, 1989.

——, *Jenseits der Nation*, Berlin: Rotbuch, 1991.

——, *Krieg ohne Schlacht, Leben in zwei Diktaturen: Eine Autobiographie*, Cologne, 1994.

45 Time in the Place of Space: Dialoguing Improvisation with Pierre Hébert

Saint-Bernard-de-Lacolle, Quebec, June 19, 2012

Interviewed by Nicholas Loess

Pierre Hébert

Born in Montreal in 1944, Pierre Hébert taught himself as a teenager how to make films, strongly influenced by the work of Norman McLaren and Len Lye; as he says to Nicholas Loess in this volume, "I saw myself as an artist using film amongst a number of things." In 1962 he began experimenting with engraving images directly onto processed 16mm or 35mm film. At the National Film Board of Canada from 1965 until 1999, in *Population Explosion* (1968) Hébert collaborated with Ornette Coleman, and, gradually in such films as *Entre chiens et loup* (1978) and *Memories of War* (1982), his work became more socially and politically involved. In 1983 he began collaborating in live performance with improvising musicians (Jean Derome, Robert M. Lepage, René Lussier, Fred Frith) and choreographers (Ginette Laurin, Rosalind Newman, Louise Bédard, and Jean-Marc Matos), finding that his own efforts to improvise within the film medium led to the development of other kinds of skills. He is currently using computers in the *Living Cinema* project with composer Bob Ostertag, and furthering his long-time interest in the relationships between animation and live action in his "Places and Monuments." In 2006 a collection of Hébert's writings on film were published as *Corps, langage, technologie*.

Key words: film; interdisciplinarity; Canada (Quebec); jazz

Nicholas Loess

Nicholas Loess' current research explores the creative linkages between film and improvisation. His recent film, the one-minute *24Progressive*, won top prize in the "Life Cycle" category at the 2012 Toronto Urban Film Festival. He is currently completing his doctorate in the School of English and Theatre Studies at the University of Guelph with the Improvisation, Community, and Social Practice research initiative. His award-winning artistic and scholarly work has been featured at conferences and festivals in Canada, USA, The Netherlands, and Romania.

Key words: music; film; interdisciplinarity; Canada

Nicholas Loess: How did you conceptualize your work when you first started making films?

Pierre Hébert: When I first started to do animation I wasn't seeing myself as a filmmaker. I saw myself as an artist using film, amongst a number of things. I was doing prints at a place in Montréal, so drawings, a little painting. One of my main references, apart from Norman (McLaren) who was clearly considering himself as a filmmaker, was Len Lye.

NL: Len Lye?

PH: Len Lye was doing film alongside all sorts of other things. He was doing sculpture. He understood himself to be an artist in a more general way, never solely as an animator. So my references were not exclusively in the field of filmmaking. There were more people who were using film and animation as just one possibility in their work … This was actually one of the reasons why I started to work with musicians. I was working more in music festivals than in animation festivals.

NL: Does this position make you more reflexive in adapting different media to different ideas to different projects?

PH: The need to use both live-action animation and animation associated together in film was a necessity and something that I was spontaneously attracted to. This created the conditions for not conforming to the classical boundaries of what animation is. It led to more freedom for integrating other forms … My film work with Jean Derome, René Lussier, and Robert [Marcel] Lepage in the eighties was quite unusual. Filmmakers are typically very precise when working with musicians. Our collaboration was more open-ended. I didn't feel like I needed to ask for specific things. They were free to do whatever they wanted as their part of the project. This was something that made me accept quite a loose framework when defining what I think animation, or an animated film should be.

NL: How did this open-endedness in the recording studio maturate into live performance?

PH: I did some drawings for a film that René was scoring. I spent quite a bit of time in the studio and there were quite a number of musicians that played on the music track. I was deeply impressed by how, on the one hand, they were improvising, and on the other hand, the way they were connected to and used the multi-track studio as an instrument. It really made me excited to see that … It became very explicit for me to try to understand how I could let their way of working influence my way of working. It really became an objective to be as free as they were in terms of physicality, and in terms of my relationship to the technological surroundings of my work.

NL: When did you start performing live-scratch animation?

PH: Jean Derome eventually joined us. He was teasing me, saying that he and René and Robert did all of the improvising and I came with my films that are already done. Our performances had led me to work much faster to add sections or change things in the performance. So the question of speed became something important in order to adjust to what they were doing ... One day, I was in the NFB cafeteria and I suddenly had this image of a projector with a loop that was long enough so that I could do work on the loose part of the loop while the projector was constantly running. This new way of doing performances was easier to handle because I considered my little set-up as an instrument. Musician friends would call me, and say, "we're playing tonight at this place," and I would come ...

NL: Bring your gear!

PH: Yup! Bring my gear as they would take their (laughs) saxophone and set up and have a gig with them. When I started to do this I was seeing myself really as a musician ...

NL: With images.

PH: With images.

NL: You must've been working on 16mm film at that time.

PH: It had to be 16mm film. There weren't many portable 35mm projectors, and film runs much faster through the 35mm projector. The piece of film would be more than twice as long. So the handling of the film with the projector eating the film that fast increased the risk of the film breaking. The other thing was that the 35mm frame is about four times as large as a 16mm frame ...

NL: There's more space for you to fill.

PH: Yeah. But it takes more time. With the 16mm frame, you do one line and you already have occupied most of the space. What you do on the 16mm frame has to be much more robust. On 35mm you can develop a sense of space, but you sacrifice time in the development of the image. Animation cannot be done as spontaneously and as directly as on 16mm ... The opening sequence to my film *Étienne et Sara* was entirely scratched on 35mm film. It was a very precise rendering of a birth of a child. It was, by far, the most precise scratch animation I've ever done. Soon after I realized that there was something absurd about this. This rendering could've been more easily accomplished using other animation techniques. What made scratch animation so interesting was its chaotic element, where you had the feeling that the energy of your body was being directly transferred through what was on the film. This transfer was all about speed and freedom. Precision removed these elements.

NL: You're talking about putting your own energy into what you're doing, and the instability and chaos of scratching on 16mm, and the speed at which you perform. You're working at 24 frames per second.

PH: Yeah.

NL: That's very fast.

PH: During a performance I would scratch one frame out of four, so there was sort of ...

NL: This chaos, instability, and spontaneity that attracts many musicians to improvised performance ...

PH: I had these improvisational musicians that I was working with regularly. They impressed me. I wanted to do the same thing that they were doing with my own image work. I stopped trying to make marks. I started to try to improvise, to animate spontaneously without having a detailed plan, without having a length of number of frames like animators would normally do. I relied on my inner feelings while I was animating ... If there was a shot I didn't like I wouldn't try to redo it. I would do something else. Looking back, even early on in my work, I can see that there was an improvisational approach. I was paying attention to the bodily relation to what I was doing ... Starting to do this live meant that my work could improve but not in terms of looking for the kind of precision and stability you find more easily in other techniques. Working live involved putting myself in such a critical situation of having to draw that quickly and not being able to rely on anything except the memory of my muscles, my hands, and my eyes. It created a totally different line of improvement of my work.

NL: So then what is the relationship between improvisation and memory in terms of your wider process and also in these moments when the film is flying by and you're not sure where you are?

PH: The relation with memory in the process of an improvisation was something I was totally conscious of. I would wish that there would be this gap in the ability of taking track of everything so it could lead me to surprising situations that appeared as problems that I had to solve. Like, I had 10 frames and I had to get this to connect with this. I was totally willing to create a situation of not being in control and not mastering the memory of everything I had done before. The other aspect of memory is more complex. I was haunted by my memory of Len Lye's images in *Free Radicals* and *Particles in Space* when I performed. I remember being unsure whether I would be quoting Lye, or if I would resist putting myself in this situation to imitate the images I have in my mind. You cannot pretend that you are always doing pure improvisation so that it would only relate to what is currently going on. This is absolutely impossible.

NL: How has your process as an improviser changed with your shift from film to video?

PH: I never quite accepted the term "new technology" as a way of declaring the appearance of a new era. There's always been this tendency to try to situate the cinema as an eternal art that could last as long as painting or sculpture. I felt uneasy with that way of seeing the cinema in terms of eternity. There was a similar sentiment for video when it took form. Artists were claiming it as an independent art. Any technologically based art is subject to the fact that at some point the technology would change radically. I left the NFB in 1999 and I knew there was no way I could afford to independently work with 35mm film. The fact that I knew that video was bound to change made it easy for me to move on from film. You cannot pretend that the technical foundations of your art will remain stable. This is an illusion. With the arrival of the first G4, and their affordability, the conditions were there for the continuation of my work.

NL: What do you think, what do you feel about improvisation as a concept and as a practice?

PH: I always had this idea that the more important ground on which an artistic work, whatever it is, in whatever field, can relate to a viewer of any kind is through the physicality of the work. Improvisation is putting this aspect in the foreground. This is one important element. I've always felt at ease with speed. I'm not a patient person, and so I like speed, and I want to take advantage to what speed allows, which involves quickly covering a lot of ground, and of course improvisation is one way that this can be implemented. Once you start to improvise you realize that you can make discoveries that would not exist otherwise. It keeps you doing it.

46 Improvisation and Theatrical Power: From Discipline to Refusal

Alan Filewod

Alan Filewod, the most prolific scholar of political theatre in English Canada, was introduced to activist theatre as a member of Newfoundland's Mummers Troupe in the 1970s, and in the 1980s, he was a founder of the Canadian Popular Theatre Alliance. Among his award-winning writings are the books *Committing Theatre: Theatre Radicalism and Political Intervention* (2011), *Performing Canada: The Nation Enacted in the Imagined Theatre* (2002), *Collective Encounters: Documentary Theatre in English Canada* (1987), and, with David Watt, *Workers' Playtime: Theatre and the Labour Movement since 1970* (2001). At the University of Guelph, his research interests include Canadian theatre history, radical political theatre, and masculinist performance in war play and reenactment. As co-director, in 2012 he presented a provocative re-staging of the long-neglected 1933 agitprop play *Eight Men Speak*, and has edited a critical edition of the play, published in 2013 by the University of Ottawa Press. "Improvisation and Theatrical Power" (2013) is a valuable overview of the different approaches to improvisation taken in Western theatre, in which it can empower the actors, reinforce (or countermand) the disciplinarity of the director–actor relationship, or feed into "a power claimed and enacted by the audience."

Key words: theatre; social activism; Canada

> DOCTOR HINKFUSS: Don't worry. Everything's under control.
>
> (Pirandello 38)

Despite its pervasive circulation as a trope of contemporary theatre practice, improvisation has been understood as a fantasy, or, as the semiotician Patrice Pavis points out in his *Dictionary of the Theatre* when addressing the relationship of improvisation to collective creation, "a myth" (181). The historical development of theatre as an integrated art form – the modernist proposal of 'theatre art'—drew upon improvisational practices as creative method, but at the same time fixed the impromptu inventiveness of improv in the regulatory structures of dramatic schema and directorial command. This was the paradox explored by Pirandello in his 1930 play *Tonight We Improvise*, in which the bombastic Dr. Hinkfuss promises an improvisational performance of a Pirandello story, but his cast rebel against the constraints of their assigned roles. Every word and intervention, including audience demonstrations, is fixed in the playscript. In theatre, Pirandello seems to suggest, improvisation is always an expression of power.

As a creative method, improv has been extraordinarily productive in channeling the creativity of actors and giving them a sense of ownership of the text. This has been particularly important in the collective approaches to script development that have been so central to the emergence of theatre cultures that challenged the authority of metropolitan repertoires and production processes in the decades after the Second World War. These were often expressed as libratory and oppositional, and the extent to which they introduced some measure of unplanned variance in performance was an index of cultural position in regards to canonical and institutional politics. Improvisation was (and is) on the one hand a technique of conservatory mastery that reinforced disciplinarity, and on the other a position of cultural oppositionality. But invariably the containment of the performance event imposes structural fixity. To dismantle that fixity is to risk negating the performance, and this has been a decided choice in contemporary political intervention theatre that refuses theatrical discipline.

The idea of improvisation has always been talismanic in the theatre because it speaks to the centrality of the actor's inventiveness from which theatre ultimately derives, as fancifully expressed in Boal's fable of the "invention" of theatre by a "prehuman woman" he names Xua-Xua, who learned to "look at herself" and in doing became human (15), "on the border of fiction and reality" (276). For two millennia, European theatre historiography accepted Aristotle's hellenocentric statement that theatre originated from improvised dithyrambs, and later historians accepted the thesis that theatre was "rediscovered" when singing monks began to improvise dialogue in the Quem Quaeritis tropes. Aethelwald's "Regularis Concordia" may be the most important early example of the textual containment process that regulated improvisation, or at least a tendency to improvise (activated by what? The excitement of the performance moment? A suffusion of worshipful joy? Performer competition?).

In these historiographic narratives, improvisation is a process that matures (according to Aristotle) into fixed structure and achieves form. We see a similar logic in the history of the commedia dell'arte, which has long exercised a powerful command on the cultural memory of theatre artists as the high moment of improvised theatre. The myth of commedia is one of an actor-centered theatre that drew upon a vast repertoire of scenarios, acrobatics, physical gestures and prankish *lazzi* to enable actors to improvise infinite variations of scenes, characters, incidents and jokes. But the memory of commedia as it has aroused theatre nostalgia is of the peak disciplinarity of the great troupes and writers of the seventeenth century, when the rustic market comedies had become court entertainment in the hands of Molière. Molière may have made the famous remark that theatre needed only two planks and a passion, but he had in fact the attention of the king and the stage of the Comédie Française, where little could be left to chance or the inclination of actors. In this, improvisation was contained as the procedural display of disciplinary skill; that is how commedia is still remembered.

Many years ago I saw this in action when I was fortunate to see Georgi Strehler's *Arlecchino, Servant of Two Masters* with the great clown Ferrucio Solieri in the lead. Strehler's adaptation of Goldoni's comedy remained in the repertoire of the Piccolo Teatro in Milan for more than half a century, and although it is now some forty years since I saw it, Solieri's audacity and physicality remain indelible in my memory. In the climactic moment of the show Arlecchino is trying to serve two offstage meals simultaneously, with plates whirling across the stage, caught, spun and sent flying in the opposite direction. Suddenly Solieri/ Arlechinno performs the classic "lazzi of the fly": Arlecchino is distracted by a fly; he follows it with his eyes and his hand; he jumps and misses it. He continues to leap around to catch the fly and eventually catches it, tears off its wings and eats it. But as he swallows it, the fly buzzes inside him and tickles him, and he stands on his hands and jumps up and down on his head to dislodge it. Time stops in the performance as the actor introduces this impromptu element. But it does not introduce chance; in fact, immediately afterwards Arlecchino realizes that his deception – of serving two masters and dinners at the same time – is about to be discovered. When he hears their approach from opposite wings, he jumps in alarm, and, in one of the greatest *coups de théâtre* I have ever seen, performs a reverse somersault and – without looking – lands in an open trunk that slams shut just as the other characters enter the stage. This was a moment that brought a house of 2000 spectators to their feet in applause. It was a remarkable stunt that the actor had practiced for four years before introducing it into the production. The actor had invented it, but in performance there was no room for error and nothing could be left to chance.

In canonical theatre practice, improvisation has been most useful as a way of unleashing actor creativity to sustain spontaneity in performance. As modernist staging increasingly emphasized the scenographic control of the stage and grounded the actor in a meaningful visual environment, that spontaneity had to be placed with fixity and precision. An actor might be creative and spontaneous but at the same time must be in the right place for the right lighting cue. This had the effect in the first half of the twentieth century to regulate improvisation, to keep it offstage and in the rehearsal hall.

For Stanislavski and his modernist contemporaries who applied the systemizations of industrial production to the theatre, the actor needed to be a creative and disciplined artist who could rediscover the performance time and again and, always guided by rigorous analysis, discover the same truth every time. Stanislavski introduced improvisational exercises in rehearsal to train actors in concentration and spontaneity, and as his principles circulated internationally in the 1920s and 30s (with a particular application in radical left modernist theatres, where they leveraged the shift from revolutionary agitprop to humanist realism), this relegation of improv to the rehearsal studio became increasingly systematized.

In the Group Theatre, which was the New York crucible of theatrical modernism, Harold Clurman advocated improvisation as a training regimen, and wrote about it briefly in his memoir, *The Fervent Years* (43–44). But the extent to which this regimen became institutionalized can be seen in John Gassner's extraordinarily influential 1949 textbook, *Producing the Play*, which became a standard handbook for collegiate and amateur theatres across North America. It reconciled rehearsal methods derived from Russian practice with the production procedures of the New York theatre economy. With sub-sections contributed by leading cadres of modernist practice, including Clurman, Lee Strasberg, Mordecai Gorelik and Marc Blitzstein, Gassner domesticated modernist theatre aesthetics and framed them in systematized and transferable production methods that emphasized the primacy of directorial analysis, Stanislavskian actor methodology, and the integration of scenography. The section on improvisation is a brief part of Clurman's contribution on "The Principles of Interpretation." Noting that the commercial theatre of the day "is unfamiliar with this method, and scornful of it," Clurman argues for the inclusion of improvisation in rehearsal processes for two reasons. "The first is to *make the actors improvise situations similar but not identical to those to be found in the play*" [italics in original] (292). This, following Stanislavski, compels the actor to use imagination to clarify the "true nature" of the role. The second type of improvisation "is based on the *doing of the actual scenes in the play with the actors using their own words* – substituting their own speech before they have committed the play's lines to memory." By doing so, Clurman explains, "the actor comes progressively closer to the play's text, till he is finally speaking the author's lines without ever having been aware of learning them at all" (293).

In the 1960s, fuelled by (mis)readings of Artaud, and inspired by the collective anarchy of the Living Theatre, the libratory theatrical resistance to this hierarchical concept of theatre as a playtext delivery mechanism advanced the idea of improvisation as collective creativity. This was to a large extent productive, as countless "alternative" troupes used improvisationally developed performances to express cultural or political specificity. But still, improvisation tended to fixity and repeatability in performance, and was subject to the (invariably masculinist) power of visionary director-auteurs. This was most visible when Peter Brook imported the methods of improvisational collective creation into the Royal Shakespeare Company in benchmark productions such as *Marat/Sade* and *US*. The tendency for improvisational theatre to coalesce around the centrality of theatrical gurus could be discerned at every point of the theatre's material spectrum, although it was a tendency fiercely contested by the feminist collectives that changed the landscape of alternative theatre practice in the 1980s.

In the disciplinary theatre – the complex of industry, professionalism, economy and canonicity that Baz Kershaw has identified as "the theatre estate" (91) – improvisation has historically reinforced regimentation. It has also produced new disciplinary regimens, in which 'improv' is a methodology to its own end. This is the trajectory that leads to the contemporary phenomenon of competitive theatre games, in which teams of improvisers compete to score points and laughs in displays of wit and skill. As a self-referential theatre practice, "improv" derives from educational drama techniques that became widespread in school curricula in the 1960s, with epicentres in the United Kingdom, Los Angeles, and Toronto. In the UK, the Theatre in Education movement saw a democratization of theatre techniques in schools as improvisation provided tools for teachers to encourage creativity. It had worldwide impact on pedagogy, principally through the writings of Dorothy Heathcote, and on theatre practice. Keith Johnstone, in his trajectory from teacher in English schools to a professorship at the University of Calgary, provided a major bridge between the educational and the professional theatre worlds; it was Johnstone who founded the concept of "theatresports" with his company, Loose Moose Theatre in 1977. At roughly the same time, improvisation had become widely circulated in North American "theatre arts" curricula through the work of Viola Spolin, whose 1963 book *Improvisation for the Theater* was one of the most influential training manuals in the history of American drama pedagogy. Its emphasis on group improv, games, and concentration exercises was a significant factor in the widespread phenomenon of collective creation as the high school students of the 1960s moved into the theatre world, many of them bypassing traditional routes of conservatory training. In Toronto, at the Ontario Institute for Studies in Education, the renowned drama educator Richard Courtney theorized improvisation in the context of cognitive science, philosophy, and pedagogical theory in his foundational 1968 book, *Play, Drama and Thought*.

Despite an explosion of techniques and applications (including therapy and workplace roleplay), the net consequence of these efforts was to institutionalize improvisation in classrooms and rehearsal halls where it is today no less assimilated into disciplinarity than it was for Stanislavski. In the theatre there has been a general sector differentiation between theatres that function as text delivery systems, where the economic necessity of short rehearsal times mitigates against extensive use of improv as a rehearsal method, and those that focus on devising, where improvisation is the channel that produces ensemble performance. If improvisation is suspended in the dialectic of libratory creativity, theatrical fixity and dramaturgical repeatability, its capacity for unplanned spontaneity emerges as a productive element of performance when it refuses disciplinarity. Perhaps the most iconic example of this is adaptive street-level interventionist performance, of masked demonstrator, clown armies and agitprop, where the dividing line between improvisation and *ad hoc* blurs.

Disciplinarity and refusal are not polarities but rather points on a spectrum of practice. They function reciprocally in the interactive performance model that Augusto Boal has called Forum Theatre. In the game structure of a theatre forum, the "spect-actor" who steps into the play to intervene in the dramatic model is improvising in a sense that is, more so than in most forms of theatrical improvisation, close to musical practice: unplanned, unrehearsed, functioning within a shared structure but with the capacity to redirect it. Forum interventions may or may not solve the problem in the moment of oppression, but a failed intervention is not therefore a performance failure. Boal has written that "I believe it is more important to achieve a good debate than a good solution because, in my view, the thing which incites spect-actors into entering into the game is the discussion and not the solution which may or may not be found" (259). Theatre forum can (and does) operate at every level of theatrical discipline, and functions most effectively with a team of trained actors and "jokers" (Boal's term for the facilitator) to establish the conditions of performance and intervention, but it refutes the most basic principle of theatrical drama, which Aristotle defined as "whole and complete." Although the "model," the play that presents a typifying simulation of an oppression, may have a dramatic structure with intervention trigger points, in the intervention phase of the performance it may never get past the first scene. For this reason, Boal states that a session of Theatre of the Oppressed never ends, "since the objective of Theatre of the Oppressed is not to close a cycle, or generate a catharsis or to bring an end to a process in development. On the contrary, its objective is to encourage autonomous activity, to set a process in motion, to stimulate transformative creativity, to change spectators into protagonists" (275).

There always remains the danger that Theatre of the Oppressed can itself be absorbed into a disciplinary framework that mitigates improvisation, but that risk is mediated by a functional theatrical refusal. Forum requires audiences who come together by shared implication in the subject of the play, a venue that opens the boundaries of house and stage, and a creative team of actors, directors, and jokers who can model the audience reality accurately, excite intervention, and adapt to audience improvisations without containing them. The social space of Theatre of the Oppressed is one defined by the intersection of theatre work and social justice activism, which means that for the most part it takes place outside of the theatre economy that organizes disciplinarity around the primacy of the authorial text and the directorial mise-en-scène. Only by (literally) unseating this authority does it establish a space in which undirected improvisation can change the course of the text. In this, Boal, like Pirandello, demonstrates that improvisation is an expression of power, but here it is a power claimed and enacted by the audience.

Works Cited

Boal, A., 1992. *Games for Actors and Non-Actors*. Translated by A. Jackson. London: Routledge.
Clurman, H., 1946. *The Fervent Years*. London: Denis Dobson.
——, 1941. Principles of Interpretation. In J. Gassner, ed. 1941. *Producing the Play*. New York: The Dryden Press. pp. 280–302.
Courtney, R., 1989. *Play, Drama & Thought: The Intellectual Background to Dramatic Education* (4th edition, revised). Toronto: Simon & Pierre.

Ethelwold [Aethelwold], 1952. Regularis Concordia. In A. M. Nagler, ed. 1952. *A Source Book in Theatrical History*. New York: Dover.

Kershaw, B., 1999. *The Radical in Performance: Between Brecht and Baudrillard* London/ New York: Routledge.

Pavis, P., 1998. *Dictionary of the Theatre: Terms, Concepts and Analysis*. Translated by C. Shantz. Toronto: University of Toronto Press.

Pirandello, L., 1987. *Tonight We Improvise and "Leonara, Addio."* Translated by J. D. Campbell and L. Sbrocchi. Ottawa: The Pirandello Society of Canada.

Spolin, V., 1969. *Improvisation for the Theater: A Handbook of Teaching and Directing Techniques*. Chicago: Northwestern University Press.

Part 7

Surprise

47 Improvised Surprise: Opening Statements

Rebecca Caines

Improvisation is hard work: it involves the exertion of continually, at times desperately, drawing on a lifetime of experience, and the simultaneous (un)working of those histories as one reacts and responds in "real time" to the alien, unexpected offers that come from collaborators and audiences during a performance. Improvisations are responsible to multiple agents. They bear the weight of intense labour and the competing pressures of simultaneous creative, social, economic, institutional, and psychological imperatives. As Viola Spolin suggests in her chapter excerpted in this section, creative spontaneity is a collaborative responsibility, as all improvisers are "inextricably bound up with every other person in the complexity of the artform." Perhaps it should be no revelation that improvisers sometimes fold under the weight of this kind of workload, releasing the unbearable pressure in a series of unexpected gestures. To surprise is "to impress forcibly by unexpectedness" (see Susan Foster, "Taken By Surprise," this volume), and it can be argued that any surprises that occur in improvisations are merely manifestations of the undeniable effect of effort in improvised forms.

Surprising moments in improvisation may come from work, but they also come from play. Mihaly Csikszentmihalyi et al. famously emphasize the sense of continuous and pleasurable "flow" that happens in play (see "A Theoretical Model for Enjoyment" in this volume), but a state of playfulness does not always flow through the players in an endless stream. It, instead, can manifest itself in shocking and sudden disruption. For Richard Schechner, certain types of play contain a sudden darkness that cannot be excised, evidencing itself in "a wisecrack, a flash of frenzy, risk, or delirium" (see his essay, this volume). He suggests in the excerpt on "Playing and Ritual" reprinted in this section that such "dark play" "subverts order, dissolves frames, [and] breaks its own rules, so that the playing itself is in danger of being destroyed ... dark play's inversions are not declared or resolved; its end is not integration but disruption, deceit, excess and gratification" (Schechner). Play in improvisation may be dark play; it is not always grounded in dialogic give and take, pass and collect, ebb and flow. Improvisations do not always move smoothly through a space; in fact, they can be contrary and disruptive, containing what Margaret Thompson Drewal calls "a whole gamut of spontaneous individual moves, ruses, parodics, transcriptions, recontextualizations, elaborations, condensations, interruptions, interventions, and more" (see her essay in this volume).

Surprise from improvised play can also be painful and contain reminders of vulnerability, fragility, and loss. UK theatre company Forced Entertainment emphasises these melancholic qualities of play, as the improvising personas in their shows enact faltering failures of language, fiascoes of narrative, and disappointments of bodies that cannot complete tasks, and that often stumble towards unseemly deaths. Forced Entertainment director Tim Etchells describes this type of play "with its transformations, its power reversals, its illogics, its joys, its potential escapes," as "nakedness, defenselessness, an exposure that does not have a name. Something beyond" (see Etchells, this volume). In Etchells's diary excerpts from the rehearsal room reprinted here, improvised play is centred in the uncontrollable and the discontinuous, where surprise takes the lead, and the performers follow.

I create community-based art practices in Australia, Canada, and Northern Ireland. In these projects, improvisation has been the main tool my collaborators and I use to build relationships between participants/artists and organisers, between elders and teenagers, between Protestants and Catholics, between the indigenous and the non-indigenous. Improvised methodologies and practices have also caused difficult or challenging surprises, taking the projects far from their origins and planned routes into uncharted and perilous places. The community projects I collaborate on deliberately use open and partial organisational structures marked by listening and experimentation, and creative workshops in the projects usually incorporate improvisational theatre and music games, improvised writing and visualisation exercises, and improvised performances and other participatory live events. My partners and I try to work carefully with these sorts of playful open scenarios in order to allow free and locally informed expression to develop, and the result is what Schechner calls "provisonality"—"the unsteadiness, slipperiness, porosity, unreliability, and ontological riskiness of the realities projected or created by playing" (see Schechner, this volume). We seek, and are changed by, surprises arising from working and playing together.

There are inherent inequities in power relations in community-based art that limit the possibility of positive surprises arising from this improvised work/play. How can surprise really be present, for example, in a room with indigenous and non-indigenous artists working together, when the inevitable and sickly predictable pressures of colonisation and economic and social devastation continue to wreak their ongoing destruction? And how can playfulness take us in new directions when historical constraints mean these directions feel as if they have already been decided? For example, sectarian segregated education institutions in Northern Ireland, and poorly funded schools in rural and Aboriginal communities in Australia, both produce young people depressingly constituted by inequities and prejudices not of their own making. What kind of project could prove it allows difference to emerge when the very physical or economic architecture of many locations denies entrance to whole sections of the population based on where they are born, how their bodies behave, or how much money they have access to? These situations all limit how "free" our improvisations could be when we build collaborative art projects.

I hold my hope in the fact that surprises force themselves through the folds and cracks as we work and play together. The most difficult and surprising moments of living often hold the most potential for learning, and therefore embody the most possibility for change. When a Protestant teenager screams with delight, "I never knew you were Catholic. I never met a Catholic before," and climbs across the table towards her workshop facilitator who has been playing theatre improvisation games with her for the past eight weeks, there is a considerable risk of physical or emotional harm. There is also unanticipated joy when they shake hands and hug, and a potential for movement against segregation and prejudice suddenly evident through this improvising relationship built on shared laughter and surprising revelation. When a community-based improvised sound and video project unexpectedly provides First Nations Lands and Resource workers in Canada with a new tool to document and preserve their interactions with their traditional lands, and thus fight back against exploitative incursions by mining companies, it is impossible to deny that dialogic, open, creative collaborations can disrupt social expectation and confront historical injustices. Of course, sometimes, the humbling reality is that surprises can occur despite, rather than because of, any one facilitator's ideas or experience. I worked with older bicycle riders in a seaside town in Australia (one of whom was my father) who politely ignored my suggestions of how to make sound art about their town, and used the tools and resources I provided in their own ways to provide new avenues for disabled and isolated residents to connect. They improvised with the recording equipment, with the bikes they built and rode, with the adults and children who were part of their group, and with the landscape and town they lived in. My work was over when their play began. The surprise was that it took me so long to catch on (Caines and Campbell, 2010).

Nicolas Humbert and Werner Penzel suggest that what matters in creative work is what they call "exchange" and "movement." They describe, for example, how when making the film *Step Across the Border* with improvising musician Fred Frith, they often "started filming in the middle of the night, responding to a new idea that had only arisen a few moments before" (see Humbert and Penzel, this volume). They contend that what is important is "an intense perception of the moment, not the transformation of a preordained plan". I believe the phrase "intense perception of the moment" beautifully contains this dual nature of improvisation as effort and play, and it describes accurately the state of suspension that is the breeding ground for the unexpected in the improvisatory act. Yet this exchange and movement also builds from grounded experience. The surprises that arise from the intense perception of the present are dark, complex, and funny but they also carry the histories, practices, and communities that shaped the improvisers' and audiences' lives. Improvising with others is to improvise with these histories. Wayde Compton's poem "DJ," reprinted in this volume, captures this movement and exchange beautifully. He describes the human interactions of a DJ and waitress and audience member caught for just a moment together, held in a sudden interaction in the web of stories and music and sound that echo back through the improvised beats of the DJ through time to ancient African story and music traditions. For Compton's characters, as for all improvisers, "now" and "then" are held together by these precious, surprising moments of unexpected connection.

Works Cited

Caines, R. and Campbell, J. 2010. *Community Sound [E]Scapes*. Improvisation, Community, and Social Practice. December 22, Guelph. [online] Available at: http://soundescapes.improvcommunity.ca/ [Accessed 6 January 2014.]

48 Playing

Richard Schechner

Richard Schechner, born in 1934, is University Professor and Professor of Performance Studies at Tisch School of the Arts, New York University. He received his
PhD from Tulane University in 1962. He is the editor of *TDR: The Journal of Per-
formance Studies*. Among his books are *Environmental Theater* (1973), *The End of
Humanism: Writings on Performance* (1982), *Between Theater and Anthropology*
(1985), *Performance Theory* (latest edition, 2003), *Performance Studies: An Introduction* (latest edition, 2013), and *A New Third World of Performance* (forthcoming).
He founded The New Orleans Group, The Performance Group, and East Coast
Artists, and his theatre productions have been seen in the US, Romania, Poland,
France, India, China, Taiwan, the UK, and the Republic of South Africa. Among his
awards are the Lifetime Achievement Award, Oslo National Academy of the Arts
(2013); the Thalia Prize of the International Association of Theatre Critics (2010); the
Lifetime Career Achievement Award of the American Theatre in Higher Education
(2008); and the Lifetime Achievement Award of Performance Studies International
(2002). In "Playing," from his 1993 book *The Future of Ritual*, Schechner writes,
"definitions are necessary for discourse," but his definition of "play" is nothing if
not wide-ranging, extending from the *Bhagavad Gita* to contemporary speculation
on the creation of "universes by the billions" from empty space.

Key words: theatre; play; cross-culture; dance; interdisciplinarity; science

[...] A coherent theory of play would assert that play and ritual are complementary,
ethologically based behaviors which in humans continue undiminished throughout life;
that play creates its own (permeable) boundaries and realms: multiple realities that are
slippery, porous, and full of creative lying and deceit; that play is dangerous and, because it
is, players need to feel secure in order to begin playing; that the perils of playing are often
masked or disguised by saying that play is "fun," "voluntary," a "leisure activity," or
"ephemeral" – when in fact the fun of playing, when there is fun, is in playing with fire,
going in over one's head, inverting accepted procedures and hierarchies; that play is performative, involving players, directors, spectators, and commentators in a quadrilogical
exchange that, because each kind of participant often has her or his own passionately
pursued goals, is frequently at cross-purposes.[1]

I cannot here unpack this unified theory-to-be. Instead, I will make one comment and
then go on to look at [two] key aspects: multiple realities [and] dark play [. ...]

Security is needed at the outset of play more than later on. Once play is underway,
risk, danger, and insecurity are part of playing's thrill. Usually there is a safety net, or a

chance to call "time out," or appeal to an umpire or other nonplaying authority who takes care of the rules. But in informal play, and in what I call "dark play," actions continue even though individual players may feel insecure, threatened, harassed, and abused. This pattern of moving from safety to danger is true of performance workshops, which need to commence in an atmosphere of "safety" and "trust" but, once underway, are places where very risky business can be explored. On a larger scale, the whole workshop-rehearsal phase of performance needs protection and isolation, a well-defined safety net, while the finished performance can move from place to place on tour, overcome many particular distractions heaped on it by audiences, and in general "take care of itself."

Maya–lila: playing's multiple realities

In the West, play is a rotten category, an activity tainted by unreality, inauthenticity, duplicity, make believe, looseness, fooling around, and inconsequentiality. Play's reputation has been a little uplifted by being associated with ritual and game theory. The defense department takes play seriously when it stages war games and simulations. The reason why play – or, more properly, playing – is a rotten category is because the multiple realities of playing are situated inside a pyramidical hierarchy of increasing reality leading from unreal make believe to "just the facts, Ma'am."

In 1945 Schutz called the multiple realities of "dreams, of imageries and phantasms, ... [of] art, ... of religious experience, ... of scientific contemplation, the play world of the child, and the world of the insane ... finite provinces of meaning," enclosing them each within its own "cognitive style" (1977:229). He explicitly denied what makes multiple realities so powerful, the systematic quality of their transformability, and claimed:

> There is no possibility of referring one of these provinces to the other by introducing a formula of transformation. The passing from one to the other can only be performed by a "leap," as Kierkegaard calls it, which manifests itself in the subjective experience of a shock.
>
> (1977:230)

I agree to the extent that reality comes bundled in discrete "packets" of energy and/or information (as physicists would say). But the absence of smooth continuity does not disallow systems of transformation from one reality to another – developing such systems is precisely the work of art (and often the work of science and religion too). It may, in fact, be the main occupation of humankind. Sometimes the passage between realities is experienced as a leap or shock and sometimes as a smooth, even imperceptible, flow. Schutz prioritized "the world of working in daily life [as] the archetype of our experience of reality. All other provinces of meaning may be considered as its modifications" (1977:230). Useful as his insights are, I don't agree with Schutz's prioritizing of realities. Playing, not "the world of working in daily life," is the ground, the matrix, birthing all experience's exfoliating multiple realities. Or, to express the same idea in a different metaphor: being is playing and "working daily life" is just one reality cookie-cut, or netted, out of playing. Working daily life is not prior or privileged; it is a culture-bound, time-bound reality and as such can appear to be "the archetype of our experience" only as the result of careful netting. Contrast this Western archetype of reality to *maya* and *lila* – Sanskrit terms for illusion and play. Maya and lila are hard words to translate because their meanings shift according to whether one is emphasizing the delights of the world, *samsara,* or the desire to end all desire, freeing one's self from the wheel of birth-death-rebirth, *moksha.* According to O'Flaherty, maya originally

> meant *only* what was real; through its basis in the verbal root *ma* ("to make") it expressed "the sense of 'realizing the phenomenal world' ... " to "measure out" the universe [,] ... to create it, to divide it into its constituent parts, to *find* it by bringing it out of chaos. ...
>
> Magicians do this; artists do it; gods do it. But according to certain Indian philosophies, every one of us does it every minute of our lives.
>
> This concept of *maya* as a kind of artistic power led gradually to its later connotation of magic, illusion, and deceit. ... It often means not merely bringing something into existence ... but manipulating the existent forces of nature or invoking the "power to create and achieve the marvelous." Thus *maya* first meant making something that was not there before; then it came to mean making something that was there into something that was not really there. The first describes the universe in the Vedic world-view; the second, the universe in the Vedantic world-view. The first is *samsaric;* the second *moksic.* In both cases, *maya* can often best be translated as "transformation."
>
> ... A similar cluster of meanings radiates from it [maya] as from the English derivatives of the Latin word for play (*ludo*) – de-lusion, il-lusion, e-lusive, and so forth – and from the word "play" itself – play as drama, as swordplay or loveplay, as the play of light that causes mirages, as the double image implicit in wordplay (as Johan Huizinga pointed out so brilliantly in *Homo Ludens*). These word clusters delineate a universe full of beauty and motion that enchants us all. All Indian philosophies acknowledge that *maya* is a fact of life – the fact of life; but some (the *moksha-oriented*) regard it as a negative fact, to be combated, while others (the *samsara-oriented*) regard it as a positive fact, to be embraced.
>
> (O'Flaherty 1984:117–19)

Lila is a more ordinary word meaning play, sport, or drama; it is etymologically related to the Latin *ludus* and from there to English ludic, illusion, elusive, and so on. Gods in their lilas make maya, but so do ordinary people, each of whom shares in the identicality of individual atman with the absolute brahman.[2] Maya and lila create, contain, and project each other: like a snake swallowing its own tail.

Maya–lila is fundamentally a performative-creative act of continuous playing where ultimate positivist distinctions between "true" and "false," "real" and "unreal" cannot be made. Psychoanalyst D. W. Winnicott, in attempting to describe the process of playing that begins in infancy, declares

> that the essential feature in the concept of transitional objects and phenomena ... is *the paradox, and the acceptance of the paradox:* the baby creates the object, but the object was there waiting to be created and to become a cathected object. ... We will never challenge the baby to elicit an answer to the question: did you create that or did you find it?
>
> (1971:89)

[...] In theatrical terms, maya–lila is the presence of the performer enacting the "not" of her role: the Ophelia who is not there, who never was there. Ophelia can only exist in the playing field between rehearsal, performers, performance, dramatic text, performance text, spectators, and readers. Or in the monsoon season performances of Raslila in India, where little boys (swarups) enact/become young Krishna, his beloved Radha, and all the *gopis* (cowherding women) who dote on Krishna, wanting to dance with him.

> With his haunting flute he [Krishna] summons the women of Braj away from their mundane occupations to come out to the forest and dance with him the mating dance, the dance of love, the *ras*; and as the peacock rotates so that his plumage will be visible to every eye, so Krishna multiplies himself to be available with an equal intimacy to every girl he summons.
>
> (Hawley 1981: 14)

In ancient Greece, Dionysus drew the women of Thebes onto the slopes of Mount Cithaeron, as Krishna drew them to the forests surrounding Brindavan. But Dionysus induced jealous frenzy for there was only one of him and so many of them, while Krishna multiplied himself limitlessly, satisfying each of the gopis who desired him. And during Raslila in Brindavan, there are as many boy Krishnas, Radhas, and gopis as are desired by the audiences who in looking at these boys see gods.

> The roles of Radha, Krishna, and the cowherd girls (*gopis*) are sanctified and dignified with the title of *svarup*, which means that the Brahmin boys who adopt them are thought to take on the very form of the personages they portray once their costumes are complete. The term applies quintessentially to Radha and Krishna, and once the two don the crowns appropriate to their roles, they are venerated as the divine couple itself.
>
> (Hawley 1981: 13–14)

These appearances are the same in principle as the Christian Eucharist, but so much less abstract, so immediate in the flesh-and-blood presence of the swarups and the acts of devotion shown to them by the thousands who gather to catch a glimpse, a *darshan*, of the divine. As gods the boys don't stop being little boys, the two realities are mutually porous. The boys/gods swat at flies, doze, giggle, or look longingly for their mothers; but they acquire sudden dignity while dancing or when reciting the lines whispered into their ears by ever-attentive priests/directors. This kind of performing-being-playing is not unique to Raslila. It constitutes an essential quality of a number of Indian performance genres.

Maya–lila is important to all aspects of Indian life, but especially decisive in theatre-dance-music. According to the *Natyasastra* (second century BCE-second century CE), the Sanskrit text dealing specifically with performance, theatre came into being as an entertainment for the gods but is enjoyed also by all classes of people. At Ramlila – an epic cycle of north India telling the story of Rama, an incarnation of Vishnu – long poles are erected, on top of which effigies of the gods-as-spectators look down on the action involving gods, men, animals, and demons. Vishnu and Lakshmi, played by two swarups, watch Rama and Sita played by two others. But Vishnu is Rama and Lakshmi is Sita, so these gods-boys double their existence, manifesting themselves before delighted, often wildly ecstatic, crowds. And from time to time the ever-observing gods intervene in the action. This is maya producing, through lila, multiple realities and comparably complex ways of participating in the drama.

Maya is the multiplicity which the world is: creative, slippery, and ongoing. Not to be too fancy about it, keeping the world existing takes a continuous playful effort on the part of Brahma or whatever god – including none – is accomplishing the acts of creation.

The cosmos itself – from the highest heaven to the Raslila or Ramlila grounds to the most ordinary of daily activities – is an immense playground. This playground is not necessarily or always a happy place. Shiva, also called *nataraj,* king of dance(rs), dances existence into being and also dances it into destruction and chaos at the end of each *yuga* or aeon.[3] Shiva's dancing creates and destroys maya and is his lila. Asserting that existence is a continuous dance is not a soft-headed metaphor for the Indians; nor is it inconsistent with contemporary theories of particle physics or cosmology as astronomers playfully construct them. For example, an article in *Science* (20 February 1987) reports:

> An analysis of localized inflation [of "black holes"] suggests that empty space may be spawning universes by the billions, without us ever knowing; was our own universe created this way? What would happen if we could somehow reproduce the conditions of the Big Bang in the modern universe? More precisely, what would happen if a sample of matter were somehow compressed into a tiny region of ultrahigh density and temperature – say 10^{24} K? ... In one solution, for example, the outside universe simply crushes the hot region into a standard black hole. However, there is a much more interesting solution in which the hot region does indeed inflate – but in a totally new direction that is perpendicular to ordinary space and time. It becomes a kind of aneurysm bulging outward from the side of our familiar universe. In fact, it quickly pinches off and becomes a separate universe of its own. ... This newborn cosmos [could then] expand to a scale of billions of light-years, producing galaxies, stars, planets, and even life.
>
> (Waldrop 1987:845)

This construction of things is very maya–lila.

Krishna, whose very name means blue-black, dark like the underside of a thundercloud, is not always or only a being of ecstatic dancing; he also has his time of bloody play, represented most clearly in the *Bhagavad Gita,* probably India's single most sacred text. To remind you of the story: the great armies of the Pandavas and Kauravas are assembled on the field at Kurukshetra. The Pandava warrior Arjuna wants to see the full array. Barbara Stoler Miller's translation takes up the story:

> "Krishna," [Arjuna says,] "halt my chariot between the armies! Far enough for me to see these men who lust for war." ... Arjuna saw them standing there: fathers, grandfathers, teachers, uncles, brothers, sons, grandsons, and friends. ... Dejected, filled with strange pity, he said this: "My limbs sink, / my mouth is parched, ... The magic bow slips from my hand, ... I see no good in killing my kinsmen in battle!"
>
> (Vyasa 1986:23–25)

Krishna then recites his great song. "You grieve for those beyond grief. ... Never have I not existed nor you, nor these kings; and never in the future shall we cease to exist'" (31). Step by step this Krishna, no longer the *bala* (boy) Krishna of Brindavan, but a great awesome Krishna, and a trickster, leads Arjuna along the path of his *karma,* toward doing that which he must do. In the tenth of his eighteen teachings, Krishna catalogs all that he is.

> "Listen," [he tells Arjuna,] "as I recount for you in essence the divine powers of myself. Endless is my extent. ... I am indestructible time, The creator facing

everywhere at once. ... I am death the destroyer of all, the source of what will be, the feminine powers: fame, fortune, speech, memory, intelligence, resolve, patience. ... I am the great ritual chant, the meter of sacred song, ... the dice game of gamblers, ... the epic poet Vyasa among sages."

(91–94)

Vyasa is the author of the *Mahabharata* of which the *Gita* is a part. In the eleventh teaching Krishna allows Arjuna a theophany:

"I see the gods in your body, O God, and hordes of varied creatures. ... I see your boundless form everywhere, the countless arms, bellies, mouths, and eyes. Lord of All, I see no end, or middle or beginning to your totality. ... Throngs of gods enter you, some in their terror make gestures of homage. ... As moths in the frenzy of destruction fly into a blazing flame, worlds in the frenzy of destruction enter your mouths. You lick at the worlds around you, devouring them with flaming mouths; and your terrible fires scorch the entire universe, filling it, Vishnu, with violent rays. Tell me who are you in this terrible form?" [... Krishna replies:] "I am time grown old, creating world destruction."

(99–103)

[...] In 1972 in Madras I saw the great bharatanatyam dancer, Balasaraswati, perform Yasoda as a solo dance. When Balasaraswati-Yasoda shook her forefinger sternly demanding that Krishna open his mouth, I laughed; but when she looked in, I saw/felt what she did, and I shuddered with terror and joy. And when she asked her son/god Krishna to close his mouth, shutting out from her all knowledge of the absolute, I too felt relief.

In even more complicated ways, the Ramlila of Ramnagar is a performance of the interrealities coexisting on different scales simultaneously. The town of Ramnagar is itself, plus the seat of the maharaja of Banaras, sponsor of the Ramlila, plus all the places where Rama's adventures take place, plus a model of India during its presumed golden age of Ramraj (when Rama was king), plus Ayodhya, the capital of Rama's kingdom, plus a pilgrimage center where for a month "god lives here" (as spectators say). On the thirtieth day of the thirty-one-day cycle, the maharaja invites the gods to dinner. As in Raslila, when the swarups wear their costumes and crowns, they are presumed actually to be the gods they represent. Mounted on splendidly decorated elephants, illuminated by continuous flares of fireworks, they arrive at the Fort, the maharaja's palace.

Thousands of common folk – usually excluded from the Fort's inner courtyard – crowd in as the maharaja and his whole family greet the gods. As a devotee of Rama the maharaja washes their feet, as host he feeds them. But even as he performs these acts, they, the boys, are being honored by the king of the place. In other words their divinity as swarups does not cancel out their existence as boys and subjects. And the maharaja is a king, I might add, who has not been "real" since 1947 when India, upon gaining independence, abolished all principalities within her borders. Still, the people of Banaras and Ramnagar treat Vibhuti Narain Singh as their king and more, hailing him with shouts of *"Hara, Hara, Mahadev!"* – "Shiva, Shiva, great god!"

Thus maya–lila generates a plenitude of performances: interpenetrating, transformable, nonexclusive, porous realities. All of these are play worlds that are the slippery ground of contingent being and experience. That is, from the Indian perspective, playing is what the universe consists of. To be "at play" is to recognize that all relationships are provisional. Ultimate reality, if there is such, is *neti*, literally "not that." To any and every specification of what such an ultimate reality might be, the answer is neti, not that. The only realities that can be experienced – personally, socially, scientifically, philosophically – are the interpenetrating, transformable, nonexclusive, porous, multiple realities of maya–lila. The Indian tradition of maya–lila rejects Western systems of rigid, impermeable frames, unambiguous metacommunications, and rules inscribing hierarchical arrangements of reality. But if reality and experience are networks of flexible constructions, dreams of dreams, unsettled relationships, transformations, and interactions, what then of "ordinary play" – children manipulating their toys, adults playing ball, and so on? These exist in India, as they do in the West, but they can suddenly, shockingly open to whole worlds of demons, humans, animals, and gods, as Yasoda found out when she looked into her son Krishna's mouth.

[...] The maya–lila notion of playing describes volatile, creative-destructive activities that are transformative, less bounded, less tame, and less tightly framed in time and space than Western play. In Hindu-Vedic terms, what is beyond play is not knowable: the atman (self) / Brahman (absolute) is unthinkable, undescribable, unexperienceable, but obtainable. To achieve *moksha* or *nirvana* or *samadhi* is to be released from the round of birth–rebirth, from maya–lila, from playing. But daily experience – the life people lead – is a flux that includes not only the grind of farming, child-bearing, and money-making but also – and on an equal basis – the categories and experiences represented by art and religion. Intense belief, ecstasy, dreaming, and fantasy are creditable among peoples living immersed in maya–lila belief systems. These are the very categories and experiences mainstream modern Western thought devalues as make believe, nonordinary, and/or unreal.

Dark play

Let me bring just a little of this home by touching on what I call "dark play." Dark play may be conscious playing, but it can also be playing in the dark when some or even all of the players don't know they are playing. Dark play occurs when contradictory realities coexist, each seemingly capable of canceling the other out, as in the double cross, or as in the Indian tale of "the Brahmin who dreamed he was an untouchable who dreamed he was a king" but who could not determine who was the dreamer and who the dreamt because each of his realities tested out as true (O'Flaherty 1984:134–35). Or dark play may be entirely private, known to the player alone. Dark play can erupt suddenly, a bit of microplay, seizing the player(s) and then quickly subsiding – a wisecrack, a flash of frenzy, risk, or delirium. Dark play subverts order, dissolves frames, breaks its own rules, so that the playing itself is in danger of being destroyed, as in spying, con games, undercover actions, and double agentry. Unlike the inversions of carnivals, ritual clowns, and so on (whose agendas are public), dark play's inversions are not declared or resolved; its end is not integration but disruption, deceit, excess, and gratification.

For all this, dark play need not be overtly angry or violent. And what might be dark play to one person can be innocuous to another. In a 1985 seminar on play,[4] I invited graduate students to write out, anonymously if they chose, examples of dark play from their own lives. I quote some of the responses:

Female: When I am feeling especially depressed or angry about the world and my life, I will play a form of "Russian roulette" with the New York city traffic: I will cross the streets without pausing to see if it is safe to do so or not – without checking the lights or the traffic. ... At the time of "play" there is a thrill in abandoning precautions and in toying with the value of life and death.

[...] *Female:* I was 16 years old and on vacation at Yosemite with my father. I climbed out over the guard rail to get a better view of the waterfall. When I realized that my father was crying for me to come back, I went to the very edge and did an arabesque. I continued balancing on one leg until he got onto his knees, crying, begging for me to come back. Ten years later, in the Sierra Nevada range I repeated the same act in front of my husband who shouted at me to think of our daughter as a motherless child. My initial inspiration for dancing on the edge was in both cases the thrill of the beauty and the danger of the dance. My father's and husband's anxiety sharpened the experience for me – the further I got away from them the closer I came to communion with some Other.

Female: I was on vacation with a friend who is not my boyfriend. During a bus ride I was teaching him a song when an old man turned to us, interested in where we came from, etc. Instantly the two of us made up a romance story of where we met, why we were there on vacation, and what we were planning to do – none of which was true. Since we both felt we were being approached as "a couple" we reacted to it as such, having a lot of fun doing so.

Male: I can achieve a flow experience by listening to music, rocking approximately in time with it, and letting my mind wander in free association. What makes this play dark is that I rock in a chair that is not a rocking chair but an over-stuffed chair. It is my body that rocks instead of the chair. My whole body enters into the flow. ... I have maintained this activity since very early childhood. I recommend it highly – and anonymously.

Leaving aside psychological interpretations of motives, personal gains, anxieties, desires played out, and so forth, what do these examples show?

First, they subvert the metacommunicational aspect of the play frame. In all cases, only some of those involved knew that playing was going on. The New York City car and truck drivers [...], the father and husband, the man on the bus are performers in the playing but they do not know they are playing. In fact, the metacommunication is just the opposite: "I, or we, are not playing," the players say to the nonplaying participants. These nonplayers – innocents, dupes, butts, anxious loved ones – are essential for the playing to continue; the reaction of the nonplayers is a big part of what gives dark play its kick. In the last example there are no coplayers and anonymity is important to the player. In [some] cases there is a high degree of physical risk. Crossing blindly through NYC traffic, and dancing on mountain ledges is playing where losing might mean dying.

Yet, I don't think any of these players are pathological. Why would they want to so endanger themselves? In only one case is there a clear instance of make believe, the con game on the bus. Rocking in a stuffed chair is an example of secret, intimate dark play. I suspect there are many more instances of this sort of secret dark play originating in early childhood and continuing right through to old age. People are cautious about sharing these kinds of solitary activities. Masking is very important – sneaking off, not being recognized, playing out selves that cannot be displayed at work, or with family. The thrill and gratification of such play is to perform anonymously, in disguise, or in a closet what one cannot do publicly "as myself."

Taken together, these examples indicate that dark play:

1   is physically risky;
2   involves intentional confusion or concealment of the frame "this is play";
3   may continue actions from early childhood;
4   only occasionally demands make believe;
5   plays out alternative selves. The play frame may be so disturbed or disrupted that the players themselves are not sure if they are playing or not – their actions become play retroactively: the events are what they are, but by telling these events, by reperforming them as narratives, they are cast as play. [...]

Conclusions

Playing is a creative, destabilizing action that frequently does not declare its existence, even less its intentions. I do not reject [Gregory] Bateson's play frame entirely – there are situations where the message "this is play" is very important. But there are other kinds of playing – like dark play – where the play frame is absent, broken, porous, or twisted. One need not accept as empirically true the maya–lila universe of multiple, contradictory realities to recognize in it a powerful performance theory. Maya–lila is not simply a version of "all the world's a stage" (a weak metaphor trivializing both art and daily living), but a dynamic system with no single fixed center, no still point or absolute referent. In this, maya–lila theory harmonizes with both contemporary science (physics and astronomy) and poststructuralist literary theory (deconstruction). Or, as O'Flaherty has it, "the illusion of art is of the same nature as the illusion of life" (1984:279).

Indeed, art and ritual, especially performance, are the homeground of playing. This is because the process of making performances does not so much imitate playing as epitomize it. From this perspective, the Batesonian play frame is a rationalist attempt to stabilize and localize playing, to contain it safely within definable borders. But if one needs a metaphor to localize and (temporarily) stabilize playing, "frame" is the wrong one – it's too stiff, too impermeable, too "on/off," "inside/outside." "Net" is better: a porous, flexible gatherer; a three-dimensional, dynamic, flow-through container.

Playing is a mood, an attitude, a force. It erupts or one falls into it. It may persist for a fairly long time – as specific games, rites, and artistic performances do – or it comes and goes suddenly – a wisecrack, an ironic glimpse of things, a bend or crack in behavior. It is "banana time" – the transformation of work into play:

> So a serious discussion about the high cost of living could be suddenly transformed into horseplay or into a prank; or a worker might utter a string of "oral autisms." The expression of themes was thus temporary, somewhat idiosyncratic excursions into the reality of play; and each protagonist experimented in his own way, and to some extent at his own pace, with these transitions from the reality of work to that of expressive behavior. ... The interspersal of "themes" among serious actions held the participants perpetually on the edge of a liminal phase – on the border of reality transformation – since none could be certain exactly when one of their number would effect the passage into an unannounced and unexpected expressive frame. ... Faced with the vista of a multitude of diverse, locally fashioned worlds of meaning, the researcher must return to intensive observation and participation to catch the emergent symbolic and organizational modes through which persons construct their

life-experiences with one another. I prefer to believe that, rather than being a cause for despair, this is a recognition of the immense capacity of human beings to come to terms with, and to express, the manifold predicaments of their social existence.

(Handelman 1976:443–45)

Handelman is on to something. But it's wrong to think of playing as the interruption of ordinary life. Consider instead playing as the underlying, always-there continuum of experience, as the maya–lila theory says. Ordinary life is netted out of playing but playing continuously squeezes through even the smallest holes of the worknet – because there is no such thing as absolute opacity, there are no totally blank walls. No matter how hard people try, play finds its way through – banana time is always with us, even in the operating theatre or on death row. But what of horrors like the Holocaust? It is as difficult for a Jew to think of Auschwitz "as play" as it was for Arjuna to consider the slaughter of the Kurukshetra war as Krishna's lila. And consider this: the very efficiency of the Nazi death camps was as extreme an example as can be actualized of "work" as the systematic erasure of playing. But, on another level, were there not jokes told in the concentration camps? Or games of various kinds played? Does thinking there were deflect or lessen the dread historicity of the Holocaust, doing disrespect to its victims and survivors? The realities of illusion can become paths into dark worlds of demons, witches, curses, black magic, illness, torture, and death. It is not easy for modern positivists to project themselves into such realities of other cultures, or back to the Salem witch trials of seventeenth-century America, or even to keep remembering the Holocaust.

Work and other daily activities continuously feed on the underlying ground of playing, using the play mood for refreshment, energy, unusual ways of turning things around, insights, breaks, openings and, especially, *looseness*. This looseness (pliability, bending, lability, unfocused attention, the long way around) is implied in such phrases as "play it out" or "there's some play in the rope" or "play around with that idea." Looseness encourages the discovery of new configurations and twists of ideas and experiences. Thus the imbalancing–rebalancing process that Barba calls attention to occurs on the mental as well as physical, psychophysical, spiritual, and metaphysical levels.

Playing occurs on several levels simultaneously. The basic ground of existence is maya–lila, an ongoing construction–deconstruction, destroying–creating. Like the theophany of Krishna, this deep play is impossible to look at (for very long) – it is as terrifying as it is exciting, as blinding as it is beautiful. In order to live our daily lives – lives of work and play in the ordinary sense – humans have constructed/invented "cultures" (see Wagner 1981). The genres of play – play, games, sports, art, and religion – are part of these cultures: they are play within culture within maya–lila. But however powerful the play genres, however "total" the work life, the basic ground of existence, maya–lila, leaks through and permeates both daily life and the play genres. So, am I proposing that maya–lila exists outside of or before cultures? Am I attempting to reintroduce some kind of transcendent force or energy? That question can't be answered yes or no, because maya–lila swallows its own tail (tale). Each culture, each individual even, creates its/her/his own maya–lila even as it/she/he exists *within* and *stands on* maya–lila. Maya–lila is not reducible to the logic of either/or choices. It is an "empty space [that] may be spawning universes by the billions, without us ever knowing" (Waldrop 1987:845).

What I can say is that it's much too limiting, too tight, too certain to build play theories around notions of play genres, identifiable "things." Of course there are play genres: efforts to contain, enslave, tame, use, and colonize playing. But presently, we need to stop looking so hard at play, or play genres, and investigate *playing*, the ongoing, underlying process of off-balancing, loosening, bending, twisting, reconfiguring, and transforming – the permeating, eruptive/disruptive energy and mood below, behind, and to the sides of focused attention. (Why not "above"? I really don't know, it's probably just cultural prejudice.) The questions we need to ask are: how, when, and why is playing invited and sustained? How, when, and why is playing denied or repressed? Is playing categorically antistructural – that is, does it always take the opposite position or role to whatever is happening at the time it erupts or is invited? Is playing autonomous – that is, will it "just happen" if nothing else blocks, cancels, or represses it?

Notes

1 See Sutton-Smith (1979:297) for his discussion of the "play quadralogue." Sutton-Smith says, it follows then that

> if language is always a *dialogue,* a situated act, and not merely a text, that all expressive forms, of which play is only one, are a *quadralogue* [sic]. They always involve at least four prototypical parties: the group or individual that stages (or creates) the event, as actors and co-actors; the group that receives this communication (the audience); and the group that directs the race or conducts the symphony (directors).

I count only three groups in Sutton-Smith's list, but to these I add a fourth, the commentators – critics and scholars – who may not even be present at the event but whose discourse affects not only future performances but the ways in which past events are received.

2 Atman is the "soul," the Self with a capital S, the imperishable whatever-it-is identical to brahman, the transcendent, universal, single absolute which a person can experience, or enter, but not describe or relate. Atman-brahman is beyond maya-lila, a cancelling out of maya-lila in a way roughly equivalent to the way antimatter annihilates matter.

3 According to Hindu mythology as told in the *Puranas,* the existence of the world is divided into four aeons, or yugas. The Indians, loving mathematics, calculated these precisely in terms of both divine and human years (one divine year = 360 human years). The Krita yuga lasts 1,728,000 human years and is a period of perfection; the Treta yuga lasts 1,296,000 years and is a truthful age; the Dvapara yuga lasts 864,000 years and is a time of diminished good; and, finally, the Kali yuga (our own time), lasts 432,000 years and is a period of darkness and calamity. One Mahayuga equals all four yugas (4,320,000 years); and 1,000 Mahayugas (4,320,000,000) is a day of Brahma.

> At the close of this day of Brahma, a collapse of the universe takes place which lasts through a night of Brahma, equal in duration to his day, during which period the worlds are converted into one great ocean. ... At the end of that night he awakes and creates anew. ... A year of Brahma is composed of the proper number of such days and nights, and a hundred of such years constitute his whole life.
>
> (Wilkins 1975:354)

When Brahma's life ends, the elements of the universe dissolve.

4 At the Department of Performance Studies, Tisch School of the Arts, New York University – where I have been teaching since 1967.

Works Cited

Handelman, Don (1976) "Re-thinking 'Banana Time'," *Urban Life* 4 (4): 33–48.

Hawley, John Stratton (1981) *At Play with Krishna*, Princeton: Princeton University Press.

O'Flaherty, Wendy Doniger (1984) *Dreams, Illusions, and Other Realities*, Chicago: University of Chicago Press.

Schutz, A. (1977) "Multiple Realities," in Mary Douglas (ed.) *Rules and Meanings*, Harmondsworth: Penguin.

Sutton-Smith, Brian (1979) "Epilogue: play as performance," in Brian Sutton-Smith (ed.) *Play and Learning*, New York: Gardner Press.

Vyasa (1986) *The Bhagavad Gita*, trans. Barbara Stoler Miller, New York: Bantam Books.

Wagner, Roy (1981) *The Invention of Culture*, Chicago: University of Chicago Press.

Waldrop, M. Mitchell (1987) "Do-it-yourself universes," *Science*, 20 February: 845–46.

Wilkins, W.J. (1975) *Hindu Mythology*, Calcutta: Rupa & Co.

Winnicott, D. W. (1971) *Playing and Reality*, London: Tavistock.

49 Taken By Surprise: Improvisation in Dance and Mind

Susan Leigh Foster

taken: 1. past tense, passive tense of the verb "to take" (*the dancer clutches the podium's microphone and twists it backward*) 2. to get into one's hands or into one's possession, power, or control (*she scoops space, getting it into her hands, then suddenly grabs the podium's edges*) 3. to catch, to copulate with, to assume, to secure, to adopt, accommodate, or apprehend (*guiding it with commanding then solicitous attention, she lowers it to the floor, then steps to the side of the now toppled support for her lecture*)

by: bye (*she waves good-bye and disappears off the edge of the stage*)

surprise: 1. to impress forcibly through unexpectedness (*she pops out from below, behind, in the midst of*) 2. to astonish, astound, amaze, or flabbergast (*she shrugs her shoulders*)

taken by surprise: the unexpected seizes control, resulting in a sexy, vertiginous encounter with the unknown, an encounter that raises issues around the workings of desire and power (*did the unexpected seize control? well, sort of, was it vertiginous? who can say? did it raise issues? whenever a body is crawling, gliding, leaping, crouching, wiggling, and kicking, all the while reading aloud from a sheaf of papers that it is clutching earnestly, issues are raised*)

improvisation: that which is *composed* extemporaneously, on the spur of the moment

Manifesto (*Phenomenologically*)

The improvising dancer tacks back and forth between the *known* and the *unknown*, between the familiar/reliable and the unanticipated/unpredictable.

The *known* includes the set of behavioral conventions established by the context in which the performance occurs, such as those of a street corner, a proscenium theater, or a lecture. The known includes any predetermined overarching structural guidelines that delimit the improvising body's choices, such as a score for the performance, or any set of rules determined in advance: for example, consecutive solos by different members of a group. The known also includes an individual body's predisposition to move in patterns of impulses established and made routine through training in a particular dance tradition as well as the body's predilection for making certain kinds of selections from a vocabulary or a sequence of movements. The known includes any allied medium with which the performance is in collaboration, such as an improvisation among musicians and dancers or an improvisation that addresses the space in which the performance occurs as an active participant. The known includes that which has already occurred previously in the performance of improvising.

The *unknown* is precisely that and more. It is that which was previously unimaginable, that which we could not have thought of doing next. Improvisation presses us to extend into, expand beyond, extricate ourselves from that which was known. It encourages us or even forces us to be "taken by surprise." Yet we could never accomplish this encounter with the unknown without engaging the known.

Manifesto (*Historically*)

The improvised is that which eludes history. The performance of any action, regardless of how predetermined it is in the minds of those who perform it and those who witness it, contains an element of improvisation. That moment of wavering while contemplating how, exactly, to execute an action already deeply known, belies the presence of improvised action. It is this suspense-filled plenitude of the not-quite-known that gives live performance its special brilliance.

History, however, keeps track almost exclusively of the known. It focuses on those human actions reiterated frequently enough to become patterns of behavior. From among this multitude of patterns, it chooses those actions that leave behind some permanent residue documenting their effects. And from among this plethora of documentation, it seizes upon those traces that lend themselves to translation into written discourse.

Histories typically suppress the improvisation that occurs consistently in all human actions. They also deny the improvisation of the historian who selects and interacts with all documentation of the past in an attempt to decipher change over time. Historical inquiry has neglected to question how certain actions slide easily across representational fields into the historical record and others are persistently unnoticed. It has tried to ignore actions resistant to written description. What would history look like if it were to acknowledge the fact of improvisation? What would a history of improvised dancing look like?

History informs us that the choreographer and dancer Marie Sallé presented her radical rendition of the Pygmalion story in London in 1734, radical because she appeared without corset or wig and because she used pantomime to tell the story without the aid of spoken or sung lyrics. According to a spectator whose description of the ballet was published,[1] she came to life as Galatea and danced an exchange with her sculptor/maker in which he demonstrated simple phrases she not only mastered immediately but also ornamented and improved upon, thereby stimulating him to present the next phrase. Imagine if this danced dialogue were improvised. Imagine the aplomb that Pygmalion would necessarily exhibit as Sallé performed a surprising response, one that required him quite suddenly to think on his feet. Imagine the suspense and involvement that viewers would have felt as they sensed the unpredictability of the exchange. Perhaps the two dancers agreed in advance to improvise their duet. Perhaps Sallé, carried away by the obvious success of her production, introduced improvised elements on opening night. Perhaps her audacious initiative escalated over subsequent performances into a full-scale improvised repartee. Perhaps none of this happened. But perhaps it did.

History informs us that Richard Bull, Cynthia Novack, and Peentz Dubble, members of the Richard Bull Dance Theatre, participated in the performance of *Making and Doing* in New York City in 1985. According to the reviewer this piece was "an exercise in inventing movement and then recalling it precisely."[2] But what does this mean and how did it work? As someone who saw the concert and also participated in an earlier version of the piece, I offer this analysis: Guided by Richard Bull's score, the dancing choreo-graphers, as though conducting a rehearsal, perform warm-up exercises, talk about their preparations, and then run through part of a "dance," each taking a solo and joining in a unison finale. This first section of the dance, seven or eight minutes in length, is then repeated to music. The dancers no longer speak, but they do perform their entire interaction, including casual conversational gestures and facial expressions. They then launch into a third repetition of the "rehearsal-dance" without music but with the original talking as the lights slowly fade to end the dance. By leading viewers through a presumed rehearsal and then re-presenting that rehearsal to music, *Making and Doing* purposefully frames all movements—the stretches of a warm-up, offhand remarks and gestures, the virtuoso execution of rhythmically complex phrases—as dance. It jostles viewers' expectations in part 1 by presenting a rehearsal onstage and in part 2 by delineating the expressivity of each minute gesture as it is performed to the music. Faithfully executing the original timing of the rehearsal, the dancers create suspenseful congruences and dissonances with the musical structure as they work to transform both pedestrian and virtuoso movement into dance.

Although the three-part structure of rehearsal, repetition to music, and second repetition guides each performance, the specific movements are always improvised. All three dancers co-choreographing the piece generate new sequences in each performance, innovating in relation to the score, to the unpredictable actions of the other dancers, and to their aesthetic judgment concerning the overall needs of the dance as it is evolving. And all this is done while attempting to remember everything they are doing in part 1 in order to repeat it in parts 2 and 3. Improvisation is also required in these sections as dancers forget portions of the material or differ in their timing of the already performed. Throughout, the dancing choreographers respond to the known and the unknown in one another and to the known and unknown about what makes a good dance. On the night I viewed the performance, the tension among what was happening, what might happen next, and how that choice would influence the overall shape of the piece electrified the performance. Viewers could watch the performance both of a dance being presented and of a dance being made at the same time.

Making and Doing, like Sallé's *Pygmalion,* comments reflexively on dancing and artmaking. Yet whereas Sallé as Galatea embodied an artistic creation whose maker watched her come to life, Bull, Novack, and Dubble each inhabited the roles of choreographer and dance. Sallé's dialogue with the sculptor entailed the introduction of movement phrases, repetition of those phrases, and variation on the steps and phrases that might lead toward the generation of yet more new movement. *Making and Doing also* involved repetition, but of a single, lengthy section of the dance. Sallé and her partner were guided in their improvisation by the codes for graceful dancing, the phrase structure and meter of the music, and the need to respond with wit and agility to one another's initiatives. They selected and combined steps from within a highly delimited vocabulary of dance steps. Bull, Novack, and Dubble, guided by an overall scenario but no specific metric specifications, attempted to choreograph an eight-minute dance, full of innovative movement drawn from the repertoires of everyday gesture and preparatory exercises as well as modern dance movement. They worked to create a trio of dynamic range, intriguing interactions, and structural integrity that could stand the test of re-viewing twice. Neither of these dances announced in advance that parts would be improvised. Viewers slowly deduced the fact of spontaneous composition from the particular quality of alertness that the dancers manifested while they were making as well as doing the dance.

What do these examples tell us? Can the fact of improvisation be informative? Are there ways to compare different blendings and assess the unique effects of the known and the unknown used in various approaches to improvisation? How could the attempt to include the improvised alter the course of historical inquiry? Are there ways to write about improvisation that establish its significance and impact without leaching from it the wonderment and critical awareness that its unexpectedness produces?

Manifesto (*Discursively*)

Within the meager discourses describing the experience of improvisation that history has left us, the terms *mind* and *body* often stand in for the known and the unknown. We read of improvisation as the process of letting go of the mind's thinking so that the body can do its moving in its own unpredictable way. But this description is an obfuscation, as unhelpful as it is inaccurate; surely, *all* bodily articulation is mindful. Each body segment's sweep across space, whether direct or meandering, is thought-filled. Each corporeal modulation in effort thinks; each swelling into tension thinks; each erratic burst or undulation in energy thinks. Each accented phrasing or accelerating torque or momentary stillness is an instance of thought. Conceptualized in this way, bodily action constitutes a genre of discourse.

If, then, bodily articulation is mindful, what quality of mindfulness does improvisation hope to transcend? The capacity to evaluate and censor? Even these faculties remain active during improvisation. Improvisation involves moments where one thinks in advance of what one is going to do, other moments where actions seem to move faster than they can be registered in full analytic consciousness of them, and still other moments where one thinks the idea of what is to come at exactly the same moment that one performs that idea. Still, both the changing of the course of things and the riding of that course through its course are mindful *and* bodyful. Rather than suppress any functions of mind, improvisation's bodily mindfulness summons up a kind of hyperawareness of the relation between immediate action and overall shape, between that which is about to take place or is taking place and that which has and will take place.

We also read in the discourses on improvisation allegations that improvisation, because of its bodily spontaneity, requires no technique. This, too, is a muddled and wrongly cast charge. Improvisation makes rigorous technical demands on the performer. It assumes an articulateness in the body through which the known and the unknown will find expression. It entails a vigilant porousness toward the unknown, a stance that can only be acquired through intensive practice. It depends upon the performer's lucid familiarity with the principles of composition. (After all, to improvise is to compose extemporaneously and composition is an arrangement into proper proportion or relation.)

Improvisation also demands a reflexive awareness of when the known is becoming a stereotype, a rut instead of a path, and it insists upon the courage and wit (also acquired talents), to recalibrate known and unknown as the performance unfolds.

Improvisation does not, therefore, entail a silencing of the mind in order for the body "to speak." Rather, improvisation pivots both mind and body into a new apprehension of relationalities.

Manifesto (*Analytically*)

In the form of its function, improvisation most closely resembles a grammatical category found in the verb forms of many languages (including classical Greek) known as the middle voice. With this particular kind of verb—and verbs are the closest of all linguistic elements to dancing—events occur neither in the active nor passive voice. The subject does not act nor is the subject acted upon. A close equivalent in the English language (which does not have middle voice) to this nonactive/nonpassive voicing is the phrase "shit happens."

The experience of middle-voicedness is perhaps most palpable when improvising with another person. Many of us have enjoyed the experience of neither leading nor following, but instead moving with, and being moved by another body. One body's weight and momentum flow into and with another body's shaping and trajectory making a double-bodied co-motion. Or both bodies, seized by the same impulse, move in tandem, never touching physically but touched by a shared sensibility about the composition's needs. Or each body, knowing so intimately the other's whims and inclinations, simply incarnates as partner. Again, throughout this experience, there are many moments when one leads or is led, thus bifurcating action into initiation and response. But there are also spectacularly lucid moments when both bodies' actions coordinate and synchronize in spontaneous ensemble.

The concept of an operation that is neither active nor passive such as the middle voice profoundly challenges hegemonic cultural values that persistently force a choice between the two. Most theories about the significance of human action depend upon the conception of an individuated and isolated self located within a body that it controls and manipulates in order to achieve self-expression and fulfill individual needs. The self within the body tells the body what to do, and the body executes those orders, sometimes reluctantly or inadequately or deviantly, but never autonomously.[3] Other theories invest the state and capital with the power to transform the body/self into a desiring machine whose every impulse only enhances the growth of capital and the all-consuming power of the state. In these models, all individual choices merely maintain the appearance of independence. On closer scrutiny, however, the structuring of individual initiatives reveals their prior co-optation by governmental or capitalist channels through which power exercises its control.[4]

In either of these models of human agency, where the self tells the body what to do, or where both self and body are subsumed by larger political and economic forces, the body is relegated to the status of instrumental object. Robbed of all vitality, much less the capacity for agency, it endures as a mute, dumb thing. The experience of improvising, however, establishes the possibility of an alternative theory of bodily agency, one that refutes the body's mere instrumentality and suggests alternative formulations of individual and collective agency.

Improvisation provides an experience of body in which it initiates, creates, and probes playfully its own physical and semantic potential. The thinking and creating body engages in action. The presence of this body, cultivated during dance classes that enhance prowess at improvisational skills, is what recalibrates ego and superego, critic and comic, attentivist and activist, and individualistic and communal impulses to build a middle voice among them. This body, instigatory as well as responsive, grounds the development of consciousness as a hyperawareness of relationalities. Each next moment of improvising, full of possible positionings, develops its choreographic significance as all participants' actions work to bring the performance into proper proportion or relation. During this playful labor, consciousness shifts from self in relation to group, to body in relation to body, to movement in relation to space and time, to past in relation to present, and to fragment in relation to developing whole. Shared by all improvisers in a given performance, this embodied consciousness enables the making of the dance and the dance's making of itself.

Power circulates through the collective actions of such improvisation. It never has the opportunity to dwell in a specific joint of the body, or alight at the site of a particular individual, or hunker down among a portion of the group. Power is repeatedly "taken by surprise" so that it can never embed itself within a static structural element that would allow it to flex into hierarchies of domination and control. In improvisation, power can only keep on the move, running as fast as it can to partner, to empower performers, never overcoming them.

Improvisation empowers those who witness it as well as those who perform it. Watching improvisation, consciousness expands out of passive reception of an event and toward active engagement in the actual making of the event. Viewers participate along with the performers in the open field of possible choices and the performers' construction and selection of those choices through which meaning is determined. The middle-voiced play of desire and power envelopes the audience and invites participation in eventing.

The recasting of power and desire that takes place during improvisation, the new conception of human agency articulated during improvisation, and the special identity of body discovered through improvisation—these are insights of crucial importance. They impact on our understanding of history and political agency, and they provide us with an enormously rich source of tactics for navigating the next millennium.

Manifesto (*Epistemologically*)

In the original presentation of this essay, I read aloud, spoke extemporaneously, and improvised choreography, speaking and dancing simultaneously.[5] I had been asked to write a speech about improvisation, to fix on paper certain thoughts about the unpredictable and deliver these verbal ideas about dance to an audience. Two contradictions held me in their clutches: (1) that a written discourse about improvisation might never incorporate its essential spontaneity; and (2) that the translation from dancing to writing might erode the power and significance of the moving body improvising. In order to extricate myself from the first contradiction, I not only added extemporized comments; I also organized the writing into trajectories of inquiry, manifestos, whose open-endedness might invite further improvised dialogues. In order to escape from the second, I improvised a dance that sometimes illustrated and other times commented upon the talking. At still other times the dancing resolutely pursued its own interests oblivious to the speaking that was taking place. In this way I hoped to create a co-motion between two discourses, speaking and dancing, as they were being composed, more and less spontaneously, together.

This essay gestures in the direction of that co-motion, its body straining between conventional prose and other writing that might depict more accurately the interaction between words and dance (*rolling up her sleeve for the fourteenth time, the dancer grins*). The essay is intended to clear a space where choreographers and scholars, together as well as separately, might begin to consider the workings of improvisation in dance and in history (*wiggling, winding down, then almost winking*). Once begun, such a talking-dancing inquiry might well last for a very long time (*she walks to the podium and rights it before exiting the stage*).

Notes

1 M***. *Mercure de France*. April 1734, pp. 770–72. For more information on Sallé, see her biography by Emile Dauer. *Une danseuse de l'Opéra sous Louis ?V: Mlle Sallé (1707–1756)* (Paris: Plon-Nourrit et Cie. 1909). For a fuller discussion of her *Pygmalion*, see my *Choreography and Narrative: Ballet's Staging of Story and Desire* (Bloomington: Indiana University Press, 1996).

2 Elizabeth Zimmer, "Richard Bull Dance Theatre," *Dance Magazine* (April 1985): 37.
3 This model of individual agency lies at the base of social-contract theories descending from those of Jean-Jacques Rousseau.
4 Michel Foucault was one of the first political theorists to advance this kind of perspective on body and agency.
5 The presentation was delivered as the keynote address of the conference "Taken by Surprise: Improvisation in Dance and Mind," organized by David Gere and Ellen Webb of the Talking Dance Project in Berkeley, California, June 10–11, 1994.

50 Seven Aspects of Spontaneity

Viola Spolin

Born in Chicago, Viola Spolin (1906–94) was raised in a family that loved music, theatre, and games. As a settlement worker at the Group Work School in Chicago, she was impressed by Neva Boyd's use of traditional game structures to cross cultural and ethnic barriers with inner-city and immigrant children. In later years, as drama supervisor at the Works Progress Administration's Recreational Project in Chicago, Spolin built upon these techniques to create "Theater Games," including these "Seven Aspects of Spontaneity" from her 1963 book *Improvisation for the Theater*: games, approval/disapproval, group expression, audience, theater techniques, carrying the learning process into daily life, and physicalisation. In 1946 she founded the Young Actors Company in Hollywood, and, returning to Chicago in 1955, she directed for the Playwrights Theater Club, worked with the Compass improvisation group, and, with her son Paul Sills, became Second City's workshop director. She continued working for years in Chicago, Los Angeles, and New York, in 1976 opening the Spolin Theater Game Center in Hollywood. In 1979 she was awarded an honorary doctorate by Eastern Michigan University. In addition to *Improvisation*, her books are *Theater Game File* (1975), *Theater Games for Rehearsal: a Director's Handbook* (1985) and *Theater Games for the Classroom: a Teacher's Handbook* (1986).

Key words: theatre; pedagogy; Second City

Games

The game is a natural group form providing the involvement and personal freedom necessary for experiencing. Games develop personal techniques and skills necessary for the game itself, through playing. Skills are developed at the very moment a person is having all the fun and excitement playing a game has to offer—this is the exact time he is truly open to receive them.

Ingenuity and inventiveness appear to meet any crises the game presents, for it is understood during playing that a player is free to reach the game's objective in any style he chooses. As long as he abides by the rules of the game, he may swing, stand on his head, or fly through the air. In fact, any unusual or extraordinary way of playing is loved and applauded by his fellow players.

This makes the form useful not only in formal theater but especially so for actors interested in learning scene improvisation, and it is equally valuable in exposing new-comers to the theater experience, whether adult or child. All the techniques, conventions, etc. that the student-actors have come to find are given to them through playing theater games (acting exercises).

Playing a game is psychologically different in degree but not in kind from dramatic acting. The ability to create a situation imaginatively and to play a role in it is a tremendous experience, a sort of vacation from one's everyday self and the routine of everyday living. We observe that this psychological freedom creates a condition in which *strain* and *conflict* are dissolved and potentialities are released in the spontaneous effort to meet the demands of the situation.[1]

Any game worth playing is highly social and has a problem that needs solving within it–an objective point in which each individual must become involved, whether it be to reach a goal or to flip a chip into a glass. There must be group agreement on the rules of the game and group interaction moving towards the objective if the game is to be played.

Players grow agile and alert, ready and eager for any unusual play as they respond to the many random happenings simultaneously. The personal capacity to involve one's self in the problem of the game and the effort put forth to handle the multiple stimuli the game provokes determine the extent of this growth.

Growth will occur without difficulty in the student-actor because the very game he plays will aid him. The objective upon which the player must constantly focus and towards which every action must be directed provokes spontaneity. In this spontaneity, personal freedom is released, and the total person, physically, intellectually, and intuitively, is awakened. This causes enough excitation for the student to transcend himself—he is freed to go out into the environment, to explore, adventure, and face all dangers he meets unafraid.

The energy released to solve the problem, being restricted by the rules of the game and bound by group decision, creates an explosion—or spontaneity—and as is the nature of explosions, everything is torn apart, rearranged, unblocked. The ear alerts the feet, and the eye throws the ball.

Every part of the person functions together as a working unit, one small organic whole within the larger organic whole of the agreed environment which is the game structure. Out of this integrated experience, then, a total self in a total environment, comes a support and thus trust which allows the individual to open up and develop any skills that may be needed for the communication within the game. Furthermore, the acceptance of all the imposed limitations creates the playing, out of which the game appears, or as in the theater, the scene.

With no outside authority imposing itself upon the players, telling them what to do, when to do it, and how to do it, each player freely chooses self-discipline by accepting the *rules of the game* ("it's more fun that way") and enters into the group decisions with enthusiasm and trust. With no one to please or appease, the player can then focus full energy directly on the problem and learn what he has come to learn.

Approval/Disapproval

The first step towards playing is feeling personal freedom. Before we can play (experience), we must be free to do so. It is necessary to become part of the world around us and make it real by touching it, seeing it, feeling it, tasting it, and smelling it—direct contact with the environment is what we seek. It must be investigated, questioned, accepted or rejected. The personal freedom to do so leads us to experiencing and thus to self-awareness (self-identity) and self-expression. The hunger for self-identity and self-expression, while basic to all of us, is also necessary for the theater expression.

Very few of us are able to make this direct contact with our reality. Our simplest move out into the environment is interrupted by our need for favorable comment or interpretation by established authority. We either fear that we will not get approval, or we accept outside comment and interpretation unquestionably. In a culture where approval/disapproval has become the predominant regulator of effort and position, and often the substitute for love, our personal freedoms are dissipated.

Abandoned to the whims of others, we must wander daily through the wish to be loved and the fear of rejection before we can be productive. Categorized "good" or "bad" from birth (a "good" baby does not cry too much) we become so enmeshed with the tenuous treads of approval/disapproval that we are creatively paralyzed. We see with others' eyes and smell with others' noses.

Having thus to look to others to tell us where we are, who we are, and what is happening results in a serious (almost total) loss of personal experiencing. We lose the ability to be organically involved in a problem, and in a disconnected way, we function with only parts of our total selves. We do not know our own substance, and in the attempt to live through (or avoid living through) the eyes of others, self-identity is obscured, our bodies become mis-shaped, natural grace is gone, and learning is affected. Both the individual and the art form are distorted and deprived, and insight is lost to us.

Trying to save ourselves from attack, we build a mighty fortress and are timid, or we fight each time we venture forth. Some in striving with approval/disapproval develop egocentricity and exhibitionism; some give up and simply go along. Others, like Elsa in the fairy tale, are forever knocking on windows, jingling their chain of bells, and wailing, "Who am I?" In all cases, contact with the environment is distorted. Self-discovery and other exploratory traits tend to become atrophied. Trying to be "good" and avoiding "bad" or being "bad" because one can't be "good" develops into a way of life for those needing approval/disapproval from authority—and the investigation and solving of problems becomes of secondary importance.

Approval/disapproval grows out of authoritarianism that has changed its face over the years from that of the parent to the teacher and ultimately the whole social structure (mate, employer, family, neighbors, etc.).

The language and attitudes of authoritarianism must be constantly scourged if the total personality is to emerge as a working unit. All words which shut doors, have emotional content or implication, attack the student-actor's personality, or keep a student slavishly dependent on a teacher's judgment are to be avoided. Since most of us were brought up by the approval/disapproval method, constant self-surveillance is necessary on the part of the teacher-director to eradicate it in himself so that it will not enter the teacher-student relationship.

The expectancy of judgment prevents free relationships within the acting workshops. Moreover, the teacher cannot truly judge good or bad for another, for *there is no absolutely right or wrong way to solve a problem:* a teacher of wide past experience may know a hundred ways to solve a particular problem, and a student may turn up with the hundred and first! This is particularly true in the arts.

Judging on the part of the teacher-director limits his own experiencing as well as the students', for in judging, he keeps himself from a fresh moment of experience and rarely goes beyond what he already knows. This limits him to the use of rote-teaching, of formulas or other standard concepts which prescribe student behavior.

Authoritarianism is more difficult to recognize in approval than in disapproval—particularly when a student begs for approval. It gives him a sense of himself, for a teacher's approval usually indicates progress has been made, but it remains progress in the teacher's terms, not his own. In wishing to avoid approving therefore, we must be careful not to detach ourselves in such a way that the student feels lost, feels that he is learning nothing, etc.

True personal freedom and self-expression can flower only in an atmosphere where attitudes permit equality between student and teacher and the dependencies of teacher for student and student for teacher are done away with. The problems within the *subject matter* will teach both of them.

Accepting simultaneously a student's right to equality in approaching a problem and his lack of experience puts a burden on the teacher. This way of teaching at first seems more difficult, for the teacher must often sit out the discoveries of the student without interpreting or forcing conclusions on him. Yet it can be more rewarding for the teacher, because when student-actors have truly learned through playing, the quality of performance will be high indeed!

The problem-solving games and exercises in this handbook [*Improvisation for the Theater*] will help clear the air of authoritarianism, and as the training continues, it should disappear. With an awakening sense of self, authoritarianism drops away. There is no need for the "status" given by approval/disapproval as all (teacher as well as student) struggle for personal insights—with intuitive awareness comes a feeling of certainty.

The shift away from the teacher as absolute authority does not always take place immediately. Attitudes are years in building, and all of us are afraid to let go of them. Never losing sight of the fact that *the needs of the theater are the real master,* the teacher will find his cue, for the teacher too should accept the *rules of the game.* Then he will easily find his role as guide; for after all, the teacher-director knows the theater technically and artistically, and his experiences are needed in leading the group.

Group Expression

A healthy group relationship demands a number of individuals working interdependently to complete a given project with full individual participation and personal contribution. If one person dominates, the other members have little growth or pleasure in the activity; a true group relationship does not exist.

Theater is an artistic group relationship demanding the talents and energy of many people—from the first thought of a play or scene to the last echo of applause. Without this interaction there is no place for the single actor, for without group functioning, who would he play for, what materials would he use, and what effects could he produce? A student-actor must learn that "how to act," like the game, is inextricably bound up with every other person in the complexity of the art form. Improvisational theater requires very close group relationships because it is from group agreement and group playing that material evolves for scenes and plays.

For the student first entering the theater experience, working closely with a group gives him a great security on one hand and becomes a threat on the other. Since participation in a theater activity is confused by many with exhibitionism (and therefore with the fear of exposure), the individual fancies himself one against many. He must single-handedly brave a large number of "malevolent-eyed" people sitting in judgment. The student, then, bent on proving himself, is constantly watching and judging himself and moves nowhere.

When working with a group, however, playing and experiencing things together, the student-actor integrates and finds himself within the whole activity. The differences as well as the similarities within the group are accepted. A group should never be used to induce conformity but, as in a game, should be a spur to action.

The cue for the teacher-director is basically simple: he must see that each student is participating freely at every moment. The challenge to the teacher or leader is to activize each student in the group while respecting each one's immediate capacity for participation. Though the gifted student will always seem to have more to give, yet if a student is participating to the limit of his powers and using his abilities to their fullest extent, he must be respected for so doing, no matter how minute his contribution. The student cannot always do what the teacher thinks he should do, but as he progresses, his capacities will enlarge. Work with the student where he is, not where you think he should be.

Group participation and agreement remove all the imposed tensions and exhaustions of the competitiveness and open the way for harmony. A highly competitive atmosphere creates artificial tensions, and when competition replaces participation, compulsive action is the result. Sharp competition connotes to even the youngest the idea that he has to be better than someone else. When a player feels this, his energy is spent on this alone; he becomes anxious and driven, and his fellow players become a threat to him. Should competition be mistaken for a teaching tool, the whole meaning of playing and games is distorted. Playing allows a person to respond with his "total organism within a total environment." Imposed competition makes this harmony impossible; for it destroys the basic nature of playing by occluding self-identity and by separating player from player.

When competition and comparisons run high within an activity, there is an immediate effect on the student which is patent in his behavior. He fights for status by tearing another person down, develops defensive attitudes (giving detailed "reasons" for the simplest action, bragging, or blaming others for what he does) by aggressively taking over, or by signs of restlessness. Those who find it impossible to cope with imposed tension turn to apathy and boredom for release. Almost all show signs of fatigue.

Natural competition, on the other hand, is an organic part of every group activity and gives both tension and release in such a way as to keep the player intact while playing. It is the growing excitement as each problem is solved and more challenging ones appear. Fellow players are needed and welcomed. It can become a process for greater penetration into the environment.

With mastery of each and every problem we move out into larger vistas, for once a problem is solved, it dissolves like cotton candy. When we master crawling, we stand, and when we stand, we walk. This everlasting appearing and dissolving of phenomena develops a greater and greater sight (perceiving) in us with each new set of circumstances. [...]

If we are to keep playing, then, natural competition must exist wherein each individual strives to solve consecutively more complicated problems. These can be solved then, not at the expense of another person and not with the terrible personal emotional loss that comes with compulsive behavior, but by working harmoniously together with others to enhance the group effort or project. It is only when the scale of values has taken competition as the battle cry that danger ensues: the end-result—success—becomes more important than process.

The use of energy in excess of a problem is very evident today. While it is true that some people working on compulsive energies do make successes, they have for the most part lost sight of the pleasure in the activity and are dissatisfied with their achievement. It stands to reason that if we direct all our efforts towards reaching a goal, we stand in grave danger of losing everything on which we have based our daily activities. For when a goal is superimposed on an activity instead of evolving out of it, we often feel cheated when we reach it.

When the goal appears easily and naturally and comes from growth rather than forcing, the end-result, performance or whatever, will be no different from the process that achieved the result. If we are trained only for success, then to gain it we must necessarily use everyone and everything for this end; we may cheat, lie, crawl, betray, or give up all social life to achieve success. How much more certain would knowledge be if it came from and out of the excitement of learning itself. How many human values will be lost and how much will our art forms be deprived if we seek only success?

Therefore, in diverting competitiveness to group endeavor, remembering that process comes before end-result, we free the student-actor to trust the scheme and help him to solve the problems of the activity. Both the gifted student who would have success even under high tensions and the student who has little chance to succeed under pressure show a great creative release and the artistic standards within the workshop rise higher when free, healthy energy moves unfettered into the theater activity. Since the acting problems are cumulative, all are deepened and enriched by each successive experience.

Audience

The role of the audience must become a concrete part of theater training. For the most part, it is sadly ignored. Time and thought are given to the place of the actor, set designer, director, technician, house manager, etc., but the large group without whom their efforts would be for nothing is rarely given the least consideration. The audience is regarded either as a cluster of Peeping Toms to be tolerated by actors and directors or as a many-headed monster sitting in judgment.

The phrase "forget the audience" is a mechanism used by many directors as a means of helping the student-actor to relax on stage. But this attitude probably created the fourth wall. The actor must no more forget his audience than his lines, his props, or his fellow actors!

The audience is the most revered member of the theater. Without an audience there is no theater. Every technique learned by the actor, every curtain and flat on the stage, every careful analysis by the director, every coordinated scene, is for the enjoyment of the audience. They are our guests, our evaluators, and the last spoke in the wheel which can then begin to roll. They make the performance meaningful.

When there is understanding of the role of the audience, complete release and freedom come to the player. Exhibitionism withers away when the student-actor begins to see members of the audience not as judges or censors or even as delighted friends but as a group with whom he is sharing an experience. When the audience is understood to be an organic part of the theater experience, the student-actor is immediately given a host's sense of responsibility toward them which has in it no nervous tension. The fourth wall disappears, and the lonely looker-in becomes part of the game, part of the experience, and is welcome! This relationship cannot be instilled at dress rehearsal or in a last minute lecture but must, like all other workshop problems, be handled from the very first acting workshop.

If there is agreement that all those involved in the theater should have personal freedom to experience, this must include the audience—each member of the audience must have a personal experience, not artificial stimulation, while viewing a play. If they are to be part of this group agreement, they cannot be thought of as a single mass to be pulled hither and yon by the nose, nor should they have to live someone else's life story (even for one hour) nor identify with the actors and play out tired, handed-down emotions through them. They are separate individuals watching the skills of players (and playwrights), and it is for each and every one of them that the players (and playwrights) must use these skills to create the magical world of a theater reality. This should be a world where every human predicament, riddle, or vision can be explored, a world of magic where rabbits can be pulled out of a hat when needed and the devil himself can be conjured up and talked to.

The problems of present-day theater are only now being formulated into questions. When our theater training can enable the future playwrights, directors, and actors to think through the role of the audience as individuals and as part of the process called theater, each one with a right to a thoughtful and personal experience, is it not possible that a whole new form of theater presentation will emerge? Already fine professional improvising theaters have evolved directly from this way of working, delighting audiences night after night with fresh theatrical experiences.

Theater Techniques

Theater techniques are far from sacred. Styles in theater change radically with the passing of years, for *the techniques of the theater are the techniques of communicating.* The actuality of the communication is far more important than the method used. Methods alter to meet the needs of time and place.

When a theater technique or stage convention is regarded as a ritual and the reason for its inclusion in the list of actors' skills is lost, it is useless. An artificial barrier is set up when techniques are separated from direct experiencing. No one separates batting a ball from the game itself.

Techniques are not mechanical devices—a neat little bag of tricks, each neatly labeled, to be pulled out by the actor when necessary. When the form of an art becomes static, these isolated "techniques" presumed to make the form are taught and adhered to strictly. Growth of both individual and form suffer thereby, for unless the student is unusually intuitive, such rigidity in teaching, because it neglects inner development, is invariably reflected in his performance.

When the actor knows "in his bones" there are many ways to do and say one thing, techniques will come (as they must) from his total self. For it is by direct, dynamic awareness of an acting experience that experiencing and techniques are spontaneously wedded, freeing the student for the flowing, endless pattern of stage behavior. Theater games do this.

Carrying The Learning Process Into Daily Life

The artist must always know where he is, perceive and open himself to receive the phenomonal world if he is to create reality on stage. Since theater training does not have its practice hours in the home (it is strongly recommended that no scripts be taken home to memorize, even when rehearsing a formal play), what we seek must be brought to the student-actor within the workshop. This must be done in such a way that he absorbs it, and carries it out again (inside himself) to his daily living.

Because of the nature of the acting problems, it is imperative to sharpen one's whole sensory equipment, shake loose and free one's self of all preconceptions, interpretations, and assumptions (if one is to solve the problem) so as to be able to make direct and fresh contact with the created environment and the objects and the people within it. When this is learned inside the theater world, it simultaneously produces recognition, direct and fresh contact with the outside world as well. This, then, broadens the student-actor's ability to involve himself with his own phenomenal world and more personally to experience it. Thus *experiencing* is the only actual homework and, once begun, like ripples on water is endless and penetrating in its variations.

When the student sees people and the way they behave when together, sees the color of the sky, hears the sounds in the air, feels the ground beneath him and the wind on his face, he gets a wider view of his personal world and his development as an actor is quickened. The world provides the material for the theater, and artistic growth develops hand in hand with one's recognition of it and himself within it.

Physicalization

The term "physicalization" as used [here] describes the means by which material is presented to the student on a physical, non-verbal level as opposed to an intellectual or psychological approach. "Physicalization" provides the student with a personal concrete experience (which he can grasp) on which his further development depends; and it gives the teacher and student a working vocabulary necessary to an objective relationship.

Our first concern with students is to encourage freedom of physical expression, because the physical and sensory relationship with the art form opens the door for insight. Why this is so is hard to say, but be certain that it is so. It keeps the actor in an evolving world of direct perception—an open self in relation to the world around him.

Reality as far as we know can only be physical, in that it is received and communicated through the sensory equipment. Through physical relationships all life springs, whether it be a spark of fire from a flint, the roar of the surf hitting the beach, or a child born of man and woman. The physical is the known, and through it we may find our way to the unknown, the intuitive, and perhaps beyond to man's spirit itself.

In any art form we seek the experience of going beyond what we already know. Many of us hear the stirring of the new, and it is the artist who must midwife the new reality that we (the audience) eagerly await. It is sight into this reality that inspires and regenerates us. This is the role of the artist, to give sight. What he believes cannot be our concern, for these matters are of intimate nature, private to the actor and not for public viewing. Nor need we be concerned with the feelings of the actor, for use in the theater. We should be interested only in his direct physical communication; his feelings are personal to him. When energy is absorbed in the physical object, there is no time for "feeling" any more than a quarterback running down the field can be concerned with his clothes or whether he is universally admired. If this seems harsh, be assured that insisting upon this objective (physical) relationship with the art form brings clearer sight and greater vitality to the student-actors. For the energy bound up in the fear of exposure is freed (and no more secretive) as the student intuitively comes to realize no one is peeping at his private life and no one cares where he buried the body.

A player can dissect, analyze, intellectualize, or develop a valuable case history for his part, but if he is unable to assimilate it and communicate it physically, it is useless within the theater form. It neither frees his feet nor brings the fire of inspiration to the eyes of those in the audience. The theater is not a clinic, nor should it be a place to gather statistics. The artist must draw upon and express a world that is physical but that transcends objects—more than accurate observation and information, more than the physical object itself, more than the eye can see. We must all find the tools for this expression. "Physicalization" is such a tool.

When a player learns he can communicate directly to the audience only through the physical language of the stage, it alerts his whole organism.[2] He lends himself to the scheme and lets this physical expression carry him wherever it will. For improvisational theater, for instance, where few or no props, costumes, or set pieces are used, the player learns that a stage reality must have space, texture, depth, and substance—in short, physical reality. It is his creating this reality out of nothing, so to speak, that makes it possible for him to take his first step into the beyond. For the formal theater where sets and props are used, dungeon walls are but painted canvas and treasure chests empty boxes. Here, too, the player can create the theater reality only by making it physical. Whether with prop, costume, or strong emotion the actor can only *show* us.

Notes

1 Neva L. Boyd, "Play, a Unique Discipline." [*Childhood Education* 10.8 (1934): 414–16].
2 "Direct communication" as used in this text refers to a moment of mutual perceiving.

51 Yoruba Play and the Transformation of Ritual

Margaret Thompson Drewal

Margaret Thompson Drewal's studies of Nigeria's many-faceted Yoruba culture reveal ritual not as an unchanging repeat performance, but as a practice that is continually adapted to changing resources, times, and circumstances; a practice that engenders transformations through play and improvisation: "innovations in ritual … do not break with tradition but rather are continuations of it in the spirit of improvisation." Trained professionally as a dancer and choreographer, Dr Drewal is a performance theorist, dance historian, and ethnographer who has studied Yoruba (West Africa) and Afro-Brazilian ritual performance, and late-nineteenth/early twentieth-century American dance and popular entertainments, including early International Expositions. Her books include *Gẹlẹdẹ: Art and Female Power Among the Yoruba* (with Henry Drewal; Bloomington: Indiana University Press, 1983) and *Performers, Play, and Agency: Yoruba Ritual Process* (New York University Press, 1989). She has also published articles in journals such as *TDR: a Journal of Performance Studies*, *African Studies Review*, *African Arts*, and *The Journal of Ritual Studies* and is the director of the 30-minute documentary *Yoruba Ritual: a Companion Video* (Indiana University Press, 1992). With special interests in the poetics and politics of performance discourse, Dr Drewal is an associate professor of performance studies at Northwestern University.

Key words: ritual; Africa; dance; Richard Schechner

Yoruba-speaking peoples number approximately twenty-five million, constituting Nigeria's second largest language group (Abiọdun 1990:64). Composed of some twenty-five distinct subgroups, which extend approximately three hundred kilometers in from the Atlantic coast, the Yoruba have a certain linguistic coherence, but in many ways they are culturally and socially diverse. This in part led J. S. Eades (1980:ix) to suggest that writing a general account of the Yoruba is foolhardy. The term "Yoruba" as a cultural designation dates only to mid-nineteenth-century colonialism (Law 1977:5). People identify with hometowns or areas first and foremost and with being Yoruba only in relation to outsiders.

Yoruba Performance: Ritual, Spectacle, Festival, Play

Throughout these pages I use the words "ritual" for *etutu*, "festival" for *odun*, "spectacle" for *iran*, and "play" or "improvisation" for *ere*. In the way Yoruba use these terms, they are not discrete, bounded categories as folklorists and anthropologists tend to think of them (Ben-Amos 1976; Handelman 1977; MacAloon 1984). Instead, they are overlapping and interpenetrating. Whether Yoruba speakers invoke one or another of the above terms in any given context is a matter of emphasis and/or orientation.

Yoruba often use ritual, festival, spectacle, and play interchangeably—which is how I use them throughout—so that any generic distinctions have to acknowledge that as categories of performance they are open and inclusive rather than closed and exclusive. My cross-application of terms in this text will no doubt disturb scholars preoccupied with genre theory and taxonomic classifications. But as Dan Ben-Amos (1976) has acknowledged, there is often a discrepancy between the analytical categories applied by scholars and those operative on the ground as applied by the "folk." Throughout I have cross-applied terms as Yoruba cross-apply them. I do this to resist readers' inadvertent attempts to impose rigid classifications, and to preserve instead the openness, inclusivity, and interchangeability of the Yoruba concepts.

The Yoruba categories of play and spectacle are broadest.[1] Yoruba conceive spectacle as a permanent, otherworldly dimension of reality which, until *revealed* by knowledgeable actors, is inaccessible to human experience. Indeed R. C. Abraham (1958:317) translates *iran* as "theatrical performance." Yoruba, however, apply the term to most religious rituals. Intrinsic to the meaning of the Yoruba word *iran* (spectacle) is repetition and transformation (Ọlabiyi Yai, personal communication, 1990). Thus *iran* derives from the verb *ran;* so, for example, *ranti (ran eti)* = to remember; *ranfa (ran Ifa)* = to recite Ifa verses; and *ranṣẹ (ran iṣẹ)* = to send a message via a messenger. In the latter case, according to Yai, the message delivered is the messenger's interpretation of the original. In each case, the repetition is a revision of whatever was repeated. The Yoruba word for a visual representation (*aworan*) is likewise based on this same root, as is the same Yoruba term used for spectator (*aworan*), the viewer of a spectacle. It is the role of knowledgeable performers to bring spectacle into the world periodically from its other-worldly domain so that it can be experienced and contemplated. In this sense, then, Yoruba spectacle is by definition restored behavior based in the embodied practices of performers.

Such performances meet all but one of John MacAloon's four criteria for spectacle (1984:243–44): 1) the primacy of visual sensory and symbolic codes, 2) monumentality and an aggrandizing ethos, 3) institutionalized bicameral roles of actors and spectators (that is, presentational action set in opposition to passive spectating), and 4) dynamism in the performance that engenders excitement in the audience. The difference is that in the Yoruba notion of spectacle *there are no fixed bicameral roles.* Yoruba spectacle is participatory; it is not set off as a unitary object of the spectator's gaze. The relationships between spectators and spectacle are unstable, one always collapsing into the other. Participatory spectacle does not set up fixed unequal power relationships between the gazer and the object of the gaze; rather, the participatory nature of Yoruba spectacle itself means that subject and object positions are continually in flux during performance.

The absence of institutionalized bicameral roles means at the same time that Yoruba spectacle does not have a destructive effect on the status of either rituals or festivals (cf. MacAloon 1984:268). This is because rituals, festivals, and spectacles are all participatory; participants move in and out of the action, moving at the same time between autotelic[2] and reflexive experience. Taussig (1987:443) has experienced this too in shamanism, "standing within and standing without in quick oscillation." Precisely for this reason, Yoruba performance accommodates optionality and individual choice much more so than do forms of spectacle, like the Olympics or those on the proscenium stage, in which the very bicameral roles about which MacAloon writes only serve to make the unified, rationalist approach to representation more thoroughly rigid and confining (Wagner 1981:116; M. Drewal 1987).

Play is a broader, more generic concept than spectacle. All Yoruba spectacle is play, but all play is not spectacle. What Yoruba mean by play, *ere* [noun] or *sere* [verb], is much more difficult to communicate because of the cultural baggage the capitalistic notion of play carries, which often sets it in opposition to work. Performing ritual is at once "hard work" and "playing."[3] What play is *not* for Yoruba is unserious, frivolous, and impotent. Yoruba have a different term for what we might call frivolous play— *yẹyẹ*—usually translated into English by Yoruba-speakers simply as "nonsense." Yẹyẹ is useless or gratuitous play, a trifle.[4] When Yoruba-speakers use the English word "play," however, it is a direct translation of *ere* or *sere*. The Yoruba presupposition is that play is dialogical in which a certain "*égalité de départ*" operates among the players (Ọlabiyi Yai, personal communication, 1990). Play—like Yoruba spectacle—is, more specifically, an engaging participatory, transformational process that is often, but not always, competitive. Below I try to evoke the transformational capacity of Yoruba play by citing particular instances and giving examples.

Yoruba Play

A Yoruba acquaintance of mine arrived at a friend's house announcing, "I made the police work today oh!" A policeman had stopped him at a checkpoint on the road to examine all his "particulars"—his driver's license, car registration, insurance, and so forth. Playing the situation, my acquaintance warned the policeman that if he turned off the car's engine, he was going to have to work (that is, to get it started again). Nevertheless, the policeman insisted that he pull over and get out. Once back in the car, my acquaintance feigned that the engine would not turn over and the car would not start. The policeman felt compelled to help him, as my acquaintance well knew when he spontaneously improvised the ruse. Since the policeman had no car at the checkpoint, it meant he had to exert himself physically. For about thirty minutes the policeman pushed the car before my acquaintance finally allowed the engine to kick in. Thanking the policeman for his help, my acquaintance was on his way again. When my friend Kọlawọle Ọṣitọla narrated this incident to me, as reported to him by our mutual acquaintance, he prefaced the story by reminding me, "you know, he is a Yoruba man." The fact of "being Yoruba" he presented as the basis for me to understand the ruse and the man's ability to pull it off.

The above example is not atypical of Yoruba tricks and ruses. Such trickster scenarios are common in the verbal arts as well as in the practice of everyday life. In one version of a popular story about the Yoruba trickster deity, Eṣu/Ẹlẹgba, he turns lifelong friends into enemies, sets fire to the townspeople's houses reducing them to ruins, and, pretending that he is going to protect the fire victims' possessions, he instead gives them away to passers-by (Wescott 1962:330–31; see also pp. 29–30). Similar scenarios abound with regard to Eṣu's Brazilian counterpart, Exu. Victor Turner (1986:54) sees Exu's potential for unexpected intrusions into Umbanda ritual as a manifestation of the danger of frame slippage. Frame slippage is dangerous because it destabilizes a situation and throws it into a zone of ambiguity. At the same time, it sets up opportunities for alterations.

But the very notion of frame slippage presupposes a "frame" from which to "slip." A frame in Erving Goffman's sense (1974) is a spatial metaphor for time, as is his use of the term "strip." Following Henri Bergson, David Parkin (1982:xxxi) has argued that such metaphors are embedded in language, where space denotes time, that is, a linear passage between fixed points that are measurable and finite. Parkin (1982:xxxi) suggested further that spatial metaphors for temporal phenomena may explain "the sway of positivist assumptions of fixity, set and measurable distance, and of observable objectivity." Frame analysis, it seems to me, exemplifies this sway, that is, our drive to isolate and identify the boundaries of situations so as to contain and control them, thereby preventing slippages and keeping the really real distinguishable from play, the serious from the unserious (Bateson 1972).

Goffman's frame analysis attempts to show how people distinguish the really real from make-believe, the indicative from the subjunctive. Play is then relegated to the latter. This model may help explain how Goffman's subjects of study attempted to structure their experience, but it cannot explain a structure of experience in which events and people are never taken to be simply what they seem. Frame analysis cannot cope analytically with a view of reality as unknowable, ambiguous, unpredictable, uncertain, and indeterminate. Indeed, indeterminacy is the very condition of the possibility of free play and is what empowers the players. It is inconceivable in frame analysis that play as the mode of everyday praxis is by definition serious and efficacious, shaping what reality is and how it is experienced. The unpredictable trickster stationed at the crossroads, whether in Nigeria or in Brazil, is a symbol of the efficacy of play, and narratives that focus on him are models *of* and *for* its practice.

What is significant is that to play a situation is to intervene in it—to transform it. When the policeman originally pulled my acquaintance's car over, he had no idea of the work he was going to do as a result. He interfered with my acquaintance, but my acquaintance reciprocated, turning the situation back on the policeman and taking pleasure in doing so. The ruse was not mere possibility cast in a "play frame"—certainly not from the policeman's point of view; it was nevertheless what Yoruba call play, what Schechner (1988) calls "dark play."

Yoruba play need not always involve ruses. In the Yoruba context, playing involves spending time with people for its own sake (indulging in time), engaging them in a competition of wits verbally and/or physically, and playing it out tactically to disorient and be disoriented, to surprise and be surprised, to shock and be shocked, and to laugh together—to enjoy. In conversations with my diviner friend and colleague Ọṣitọla, he would often insist, "All work and no play makes one become dull," in order to appeal to my Western perception of an unplayful Jack as "a dull boy." The following incident was a spontaneously improvised riddling encounter in which Ọṣitọla and I collaboratively explored our working relationship (taped interview #82.71). Recapping what we, together with Henry Drewal and John Pemberton III, had just discussed,

I reiterated:	So when a six-year-old child goes through [an Itẹfa ritual], it is his mother who goes with him.
Ọṣitọla:	Yes, his mother.
Me:	He would be touching his head to each of those *ebe* [earthen mounds prepared with medicines].
Ọṣitọla:	Yes, but ...
Me:	And the mother would follow.
Ọṣitọla:	Will follow ...
Me:	And touch her head to ...

Ọṣitọla:	She will help him. She will be the helping hand. And, yes, any more questions? [Laughter.] Yes. The mother will be doing the work of the wife. And the question is, when you marry how will you [that is, me—a wife] have authority with the Ifa? That is the next question. Uh huh?
Me:	Uh huh. [Laughter.]
Ọṣitọla:	The question, I know that is the …
Me:	Well, answer! [Laughter] Answer your own question now!
Ọṣitọla:	Um um. Is it my question or your question? [Laughter.]
Me:	Well, I'll take it. I'll take it.
Ọṣitọla:	No! Who owns that question? [Uproarious laughter.] Well, I keep the answer within me.
Me:	You own the question.
Ọṣitọla:	Then I keep the …
Me:	I second the question. I will second the question.
Ọṣitọla:	I thank you for seconding my question, then I will take the answer for myself. [Laughter.] Because when I own the question, then I have to hold the question because I need the answer. [More laughter.] Then I will have to keep the answer for myself. [We laugh again.]
Henry:	That means we can't let him [Ọṣitọla] ask any more questions. [Laughter.]
Me:	No, we can't let him ask any questions because we will never know the answer.
Ọṣitọla:	Uh huh! So, maybe, I want you to ask the question, then I [will] give the answer.
Me:	Ah ha!
Ọṣitọla:	Let's agree it's not my question now, then you ask the question.
Me—resuming with *my* question:	So it's the mother that goes through the ceremony with the six-year-old son. What happens again when he is married?
Ọṣitọla:	When he is married?
Me:	And takes a wife?
Ọṣitọla:	When—thank you!—when he has married the wife, we have to associate the wife with the Ifa like this [… etc.].

Such play is reflexive. In the case above, it was about our mutual roles as—to use Ọṣitọla's creative English—"questionaire" (someone who has questions like a millionaire has millions) and respondent. By mutual agreement the ownership of the question was transferred to fit the roles we had set up for ourselves in the process of the doing. In this kind of play, nobody formally wins or loses, although Yoruba play is an exercise of power and it is fundamentally exploratory. The trajectory of the process, as well as the outcome, is unpredictable.

The object is to turn one condition into another through a series of exchanges that bring revelations, altered perceptions, or even a reorientation of the participants. It is the process itself that is critical, whereby each spontaneous response turns on the previous one and to some degree directs the one that follows. This process is also at times autotelic. When it involves competition between people, the activity itself organizes their relationships.

Such play is integral to the practice of everyday life, a "mode of activity" occurring at any time or any place (Schwartzman 1982:328; Schechner 1988). Over years of research,

Yoruba friends have time and again advised me to "play with people" as a strategy "to get what you want," i.e., to do successful research. What they meant is that in order to establish the kind of relationship with people in which there is an open exchange of ideas and points of view—a prerequisite for working successfully with them—it is crucial to engage in play.

People who do not know how to play will ultimately be tricked because the play will proceed in any case without their awareness. Westerners, for example, are not generally known for their ability to play. Consequently, there is a well-known saying in Yorubaland that "you can always get a white man to fool." Or, more literally, you can easily "circumcise a white man" without his realizing it (*d'ako fun oyinbo*). Individual acts such as this may not have subverted colonialism, but could on occasion undermine a colonialist.

Play as a mode of activity is by nature tactical. It also demonstrates how individuals handle themselves and manipulate situations. Engaging in competitive play is probing; it probes individuals' personalities and ways of operating, revealing at once their strengths and weaknesses. As keen observers of human behavior, Yoruba are also extremely conscious of the value of exposing opponents and of the dangers of being exposed oneself. The Yoruba concern with appearances is expressed in their acute awareness of *oju aye*, "the eyes of the world" (Adedeji 1967:62). The implications of probing individuals' ways of operating transcends any notion of a bounded "play frame." Play in the Yoruba sense is an interactive exploration of the inner heads (*ori inu*) of the players, a creative, engaging, ongoing strategy for testing the stuff opponents are made of. The insight one gains in this kind of play is applicable to any life situation.

The Play of Ritual

Yoruba rituals (*etutu*) are propitiatory performances for the deities, ancestors, spirits, and human beings. They propitiate, or "cool" (*tu*), in that they entail both sacrifice (*ebo*) and play (*ere*), and in this they are socially and spiritually efficacious. What an *etutu* shares with the Indo-European root of ritual, *ri*—apart from its sacred dimension—is the notion of counting or enumerating (see Klein 1967:1351). Thus Yoruba specialists went on at great lengths enumerating the order of discrete segments (*aito* or *eto*) that make up their conceptual models of particular *etutu*. As a broad category of performance, the Yoruba concept of ritual subsumes annual festivals (*odun*), weekly rites (ose), funerals (*isinku*), divinations (*idafa*), and initiations and installations of all kinds—known by various Yoruba names according to the particular context.[5] Performances in each sub-category vary radically from place to place and from time to time. When Yoruba "perform ritual" (*se etutu*) they often say in English that they are going to "play." The concept has endured even in Yoruba-derived ritual practices in Brazil.[6]

In relation to ritual, what I understand Yoruba to mean by "play" is, more specifically, that they improvise. I do not use the term "improvisation" strictly in relation to music and dance, although in certain rituals Yoruba name and frame such activities as "play." In reference to ritual practice broadly, I use the term "improvisation"—as Yoruba use the English word "play"—to refer to a whole gamut of spontaneous individual moves: ruses, parodies, transpositions, recontextualizations, elaborations, condensations, interruptions, interventions, and more.

Improvisations are easiest to spot cross-culturally when they involve the incorporation of mass-produced items into new contexts for which they were never intended, as for example when maskers wear Western tuxedos, imported latex Halloween false faces, or World War II gas masks and sneakers, or when they carry pocketbooks in their hands and assemblages of plastic toys on top of their heads. In a similar vein, an Egungun masker in the Ẹgbado Yoruba town of Imasai in 1978 used his raspy, guttural spirit voice to speak Pidgin English in imitation of a popular Nigerian radio and television comedian named Baba Sala.

More difficult to recognize, unless the observer knows carving styles over a wide area, are masks produced in neighboring cultures, such as masks made by Ibibio people of southeastern Nigeria for foreign tourists, but used in ritual by Yoruba performers. As representations of ancestral spirits, such masks refer to the past, but the newly incorporated items mark divergence from the conventional rather than similarity to it. In this sense, each mask is a "formal analogue to the dialogue of past and present" in which the past as referent is modified, signaling new meaning (Hutcheon 1988:24–25).

As in the ruse my acquaintance pulled on the police or in my agreeing to agree with Ọṣitọla that his question was really my question, the subjunctive gives way to the indicative by playing a situation, a code, a learned conventional pattern, or a form. The performance is a restoration of an earlier performance and, at the same time, a new actualization (Schechner 1985:35–116). I believe it is not purely coincidental that the Yoruba word for spectacle is the same word used to speak of a generation of people born into the world at the same time.[7] In ritual performance as in the notion of descent, there is at once a continuity and a transformation. A World War II gas mask becomes the spirit's face, or plastic dolls become spiritual accoutrements. They do so in synthesizing practices. Mere possibility or potential becomes a newly synthesized representation. When new syntheses are popular, they can spread widely, effecting change in the entire masking complex. In such cases, the new synthesis may eventually become conventional.

Unfixed and unstable, Yoruba ritual is more modern than modernism itself. During the 1970s, oil revenues brought prosperity, increasing the economic power of Nigerians to stage rituals in urban areas, for example. In Lagos, a cosmopolitan city, masks became posh and elaborate, made of imported damask, brocade, and velveteen. One I saw in the Ẹgbado Yoruba town of Ilaro in 1977 was sewn with about sixty meters of velveteen— longer than the house where it was stored—reflecting the combined cash contributions of lineage members (according to two men in the household). If verticality in New York City speaks visibly of corporate power (Kirshenblatt-Gimblett 1983:186), then the horizontality of these masks called *baba parikoko* visualizes another kind of corporate power for Yoruba—large cohesive descent groups.

Baba parikoko masks represent spirits of "the original" Egungun lineages in the town. Each has a personal name deriving from lineage praise epithets (*oriki*). When *baba parikoko* parade around the town in slow, stately fashion, other family masks accompany them to carry and position their trains, to translate their gestures, and to chant their personal praise epithets. The procession acquires power and eminence for the masks, and by extension for the lineage they represent, through sheer visibility in space. In procession, the entourage becomes a monumental spectacle, particularly as a *baba parikoko's* enormous flexible form continually changes. The performance is an exercise of power that constructs for the participants a sense of self, both individually and collectively (Tuan 1977:173, 175). Many different groups representing various lineages parade the town simultaneously—but not as a unified group—thereby setting themselves competitively against each other.

Since ritual is at various levels a joint sacrifice, the amount of money participants put into their performances should ideally represent their economic conditions at that moment. As economists see it, people invest their incomes in ceremonies such as funerals and installations to reinforce relations of seniority and patronage as a strategy for competing for wealth and influence. In her study of Yoruba economics, Sara Berry (1985:192–94) concludes that such strategies "promoted unproductive patterns of accumulation and resource use and management." Thus people dissipate their surplus pursuing the means of competition rather than building the means of production, in a process that has mitigated against unimodal economic development and one that, in her words, "is not likely to be arrested by the unilateral action of any single class, community, or institution." But investing income in performance is "unproductive" according to whose system of values? Economic prosperity in the 1970s during Nigeria's oil boom did not necessarily make costumes and performances better, but it enabled them to proliferate and flourish. Likewise, *baba parikoko* masks took on monumental proportions during the peak of Ilaro's cocoa industry in the early 1950s. The monumentality of the form was itself a revision: an improvisation that was contingent on economic conditions at the moment of its creation.

When Yoruba people say that they perform ritual "just like" their ancestors did it in the past, improvisation is implicit in their re-creation or restoration. Innovations in ritual, then, do not break with tradition but rather are continuations of it in the spirit of improvisation. In practice, improvisation as a mode of operation *destabilizes* ritual—making it open, fluid, and malleable. The progression of the action as well as the meanings it generates are unfixed, "trajectories obeying their own logic" in de Certeau's words. These trajectories have a dialectical relationship to each individual's conceptual model of a particular ritual, and, in a kind of ongoing process of evaluation, a lot of the discussion *about* ritual centers on discrepancies between those models and what in fact "happened."

Since what Yoruba performers "do" in ritual reflects their assessments of the moment, it would be naive and reductionistic to think of their performances as a preformulated enactment or reenactment of some authoritative past—or even as a reproduction of society's norms and conventions. As I attempt to show, Yoruba ritual is not a rigid structure that participants adhere to mindlessly out of some deep-seated desire for collective repetition in support of a dominant social order. If that were true then perhaps culture itself should be defined as hegemonic. And if the Yoruba perception of the white man's general incapacity to engage in play, or even to recognize it, can be taken as empirical evidence, it suggests that more attention should be given to improvisation as praxis and to its potential to test propriety, to challenge convention, and even to commandeer and transform ritual structures.[8] [...]

Notes

1 All Yoruba festivals are spectacles, but not all rituals. Divination rituals, for example, are not usually called spectacle, because they are private, small, and sedate. However, when rituals are public and the intention of the organizers is to amass people, attempting to attract the entire community as well as strangers from other places, they can also be referred to as spectacles. A well-known saying about the rituals of the Gẹlẹdẹ masking society, performed to "cool" or appease spiritually powerful women, declares: "the eyes that have seen the Gẹlẹdẹ have seen the ultimate spectacle" (H. Drewal and M. Drewal 1983). The number of spectators such spectacles draw is considered indicative of their success as rituals.

2 In Csikszentmihalyi's words (1975:181), "a matching of personal skills against a range of physical or symbolic opportunities for action that represent meaningful challenges to the individual."

3 *Ere* is also pronounced *ire* and *are*, depending on the geographical area (Abraham 1958:314).

4 Thus, when Yoruba say *o nṣe yẹyẹ*, the phrase is often translated into English as "he is making nonsense," as opposed to *o nṣ'ere [nṣe ere]*, "he is playing."

5 *Ọdun* literally means "year" but, when used in conjunction with performances of Ifa or Oṣugbo (*odun Ifa, odun Oṣugbo*) refers more specifically to the annual festivals of Ifa and Oṣugbo. Similarly, *ọsẹ* literally means "week," but is also used to speak of rituals performed weekly—*ọsẹ* Ifa and *ọsẹ* Oṣugbo, for example. Apart from the temporal spacing between each ritual repetition, the main difference between weekly rites and annual festivals is one of scale and expense.

6 As Omari (1984:25) notes, "public festivals (*xire*, Yoruba for play, gala, party) provide an opportunity for aesthetic and theatrical display. Initiates are able to be 'onstage' and the focus of attention for a time. When viewing these attempts to please the Orixa [Yoruba deities] through a rich and colorful exhibition of beautiful and unusual costume elements, an etic interpreter will discern a competitive aspect to Afro-Bahian ritual art—attempts by initiates to outdo 'sisters' or fellow initiates with their display."

7 Ọlabiyi Yai (personal communication, 1990) tells me that the uses of *iran* as both generation and spectacle can be traced to the verbal radical *ran*, which at once entails repetition and transformation.

8 Turner (1977:40; 1982:32, 55; 1986:123–38) has acknowledged these capacities of play, but tends to associate them more with so-called "liminoid" phenomena, like Mardi Gras. Thus, "*liminal* phenomena, many, on occasion, portray the inversion or reversal of secular, mundane reality and social structure. But *liminoid* phenomena are not merely reversive, they are often subversive, representing radical critiques of the central structures and proposing utopian alternative models" (1977:45).

Works Cited

Abiọdun, Rowland. 1990. The Future of African Art Studies: An African Perspective. In *African Art Studies: The State of the Discipline, Papers Presented at a Symposium Organized by the National Museum of African Art, Smithsonian Institution, September 16, 1987*, pp. 63–89. Washington, D.C.: National Museum of African Art.

Abraham, R.C. 1958. *Dictionary of Modern Yoruba*. London: University of London Press.

Adedeji, Joel A. 1967. Form and Function of Satire in Yoruba Drama. *Odu* 4(1): 61–72.

Bateson, Gregory. 1972. *Steps to an Ecology of Mind*. New York: Ballantine Books.

Ben-Amos, Dan, ed. 1976. *Folklore Genres*. Austin: University of Texas Press.

Berry, Sara. 1985. *Fathers Work for Their Sons: Accumulation, Mobility, and Class Formation in an Extended Yoruba Community*. Berkeley: University of California Press.

Csikszentmihalyi, Mihaly. 1975. *Beyond Boredom and Anxiety*. San Francisco: Jossey-Bass.

Drewal, Henry John and Drewal, Margaret Thompson.1983. *Gẹlẹdẹ: Art and Female Power among the Yoruba*. Bloomington: Indiana University Press.

Drewal, Margaret Thompson. 1987. From Rocky's Rockettes to Liberace: The Politics of Representation in the Heart of Corporate Capitalism. *Journal of American Culture* 10(2): 67–80.

Eades, J.S. 1980. *The Yoruba Today*. Cambridge: Cambridge University Press.

Goffman, Erving. 1974. *Frame Analysis*. New York: Harper & Row, Publishers.

Handelman, Don. 1977. Play and Ritual: Complementary Frames of Metacommunication. In *It's a Funny Thing: Humour*, eds. A. J. Chapman and H. Fort, pp. 185–92. London: Pergamon.

Hutcheon, Linda. 1988. *A Poetics of Postmodernism: History, Theory, Fiction*. New York: Routledge.

Kirshenblatt-Gimblett, Barbara. 1983. The Future of Folklore Studies in America: The Urban Frontier. *Folklore Forum* 16(2): 175–234.

Klein, Ernest. 1967. *A Comprehensive Etymological Dictionary of the English Language*. Vol. II. Amsterdam: Elsevier Publishing Company. 16(2): 175–234.

Law, Robin. 1977. *The Oyo Empire c. 1600–1836*. Oxford: Clarendon Press.

MacAloon, John J. 1984. Olympic Games and the Theory of Spectacle in Modern Societies. In *Rite, Drama, Festival, Spectacle: Rehearsals Toward a Theory of Cultural Performance*, ed. J. MacAloon, pp. 241–80. Philadelphia: ISHI.

Parkin, David. 1982. Introduction. In *Semantic Anthropology*, ed. D. Parkin, pp. xi-li. London: Academic Press.

Omari, Mikelle Smith. 1984. *From the Inside to the Outside: The Art and Ritual of Bahian Candomble.* Monograph Series, no. 24. Los Angeles: Museum of Cultural History, UCLA.

Ọṣitọla Kọlawọlẹ. #82.71. Taped discussion, 20 June 1982.

Schechner, Richard. 1985. *Between Theatre and Anthropology.* Philadelphia: University of Pennsylvania Press.

———. 1988. Playing. *Play and Culture* 1(1).

Schwartzman, Helen B. 1982. *Transformations: The Anthropology of Children's Play.* New York: Plenum Press.

Taussig, Michael. 1987. *Shamanism, Colonialism, and the Wild Man: A Study of Terror and Healing.* Chicago: The University of Chicago Press.

Tuan, Yi-Fu. 1977. *Space and Place: The Perspective of Experience.* Minneapolis: University of Minnesota Press.

Turner, Victor. 1977. *The Ritual Process: Structure and Anti-Structure.* Ithaca: Cornell Paperbacks Edition.

———. 1982. *From Ritual to Theatre: The Humane Seriousness of Play.* New York: Performing Arts Journal Publications.

———. 1986. *The Anthropology of Performance.* New York: Performing Arts Journal Publishers.

Wagner, Roy. 1981. *The Invention of Culture.* Revised and expanded. Chicago: University of Chicago Press.

Wescott, Joan. 1962. The Sculpture and Myths of Eshu-Elegba, the Yoruba Trickster. *Africa* 32: 336–53.

Yai, Ọlabiyi. 1990. Personal communication.

52 Play On: Collaboration and Process

Tim Etchells

In his book *Certain Fragments* (Routledge 1999), Tim Etchells writes about his work as artistic director of Forced Entertainment, a theatre company founded in 1984. His other books include the collection *Endland Stories* (Pulp Books 1999), *The Dream Dictionary for the Modern Dreamer* (Duck Editions 2001), and a novel, *The Broken World* (Heinemann 2008). He has curated several festivals and exhibitions, and, in recognition of his writing about contemporary performance, as well as his work in the field, in 2007 he was awarded an honorary doctorate by Dartington College of Arts in southwest England. From 2004 to 2007 he was a Creative Research Fellow at Lancaster University, and was the Legacy: Thinker in Residence at London's Tate Research and LADA 2009–10. A professor of performance writing at Lancaster University, he collaborates with performance maker and writer Matthew Goulish on the imaginary think tank, Institute of Failure. "Play On" reveals Etchells as an artist concerned with improvisation at its most essential: "because I trust discoveries and accidents and I distrust intentions."

Key words: theatre; performance art; UK

This piece was written for and first presented at a seminar on play and performance in Leuven, Belgium in January 1998. The considerably expanded version here makes use of material I presented in Wolverhampton during a paper I gave there in 1995 on creative process and collaboration. The essay is a fragmented, speculative account of our own process, an anatomy of collaboration and an investigation of the role of play itself as a force of transformation, subversion and resistance.

A Warning

It is almost inevitable that in trying to write about play, I will write very often about death.

A memory. I saw a performance by a colleague of ours.[1] She'd been collaborating with someone, a friend of hers, he'd been ill when they started—HIV—but after they showed the work some times in public he got very ill. He was in hospital and she used to go and work with him there—they taped a lot of stuff on video—he clearly wasn't going to get out again—they figured he could be in the piece, you know, on video. So by the time I saw the performance the guy was dead already. Not long dead—a month, probably, maybe even less. And F was trying to show the work in public for the first time since he died and she was dealing with her grief in the piece and it showed and someone said to me that really she should have been home in bed. It was brave and fucked-up. It was raw and sometimes it didn't make much sense. And it might even have been embarrassing except that death and loss hung over the piece so strongly you could never exactly dismiss it.

Anyway. One thing about it that really held a charge was the video material of the guy acting from his hospital bed. In these scenes he was dressed in some frivolous cape or costume, gesturing faintly, laughing, or he was moving round the hospital room, making some great long speech from the text, an IV drip on a wheeled trolley thing plugged into his arm, a cheap plastic crown on his head and a wooden sword in his other hand, his arm as thin as death. It was absurd. A background of medical machines. I can't tell you how beautiful that was. To see him so obviously close to dying and yet still committed to the act of pretending—to see him playing—to see him acting—to see him give life to some fictional part of himself—in the ruins of his body. I admired that—it was funny and a bit scary—I think I liked it because it was resistant—I liked it that even as the real world of biology and material facts were catching up with him fast this person wasn't paying much heed—he was playing, changing the world in this (I want to say frivolous) way. But I don't mean frivolous.

> My love—
> It's not frivolous to challenge the hard logic of biology or material facts with the soft and mutable logics of play—play with its transformations, its power reversals, its illogics, its joys, its potential escapes …
> It's not frivolous to think that even as we die we're creatures of fiction and pretending, that we're not simply 'facts' or biology, that we may not be contained by either. I don't think it is frivolous to insist that, even as one dies, one is multiple, playful, partial, strategic and indeed fictional.
> I learned that from F, and from M, if I didn't know it already.

Shopping

My son Miles (aged 4 at the time) is loading the bath with more and more ridiculous plastic items, dropping them into the water and on top of me—blue ducks, yellow guns, giant clocks, alligators, wind-up fish—asking 'do you want some more toys dad?'

An adult body, surrounded by the props and objects of children's play.

These last few years are those in which the bedroom has half-filled with strange animals and plastic figures, in which most of the stories I have read feature talking mice and animate trees and in which our late-night motorway journeys are soundtracked by the delights of 'Heads, Shoulders, Knees and Toes'.

Years in which the rehearsal studio has come more and more to resemble Miles's room—a playhouse: balloons, large inflatable hammers all from *Showtime* (1996) rehearsals, costumes for dressing up—as trees, as gorillas, as a horse, as a ghost, as a dog, as a thief …

Miles wanted to know if there was a shop you could go to if you were frightened of dying. He was scared to die and just wanted to know.

Process (1)

They had this unspoken agreement that no one would bring anything too completed to the process—a few scraps or fragments of text, an idea or two for action, a costume, an idea about space, a sketched-out piece of music—everything unfinished, distinctly incomplete—so there'd be more spaces for other things to fill in … more dots to join.

They talked about the way that half-demolished or half-built houses were the best places to play … so much incompletion in the spaces, so much work (imaginative, playful, transformative) to be done. They liked this kind of mental space for themselves to work in, and they liked to leave some of it for the public too.

The process they used was chaotic, exploratory, blundering. A question of going into the rehearsal room and waiting for something to happen. Waiting for something that amused, scared, hurt, provoked or reduced one to hilarity. A starting-point could be anything—a record, a second-hand suit of a particular kind, a list of different kinds of silence, two imaginary scenes from a soap opera, a blackboard, the gesture of someone they had seen in the street, a hasty construction of a space in which to work—any of these things could be a major clue, alone, or in some unexpected combination. It was important that no one did their homework too well—that no element of the theatrical language might substantially precede any other—so that any element could lead.

For years they couldn't quite bring themselves to use the word 'improvising'—they'd call it messing about, having a bit of a run around in the space, playing around. In any case often the best of these 'improvisations' would start without anyone noticing—during lunch break perhaps when someone might get up and start messing about in the performance area—waving a gun maybe, trying out some text. Then someone else would join in and someone else, and someone else. Before long they'd be somewhere else too—pushing the material into unexpected territory. It seemed fitting that these good improvisations so often began in the blurred space between lunch break and performance, between the everyday and the fantastic.

Most recently they talked about 'trying to get themselves into trouble'. An antidote to the skills and strategies they'd built up, a way of avoiding their own conventions … getting into trouble was something you achieved by working too hard and too late, through exhaustion, confusion, delirium, drink and the rest of it, by sticking to the ridiculous randomness of the process—'getting into trouble', i.e., like pushing the work so you find yourselves in a territory beyond the one you know—by following a loose associative logic, by playing with no regard, in the first place, for sense.

'Nice Cop/Nasty Cop'

For a few days they'd play almost without thinking, doing, well, whatever came to mind. Improvisations (they finally got used to the word) were long and relatively unstructured. The mood would be, well, 'see what happens … '.

But after days of this the discoveries (or antics) of the week would be scrutinised. The video-tapes of improvisations would be played back and discussed, and a process of interrogating the material might begin. They'd ask the questions that were largely denied until this point: what is that doing there? What might that mean? What does this imply about structure? Would this work be sustainable as a 'show'? What is missing from it? What does it remind one of? … and they'd make demands of the material—for more sense (or less), for more joy (or less), for more pain (or less), for more intelligence (or less).

After a day or two of this kind of talk they'd go back to playing again. Forget what they'd just said. Or half forget about it. More days of play, more days of 'anything goes'.

Then back to questioning again.

This routine of nice cop/nasty cop, the tactic so beloved of interrogators the world over, kind of suited them too. It seemed a good way of teasing stuff from the unconscious and working it. But even playing nasty cop there was a certain lightness to the way they operated. To bring down a conceptual grid or frame onto what they were doing, but then to take it off again and replace it with another one. In this they were, at best, speculative and pragmatic. They had no dogma (or they tried to have none)—they were only interested in 'what worked' (what worked for them, in this place in history, culture and time). They tried not to get stuck in one logic—they tried to keep it moving, playful, nimble.

They talked about the difference between arriving at a decision and making a decision. The difference between coming to a decision and forcing one. They always preferred the former approaches—the meandering (with a strange certainty that you dare not trust) towards the things that they needed but could not name in advance.

The sign they lived by: 'You know it when you see it.'

1985

One night in the kitchen of the house where they lived on Langsett Road, one of them put his hands to his face and pretended to cry—a broken sobbing that was somehow very realistic. A couple of people were at the cooker—making dinner—they heard the noise and turned around, concerned—he sobbed a few-more times, then took his hands down and smiled, soon they were all laughing.

After that there was always crying in the work, more or less—sometimes ludicrous cartoon-style weeping, sometimes soft and gentle sobs, sometimes foolish tears splashed out of water bottles.

Oh, and yes, there was quite often real crying in the kitchen too, and in bedrooms, and hotel rooms and in cars and in all of the other locations that God and capitalism saw fit to provide for the glorious movie of their lives.

Tears then. Between the real and the fictional.

Play (1)

Play as a state in which meaning is flux, in which possibility thrives, in which versions multiply in which the confines of what is real are blurred, buckled, broken. Play as endless transformation, transformation without end and never stillness. Would that be pure play?

Perhaps the closest they ever got to it was in *12am Awake & Looking Down* (1993).

There were five performers with a vast store of jumble-sale clothing and a pile of cardboard signs which bore the names of characters—real, imaginary, from fiction, from history—characters that came from the great crowd of some scrappy urban collective unconscious—a crowd containing FRANK (DRUNK), THE EX-WIFE OF THE EX-PRESIDENT OF THE UNITED STATES, A BLOKE WHO'S JUST BEEN SHOT, A 9-YEAR-OLD SHEPHERD BOY, AN EU TRADE NEGOTIATOR, LEAH BETTS and A BOXER WITH A TORN RETINA.

By changing costumes and changing names the performers ventured endless possibilities for and of themselves, and the constant rearrangement of character, signs, costume and spatial positions worked like a narrative kaleidoscope—throwing up stories, potential stories, meetings, potential meetings, coincidences ...

JACK RUBY crosses the stage his hands under his coat as AN AIR STEWARDESS FORGETTING HER DIVORCE sits crying, wrapped in a towel ... THE

HYPNOTISED GIRL stares into space as A YOUNG WHITE RACIST ELECTRICAL ENGINEER makes a hasty Fascist salute ... ELVIS PRESLEY THE DEAD SINGER walks over the stage and AN ANGEL, SENT FROM HEAVEN TO THE EARTH stalks him, following ... and at the sides of the stage there were always further performers changing costumes, choosing signs, watching the action for an opportunity or a space.

Richard Foreman speaks about his pieces as 'reverberation machines'. In the studio I would watch *12am* as a kind of endless coincidence machine—I would watch it for hours—unable to stop it somehow—always eager to see what it 'threw up' next, what they did next, what they thought of next ... I was always gripped by the process of them playing—watching them think, watching them stuck, watching them try, watching them find ... the world is constant invention, constant flux.

And there were times when I would look at it and think this is terrible—this is just the empty Fragments of 2,000 stupid stories colliding with each other—there's no meaning in it, just the noise left in the machine of culture ... and then FRANK (DRUNK) would take a curious look at BANQUO'S GHOST and meaning would happen, like electricity between two lovers who are kissing goodnight, car alarms ringing, and there'd be nothing I could do to stop that.

Between the meaningless and the very highly charged.

Collaboration (1)

Is collaboration this: the 12 years' endless proximity to other people, physical, vocal, all day and into the night, watching people fade in and out of coherence and concentration—an intimacy that approaches that of lovers who now no longer bother to close the bathroom door whilst shitting? We are in the rehearsal space at 2am still talking and arguing about how it works or doesn't work and X is asleep on the floor, face up, mouth open, arms by his side while the remainder of us talk. When he wakes we will joke a little and continue. Change the furniture, clothes, haircuts and this scene could be any time this past decade. A sharedness that doesn't have a name.

Or is collaboration this: a kind of complex game of consequences or Chinese whispers—a good way of confounding intentions?

If the process of direction in the theatre most usually has at its heart the interpretation of a text and the fixing of a set of meanings in it, the staging of one interpretation out of many possible ones—perhaps we had in mind something utterly different—of theatre or performance as a space in which different visions, different sensibilities, different intentions could collide.

In an unpublished essay John Ashford, now head of The Place Theatre, once called experimental theatre 'a compromised art ... a mucky, mutable, dirty, competitive, collaborative business', and we always liked the quote, recognising in it the great mess of our own process but also appreciating the fine word compromise—no clean single visions in our work, no minimalist control freak authorial line—since by collaboration—impro, collage, the bringing together of diverse creativities—one gets an altogether messier world—of competing actions, approaches and intentions.

What does Elizabeth LeCompte say somewhere about her work with The Wooster Group—about her job being to build the frame around the performers' lives?

And once again: is collaboration just a good way of confounding intentions? I think so, and because I trust discoveries and accidents and I distrust intentions, I sit at the computer and I make a list of the misunderstandings and misrecognitions in our collaborative process, celebrating these above the instances of clear communication:

(1) I give instructions for impro to the performers but they are misheard—I have no idea what the people on-stage think they are doing—most of it is ridiculous but there is a moment that no one could have expected or predicted and it is wonderful.
(2) A performer tries something in impro but it is mis-seen or mis-recognised by the others on-stage—the others grab firmly on the wrong end of the stick and something brilliant happens.
(3) The composer mis-sees what we have done and writes music which we did not expect. I love it.
(4) I mis-see the performers—projecting onto them a narrative and intention which they do not have—for ages Terry is at the back of the space talking into the disconnected telephone as the impro continues around her. I have made up a whole story about who she is and what she is talking about but when the scene around her quietens down I can hear snatches of her talking and I am shocked to find that she is simply replaying a conversation with an accountant or a bank manager that she had some 10 minutes earlier on the real phone in the office:
'Yes … I can understand your position, but I don't accept that the delay is my problem or my responsibility … yes … yes … May 23rd … no … '

I stare at her—unable to admit for ages that I was so completely wrong, but enjoying the revelation.

Collaboration then not as a kind of perfect understanding of the other bloke, but a mis-seeing, a mis-hearing, a deliberate lack of unity. And this fact of the collaborative process finding its echo in the work since on-stage what we see is not all one thing either—but rather a collision of fragments that don't quite belong, fragments that mis-see and mis-hear each other. A kind of pure play in that too.

In *Hidden J* (1994) Richard as drunk git English bloke on his way back from a wedding; Cathy and Rob as gibberish speakers from war zone broken Europe; Claire sat at the front with this sign saying LIAR around her neck; Terry as frivolous narrator who can't even decide what century all this happened in. None of them in the same show really, or the same world, battling it out for space and the right to speak or own what is happening—a piece of contradictory intentions, brutal fragmentation.

Collaboration for them then was never about perfect unity but about difference, collisions, incompatibilities.

Everybody Join In

A great rushing joy in the game of dying from our piece (*Let the Water Run its Course*) *to the Sea that Made the Promise* (1986)—four players—two large bottles of tomato ketchup for blood—and a soundtrack of bad American TV, cut up and channel-hopping fast, the channel hops sound like gunshots …

The contest is to see who can act out the best movie deaths—the deaths getting ever more glorious, more bloody, more violent, more romantic—and the glee of the game was always infectious—like everyone watching just wanted to join in. There was a moment of hesitation for the performers—like, 'Do I really have to get that revolting stuff all over me again?'—but then they'd bite the imaginary bullet, get the first spray or great dollop of ketchup on them and then surrender sense, give in, abandon … go all the way—throw themselves into it, pure glee.

Everybody Pause

And then inside the game there would also be these moments of pause or reflection.

> When the players would take a look at each other and think about what was happening. Thinking 'what if this were real?' or else 'what are we really doing here?'
>
> A flickering—between real time and play time—between the idea of action with no consequence and the fact of action that hurts.
> And then back to the game again—doubled speed, gleeful commitment.
>
> For them there were always these numerous semi-stops, hiccups, breaks in the flow of the performance, moments where one game stopped, broke, exploded, slipped into or behind another.
>
> There were the kind of contemplative stops in *Let the Water* … where the players would cease their game for a moment and consider its consequences.
>
> And there were the kind of strange interludes where people committed to one task for more or less a whole performance would give it up for a while and do something else.

All through *Showtime* Cathy pretended to be a dog—on her hands and knees in an old overcoat, with a ludicrous dog's head mask (I can't remember where we got it from—some crap costume hire place—the kind of costume no one else had ever hired). Anyhow, Cathy as this disruptive dog—'scampering' and barking throughout all the other scenes—a truly unhelpful presence—and then at a certain point Claire decides to interview the dog—she sits down next to Cathy, asks her if she minds answering a few questions, she points the microphone to the dog and Cathy answers in her own voice 'No, no, I don't mind'.

And for a while Cathy talks and answers the questions and you can't be sure if this is 'Cathy' or the 'Dog' that is meant to be answering. And then Claire says, at a certain point, 'Cathy don't you think it's about time you took that dog's head off now?' and the dumb blank dog looks at us (questioningly) and Cathy's hands come up and lift off the dog's head and we see her face for the first time in the piece—must be about 50 minutes into it—and she's sweating and still a little out of breath I think but the only thing that's for certain is that, in the ruins of the dog game, she is more present than she ever could have been if she'd just walked onto the stage and sat down—Cathy is very here, and very now, very here and now, in the ruins of the Dog game she's very present.

The game pauses and it's like you need to see her take the dog's head off in order to even begin to understand what it was, what it meant to pretend that dog for so long, like only now, when the head comes off and the game stops can you measure it, and as Cathy talks (death again: a long slow story about how she would commit suicide if she were going to do it) we measure the distance/difference between real and fictional, human and animal, real time and playtime …

A strange reassertion of the game; when she's completed her long suicide story Cathy puts the dog's head back on again. And remains as the 'Dog' for the rest of the performance.

Simon Says Watch

In the ketchup/movie deaths game from *Let the Water*, and in so many others they played on stage, there were always people watching as well as people doing. These figures stood looking on, assessing the performance of their colleagues, encouraging them, spurring them on, looking on with concern or bemusement, awaiting their own turns.

They loved this mixing of the hot and the cold—those doing and those watching—they loved this flickering, or this co-presence, this flickering of real time and play time.

They saw a tape of a James Brown encore routine in which Brown was down on his knees and out of his mind with emotion singing 'Please, please pleaaaaaaase, pleeeeaaaaaasse!', whilst his minders-cum-trainers-cum-bodyguards were looking on in concern, like 'James has really gone too far tonight … '. And on the tape the minders tried to stop him, tapping him on the shoulder as if to say 'Come on, that's enough, get back to the dressing room' but Brown would not give it up and the minders were shaking their heads and Brown was sweating and shaking and screaming singing 'Please, please pleaaaaaaase, pleeeeaaaaaasse!' And of course he only seemed so very very into it because the guys behind him were so very very cool and distant, not into it at all.

Again, this hot and cold, this doing and watching from the stage.

Simon Says Stop

Perhaps the strangest moment of any of these games was when they stopped. Because in the stopping was always the time for measuring how far things had gone, how much the world had changed because of the game.

They were tempted to think of endings in performance as a kind of return—a point at which the travellers, sent out to discover things in a strange imaginary country, had finally come back. In shamanic performance this journey is taken as literal—performers sent out (or in or down) on a journey to the spirit world, a task that has real consequences, real dangers, a return that can bring real gifts. Performance then as going out, and coming back changed.

The audience-cum-witnesses want to measure the distance (or feel the proximity) between their world and the other. Listen: water dripping into the pool from the desolate gantries at the end of Impact Theatre and Russell Hoban's extraordinary piece *The Carrier Frequency*—a portrait of a flooded world, post-holocaust. After the piece has ended people somehow can't resist the temptation to come and stick their fingers in the pool, testing the limits, as if the feel of the water on their fingers might take them that bit further to the place that they've just seen. Or the end of our own *Speak Bitterness* (1995)—where the audience often gather at the long long table to examine the text which is strewn all across it—were they really reading stuff from that? Is there anything we missed? Just how does it feel to stand here and look out?

Pina Bausch

Performance as a way of going to another world and coming back with gifts.

For me, ending performance was always about crossing the line between worlds, or passing on the chance to cross it; refusing to come back. The five or six curtain calls closing Pina Bausch's *Cafe Muller* which I saw in summer '93 were almost pure refusal.

Here the gazes of the dancers (Bausch included) were as stern and distant and as lost in private pain as they had been throughout the performance—there was no returning in it, or only a nod to that, as though the image-world could not be quit, its psychic residue too strong.

Perhaps blurring, uncomfortable endings such as this one are the best—they stay with us, after all, and if Bausch's dancers cannot leave off, cannot shrug off their journey, then somehow, neither can we.

Central to the charge of these difficult endings and at stake in all performance endings is the negotiation of *where* the events we have witnessed will have their consequence. In real or imaginary space? What will be the transfer? How will it take place? How and where will these things mean?

At a workshop presentation years ago I watched a performer remove all his clothes and stand motionless before us for a minute. As an action it meant next to nothing (too meaningful!) but the audible sighs of relief from the performer once he'd retreated to the dressing rooms (sighs on the edge of laughing and crying, sighs on the very edge of the performance itself) were as gripping as anything I've witnessed. Those sighs were the marking of the journey from the play-space to the real, inscribing consequence.

Play (2)

Play is charged, it resonates, because it is a stupid dog (like the one in *Showtime*) worrying at the edges of what is real and what is not … playing at the edges of what is real and what is not, disrupting the borders between the so-called real and the so-called fictional.

I wondered:

What game might you play using 2 men, a bottle of whisky, a blindfold and a gun?

What game might you play with a pile of jumble-sale clothing and a record slowed down to 16 rpm?

What game might you play with four women and a disconnected telephone?

Sometime when we're touring (now maybe, years ago maybe, impossible to say). Two people, whose names can't be mentioned, end up staying with people from the venue. They have to share a room. They aren't together but it isn't a problem. They get put in the kids' room—the kids must be away or something. They sit in the room talking—it's very late already—bright painted walls, pictures, a mobile of clouds and space rockets. There are bunk beds. They end up fucking. The bed is too small. There are toys in it.

To be naked in this room is a strange thing. Sex in there is a kind of time travel. A loosening of the borders between what's real and what is not. Your body changes shape and size. They are watched by the toys.

Miles one night (years later?) couldn't sleep, he calls me in. He's very scared. He looks to the toys in the corner of the room and says 'Tigger and one of the rabbits are ignoring me'—I love it that what bothers him is not the life in these animals—they could be laughing, singing, dancing or whatever, he wouldn't mind—it's just that they're ignoring him.

Another time: again Miles can't sleep: he calls D into the room—he says the doors and handles of the cupboard are 'making him think that they are eyes and a nose'.

Letter

My darling,

> We talk as if the real and the playful were separate. But we know that isn't true.
> After *Psycho* the shower is not the same place. After the game we played endlessly one rainy Saturday afternoon, rushing in and out of the front room pretending to be monsters the house is not the same place …

A childhood memory—endlessly devising the rules and the systems of unplayable games. They had one game that was to be played all through the streets of the area where they lived. There were supposed to be two teams, each team was supposed to hide something—a matchbox—the other team had to find it. There was a crazed complicated system of clues and questions provided by each team. Their own plan was to hang the matchbox on a thread, down inside a drain by the side of the road. They even talked about ageing or dirtying the thread so it would not be visible. … They talked about the game several times, always adding new rules, new locations through the streets, but obviously, never really got round to playing it.

At the same time a friend and I found an old butcher's chopping knife—a big ugly thing—too rusty to be sharp but quite suggestive of violence at least. We took the knife-thing to school in a polythene bag—we must have been 8 or 9 years old—and tried burying it in some bushes at the edge of the playground.

At the same time—playing in the newly built houses on the edge of the estates. Burying things in the foundations—pictures, objects, broken things. What might some archaeologist of the future make of these strange secreted offerings?

In all of these games there was perhaps one thing in common—the sense of the game as a secretive intervention in everyday life. Just to think—the same streets that people lived, loved and died on were to them the arena for these games. And after their games the streets were not simply safe or normal any more. The playground was a changed place with a large knife buried at its edges. The families that moved into the new houses suffered strange dreams, unwitting victims of the aimless voodoo practised by us.

Those games were rewriting the everyday. Quite simply: changing the world by any means necessary.

Nights

We had a similar approach when we were making *Nights in this City* (1995 and 1997)—a mischievous guided coach tour of Sheffield and then, in a second version, of Rotterdam.

In trying to determine the route for the coach in Rotterdam we are helped by many people who live and work there.

We start by asking them questions like: 'Where is the tourist centre of the city?' 'Where is a rich neighbourhood?' 'Where is a poor neighbourhood?' 'Where is an industrial area?'

But these boring questions get the boring answers they probably deserve. We do not find what we are looking for. We switch to another tactic. Richard and Claire are talking to one of our helpers. They ask her:

> If you had killed someone and had to dump the body where would you take it?
> If you had to say goodbye to a lover where in this city would you most like to do it?
> Where in this city might be the best place for a spaceship of aliens to land?

This is what you might call *our* geography.

We think of this project like a strange writing onto the city—a playful and poetic reinvention—like you can take the city and project on top of it using words—of course the text contains hardly any facts about the city—it's not an official tour in that sense—it's much more playful. We are driving the streets of Rotterdam and pretending that it is Paris.

What's the quote of Baron Munchausen that Terry Gilliam uses in his film? the Baron's motto, or his favourite saying—OUT OF LYING TO THE TRUTH—that could very well be our strategy here.

Rewriting the everyday.

Process (2)

Peggy—You talked at one point about artists themselves needing to fall into (or for) their work, (or into the territory of their work, beyond their initial agendas)—to let it take them somewhere unknown, to surrender to that, or to respect that, to go with the work to a new place—an ethical need. That made me smile because we've long asked ourselves, when working on performance projects, having amassed some material by random collection and impro and accident and intention, and having worked with it a little, we have long asked ourselves the question: 'What does it want?' 'What does it need?' Anthropomorphising the work as if it had desires of its own. As if the fragments of the work in this early stage are a note (for Alice) saying 'follow me'.

Friends have sometimes reminded us that it is really our desires we ought to be considering and not those of a dubious non-existent entity—and we laugh with them at our deferral/projection to this 'it' but at the same time we know there is also an 'it'—a collection of objects, texts and fragments which resonate in certain ways (in particular circumstances, personal, historical, cultural)—and which in combination really do (I think) make demands, demands that have to be heeded if the work is to be worth making and sharing.

Collaboration (2)

Is collaboration this: four people in the room drunk and tired, treading again through an argument about the structure of the show, an argument which we've already had 100 times in the last week and for which all of us, by now, know all of the parts and yet are always coming back in circuits to the same stalemate stand-off conclusions about how and why the show does not work and will not work? There is a word for these too familiar arguments—we call them the loop, arguments that soon are shorthand and can be indicated simply with a gesture: the circling of a hand.

> Yes, someone says, it should really work like that. But the thing is, when Claire stands there we have no way of knowing what the fuck is going on. It can't just happen.
>
> So we have to go into a text. That'll help.
>
> But we tried a text there (three weeks ago) and I can tell you it doesn't work.
>
> Yes that's right. A text can't help. Claire just has to stand there.
>
> But the thing is, when Claire stands there we have no way of knowing what the fuck is going on. It can't just happen ... (etc.)

And now we're into the loop. For every group a process, and for every project a loop. Maybe collaboration is simply the process of developing new words for the strange situations in which a group can find itself.

The loop is the heart of the show, a wall you hit your heads against until you are senseless, gibbering and tired of it, tired of it, tired of it. And strangely it seems sometimes that the worst thing of all is that the loop must be tackled in public, with the group, through speech, discussion. So many times in the process I begin to envy the solitude of writers and painters—who surely have their loops but at least aren't condemned to sit up forever and talk about them. Worse than Beckett, worse than Sartre. After two months of working on the show I can chant you the loops in my sleep.

Drawing In

Cathy's long suicide story in *Showtime* comes right after she has removed the dog's head. Claire asks her, if she *were* going to commit suicide, how exactly she would chose to do so. The answer draws the audience in softly—a long and intimate pornography of detail; of running the bath, and of lying in it to watch some TV, of listening to a favourite song, of sticking her toes into the taps, of listing her favourite people, favourite books and favourite places, and of waiting for the electric bar fire to glow a perfect orange before lifting it up and dropping it into the water where she lies ...

When Cathy has finished Claire tells her 'Thank you', and at that point Terry—dressed as a pantomime tree, and coming straight out of 10 minutes' stillness—makes her outburst. From inside her absurd brown-painted cardboard costume—a cylinder with stupid holes for arms and eyes—she yells at the audience, gesticulating like a psychopath, thick with vehemence, breaking the mood:

> 'What the fuck are you looking at? What the fuck is your problem? Fuck off! Voyeurs! There's a fucking fine line and you've just crossed it. Where's your human decency? Call yourselves human beings? Why don't you fuck off, piss off, cock off, wankers, voyeurs. Fuck off. Go on, pick up your things, pick up your coats and your fucking bags and bugger off just fucking cocking buggering wank off ... '

They had this game with the audience, that's for sure. A game of drawing them in and pushing them away.

Like your presence at this event had to cost something.

Claire

Claire takes her seat at the start of *Hidden J*. She comes out before the audience on her own. She's first out. She takes the cardboard sign which is lying on the chair—she puts it round her neck, it says: LIAR.

> She settles in her seat. Looks those watching in the eyes.
> It's hard to look at her, since in looking you contribute to her shaming.

Like Claire fell victim to some backstage dispute in the company—they sent her out here to be humiliated for a while before the piece really starts. Soon the others come out— they start building the set. Claire is in position like she is holding the fort, bearing the weight of the audience's attention, but all she may do is sit there and suffer their gaze. To be in the audience here is, simply, to objectify and humiliate Claire. She sits there for most of the piece. Our watching is never without a kind of ethical problem.

Go Too Far

In *Club of No Regrets* (1994)—Robin and Cathy bound and gagged with industrial tape near the beginning—the actor/hostages that will enact this evening's spectacle. Cathy and Richard as their brutal captors come clumsy don't-give-a-shit stagehands—they point toy guns at the hostages' heads, look to the audience as if to say 'What shall we do with these two ... how far would you like us to take them tonight ... '.

In previews through the summer of 1995 we had friends tell us again and again that they liked the work, they liked the violence and extremity of the piece, they liked it but they wanted more. We should go further. They wanted more.

The chairs routine was already dangerous. It was before we had the rubber floor and the studio floor was lethal once wet. We hadn't even worked out how to do the taping-up properly so sometimes people got taped in such a way as they couldn't protect themselves when falling. Most often when supposedly watching that section I couldn't even look. I remember D coming in to watch it one time, the only person I recall saying, 'Really, why are you doing this to each other ... '. She was probably crying.

But everyone else wanted more.

What is it about those human persons who, as Richard says in *Showtime,* 'Like to sit in the dark and watch other people do it'?

People (like me and maybe you) who will pay money to sit down and watch others act things out, pay money to see pretending. And people (like me, and maybe you) who want to see more pain than anything else. The death scene. The crisis. The agony. The anger. The grief. Done convincingly, done with distance or irony, but done none the less.

And if the performers sometimes stop and ask themselves, in the middle of the game, 'What is this, really?' No surprise that the work will sometimes turn on its audience and ask them, simply, 'What was it that you wanted to see? What did you demand?' 'What was it that you wished for when you came inside tonight?'

One time when they showed the durational *Speak Bitterness* (six hours of confessions from behind the long table, with an audience that was free to come and to go at any point)—it was Amsterdam—the audience came in at the beginning and then, to their horror, more or less, hardly anybody left. After two hours they were pretty well out of material. They were making things up, inventing frantically, shifting the tone around as if somehow they might figure out what these people needed, what they wanted, what for them would be enough. It was desperate, slipping into hysterical humour very often. A small space—so small you could count the audience, you could see every move they made. He remembered an endlessness of eye contact, of enquiry from him to them—and in the end all he was thinking was, 'What do you want, what do you want, why don't you leave us ... there's no release in this ... '. It became the most fascinating night. Truly fantastic.

Afterwards he talked to some people from the audience. This guy said:

> I felt I got to see you all for the performers you would like to be, and for the performers that you really are and for the people you would like to be and for the people that you really are ...

And with that he realised—the desire, really, was for nakedness, defencelessness. An exposure that does not have a name. Something beyond.

Teasing

They had this game with the audience, that's for sure. A game of drawing them in and pushing them away. Teasing them with meaning, teasing them with narrators and central figures who would appear to be helpful but who would really say little to guide them through the mess.

Teasing them with certainties that would collapse. Teasing them with chaos, preposterous ineptitude.

Teasing, teasing. The kind of teasing that a confident audience would love and respect.

Did I tell you that account I read of hippies in Haight Ashbury—in the late 60s—they were so fed up with the coach loads of tourists gawking, staring from the windows of their buses that they took to carrying mirrors—when a bus full of tourists would go by the hippies would takes out their mirrors and hold them up to the buses—asking the people on board to simply look at themselves.

What was it you wanted to see?

Did you dream of a looking that had no consequence, no ethical bind, no power inherent in it, no cost?

You won't find that here.

You Play with what Scares You

Watching Richard holding Robin in *Showtime* rehearsals, the lurid guts (a can of Heinz Spaghetti tipped into his hand and clutched to his belly) oozing out of Robin, Robin dying.

It was the same summer that Richard's brother drowned. I mean it was only a few weeks before that Richard's brother had died and Richard was already back in rehearsals and now he was just holding Robin leaning against the blue and red kids' playhouse that was a part of the set, holding him, watching him saying nothing, trying to comfort him unable to speak as Robin played this big stupid death scene.

It must have been apparent at some moment that Richard was going to spend whole sections of the show holding Robin like that, in the way that he hadn't been able to hold Chris. I don't think we ever talked about it. Not much anyway. I think we all knew what it was. And we dedicated the show to Chris in a very quiet way.

You play with what scares you and you play with what you need.

At the end of the same show Richard with a timebomb strapped to his chest, making wishes, waiting for it to go off—things he'd like to have done, goodbyes he would like to have said … Waiting to die.

You play with what scares you and you play with what you need.

Antwerp 1998. I ask the women that I'm working with to write death threats—the kind of thing you could leave on an answer-phone—invasive, vicious, unsettling—the kind of thing that makes a house feel poisoned or unsafe. They start writing—they look puzzled at first, hunched over notepads, then after a time the first one starts smiling—this glee that she has thought of something really unspeakable and vile. Then the next one starts smiling, laughing almost, a similar feeling—there are curious looks passing between them. They hunch closer over the papers. A strange exam.

Later I ask them to play the death threats into the disconnected phone I've placed in the centre of the performance space. They come up one by one, a little nervously and then read from their papers—picking up the phone and spouting viscous vile threats, rape threats, burglary threats, I'm-watching-you-from-under-the-table messages—a festival of invasion. And as each one takes a turn to come forwards and leave their messages the reactions from the others swing wildly—from nervous laughter, to silent horror, to expressions of disgust (that one went too far, that's too much) and back to fascinated staring, to laughter again—switching between these things …

Afterwards we talk about this strange game of scaring each other—of tapping into fear. We notice that all of them, by implication, cast themselves as men whilst leaving their messages, cast themselves, in effect, as their own victims—not a part of my instructions.

Playing as a game of sitting in the house with all the lights switched out at midnight, just to prove that you can do it.

Or the game Michael used to play with his sister—playing their parents' record collection at 16 rpm in part to guess the tunes, but more just to frighten each other with the devil voices and from-hell tunes they told each other they could hear. You play with what scares you.

Three Letters

Dear Miles,

When I faxed you several times from America it was around the time of your 4th birthday and I mostly sent stories—stories about you, imaginary exploits, pirates, goodies and baddies, super heroes, transformations, magic.

Then one time I decided to write you a letter saying what exactly we had been doing—performing a show, going to a party all night, staying up to see the sunrise from a hill called Twin Peaks. Mad drunken dawn. I liked sharing this with you—in language I thought you might just understand—strange sights and excitements, adventures in a way—but when we spoke a few days later on the phone you asked me only 'why wasn't it a story?'

You wanted fiction.

I'm not sure what stories are now. Are they a means of escaping? Or of learning? Or of organising the world? A way of projecting oneself into imaginary victory and pain.

Miles—how come the stories you like are all about victory—how come the goodies always have to win? Miles—how come the stories you love always end with bedtime, or a birthday meal, or the violent and comical defeat of the villains, or a final coming home? Because you're building yourself?

Miles—How come the stories I like are falling to pieces—stories scarcely worthy of that name. In them the world is badly organised, in them an ending is something that wants to happen but cannot, in them good isn't easily told from bad, in them the world aches and goes on aching. How come the stories we in Forced Entertainment love are built on shifting sand and made of channel-hopping? Because we've been in the world a little longer than you? Perhaps, perhaps. I don't know.

I am thinking of you.

Tim.

Dear Miles.

I'm sorry for firing so many questions at you in that letter before. I didn't mean to. Next time I'll just send a story.

Best wishes—Tim

Dear Miles,

There was once a woman who gave birth to two daughters, and brought them up alone, far from everything. For twelve years she kept the truth of the world from them, sparing them all of the unpleasant things that might spoil their childhood, and then on their 12th birthdays she sat them all down and told them everything ... she told them about darkness and the things that happen in it, she revealed the truth about the false-nose gunman, about the cellar and the shapes that lived in it, about codes and signs of regret, she told them about economies of scale and diseconomies of scale, she told them how the past lives on in the present, she told them about ghosts, about sexual pleasure and how it is obtained, she told them stories of entrapment and enchantment, she taught them to count in numbers, she taught them bad words and good words and she spared them nothing.

It took her a whole night to tell them, through the dark and into the fleeting hours of morning, she told them about ships at sea which encounter ice, about the boiling point of blood and the breaking point of bones, she told them about stories and what their uses were, she told them how to hurt people, and how people got hurt. She revealed the true law of desire.

She taught the meaning of the words 'uncanny' and 'impossible', she told them about Nixon and the strange quiet that sometimes falls in the middle of a big city, she taught them Truth Dare Kiss and Panic, she told them about game shows about sky and sea, about telephone wires, about noises and voices, and how men and women really die.

Thinking of you.
Tim.

Process (3)

Watching back the video-tapes. Checking to see what happened in some improvisation or another, trying to register exact combinations, coincidences, structures. So that the spur-of-the-moment games and accidents could (later) be transcribed and re-presented.

They often wondered what making the work had been like before the video camera, but, try as hard as they might they could not remember. It was a constant companion to them and the store cupboards filled up with crudely lodged, half-incomprehensible tapes.

Some days they ran out of blank video-tape. No one could be bothered to walk into town to buy fresh supplies. They'd go to the cupboard and select an old tape from the unofficial archive—how about *Emanuelle* (1992) number 22?—may as well tape over that—sure— another gap in the history ... another store getting more and more provisional, fragmented.

Simon Says Go Too Far

In any game there was always the pull to the edges. That question of 'What's the furthest you can go inside the structure of this game?' or 'What would a rule break consist of here?' or simply 'How far could one go with this?' or 'How can we collapse this?'

So in *Hidden J* the pretty game of opening and closing the curtains of the tiny house centre-stage gave rise in the end to a whole section of the piece performed in private and obscured from the audience—where only the sound of Cathy's volatile emotional phone calls in a made-up foreign language could be heard from just behind those curtains—a six- or seven-minute harangue of hysteria in which all one could see was the other performers, nervous, bored, distracted, waiting for her to stop, considering the awful sound of what she was doing ... and their inability to see it.

Go too far. Go too far. So that in the game of playing dead, in the end two of them go down and stay down for 15 minutes. Not playing at all, or playing too much.

Go too far, go too far. The scenes repeated in *Club of No Regrets* getting faster and faster, the clumsy special effects of blood and smoke and water and leaves getting piled on the scene like a storm.

> Isn't that the constant frustration for play? That it isn't real?

> No surprise then that play always dreams of its other. The thing has aspirations.

> Go too far, go too far. More storm. More storm. More storm.

So that there were always some players who don't know when to stop. Who'd be left out there in fiction or in play, getting too involved in it, getting confused. Remember Dennis Hopper's character in *The Last Movie*—a minor actor who stays behind in a Mexican town where a film crew have been shooting a western—the locals get into the whole movie thing—they want to play too—they build cameras and film lights from wood and string—they want to stage gunfights, fist fights—but they don't understand about pulling the punches—people get hurt, they want Hopper to teach them, they want, they want, they want someone to die.

And the stories of Hopper making the movie. Sam Fuller (or someone) going down to see him on-set—the cabins deserted, finding Hopper tripping naked in the woods, with a gun ... out of control.

Go too far, go too far.

Cathy yelling and yelling the longest list of confessions in *Speak Bitterness*—'we shouted for so long it didn't even sound like our own voices anymore ... ' Her yelling like ice being poured right down your spine. 'We never never never wanted kids anyway.' Not even a fucking game any more.

Richard in impro for *Pleasure* (1997). Claire lying 'dead' on the ground in front of him. He covers her head with a jacket, then pulls her underpants off. Sits staring at her cunt.

> Not even a game anymore.

> Go too far. Go too far. Go too far.

> Edges of the game—where it comes back to the real. Back to blank facts. The material. What is, here. Now.

> The game is in dialogue with the now. It cannot escape it.

> A room in Antwerp. Laptop and MTV. Words. Voices.

> Stillness.

> Game over.

Notes

1 *Recognition*, Fiona Templeton, 1994.

53 Step Across the Border (DVD Liner Notes)

Nicolas Humbert and Werner Penzel

Throughout their early years, both Werner Penzel and Nicolas Humbert were active in music, writing, and the visual arts. Penzel worked with the Brazilian theatre company Oficina, studied at the Munich Film School, and travelled through South America, North Africa, India, and Japan throughout the 1970s. Humbert, very influenced by French surrealism in his writing, painting, and Super-8 films, also studied at Munich before the two founded their own production company in 1987, Cine Nomad. Their films for Cine Nomad have been internationally acclaimed: *Middle of the Moment* (1995) follows modern nomads the North African Tuaregs, a circus company, and the writer Robert Lax, and they pay homage to Lax once more in *Three Windows* (1999). Chance, coincidence, and improvisation are the recurring narratives of their films. *Step Across the Border* (1990) focuses on Fred Frith's days as a nomadic improviser; it won numerous awards and in 2000 was voted by Cahiers du Cinema film critics in Paris to be one of the 100 most important films in cinema history. "How can one describe their work succinctly?" asks Jean Perret of the Visions du Réel film festival. "It is a quest—to the rhythm of the nomads—beyond the bounds of gravity."

Key words: cinema; nomadism; interdisciplinarity; improvised music; Fred Frith

In *Step Across the Border* two forms of artistic expression, improvised music and cinema direct, are interrelated. In both forms it is the moment that counts, the intuitive sense for what is happening in a space. Music and film come into existence out of an intense perception of the moment, not from the transformation of a preordained plan. In improvisation the plan is revealed only at the end. One finds it. The other connection concerns the work method: the film team as band. Much as musicians communicate via the music, our work, too, was realized within a very small and flexible team of equals. What mattered was exchange. And movement. Sometimes we started filming in the middle of the night, responding to a new idea that had arisen only minutes before. We had a fundamental feeling for what we wanted to do, for what kind of film this should be. And we followed that feeling. It was all very instinctive …

Do you know a white rabbit who, playing trumpet, circles the world on his flying carpet?

May be you have met him somewhere already, in Zurich, London, Leipzig, Tokyo or New York. That at least was about the route we took and what resulted from it was the black-and-white wink of an eye at the symphonic connection between subways, storms and electric guitars.

An American critic wrote: 'Fred Frith's music makes your jaw drop, your feet dance, and your neighbours move.'

Also starring: several telephones, puddles, scarecrows, saxophones, orchestrated cities and motors.

A music film.

54 DJ

Wayde Compton

Born in Vancouver in 1972, Wayde Compton is the director of The Writer's Studio at Simon Fraser University, and teaches English composition at the Emily Carr University of Art and Design. He is a co-founder, with David Chariandy and Karina Vernon, of Commodore Books, the first black-oriented press in Western Canada, which has published such authors as Troy Burle Bailey, Fred Booker, Crawford Kilian, and Addena Sumter-Freitag. In 1996, Compton wrote the semi-autobiographical poem "Declaration of the Halfrican Nation," and his books include poetry—*49th Parallel Psalm* (1999) and *Performance Bond* (2004)—and non-fiction—*After Canaan: Essays on Race, Writing, and Region* (2010). He is also the editor of *Bluesprint: Black British Columbian Literature and Orature* (2001), the first comprehensive anthology of black writing from British Columbia. Compton performs turntable-based sound poetry in the duo The Contact Zone Crew with Jason de Couto, and is a co-founding member of the Hogan's Alley Memorial Project, an organisation dedicated to preserving the public memory of Vancouver's original black community. In what might be seen as a contemporary revision of a jazz poetry tradition, Compton depicts the improvising titular character of "DJ" (1999) as a keeper of ancient knowledge.

Key words: Canada; African Canadian; poetry; community

> stimulator of the inner simulacra
> > turner of the worlds
> lobe and hip at one with the word
> > conduit of the herd
> shepherd of the unheard
> > hands on the vinyl
> needle in the curve
> > turntable arm prosthetic
>
> phantom limb pinning down the intersections—
>
> jungle and house   soul and techno   euro and rhythm and blues
> cues the anticipation
> > plays our feet and strums our blood
> alcohol permeates the paradigmatic
> > digs his fingers into static
> crossfades the synth with beaten blood
> > like a clock of tactic

turns the syntagmatic backwards
                            scratches 'bring that beat back'
catches
       the loop on the off
beat   matches
            that per minute mix like magic
makes the walls shake and the bass roll dashes
                         your soul
against the table's glasses
              the waitress passes

on the next round she wades in
delivers sapphires of liqueur
under black light
gets our orders all wrong
we pass and swivel and change chairs
to put the drinks wrongside right
the waitress wades back through the bass   the mix
the sound's humidity
the tindery contagion of humanity and electricity
touching touching
and she's gone

a hand on the texts and tomes   the keeper
spins limbs   the griot
holds in his collection the keys to corporeal
wisdom   this body of texts
these twelve-inch tablets of counterclock wiseness   the old
school warmth of vinyl and tubes   the blues
in the hyperbolic hip hop and trickster electronica
more singles in the crates than scrolls in the ancient library
of Alexandria

castanets
from hinges
snare drum
from this splintered jamb
bass from pane
we kick the damn
door down   chant
from chastisement
sticks
from names that wound
like a clock past tense wound
recyclers
scavengers
swallowers
excreters
of sound

dip
the divine stylus   drop
the needle
flip
through files
for the right disc   switch
the crossfader to the left side
snare
knock knocking   lift
the right
drop it   drop
the needle on the next
cut cutting
rock
knock knock knocking
Papa   Labas
open the doors
straddle the roles
dip   your oar
of ear
or ear
d'or
pan west
then north
then on   and on
back back wards and back to back
ear we are
ear for or
rockin in
our fly new gear
our hype blue camouflage

Part 8

Hope

Epilogue: Hope and Improvisation

William Parker (Centeringmusic 2013)

Born in 1952 in the Bronx, New York, William Parker studied bass with Richard Davis, Art Davis, Milt Hinton, Wilbur Ware and Jimmy Garrison, and emerged on the New York scene playing with Bill Dixon, Charles Tyler, Charles Brackeen, Don Cherry, Milford Graves, Jemeel Moondoc, and many others. He was the bassist with the Cecil Taylor Unit from 1980 to 1991, and in the early nineties began concentrating on composing for his own groups, In Order To Survive, and The Little Huey Creative Music Orchestra. He has become known not only for his playing and composing, but also for his many writings, his teaching, and his mentoring of younger musicians. In "Hope and Improvisation," Parker reveals the motivating force of his art; improvisation, like hope itself, is a way of penetrating to the truth of who and what we are, in the moment, singularly and together. Improvisation, like hope, can turn mistakes into miracles, and Parker has brought from his decades of creating music "the hope that all human beings may find their true self, not the corporate or designer self but the true self that runs neck and neck with the wind, the stars and the sky."

Key words: jazz; Europe; interdisciplinarity; pedagogy; poetry

Hope

(I)

> What is hope?
> It is the ability to forgive
> The ability to grow
> The ability to know and see the unknown
> To believe in what we can't see
> To trust our feelings
> Hope never doubts the music
> Like flowers in the snow
> Like a lake in the middle of the desert
> Hope is having compassion for those who hate us.
> Hope is idealism over practicality
> Not once but every time
> Hope is seeing the sky in-between all the tall buildings on a Sunday evening

(2)

She hopes, he hopes, they hope, we hope.
Is hope a dream? A vision or a short story
I hope one day the sad goes away
And the happiness will come and stay
I hope the lie will die
And Truth will never fade away
I hope every child gets to fly
And every bullet and every bomb turns to dust
As of
Yesterday
And every millionaire, billionaire
Gangster, businessman, politician
Realizes that they are not the only people on earth
I hope they realize that humans are fragile
They are more important than making money
That success in life is no war and no imperialism
See the poetry in the living
Little Huey poet from the south Bronx

Improvisation

Improvisation is joy! Improvisation is a spirit, it is a living thing, and it is a being that alters our reality, a natural force like the wind, ocean, and rain. Improvisation is a bird in flight, it is also gravity. Improvisation is a language that embellishes our movements as we make it through life. Improvisation is a ritual that helps us to seek the higher self. A kinetic flow that allows us to reach for limitless landscapes of possibility using the known and unknown. The minute we become familiar with the unknown it becomes the known. Another unknown fact replaces the old one and it continually regenerates itself. When improvisation is activated it changes shape, assuming a different identity, a different face, than the one it started with. Musical improvisation is a system of magical formulas that can be studied but never figured out because they change second to second. At the same time improvisation is an exact science the same way love is an exact science. Improvisation is the yeast that makes music rise. Improvisation is a series of mistakes that turn into beautiful statements or poems. If we make thousands of these mistakes they are no longer mistakes; they turn into miracles. They become ways of life. Improvisation means different things to different people. It means only one thing to the creator. How far do we go into a musical improvisation before our musical training steps in and says the dreaded words "this is not music." Echoes of the phrase "they are not human beings" (how cruel). Which came first, music or improvisation? How far will you take the music? How far will you follow it anywhere, or will you say, "I am the musician, the music must follow me?" Does it lead you, or do you lead it? What is music to one is not music to another. Where one person stops, another begins. Your outtakes may be my first choices. Music is a living breathing entity that is not to be enslaved; it must maintain its autonomy. Improvisation is an exact science, precise and exquisite. A good improvisation is in tune with Raindrops dancing through leaves and in time with the sun setting and rising. Improvisation, like the soul, is something that can be reincarnated. Improvisation is the key to eternal beauty of tomorrow: it is curiosity, creativity, and happiness. There are millions of ways to improvise, but only one key to heaven. It is the core that runs through our lives daily. Improvisation is making up poems on the spot and spotting angels on their way to the grocery store and inviting them into our hearts. Improvisation is acceptance of the mystery not ownership. It is playing the right thing at the right time every time one engages in a musical setting, whether that setting is solo duo trio or large ensemble or inter-galactic orchestra. Improvisation is sound silence, a shooting star, a butterfly and an eagle all at the same time.

Hope

What is hope? Is it the question, the answer, the illustrator, and the illustration? They say whenever a baby is born hope is born, a chosen one comes to save the world to renew us, to bring us to our feet. The chosen one's name is hope. Some others say hope is born every time we forgive each other, every time we conquer a fear or grow as human beings. Hope is both a living entity and a fundamental concept of freedom (tomorrow will be a better day). So, is hope the blues? Is hope the spiritual, the gospel hymn, the Gregorian chant or the pentatonic temple? Hope is at the center of all positive or negative action. It is detached from human wants and desires such as *I want that toy, I hope it doesn't rain, I hope I don't get caught*. Hope is the reason we get up in the morning and are moved to think to feel and become obsessed with life and music. Hope is a breathing living thing that resides inside all of us. It is present in all nature and is the voice we hear in anything that is beautiful. It outlines all the possibilities of vibration on a profound level. Hope is often materialized in the faces of children. Some are black and have swollen stomachs due to lack of food. Others have swollen stomachs because of too much food. When children grow up, where does the hope go? Is it outgrown like a pair of shoes or has it gone to sleep? Or is it lost somewhere inside of us? Does a vanished hope turn into capitalism, evangelism, or does it become the tea party? The science of faith is based on the hope that all human beings may find their true self, not the corporate or designer self but the true self that runs neck and neck with the wind, the stars, and the sky. Hope is the thing that transforms us to our greater self and allows us to go on for another day. We live in the now but the precursor to the moment is the anticipated tomorrow that ceases to exist the second it is born. Hope is active. It is not about sitting around waiting for the sun to rise, it is the realization that the sun never sets. What is this mysterious thing that some believe can save the world and inspire human beings to bring the lost compassion back in the cities and for once give the Gold! to the poor who later find out that the only true gold is love? At the same time, we are looking for a brighter tomorrow that does not contain inflated egos or competition, a tomorrow that could strive for peace and unity among brothers and sisters. Hope is present this moment like no other moment in history. The grass is not greener on the other side. At the same time that I am in my shining hour, someone else is suffering, imprisoned, and struggling for survival. **So what is Hope?** It is the sound of Grachan Monchur's trombone at its peak; it is flowers coming up between the cracks in the sidewalk when it has not rained for weeks. Hope is music, poetry, dance, and painting.

Coda: Hope/Improvisation

Hope is the shell, improvisation is the fruit, and music is the entire universe. Improvisation believes: it is having faith that if we fall, music will catch us and we will make the transition into the tone world. Understanding that it is natural law, we are not lost, the map is precise, and it always gets us there. We are brilliant. The theory is that if we play long enough and hard enough the ballad will come. If we play soft enough the hurricane will rip and the tornado will swirl. (Do hurricanes and tornadoes improvise as well?) I don't know, but I do hope that every child in the universe will be nourished and the earth will enlighten us. Those who get it will rise and sing and dance until the message is heard. Each time we play music we step into the garden of the lord and it is a deep blessing. In the cosmos is music spelled H-O-P-E. Improvisation is music and music is improvisation. Sound is silence. As we look into the SON we see the SUN. We stop asking and begin to accept, we begin to live, to be. We are the answer.

Index

Plains Indians 71–72
play: improvisation as 383–85; multiple
    realities of 386–92, 394; quadralogue 386,
    396n1; and ritual 386; in theatre 27–31,
    424–40; Yoruba 414–21, 422n8 *see also*
    dark play
Pleasants, Henry 225, 228
Plessy v. Ferguson 322, 329, 333
poetry 247–49, 233n2, 362–63, 443–45; Beat
    195, 232; collaborative 101, 109–12, 114;
    jazz 195
politics: and improvised music 63–64, 350; and
    theatre 79–86, 124–33
polyrhythm 74, 224, 226, 228–30, 251
Porter, Cole 65
Potter, Sally 268, 270–71, 276n4
Pound, Ezra 193, 195, 197, 258
Powell, Bud 229
Pozo, Chano 235n54
Prévost, Eddie 198n13, 263, 271
Priester, Julian 302, 310
"Princess" 37–39, 87–88
prosody 224, 229, 231–32, 233n2
psychogeography 176–80
punk: movement 183, 185

Queen Latifah 183, 186n11

R&B (rhythm and blues) 19, 232, 244, 260n31,
    443. *see also* blues.
race 2, 9–15, 188, 190–91; and bebop 232;
    and dance 138–39; and experimental music
    296–97, 308; and improvisation 2, 188, 190–91;
    intersections with gender 267–77; and
    politics 321–33, 362–63; and theatre 124–25
racism 190–93, 198n18, 308, 321–33, 362–63
ragtime 191, 224, 256, 344, 346
Rainer, Yvonne 135–37
rap 148, 181–85, 244, 338–39, 362–63 *see also*
    hip-hop
rebellion 330, 332, 341; improvisation and
    9–10, 14–15, 82, 301 *see also* revolution
recorded: vs live 12, 182, 195, 357–60,
    362–63, 370
Redman, Don 337, 344–45
Reid, Rufus 88
revolution 362–63: and theatre 82–86, 121–22
Richards, Keith 13–14
risk 322–23
ritual 323–28; Yoruba 419–21, 422n5
Roach, Joseph 112
Roach, Max 13, 194, 199nn24, 31, 227–29,
    233n12
rock 20; authenticity 358–59; 'n' roll 13–14;
    progressive 272
rock climbing: and flow 147, 152, 154–57,
    159–60

Rock Steady Crew 182
Rodríguez, Diane 130–31
Roelofs, Annemarie 268, 270, 272–73, 276n4
Rollins, Sonny 232
Rose, Tricia 148, 198n18
Rosenthal, Rachel 4
Rudd, Roswell 313
rupture 10, 148, 183–84
Rutherford, Paul 298, 309
Rypdal, Terje 306

Sahlins, Bernie 93
Sallé, Marie 399–400
Salt and Pepa 182
"Salt Peanuts" 38–39, 87–88
San Francisco Mime Troupe 126, 130, 132
Sanders, Pharoah 308
Sauer, Heinz 306
scat 229, 231, 233n9, 234n32, 250
Schechner, Richard 322–25, 383–84, 417
Schoenberg, Arnold 342
Schoof, Manfred 298, 300–302
Schubert, Franz 71–72, 78nn14–15
Schweizer, Irène 263, 266, 268, 271–73, 276n4,
    298, 300, 302
Scott, Lincoln 136
Second City, The 93
self: listening and 19–23, 24n11, 25nn19–20
senses: listening and 18–20, 24nn10–11,
    24–25n17, 25–26n31
Sharrock, Sonny 292
Shaw, Artie 244
Shepp, Archie 228, 305, 310, 312
Showtime 425, 430, 432, 435–37
silence: in music 13, 18, 305, 308–9, 315–16,
    451–52; in theatre 27–31, 123, 237, 281
Silver, Horace 232
simultaneous dramaturgy 79–81
Sir Mix-a-Lot 183
Situationists 148
Skidmore, Alan 306
slavery 14, 223, 246–49, 253–54, 265, 293–94,
    299, 330; and blues music 336, 338
Sleeping Giants 101, 111–14, 115n4
solos: in bebop 224, 226–30, 233n21, 251–52; in
    improvised jazz 37–42, 45–46, 48–49, 49n3,
    61, 74, 87–88, 91, 196; in jazz 343–44
Special Ed 183
Spindarella 183
Smith, Bessie 337, 345
Smith, Mamie 338
Smith, Wadada Leo 296, 305–7, 312, 318n35
Spolin, Viola 377, 383
Stanislavski, Constantin 376–77
Stein, Gertrude 193, 195, 197, 255–58, 260n45
Stevens, John 267, 298, 300
Stevens, Wallace 25n19, 193, 197